MEDIEVAL FOLKLORE

An Encyclopedia of
Myths, Legends, Tales,
Beliefs, and Customs

MEDIEVAL FOLKLORE

An Encyclopedia of
Myths, Legends, Tales,
Beliefs, and Customs

Volume 1: A–K

Carl Lindahl
John McNamara
John Lindow
Editors

ABC-CLIO
Santa Barbara, California
Denver, Colorado
Oxford, England

Library of Congress Cataloging-in-Publication Data

Medieval folklore: an encyclopedia of myths, legends, tales, beliefs, and customs / Carl Lindahl, John McNamara, and John Lindow, editors.
    p. cm.
Includes bibliographical references.
ISBN 1-57607-121-9 (hardb. : acid-free paper)
1. Folklore—Encyclopedias. 2. Civilization, Medieval—Folklore—Encyclopedias. I. Lindahl, Carl, 1947– II. McNamara, John. III. Lindow, John.
GR35 .M43 2000
398'.03—dc21   00-00913

06 05 04 03 02 01 00   10 9 8 7 6 5 4 3 2 1 (cloth)

ABC-CLIO, Inc.
130 Cremona Drive, P.O. Box 1911
Santa Barbara, California 93116-1911

This book is printed on acid-free paper ∞.
Manufactured in the United States of America

Contents

Contributors and Their Entries, ix
A–to–Z List of Entries, xix
Preface, xxiii
Acknowledgments, xxxi
A Note on Orthography, xxxiii

Volume 1: Entries A to K, 1
Volume 2: Entries L to Z, 575

Index of Tale Types, 1073
Index of Motifs, 1077
General Index, 1085

Illustration information—see page 744

Contributors and Their Entries

Louis Alexander
Attorney at Law
Sugar Land, Texas
    Law

Alexander Argüelles
Handong University
Pohang, Republic of Korea
    Dreams and Dream Poetry

Samuel G. Armistead
University of California at Davis
Davis, California
    Ballad
    Hispanic Tradition

Michele Bacci
Scuola Normale Superiore
Pisa, Italy
    Icon
    Votive Offerings

E. J. W. Barber
Occidental College
Los Angeles, California
    Spinning and Weaving

Pamela Berger
Boston College
Chesnut Hill, Massachusetts
    Grain Miracle

Karen Bezella-Bond
Columbia University
New York, New York
    Games and Play

Bettina Bildhauer
Pembroke College,
  University of Cambridge
Cambridge, England
    Blood

Zoe Borovsky
University of Oregon
Eugene, Oregon
    Sagas of Icelanders

Betsy Bowden
Rutgers University
Camden, New Jersey
    Cato's Distichs

Nancy M. Bradbury
Smith College
Northampton, Massachusetts
    Havelok
    Romance

Erika Brady
Western Kentucky University
Bowling Green, Kentucky
    Augustine of Hippo, Saint

Dorothy Ann Bray
McGill University
Montreal, Canada
    Patrick, Saint
    Wells and Springs

Nicholas N. Burlakoff
Southwest Planning Assoc., Inc.
Yonkers, New York
    Ships

†Pack Carnes
Lake Forest College
Lake Forest, Illinois
    Fable
    Marie de France

Jane Chance
Rice University
Houston, Texas
    Christine de Pizan
    Mythography

Nicola Chatten
University of Saint Andrews
Fife, Scotland
   FABLIAU

Geert H. M. Claassens
Katholieke Universiteit Leuven
Leuven, Belgium
   CHARLEMAGNE

Albrecht Classen
University of Arizona
Tucson, Arizona
   CRUSADES
   FOREIGN RACES
   NIBELUNGENLIED
   SARACEN PRINCESS
   TANNHÄUSER
   WOLFRAM VON ESCHENBACH

Lawrence M. Clopper
Indiana University
Bloomington, Indiana
   MIDSUMMER

Joyce Coleman
University of North Dakota
Grand Forks, North Dakota
   MALORY, SIR THOMAS
   ORALITY AND LITERACY

Melinda Sue Collins
Indiana University
Bloomington, Indiana
   ACCUSED QUEEN

Lisa H. Cooper
Columbia University
New York, New York
   TOURNAMENT

Stephen D. Corrsin
Wayne State University
Detroit, Michigan
   SWORD DANCE

Deborah Crawford
Phoenix College
Phoenix, Arizona
   GLASTONBURY
   JOSEPH OF ARIMATHEA,
     SAINT

Fabrizio Crivello
Scuola Normale Superiore
Pisa, Italy
   BOOKS OF HOURS

Hilda Ellis Davidson
University of Cambridge
Cambridge, England
   GIANTS
   OTHERWORLDLY JOURNEY
   SUPERNATURAL WEAPONS
   SWORD
   VALKYRIES
   WOMAN WARRIOR

Linda Davidson
University of Rhode Island
Kingston, Rhode Island
   JAMES THE ELDER, SAINT
   LIBER SANCTI JACOBI
   PILGRIMAGE

Giuseppe C. Di Scipio
Hunter College,
   City University of New York
New York, New York
   DANTE ALIGHIERI
   DECAMERON
   ITALIAN TRADITION
   NOVELLA

Peter Dinzelbacher
Universität Salzburg
Salzburg, Austria
   HARROWING OF HELL
   HELL
   PURGATORY

Graham N. Drake
State University of New York at
  Geneseo
Geneseo, New York
  HOMOSEXUALITY (MALE)
  KNIGHTS TEMPLAR

Thomas A. DuBois
University of Wisconsin
Madison, Wisconsin
  BALTIC TRADITION
  CROSS
  FINNIC SONG
  FINNO-UGRIC TRADITION
  SAUNA
  SKIS AND SKIING

Joseph J. Duggan
University of California at Berkeley
Berkeley, California
  CANTAR DE MIO CID
  CHANSON DE ROLAND

Maryjane Dunn
Independent Scholar
Lufkin, Texas
  JAMES THE ELDER, SAINT
  LIBER SANCTI JACOBI
  PILGRIMAGE

Bradford Lee Eden
University of Nevada, Las Vegas
Las Vegas, Nevada
  ADVENT
  BOWED STRINGS
  BOY BISHOP, FEAST OF THE
  CANDLEMAS
  CHRISTMAS
  DANCE
  DRUMS AND PERCUSSION
  FOLK MUSIC AND
    FOLKSONG
  FOOLS, FEAST OF
  GARDEN OF EDEN
  LUTE
  NEW YEAR'S
  ZITHER

Mary Agnes Edsall
Columbia University
New York, New York
  WINE

J. K. Elliott
University of Leeds
Leeds, England
  JESUS CHRIST
  JOSEPH, SAINT
  PETER, SAINT
  PILATE
  VIRGIN MARY

Deanna Delmar Evans
Bemidji State University
Bimidji, Minnesota
  NINE WORTHIES

Jonathan Evans
University of Georgia at Athens
Athens, Georgia
  DRAGON

Cathalin B. Folks
Pellissippi State Technical
  Community College
Knoxville, Tennessee
  BEHEADING BARGAIN
  GAWAIN
  LOATHLY LADY
  MORGAN LE FAY

Judith Gilbert
Language and Culture Center,
  University of Houston
Houston, Texas
  MERMAID

Stephen O. Glosecki
University of Alabama
  at Birmingham
Birmingham, Alabama
  BEAR
  SHAMANISM
  SHAPESHIFTING
  TOTEM
  WOLF AND WEREWOLF

Peter Goodrich
Northern Michigan University
Marquette, Michigan
> MERLIN

Cynthia Whiddon Green
University of Houston
Houston, Texas
> BAGPIPE
> HARP

Valdimar Tr. Hafstein
University of California, Berkeley
Berkeley, California
> DWARFS

Mark C. Hanford
Independent Scholar
Waltham, Massachusetts
> WIZARD

William Hansen
Indiana University
Bloomington, Indiana
> HAMLET

Susan Haskins
Independent Scholar
London, England
> MARY MAGDALEN

Thomas Head
Hunter College and
   The Graduate Center,
City University of New York
New York, New York
> OTTER
> RELICS

Lars Hemmingsen
University of Copenhagen
Copenhagen, Denmark
> ATTILA AND THE HUNS
> MIGRATIONS, AGE OF

Elissa R. Henken
University of Georgia at Athens
Athens, Georgia
> DAVID, SAINT
> GERALD OF WALES
> GILDAS
> MAELGWN GWYNEDD
> MAP, WALTER
> NENNIUS
> OWAIN
> OWAIN GLYNDŴR
> SLEEPING KING
> WELSH TRADITION

Constance B. Hieatt
Essex, Connecticut
> FOODWAYS

Elliott Horowitz
Ramat-Gan, Israel
> JEWS, STEREOTYPES OF
> PURIM

Nicholas Howe
Ohio State University
Columbus, Ohio
> ANGLO-SAXON CHRONICLE

Bonnie D. Irwin
Eastern Illinois University
Charleston, Illinois
> ASSASSINS NIZARI
> ISMAᶜILIS
> FRAME TALE
> HARUN AL-RASHID
> SEVEN SAGES
> THOUSAND AND ONE NIGHTS

Madeleine Jeay
McMaster University
Hamilton, Canada
> JOAN OF ARC, SAINT
> MARRIAGE TRADITIONS
> RITES OF PASSAGE

Karen Louise Jolly
University of Hawaii at Manoa
Honolulu, Hawaii
  CHARMS
  MAGIC

Leslie Ellen Jones
Independent Scholar
Los Angeles, California
  DRUIDS
  FAIRIES

Malcolm Jones
University of Sheffield
Sheffield, England
  BESTIARY
  BURIAL MOUNDS
  COCKAIGNE, LAND OF
  CUCKOLD
  DANCE OF DEATH
  DOGHEAD
  EULENSPIEGEL
  FOOL
  FOOLS, FEAST OF
  GREEN MAN
  ICONOGRAPHY
  MANUSCRIPT
      MARGINALIA
  MISERICORDS
  NAMES, PERSONAL
  PHALLIC IMAGERY
  PUNISHMENTS
  SCATOLOGY
  SHIPS
  SILENCE
  TRICKSTER
  WILD MAN
  WORLD TURNED
      UPSIDE DOWN

Henryk Jurkowski
Theatre Academy
Warsaw, Poland
  PUPPETS, PUPPET PLAYS

Marianne E. Kalinke
University of Illinois at Urbana-
Champaign
Urbana, Illinois
  RIDDARASÖGUR

Merrill Kaplan
University of California at Berkeley
Berkeley, California
  RUNES AND RUNIC INSCRIPTIONS

Richard Kieckhefer
Northwestern University
Evanston, Illinois
  MAGIC MANUALS
  NECROMANCY AND NIGROMANCY
  WITCHCRAFT

Samuel Kinser
Northern Illinois University
DeKalb, Illinois
  CARNIVAL
  MASKING

Norris J. Lacy
Pennsylvania State University at
University Park
University Park, Pennsylvania
  ARTHUR
  CHRÉTIEN DE TROYES
  GRAIL
  TRISTAN AND ISEUT

Eve Levin
Ohio State University
Columbus, Ohio
  SLAVIC TRADITION, EAST

Shimon Levy
Tel Aviv University
Tel Aviv, Israel
  PASSOVER HAGGADAH

Carl Lindahl
University of Houston
Houston, Texas
    ACCUSED QUEEN
    BECKET, SAINT THOMAS
    CHAUCER, GEOFFREY
    ENGLISH TRADITION:
        MIDDLE ENGLISH PERIOD
    FOLKLORE
    FOLKTALE
    GUINEFORT, SAINT
    LOATHLY LADY
    MARIE DE FRANCE
    MOTIF
    MYTH
    PEASANTS
    TRICKSTER
    VALENTINE'S DAY, SAINT
    WANDERING JEW

John Lindow
University of California, Berkeley
Berkeley, California
    BERSERKS
    BURGUNDIAN CYCLE
    SCANDINAVIAN MYTHOLOGY
    SNORRI STURLUSON'S EDDA
    THOR
    WILD HUNT

Timothy J. Lundgren
University of Michigan
Ann Arbor, Michigan
    OUTLAW
    ROBIN HOOD

Emily Lyle
The University of Edinburgh
Edinburgh, Scotland
    THOMAS RHYMER

Patricia Lysaght
University College Dublin
Dublin, Ireland
    BELTANE
    LUGNASA
    SAMHAIN

Elizabeth MacDaniel
Clarion University
   of Pennsylvania
Clarion, Pennsylvania
    MANDEVILLE'S TRAVELS
    TRAVEL LITERATURE

Ulrich Marzolph
University of Göttingen and
Enzyklopädie des Märchens
Göttingen, Germany
    ARABIC-ISLAMIC TRADITION

Adrienne Mayor
Independent Scholar
Princeton, New Jersey
    FOSSILS
    GRIFFIN
    LABYRINTH
    SEVEN SLEEPERS OF EPHESUS
    SIBYL

Cynthia Marshall McNamara
Southwest College, Houston
Community College System
Houston, Texas
    NUNS

John McNamara
University of Houston
Houston, Texas
    ANGELS
    BEDE THE VENERABLE
    BRIGID, SAINT
    CÆDMON
    DREAMS AND DREAM POETRY
    ENGLISH TRADITION:
        ANGLO-SAXON PERIOD
    EXEMPLUM
    FABLE
    MONKS
    OUTLAW
    SCOTTISH TRADITION

Binita Mehta
Independent Scholar
London, England
    PRESTER JOHN

Daniel F. Melia
University of California, Berkeley
Berkeley, California
  EPIC
  ORAL THEORY
  ULSTER CYCLE

Wolfgang Mieder
University of Vermont
Burlington, Vermont
  BLASONS POPULAIRES
  PROVERBS

Michelle Miller
University of Houston
Houston, Texas
  PLOW AND PLOWING
  SIR GAWAIN AND
    THE GREEN KNIGHT

Robert Mills
Pembroke College,
  University of Cambridge
Cambridge, England
  FUNERAL CUSTOMS AND
    BURIAL RITES
  MEMENTO MORI

Stephen A. Mitchell
Harvard University
Cambridge, Massachusetts
  FORNALDARSÖGUR
  SCANDINAVIAN TRADITION

Joseph Falaky Nagy
University of California
  at Los Angeles
Los Angeles, California
  IRISH TRADITION

Tara Neelakantappa
Columbia University
New York, New York
  INNS AND TAVERNS

Paul B. Nelson
Indiana University
Bloomington, Indiana
  SWAN KNIGHT

W. F. H. Nicolaisen
University of Aberdeen
Aberdeen, Scotland
  NAMES, PERSONAL

John D. Niles
University of California, Berkeley
Berkeley, California
  BEOWULF

Dáithí Ó hÓgáin
University College Dublin
Dublin, Ireland
  CELTIC MYTHOLOGY
  FENIAN CYCLE

Lea Olsan
University of Louisiana
  at Monroe
Monroe, Louisiana
  MEDICINE

Alexandra H. Olsen
University of Denver
Denver, Colorado
  APOLLONIUS OF TYRE
  CONFESSIO AMANTIS
  ROBERT OF SICILY

Ward Parks
Avatar Meher Baba Trust
Amednagar, India
  FLYTING

Evelyn M. Perry
Framingham State College
Framingham, Massachusetts
  THIEVES AND ROBBERS

Leander Petzoldt
Institut für Europäische Ethnologie
  und Volkskunde
Innsbruck, Austria
German Tradition
  SATAN
  SPIRITS AND GHOSTS

Ruth Petzoldt
Universität Regensburg
Regensburg, Germany
VAMPIRE

Chiara Piccinini
Scuola Normale Superiore
Pisa, Italy
GARGOYLES

Éva Pócs
Hungarian Academy of Sciences
Budapest, Hungary
HUNGARIAN TRADITION

Gillian S. Polack
Australian National University
Canberra, Australia
CHANSON DE GESTE
WILLIAM OF ORANGE

Liam Purdon
Doane College
Crete, Nebraska
INVESTITURE

Catharina Raudvere
Lund University
Lund, Sweden
NIGHTMARE

Velma Bourgeois Richmond
Holy Names College
Oakland, California
AMICUS ET AMELIUS
GUY OF WARWICK

Brynley F. Roberts
Former Librarian,
National Library of Wales
Aberystwyth, Wales
ANNWFN (ANNWN)
ARTHURIAN LORE
BRUTUS
CAMLAN
GEOFFREY OF MONMOUTH
GERAINT AB ERBIN
GODODDIN, Y
GWYNN AP NUDD

LEAR, KING
MAP, WALTER
MAXEN WLEDIG
MYRDDIN
NENNIUS
PEREDUR, SON OF EFRAWG
TALIESIN
TRIADS OF THE
ISLAND OF BRITAIN
WELSH TRADITION

Nicola Royan
University of Glasgow
Glasgow, Scotland
ANDREWS DAY, SAINT

Miri Rubin
Pembroke College, Oxford
Oxford, England
EUCHARIST

Joyce E. Salisbury
University of Wisconsin
Green Bay, Wisconsin
BESTIALITY
SEXUALITY

Sandra M. Salla
Lehigh University
Bethlehem, Pennsylvania
CAROL
FAIRY LOVER

Francesca Canadé Sautman
The Graduate Center,
The City University of New York
New York, New York
ANNE, SAINT
FRENCH TRADITION
LESBIANS
PARDON, LETTERS OF

Michèle Simonsen
University of Copenhagen
Copenhagen, Denmark
ANIMAL TALE
UNIBOS

Jacqueline Simpson
Past president, Folklore Society
   (England)
Worthing, England
   AMULET AND TALISMAN
   EVIL EYE
   GEORGE, SAINT
   SUTTON HOO

Leigh Smith
University of Houston
Houston, Texas
   CATHERINE OF ALEXANDRIA,
      SAINT
   COURTLY LOVE
   KNIGHT
   RICHARD THE LION-HEART
   UNICORN

John Southworth
Independent Scholar
Ipswich, England
   MINSTREL

Lorraine K. Stock
University of Houston
Houston, Texas
   BAL DES ARDENTS
   CHARIVARI
   GODIVA, LADY
   WILD WOMAN

Kathleen Stokker
Luther College
Decorah, Iowa
   OLAF, SAINT

Jeff Sypeck
University of Maryland
College Park, Maryland
   ORDEAL

Timothy R. Tangherlini
University of California,
   Los Angeles
Los Angeles, California
   BLACK DEATH
   EDDIC POETRY
   LEGEND

Sandra H. Tarlin
University of Houston
Houston, Texas
   JUDITH

Wade Tarzia
Naugatuck Valley
   Community College
Waterbury, Connecticut
   FEUD

Elizabeth Tucker
Binghamton University
Binghamton, New York
   CHILDBIRTH

Martin W. Walsh
University of Michigan
Ann Arbor, Michigan
   DRAMA
   FESTIVALS AND CELEBRATIONS
   HARVEST FESTIVALS AND
      RITUALS
   MARTINMAS

Andrew Welsh
Rutgers University
New Brunswick, New Jersey
   CULHWCH AND OLWEN
   MABINOGI
   RIDDLE

David Williams
McGill University
Montreal, Canada
   SAINTS, CULTS OF THE

Myra Corinne Williams
University of Houston
Houston, Texas
   PUNISHMENTS

Lee Winniford
University of Houston
Houston, Texas
   BECKET, SAINT THOMAS
   DANCE

Roger Wood
Central College, Houston
Community College System
Houston, Texas
    PEASANTS' REVOLTS

Eli Yassif
Tel-Aviv University
Tel-Aviv, Israel
    GOLEM
    JEWISH TRADITION
    JUDAH THE PIOUS
    LILITH

A-to-Z List of Entries

Volume 1

Accused Queen
Advent
Amicus et Amelius
Amulet and Talisman
Andrew's Day, Saint
Angels
Anglo-Saxon Chronicle
Animal Tale
Anne, Saint
Annwfn
Apollonius of Tyre
Arabic-Islamic Tradition
Arthur
Arthurian Lore
Assassins Nizari Isma^cilis
Attila and the Huns
Augustine of Hippo, Saint

Bagpipe
Bal des Ardents
Ballad
Baltic Tradition
Bear
Becket, Saint Thomas
Bede the Venerable
Beheading Bargain
Beltane
Beowulf
Berserks
Bestiality
Bestiary
Black Death
Blasons Populaires
Blood
Books of Hours
Bowed Strings
Boy Bishop, Feast of the

Brigid, Saint
Brutus
Burgundian Cycle
Burial Mounds

Cædmon
Camlan
Candlemas
Cantar de mio Cid
Carnival
Carol
Catherine of Alexandria, Saint
Cato's Distichs
Celtic Mythology
Chanson de Geste
Chanson de Roland
Charivari
Charlemagne
Charms
Chaucer, Geoffrey
Childbirth
Chrétien de Troyes
Christine de Pizan
Christmas
Cockaigne, Land of
Confessio Amantis
Courtly Love
Cross
Crusades
Cuckold
Culhwch and Olwen

Dance
Dance of Death
Dante Alighieri
David, Saint
Decameron

Doghead
Dragon
Drama
Dreams and Dream Poetry
Druids
Drums and Percussion
Dwarfs

Eddic Poetry
English Tradition: Anglo-Saxon
    Period
English Tradition: Middle English
    Period
Epic
Eucharist
Eulenspiegel
Evil Eye
Exemplum

Fable
Fabliau
Fairies
Fairy Lover
Fenian Cycle
Festivals and Celebrations
Feud
Finnic Song
Finno-Ugric Tradition
Flyting
Folk Music and Folksong
Folklore
Folktale
Foodways
Fool
Fools, Feast of
Foreign Races
Fornaldarsögur
Fossils
Frame Tale
French Tradition
Funeral Customs and Burial Rites

Games and Play
Garden of Eden
Gargoyles
Gawain
Geoffrey of Monmouth

George, Saint
Geraint ab Erbin
Gerald of Wales
German Tradition
Giants
Gildas
Glastonbury
Godiva, Lady
Gododdin, Y
Golem
Grail
Grain Miracle
Green Man
Griffin
Guinefort, Saint
Guy of Warwick
Gwynn ap Nudd

Hamlet
Harp
Harrowing of Hell
Harun al-Rashid
Harvest Festivals and Rituals
Havelok
Hell
Hispanic Tradition
Homosexuality (male)
Hungarian Tradition

Icon
Iconography
Inns and Taverns
Investiture
Irish Tradition
Italian Tradition

James the Elder, Saint
Jesus Christ
Jewish Tradition
Jews, Stereotypes of
Joan of Arc, Saint
Joseph, Saint
Joseph of Arimathea, Saint
Judah the Pious
Judith

Knight
Knights Templar

Volume 2

Labyrinth
Law
Lear, King
Legend
Lesbians
Liber Sancti Jacobi
Lilith
Loathly Lady
Lugnasa
Lute

Mabinogi
Maelgwn Gwynedd
Magic
Magic Manuals
Malory, Sir Thomas
Mandeville's Travels
Manuscript Marginalia
Map, Walter
Marie de France
Marriage Traditions
Martinmas
Mary Magdalen, Saint
Masking
Maxen Wledig
Medicine
Memento mori
Merlin
Mermaid
Midsummer
Migrations, Age of
Minstrel
Misericords
Monks
Morgan le Fay
Motif
Myrddin
Myth
Mythography

Names, Personal
Names, Place

Necromancy and Nigromancy
Nennius
New Year's
Nibelungenlied
Nightmare
Nine Worthies
Novella
Nuns

Olaf, Saint
Oral Theory
Orality and Literacy
Ordeal
Otherworldly Journey
Otter
Outlaw
Owain (sixth century)
Owain Glyndŵr

Pardon, Letters of
Passover Haggadah
Patrick, Saint
Peasants
Peasants' Revolts
Peredur, Son of Efrawg
Peter, Saint
Phallic Imagery
Pilate
Pilgrimage
Plow and Plowing
Prester John
Proverbs
Punishments
Puppets and Puppet Plays
Purgatory
Purim

Relics
Richard the Lion-Heart
Riddarasögur
Riddle
Rites of Passage
Robert of Sicily
Robin Hood
Romance
Runes and Runic Inscriptions

Sagas of Icelanders
Saints, Cults of the
Samhain
Saracen Princess
Satan
Sauna
Scandinavian Mythology
Scandinavian Tradition
Scatology
Scottish Tradition
Seven Sages, The
Seven Sleepers of Ephesus
Sexuality
Shamanism
Shapeshifting
Sheela-na-Gig
Ships
Sibyl
Silence
Sir Gawain and the Green Knight
Skis and Skiing
Slavic Tradition, East
Sleeping King
Snorri Sturluson's *Edda*
Spinning and Weaving
Spirits and Ghosts
Supernatural Weapons
Sutton Hoo
Swan Knight
Sword
Sword Dance

Taliesin
Tannhäuser
Thieves and Robbers
Thomas Rhymer

Thor
Thousand and One Nights
Totem
Tournament
Travel Literature
Triads of the Island of Britain
Trickster
Tristan and Iseut

Ulster Cycle
Unibos
Unicorn

Valentine's Day, Saint
Valkyries
Vampire
Virgin Mary
Votive Offerings

Wandering Jew
Wells and Springs
Welsh Tradition
Wild Hunt
Wild Man
Wild Woman
William of Orange
Wine
Witchcraft
Wizard
Wolf and Werewolf
Wolfram von Eschenbach
Woman Warrior
World Turned Upside Down

Zither

Preface

Fully five centuries after their passing, the Middle Ages have never been more popular than they are today. Their heroes—King Arthur, Joan of Arc, Robin Hood—are named by twenty-first century Americans as often as any hero now alive. Their supernatural villains—dragons, giants, dwarfs, witches—are the stuff of contemporary fairy tales, fantasy novels, and live-action role-playing games. Their lovers—Tristan and Iseut, Guinevere and Lancelot—persist as major figures in romantic opera and contemporary film. The focal image of today's fantasy world—the multi-turreted castle standing at the center of a Walt Disney theme park—is based upon modern notions of a medieval castle. No past era is more clearly and pervasively a part of our own than the Middle Ages.

More than any other aspect of medieval life, we know about its folklore—its traditional festivals, such as Carnival and the Feast of Fools; its courtly and martial games, including tournaments and lovers' serenades; its customs and beliefs, exemplified by the healing rituals of French and English kings; its extraordinary gods and heroes, such as Thor and Cú Chulainn; and its enduring legends, as expressed in such epics as *Beowulf*, the *Cantar de mio Cid*, and the *Chanson de Roland*.

Yet for all the present-day excitement generated by the medieval world, most of our impressions of its folklore come from the imaginative reconstructions of the past 200 years—from Victor Hugo's *Notre Dame de Paris* to Disney's *Hunchback of Notre Dame*, from Richard Wagner's *Ring of the Nibelungs* to recent *Thor* comic books, from Alfred, Lord Tennyson's *Idylls of the King* to T. H. White's *Once and Future King*. Most twenty-first-century Americans, asked what strikes them about this period, would mention a postmedieval stereotype—for example, the gargoyles of Notre Dame Cathedral in Paris, as much the products of the nineteenth-century architect Eugène Viollet-le-Duc as of any medieval sculptor; or the tale of how Robin Hood saved England from the clutches of King John, though this scenario owes more to Sir Walter Scott than to twelfth-century English intrigue.

This encyclopedia seeks to reach beyond such modern imaginings to capture a sense of medieval folklore in its own time. Our work is dedicated to the conviction that no matter how exciting our fantasies about the Middle Ages may be, the real thing was even more engaging. This book assumes the daunting task of presenting the folk cultures of medieval Europe in their own light and on their own terms. To that end, we asked our authors to craft their contributions according to some basic premises of current folklore studies.

Some Guiding Premises for the Study of Medieval Folklore

As imperishable as the heroes of medieval folklore seem to be, there is nothing more protean, volatile, and elusive than folklore itself. A much fuller description of the qualities of folklore is available in the entry Folklore in this encyclopedia. Here, we set out some of the premises that most informed us in planning the encyclopedia.

Because folklore changes over time, medieval folklore should not be confused with earlier or later folkloric expressions. In the nineteenth century, when the term *folklore* was coined, many people assumed that folklore, like a fossil, preserves a frozen image of the ancient past. If one accepts this premise, then the folklore of any given time will be essentially the same in form, function, and meaning as the folklore of any other. To the contrary, through close observation, folklorists have noted that folklore tends to be extraordinarily dynamic, extremely prone to change with changing times and environments.

In describing medieval folklore, contributors often mentioned related phenomena from earlier or later periods, sometimes to demonstrate significant continuity, sometimes to demonstrate crucial differences over time in the development of a given custom, tale, or belief. We asked them to provide clarity to our readership by being very specific in dating and characterizing both medieval and nonmedieval phenomena.

Because folklore serves as the foundation for most other forms of cultural expression, it is so powerful, relevant, and pervasive that it will leave its traces even in the most official culture. Most medieval folklore comprised ephemeral acts and perishable expressions: oral tales, customs recorded only incidentally in writing, sung and instrumental performances delivered without the aid of musical notation, dances so often known to us now only by a drawing or a woodcut capturing only one frozen motion of the whole. Thus, many of the fullest and most vital expressions of medieval folklore disappeared centuries ago.

Nevertheless, folklore is such a pervasive force that even such a formal, official cultural phenomenon as law will reflect unofficial folk custom. Therefore, an entry on Law is included in this work. Similarly, because the official process of canonizing a saint also relied upon and incorporated folk customs, our entry Saints discusses both the official and unofficial aspects of the canonization process, just as the entries Feud and Ordeal consider both the official legal nature and the folkloric expressions of these phenomena.

Also, because all human groups and complex cultural activities possess their unofficial sides, folklore is everywhere, not merely limited to a certain social layer— it is not, for example, restricted to poor, rural populations or to the Celts. Not only peasants, but also knights possessed and practiced folklore in the Middle Ages. Therefore, this encyclopedia contains entries describing the traditional practices of both groups. Entries such as Courtly Love and Tournament, for example, treat aristocratic play traditions, while the entries Harvest Festivals and Rituals and Midsummer devote themselves more pointedly to lower-class entertainments. Many entries, such as Carol, Dance, and Foodways, treat both upper- and lower-class expressions of traditional culture.

Because folklore is so strongly influenced by its environment, the study of folklore must proceed hand in hand with the study of its cultural context. Folklore inevitably changes when transmitted from one distinctive cultural environment to another. Thus the Welsh King Arthur (treated in the entry Arthurian Lore) is a figure distinctly different from the Arthur described in the twelfth-century French works of Chrétien de Troyes (see the entries Arthur and Chrétien de Troyes), who in turn differs from the king as depicted at the end of the fifteenth century in England (see Malory, Sir Thomas). Each of these figures embodies images and attitudes concerning kingship that are based on the folkloric traditions of its respective time, author, and audience. To begin to understand the folkloric meaning of these different Arthurs, it is necessary to know something about their various cultural milieux.

The editors have devoted as much space as possible to treating the largest tradition areas of medieval Europe as defined by common history, language, and other culture traits. Readers of this encyclopedia are urged to get a sense of the diversity and complexity of the period by browsing the entries Arabic-Islamic Tradition, Baltic Tradition, English Tradition (both the Anglo-Saxon Period and the Middle English Period), Finno-Ugric Tradition, French Tradition, German Tradition, Hispanic Tradition, Hungarian Tradition, Irish Tradition, Italian Tradition, Jewish Tradition, Scandinavian Tradition, Scottish Tradition, Slavic Tradition (East), and Welsh Tradition.

The Entries

Following the precepts outlined above, we asked our contributors to structure their entries in a format designed to peel away postmedieval preconceptions and to recover as much as possible of the medieval folkloric world. Authors were to begin their articles with "the most concrete and least contestable evidence" so that readers would soon gather how much (or more often, how little) information is available to us, as well as the nature of that evidence.

In order to conserve space and maintain a steady focus, the editors have devoted relatively little space to discussing ways in which medieval folklore reflects ancient culture or presages traditions practiced today. Our aim is, rather, for the reader to experience the medieval phenomenon, to the very limited extent that it is possible to do so from such a vast remove in time. To this end, we asked contributors—even those writing about phenomena well documented in ancient times—to begin by presenting the most relevant medieval information. Medieval folklore would thus appear as a vital entity in its own right rather than as it has so often been interpreted—as a final footnote to an ancient practice, more important for what it suggests concerning distant origins than for what it reveals about medieval life.

The contributors responded creatively and in highly varied fashion, and we have striven to preserve the integrity of their individual voices, methodologies, and approaches. Some entries, such as Norris J. Lacy's entry Arthur and Brynley F. Roberts's entry Arthurian Lore, are impeccable models of precision in which the authors scrupulously lay out all the known facts and resist generalization. Other entries, such Stephen O. Glosecki's entry Totem, address phenomena that we cannot even prove to have existed in the Middle Ages, yet they do so in ways that clearly distinguish evidence from speculation. Although authors vary enormously in their willingness to speculate, the editors have attempted to minimize those differences by asking contributors to supply their most speculative interpretations at the end of each entry.

Each author was asked to provide a narrative bibliography. In the section titled "References and further reading," which appears at the end of each entry, the authors guide the reader to major approaches to and sources of information on the subject. The authors' descriptions and evaluations of these works are usually sufficiently specific to help readers decide which books are most relevant to their particular purposes.

Audience

This encyclopedia is the first of its kind. General works, including the *Dictionary of the Middle Ages* (13 vols., edited by J. R. Strayer, 1982–1989) and *Funk and Wagnalls Standard Dictionary of Folklore, Mythology, and Legend* (2nd ed., edited by Maria Leach, 1960), include medieval folklore as part of their overall designs. More specific reference tools, such as *The Arthurian Encyclopedia* (2nd ed., edited by Norris J. Lacy, 1996), discuss the medieval and folkloric dimensions of their particular topics. But no previous encyclopedia has devoted itself both broadly and exclusively to the subject of medieval folklore. Aware of the unique nature of our project, we attempt to address three distinct audiences:

Those who are entirely new to the academic study of both folklore and the Middle Ages. We assumed that this population would make up our largest audience. Accordingly, we strove for precision in language and clarity in presentation, as well as to characterize and define those concepts and terms that are not generally known outside the fields of folklore and medieval studies.

Those who have studied medieval culture but who have little knowledge of folklore, and vice versa. The encyclopedia treats two areas of great appeal for nonspecialists even in the academic world. The fact is that the great majority of specialists in both medieval studies and folklore studies know very little about the other discipline. Thus, this encyclopedia relies on a core group of contributors who are adept in both fields and who are committed to and experienced in reaching out to those who are novices in either.

Those who are specialists in both medieval studies and folklore. Because there has never previously been an encyclopedia of medieval folklore, we designed these volumes to serve as a site for consolidating a body of information currently available only in widely scattered sources. Each major article is structured to give a general survey of its topic; in sum, the two volumes present a larger body of specific information on medieval folklore than can be provided by any other book currently in print.

The bibliographical discussions that follow each entry reflect our concern with all three audiences. In most entries, the section labeled "References and further reading" presents texts of interest to novices and experts alike and gives sufficient information about the various books and articles to indicate which are most useful to beginners.

Scope

Because the encyclopedia was designed to present not only individual items of lore but also their social and cultural contexts, the editors could have created a work many times the length of this one and still not have come close to exhausting our subject. Necessarily, then, the encyclopedia has been limited in its scope. These are the work's most significant boundaries:

1. The encyclopedia is limited in geographic range: it concentrates on European folklore. Furthermore, the editors, bearing in mind an English-reading audience, focus more intently on England, Ireland, Scotland, and Wales than on other medieval cultures. The cultures that most strongly influenced and interacted with medieval Britain and Ireland—French, West Germanic, and Scandinavian—received somewhat less detailed but still substantial treatments. Arabic-Islamic, Baltic, East Slavic, Finno-Ugric, Hispanic, Hungarian, Italian, and Jewish folk cultures also figure significantly in this encyclopedia, but the scope of our project did not allow us to extend far beyond the boundaries of Europe. Thus, medieval Africa, East Asia, and South Asia are little mentioned.

2. In terms of time, we have concentrated on the period 500–1500 C.E. The relatively few people who died or events that transpired before 500 that are treated here—St. Peter and St. Augustine of Hippo, for example, or Attila and the Hunnish invasion of Rome—are discussed for their enormous influence on medieval folk traditions rather than for the ways they influenced and were influenced by premedieval folklore. On the opposite end of the time line, we have included a significant amount of postmedieval information, almost all of it from the sixteenth century, for two reasons: such records are often substantially richer than medieval records, and they provide information of special value for certain cultural regions, such as the Baltic and Finno-Ugric, in which medieval traditions continued largely unchanged into and sometimes beyond the sixteenth century.

3. Even within our areas of greatest concentration, we make no claim of completeness. An encyclopedia of this size could easily have been devoted exclusively to the folklore of medieval saints, yet this encyclopedia contains separate entries devoted to fewer than 20 such saints. Again, the folklore of medieval royalty could have handily filled two volumes, yet this work devotes separate entries to only four historical rulers, Attila, Charlemagne, Olaf (who was also a saint), and Richard the Lion-Heart, as well as one legendary king, Arthur. In similar fashion, the encyclopedia treats most of its major categories by devoting individual entries to a few of the most representative examples and discussing others in more general fashion. For example, there are separate articles on some wild animals (see, for example, Bear, Otter, and Wolf and Werewolf) as well as some legendary beasts (see Griffin and Unicorn), but clerical lore concerning other animals is discussed in the entry Bestiary, and the entries Animal Tale, Bestiality, and Gargoyles also bring together significant amounts of medieval animal lore.

Finding Information

Although no encyclopedia, including this one, could present an exhaustive treatment of medieval folklore, these two volumes do offer the reader access to some of the most important aspects of the folk traditions of medieval Europe, and they also introduce some of the major current methods and tools of folklorists.

The encyclopedia contains three classification systems for guiding readers to the information that they seek: first, the entries themselves, listed in alphabetical order; second, the list of cross-references following the heading "See also" at the end of each entry; and, third, the general index, found at the end of volume 2. Although the encyclopedia contains only 306 entries, it makes significant reference to thousands of aspects of medieval folklore. For example, Melusine, an otherworldly being featured in late-medieval French romances, does not have an entry devoted exclusively to her, but she does figure significantly in the entries on Fairies, Fairy Lover, Mermaid, and Myth; all of these references can be found by consulting the general index.

Finally, readers interested in folk narrative have five means of finding information on a desired topic: in addition to the three tools just listed, there are separate type and motif indexes provided in volume 2 just before the general index. Thus, readers interested in the tale known to folklorists as "The Dragon-Slayer" can find references not only in the general index but also in the tale type index, where "The Dragon-Slayer" is listed as type AT 300, and the motif index, where motif B11.11, "Fight with dragon," refers to an important element in this particular tale.

Tools for Folklore Study

This encyclopedia focuses primarily on expressions of folk culture and consequently devotes a relatively small amount of space to the theories and methods of folklorists. Nevertheless, certain articles were designed wholly or largely to convey information about the principles, methods, and theories of folklorists. The entry Folklore defines the field and describes some of its major contemporary approaches and methods. The entries on certain folklore genres— Blasons Populaires, Folktale, Harvest Festivals and Rituals, Legend, Myth, and Proverbs in particular—discuss some of the major past perspectives in the history of folklore studies as well as some of the more recent scholarly approaches. The bibliographies accompanying these entries provide helpful references for the continued study of medieval folklore.

In addition, the entries on Folktale and Motif discuss traditional approaches to the classification and comparative study of folk narrative. Folktale discusses the concept of the tale type, and Motif assesses the uses and weaknesses of the concept of the motif. Because many authors who wrote about folk narratives use the tale type numbers developed by Antti Aarne and Stith Thompson in their *The Types of the Folktale* (3rd ed., 1961) as well as the motifs classified in Thompson's *Motif-Index of Folk-Literature* (2nd ed., 1955–1958), we have provided a tale type index and a motif index at the back of the book. Readers new to the study of types and motifs should read the entry Folktale before consulting the type index, and the entry Motif before consulting the motif index.

Our most persistent attempt to infuse folklore studies into this encyclopedia lies in structuring the entries in ways that encourage readers to "think folkloricly," to consider folklore as a living process that both reflects and influences its social and cultural environment. We encourage readers to browse through this encyclopedia, reading the entries on culture areas (Baltic Tradition and Welsh Tradition, for example) and social groups (Knight, Monks, Nuns, Peasants) to consider how folklore reflects both its broadest cultural contexts and the specific values of the group that creates it; and surveying the entries on folklore genres (Animal Tale, Blasons Populaires, Folk Music and Folksong, Folktale, Harvest Festivals and Rituals, Legend, Myth, Proverbs, Riddle) as well as the medieval literary and performance genres in which so much folklore is embedded (Drama, Flyting, Puppets and Puppet Plays, Romance). If the folklore of the Middle Ages lies beyond the experience of us all, the combined efforts of more than 100 authors will bring readers closer to those vanished traditions than any other work currently available.

Acknowledgments

The editors gratefully acknowledge their sources of funding and project support. In 1993, 1996, and 1999 the University of Houston supplied Limited Grants in Aid, allowing the coeditors to retain Katherine Oldmixon, Sandra Jordan, and Myra Williams to perform editorial work related to this project. University of Houston English Department chairs Harmon Boertien and Wyman Herendeen generously supported the work by providing materials, computers, and services that would have been extremely difficult for us to do without. University of Houston English Department office manager Lynn Dale, Barbie DeVet, and Andrea Short performed numerous acts of assistance and kindness. Dean Lois Zamora of the University of Houston's College of Humanities, Fine Arts, and Communication assisted the project with allotments to help retain Myra Williams. Eric Granquist and Dan Jackson of the college's Computing Support Office contributed time and expertise to help establish a server and database for the project. David Rossi of the English Department Computer Writing Lab volunteered assistance in a number of technical matters.

We further acknowledge Gary Kuris, who first conceived of the project; Samuel Armistead, Michael Chesnutt, W. F. H. Nicolaisen, and J. Michael Stitt, who contributed substantially to the early planning; William Gillies, who generously reviewed the Pictish and Gaelic sections in the article on Scottish Tradition; and the members of our advisory board: Elissa R. Henken, Malcolm Jones, Samuel Kinser, Ulrich Marzolph, Stephen A. Mitchell, Brynley F. Roberts, Eli Yassif, and the late W. Edson Richmond.

Once more, we thank our contributors, whose names are listed beginning on page ix, both for sharing their expertise and for extending their patience throughout the long process of preparing this encyclopedia.

Among the people who gave generously of their time, we would particularly like to thank Elissa R. Henken, Malcolm Jones, and Brynley F. Roberts, who, together, are responsible not only for writing nearly one-seventh of all the entries that appear in this encyclopedia but also for offering considerable aid and advice on other aspects of the encyclopedia, recommending and contacting potential contributors, locating illustrations, and offering much-needed criticism.

Sabrina Sirocco of the University of California, Berkeley, and Jack Hall, James Williams, and Malcolm Williams of the University of Houston generously provided translations of seven entries initially written in German. Gerida Brown of the University of Houston's M. D. Anderson Library volunteered extensive time and expertise to check bibliographical citations.

Graduate and undergraduate students at the University of Houston provided exemplary editorial services: Katherine Oldmixon, Sandra Jordan, and Myra

Williams gave the project far more than their grant moneys ever compensated them.

Former students Erin McAfee, Dr. Leigh Smith, Andrea Tinnemeyer, and Dr. Lee Winniford performed extraordinary eleventh-hour research.

Copyeditor Kathy Delfosse and Todd Hallman and Martha Whitt of ABC-CLIO furthered the enterprise with an extraordinary mixture of expertise and inexplicable good humor.

A Note on Orthography

In adapting foreign language text, we have tried to follow a principle of using forms most familiar to a nonspecialist audience and have aimed for consistency only within a given language, not across languages. Thus, for example, we have eliminated acute accent marks from Old Norse and retained them in Old Irish (but kept ö in Old Norse because it is frequently found in the familiar title *Völsunga Saga*). We have also uniformly edited personal and geographic names to the forms found in *Webster's New Biographical Dictionary* and *Merriam Webster's Geographical Dictionary*, even when this principle caused us personal distress (e.g., Harold Hardraada, a form in which only two of the five syllables might reasonably be defended and that otherwise vanished with Victorian scholarship). We have, however, kept the original orthography of words and titles in the bibliographies following the entries, which means that a reader might encounter, for example, *Gisli's Saga* in the text and *Gísla saga* in the references.

We fully recognize that this system is imperfect, that it could never pretend to be fully consistent, and that our application of it may not have been faultless, but we believe that it was nevertheless the best way to serve the various groups we perceive to be the audience of this encyclopedia.

Accused Queen

Most often, a woman who is first abused in her parents' home and later slandered and otherwise persecuted in the home of her husband; more rarely, a woman falsely charged with adultery; a common figure in late-medieval romances, chronicles, and saints' lives, also known as the Calumniated Woman.

"The Maiden without Hands"

Tales about a woman victimized first as a daughter and then as a wife began to appear in force in thirteenth-century chronicles (*The Life of Offa I*, a Latin text written in England) and legendary romances (such as the French *La belle Helene* and *La manekine*) and grew progressively more popular as the Middle Ages wore on. The general plot has remained a staple in oral tradition into the present century; the oral form of the accused queen tale is identified by folklorists as "The Maiden without Hands" (AT 706).

In the most common medieval versions, the protagonist undergoes two threats of death and two long exiles before she is finally reunited with both the family of her birth and the family of her marriage. One of the earliest versions of the full-blown plot, Philippe de Remi's *La manekine* (French, c. 1270), presents particularly striking correspondences with the modern folktale:

The king of Hungary promises his dying queen that he will remarry only when he finds a woman who looks just like her. No such woman can be found outside the household, so the king's councilors, clamoring for a male heir, tell the king to marry his daughter Joie, his only child. At first reluctant, the king develops a love for his daughter and sets a wedding date. Joie cuts off her own hand to avoid the marriage. The king has her condemned to death, but sympathetic courtiers save her from her fate and set her out to sea in a sail-less, rudderless boat.

Joie prays, and divine guidance brings the boat ashore in Scotland, where she attracts the attention of the Scottish king. She will not reveal her name or family origin to him, so he calls her *La manekine* (Mannequin). Her silence, however, does not prevent him from falling in love with her, and the two are married in a joyous celebration that only the king's mother refuses to attend.

Five months after Manekine becomes pregnant with the king's child, he travels to France to join in a tournament, leaving her in his mother's care. Manekine gives birth to a son and has a letter sent to her husband announcing

1

the birth. The evil mother-in-law intercepts the letter and replaces it with an announcement that Manekine has given birth to a monster. When the king receives the news, he replies with a letter instructing that mother and child be kept safe until his return, but his mother again replaces the original letter, this time with one ordering mother and son to be burned alive. Sympathetic councilors intervene and have two mannequins burned, while Manekine and her son are sent off secretly in a rudderless boat.

The boat lands in Rome, where a senator takes care of the mother and son. Meanwhile, the Scottish king learns the truth about his wife, imprisons his cruel mother, and sets off on a seven-year quest to find Manekine. He stops at the Roman senator's house, recognizes Manekine through a ring that he had given her (now worn by her son), and the two are reunited.

Another reunion is in the making. After many years Manekine's father, the king of Hungary, repents his desire to marry his daughter, and he goes on pilgrimage to Rome to seek absolution from the pope. He finds his daughter in Rome, and when the two are reconciled, his daughter readopts her birth name, Joie. The pope announces that Joie's severed hand has been found in the baptismal water, and God's voice orders the pope to reattach it. All live whole and happy.

Among the dozens of medieval romances and chronicles following this basic plot are fourteenth- and fifteenth-century works in German (*Mai und Beaflor*, Jason Enikel's *Weltkronik, Königstochter von Frankreich, Herzog Herpin*), French (*La comtesse d'Anjou, Alixandre roy de Hongrie, Yde et Olive*), Catalan (*El rey de Hungria*), Italian (*Regina Oliva, Novella della figlia del re di Dacia*), English (*Emare*, Chaucer's "Man of Law's Tale," and Gower's "Tale of Constance"), and Latin (*Ystoria regis Frachorum*).

A comparison of *La manekine* with recent oral folktales reveals extraordinary similarities, but also significant differences. This is the general outline of "The Maiden without Hands":

1. *Mutilation:* A maiden's hands are cut off to punish her for refusing to marry her own father or brother (or the maiden lops off her own hands, eyes, or breasts and sends them to her incestuous suitor, who has admired them; or a father carelessly sells his daughter to the devil, who forces him to cut off her hands; or a malicious sister-in-law effects the mutilation by slandering the maiden to her brother). The maiden is cast out.
2. *Royal marriage:* A king (usually out hunting) finds her in the woods, takes her home, sometimes has silver hands fashioned for her, and marries her. While her husband is away she bears a child and sends a letter to the king announcing the birth.
3. *Calumniation:* However, she is cast forth again because her resentful mother-in-law (or jealous sister-in-law, depraved father, or the devil) exchanges the letter, substituting one falsely accusing her of giving birth to a changeling (or of eating her infant). When her compassionate husband sends a message ordering that his wife be cared for, the villain exchanges that letter for one commanding that she be put

to death. Because of her incomparable beauty and gentleness, the would-be executioners are unable to kill the queen and instead exile her.

4. *Restoration:* While in the wilderness for the second time, her hands are miraculously restored, and she is reunited with her family.

La manekine and the other medieval accused queen romances most closely resemble the modern oral folktales in the central episodes, involving the cruel mother-in-law and the substituted letters, which have remained the most stable parts of the story for more than seven centuries. In other respects the differences between medieval and modern versions are many and striking. One of the major atmospheric differences is that the medieval woman usually undergoes two exiles in an open boat, while the märchen victim wanders in a forest. Other changes in the plot over time concern significant differences in treating issues of gender, sexuality, and maturity.

In the modern folktale incest is one of many possible causes for the exile of the innocent daughter, but in medieval romance the father's attempt to marry his daughter is almost always the cause. Sometimes, as in *La manekine*, the father is pushed toward incest by councilors who desire an heir. Sometimes, as in *Mai und Beaflor*, his long grief over the death of his wife slowly transforms into desire for his daughter. Elsewhere the king seems to go mad with sudden passion, as in *La comtesse d'Anjou*, where he conceives a great desire for his daughter as they play chess together. In other cases, as in *La belle Helene* and *La figlia del re di Dacia*, the devil infects the king with lust. In only a few of the romances is the incest motive missing, but they are among the most famous: Chaucer's "Man of Law's Tale," Gower's *Confessio Amantis*, and the Italian *Il pecarone*.

Second, though mutilation is common enough in medieval versions, it is not as common as in modern oral versions of "The Maiden without Hands"; furthermore, the medieval heroine—like Manekine, who cuts off her hand, or the heroine of Enikel's *Weltkronik*, who claws at her face until she looks "like the devil"—most often mutilates herself, whereas in the majority of oral tales the father or the devil mutilates the child. Thus, the typical medieval father is a sexual predator; the most common folktale father, a physical abuser of his child. By and large the romance heroine is slightly stronger than the märchen heroine in taking her fate into her own hands, so to speak. She may attempt to gain control over her situation, desperately, through self-mutilation, but also sometimes, less self-destructively, through a clever escape (as in the Latin *Columpnarium*) occasionally (as in the French *Yde et Olive*) disguised as a man. The romance heroine could be fairly characterized as more "grown up" than the oral folktale maiden.

A third major difference further points to the adult nature of the medieval heroine. Although the most stable part of the medieval and modern tale is the wicked mother-in-law who substitutes the letters, Margaret Schlauch has pointed out that in the later Middle Ages a male villain tended to enter the plot to subject the queen to further slander. In such romances the female persecutor is aided, either purposely or incidentally, by a male: in *Valentine and Nameless* the malign mother-in-law's accomplice is a reprobate bishop; in Chaucer's "Man of

Law's Tale" Constance is calumniated first by the lustful knight (for murder) and later by her mother-in-law (for monster birth). In such romances, nonincestuous, adult sexuality supplements or replaces the father-daughter relationship.

Chronicle, Ballad, and Late Medieval Romance Accounts

The false charge of adultery occurs independently in chronicle accounts before the first surviving version of "The Maiden without Hands" appears. Queen Gunhilda (also Gunhild), daughter of the English King Canute (also Cnut) the Great and wife of the German Emperor Henry III, is an early example. Married in 1036, Gunhilda died of the plague in 1038, apparently never having been the object of calumny. But writing circa 1125, the English chronicler William of Malmesbury relates that after years of married life Gunhilda was accused of adultery by a massive antagonist. The queen's champion was a young boy who succeeded in defeating her accuser, after which Gunhilda left her husband and entered a convent. (The story of Gunhilda later appears in ballad form in the seventeenth-century English "Sir Aldingar" and the sixteenth-century Danish "Ravengård og Memering.") A thirteenth-century French chronicle of the life of Edward the Confessor recounts a very similar story but identifies the champion as a dwarf named Mimecan. The account of St. Cunigund (married to Emperor Henry II in the early years of the eleventh century) partakes of many of the same motifs: calumniated wife; woman slandered as adulteress; physically abusive husband; trial by ordeal (walking barefoot over hot plowshares, carrying hot iron in her bare hands). As they must in märchen and ballads, wives in chronicles and saints' lives must fend off degenerate acquaintances, spousal battery, and slander and must avoid being burned to death. But unlike folktale wives, those in chronicles and hagiography often refuse to stay with their cruel husbands. The near absence of children in these narratives stands in stark contrast to the maiden without hands tales and romances, in which the children of the accused queen play an important role, motivating the plot and heightening pathos in the narrative.

Yet many later medieval romances incorporate the charge of adultery. When the mother-in-law is replaced as the persecutor, often the nature of the persecution changes. In such romances as *Hirlanda of Brittany* and *Charles le chauve* the villainous brother-in-law and the false steward, respectively, level the familiar folktale charges (animal or monster birth and infanticide), but increasingly a new slander takes center stage. The supremely persecuted Hirlanda, accused of giving birth to a monster and of murdering her child, is further vilified as an adulteress. The new charge of infidelity occurs frequently in calumniated woman romances, including a number of fourteenth- and fifteenth-century works: *Syr Tryamore*, *The Erle of Toulous*, *Valentine and Orson* (part of the Charlemagne cycle), and *Theseus de Cologne* (a long romance with three calumniated women). An earlier work, Ulrich von Zatzikhoven's Middle High German *Lanzelet*, belongs to the Arthurian cycle and is unusual in its depiction of Guinevere as an accused queen charged with the treasonous act of poisoning a knight. In these and many others of roughly the same period, the villain has become a power-hungry courtier, and his slander of choice is the charge of infidelity, while the heroine remains virtuous and sorely tried, perhaps even the victim of physical abuse. *Valentine and Orson*'s beautiful pregnant Queen Bellissant rebuffs the lustful archbishop of Constantinople, resulting in his denouncing her as an adulteress and a traitor; her credulous husband (the emperor) savagely beats her before the court, deaf to her pleas for mercy for herself and her unborn child. However, the accused queen's role as blameless sufferer did not mean that she always met abuse passively, or even with pragmatic resignation. For example, in *Valentine and Nameless*, Queen Phila's mother-in-law and her accomplice, the false bishop, accuse the queen of infanticide. When the bishop affirms that Phila told him in the confessional that she had committed the crime, the outraged young queen yanks his hair, vigorously refuting his testimony. *Charles le chauve*'s pregnant Queen Dorame is subjected to a tiresome and protracted suit by the lustful steward Butor: first he falsely reports her husband's death, then he tries to win her with logic, and when that tactic fails he tries to rape her. Dorame is fiercely chaste, however, and in the struggle she knocks out several of his teeth. Spirited persecuted heroines like Phila and Dorame have proven hardy, retaining salience for hundreds of years and inspiring late-twentieth-century writers of poetry and prose as they formerly caught the imagination of storytellers, ballad singers, chroniclers, and romance writers.

See also: Folktale; Lear, King; Swan Knight

References and further reading: In addition to "The Maiden without Hands" (AT 706), the theme of the Accused Queen appears in its subtypes "Help of the Virgin's Statue" (AT 706A), "Present to the Lover" (AT 706B), and especially "Lecherous Father as Queen's Persecutor" (AT 706C), as well as in such other types as "Our Lady's Child" (AT 710); "Crescentia" (AT 712); "Brother and Sister" (AT 872*); "The Innocent Slandered Maiden" (AT 883A); and "The Lecherous Holy Man and the Maiden in a Box" (AT 896). For other medieval treatments of this theme, related to "The Maiden Who Seeks Her Brothers" (AT 451), see the entry Swan Knight in this encyclopedia.

The most thorough treatment of the Calumniated Woman in folktale and romance is still M. Schlauch, *Chaucer's Constance and Accused Queens* (1927), which despite its antiquarian assumptions about societal development, presents a very useful analysis of the primary material. Excellent comparative studies of the medieval versions are A. B. Gough, "The Constance Saga," *Palaestra* 23 (1902), and H. Suchier's discussion of *La manekine* in his edition of the *Oeuvres poétiques de Philippe de Remi, sir de Beaumanoir*, 2 vols. (1884). I. Gnarra, *Philippe de Remi's La Manekine: Text, Translation, Commentary* (1988), presents the text in French with facing-page English translation and provides a fine discussion of related medieval versions of "The Maiden without Hands." Another particularly useful discussion and edition of a medieval version of AT 706 is E. Rickert, ed., *The Romance of Emare* (1906). Commentary on Emare is updated in A. Laskaya and E. Salisbury, *The Middle English Breton Lais* (1995), which also includes an edition, with commentary, of the *Erle of Toulouse*. N. D. Isaacs, "Constance in Fourteenth-Century England," *Neuphilologische Mitteilungen* 59 (1958), provides useful comparisons of Chaucer's and Gower's versions. For help in locating editions and criticism of the English Accused Queen romances, consult J. Rice, *Middle English Romance: An Annotated Bibliography, 1955–1985* (1987). "Sir Aldingar" appears as ballad 59 in F. J. Child, *The English and Scottish Popular Ballads*, 10 vols. (1882–1898); Child supplies fine notes on the medieval chronicle sources and the postmedieval European ballad traditions relating to the story of Gunhilda.

C. Velay-Vallantin, *L'histoire des contes* (1992), discusses the long-range histories, medieval to modern, of "The Maiden without Hands" and another important medieval Accused Queen tale, "Ste. Geneviève of Brabant" (a variant of AT 883A, "The Innocent

Slandered Maiden"). Perhaps the most interesting recent work on postmedieval persecuted heroine narratives has been carried out by feminist scholars, with one of the most useful works C. Bacchilega, ed., *Perspectives on the Innocent Persecuted Heroine in Fairy Tales*, special issue, *Western Folklore* 52 (1993). Perspectives range from structural analysis to neo-Marxist theory, but the primary focus is on issues that feminist scholars have traditionally found significant, such as power relationships and violence. A slightly more recent but significantly more accessible work is M. Warner, *From the Beast to the Blonde: On Fairy Tales and Their Tellers* (1994). Warner's scope is wide, ranging from medieval tales to late-twentieth-century poetry and cinema; the Calumniated Woman and the Maiden without Hands figure large in the work.

—*Melinda Sue Collins and Carl Lindahl*

Advent

A time of preparation for the celebration of Christ's birth on December 25, generally the four-week period prior to Christmas.

From very early times, just before the onset of Advent there were festivals and celebrations associated with the autumn harvesting of crops, the slaughtering of livestock, and the preservation of foodstuffs for the long winter ahead. Among the numerous such festivals held throughout Europe, the Celtic Samhain—which developed into Halloween—is a good example of the ways people during the Middle Ages and beyond celebrated the harvest time with feasting while at the same time observing a time when otherworldly beings could enter the natural world. With the coming of Christianity to the north, such celebrations were assimilated to the Church calendar: Samhain coincided with All Saints' and All Souls' Days (November 1 and 2) as a time of experiencing the presence of those gone to the afterlife, and Advent actually began on the Sunday closest to St. Andrew's Day, the last day in November.

In the fourth century, when the Church fixed the date of Christ's birth on December 25, the concept of a spiritual time of preparation for this feast began to be developed. In the Gallic Church this time period took on a penitential character and was called *Quadragesima Sancti Martini*, the Forty Days' Fast of St. Martin, in honor of the Feast of St. Martin on November 11, when this fasting period would begin. On the other hand, in the Roman Church, the mood was one of festive and joyful preparation for Christ's birth, and by the sixth century, the focus was on a series of sermons or homilies on this theme. By the eighth century, when the Frankish Church accepted the Roman liturgy, the penitential seven-to-nine-week Advent observance of Gaul clashed with the festive four-week Advent celebration of Rome. By the thirteenth century, a long period of compromise had eventually determined the current mode for celebrating Advent, combining the four-week time period of Rome and the penitential character of Gaul, though the fasting obligations were not as severe as those of the Lenten observance.

During the medieval period Advent also came to be designated as the beginning of the Church year. The annual cycle begins with Christ's birth; it continues through the year with his Passion, Resurrection, and Ascension, the coming of the Holy Spirit, and the celebration of the Church Triumphant; and it concludes with the ceremonies during All Saints' and All Souls' Days, invoking the remembrance of those who have already passed away.

This leads to the subject of the Second Coming of Christ. Medieval Christians viewed Advent not only as a time of waiting and expectation before Christ's birth but also as analogous to the present time of waiting and expectation before Christ's Second Coming. Partly due to the analogies among these cyclical religious moments of expectation and fulfillment, Advent came to be regarded as the beginning of the Christian church year—a period encompassing the life of Christ, the life of the Church, and the eventual return of Christ to his people on earth.

The most visible symbols of the Advent season in modern times are the Advent wreath and the Advent calendar. The Advent wreath, on which four candles are lit progressively, one more each week, during the four weeks of Advent, originated in the sixteenth century among German Lutherans. The Advent calendar has been developed to assist children in the preparation for Christ's birth through a combination of pictures, symbols, and treats hidden behind "doors" on a large cardboard house, to be opened once a day until Christmas.

See also: Christmas; Harvest Festivals and Rituals; Martinmas; Samhain
References and further reading: Sources of information on Advent include F. X. Weiser, *Handbook of Christian Feasts and Customs* (1958), and M. Ickis, *The Book of Religious Holidays and Celebrations* (1966).

—*Bradford Lee Eden*

Amicus et Amelius

One of the most popular stories of the Middle Ages, from the early eleventh to the fifteenth centuries, with versions in Latin, French, English, Italian, Spanish, Dutch, German, Norse, and Welsh; also a designation for a widespread group of related postmedieval folktales (AT 516C).

There are two groups of such stories: those in which the characteristics of romances predominate, and those that more closely resemble saints' lives. Both treat the ideal of friendship between two knights, include the ultimate test of child sacrifice, and have a strong didactic argument, but the moral exposition and details of the action differ, and there is much disagreement about interpretation.

The major romance versions, which vary widely and are mostly unrelated by source, include *Amys et Amillyoun* (Anglo-Norman, thirteenth century) and *Amis and Amiloun* (Middle English, fourteenth century): Amis and Amiloun are conceived on the same night and born on the same day. Sons of barons of Lombardy, the boys are so much alike in virtue, strength, beauty, and courtesy that none can tell them apart. They are adopted by the duke of Lombardy at the age of 12, swear eternal friendship, become knights at the age of 15, and are much admired and honored at court. When Amiloun returns home after his father's death, he has two exact golden cups made as mementos (and potential tokens of recognition) and presents one to his sworn brother Amis. Inevitably such praised young knights incur the envy of the jealous steward, who betrays

Amis, after he reluctantly became the lover of the duke's daughter Belisaunt, a forth-putting maiden.

The hero denies the charge and is allowed a chance for judicial combat. Belisaunt and her mother offer themselves as hostages. Amis, afraid to fight because he would have to perjure himself, seeks his friend Amiloun, and the two exchange places. Amis sleeps with a sword of chastity (motif T351) between himself and Amiloun's wife, pleading illness.

Amiloun goes to the duke's court and fights, even though a voice warns that he will be punished with leprosy. He kills the steward and tells Amis, who returns and marries Belisaunt and ultimately becomes duke. Amiloun explains his actions to his own angry wife, who later drives him away when he develops leprosy. Accompanied by his nephew Amoraunt, Amiloun travels about as a beggar. Amis sends wine to him in his token cup, and Amiloun takes it in his duplicate cup. Amis believes that the leper has injured his friend and attacks him, until he recognizes his sworn brother, whom he treats kindly.

After a year both friends dream that Amiloun can be cured of leprosy by being washed in the blood of Amis's children (S268). Belisaunt agrees; Amis cuts the children's throats, and Amiloun is healed. Friendship triumphs as the highest good; the children are found alive in the nursery. Later the friends return to Amiloun's country and punish his evil wife. Amis and Amiloun die on the same day and are buried in Mortara, or in some romances, Amiloun returns to live with Amis.

The hagiographic version is older; the Latin *Vita Amici et Amilii* dates from the twelfth century, the French *Ami et Amile*, from circa 1200. Both are set in the eighth century, at the time of Charlemagne. The French version is stylistically similar to chansons de geste, and its details are closely tied to religion. Two fathers, one Germanic and one from the Auvergne region of France, take their boys to Rome in response to a dream; Amicus (Ami) and Amelius (Amile) become fast friends on the journey. They are baptized by the pope, who gives them identical cups as mementos. The two separate to sort out inheritance but soon seek each other. Each meets a pilgrim, who believes there is only one because they are so alike; not recognizing each other, they almost fight, but they then swear friendship on the hilt of a sword that contains relics.

At court Charlemagne receives and honors both. It is Amelius who loves the forward princess, and the steward accuses him of robbing the treasury. Amicus offers to substitute for him in the judicial combat, and the two change places. Realizing that he will be guilty of murder, Amicus tries to resolve the conflict but has to kill the steward. His leprosy is explained as God's chastisement of those he loves. Amicus's wife tries to kill him, but he flees to Rome, where Amelius meets him and recognizes him through the cups. The angel Raphael explains that the blood of Amelius's children will cure the leprosy. Amelius, after sustained self-questioning, decides to make the sacrifice. As the friends go to church in thanksgiving, bells ring to announce the miracle of healing. They find the children restored by the Virgin Mary, and devils enter Amicus's wife and kill her. Later the friends join Charlemagne's army against Didier in Lombardy and are killed at Mortara. They are buried in separate churches; miraculously, the two are united in one place. After his victory

Charlemagne leaves priests and clerics to care for the tomb of Amicus and Amelius.

Rodulfus Tortarius's Latin poem (before 1175) refers to the sword of the epic hero Roland, but otherwise it is largely classical and pagan in references and attitude. The Anglo-Norman and Middle English romances contain many details of Christian belief. Many postmedieval folktales share significant traits with the medieval versions of the story of Amicus and Amelius. The widespread folktale "The Twins or Blood Brothers" (AT 303) parallels the medieval narrative: it features males who look identical, were born on the same day, and are separated in their travels, and it incorporates the motifs of the life tokens (E761) and the separating sword. The concluding episode of the medieval tale, centering on sacrifice and revivification of the children, is echoed in the oral folktale "Faithful John" (AT 516, 516C).

See also: Folktale; Romance; Sword

References and further reading: Good summaries of the various versions and their histories are found in M. Leach, ed., *Amis and Amiloun,* Early English Text Society 203 (1937), and F. Le Saux, *Amys and Amylion* (1993), both editions of Middle English versions of the tale. In his introduction Leach argues that the romantic version was earlier, pagan, and closer to folktale. Leach incidentally summarizes J. Bédier, *Les légendes épiques* (1908–1913; 1914–1921), who thought that the original was feudal and hagiographic, and L. Gautier, *Les épopées français* (1878–1897). W. Calin, *The Epic Quest* (1966), argues a doctrinal core in the Old French chanson de geste. V. Richmond, *The Popularity of Middle English Romance* (1976), makes the case for friendship shown as part of Christian experience in the world, while S. Crane, *Insular Romance* (1986), insists upon the secular ideal of friendship. C. Fewster, *Traditionality and Genre in Middle English Romance* (1987), reviews several versions and questions of genre. Major studies of related oral folktales, incorporating discussions of the medieval tales, include K. Ranke, *Die zwei Brüder,* Folklore Fellows Communications 114 (1934), and E. Rösch, *Der getreue Johannes,* Folklore Fellows Communications 77 (1928).

—*Velma Bourgeois Richmond*

Amulet and Talisman

Words that first appeared in European languages late in the Middle Ages to denote material objects thought to have some mysterious power to protect their owners from misfortune, disease, or witchcraft or to bring them wealth, success, and good luck.

There is considerable overlap between the two terms, and those scholars who do differentiate between them do not agree on their definitions. Some use *amulet* for "a passive protector or preventive charm" and *talisman* for one that has an "active principle" and "positive power" to procure a fortunate result. Others say an amulet is necessarily small enough to be carried on the person or worn as jewelry, whereas a talisman can be any size; others, that *amulet* is the broader term and can be used of anything, however natural or homely, which is thought to bring healing, protection, or luck—for example, a holed stone, a piece of coral, a wolf's tooth—whereas *talisman* has the more restricted meaning of an elaborate device constructed according to the rituals of learned magic. One reason for the difficulty is that the same object or class of objects can fulfill both functions. Astrological figures were often protective as well as active, while other objects changed their roles over time—a horseshoe on a Tudor door was a defensive measure against witchcraft, but on a modern wedding cake it is expected to confer good luck.

Talisman, the more closely definable term, entered English in the 1630s as a rendering of the Byzantine Greek *telesm*, the name for a magic statue defending a city or some hidden magic object to protect a building from harm. However, the Greek *telesm* was itself borrowed from Arabic *tilsam*, a metal plaque, jewel, or parchment bearing astrological designs, words, or letters that harness the powers of the planets and stars and the spirits associated with them. This astrological meaning persists in most seventeenth-century uses of the word, though in the nineteenth century (perhaps under the influence of Sir Walter Scott's famous novel *The Talisman*) it came to be used far more loosely.

Astrological talismans were based upon elaborate systems of occult knowledge; these were most fully developed by Renaissance intellectuals, such as Cornelius Agrippa (1486–1535) and John Dee (1527–1608), but their individual components were already present in the Middle Ages. One was the ancient idea, systematized by Bishop Isidore of Seville (c. 560–636), that all precious and semiprecious stones had "virtues" beneficial to the wearer—either for healing or for conferring power. Thirteenth-century lapidaries claim, for example, that any man wearing a ruby will be received with honor wherever he goes and can never be defeated in games or in battle; that the sapphire "is good for kings, queens, and great lords," gives deep joy, wisdom, and chastity to whoever gazes at it, and breaks iron fetters; and that the emerald "multiplieth a man's goods."

Such powers were increased by sacred words and symbols engraved on the gem or its metal setting. Names of God and of angels were especially potent; some were Hebrew, including the tetragrammaton *JHVH* (the letters forming the name of God), others Greco-Egyptian, others Arabic. Some were the initials of words, such as AGLA, for *Atha Gebri Leilan Adonai* (Thou art mighty forever, O Lord); others depended on numerology, since all individual letters had been assigned numbers. Thus, many rings have been found bearing the word ABRAXAS, the name of God, according to the Gnostic Basilides of Alexandria (fl. c. 125); its Greek letters have the value 365, supposedly corresponding not only to the days of the year but also to the number of eons, of ranks of angels, and of bones in a human body. Abraxas was represented as a bird-headed figure with snakes for legs; old gems with this image were reused in medieval times—for example, the intaglio ring buried with Bishop Seffried of Chichester (Sussex), who died in 1151. The names ascribed to angels and demons, by which they could be invoked and their powers harnessed, became increasingly numerous and fantastic throughout the period. At the beginning of the thirteenth century Michael Scot had already listed some whereby demons could be imprisoned inside a ring or bottle.

Arithmetical magic spread with Islamic culture into Europe. Each of the seven planets had its "magic square" of numbers so arranged that in whichever direction they were added the result was the same. There were also "letter squares," most famously the classical *ROTAS-OPERA-TENET-AREPO-SATOR*, which, when arranged in box form,

```
R  O  T  A  S
O  P  E  R  A
T  E  N  E  T
A  R  E  P  O
S  A  T  O  R
```

delivered the same five-word sentence, vertically as well as horizontally, backward from the bottom as well as forward from the top. (The sentence has many possible translations, one of which is "Sator the plowman performs the work of wheels.") And the pattern can also be manipulated to yield the Christian message *PATER NOSTER A O*. It was said to extinguish fires if written on a wooden tablet and thrown into the flames.

An important symbolic pattern was the six-pointed star, which was called the Shield of David in Hebrew and Solomon's Seal in Arabic and in Byzantine Greek, it was the sign of Solomon's legendary authority to make demons serve him. Another was the five-pointed figure variously known as the pentagram, pentacle, or pentalpha (that is, five A's). It is first found in ancient Greece and the eastern Mediterranean as a decorative pattern, and to Gnostics and Neoplatonists in the early centuries C.E. it symbolized the perfect universe (four elements plus spirit). It reached medieval Europe via Jewish and Arab culture and was reinterpreted as representing the five wounds of Jesus—a symbol guaranteed to put demons to flight. In the poem *Sir Gawain and the Green Knight* it is painted on the hero's shield, presumably with defensive intent, though the poet does call it Solomon's Sign, implying knowledge of its talismanic function.

Solomon was respected as a virtuous wizard in medieval times, and manuals of magic were falsely ascribed to him, such as the famous *Key of Solomon*. These contained many designs for talismans to be inscribed on metal plaques under astrological conditions, with much prayer and invocation of spirits. Typically they would include a pentacle inscribed within a circle and surrounded by sacred words. They were used for finding treasure, winning women's love or great men's favor, destroying enemies, and the like.

Terms for "amulet" entered European languages at the end of the Middle Ages. The word *amulet* itself is of unknown derivation; however, the class of objects it applies to is extremely ancient. In fact, there has probably never been a period of history or prehistory during which people did not regard certain things as worth keeping for religio-magical protection against sickness, poison, spells, the attacks of enemies or wild animals, or simple bad luck. At their simplest these are natural objects such as animal teeth, horns, claws and bones, pointed stones, holed stones, and fossils of striking appearance; or they may be older human-made items no longer recognized as such and therefore credited with magical powers: stone axes to ward off thunderstorms, flint arrows to detect poisons, Romano-British glass rings interpreted as "snake stones" with healing powers. Various substances were regarded as intrinsically effective, notably coral, jet, and amber, as described by Pliny and other ancient authors. Medieval amulets containing some of these substances include the jet pendants made at Santiago (including, alongside religious items, old magic symbols such as eyes and hands) and the coral beads popular in Italy to ward off the evil eye from children. Museums, understandably, tend to display the more artistic and expensive amulets—for example, those where the protective object is mounted in silver or gold. Simple items are in any case likely to have perished. It is only in specialist collections such as the Pitt-Rivers Museum (Oxford) and the Horniman Museum (London) that one can see such things as a mole's paw carried by a farm laborer in the 1920s to ward off cramp and wonder how many medieval peasants may have done the same.

Folklorists have given special attention to amulets with proven precedents in pre-Christian culture. Representations of eyes have been used since ancient Egypt, especially in Mediterranean countries, and are probably related to the blue bead with an eye-like pattern widely used in the same regions. In ancient Rome the phallus brought good luck and warded off the evil eye, as its successor, the red or silver "Neapolitan horn," did in medieval Italy and still does. The pagan origins of mermaid and sea-horse figures as charms are also clear. Certain gestures were thought to ward off evil, notably making "horns" by extending the index and little fingers, the rest being folded; making "the fig," a sexual gesture, by thrusting the thumb between clenched fingers; and (in some countries) extending the hand palm outward. Small metal or bone hands making these gestures were worn as pendants.

But it must not be forgotten that throughout medieval Europe there were innumerable Christian objects worn or kept in the home as safeguards against misfortune; to assist in sickness, childbirth, or danger; or as a guarantee that one would not die suddenly and unshriven: medals, crosses, pilgrim badges, saints' emblems, ribbons or strips of paper alleged to be the exact length of Christ's body, papers inscribed with religious texts and sewn up in a pouch, wax disks stamped with the Lamb of God, and many more.

Naturally, it is usually the finer specimens that survive. Among many examples, one could cite the fifteenth-century Scottish Glenlyon brooch, bearing the names of the Three Magi and Christ's dying words, *consummatum est* (it is finished), which (according to various medieval texts) protect the wearer from bleeding, fever, thieves, epilepsy, storms, danger while traveling, and sudden death. A gold pendant discovered in 1985 near Middleham Castle in Yorkshire is engraved with representations of the Trinity, the Nativity, and various saints, and also with *JHVH* and the word *ANANYZAPTA*, supposed to cure epilepsy and drunkenness and to prevent "an evil death"; it also bears a large sapphire, a gem with many medicinal and protective powers. It is hollow and contains fragments of rich embroidery, presumed to be relics. In medieval Catholic culture, artifacts such as these were devotional objects. Protestant critics called them "superstitious idols," and now scholars categorize them as amulets.

See also: Charms; Evil Eye; Magic; Relics

References and further reading: Traditional distinctions between "amulet" and "talisman" may be found in the articles on them in *Funk and Wagnalls Standard Dictionary of Folklore, Mythology and Legend,* ed. M. Leach (1949). For general surveys of medieval magic, see the relevant volumes of L. Thorndyke, *A History of Magic and Experimental Science* (1923–1958), and R. Kieckhefer, *Magic in the Middle Ages* (1990). For amuletic and talismanic jewelry, see J. Evans, *Magical Jewels of the Middle Ages and the Renaissance* (1922); F. T. Elworthy, *The Evil Eye* (1895); and J. Cherry, *The Middleham Jewel and Ring* (1994).

Descriptions of other amulets continuing medieval traditions will be found in E. Ettlinger, "British Amulets in London Museums," *Folklore* 50 (1939), and "The Hildburgh Collection of Austrian and Bavarian Amulets," *Folklore* 76 (1965); and V. Berry, "Neapolitan Charms against the Evil Eye," *Folklore* 79 (1968). For Jewish occultism, see G. Scholem, *Major Trends in Jewish Mysticism* (1941) and *Kabbalah* (1974). Popular accounts of various occult systems can be found in R. Cavendish, *The Black Arts* (1967), and long excerpts from medieval and later magic manuals can be found in I. Shah, *The Secret Lore of Magic* (1957). Chapters 9 and 10 of N. Cohn's *Europe's Inner Demons* (1975) assess the Church's attitude toward ritual magic.

—*Jacqueline Simpson*

Andrew's Day, Saint

The feast day for St. Andrew the Apostle, November 30, which was notable in the Western Church calendar for its proximity to Advent.

St. Andrew was believed to have been martyred around 60 C.E. on a cross in Patras, Greece, whence his relics were taken to Constantinople. He remains the patron saint of Patras, and his feast day is still important in Greek Orthodox liturgy, although earlier practice of his cult in the East is unclear. Claimed as the first evangelist of Georgia, Russia, and Ukraine, Andrew is also revered in Russian Orthodoxy. The cult of the saint came to the West in the fourth century, partly through the efforts of St. Ambrose, who presented relics, now lost, to his church in Milan. The cathedral in Amalfi, Italy, gained relics around 1208, and there, since 1304, both the clergy and lay folk have claimed that on days associated with St. Andrew, a liquid forms in a vessel suspended over the area known as the Apostle's tomb.

St. Andrew is also the patron saint of Scotland. According to early legend St. Andrew appeared to King Hungus in a dream, promising him victory over his enemies. In the meantime, an angel appeared to St. Rule (or Regulus), directing him to take relics of St. Andrew somewhere in the northwest, though not telling him specifically where. During St. Rule's travels, the angel later directed him to stop in Fife, Scotland, where the saint built the church of St. Andrews for the relics. Moreover, since King Hungus had already had his vision of St. Andrew, St. Rule was particularly welcome when he turned up with the relics at Kinrymont.

Despite the saint's importance, popular customs connected particularly with his feast day are rare. In Scotland, to honor the saint's patronage on his feast day, men and boys would trap rabbits and squirrels for "Andermas" dinner. Andermas dinner appears to have originated as a medieval custom, although time lines are of course a bit blurred in rural Scotland. The practice is also found in England from early times, and in postmedieval times, in shires where the saint's day marked a lace makers' holiday, mumming was also found.

See also: Advent; Relics; Saints, Cults of the; Scottish Tradition
References and further reading: There has been quite a bit of research on this area recently, including M. Ash and D. Broun, "The Adoption of St. Andrew as Patron Saint of Scotland," in *Medieval Art and Architecture in the Diocese of St Andrews*, ed. J. Higgit (1994); S. Taylor, "The Coming of the Augustinians to St. Andrews and Version B of the

St. Andrews' Foundation Legend," and D. Broun, "The Church of St. Andrews and Its Foundation Legend in the Early Twelfth Century: Recovering the Full Text of Version A of the Foundation Legend," both in *Kings, Clerics, and Chronicles in Scotland, 500–1297: Essays in Honour of Marjorie Ogilvie Anderson on the Occasion of Her Ninetieth Birthday*, ed. S. Taylor (2000). References to apparently medieval Andermas customs may be found in U. Hall, *St Andrew and Scotland* (1995); F. M. McNeil, *The Silver Bough*, vol. 3 (1961); and C. Hole, *British Folk-Customs* (1976).

—*Nicola Royan*

Angels

God's heavenly helpers who bring messages to earth and in various ways provide aid and protection to humans, named from the Greek word for "messengers," which was based on the Hebrew word with the same meaning.

Biblical Angels

Angels have a long biblical history. A "messenger of Yahweh" appears in numerous places in the Hebrew Bible, appearing to Hagar in the desert, preventing Abraham from sacrificing Isaac, speaking to Jacob in a dream and to Moses at the burning bush, and leading the Israelites through the Red Sea. The messenger is usually alone, but exceptions include the two angels who rescue Lot from Sodom and those that Jacob sees in a dream going up and down the ladder to heaven. Eventually, some angels are given names: Raphael, who helps Tobit and his sons; Gabriel, who flies to Daniel as part of his vision; and Michael, described by Daniel as a "prince," who strives with the prince of Persia on behalf of Israel. These angels are all friends to the Chosen People, of course, but some figures may be fearful instruments of divine justice. Such is the case with

Angel climbing Jacob's ladder; a twelfth-century illustration from Herrad of Landsberg's Garden of Delights. (*Reproduced from Gérard Cames,* Allégories et symboles dans l'Hortus deliciarum, *Leiden, 1971*)

the great winged creatures and the fiery sword that God posts outside Eden after expelling Adam and Eve.

The Christian New Testament continues this rich tradition of angels. Gabriel announces the coming births of both John the Baptist and Jesus; angels sing in the heavens at the birth of Jesus, and one tells the shepherds of the event; an angel appears to Joseph in a dream, reassuring him that Mary will give birth while still being a virgin; the angel reappears to Joseph in another dream warning him to flee with Mary and the child to Egypt; angels minister to Jesus after his temptation; at the Mount of Olives an angel comes from heaven to give Jesus strength during his agony; and angels by his empty tomb proclaim that he has risen from the dead. In the traditions of the early Church recorded in the Acts of the Apostles, angels also figure prominently in such instances as releasing Peter and John from prison, assuring Paul in a dream that his ship to Rome will arrive safely despite a terrible storm, and striking the proud Herod Agrippa with a horrible disease in which worms eat him alive. Numerous angels appear in the Revelation, or Apocalypse, especially Michael as leader of the forces that defeat Satan. On Judgment Day angels will separate the saved from the damned, leading the blessed to their heavenly reward. Thus, angels become far more than messengers, serving as powerful agents of divine power in both Jewish and Christian biblical traditions.

Early Medieval Angels

The popularity of angels continued to promote a rich lore in early and medieval Christian culture. Thus, by the second and third centuries, even theologians such as Clement of Alexandria (fl. c. 200–215) and Origen (fl. c. 222–254) recognized the special function of guardian angels in protecting humans, and Origen claimed that each person had a good angel on one side and a bad angel on the other, perhaps reflecting the dualistic tendencies in pre-Christian popular religion from the East (e.g., that associated with the followers of Mani). In the fourth-century Apocalypse of St. Paul, a man living in the saint's former house in Tarsus is visited by an angel who tells him to dig under the house and publish what he finds there. Twice he refuses to believe the angel, and so the third time the angel appears and scourges him, forcing him to break up the foundation of the house and there find a marble box. Terrified, he takes the box to a judge, who in turn sends it to Emperor Theodosius. When the emperor opens it he discovers St. Paul's own Revelation. In it Paul describes being transported to the Third Heaven where, among other things, he learns that dwelling within "every man and woman" there resides a guardian angel who reports each night to God about the person's good or sinful deeds during the day. By God's order, these guardian angels protect the virtuous who have renounced the world and seek to convert or inspire repentance in sinners who are "caught in the snares of the world." Later in the narrative, after viewing the torments of the damned in hell, St. Paul and St. Michael, together with other angels, ask God to relieve the sufferings of these sinners for a day—a motif that became common in many later visions of hell. The Apocalypse of St. Paul became so popular that it was translated into virtually all European languages, and it did much to spread lore about angels as well as influence later visions of the afterlife.

Although there was some biblical mention of various orders of angels, it was the *Celestial Hierarchy* of the Pseudo-Dionysius (late fifth or early sixth century) that was most influential in schematizing these orders for medieval tradition. Whoever the author was, he claimed to be Dionysius the Areopagite who was converted by St. Paul himself, and thus his *Celestial Hierarchy* appeared to have authority extending back to the apostolic age, an authority that was not seriously questioned until the end of the Middle Ages. In this work, not only is God seen as a Trinity, but there are three trinities of angelic orders, each with three further orders, all arranged in a hierarchy. At the top are seraphim, cherubim, and thrones; next come dominations, virtues, and powers; and finally principalities, archangels, and angels. Originally written in Greek, this scheme entered the West through the Latin translation of Abbot Hilduin of Saint-Denis (827), which also contained a legendary biography of the author, and then through the even more widely influential translation made by John Scotus Erigena (860–862) at the request of Charles the Bald.

Popular Cults

In the meantime the Church had become increasingly anxious about popular cults of angels, which spread rapidly and took various local forms. Thus, after earlier warnings had done little to stop such devotions to the angels, the Lateran Synod of 745, followed by subsequent councils, officially condemned as idolatry the popular tendency to name angels, thereby personalizing them as local spirits. Nevertheless, the Church did allow the naming of and devotion to the biblical angels Gabriel, Raphael, and Michael, along with Uriel. Though Uriel was not named in the Bible, he was sanctioned by ancient Jewish tradition and figured prominently in the mid-second-century Apocalypse of St. Peter, which as part of the apocryphal New Testament enjoyed great popularity and influence in the Middle Ages. Another exception, according to Jacobus de Voragine's *Legenda aurea* (The Golden Legend, c. 1260), was John the Baptist, whom many called an angel since he performed the function of an angel in proclaiming the coming of the Son of God.

The earliest known angelic cult sanctioned by the Church focused on the Feast of St. Michael and the Angels (September 29), especially after the widely reported apparition of St. Michael at Mount Gargano in Italy (c. 490); both Mount Gargano and Mont-Saint-Michel in France, where a later apparition took place (708), became the sites of famous monasteries dedicated to his cult. According to the earliest version of the *South English Legendary* (thirteenth century), popular tradition related that shortly after his first miracle at Mount Gargano St. Michael killed with lightning bolts some 600 Saracens who were attacking Christians at his mount—an example of the saint's military function and his association with mountains and hills. (Numerous churches dedicated to St. Michael are situated on high places.)

But perhaps St. Michael's most unusual miracle is his saving a pregnant woman in the sea. In the *South English Legendary* we read that a church of St. Michael was built on a mount at Toumbe, which was located "in the great sea" and thus only accessible to pilgrims at low tide. On the feast day of the saint a group of worshippers was making the crossing to the shrine when the tide suddenly came rushing in. All escaped the swift current except for a pregnant woman who could not keep up with the others. Yet through the help of St. Michael in his role as guardian angel ("guod wardein"), she floated on the turbulent waters, gave birth to her baby amid the waves, and survived in the sea with the infant for a whole year on fish and water provided by the saint.

Angels likewise affect individuals on a very personal level, either as protectors or as enforcers. Thus, according to Gregory the Great's immensely popular *Dialogues* (c. 593), a certain Equitus, disturbed by sexual temptations, had a nocturnal vision in which he was made a eunuch with an angel mysteriously in attendance, and afterward Equitus was no longer troubled. In *The Golden Legend*, after St. Catherine (Katherine) of Alexandria has been severely tortured angels treat her wounds and feed her in prison, and one of the angels later destroys the torture wheel that had caused her such suffering. Even so, angels could also deal harshly with saints when necessary, as Adomnán relates in his *Life of St. Columba* (c. 697) that when the saint did not want to follow an angel's directions, the angel struck him with a whip, leaving a blue mark as a sign of his punishment.

There are numerous legends in which "reliable witnesses" are reported to have had visions of saints being carried to heaven, at the very moment of their deaths, by crowds of angels. In his *Dialogues*, Gregory relates that no less a person than St. Benedict himself saw the soul of Bishop Germanus of Capua borne by angels to heaven "in a ball of fire." Bede's *Ecclesiastical History of the English People* (731), one of the greatest achievements of medieval historical writing, is filled with such accounts, all reported by (or at least to) reliable persons. For example, Bede relates that Egbert, "a most reverend man," reported that he was told by an eyewitness that St. Chad's soul was carried to heaven by angels. Bede goes on to say that "whether [Egbert] was speaking of himself or of another is uncertain, but what cannot be uncertain is that whatever such a man said must be true" (Bk. 4, ch. 3). In a later chapter (Bk. 4, ch. 23) Bede tells of a nun named Begu who lived in a monastery 13 miles away from the monastery over which St. Hilda presided as abbess. Despite this distance Begu saw the saint carried upward at the moment of her death in a great light, guided by angels to her heavenly reward. Lest this account seem to be founded on the testimony of Begu alone, Bede goes on to cite other witnesses as well. In such narratives we see a feature that folklore scholars recognize as common in legends, whether medieval or modern: the claim that

The devil enchained by two angels: a twelfth-century illustration from Herrad of Landsberg's Garden of Delights. *(Reproduced from Gérard Cames,* Allégories et symboles dans l'Hortus deliciarum, *Leiden, 1971)*

however much the story may exceed our normal experience, it is "really true"—a claim that is generally supported by the statement that it happened to the person recounting the experience or was witnessed by some reliable person who told the story to the narrator.

Such claims are especially important in yet another kind of popular legend involving angels, the account of an out-of-body experience in which a human is guided by angels to a vision of the afterlife. Following the second-century Apocalypse of St. Peter and the fourth-century Apocalypse of St. Paul there are numerous visions of heaven and hell in the Middle Ages (and of purgatory after the twelfth century), long before Dante's *Divine Comedy* in the fourteenth century. Bede gives two of these in his history, the visions of Fursa and of Dryhthelm. In the first, Fursa is led safely by angels through fires tormenting the damned, though at one point an evil spirit throws one of the damned against Fursa, burning him on the chin and shoulder. An angel explains that the burn is punishment for Fursa's earlier having accepted property from someone he knew to be a sinner. When Fursa returns to this world he bears the scars for the rest of his life, clear evidence of the truth of his account of his experience. In the case of Dryhthelm, we have a man who appears to die and is guided and protected by an angel through terrifying images of hell, whose torments include extreme cold as well as heat, until he returns to life and relates his vision to the holy monk Hæmgisl, who in turn relates it to Bede.

In some of these visions the angelic guide comments at length on the specific sins that have landed sinners in hell. For example, in the *Vision of Wetti* (824) the angel mentions various sins but focuses on those of a sexual nature, especially sodomy: "Again and again the angel introduced a discussion of sodomy ... five times and more he said that it should be avoided." While he does not define the sin specifically, commenting only that it is "contrary to nature," the angel does make it clear that

> not only does the violent contagion of this creeping disease infect the polluted soul of males who lie together, but it is even found in the ruin of many couples. Stirred up in madness by the instigation of devils and changed by the vexation of lust ... married ones change an immaculate marriage bed into a stain of disgrace as they prostitute themselves with devils.

This stress on sexual sins parallels the growing attention to them in contemporary penitential manuals for priests hearing confessions, and despite the qualification about married couples, his particular preoccupation with sodomy may be connected to the monk Wetti's urging—also in his vision—that his fellow monks (and nuns) undergo serious reforms of their practices in his time. It is worth noting that Wetti's admonitions are given special force by being put in the mouth of the angel guiding him through the afterlife.

This mention of devils also shows the medieval depiction of devils as fallen angels, following the great narratives of the war in heaven, won by St. Michael and the good angels when they cast Satan and the evil angels down to hell. Although rooted in the biblical Revelation, this story was greatly elaborated in the Middle Ages—for example, in the ninth-century Anglo-Saxon poem, *Gen-*

esis B, whose narrative power bears comparison with John Milton's *Paradise Lost*. These evil angels, or devils, frequently appear in medieval saints' lives as enticing tempters or dreadful enemies testing the virtue of the holy men and women who resist them (e.g., in Athanasius's fourth-century *Life of St. Anthony*, which, through Evagrius's translation, became a model for such narratives throughout Europe). Although guardian angels usually defeat devils and drive them away from the virtuous, sometimes the angels concede victory to their enemies. Bede tells of a young man who remains adamant in his life of sin despite all efforts to reform him. Shortly before his death he sees himself surrounded by hideous devils, the chief of whom is holding a large dark book detailing all his sins. Two angels appear with a very small white book containing the man's good deeds, but when they see the size of the devil's book they withdraw, and the devils drive the sinner down to hell.

Despite official Church efforts to control the views of the faithful about angels, including the fallen angels, popular lore extended the presence and powers of these figures into areas far beyond ecclesiastically accepted measure. In the *South English Legendary* both good and evil angels are believed to cause dreams, with nightmares being inspired by evil angels. These same evil angels lie with women and get them pregnant, or, having taken the shapes of women, they lie with men. Evil angels are also known to have special power in the woods, where they are better known as elves. Moreover, evil angels could sometimes assume an ethnic or even political significance. According to Felix's eighth-century *Life of St. Guthlac*, the saint, apparently living in a border area in England, spends a terrible night tormented by evil angels whom he recognizes as devils because they are shrieking in Welsh.

The earliest pictorial images of angels present them in glorified human forms, as wingless young men, often surrounded by bright light. In antiquity these figures sometimes appeared wearing the togas of Roman senators, thus conferring on them a conventional sign of dignity. In the Middle Ages the toga was often replaced by such signs of authority as a diadem, scepter, or codex. In the late-medieval mystery plays angels could be dressed in garments suggesting a liturgical function associated with the time of the dramatic action in the Church calendar. Art historians have traced the iconography of winged angels to the classical sculptures of Nike, goddess of victory, as these figures emerged in the fourth century. Seraphim could be recognized by their six wings (perhaps covered with eyes) and the color red, while cherubim had four wings and their color was the blue of the heavens. Whereas biblical angels were always masculine, in the Middle Ages they became idealized forms of beauty, and in Renaissance paintings angels began to take on feminine qualities.

See also: Bede the Venerable; Hell; Iconography; Saints, Cults of the; Satan; Spirits and Ghosts

References and further reading: Despite the contemporary popularity of books on angels, few are scholarly accounts, and for angel lore in the Middle Ages it is best to go to the primary sources. Angel lore may be found throughout collections of saints' lives, but there is usually a special concentration on such lore in the life of St. Michael. See J. de Voragine, *The Golden Legend: Readings on the Saints*, trans. W. G. Ryan, 2 vols. (1993), and C. Horstmann, ed., *The Early South English Legendary*, Early English Text Society, Original

Series 87 (1887; rpt. 1987). For Gregory and Bede, see O. J. Zimmerman, trans., Saint Gregory the Great, *Dialogues*, Fathers of the Church 39 (1959), and B. Colgrave and R. A. B. Mynors, ed. and trans., *Bede's Ecclesiastical History of the English People* (1969). Numerous accounts of angels, both good and evil, appear in E. Gardiner, ed., *Visions of Heaven and Hell before Dante* (1989).

—John McNamara

Anglo-Saxon Chronicle

Annals of English history spanning the years from around 60 B.C.E. to 1154 C.E. and found in four major manuscript versions, conventionally designated as Parker (A), Abingdon (B and C), Worcester (D), and Peterborough or Laud (E).

Although these versions differ in some respects, their similarities are sufficiently strong that they are known collectively as the *Anglo-Saxon Chronicle*. Written in Old English, they share a core of material, the so-called Common Stock, that dates to the beginning of their composition during the reign of King Alfred in the 890s. The Common Stock draws heavily on written and oral sources; it begins the record of English history with Julius Caesar's attempted conquest of the island and focuses on ecclesiastical, political, and military events through 891. Whereas accounts of early history necessarily derive largely from written sources, with some material from oral tradition, as continuations of the *Chronicle* become more contemporaneous with the events they record, from the early 900s through 1154, they rely heavily on orally circulating stories and thus become more valuable to those working in medieval folklore.

The *Chronicle* contains a great wealth of information about the cultural practices and beliefs of the Anglo-Saxons scattered throughout its versions because its compilers went far beyond the expected record of political and religious conditions. They included events that affected daily life in early medieval England, such as the activities of outlaws and others on the social margins; the effects of severe weather on crops and domestic animals; outbreaks of murrain and other pestilence; fires in major urban areas; unusually high or low tides along the coastline and rivers; atmospheric conditions such as the aurora borealis; and noteworthy celestial occurrences such as eclipses, comets, and astronomical portents. For example, the E version entry for 1117 records that on the night of December 16 the sky was as red as if it were on fire. The chronicler notes this disturbance of the natural order immediately after recording the oppressive taxation policies of King Henry I. The audience of the *Chronicle* is thus invited to see this natural portent as a sign of divine displeasure with Henry's rule. Thus, contemporary interpretations of such events often appear in entries and are of particular interest.

The *Chronicle* also contains information about the origins and ancestors of the Anglo-Saxons. It records the migration of the Germanic tribes to Britain in 449 C.E. as well as extended genealogies (at various entries) that trace English rulers back to Germanic chieftains and divinities of continental Europe. The appearance of genealogies in the *Chronicle* indicates the importance of popular beliefs about ancestry, particularly the lasting value of such names as Woden and Geat, who lent legitimacy to the political power of those claiming such ancestry during the period.

Only the Peterborough (E) version of the *Chronicle* continues to record events beyond 1080, 14 years after the Norman Conquest. Until it ends in 1154, this version vividly records the Norman occupation of England from a native perspective. These later entries are of special value for the study of Anglo-Saxon beliefs, customs, and practices as they were affected by the pressures of Norman rule.

See also: English Tradition: Anglo-Saxon Period; Wild Hunt
References and further reading: A new multivolume edition, under the general editorship of D. Dumville and S. Keynes, will supplement C. Plummer and J. Earle, *Two of the Saxon Chronicles Parallel* (1892). For translations, see D. Whitelock et al., *The Anglo-Saxon Chronicle* (1962), and M. Swanton, *The Anglo-Saxon Chronicle* (1996). For background, see A. Gransden, *Historical Writing in England, c. 550 to c. 1307* (1974).

—*Nicholas Howe*

Animal Tale

A fictional oral narrative in which animals perform the principal plot actions.

As a folklore genre, animal tales are distinct from the closely related genres of mimologisms and etiological legends. Mimologisms are verbal expressions and dialogues, sometimes introduced by a very short narrative, that interpret the sounds of animals in humorous ways. Etiological legends relate events, supposed to have taken place once in the distant past, to explain particularities of the animal and natural world still observable nowadays—for example, to tell why the bat is blind and flies only at night (AT 222A, a version of which appears as the twenty-third tale in the *Fables* of Marie de France), or to explain why the bear has no tail (AT 2, "The Tail-Fisher").

In certain cases animal tales so closely resemble etiological legends that they share the same plot, although the two genres put that plot to different uses. Medieval versions of "The Tail-Fisher," for example, pit the fox against the wolf: the fox convinces the wolf to use his tail as a fishing line. As the wolf sits on a hole in a frozen pond, waiting for the fish to bite, ice forms around his tail and traps him. Farmers arrive and beat the wolf; in order to survive he has to cut off his own tail. The version just summarized comes from the medieval *Roman de Renart*, a twelfth-century collection of fictional tales. But in some modern oral traditions the tale is told about a bear, and after the bear loses his tail in the ice, the narrator ends by explaining that this is why, today, bears have no tails.

Like "The Tail-Fisher," most animal tales feature two major characters. And, also like "The Tail-Fisher," most are simply structured stories of deceit involving two basic plot actions. First, there is the deceit or deception (the fox tricks the wolf into using his tail as a fishing line); second, the outcome, a sudden ending (the wolf is beaten and loses his tail). In the actual practice of storytelling, however, a narrator may string together many such short tales into long narratives. Because the episodes are all similar in structure, they may occur in any order, thus allowing gifted performers great freedom to compose their own chains of episodes. Nevertheless, some chains have proved remarkably stable in practice. For example, in both medieval literature and in recent oral tradition "The Tail-Fisher" is often prefaced by "The Theft of Fish" (AT 1), in which a hungry fox plays dead; fishermen find him in the road and, eager to skin him, throw him into their fish basket (or in the *Roman de Renart,* a cart full of eels); as the fishermen make their way home, the fox throws the fish out of the basket and then escapes to eat them.

The animal tales of oral folk tradition are organized around a few clear semantic oppositions: physical weakness combined with cunning conflicts with physical strength combined with stupidity. Wild animals conflict with domestic animals. These two sets of oppositions generally coincide, as both stupidity and savagery are stigmatized while cunning and domesticity are valorized. In European tradition strength and stupidity are most often embodied in the figure of the wolf, though in the Nordic countries the bear frequently fills this role. The trickster par excellence is the fox, but his status is more ambiguous. When opposed to domestic animals, he represents physical strength and is sometimes the loser, but when opposed to the wolf or bear, he is the embodiment of cunning, thus acquiring some of the traits normally attached to the human/domestic sphere.

In medieval literature animal tales were told for moral and edifying purposes, in fables and exempla; for didactic purposes, in bestiaries; but above all, for comic and satiric purposes, in the vast cycle of Reynard the Fox: the immensely popular and influential *Roman de Renart* (1174–1250), its antecedents in clerical Latin poetry, and its many continuations into the fifteenth century.

Fable and Exemplum Traditions

The oldest literary versions of animal tales in Western tradition are the medieval collection of fables called *ysopets* or *Romulus,* which transmit and adapt the fables of classical antiquity (Aesop and Phaedrus) throughout the Middle Ages. Generally speaking, the fable, of learned origin and cultivated by clerics, is written to convey a moral message; the animal tales of oral folk tradition, on the contrary, tend to be told for entertainment. This difference affects their respective narrative structures. For example, fables tend to end with a pointed moral, whereas animal tales seldom do.

Although medieval fables ultimately derive from the antique fables of Aesop and Phaedrus, a number of them are retellings of animal tales from folk traditions. Compilers of fable collections used a variety of sources. A case in point is the *Fables* of Marie de France, possibly the first such collection to appear in a European vernacular. It includes 20 stories derived from classical fable tradition as well some 12 fabliaux, but the remainder are animal tales rooted in medieval oral folk traditions. Three of the folk-derived fables feature the fox: "The Cock and the Fox" (AT 6), "The Fox and the Dove" (AT 62), and "The Fox and the Bear" (AT 36). Significantly, all three tales also appear in the major beast epic collections *Ysengrimus* and *Renart.* Eight others commonly associated with folk tradition feature the wolf. In contrast to the fox tales, the wolf tales seem to have come more immediately from clerical sources. In these tales animals fast, officiate at mass, and serve as bishops! One of Marie's wolf fables (no. 90) follows the plot of the popular tale of "The Wolf and the Seven Kids" (AT 123).

After 1250 medieval fables featuring the fox and the wolf are likely to borrow from the widely popular *Roman de Renart* rather than directly from folk tradition. For example, the *Liber parabolarum* (Book of Parables) by Odo de Cheriton contains 116 fables, of which 15 can be traced back to classical tradition through the *Romulus* and others to bestiaries, while several are connected with the cycle of Reynard the Fox. For example, Odo's fable 74 is the tale of "The Tail-Fisher" (AT 2). Fable 23, "De fraudibus vulpis et catti" (On the Tricks of the Wolf and the Cat), is a folktale: the cat's only trick saves him. When in danger, the cat climbs up the tree, whereas the fox is captured in spite of his many tricks (AT 105, "The Cat's Only Trick"). The protagonists of this fable are given the names—Reynard the Fox and Tibert the Cat—earlier bestowed upon them in the *Roman de Renart,* although the story itself does not appear in the *Roman.* Fables by Jean de Sheppey (between 1354 and 1377) include such narratives as "Lupus et vulpes in lardio" (The Wolf and the Fox in the Larder), a version of the popular animal tale "The Wolf Overeats in the Cellar" (AT 41, also found in the fables of Odo of Cheriton).

Preachers often employed animal tales in their sermons, first exploiting the entertaining features of the folktale to gain the attention of the audience and then shaping the tale to underscore moral points. Such tales, known as exempla, became increasingly popular in the later Middle Ages. The French exemplum collection *Chastoiement d'un père à son fils* (A Father's Warning to His Son) includes the tale of the wolf and fox in the well (AT 32). The *Chastoiement* is a translation of the eleventh-century *Disciplina clericalis* by Petrus Alfonsi, a Spanish Christian converted from Judaism. Alfonsi, in turn, had borrowed the tale from the Talmudic commentator Rachi. Through such channels, many Jewish and Arabic tales entered the written traditions and influenced the oral traditions of medieval Europe, especially from the thirteenth century forward, as the Latin tales were translated into European vernaculars.

The *Roman de Renart*

The animal tales of medieval written tradition are most richly represented by the vast and complex literature centered around the figure of Reynard the Fox.

Questions concerning the relationship between oral folk tradition and the *Roman de Renart,* as well as the *Roman's* sources of inspiration in general, have given rise to violent scholarly disputes. It is now clear that the animal tales written in Latin in poetic form by clerics and monks had a decisive influence. The earliest of these, "Ecbasis captivi" (The Escape of a Captive, written in 937), depicts animals and scenes later found in the *Roman de Renart.* Two centuries later appears *Ysengrimus,* a long satirical poem by the monk Nivard of Ghent (1149) and a direct precursor of *Renart. Ysengrimus* portrays the exploits of the fox Reinardus and his sustained feud with the wolf Ysengrimus; this is the earliest work in which animals are given personal names. In content and structure *Ysengrimus* displays strong similarities with the later *Renart.* For example, *Ysengrimus* contains a sequence of four episodes that would later appear, in the exact same order, in the earliest branch of the Renart cycle (branch II): Renart and the cock, Renart and the titmouse (though the role of titmouse is filled by a cock in *Ysengrimus*), Renart's insult of Isengrin's cubs, and his rape of Isengrin's wife.

These early animal epics in the form of Latin poetry are themselves inspired by Aesopian fables, but they are amply developed and are given an ecclesiastic twist through such features as the wolf dressed as priest, which was a widespread religious topos in the Middle Ages.

Although undeniably influenced by the *Ysengrimus*, the *Roman de Renart* displays some distinctive innovations. Written in the vernacular, it appeals to a much larger audience, more interested in laughter than in philosophical and moral speculations. Plot and characters are no longer confined to monastic life.

Roman de Renart is not a unified work. Rather, it is a cycle of independent poems in the French vernacular, centered around the trickster figure of Reynard the Fox. These poems, called "branches," were composed at different times by different authors, most of them anonymous. Sometimes they relate a single episode, and sometimes a string of episodes. Although they sometimes refer to each other, these poems were meant to be read independently and therefore often overlap or contradict each other. The numerical order of the branches established by Ernest Martin in the 1880s is still used by scholars for practical purposes, although it differs both from the chronology of the events in the narration and from the presumed chronology of their writing.

As early as the thirteenth century copyists tried to assemble the branches into comprehensive collections. Three different collections survive from the Middle Ages, none of which contains all 28 of the branches identified by scholars today. The choice of branches and their order of appearance are also different in the three collections. Furthermore, even the total of 28 branches is misleading because some branches (e.g., V) have been subdivided into subbranches a and b, each of which may be counted as a separate branch.

In a scene reminiscent of the Roman de Renart *and Chaucer's "Nun's Priest's Tale," a woman watches as a fox runs off with a rooster in its jaws. (Walters Art Gallery, MS 88, fol. 155r)*

The earliest 6 branches were written between 1174 and 1178, another 12 between 1178 and 1205, and yet another 12 between 1225 and 1250. These three groups total about 25,000 lines.

The earliest six branches (II–Va, III, V, XV, IV, XIV) constitute the sections of the *Roman de Renart* that most strongly parallel the tales of oral folk tradition. In branches II and Va, the oldest poem of the *Roman* (1174–1177), written by a cleric, Pierre de Saint-Cloud, Renart catches the cock Chantecler by inducing him to crow with his eyes closed; Renart leaps and seizes the cock in his jaws (AT 61). Chantecler escapes by persuading Renart to talk and taking advantage of the situation to fly out of the fox's mouth (AT 6). Defeated by the cock, the fox then tries to beguile the titmouse into closing his eyes and kissing him, claiming that King Noble, the lion, has ordered peace among all animals. Suspicious, the titmouse touches Renart with a twig, and the fox snaps at it. The titmouse escapes unharmed (AT 62, "Peace among Animals"). Renart, pretending to make friends with Tibert the cat, proposes that the two run a race; Renart's plan is to steer Tibert into a trap, a pit dug in the path by a peasant; Tibert sees the pit and swerves just in time, but eventually steers Renart into it (AT 30). Renart flatters Tiecelin the raven into singing. Tiecelin drops his cheese and Renart gets hold of it (AT 57). The poem then turns to the origin of the mortal feud that opposes Renart and Isengrin the wolf. One day Renart finds himself by accident in the wolf's den, and Hersent, Isengrin's wife, makes advances to him. Renart embraces her, but fearing the return of Isengrin, he soon leaves, after having stolen her food and insulted her cubs. The cubs reveal their mother's behavior to their father. Isengrin forces Hersent to help him catch Renart. Renart flees to his den. Isengrin and Hersent pursue him with such speed that Hersent gets trapped, with her head in the den and her hindquarters outside. Renart goes out through another entrance and rapes her, while insulting Isengrin, who is witness to the scene.

In branch III Renart plays dead on the road. A peasant takes him up and throws him in his wagon, which is full of eels, and Renart throws them one by one out of the wagon (AT 1, "The Theft of Fish"). Isengrin, pursued by dogs, takes refuge in a monastery and puts on monk's robes. Renart induces him to catch fish with his tail through a hole in the ice. The wolf's tail freezes fast, and when he is attacked and tries to escape, he loses his tail (AT 2, "The Tail-Fisher").

In branch V Renart helps Isengrin steal a ham, but the wolf tricks him and eats it alone. Renart tries in vain to eat the cricket. In branch XV Renart and Tibert the cat find a sausage. Tibert tricks Renart into letting him carry it, climbs up a cross, and eats the sausage alone. In branch IV (written in 1178), Renart dives in the well of the monastery, mistaking his reflection for his wife Hermeline (AT 34). When Isengrin arrives, Renart pretends that he is in heaven, inducing Isengrin to descend into the well in one bucket, thus bringing Renart up in the other one (AT 32). Branch XIV (written in 1178) features Renart and Tibert in the cellar (AT 41); Renart plays tricks on Primaut, a wolf whose adventures are very similar to those of Isengrin.

After 1178 the poems of the cycle diverge substantially from oral traditional animal tales and take on themes related to professional life and upper-class society. Branch I (1179) is devoted to the trial of Renart; branch VI (1190) to his duel with Isengrin and his becoming a monk; branch XII (1190) to Renart and Tibert in the cloister; branch VIII (1190) to Renart's pilgrimage; and branch Ia (1190–1195) to the siege of Renart's den Maupertuis. In branch Ib (1195) Renart becomes a *jongleur*; in branch VII (1195–1200) Renart confesses; in branch XI (1196–1200) he becomes emperor. Branch IX (1200) presents Renart, the peasant, and the bear; branch XVI, Renart's will; and branch XVII (1205), Renart's death and burial.

Characters in the *Roman de Renart*, especially in the earlier branches, are described as both humans and animals. Renart is a seigneur who owns a fortified castle, Maupertuis, and a fief and who fights a duel with Isengrin. The society around him is a close reflection of the feudal world of the twelfth century. Yet he has to crawl on four legs through the kitchen garden in order to catch a chicken. The other protagonists, too, have their traditional animal characteristics: Brun the bear is clumsy and greedy; Tibert the cat is agile, fastidious, and hypocritical; Chantecler the cock vain and protective; and Bernart the donkey immensely credulous and silly. This does not apply to the female protagonists, however. Queen Fiere, the lioness, is as noble and beautiful as a queen in an Arthurian romance, Renart's wife Hermeline appears largely in the role of devoted wife and mother, Isengrin's wife Hersent is as sensuous and unfaithful as the wives in fabliaux—but these traits do not reflect the characteristics of their animal species in folk tradition.

From its very beginning the *Roman de Renart* displays both a comical and a satirical aspect. The balance between these two aspects changes progressively, from the more comical to the more satirical. The earliest branches, closer to folklore, introduce a strong parodic element alongside the simple comedy of traditional animal tales. Writers of the *Roman de Renart* continually parody the scenes and rhetorics of courtly literature, chansons de geste, legal procedures, and other realms of refined aristocratic and ecclesiastical life.

The *Roman de Renart* has had many continuations, new poems that can be considered as new branches in a way, but whose style and purpose infuse the figure of Renart and his adventures with more and more satire and less overt comedy. The characters also become increasingly anthropomorphic. In *Renart le bestourné* (1261), Rutebeuf delivers a violent attack on friars, as does the anonymous poem *Le couronnement de Renart* (1263–1270). *Renart le nouvel* (1289), by Jacquemart Gielée, is a long allegoric and didactic poem, a prose adaptation often copied and published in the course of the following 300 years. New branches are composed in the fourteenth century. The anonymous *Roman de Renart le contrefait* (1319–1342) is an enormous work of encyclopedic knowledge.

The first six branches of the *Roman de Renart* inspired *Reinhart Fuchs*, written about 1190 in Alsatian, a German dialect, by Heinrich le Glichezâre. A new branch of *Renart* developed in Italy: *Rainardo e Lisengrino*, written in Franco-Italian dialect in the thirteenth century.

English-language versions of the Renart tales are relatively rare before the fifteenth century. The short thirteenth-century poem "The Fox and the Wolf" relates the story of Renart and Isengrin in the well. Renart next appears in the last years of the fourteenth century in Chaucer's "Nun's Priest's Tale," a free adaptation of the episode of Renart and Chantecler the cock.

King Noble, the lion, sits by as Renart pursues his sexual appetites. From a thirteenth-century manuscript of Renart le nouvel. *(Reproduced from Kathryn Gravdal,* Ravishing Maidens: Writing Rape in Medieval French Literature and Law, *Philadelphia, 1991)*

The popularity and diffusion of the *Roman de Renart* has been especially strong in the countries north of France. The Flemish poem *Reinaert de Voes* (c. 1250), which combines and translates several French branches, inspired a prose adaptation in Dutch (published 1479). The Dutch versions was in turn translated into English by Caxton under the title of *History of Raynard the Fox* (1481) and became the source of a number of German and Scandinavian translations and reworkings in subsequent centuries, even serving as the main source of inspiration of Goethe's *Reinecke Fuchs*.

Numerous allusions in chansons de geste, fabliaux, and other literary works testify that by the twelfth century all classes of society were already very familiar with the tales of Renart. A verse in Gautier de Coincy's *Miracles de Notre-Dame* implies that scenes from the Renart epic were painted even in priests' houses (Pocquet ed., col. 59, vers. 168–172). The extraordinary popularity of the animal epic created around the figure of the trickster fox is perhaps best attested by the fact that since the thirteenth century the personal name of the protagonist, *Renart* (adapted from the German name *Raginhard*, "He who wins through cunning"), has replaced *goupil* to mean "fox" in the French language—and has become the basis of another French word, *renardie* (hypocrisy or craftiness).

Renart the trickster is cruel, unscrupulous, vicious by inclination as much as by necessity, and, above all, cunning. Originating partly in the animal tales of medieval folklore, but mostly in the learned Latin animal poems written by clerics influenced by the fables of Phaedrus, the *Roman de Renart* and its continuations have become the most powerful expression of the satiric spirit of the Middle Ages. Progressively, the trickster figure of Reynard the Fox becomes the symbol of cunning and of hypocrisy, two aspects of evil, one of the major preoccupations of medieval culture.

See also: Bestiary; Exemplum; Fable; Marie de France; Trickster

References and further reading: The text of *Ysengrimus* has been translated into German by A. Schoenfelder, *Isengrimus, das mittelalterliche Tierepos aus dem Lateinischen verdeutscht* (1955), and into French, together with a commentary, by E. Charbonnier, *Recherches sur l'Ysengrimus: Traduction et étude littéraire* (1983). E. Martin's edition, *Le Roman de Renart*, 3 vols. (1882–1887), established the tradition of dividing the *Roman* into branches indicating their independent origins, and his system is still in use today. J. Dufournet, *Le Roman de Renart* (1985), provides a new edition of the texts together with a translation into modern French. An English translation is provided by P. Terry, *Renard the Fox* (1984). Marie de France's *Fables* have been translated into English several times, by J. Beer, *Medieval Fables* (1981); M. L. Martin, *The Fables of Marie de France: An English Translation* (1984), which supplies the original French with English prose translations; and H. Spiegel, *Marie de France: Fables* (1987), which provides a facing-page English verse translation for the French original. E. B. Ham's edition of Rutebeuf's *Renart le bestorné*, University of Michigan Contributions in Modern Philology no. 9 (1947), must be completed with the corrections offered by E. Faral in his review in *Romania* 70 (1949). "The Fox and the Wolf" appears in many editions, notably J. A. W. Bennett and G. V. Smithers, eds., *Early Middle English Verse and Prose* (1968). See also E. Arber, ed., *The History of Reynard the Fox,* translated and printed by William Caxton (1842). The preferred edition of and most exhaustive commentary on Chaucer's "Nun's Priest's Tale" is D. Pearsall, *Chaucer, The Nun's Priest's Tale,* Variorum Edition of the works of Geoffrey Chaucer, vol. 9, part 9 (1983). K. Sisam, ed., *The Nun's Priest's Tale* (1927), makes Chaucer's tale available in modern English.

M.-L. Tenèze, *Le conte populaire français: Catalogue raisonné*, vol. 3: *Contes d'animaux: Introduction* (1976), provides a most rigorous analysis of animal tales as a folklore genre. K. Krohn's "Bär (Wolf) und Fuchs: Eine nordische Tiermärchenkette," *Journal de la Société finno-ougrienne* 6 (1889), maps the elaboration and dissemination of the bear (fox)/wolf folktale chains throughout Europe. L. Sudre, *Les sources du Roman de Renart* (1893), provides interesting material about animal tales, although his views about the folkloric sources of the *Roman de Renart* have not been accepted since Foulet's refutation. L. Foulet's *Le Roman de Renart* (1914) still provides the definitive survey of the compositional history of the poem and argues convincingly for the predominance of learned sources over oral tradition. His viewpoint is partly contested by A. Graf, *Die Grundlagen des Reineke Fuchs,* Folklore Fellows Communications 38 (1920). J. Flinn, *Le Roman de Renart dans la littérature française et dans les littératures étrangères du moyen âge* (1963), provides a very thorough survey of all the texts, adaptations, and translations that spread the fame of the *Roman de Renart* throughout medieval Europe. H.-R. Jauss, *Untersuchungen zur mittelalterlichen Tierepik* (1959), delineates traces of oral performance poetry and written poetry in the French and the German/Flemish *Renart* texts. The anthology volume *Aspects of the Medieval Animal Epic,* Mediaevalia Lovaniensia, series 1, studia 3 (1975), provides a number of more specialized studies, noteworthy among which are G. Van Dievoet, "Le *Roman de Renart* et *Van den Vos Reynaerde*: Témoins fidèles de la procédure pénale aux XIIe et XIIIe siècles?" and O. Jodogne, "L'anthropomorphisme croissant dans le *Roman de Renart*." E. Suomela, *Les structures narratives dans le Roman de Renart* (1981), compares *Ysengrimus* and the *Roman de Renart* in the light of modern narratology. K. Gravdal,

Ravishing Maidens: Writing Rape in Medieval French Literature and Law (1991), studies the remarkable correspondences between Renart's rape trial and the judicial conflicts of the twelfth and thirteenth centuries. K. Varty, *Reynard the Fox: A Study of the Fox in Medieval English Art* (1967), provides an interesting survey of the visual dimensions of the Renart story in medieval culture.

—*Michèle Simonsen*

Anne, Saint

According to ancient and medieval legend, the mother of the Virgin Mary, and therefore grandmother of Jesus.

Although she is not mentioned in the New Testament, St. Anne and her husband St. Joachim are named as the parents of the Virgin Mary in the second-century apocryphal Gospel of James, also known as the Protevangelium, or Earlier Gospel, since it treats of events before the Virgin Mary's conception and the birth of Jesus as related in the canonical gospels. According to the Gospel of James, Joachim and Anne were unable to have children, and he retreated to the wilderness until receiving a sign from God, while Anne remained at home singing songs of sorrow and praying. Both were subsequently visited by angels declaring God's favor, and when Joachim hurried home he was embraced by his wife Anne, who told him she was to become pregnant through a miracle. After Mary is born Anne takes her to her room, which she has made into a kind of sanctuary, where she nurses and cares for her until the child's presentation in the temple a year later; Mary spends another two years in Anne's sanctuary before her parents place her as a virgin in the temple at age three.

No doubt aided by the developing devotion to the Virgin Mary, Anne herself came to be venerated as a saint in the early Church. Justinian had a church built for her in Constantinople, and by the tenth century a feast honoring her miraculous conception was being celebrated in Naples. The practice soon spread to northern Europe. She continues to be venerated in parts of Europe and Canada.

In medieval Italy she was revered by embroiderers, who kept her feast day under penalty of seeing their labor destroyed, a practice also followed by washerwomen. She was the great intercessor for women in childbirth, but she has also been a patron to woodworkers, seamstresses, and seafarers; Hugh of Lincoln became her devotee while threatened by a storm at sea. According to the *trinubium* tradition, Anne was married subsequently to Cleophas and Salome after Joachim, a tradition criticized by some Church Fathers but accepted by Peter Lombard and Guillaume Durand. She thus gave birth to holy progeny, including the two other Marys, Mary Jacobus and Mary Salome; and from them, to James the Lesser and the Greater, John the Evangelist, Simon, and Jude, all offshoots of one sacred tree of which Anne was the root. This tradition also gained wide circulation because it was related in Jacobus de Voragine's immensely popular *The Golden Legend* (c. 1260).

Her position in folk religion derives from a variety of symbolic associations, including verbal plays and the Latin meanings of her name, linking her to the year (*annus*) and thus to the figure of Anna Perenna (who personified the year in Roman popular tradition) and, in a pun on the French word *ane*, to a humble beast, the ass.

Her legend was widely known through the Middle Ages in several traditions focusing on her belatedly fertile marriage to Joachim. A unique French text, the *Romanz de Saint Fanuel et de Sainte Anne et de Nostre Dame et de Nostre Seigneur et de ses Apostres* (Romance of St. Fanuel, St. Anne, and Our Lady and Our Lord and His Apostles), which is extant in eight different manuscripts and alluded to indirectly in Wace's poem *The Conception of Our Lady*, tells us that she was not "engendered by a man" and had no mother but, rather, was carried in the thigh of a holy man, Fanuel, and "impregnated" after he wiped the juice of apples endowed with curative power on it. Anne, the girl born of this wonder, was exposed in an empty eagle's nest, where she grew up and whence she instructed the king's seneschal, Joachim, to spare the deer he was about to strike, so impressing him that he married her.

St. Anne was invoked by woodworkers, especially joiners and turners, and one of the lead tokens used by guilds and societies represents her instructing the Virgin in reading on one side (a characteristic feature of the medieval iconography of St. Anne) and with the compass and other measuring instruments on the other. This association has been variously ascribed to the profession of her son-in-law Joseph or to the notion that she made the first true tabernacle.

She was also associated with the grapevine from the time of John Damascene who wrote of her bringing forth a fertile vine, producing a delicious grape, and this power is also invoked in the litanies of the church of Apt, which claimed to have Anne's relics from the time of Charlemagne.

She was also credited with many healing and curative powers. They appear in a list compiled by the German monk Johannes Trithemius in the sixteenth century. Besides those mentioned, she cured melancholics, protected those among enemies or thieves, guarded against sudden death and assisted the dying, and was invoked against plagues. Water consecrated to St. Anne's worship held a wonderful healing value in France, Italy, England, and Germany: it lessened fevers and helped parturients and those who had lost their minds. Finally, in many parts of France she was associated with wells and springs and consequently with the regulation of drought.

See also: Saints, Cults of the; Virgin Mary
References and further reading: For the treatment of St. Anne in history and iconography, see K. Ashley and P. Sheingorn, eds., *Interpreting Cultural Symbols: Saint Anne in Late Medieval Society* (1990), especially F. Canadé Sautman, "Saint Anne in Folk Tradition: Late Medieval France," for a detailed discussion of St. Anne in folklore, and G. M. Gibson, "Saint Anne and the Religion of Childbed: Some East Anglian Texts and Talismans."

—*Francesca Canadé Sautman*

Annwfn [Annwn]

The otherworld in Welsh mythology and folklore, probably either *an-* (intensive prefix) and *dwfn* (deep), thus "very deep," or *an-* (negative) and *dwfn* (world), thus "not world."

Annwfn is sometimes located across the sea, and both real offshore islands and unspecified islands are portrayed as the otherworld. For example, in the Four Branches of the Mabinogi, Gwales (an island now called Grassholm off the Pembrokeshire coast), where time stands still, is the scene of an extended sojourn of feasting and pleasure, while in an early poem in the Book of Taliesin, "Preiddau Annwfn" (The Spoils of Annwfn), the otherworld is an unnamed island (unless Ynys Wair, now Lundy Island in the Bristol Channel, is intended). In this poem Arthur leads an expedition to the otherworld to win a treasure and to rescue a prisoner. "Three shiploads we went; save seven none returned" from this expedition to the island, which is given a number of descriptive titles: Fortress of Intoxication, Four-Cornered Fortress, Glass Fortress (a title that recalls an account in the *Historia Brittonum* [History of the Britons] of a raid upon a glass tower in the ocean from which only one shipload escaped). In other sources Annwfn is contiguous with this world, and the passage from one to the other is analogous to traveling from familiar to unfamiliar territory, becoming lost. Thus, in the First of the Four Branches of the Mabinogi, during the course of a hunt near his own court Pwyll becomes separated from his friends; he encounters the king of Annwfn and accompanies him to the otherworld. This appears to be a feature transmitted to Arthurian romance, in which hunts and journeys through forests are frequently the prologues to magical encounters. Mounds are often liminal areas where the boundaries between the two worlds become blurred. For example, the Mound of Arberth in the Four Branches of the Mabinogi is a place where mortals encounter otherworldly persons. Peredur meets an otherworldly lady who directs his journey and whom he "marries" at a mound. The magical properties of other hills are recorded in Welsh folklore: Crug Mawr (Cardiganshire), Cadair Idris (Meirionethshire), Glastonbury Tor. Though there is no suggestion that Annwfn may be entered through such hills or mounds, it is nevertheless frequently regarded as being underground and may be entered through caves, lakes, bogs, or other orifices.

All these locations—islands, unfamiliar territory, underground dwellings—have been considered the homes of the fairies throughout medieval and into modern Welsh folklore. In west Wales the "Children of Rhys Ddwfn" was a name for the fairies whose home consisted of islands lying a short distance off the coast of Pembrokeshire. Gerald of Wales recounts the sojourn of a man named Elidyr in fairyland, a delightful land of meadows and woods that he reached through a dark underground tunnel. Stories of fairy rings and fairy dances are common throughout Wales, and a number of late-medieval poems have as their theme tales of travelers becoming lost in the marshes and bogs of the Welsh hills and of being led astray by the fairies.

Annwfn is usually conceived of as a single kingdom, subject to the same tensions as this world. In the First of the Four Branches of the Mabinogi, although Arawn, head of Annwfn, is king of Annwfn, he is, nevertheless, challenged by Hafgan, "a king in Annwfn," presumably a *subregulus*, if, indeed, such strictly realistic approaches to this type of story are appropriate. There are other references in Welsh to the head of Annwfn (*Pen Annwfn*); however, this title is not always applied to the same figure.

Annwfn is not the world of the dead. In a poem in the Book of Taliesin the otherworld is portrayed as a land of feasting and never-ending pleasure, a place whose inhabitants are harmed by neither plague nor age. The same concept underlies the story of Arthur's passing to the Isle of Avalon to be healed of his wounds after his last battle. The timeless feast at Gwales is typical of views of Annwfn and is reflected in the sixteenth-century *Life of St. Collen,* when the saint ascends Glastonbury Tor to meet Gwynn ap Nudd, "king of Annwfn and the fairies." He finds awaiting him the fairest castle he has ever seen, the finest retinues of courtiers and musicians to welcome him, and the most luxurious table imaginable. Annwfn became equated with hell, and its people with devils (as is made clear in references in the story *Culhwch and Olwen*), and Collen, recognizing the illusion that was intended to ensnare him, sprinkled holy water over all, causing the castle and its folk to disappear.

See also: Celtic Mythology; Gerald of Wales; Gwynn ap Nudd; *Mabinogi;* Peredur, Son of Efrawg; Taliesin
References and further reading: P. Mac Cana, *Celtic Mythology* (1970); J. Rhŷs, *Celtic Folklore* (1901); R. S. Loomis, *Wales and the Arthurian Legend* (1956); P. Sims-Williams, "Some Celtic Otherworld Terms," in *Celtic Language, Celtic Culture,* ed. A. T. E. Matonis and D. F. Melia (1990).

—*Brynley F. Roberts*

Apollonius of Tyre

A classical romance that remained popular throughout the Middle Ages and Renaissance; also, the first romance in English.

Apollonius of Tyre probably derives from Hellenistic times, since the names of the characters and settings are from Greece and Anatolia. The first Latin reference to this work is in the *Carmina* of Venantius Fortunatus (written c. 566–568). Fortunatus compares his wanderings with those of Apollonius. The earliest surviving version is the Latin prose *Historia Apollonii Regis Tyri* (Story of Apollonius, King of Tyre) in ninth-century manuscripts. There are numerous medieval Latin versions, including a brief poem in the *Carmina Burana* (1230–1250) and a version in the fourteenth-century *Gesta Romanorum* (Deeds of the Romans), and there are translations and adaptations in almost all the European vernaculars, including Hungarian. The most famous Renaissance retelling of *Apollonius* is Shakespeare's *Pericles* (1607), and T. S. Eliot's "Marina" is a modern version.

The earliest English version is a fragmentary eleventh-century Old English prose work. This version and a 1,737-line version in John Gower's *Confessio Amantis* (The Lover's Confession) are of the greatest interest to students of the English Middle Ages.

Apollonius is a story that deals with the trials and triumphs of virtuous love. The story begins in folktale fashion, *"Fuit quidam ..."* [There was once ...]. The cruel king Antiochus of Antioch is living incestuously with his beautiful daughter and putting all her suitors to death. Apollonius discovers the father-daughter incest, and Antiochus tries to assassinate him. Apollonius flees to sea and is shipwrecked in Cyrene, where he marries the daughter of King Architrates.

On their voyage home, the young wife gives birth to a daughter during a tempest and apparently dies. Her body is placed in a coffin and thrown overboard, but it washes ashore near Ephesus. She is revived by a physician and placed in the temple of Artemis. Apollonius entrusts his infant daughter to foster parents in Tarsus and returns to Tyre. His daughter, Tharsia, grows up beautiful and accomplished and incites the hatred of her foster parents, who decide to kill her. She is kidnapped instead by pirates, who sell her to a brothel keeper in Mytilene. She manages to preserve her virginity. When Apollonius returns to Tarsus 14 years after he left his daughter there, he is told that Tharsia is dead and falls into a deep despair. He puts out to sea, and a tempest drives the ship to Mytilene. Apollonius and Tharsia are reunited. Apollonius is instructed in a dream to go to Ephesus, and in the temple of Artemis he meets his wife. The family is reunited and lives long and happily thereafter.

The Apollonius story is little discussed by modern scholars. The Old English version is found in a manuscript of Wulfstan's *Homilies* and copied by the same scribe. This version of *Apollonius* is the first romance in English. This preeminence is especially noteworthy because Old English prose otherwise consists of chronicles, homilies, and documentary materials. The presence of this romance amid such disparate genres suggests that the taste for literature of entertainment including wonders and sensationalism existed before the conquest as well as after. There seem to be relatively few connections between the story of Apollonius and Old English poetry such as *Beowulf*. As a hero, Beowulf, always eager for confrontation, diverges sharply from Apollonius, who flees in disguise.

Apollonius contains interesting threads common to both the Old and Middle English periods (e.g., love between members of the upper classes of the kind popularized by the romances of Chrétien de Troyes). The Old English *Apollonius* has more in common with Gower's version in the *Confessio amantis* than with most other works in Old English literature.

Gower's narrative "The Tale of Apollinus" is little discussed. The tale occupies most of the *Confessio*'s Book 8, which is devoted to the laws of marriage and includes three stories of incest as prologue to the story of Antiochus: namely those of Caligula, Amon, and Lot. At the end of Book 8, Amans (the Lover) meets Venus for the second time and learns that his love cannot prosper because he is old. Although the tale of Apollonius is always structurally loose, Gower emphasizes parallels—especially those parallels concerning three father-daughter relationships between: Antiochus and his daughter; Archistrates and his daughter; Apollonius and Tharsia. The tale is related to the end of Book 8 primarily through its exploration of the theme of natural and unnatural love. It is related to the *Confessio* as a whole through its theme of love that unites passion and reason.

Like all Greek romances, *Apollonius of Tyre* includes many stock motifs, situations, and characters that are common in folk tradition: long voyages that reveal the sea as a metaphor for the transience of life; tempests; shipwrecks; pirates; wicked foster parents; prophetic dreams; separations and reunions; love affairs; virginity miraculously preserved. In one episode set in Cyrene, the shipwrecked Apollonius is befriended by a compassionate fisherman; this is a motif found in many Greek romances. A study of these elements both in the Latin *Apollonius* and in vernacular works would demonstrate the folklore roots behind the written medieval versions.

See also: *Confessio amantis;* Romance
References and further reading: The earliest Latin version is edited by G. A. A. Kortekaas, *Historia Apolonji Regis Tyri* (1984). The Old English version is edited by P. Goolden, *The Old English "Apollonius of Tyre"* (1958). John Gower's version is found in *The Works of John Gower*, vol. 3, ed. G. C. Macaulay (1901). A. H. Smyth provides summaries of all the vernacular versions of the story in *Shakespeare's* Pericles *and* Apollonius of Tyre: A Study in Comparative Literature (1898). There are few studies devoted to the Old English *Apollonius* except A. R. Riedinger's "The Englishing of Arcestrate: Woman in *Apollonius of Tyre*," in *New Readings on Women in Old English Literature*, ed. H. Damico and A. H. Olsen (1990), which contrasts Arcestrate (daughter of Archistrates) to the lady of heroic literature. In "John Gower's *Apollonius of Tyre: Confessio amantis*, Book VIII," *Southern Review* 15 (1982), P. Goddall discusses the structure of the tale. A. H. Olsen's "Literary Artistry and the Oral-Formulaic Tradition: The Case of Gower's 'Apollonius of Tyre,'" in *Comparative Research on Oral Traditions*, ed. J. M. Foley (1987), discusses the debt to oral-formulaic tradition in a tale by this seemingly most literate of poets.

—*Alexandra H. Olsen*

Arabic-Islamic Tradition

The folkloric culture of the peoples of the Islam-dominated Mediterranean and Middle Eastern regions.

The defining basis of Arabic-Islamic tradition resides in the religious concepts of Islam, which originated against the backdrop of Judaism and Christianity in pagan Arabia. As Islamic culture spread into regions beyond Arabia, it absorbed and integrated traditions of various origins, ranging from Greek and Persian antiquity to the North African Berber cultures.

History

When the Arabs entered the theater of international history at the beginning of the seventh century, the culture of the Arabian Peninsula was dominated by tribal structures. Pagan religion focused on a central sanctuary in Mecca, including the sacred black stone incorporated in the Kaaba as well as the holy well Zamzam that, according to tradition, was dug by Abraham. While essentially polytheistic, pre-Islamic Arabic paganism had developed a certain hierarchy of deities, founding a nucleus for the subsequent development of the strict Islamic monotheism. Popular religious practices included such elements as charms and divination exercised by various means, such as interpreting lines in the ground (geomancy) or marks on the shoulder blade of a sheep (scapulimancy). Belief in supernatural beings was widespread, particularly in the demonic beings known as jinn (source of the English "genie") often associated with desert wells, as well as the cannibal ʿifrît or ghûl (source of the English "ghoul").

The mission of the prophet Muhammad (d. 632) resulted in the propagation of the religion of Islam (*islâm*, "absolute submission") and the constitution of a new era, initiated by Muhammad's exodus (*hijra*) from Mecca to Medina in the year 621. The obligation to spread the new religion (*jihâd*, "holy war") soon became a unifying force, supplying to the Arabs an overwhelming military verve.

Tending trees in arid country, from a thirteenth-century Arabic manuscript. (Al-Qazwini, The Wonders of Creation, *BN MS Arabe 5847, fol. 138r)*

Arabic conquests in the first century of the new era included North Africa and Spain in the West and the Levantine, Mesopotamian, Caucasian, and Iranian territories in the East. In Western Europe the Islamic onslaught was only reversed by the battles at Tours and Poitiers in present-day France in the year 732. Even though the Christian rulers soon strove to regain the Andalusian territories *(reconquista)*, the last remaining Islamic kingdom in Granada was not conquered until 1492, when Isabella of Castile and Ferdinand of Aragon prevailed. Their conquest and the ensuing political stability also resulted in the release of organizational and financial resources that enabled Christopher Columbus to explore the Americas. Meanwhile, other Mediterranean regions, such as Sicily and Malta, had also experienced periods of Islamic domination. Moreover, in the course of the fourteenth through the sixteenth centuries, the eastern Mediterranean regions of Anatolia and the Balkans had been conquered by the Islamic Ottoman dynasty, whose progress toward central Europe was halted in 1683 when the Ottoman army was kept from conquering Vienna. In Palestine and the Levant, the Crusades (beginning in 1096) not only resulted in the temporary conquest of Jerusalem and the occupations of territories of the Holy Land (until 1291, when the last Christian fortress fell to Islam) but also served as a unique opportunity for cultural contact between the medieval European and Arabic-Islamic cultures.

Cultural Contacts

In terms of cultural heritage, Arabic-Islamic tradition is a sibling of Christian European traditions. In addition to translating, researching, discussing, and preserving ancient Greek scientific heritage, it also incorporated constituents of other cultures, such as of the partly hellenized Iranian tradition that in turn also drew on elements of Indo-Iranian origin. Thus, beyond exposing the West to its own distinct characteristics, Arabic-Islamic culture also served as the predominant vehicle for the preservation of previous cultural heritage and as a channel for transmitting knowledge of the ancient world to the West. Areas of cultural contact include military confrontations as well as commercial relationships and peaceful coexistence in a multicultural environment.

Notably, the Islamic dominion of Spain constituted a period of productive cultural contact. In an atmosphere of religious tolerance, Arabic scientific works were translated into Latin, often with the active cooperation of Jews converted to Christianity. Medieval trade relations resulted in numerous contacts that show traces of Eastern influence far beyond the obvious, even as far north as Iceland. Even warfare, though dominated by the perception of the Islamic enemy as brutish and bloodthirsty (consider, for example, the "Saracen" as portrayed in the *Chanson de Roland*), also contributed to transmitting notions of an educated and chivalrous cultural counterpart as exemplified in the noble Saladin (Salah ad-Din, ruled 1169–1193), founder of the Ayyubîd dynasty and legendary opponent of the English king Richard the Lion-Heart during the Third Crusade.

The knowledge passed on from or via the Arabs to medieval Europe predominantly relates to philosophy, the natural sciences (notably algebra, astronomy, and alchemy), medicine, geography, and architecture. Islamic artistic influences on Europe included love poetry and the concept of courtly love. Arabic-Islamic tradition possessed wandering poets and singers; whether these served as models for the European troubadour is a subject of some debate. The phenomenon of the English morris dance obviously relates to a tradition of Islamic Spain, the Andalusian *morisco*, or morris ("Moorish") dance, recorded as early as 1149. Above all, cultural contacts between the Arabic-Islamic cultural sphere and Christian Europe can be traced in numerous instances of narrative literature.

Popular Literature

The most influential of all works of narrative literature transmitted to the medieval West through Arabic-Islamic culture is the collection known by the name of its two protagonist jackals, *Kalila and Dimna*. Originating from the Indian *Panchatantra* (Five [Books of] Wisdom), the book was first brought to Persia by Burzoy, physician to the Achaemenid ruler Anosharvan (531–579). From a middle-Persian translation, now lost, Abu Muhammad ibn al Muqaffa͏ᶜ in the eighth century prepared an Arabic adaptation, which in turn was translated into Greek (eleventh century), Hebrew (early twelfth century), and Spanish (mid-thirteenth century). The Latin version, *Directorium vitae humanae* (Guide Book for Human Life), prepared about 1270 by the converted Jewish author John of Capua, became the source of a large number of translations into European vernacular languages.

Kalila and Dimna contains narratives that might best be termed instructive stories (exempla) or, since they often deal with animal characters, fables. The narratives are linked by a frame story that serves as an umbrella bringing together tales featuring various protagonists and dealing with various topics. In *Kalila and Dimna*, as in other similar works, the frame story consists of a conversation or dispute, in the course of which exemplary tales are employed by the opposing parties in order to illustrate their relevant points. Other influential Arabic-Islamic frame tales include the religious romance *Barlaam and Josaphat*, an adaptation of the Indian legend of Buddha, and the *Sindbâd-nâme/Syntipas*, an originally Persian collection of tales about the wiles of women, anonymously translated into Latin in the early twelfth century as *Historia septem sapientium* (History of the Seven Sages). In medieval Western literature the Eastern narrative device of the frame story appeared in a wide range of works, including Chaucer's *Canterbury Tales* and Boccaccio's *Decameron*. The *Disciplina clericalis* (Clerical Discipline), compiled in the early twelfth century by Petrus Alfonsi, a Spanish Jew converted to Christianity, draws heavily on material originating from Arabic-Islamic tradition. The *Disciplina clericalis* was the first European collection of short narratives and was highly influential in inaugurating a new genre in European literature.

While the above-mentioned collections exemplify scholarly, written tradition, there is evidence indicating that oral tradition also contributed much to the transmission of Arabic-Islamic popular narratives to the medieval West. The most famous of all Eastern frame tales is the *Thousand and One Nights*, commonly known as *The Arabian Nights*. It begins when King Shahzamân becomes aware of his wife's sexual infidelity, kills her, and travels to visit his brother Shahrayar. There, he remains depressed until by chance he notices that his brother's fate is by no means different. When both set out on a journey, they are forced to make love to a woman who is being kept by a demon in a chest; her

Dome of the Rock, Jerusalem, one of the holiest shrines in Islam, built circa 700. (Hanan Isachar/Corbis)

ability to seduce men even when guarded by a supernatural being demonstrates to the brothers the ultimate success of the wiles of women. Shahrayar subsequently decides to distrust women altogether, kills each of his wives after her wedding night, and is reformed only after Shahrazad manages to stay alive and win his trust with 1,001 nights of storytelling. The Italian authors Giovanni Sercambi (1348–1424) and Ludovico Ariosto (1474–1533) present evidence that some version of this frame story was known to medieval Italy. In Sercambi's *Novella d'Astolfo*, a king, made melancholic by his wife's infidelity, recovers after undergoing an adventure similar to that experienced by the two royal brothers Shahrayar and Shahzamân when they made love to the woman kept in the chest. The story of King Jocondo and his brother Astolfo being deceived by their respective wives in Ariosto's *Orlando furioso* (canto 28) is also reminiscent of the frame story of the *Thousand and One Nights*.

In medieval epics, particularly Wolfram von Eschenbach's *Parzival* and the anonymous travel romance *Herzog Ernst*, a number of narrative motifs from Arabic-Islamic tradition appear, of which the most popular ones are the magnetic mountain and the city of brass. Besides exempla, fables, märchen, and elements of chivalrous romance, even comic narratives can be shown to have been transmitted from Arabic-Islamic tradition via Latin versions to the West. A case in point is the work of Jacques de Vitry, who served as bishop of the Palestinian town of Acre between 1216 and 1227. His collections of sermons, particularly the *Sermones feriales et communes* (Holiday and Saint's-Day Sermons) and the *Sermones communes vel quotidiani* (Saint's-Day and Everyday Sermons), preserved in their original Latin, contain a number of short narratives of Arabic origin, such as the one about the peasant who fell unconscious when smelling roses but was revived by smelling dung. A number of Jacques de Vitry's anecdotes are introduced by the remark "*Audivi ...*" [I have heard ...], strongly suggesting that he relied on oral sources. The above anecdote in later European tradition appears in the genre of fabliaux (French humorous verse narratives) as *Le vilain mire* (The Peasant Doctor) and serves as a reminder that the fabliaux as well as other short medieval narrative genres might well contain elements retaining Arabic-Islamic influence.

Trade and diplomatic relations exerted great impact on the transmission of popular narratives, even in clerical circles, as demonstrated by the papal secretary Poggio Bracciolini's *Liber facetiarum* (Book of Comic Tales), compiled around 1450 and containing numerous anecdotes of Arabic-Islamic origin. A convincing example of the lasting impression of medieval Arabic jocular tradition is the fact that the Sephardic Jewish community expelled from Spain after the Christian conquest in 1492 and ultimately settling in the Balkans even today remembers the popular Arabian trickster character Juha under his original name.

See also: Crusades; Frame Tale; Harun al-Rashid; Hispanic Tradition; Jewish Tradition; *Seven Sages, The; Thousand and One Nights*

References and further reading: The comprehensive survey of contemporary Islamic popular belief published by R. Kriss and H. Kriss-Heinrich, *Volksglaube im Bereich des Islam*, 2 vols. (1960), is also very useful for understanding the traditions of earlier periods, for which B. Shoshan's *Popular Culture in Medieval Cairo* (1993) supplies a thorough, focused study.

Numerous aspects of the transmission of popular culture have been treated in the published proceedings of a number of international scholarly symposia, such as *Orientalische Kultur und europäisches Mittelalter* (Miscellanea Mediaevalia 17, 1985), *Die Begegnung des Westens mit dem Osten* (1993), *Kommunikation zwischen Orient und Okzident: Alltag und Sachkultur* (1994), and *The Arab Influence in Medieval Europe* (1994). Literature in general is the focus of M. R. Menocal's *The Arabic Role in Medieval Literary History* (1987), while E. L. Ranelagh's *The Past We Share* (1979) is still a useful introduction into the Middle Eastern ancestry of Western folk literature. Details concerning the context of the *Arabian Nights* are contained in R. Irwin's very readable companion, *The Arabian Nights* (1994). U. Marzolph's *Arabia ridens,* 2 vols. (1994), contains a chapter dealing extensively with the transmission of comic narratives. Arabic-Islamic popular literature is catalogued in H. El-Shamy's *Folk Traditions of the Arab World,* 2 vols. (1995), while M. C. Lyons, in his *The Arabian Epic,* 3 vols. (1995), supplies a comprehensive survey of the ten most representative epics in Arabic-Islamic tradition.

—Ulrich Marzolph

Arthur

Legendary British hero and king, savior of Britain during a turbulent period.

Arthur's story is historically linked with events following the Roman withdrawal from Britain around 410 C.E., but evidence concerning his very existence is scattered and contested. There clearly was never a historical King Arthur with a Round Table and a castle known as Camelot, but there may well have been one or many historical figures whose exploits provided the germ of the legend that was to develop.

Early Traditions

Early documents that could shed light on the genesis of the legend are scarce. Gildas, the sixth-century author of *De excidio et conquestu Britanniae* (On the Ruin and Conquest of Britain) discusses the Saxon invasion of Britain after the Roman departure and notes that those wars culminated in the "siege of Mount Badon," a battle that would later be attributed to Arthur. Gildas does not, however, mention Arthur by name, a fact that some scholars have taken as evidence of Arthur's nonexistence.

The first reference to Arthur may have been made around 600 C.E. in a Welsh composition titled *The Gododdin,* which praises a certain warrior but adds that "he was no Arthur." This reference, which may have been added to the work later, nevertheless demonstrates that Arthur was already reputed to be an extraordinary, if not legendary, military figure. His fame would grow steadily. In the ninth century, the *Historia Brittonum* (History of the Britons), perhaps by a Welsh cleric named Nennius, names Arthur and enumerates his major battles, but he is described not as a king but as a *dux bellorum* (war leader). Only in the twelfth century would he become *King* Arthur. It was at that time, with Geoffrey of Monmouth's *Historia regum Britanniae* (History of the Kings of Britain, c. 1138), that Arthur received for the first time a full biography that includes his conception, birth, youth, conquests, marriage, and an extended period of peace. From Geoffrey the legend of Arthur spread throughout Europe, and the king would quickly become a figure of romance and overt fiction. That is the King

Arthur we still know, but that status itself says nothing either for or against his historical existence.

Debates on Arthur's Life and Death

This last question—whether or not Arthur had actually lived—was often and hotly debated during the Middle Ages. Chroniclers disagreed with one another; Robert Mannyng of Brunne, John Hardyng, and other chroniclers accepted him, sometimes uncritically, as real, while others, like William of Newburgh, concluded that he was a creation of fiction or legend. Still others assumed that beneath an overlay of fanciful elaborations there was a kernel of truth. Among them was William of Malmesbury, who attested to his belief in Arthur's historicity by lamenting the fact that reality had been obscured or contaminated by so many fictional details.

Differences of opinion concerned not only Arthur's existence but also his character and the legitimacy of his rule. Geoffrey's *Historia* presented Arthur as an enemy of the Scots, and the Plantagenets in effect claimed Arthur as an English king. These developments presented a dilemma to Scottish chroniclers. Until the very late Middle Ages, most expressed admiration for Arthur, although John of Fordun, in his *Chronica gentis Scotorum* (Chronicle of the Scottish People, 1385), suggested that Scots (such as Gawain and Modred, or Mordred) and not Arthur should have occupied the throne. During the fifteenth century and beyond, many Scottish chroniclers (such as Hector Boece in 1527) dismissed or condemned Arthur as a corrupt and illegitimate ruler.

Debates concerning Arthur were influenced by historical events, most notably by the ostensible discovery at Glastonbury Abbey around 1191 of Arthur's body and that of his queen. Gerald of Wales (in his *De principes instructione*, 1193) tells us that Henry II, having learned from a Welsh bard the location of the bodies, informed the abbot, who before long ordered excavations in the abbey cemetery. Found were a large lead cross, whose inscription identified the spot as the grave of Arthur and his queen, and the remains of a man and a woman. It was concluded that the king had been discovered. The bodies were removed to a tomb before the altar in the abbey church, where they remained until the monasteries were dissolved during the sixteenth century. At that time they disappeared. The lead cross has also disappeared, although we have a 1607 drawing of it published in William Camden's *Britannia*.

Scholars have not agreed about the historical value of this discovery. Many, suspicious of motives—Glastonbury Abbey had burned in 1184 and needed money for rebuilding—have declared it a hoax intended to attract pilgrims and therefore income. Others have argued that the burial was clearly earlier than the twelfth century, though in the present state of our knowledge it is impossible to date it to the "Arthurian era" of post-Roman Britain.

In any event this discovery is important for several reasons. The English, Welsh, and Scottish rulers all had a stake in claiming the legendary Arthur as their own. The Plantagenets, as noted, were particularly intent on doing so, a fact that may account for Henry's privileged information about the grave. In the next century, after claiming Arthur's crown from the Welsh in 1278, Edward I held an elaborate ceremony at Glastonbury, during which the bodies were displayed as one might display the holiest of relics. The ceremony was an important effort by Edward to establish himself as Arthur's legitimate successor.

For legend and folklore, the importance of the 1191 discovery is that the grave, if authentic, would by definition shatter the belief in Arthur's return. From the early Middle Ages on, many believed that Arthur had not been killed but only gravely wounded and that he had been taken away (to a cave or to a place named Avalon, most frequently identified with Glastonbury). He would eventually return in the hour of Britain's greatest need. (Arthur is only one among a number of legendary figures around whom such beliefs coalesced; folk-lorists know the motif as culture hero's expected return, motif A580.) A narra-tive written by Hermann of Tournai in 1113 documents the belief, which must have existed much earlier. Hermann reported that during the course of a reli-gious observance, violence broke out because someone dared to contend that Arthur was really dead. The growing legend of Arthur's survival is attested as well by others, including William of Malmesbury, who in 1125 wrote in his *Gesta regum Anglorum* (Deeds of the Kings of England) that "Arthur's grave is nowhere beheld, so that ancient songs say that he is still to come." A great many writers rejected this element of the Arthurian story, and Caxton's version of Sir Thomas Malory's *Le Morte Darthur* (printed 1485) leaves the question open, but the notion of the "once and future king" persisted in literature and thrived in the popular imagination.

The death of Arthur, from William Copland's 1557 edition of Le Morte Darthur. *(British Library)*

The question of Arthur's existence or nonexistence did not diminish his appeal as a literary and legendary figure, either during the Middle Ages or since. Geoffrey's text was adapted into French by Wace in 1155 in his *Roman de Brut* (Romance of Brutus). Soon afterward the Arthurian court was transformed into the setting for courtly fiction. The greatest French author of romances, Chrétien de Troyes (fl. 1165–1191), set all five of his major works in an Arthurian context, but even as he made the Arthurian court into a powerful symbol of chivalric accomplishment he diminished the king himself. He remade Arthur into an often ineffectual and sometimes almost comical figure, though, paradoxically, a virtuous and respected one as well. (Some scholars have suggested that this transformation is the natural result of a French author writing of a British king.) In Chrétien Arthur is a secondary figure, and the romances center on particular knights of the Round Table—Lancelot, Yvain, Gauvain, Perceval, and others. Even in biographical (as opposed to episodic) romances, the same principle holds in part; in the French Lancelot-Grail cycle (c. 1215–1235) and in Sir Thomas Malory's *Le Morte Darthur* (c. 1470) the authors concentrate on Arthur until his kingdom is firmly established and then focus primarily on other knights and their adventures. Arthur thereafter remains an inspirational but often peripheral figure.

Arthur's Character and Popularity

Arthur's virtues, of which there were many, and his vices, which were generally considered few, vary from text to text. He is almost always presented as compassionate and generous. He is rarely wrathful, although the Middle English alliterative *Morte Arthure* (late fourteenth century) is a dramatic exception; nor is he a notably proud person, except when he is presented as a conqueror. He is generally faithful to his knights and to his queen, but there are glaring exceptions to the latter generalization. He lies with more than one woman besides his wife, and in some texts he cruelly rejects Guinevere in favor of the False Guinevere, an impostor. More commonly, though, even when he is required (by law, by his barons, or by his own judgment) to arrest or reject the queen, he does so with more sorrow than anger. The majority of authors after Chrétien follow him in presenting a spiritually imperfect king, and the French *Queste del saint Graal* (Quest for the Holy Grail, c. 1225) dramatizes the spiritual imperfection of Arthur and his court by emphasizing the superiority of the Grail ideal.

Yet it is apparent that the Arthur who maintained a strong hold on the popular imagination was the great, pious, generous, and compassionate king, not the weak, indecisive, and morally flawed figure. When Jacques de Longuyon (early fourteenth century) proposed a list of heroes to be respected and emulated, he included Arthur among them. He listed Nine Worthies: three pagans (Hector, Julius Caesar, and Alexander), three Christians (Charlemagne, Arthur, and Godfrey de Bouillon), and three Jews (Joshua, David, and Judas Maccabaeus). Here, despite his frequently ambiguous and occasionally negative depiction in literature, Arthur served as a symbol of glory, valor, and virtue, and the Nine Worthies (or often the Three Christian Worthies) were the frequent subjects of literary depictions as well as depictions in painting, tapestry, and other forms.

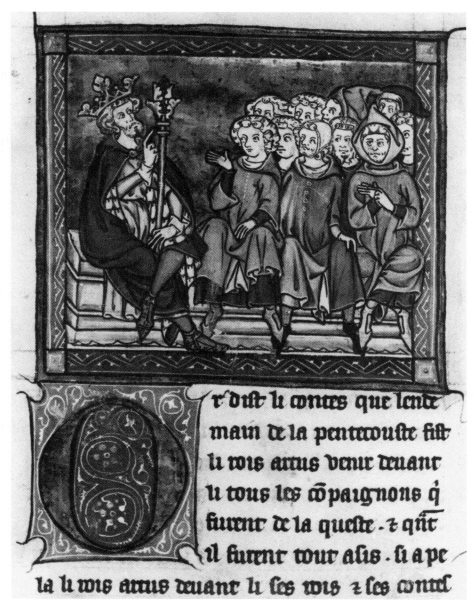

Arthur convokes the Grail questers. (Reproduced by courtesy of the Director and University Librarian, the John Rylands University Library of Manchester; French MS 1, fol. 114v)

Whatever the fact of Arthur's existence, his appeal was so strong that reality began to imitate legend, and beginning in the thirteenth century Arthurian enthusiasts organized chivalric pageants called "Round Tables." Including jousts, feasting, and other activities, these pageants often featured participants who assumed Arthurian names and coats of arms. In 1446 René d'Anjou even built an "Arthurian" castle for the event.

Theories of Origin

Given the enduring popularity of the legend, it is unsurprising that the search has continued for a historical Arthur or for the historical models around whom his legend coalesced. There have been theories of a northern Arthur, a Welsh Arthur, even occasionally a Continental Arthur. Among the theories that attempt to explain the genesis of the legend, two have received a good deal of attention in recent years. These two, which are not mutually exclusive, are the Riothamus theory and the "Sarmatian Connection."

The former, suggested as early as 1799, by Sharon Turner, has been developed most systematically by Geoffrey Ashe. The notion concerns "Riothamus" (the word *riothamus* is an honorific meaning "high" or "supreme king" rather than a proper name). Indeed, a British high king called Riothamus is known to have existed. He crossed the channel in 468 C.E. to conduct military operations against the Britons' enemies in Gaul, as Geoffrey of Monmouth's *Historia* tells us Arthur did. This Riothamus (who may be identifiable with one Lucius Artorius Castus) is the only Briton of his time who figures in Continental records. He thus may be either "Arthur" or, at least, the historical figure around whom the Arthurian legend crystallized.

The so-called Sarmatian Connection concerns horse nomads sent to Britain from Eastern Europe as auxiliaries for the Roman army. It is thought that their customs and beliefs may well have been merged with stories of an emerging hero to shape the Arthurian legend as we would come to know it. Among the striking connections with the Arthurian story are the symbolism of an upright naked sword (reminiscent of the sword in the stone), battle ensigns carrying the image of a dragon, and sacred cauldrons (perhaps related to the Grail) used in rituals.

Despite the appeal of these and other theories, the majority of scholars remain skeptical, and there are those who assert that the truth behind the Arthurian legend is unknowable. Thus far, that is correct.

See also: Arthurian Lore; Chrétien de Troyes; Geoffrey of Monmouth; Grail; Nine Worthies; Sleeping King

References and further reading: On all aspects of the Arthurian legend, from "The Arthur of History" by K. H. Jackson to "The Oral Diffusion of the Arthurian Legend" by R. S. Loomis and to studies of the major authors and texts, see R. S. Loomis, ed., *Arthurian Literature in the Middle Ages* (1959), still a standard and valuable resource, even though many of the chapters have been supplanted by more recent work. J. Morris, *The Age of Arthur* (1973), studies the "Arthurian period" itself and the origins of the legend; it is a useful but not entirely reliable guide to its subject and so must be consulted with caution.

For information about Arthurian origins and chronicles as well as the king's treatment in literature and art, see N. Lacy, ed., *The New Arthurian Encyclopedia*, updated ed. (1996); entries (by various authors) include "Arthur, Character of," "Arthur, Origins of Legend," "Chronicles, Arthur in," and "Chronicles, Scottish," as well as entries devoted to individual chroniclers and authors. R. Fletcher, in *The Arthurian Material in the Chronicles, Especially Those of Great Britain and France* (1906; rpt. 1966), offers excerpts and discussions of the chronicles related to Arthur. R. Bromwich, A. O. H. Jarman, and B. Roberts, eds., *The Arthur of the Welsh* (1991), is an essential contribution to our knowledge of the historical background and of Welsh Arthurian literature as well; see especially the valuable assessment of the chronicle material and historical documents by T. Charles-Edwards, "The Arthur of History."

R. Morris, in *The Character of King Arthur in Medieval Literature* (1982), offers a thorough account of Arthur's representation in British and Continental sources, ranging from the facts of his birth, reign, and death to his "Personal Attributes" (ch. 7). C. Dean's *Arthur of England: English Attitudes to King Arthur and the Knights of the Round Table in the*

Middle Ages and the Renaissance (1987) presents a full and perceptive account of the complexities of Arthur's reputation among the English.

The search for a historical Arthur is the subject of a vast literature, varying from impressive scholarly treatises to fanciful hypotheses. Among the skeptics concerning the subject is D. Dumville, who in "Sub-Roman Britain: History and Legend," *History* 62 (1977), offers a strong condemnation of most efforts up to that time to locate a reality behind the legend. However, his skepticism only temporarily interrupted such efforts, and in 1985 G. Ashe, in *The Discovery of King Arthur*, argued for Riothamus as the possible model for Arthur. The most recent refinements of the Sarmatian Connection are offered in C. S. Littleton and L. Malcor, *From Scythia to Camelot* (1994).

—*Norris J. Lacy*

Arthurian Lore

Traditional narratives and motifs, attitudes, and beliefs associated with Arthur, his court, and his followers.

The legend of Arthur was one of the most productive themes of medieval literature in Western Europe. Grounded in popular beliefs in the Celtic-speaking regions of Great and Little Britain—primarily Wales, Cornwall, and Brittany—Arthurian tales were adapted first by Norman, Anglo-Norman, and French authors and then by others, especially German and English. Arthurian lore is preserved mainly in literary narrative genres—histories, *vitae sanctorum* (saints' lives), prose and verse romances, poems—and its stories and episodes are therefore found at some remove from their primary oral forms.

Nevertheless, though the legend takes many forms in various cultural contexts, it has some salient features. There is a core Arthurian entourage and a number of characteristic types of adventure (hunts; quests; journeys to unknown regions; combats with monsters, giants, hags, or with other knights). There developed an Arthurian ethos of service and magnanimity centered upon Arthur's court. But the two themes that caught the imagination of writers and of their audiences (leaving aside the related but independent Merlin and Grail legends) were the abduction of Arthur's wife Guinevere and, especially, Arthur's final defeat, death, and prophesied return. These became the enduring features of the legend, which developed on the one hand into one of the great tragedies of world literature and on the other into a symbol of renewal and restoration.

Early Fragments of Legends

The earliest Arthurian texts derive from Wales and are written in Welsh or Latin. In these Arthur assumes a range of roles: he is variously termed hero, warrior, king, emperor, or simply leader. The ninth-century *Historia Brittonum* (History of the Britons), written in southeast Wales and often attributed to Nennius, has two stories of Arthur in a section describing some of the *mirabilia* (wonders) of Britain. Both seek to explain the names of features in the topography of south Wales, and it is possible that the Arthurian associations are secondary. One explains the name of a spring in present-day Herefordshire, Llygad Amr, "The Eye [i.e., fountain] of Amr [or Anir]," now Gamberhead, by identifying it as the spot where *Arthur miles* (Arthur the warrior) killed his own son Amr. Amr's grave, a tumulus, is nearby and cannot be accurately measured.

Although this son is named again in a later Welsh romance, he does not appear to be a traditional character, and he seems to have been created from the place name. In this instance, a common motif may simply have been given an Arthurian context.

The other wonder is Carn Cabal (now Corn Gaffallt), a stone atop a cairn above the Wye valley in Builth, which bears the footprint of Arthur's dog Cabal (Cafall, in modern Welsh orthography), impressed upon it during the hunt for the boar Porcum Troit. This familiar explanation of a peculiarly marked stone is linked to another common motif, for though the stone may be removed it always returns to its original location. The Arthurian association provides a more specific context. *Cafall* is Old Welsh for "horse," and as the name of Arthur's hound it reflects the gigantic size of the dog and, by implication, of its owner. These two stories are the earliest examples of a widespread element in Arthurian folklore, the use of Arthur's name to identify topographic features. In 1113 Hermann of Tournai noted Arthur's Chair and Arthur's Oven in the West country, and there are scores of later examples throughout Britain. Nevertheless, it cannot be assumed that every Arthur's Seat, Quoit, Bed, or Stone had an onomastic tale attached to it, though they are certainly evidence of the popularity and magnetism of Arthurian associations.

The Earliest Surviving Welsh Tales

The hunting of the boar Porcum Troit (named Twrch Trwyd or Trwyth, in Welsh) by Arthur and his men was, however, a well-established tale. It forms a major part of the eleventh-century Welsh story "How Culhwch Won Olwen" (*Culhwch and Olwen*). Twrch Trwyth is there said to have been a king transformed into a swine for his sins. Between his ears are the shears and comb that the hero Culhwch must obtain to shave his future father-in-law, the giant Ysbaddaden, before the wedding feast. The hunt takes Arthur, who is Culhwch's kinsman and helper, and his men from Ireland across south Wales to the Severn valley and thence along the Cornish peninsula until the boar is driven off the cliffs of Land's End and his magic implements snatched away. Hunts of magic animals, boars and stags especially, are frequent in Celtic legends, often as a means of leading the hero to an arranged tryst or enchantment, but the tale of Twrch Trwyth is of a boar hunted for its own enchantment and for the capture of magic talismans (though into this narrative have been interwoven a host of onomastic elements).

Culhwch and Olwen, the earliest extant Arthurian story, has other characteristic Arthurian episodes: journeys to free prisoners and to gain treasures; combats with monsters, giants, and witches—all in a magical, supernatural world. Although they have been brought together within a single narrative about winning the giant's daughter, no doubt many if not all of these adventures had an independent existence. In addition to the hunting of Twrch Trwyth (one of two boar hunts found in the tale), *Culhwch and Olwen* contains at least two other quests that belonged to earlier traditions: the first of these is the release of Mabon son of Modron, originally divine beings (the Maponos and Matrona whose names are found on Romano-British altars), from his prison in Caerloyw (which may mean "shining fortress"), in Gloucester. The second is the expedition to Ireland to win the cauldron of Diwrnach the Irishman. The two quests echo a ninth- or tenth-century Welsh poem "The Spoils of Annwfn," apparently spoken by the archetypal bard Taliesin. The poem recalls a disastrous expedition undertaken by Arthur, in his ship Prydwen, and two other shiploads of men to Annwfn, the Welsh otherworld—variously called here the Glass Fortress, the Fairy Fortress, and the Fortress of Intoxication—from which only seven men returned. The allusions to the features of the otherworld are similar to those found in early Irish literature, but the purpose of the voyage was to free a prisoner, Gweir, and to win the richly ornamented cauldron of the head of Annwfn; kindled by the breath of nine maidens, its peculiarity was that it would not "boil the meat of a coward." The same cauldron, now that of Dyrnwch the giant, is listed elsewhere as one of the 13 treasures of Britain, all of which appear to be, in origin, otherworld talismans. It seems likely that Diwrnach's cauldron in *Culhwch and Olwen* is another version of the same story, one that seems to have been a common type: of expeditions to win otherworld treasures—even if, in *Culhwch and Olwen*, Ireland has replaced Annwfn as the site of the cauldron. Taliesin is not usually one of Arthur's followers, but a number of other characters named in the list in *Culhwch and Olwen* reappear in another early dialogue poem in which Arthur, seeking entrance at the gate of a fort, is made to declare the worth of his men. What follows is a catalog of heroes and warriors—pride of place being given to Cai (Kay) and Bedwyr (Bedivere)—and a series of allusions to their exploits against human enemies and supernatural monsters and hags. Another poem describes the heroism of Emperor Arthur in a human battle. Even more allusive are references to Arthur in the Welsh Triads of the Island of Britain. The general outlines of the persona of Arthur remain unchanged, but there are hints of an extensive lost Arthurian literature.

Arthur in the Saints' Lives

Supernatural combats are portrayed in a negative way in some saints' lives of the twelfth century. In these renditions of combat in saints' lives, written in Latin but using Welsh and Breton traditions, Arthur, often *quidam tirranus* (a certain king), now fights but fails to slay dragons. He challenges his rivals, no longer giants but monks or hermits. No longer victorious, he is discomforted and ridiculed. He is not heroic but avaricious and jealous. The nature of the Arthurian adventure has not changed, but the narrator has; rather than a writer of heroic poetry, the author is a cleric presenting his story to reflect the viewpoints of the saints, Arthur's rivals from ecclesiastical folklore. The saint challenges Arthur to win not his kingdom but, rather, the loyalty of Arthur's followers; this he accomplishes by overcoming Arthur and all he stands for. In making Arthur the villain of choice, the authors are acknowledging his importance; in this inverted sense, the *vitae sanctorum* are evidence of the same Arthurian lore as the early Welsh poems and *Culhwch and Olwen*.

Most of these episodes may be no more than conventional composed stories in which Arthur fills the slot of the stereotyped villain, but the *Life of Gildas* (c. 1130), by Caradog of Llancarfan, has two episodes that appear to be genuine fragments of Arthurian lore. One concerns the long-standing enmity of Arthur and Hueil, Gildas's brother; this rivalry also appears in the writings of Gerald of Wales and survives as a Welsh folktale at least as old as the sixteenth century. The second is the earliest account of the abduction of Arthur's wife (called Guennuvar by Caradog and generally known as Gwenhwyfar in Welsh): Melwas, king of *aestiva regio* (the summer country), carries the queen to Glastonbury, which the author calls *Urbs Vitrea* (Glass City). After a year's search, Arthur learns that she is a captive in Glastonbury and besieges the city to win her back. Gildas intervenes to have Gwenhwyfar returned to Arthur peaceably. The fact that the hero saint outshines Arthur by restoring Gwenhwyfar without a fight demonstrates that this particular version of the story is steeped in clerical values. Yet the abduction theme recurs constantly in Arthurian literature: in an obscure Welsh dialogue poem, in the *Lancelot* of Chrétien de Troyes (where the abductor is Meleagant and the rescuer Lancelot, her lover), and in later romances.

Geoffrey and Other Twelfth-Century Treatments

In Geoffrey of Monmouth's *History of the Kings of Britain* (c. 1138), the queen's infidelity with Arthur's nephew Modred (in Welsh, Medrawd) and the latter's treachery are the cause of the final battle of Camlan, where Arthur is killed. Geoffrey created a potent mix of Welsh legend and tradition, classical and contemporary Latin writings, and creative imagination to present Arthur, the European emperor. Beneath this portrayal can be found some nuggets of genuine tradition: Arthur's sword Caliburnus (Excalibur), forged in the otherworld; Prydwen, his shield (not his ship, as in "The Spoils of Annwfn"); his wife and companions. Arthur fought the giant Ritho, who claimed his beard for his cloak of pelts (as Arthur had shaved the beard of Dillus in *Culhwch and Olwen*), and the obscene giant of Mont-Saint-Michel. Making Modred play the role of Melwas may be Geoffrey's error, and the battle of Camlan may not have been the result of any enmity between Arthur and Modred, but that the battle was the traumatic catastrophe of the Welsh Arthurian legend seems clear in the light of allusions found in the Triads, *Culhwch and Olwen*, and poetry. It became the focus for related incidents and developed its own group of traditions. Geoffrey claims that Arthur was taken to *Insula Avallonis* (the Isle of Avalon) to be healed of his wounds, a circumspect allusion to the belief in his eventual return. In his poem *The Life of Merlin*, Geoffrey developed the theme of Arthur's passing after Camlan, and his description of the "island of apples," ruled over by nine sisters who recall the nine maidens of the poem "The Spoils of Annwfn," and of the healing powers of Morgen, the chief of them, accurately reflects Irish and Welsh descriptions of the otherworld.

One of the Welsh "Stanzas of the Graves" (in the Black Book of Carmarthen) merely states that a grave for Arthur would be a wonder of the world, presumably because he had not died, but Geoffrey's contemporary William of Malmesbury, writing in 1125, is clearer, stating that "the grave of Arthur is nowhere to be seen, and that ancient songs prophesy his return," a belief that was given powerful expression when a near riot erupted in Bodmin, Cornwall, because some visiting monks were foolish enough to voice their doubts, according to the 1113 account given by Hermann of Tournai. Other twelfth-century writers, including Henry of Huntingdon, Gerald of Wales, and Étienne de Rouen, refer to this belief, which was to become the most abiding piece of Arthurian folklore. The earliest narratives of the king's survival, those of Geoffrey of Monmouth and Wace, tell of Arthur's passing to an otherworld island to be healed of his wounds and to await the hour and occasion of his messianic return. A more popular form of the theme is the cave legend of the sleeping lord. The earliest of these stories is related by Gervase of Tilbury in his *Otia imperialia* (Imperial Pastimes, c.1211), which locates the cave in Mount Etna, Sicily, but a sixteenth-century Welsh chronicler provides the earliest evidence locating the legend in Wales, at south Cadbury.

Romance Traditions

Some familiar Arthurian themes are found for the first time in French romances. Arthurian stories, and perhaps an Arthurian legend as a frame of reference and context for them, were clearly well established in early and medieval Britain, as the narratives and allusions found in Welsh and in Latin attest. Arthurian heroes, stories, and ambiance apparently had a particular appeal for Normans in England, Wales, and Brittany, and these were transmitted to the French and Anglo-Norman cultural environments where Arthurian romance, verse, and, later, prose flourished, but it cannot be assumed that either the plots or all the episodes contained in the romances have a Welsh or other Celtic origin or that anything more has been borrowed in many cases than a traditional Welsh or Breton personal name. Wace, in *Roman de Brut* (Chronicle of Brutus, 1155), is the first to refer to the Round Table, established to prevent discord over claims of precedence at court and about which "Britons tell many wondrous tales," he claims. No such tales, however, have survived.

Stories of Arthur's begetting and boyhood may have been an element in his legend, but the celebrated incident of the Sword in the Stone, whereby Arthur's claim to royal leadership is confirmed when he alone is able to withdraw a sword from a block of stone, occurs first in Robert de Boron's *Merlin* (early thirteenth century). But French Arthurian romance has types of tales that can be more easily paralleled in Celtic stories. The most common of these are the hunt of the white stag, the transformed hag, journeys to enchanted castles and forests, magic fountains and mists, quests for wondrous objects, and the wasteland. These "Arthurian commonplaces" derive from Celtic mythological themes that may or may not have been associated with Arthur in their native, primary forms but that were part of the totality of Brythonic narrative themes and motifs that together with Arthurian elements gave medieval Arthurian romance its particular flavor.

That Arthur and some close companions—Cai (Kay), Bedwyr (Bedivere), Gwalchmai (Gauvain, Gawain)—were popular folklore figures is clear. Stories about them can be retrieved, complete or in allusions. What is more debatable is whether this Arthurian lore was so many individual pieces or whether they existed within a legendary frame. Most Arthurian stories center on widespread motifs—combats, monsters, witches, and the like—and they are, therefore, movable. But the fixed elements—including the abduction and loss of Guinevere, the battle of Camlan, the death and return of Arthur, and an ethos of service found even in *Culhwch and Olwen* and the *Life of Cadoc*—suggest that one can refer to an early Arthurian legend. Whether any of this has a historical basis is irrelevant. Much of what is said of Arthur, even in the Latin chronicle texts, is expressed in terms that are recognizable as popular themes and motifs of myth and folktale.

See also: Annwfn; Arthur; Camlan; *Culhwch and Olwen*; Geoffrey of Monmouth; Gerald of Wales; Merlin; Myrddin; Nennius; Taliesin

References and further reading: The literature on Arthur and his legend is enormous and expands annually. Welsh Arthurian literature is fully discussed and extensive bibliographic references are provided in R. Bromwich, A. O. H. Jarman, and B. F. Roberts, eds., *The Arthur of the Welsh* (1992). The edition of *Culhwch and Olwen* (1992) by D. S. Evans and R. Bromwich has much information on the Arthurian episodes in the tale. R. Bromwich, *Trioedd Ynys Prydain*, 2nd ed. (1978), is the best encyclopedic guide to traditional elements in medieval Welsh narrative, but see also P. C. Bartrum, *A Welsh Classical Dictionary* (1993). For the saints' lives, see C. G. Loomis, "King Arthur and the Saints," *Speculum* 8 (1933). E. K. Chambers, *Arthur of Britain* (1927; rpt. with supplementary bibliography. 1969), is still useful for its discussions of folklore elements in the legend. L. A. Paton, *Fairy Mythology of the Arthurian Romances* (1903), is now rather dated. The relationship of episodes in French romance with earlier Celtic stories is a vexed question. R. S. Loomis, *Arthurian Tradition and Chrétien de Troyes* (1949), overstates the case, but R. Bromwich, "Celtic Elements in Arthurian Romance: A General Survey," in *The Legend of Arthur in the Middle Ages*, ed. P. B. Grout et al. (1983), is a well-balanced discussion. G. Ashe, *A Guidebook to Arthurian Britain* (1983), is a useful reference book to topographic legends.

—*Brynley F. Roberts*

Assassins Nizari Isma'ilis [Nizari Isma'ilis]

A medieval Shi'i Muslim sect known for their use of political assassination.

The Isma'ilis take their name from Muhammad ibn Isma'il (d. 760 C.E.), who, although he predeceased his father Ja'far al-Sadiq, was accepted by many as having achieved the high spiritual state of imam. The Nizari branch is named for Abu Mansur Nizar (d. 1095), a caliph of the Fatimid dynasty. The Isma'ilis inhabited many regions of the Middle East in the medieval period, but their authority was centered in Syria and Persia, which came under their control when Hasan-i Sabbah seized the Fortress of Alamut in 1090. Outnumbered by Sunni Muslims and beset by schisms, the Isma'ilis turned to political assassination in the Fatimid (909–1171) and post-Fatimid periods as a means of self-preservation. Training for these missions took place in secret, apparently in several of the fortresses controlled by the Nizaris, but the assassinations were often public and spectacular, inspiring many legends about the Nizaris and their leaders.

Contrary to European legend and history, most Nizari assassinations were directed at other Muslims, and the term *Assassin* derives from *hashishiyya*, first used to described the *fida'is* in the twelfth century. Although the term literally means "hashish user," it is now believed to have been used by other Muslims as a broad insult meaning "social outcast" or "irreligious." Persian Isma'ilis were rarely if ever referred to by this term; they were more commonly known as *mulhidun* (apostates). Nonetheless, *Assassin*, first used in a European chronicle by Burchard of Worms in 1175, became the common Western term for all Nizaris.

Legends concerning the Nizaris were not limited to Western traditions. Muslim legends also circulated, particularly in the twelfth and thirteenth centuries, when the Nizaris attained political prominence in Persia and Syria. Though the Nizaris were too few to undermine Sunni authority, their great influence led to exaggerated tales of their training and exploits. The Sunni legend tradition consisted of attributing all assassinations to Nizaris, thus magnifying the strength of the sect and its impact on the medieval Muslim political scene. As the Frankish crusaders came into contact with Muslims, stories of the efficient Assassins spread into European lore. Stories that they targeted Christians became more and more prevalent, and many deaths during the Crusades themselves were attributed to the Nizari Assassins.

Europeans, not able to understand the Shiʿi martyrology that would cause one to willingly sacrifice one's life in a murder attempt, created tales of young men trained as assassins in compounds where their minds were controlled by drugs. That addicts would be neither efficient nor effective as assassins was not considered as the legends were perpetuated both in oral tradition and in historical texts, such as that of Arnold of Lübeck (d. 1212). Western legend combined the Shiʿi belief that martyrs immediately entered Paradise and the Persian tradition of planting lavish gardens into images of hedonistic training centers where the drug-crazed young Assassins were deluded into believing that Paradise existed on earth and that if they completed their missions, they would be allowed to return to it.

Loyalty to the Nizari movement became in legend loyalty to a single leader, Rashid al-Din Sinan (d. 1192), also known as the Old Man of the Mountain. Henry of Champagne was purportedly treated to a demonstration in 1194, when the Old Man of the Mountain ordered his followers to commit suicide by leaping off the wall of his fortress. This story is believed to have been inspired by a late romance in which Alexander the Great intimidated an enemy by ordering troops to commit suicide. By the end of the thirteenth century the legend was widely accepted enough to be included in chronicles, and the loyalty of the Assassins was so renowned that Provençal troubadours adopted them as role models for lovers, who declared themselves to be as devoted as Assassins. Ibn Jubayr and other Arab historians apparently adapted the death-leap story from its European origins into Arabic chronicles as well, where it supported the notion that the Nizaris were fanatical.

Originally separate legend strands, the hashish addiction, Paradise fantasy, and suicide cult became facets of one story and were granted historical authority in the writings of Marco Polo (1254–1324) and his scribe Rustichello. Polo stopped at the Persian fortress Alamut on his travels; there he claimed to have heard several reports concerning the Old Man, inexplicably in Persia instead of Syria, who convinced his young adherents that his garden was indeed Paradise. The Assassins were administered an opium potion that enhanced their fantasies and enabled them to be manipulated into killing the Old Man's enemies in order to regain access to Paradise. Most subsequent renderings of Assassin legends can be traced back to Marco Polo's composite version of the fourteenth century.

See also: Arabic-Islamic Tradition; Crusades; Travel Literature

References and further reading: Recent Assassin scholarship has concentrated on separating history from legend. F. Daftary, *The Assassin Legends: Myths of the Isma'ilis* (1994), identifies many of the Arab legends and explains their reinterpretation by Europeans. J. von Hammer-Purgstall, *The History of the Assassins, Derived from Oriental Sources* (1835; rpt. 1968), provides several examples of the legends but also includes scholarship since amended by others. E. Burman, *The Assassins* (1987), and B. Lewis, *The Assassins: A Radical Sect in Islam* (1968), examine the European legends. All of the above contain the entire passage from Marco Polo's *Travels.* L. Hellmuth, *Die Assassinenlegende in der österreichischen Geschichtsdichtung des Mittelalters* (1988), explores the possibility of influence on these legends from romance traditions. For more information on hashish and the use of the term *hashishiyya*, see F. Rosenthal, *The Herb: Hashish versus Medieval Muslim Society* (1971).

—Bonnie D. Irwin

Attila (406?–453) and the Huns

The single most impressive figure of the Age of Migrations, in terms of his impact on European culture as well as his continued life in medieval epic and legend.

Attila ruled the Huns in Europe from 436 to 453 C.E. He was, however, not the first ruler of the Huns in Europe, but the last. The Huns, or as the Chinese annals call them, the Hsiung Nu, were Asiatic horse nomads with a taste for warfare and plunder. Their long trek west began when the Chinese built the Great Wall to keep them and similar peoples out. They appear for the first time in European records when Dionysius "Pinax," a Greek geographer who had come to study in Rome, records their presence at the Caspian Sea. In the late third century they left some traces in northern Iran. In 375 they overran the Goths in Ukraine and opened the Age of Migrations, but chances are that they had already made their presence felt in southern Russia for a while, even though we have no records of it.

We have no idea who ruled the Huns in 375; only about the year 400 do names begin to crop up. The first ruler we hear of is Gainas (perhaps Geoffrey of Monmouth's Guanius), who does not, however, seem to have been a king and who may have been Gothic rather than Hunnish. The first Hunnish king we know of is Huldin or Uldin (ruled c. 400–406), who, in Danish legend, may have become Haldan, and in *Beowulf* Healfdene, founder of the Skjoldung (*Beowulf*: Scylding) dynasty. His coregent Charaton left no traces in legendary history. The next generation counted the coregents Roas and Uptar or Octar. Roas or Rugilas (ruled c. 415–436), the son of Huldin, is second only to Attila in the heroic legends. According to Niels Lukman, he appears in *Beowulf* as Hrothgar and in Danish historical legend as Roar or Roe, in the Icelandic *Skjöldungsaga* as Roas, and in German heroic legend as Rüdiger, but variant names appear, such as Ruother or Rother.

It was Octar who overran the Burgundians around 430 and thus won his own place in Germanic historical legend. It was also he who attacked Cologne, although he has been replaced by Attila in the legend of St. Ursula (who, according to the tenth-century account, was captured by the Huns and martyred when she refused to marry their chief). Octar died of excessive feasting, a fate that was also to befall Attila.

After Roas and Octar, the coregents Attila and Bleda came to power in 436. It is, and will probably forever remain, a riddle what Attila did in the early years of his rule, except that we know that he soon got rid of Bleda. It has been conjectured that he extended his rule all the way to Scandinavia, where he was to be celebrated in the Viking Age not only under the name Atli in the *Edda* poems, some of them composed as far away as Greenland, but also perhaps under a Nordic "alias," King Adils of Sweden. In *Beowulf* he appears as Eadgils.

The end of Attila's, and the Hunnish, dominion followed the battle at the Catalaunian Fields somewhere in southern France in 451. An unorthodox alliance of Romans and Germans summoned the power necessary to check the advance of the Huns. Reportedly Attila had already mounted the pyre to be cremated alive rather than face defeat, when the tides of the battle turned sufficiently for him to effect a retreat. In 453 he died of a hemorrhage at his wedding—not exactly the first such—to a Germanic woman, according to the Byzantine diplomat Priscos. Reportedly he had more than 60 sons, although we know the names of only 2.

The death of Attila marked the end of Hunnish domination. The alliances he had carefully made with various Germanic peoples, usually by threat, fell apart, and an anti-Hunnish alliance was formed under Ardarich, king of the Gepids. This new alliance met the Huns in battle in 454 or 455 and defeated them. The last Hunnish king to leave any traces in heroic legend was Attila's son Ellac, who ruled the remains of the Hunnish kingdom northeast of the Black Sea. According to Lukman, he appears as Halga in *Beowulf* and Helgi in Norse-Icelandic and Danish historical legend. It was also from this kingdom that Chinialon emerged in 549 with an army of 12,000 Huns to burn and plunder in the Balkans. It may be he who was later remembered in legend as Hinieldus or Ingeld.

See also: Burgundian Cycle; Migrations, Age of; *Nibelungenlied*
References and further reading: A comprehensive scholarly account is F. Altheim, *Geschichte der Hunnen*, 5 vols. (1960–1962). A fine introduction to the Huns and their history and culture is J. O. Maenchen-Helfen, *The World of the Huns* (1973). N. C. Lukman, *Skjöldunge und Skilfinge* (1943), identifies the Nordic legendary kings as the Migration Age rulers near the Danube.

—*Lars Hemmingsen*

Augustine of Hippo, Saint (354–430)

Bishop and saint, designated one of the four principal Doctors of the Catholic Church.

Augustine was born in Tagaste, Numidia (North Africa), to a pagan municipal official and a Christian mother. His spiritual journey toward conversion, culminating in his baptism in 387, is recounted unforgettably in the *Confessions*. His written works were so extensive that his biographer and cataloger Possidius claimed that no single person could read them all. His influence on Christian theology has been incalculable, but perhaps equally pervasive has been his influence on what might be termed the "flavor" of medieval Christian culture.

The nature of Augustine's ethnic origin has been a matter of scholarly debate: fourth-century Numidians appear to have been closely related to modern Berbers. Although she was a devout Christian, Augustine's mother had been reprimanded for maintaining graveside rituals of pagan origin (*Confessions* 6, 2); her name, Monica, may derive from that of a Numidian mother goddess. Augustine's education was rigorously classical, but certain preoccupations and values evince African influence: ecstatic intensity of emotional attachment directed toward the divine as well as the human, and a portentous sense of the created world as a kind of text from which universal meaning may be inferred, whether by divinatory interpretation or the construction of elaborate allegorical schema.

Augustine was an acute observer of human behavior; his interest in traditional belief was intellectual, practical, and on occasion personal. The critical point in his conversion occurred when he was in the depths of a spiritual crisis and heard a nearby voice chanting, "Take up and read; take up and read." His first reaction was to consider whether this might not be part of some children's game. His decision to take the advice of the mysterious voice as a prompting to a bibliomantic ritual—opening the Bible and reading the first passage he saw—resulted in his emotional breakthrough to belief.

Official Christian teaching as *doctrina publica* had emerged toward the end of the second century and was thus relatively recent in Augustine's time, and the process of shaping a central core of belief distinct from "optional" beliefs and practices (comprising what Adolph Harnack has called "Christianity of the second rank") was still being negotiated. A conscientious pastor after his conversion, Augustine was especially concerned with the necessary process of riddling through pre-Christian traditions of belief to determine which would support the new faith, which might undermine it, and which might be "baptized" through allegorical reinterpretation. A skilled rhetorician as well as a scholar, he was preoccupied with the distinction between orality and the written word: he was fascinated by his mentor Ambrose's habit of reading without moving his lips (*Confessions* 6, 3).

Augustine's concern with folklore is expressed in the three primary roles of his life. As a theologian, his absorption in consensual symbols as a vehicle for both meaning and communion, human and divine, is most movingly set forth in the dialogue *De magistro* between himself and his son Adeodatus, whose mother was a woman with whom Augustine had a relationship before becoming a priest. In their conversation, in a manner both serious and playful, Augustine demonstrates both the necessity for symbolic communication and its limitations. Although he claims "I am afraid I shall appear ridiculous, because I set out on so long a journey with the consideration of signs and not of the realities they signify," he concludes "there is absolutely nothing that can be taught without signs."

As a preacher, he made daring rhetorical use of popular beliefs, especially in his oral commentaries on the Psalms. For example, glossing the line "the voice of the Lord perfecting the stags," Augustine alludes to the popular belief that a stag could draw serpents from their dens by means of the sweetness and power of its breath, illuminating an otherwise opaque verse (one that is, in fact, a mistranslation). The "perfected" stag becomes an image for the power of Christ over calumny, "for the voice of the Lord has above all led to perfection those who know how to control and discountenance enemy tongues" (*Enarrationes*, Psalm 28).

Third, as an ecclesiastical administrator, he attempted to define criteria by which orally transmitted accounts of miraculous "wonders," the "urban legends" of his time, could be evaluated with both intellectual rigor and reverence—an issue still unresolved in our own day. Although early in his conversion he averred that the time of miracles had passed, in later life he was sufficiently impressed by a series of cures resulting from contact with shrines to the holy in his domain to institute a formal procedure for documenting each event, requiring a written affidavit from the recovered patient to be proclaimed in church and later filed in the bishop's library, thus ensuring that any exaggerations or garbling of the account in oral circulation could be checked against this first-person testimony.

In his great work, *The City of God*, he related miracles that could be verified from his own time and locale. For example, he related a story of a kind familiar to folklorists: a fellow townsman of Hippo, a tailor named Florentius, lost his coat, prayed to the Twenty Martyrs for a new one, was ridiculed by the young men of the town, found a fish on the shore, and took it to a cook, who cut it open to find inside the fish a gold ring. Thus, the tailor got his new coat through a miracle (22, 8). Similar material of interest to folklorists in that same work would include his discussion of Adam and Eve's realization of their nakedness after the Fall, which involuntarily "moved" their sexual organs with lust (14, 17); his speculations about the origin of giants through intercourse with ordinary women (15, 23); the abominations of rites of the Great Mother, as celebrated by castrati (7, 26); his description of pagan hydromancy as a form of divination in which the images of gods (actually demons) appeared in water (7, 35); and the helpful information that peacock's flesh has antiseptic power (21, 4).

Approached on his deathbed by a dream-prompted sufferer hoping for a miraculous cure, Augustine remarked wryly that if he had such powers he would apply them to his own affliction—but he laid gentle hands on the man nonetheless.

See also: Saints, Cults of the

References and further reading: The best introduction to Augustine's life and times remains P. Brown, *Augustine of Hippo* (1967). Most contemporary translations of Augustine's writings are based on texts found in J.-P. Migne's *Patrologia Latina* (1844–1864) or the more limited *Corpus scriptorum ecclesiasticorum Latinorum* (1866ff.). The *Confessions* can be found in many translations; a satisfactory recent work is that of H. Chadwick (1991). For the text of Augustine's *Expositions of the Psalms*, see D. E. Dekkers, O.S.B., and J. Frepont, eds., *Sancti Aurelii enarrationes in Psalmos*, which closely follows that of Migne's *Patrologia* (vols. 36 and 37), which is standard. A partial translation happily lacking in self-conscious archaism is that of Dame Scholastica Hebgin and Dame Felicitas Corrigan, in the series Ancient Christian Writers (1961). A translation of *De magistro* can be found in *Augustine: Earlier Writings*, ed. J. H. S. Burleigh (1953). The classic translation of *The City of God* is by M. Dods (1950), though several others are now available.

—Erika Brady

Bagpipe

A musical instrument of unknown but ancient origin.

Suetonius attests to Nero's ability on the bagpipe, Procopius writes that the bagpipe was used by the imperial Roman army, and historians suggest that the Roman soldiers introduced the bagpipe into England. Two distinct types of the bagpipe have been documented in medieval Europe: the conical chanter, which produced a loud piercing sound, and the cylindrical chanter, which gave off a soft buzzing tone. Although both single drone and droneless pipes were played in the Middle Ages, the multidrone bagpipe common today seems to be a postmedieval invention.

The bagpipe is considered predominantly a folk instrument in Western European traditions, and its music accompanied weddings, dances, and festivals. The instrument did maintain a connection to royalty: in 1290, for example, Edward I of England memorialized his queen Eleanor by having bagpipes play while crosses dedicated to her memory were erected. It was also common practice for pipers to accompany religious pilgrims. In the early fifteenth century, Thomas Arundel, archbishop of Canterbury, remarked that bagpipes could drive away a pilgrim's hurt, and Chaucer's Miller seems to accurately reflect this practice as he pipes the pilgrims forth to Canterbury.

The bagpipe possessed traditional associations with gluttony, animal lust, and the male genitals. Carved images of pigs with bagpipes can be found at Beverley Minster in England and at Melrose Abbey in Scotland. According to a chronicle of Bruges, Belgium, for the years from 1477 to 1491, when crimes and executions rose at an alarming rate, one of the worst criminals was a musician "called Anthuenis, and he was known as a soothsayer, who used to play the bagpipes, and he was put to death for things that are better not reported."

The manuscript evidence, however, such as *Très riches heures* and the *Cloisters Apocalypse*, depicts both shepherds and angels playing bagpipes at Christ's birth. Such a wide range of associations highlights the diverse attitudes displayed toward the bagpipe by Western medieval culture.

See also: Folk Music and Folksong

References and further reading: E. Winternitz, *Musical Instruments and Their Symbolism in Western Art* (1979); R. Hoppin, *Medieval Music* (1978); E. Block, "Chaucer's Millers and Their Bagpipes," *Speculum* 24 (1954); J. Gellrich, "The Parody of Medieval Music in 'The

Wedding Dance in the Open Air, *mid-sixteenth-century painting by Pieter Brueghel the Elder; note the bagpipe player at the right in the painting. (Francis G. Mayer/Corbis)*

Miller's Tale,'" *Journal of English and Germanic Philology* 73 (1974); R. Boenig, "The Miller's Bagpipe: A Note on *The Canterbury Tales* A565–566," *English Language Notes* 21(1983); R. Strohm, *Music in Late Medieval Bruges* (1985).

—Cynthia Whiddon Green

Bal des Ardents

The "dance of the burning men," one of the most infamous incidents in the late-fourteenth-century reign of France's King Charles VI, which was less a ball than a *danse macabre*.

The Bal des Ardents occurred on January 28, 1393, at a festivity celebrating the wedding of two members of the royal household, hosted by the king at the Hotel de St. Pol, one of the favorite residences of Charles and Queen Isabeau. The bride was one of the queen's favorite ladies-in-waiting. Six members of court, one of whom was Charles himself, dressed in costumes and performed a dance as an entertainment for guests at the reception. Either by accident or by design the flammable costumes ignited, and four of the dancers died of the burns. Although the king fortuitously escaped death, the incident caused a scandal because of the tragic but avoidable deaths of four participants. While the general outlines of the story remain similar from account to account, there are significant inconsistencies in the details about the event supplied in the respective versions written by contemporary chroniclers of affairs of court during Charles VI's late-fourteenth-century reign.

One royal chronicler, the Monk of St. Denis, interprets the event as a charivari. The Monk emphasizes that the party celebrated the third marriage, to a German lord, of one of Queen Isabeau's favorite ladies-in-waiting. Remarriages and marriages to outsiders or foreigners were both violations of social taboos that could precipitate the enactment of charivari, a ritual of humiliation aimed at transgressors against local socio-sexual mores. After generally condemning the practice of humiliating remarrying widows by means of a charivari, the Monk of St. Denis reports that King Charles VI and five other courtiers nevertheless planned a spectacle directed at the newlyweds being feted. The masked dancers entered the hall in frightful disguises that rendered them unrecognizable. In line with his earlier censorious remarks, the Monk thus implies that the dance of Charles VI and his costumed cohorts was a charivari. This chronicler profoundly criticizes the behavior of the king and his courtiers, especially their disgraceful postures, obscene gestures, and bestial cries, which he compares to the howling of wolves. When somebody, either accidentally or purposefully, tossed a spark toward one of the charivari participants, the danc-

Le Bal des Ardents, from a manuscript of Jean Froissart's Chroniques, *1472. (Giraudon/Art Resource, NY)*

ers' highly flammable costumes ignited. Of the six charivari participants, only the king and one other dancer survived; the other four participants died painfully of their burns. As the Monk reports the Bal des Ardents, the perpetrators of the purported charivari, not the newlyweds, became the inadvertent victims of their own guising, a sign, in his opinion, of poetic justice and divine retribution. Regardless of the actual intent of Charles VI and the other dancers, the Monk's implication that the dancing at this wedding feast constituted a charivari permits him to reaffirm recent ecclesiastical critique of the custom and to criticize the monarch's foolish lack of decorum.

But the most famous account of this event, by Jean Froissart in his late-fourteenth-century *Chroniques*, does not mention the motif of charivari and instead emphasizes the specific costumes worn by the dancers in what may have been meant only as an entertaining masque. In Froissart's chronicle Charles VI and the other five courtiers impersonated *hommes sauvages* by wearing highly flammable costumes that resembled the body fur of the legendary medieval Wild Man. Froissart adds specific details about the guests, emphasizes the preventive measures taken to ensure the dancers' safety (torches or other sources of fire were forbidden during the dance), and mentions that the dancers, with the exception of the king, were attached to each other. Froissart also adds material about the spectators' marveling reactions to the dance and explains that, separated from the other Wild Men and passing by his wife, the king walked over to a group of female guests at the party and engaged in a conversation with the duchess of Berry. (Though the duchess was the king's aunt—her husband the duke of Berry was Charles's uncle—she was the youngest woman at the reception.) Of all the chroniclers, Froissart provides the most detail about the occasioning of the fire and identifies the cause of the blaze: the king's brother, Duke Louis of Orléans, arrived late and carried a torch to the dancers for closer inspection and (either accidentally or deliberately) set off a conflagration. Igniting one costumed link in this human chain lit them all. Pandemonium broke out among the horrified guests. When the dancers caught fire, the duchess of Berry protected the king by covering him with her dress, thus saving his life. The only survivors of the debacle were the king and one other dancer, who threw himself into a tub of fresh water used for rinsing flasks and goblets and thus doused the flames.

Whereas the Monk focuses his critique on the practice of charivari in his account, Froissart's version is more concerned with the inadvisability of the king's having participated in the dance; the significance of the specific folk figure being impersonated in the furry costumes, the Wild Man of the woods; the way the king escapes being burned, by perhaps-unsuitable engagement with a young woman; the culpability of the king's brother; and the ensuing scandal when news of the tragedy spread throughout Paris. Froissart's version of the Bal des Ardents seems designed to excoriate the monarch responsible for the tragedy that occurred at a wedding party he hosted.

See also: Charivari; Dance; Wild Man
References and further reading: For the Monk's version, see *Chronique du Religieux de Saint-Denys, contenant le Regne de Charles VI, de 1380 à 1422*, ed. M. L. Bellaguet, vol. 2 (1840).

For Froissart's version of the same event, see *Oeuvres de Froissart: Publiées avec les variantes des divers manuscrits par chroniques*, ed. K. de Lettenhove, vol. 15 (1870–1875). For the significance of the Bal des Ardents in the history of Charles VI's reign, see B. Tuchman, *A Distant Mirror: The Calamitous Fourteenth Century* (1978), and F. Autrand, *Charles VI: La folie du roi* (1986).

—*Lorraine K. Stock*

Ballad

A relatively short, orally transmitted, narrative song, common in postmedieval traditions, but scarce in surviving medieval records.

Such songs certainly existed in Western Europe as early as 1200 and perhaps even earlier, but we know very little, if anything, about the prehistory of the surviving ballads: their origins and their immediate antecedents are shrouded in mystery. Depending on geographical area, epic poetry, sagas, metrical romances, the traditional lyric, and other genres purveyed by minstrels may well have played a significant part in the ballad's origins. The term *ballad* (from French *ballade*, a dancing song, and late-Latin *ballare*, "to dance") suggests a song performed as accompaniment to a dance. The connection was stressed, perhaps overstressed, long ago by Johannes Steenstrup, who argued that ballads as we now know them grew from dance songs. But there are plenty of medieval testimonies to narrative dance songs (e.g., in Scandinavia and Germany), dances are mentioned as the context of ballad narratives in various traditions, and ballads still continue to be performed as dance songs in certain conservative areas on the periphery of Europe—such as the Faroe Islands, Azores, and La Gomera (Canary Islands)—as they still were in certain Spanish villages until early in the twentieth century. The dance performance context cannot, however, explain the origins of all ballads, or even of any one ballad tradition, to the exclusion of other interacting factors.

Ballads differ significantly in form and in character from one linguistic tradition to another, but even so there are also striking similarities, and many ballad narratives have, until recently, been sung in genetically related, though metrically diverse, poems over the length and breadth of Europe. Whatever their ultimate origins, we are probably justified in viewing the various subtraditions of medieval European balladry as at least partially interrelated manifestations of a single genre. Colin Smith's incisive characterization of Spanish ballads could just as accurately be applied to various other branches of the medieval European tradition:

> stylistic compression, … bluntness, terseness and dramatic power, … extreme plainness of language bereft of elaborate simile, metaphor and other rhetoric … [a] genius for understatement and for evocation by silence, … implicit rather than explicit. … The ballads are not exemplary or didactic, … there is no preaching … [they] lack … religiosity.

Roderick Beaton's equally apposite description of Greek ballads also rings true for numerous other traditions:

> Very few Greek songs … are either charming or simple. Most are formal and highly organised, although … these characteristics are not always immediately apparent. The ideas they express are complex, often hauntingly elusive; and alongside their lyricism and fine imagery there is a violence and an uncompromisingly pragmatic outlook which are not easily sentimentalised.

While many ballads—a majority—must have been composed in later centuries, a substantial number even of ballads sung today (or at least sung up to the early years of the last century) can be documented in medieval variants or, on other grounds, can be reasonably characterized as probably (or very possibly) of medieval origin. In the latter case, for example, are ballads that tell in detail of little-known but demonstrably historical events not easily gleaned from written sources or, again in certain cases, ballads that share the same plots and some as yet undetermined relationship with other traditional or traditionalized medieval narratives (such as epics and romances). Likewise a ballad in traditional style, first recorded in writing in, say, the sixteenth century, can in certain instances be assigned a putative origin in the fifteenth century or even earlier. Obviously, such identifications need to be approached with the greatest caution and in most cases must remain provisional. Ballads recorded in distinctive readings or in unique text-types in archaic lateral areas (in Gottschee; among Volga Germans; on Spanish and Portuguese Atlantic islands; in Judeo-Spanish communities; among Székeley and Moldavian Hungarians) can, in some cases and in combination with other evidence, provide additional if indirect witnesses to a ballad's possible currency during the Middle Ages. Wide geographic distribution of a given text-type may also suggest the possibility of an early origin but cannot be taken as proof without the presence of additional corroborative evidence. The present survey will proceed through Western Europe, roughly from north to south, from Scandinavia to the Iberian Peninsula, and thence to Hungary.

See also: Carol; Dance

References and further reading: R. Beaton, *Folk Poetry of Modern Greece* (1980), quotation above from pages 7, 19; R. W. Brednich, L. Röhrich, and W. Suppan, *Handbuch des Volksliedes*, 2 vols. (1973–1975); W. Danckert, *Das europäische Volkslied* (1970); W. Entwistle, *European Balladry* (1951); O. Holzapfel, J. H. McGrew, and I. Piø, *The European Medieval Ballad* (1978; abbreviated EMB); E. Seemann, D. Strömbäck, and B. R. Jonsson, *European Folk Ballads* (1967); C. Smith, "On the Ethos of the *Romancero viejo*," in *Studies of the Spanish and Portuguese Ballad*, ed. N. D. Shergold (1972), quotation above from page 13; J. C. H. R. Steenstrup, *The Medieval Popular Ballad* (1968).

Scandinavia (Denmark, Norway, Sweden, Faroe Islands, Iceland)

A good number of Scandinavian ballads can confidently be considered of medieval origin, and the fact is commonly acknowledged in the titles of pertinent publications. There is also documentary evidence: according to a Swedish chronicle account for 1471, just before the Battle of Brunkenberg, the Swedish army "greatly comforted themselves" by singing "The Ballad of St. George" (SMB 49). Ballad fragments in Danish show up as early as the first half of the thirteenth century; for example, the famous "Rune Verse" (c. 1300): "drømde mik en drøm i nat / um silki ok ærlir pæl" [Last night I dreamt a dream / of silk and noble furs]. Medieval church paintings at Floda in Sweden and a fifteenth-century Danish map made by Claudius Clavus Svart are captioned by verses that appear later in postmedieval ballads; records of the church at Solum in Norway also contain such verses.

Svend Grundtvig's 12-volume *Danmarks gamle Folkeviser* (Denmark's Ancient Folk Ballads, abbreviated *DgF*) was the pioneering scholarly effort to assemble postmedieval texts and correlate them with medieval evidence; Grundtvig's influence was enormous, serving as the inspiration for Francis James Child's *English and Scottish Popular Ballads*. The older Scandinavian ballads concern events in medieval history; evoke a medieval social context; embody narratives already known to earlier epics, sagas, and romances; and perpetuate beliefs in magical phenomena and supernatural creatures (trolls and giants) characteristic of rural societies that continued to harbor a medieval folkloric heritage. Full ballad texts are amply attested in aristocratic Danish and Swedish manuscripts (*adelsvisebøger*) starting in the 1500s. The earliest, to my knowledge, is the beautiful little heart-shaped *Hjertebogen* (1553–1555). Norwegian records are later; they contain some 21 ballads written in the seventeenth century, but richer documentation exists only in texts recorded from folk tradition in the early nineteenth century and later. The Danish "Erik Emuns drab" (The Murder of King Emun; *DgF* 116) alludes to an event of 1137. But when was it composed? "Elveskud" (Elfshot; *DgF* 47), in which the protagonist dies after dancing with an elf-maiden, is first recorded in Karen Brahe's folio manuscript (c. 1570), has analogs all over Western Europe (in England, Brittany, France, Italy, and Spain and among Spanish Jews), and—because of its association with a widespread medieval folk belief—must certainly be medieval in origin. The "Bjarnarsonar" (The Sons of Björn), known only in Iceland, recounts a historical happening in Norway in the early thirteenth century, but questions have been raised about the exact dating, which could be considerably later (c. 1500). The names of such celebrated medieval heroes as Sigurd, Hagen, Charlemagne, and Roland continue to be heard in the still-vital Faroese dance tradition; however, these ballads probably represent re-rhymings of late-medieval prose texts. Whatever the exact details of dating may be, many older Scandinavian ballads impart an unmistakably medieval aura. The Scandinavian repertoire also comprises an extensive body of ballads composed in relatively recent times. The classic collection—which served as a model for Child's *English and Scottish Popular Ballads*—is Grundtvig's *DgF*, but comprehensive Norwegian and Swedish collections are also under way. The repertoire of Swedish-speaking communities in Finland should also be taken into account.

See also: Scandinavian Tradition
References and further reading: B. R. Jonsson et al., *Types of the Scandinavian Medieval Ballad* (1978; abbreviated *SMB*), offers a crucial starting point for studying Scandinavian balladry. See also B. R. Jonsson, *Svensk balladtradition* (1967), "The Ballad in Scandinavia," in *The European Medieval Ballad*, ed. O. Holzapfel (1978; abbreviated *EMB*), and *Sveriges medeltida ballader* (1983–), a comprehensive collection in progress soon to supercede A. Noreen and J. A. Lundell, *1500- och 1600-talens visböcker* (1900–1915). Also by Jonsson, "Oral Literature, Written Literature, and the Ballad," in *The Ballad and Oral Literature,* ed.

J. Harris (1991), proposes that the ballad was introduced to Scandinavia through the Norwegian courts. V. Ólason, *The Traditional Ballads of Iceland* (1982), is an enormously useful, authoritative treatment of Icelandic ballads. For the earliest Norwegian ballads, see R. Kvideland and H. Johnsen, eds., *1600-tals viser: Eit handskrift fra Roldal* (1976). See also P. Abrahamson and E. Dal, *The Heart Book* (1965); O. Andersson, *Finlands svenska folkdiktning*, vol. 5 (1934); E. Dal, *Danish Ballads and Folk Songs* (1967); S. Grundtvig et al., *Danmarks gamle Folkeviser*, 12 vols. (1853–1863; rpt.1966–1976; abbreviated *DgF*); S. Grundtvig and J. Block, *Corpus Carminum Færoensium*, 6 vols. (1941–1972); A. Olrik, *A Book of Danish Ballads* (1939). Very useful is L. E. Syndergaard, *English Translations of the Medieval Scandinavian Ballads: An Analytic Guide and Bibliography* (1995).

Germany, Holland, Flanders

Two Latin verses (and their refrain), attributable to an incident supposed to have occurred in 1020, may possibly document the first known German ballad (and perhaps the first known European ballad). The lines come from the account of the "Dancers of Kölbigk" (motif C94.1.1), a tale concerning a group of young people who dance and sing in a churchyard during Christmas and are cursed to continue dancing while holding each other's hands for the entire following year. This is the song that they are reported to have sung while dancing:

> Equitabat Bovo   per silvam frondosam,
> Ducebat sibi   Merswinden formosam.
> Quid stamus?   Cur non imus?

> [Bovo rides through the leafy wood, taking beautiful
> Merswind with him. Why are we stopping?
> Why don't we go on?]

The first half line, in which the protagonist rides forth—to encounter his fortune, his adventures, his fate—is typically balladic, appearing in such postmedieval examples as "Es reitet en Reiter durch grünen Wald" [There rides a rider through the greenwood].

The best tool for locating early German ballads is the extensive 10-volume collection begun by John Meier and incorporated in *Deutsche Volkslieder mit ihren Melodien* (German Folksongs with Their Melodies, abbreviated *DVM*).

Several German ballads rework episodes from early Germanic heroic poetry: "Das jüngere Hildebrandslied" (The Later Song of Hildebrand, *DVM* 1), known in two fifteenth-century manuscripts and many sixteenth-century German and Dutch printings; "Ermenrichs Tod" (Ermenrich's Death, *DVM* 2), surviving in a lone Low German broadside version (c. 1560); and "Der Jäger aus Griechenland" (The Hunter from Greece, *DVM* 5), pertaining to the epic cycle of Wolfdietrich and preserved in a single early-nineteenth-century Dutch redaction. "Die Meererin" (The Seaside Girl, *DVM* 4), on the motif of the long-lost sister, from the archaic German speech island of Gottschee (Slovenia), exhibits striking agreements with the Hispanic ballad "Don Bueso y su hermana" (Don Bueso and His Sister). Both, in turn, agree in numerous details with the medieval Bavarian-Austrian epic *Kudrun* (c. 1230). The ballads need not derive directly from this work, but possibly go back to a medieval balladic archetype also reflected in the epic poem. "Der edle Moringer" (The Noble Moringer, *DVM* 12), printed in 1497—about a husband's return from war to interrupt his wife's second wedding—tells the same story as the Spanish "Conde Dirlos" (Count Dirlos), printed circa 1510. This vastly diffused Odyssean story was certainly circulating in ballad form in various European contexts during the fifteenth century, and even, perhaps, much earlier. "Die Königskinder" (The King's Children, *DVM* 20)—the Hero and Leander story—is first documented in a German fragment, with music, from 1540 and was surely in wide circulation long before. The citation of a single verse, "Elzeleyn lipstic elzeleyn" [Dearest little Elsa], dates from around 1480. The earliest known German texts of "Der Mädchenmorder" (The Killer of Maidens, *DVM* 41)—in which a young woman kills a suitor who attempts to murder her—are in printed broadsides dating from 1550 to 1565, but the Dutch *Halewijn* redaction, though of a much later date (between 1783 and 1854), doubtless represents an earlier and more interesting stage in the ballad's development. The earliest Danish versions of "Kvindemorderen" (The Killer of Women, *DgF* 183) also date from the sixteenth century (the earliest, from Karen Brahe's manuscript), and their Spanish counterpart, "Rico Franco," was first printed in Amsterdam around 1548. In somewhat later testimonies and also in modern texts, we know similar narratives from England, France, Italy, Portugal, Hungary, and Spain, including among the Spanish Jews. Clearly here, too, we have an early ballad narrative whose roots were already firmly planted over a wide area during the Middle Ages. German texts of "Der König von Mailand" (The King of Milan, *DVM* 67) were all collected quite late (from the early nineteenth century on), including a good modern version from the archaic Volga German settlements. Its English-Scottish counterpart, "Lady Maisry" (Child 65), is correspondingly late, and the earliest witness to the Hungarian "Dishonored Maiden" is from the mid-nineteenth century (1857–1872), but the Spanish tradition's "Conde Claros fraile" (Count Claros in Friar's Garb), first printed in 1550, assures us that its German, English, and Hungarian congeners all belong to a very early tradition. In a similar case is "Die Königstochter im Heeresdienst" (The King's Daughter in Military Service, *DVM* 95), represented by modern versions collected in the archaic community of Gottschee. There are very close analogs in Hungarian (solely from a marginal population in Moldavia), in Romanian, and in various Slavic traditions, as well as in Italian and French. To my knowledge, all were collected from the modern tradition. An essentially identical story, "La doncella guerrera" (The Warrior Maiden), is known in many Hispanic subtraditions, but all the full texts, like their pan-European relatives, have been collected in recent times. Yet two complementary Portuguese and Judeo-Spanish witnesses confirm beyond doubt the ballad's early provenience. Two dramas (dated 1561 and 1567) by the Portuguese playwright Jorge Ferreira de Vasconcelos (1515?–1585?) embody brief but incontrovertible citations. The better of the two, dating from 1567, reads: "Pregonadas son las guerras / de Francia contra Aragone! // Como las haría, triste, / viejo, cano y pecador?" [War has been proclaimed / between France and Aragon! // Woe is me! How could I go to fight, / old and gray-haired sinner that I am?] (Michaelis, page 146). These unique Portuguese testimonies are confirmed by an identical eastern Judeo-Spanish citation of the first half line, "Pregonadas son las guerras," used as a tune indicator in a collection of Hebrew hymns dating from 1599 (S. G. Armistead and J. H. Silverman, "Antiguo romancero," no. 53). For the present purposes, one of the most significant aspects of the German tradition is the prevalence of archaic ballad repertoires in the varied German communities that existed in Eastern Europe prior to World War II (in Gottschee, Banat, Siebenbürgen, Volga Republic).

See also: Burgundian Cycle; Judith; *Nibelungenlied*
References and further reading: The basic collection remains J. Meier et al., *Deutsche Volkslieder mit ihren Melodien: Balladen*, 10 vols. (1935–1992; abbreviated *DVM*); crucial for the study of German balladry is O. Holzapfel's indispensable text-type index found in volume 10 of *DVM*. R. W. Brednich et al., *Gottscheer Volkslieder* (1969); M. Haavio, *Essais folkloriques* (1959); and J. Kunzig and W. Werner, *Volksballaden und Erzähllieder* (1975), document the German ballads of Eastern European cultures; see also J. Meier, *Balladen*, 2 vols. (1964); L. Röhrich and R. W. Brednich, *Deutsche Volkslieder*, 2 vols. (1965–1967).

England and Scotland

There is plenty of evidence of a ballad tradition in the British Isles before 1500; most of the evidence can be found in Francis J. Child's monumental work, *The English and Scottish Popular Ballads*, which provides not only all the texts that Child could amass but long introductory notes discussing the relationship between a given British ballad type and its antecedents in medieval romances, chronicles, and other sources, as well as its analogs in other European traditions. "Judas" (ballad 23 in the Child collection) dates from around 1250; it is far older than the other surviving medieval texts, which are recorded in fifteenth-century manuscripts or sixteenth-century prints. Among these are "Riddles Wisely Expounded" (Child 1, c. 1444–1445), "St. Stephen and Herod" (Child 22, c. 1450), "Robyn and Gandeleyn" (Child 115, c. 1450), and two Robin Hood ballads (Child 119, 121). Early-sixteenth-century printed texts include the "Gest of Robyn Hode" (Child 117). "The Battle of Otterburn" and "Chevy Chase" (Child 161, 162), known in sixteenth-century manuscripts, both reflect a historical event of 1388. "Arthur and Cornwall" (Child 30), probably based on a medieval English minstrel's reconfiguration of the twelfth-century French epic, *Pèlerinage de Charlemagne* (Charlemagne's Pilgrimage), and "Sir Aldingar" (Child 59), with plentiful analogs in medieval sources as well as in traditional balladry, are both from the famous mid-seventeenth-century Percy manuscript. There are many ballads from later oral tradition that go back to medieval analogs or have early parallels in other ballad traditions. The hauntingly magical "King Orfeo" (Child 19), sung in 1880 by an old man on the Shetland Islands, perpetuates a Scandinavian refrain in Shetland Norse and is genetically related to the Middle English lay of *Sir Orfeo* (and its various medieval congeners). Thomas Rhymer's adventures with the Queen of Elfland ("Thomas Rymer," Child 37) certainly derive from the mid-fifteenth-century romance *Thomas of Erceldoune*. "Clerk Colvill" (Child 42) is related to the Scandinavian "Elveskud" (c. 1550) and the archaic Spanish and Judeo-Spanish "Muerte ocultada" (Hidden Death). Other ballads having early congeners in different European traditions—though this need not indicate that their British manifestations are necessarily medieval in origin—are "Lady Isabel and the Elf-Knight" (Child 4), "Hind Horn" (Child 17), "Young Beichan" (Child 53), "Fair Annie" (Child 62), "Lady Maisry" (Child 65), "Lord Thomas and Fair Annet" (Child 73), "Baffled Knight" (Child 112), "Mother's Malison" (Child 216), and "Our Goodman" (Child 274). Venerable versions of medieval (or putatively medieval) English-Scottish ballads have survived in the overseas traditions of Canada and the United States: "Riddles" (Child 1), "Lady Isabel" (Child 4), "Hind Horn" (Child 17), "King Orfeo" (Child 19), "Thomas Rymer" (Child 37), "Young Beichan" (Child 53), and various others.

See also: Accused Queen; Robin Hood; Scottish Tradition; Thomas Rhymer

References and further reading: The starting point for early ballad studies is F. J. Child, *The English and Scottish Popular Ballads*, 5 vols. (1882–1898; rpt. 1965). Indispensable supplements are B. H. Bronson, *The Traditional Tunes of the Child Ballads*, 4 vols. (1959–1972); T. P. Coffin and R. de V. Renwick, *The British Traditional Ballad in North America*, 2nd ed. (1977); and G. A. Morgan, *Medieval Ballads: Chivalry, Romance, and Everyday Life* (1996).

Brittany

Mary-Ann Constantine has said that some Breton ballads "must have had a long period of … stable transmission before surfacing onto paper in the mid-19th century," yet many, in line with their recent moment of collection, give the impression of a relatively late tradition. No mention of early-medieval Britain survives—seaborne English pirates are seen as the Bretons' enemies—and French influence on the ballads is pervasive. All the same, the Breton tradition is of great value historically, and several text-types of ultimately medieval extraction persist. The crown jewel of these is "Lord Nann," which reflects a more archaic stage of "Le roi Renaud" (King Renaud) than any known French form. "The Saracens" follows the French "Escrivette," which, with its Catalan and Italian congeners, has ancient origins.

References and further reading: M.-A. Constantine, *Breton Ballads* (1996), brilliantly puts the tradition in perspective. F. M. Luzel, *Chants et chansons populaires de la Basse-Bretagne*, 4 vols. (1971), is the basic collection; H. de la Villemarqué, *Barzaz-Breiz: Chants populaires de la Bretagne* (1845; rpt. 1963), full of romantic reworkings, if not falsifications, is always to be used with great caution.

France (French, Provençal, French Canadian)

At first glance Gallo-Romance balladry may seem late and predominantly lyrical rather than narrative. In a cultured Gallic tradition, informed by the eighteenth-century Enlightenment, the *chanson populaire*, often as not in some local patois, never had the national and cultural resonance that ballads called forth in Scandinavia, Iberia, Greece, or Finland. Except for George Doncieux's, most collections hardly distinguish between narrative and lyric songs. Yet France was a crucial center for the diffusion of medieval balladry, and if we see French balladic tradition in relation to the neighboring traditions that it profoundly influenced long before it was ever consecrated in writing, it emerges as being of venerable antiquity. Possible antecedents of French ballads may have been the medieval *chansons de toile*, sung by weavers, and perhaps also the *pastourelles*, but in contrast to Iberia and Germania there is no trace in the *chansons populaires* of the rich epic tradition of medieval France. One of the early written texts of a French ballad is "Gentilz gallans de France" (Noble Gallants from France), from a late-fifteenth-century manuscript. Its modern French derivatives are rare and contain lacunae, but the ballad had doubtless reached Spain long before 1605, when its earliest known Spanish version was published (S. G. Armistead et al., *El romancero judeo-español en el Archivo Menéndez Pidal* [abbreviated CMP], 12). Another ballad, on a husband's return from war, is "Le prisonnier de Hollande," which, with its widely known refrain "Auprès de ma blonde," seems only too modern, but its genetically related Hispanic counterpart "La vuelta del marido" (The Husband's Return, CMP 11), was already known in 1550, as documented in verses absorbed by another ballad and confirmed by a Jewish-Spanish tune marker, "Arbolera tan gentil" (Noble Tree), dating from 1555 (S. G. Armistead and J. H. Silverman, *Folk Literature of the Sephardic Jews* [abbreviated FLSJ], II, 35; "Antiguo romancero," no. 12A). The French ballad "L'assassin" (The Murderer) is rare now on its native soil, but it is better known in Italy as "Il marito gustiziere" (The Husband as Executioner; Constantino Nigra, *Canti popolari del Piemonte*, no. 30), and by the end of the 1400s it had already migrated to Spain, where this unpleasant story of mortal vengeance against an unfaithful wife was defamatorily applied to a historical personage, Bernal Frances, a hated general in the service of Ferdinand and Isabella (CMP M9). French narrative songs have greatly influenced the balladry of Italy, particularly in the North, because of strong linguistic affinities. The distinctive Provençal tradition is crucially important in providing a bridge to the Hispanic repertoire of Catalonia.

French Canada offers a more archaic tradition than does the homeland, including various songs whose early origins are further vouched for by sixteenth-century Spanish congeners. Traditional French ballads are also known in the Cajun tradition of Louisiana, though they are much rarer than in Canada. They were also still sung early in the twentieth century in the Indiana enclave of Vincennes.

References and further reading: There is no text-type index for French balladry. G. Doncieux, *Le romancéro populaire de la France* (1904), remains the most useful collection, despite its flawed, indeed impossible, premise of reconstructing original prototypes on the basis of modern readings. But important documentation is brought together in L. Vargyas, *Hungarian Ballads and the European Ballad Tradition*, 2 vols. (1983), which lists French parallels of Hungarian ballads, and also by H. Binder, who examines French-German ballad relationships in "Deutsch-französische Liederverbindungen," in *Handbuch des Volksliedes*, 2 vols. (1972–1975). For the Canadian tradition, see M. Barbeau, *Le rossignol y chante* (1962); for Indiana, C. R. Berry et al., *Folk Songs of Old Vincennes* (1946); for Cajun Louisiana, H. Oster, "Notes on Some Classic French Folk Ballads … in Louisiana," in *Studies in Comparative Literature*, ed. W. F. McNeir (1932). See also G. Paris, *Chansons du XVe siècle* (1875).

Italy

The first evidence of Italian ballads appears toward the mid-1400s, when "Giù per la via lunga" (Down the Long Street), a narrative song no longer alive in the modern tradition, is documented in various manuscripts. "Il falso pellegrino" (The False Pilgrim), in which a disguised husband returns to test his wife's fidelity, is quoted fragmentarily in a play written in 1536. There is a 1629 citation of "Il testamento dell' avvelenato" (The Poisoned Man's Will, similar to "Lord Randal," Child 12). The vast majority of ballads are known only in eighteenth- and nineteenth-century witnesses. "Figlia del re" (King's Daughter), "Eroina" (Brave Girl), "Sposa morta" (Dead Wife), "Occasione mancata" (Lost Chance), and "Repliche di Marion" (Marion's Answers) (nos. 8, 13, 17, 71, and 85 in Constantino Nigra's *Canti popolari del Piemonte*) all have sixteenth-century Spanish counterparts, suggesting common origins in late-medieval prototypes. (The Italian songs do not derive from the Spanish.)

References and further reading: There is no text-type index for Italian ballads. C. Nigra, *Canti popolari del Piemonte* (1957), remains the basic point of reference. It gives the tradition a decidedly northern slant but is counterbalanced by G. B. Bronzini, *La canzone epico-lirica nell'Italia centro-meridionale*, 2 vols. (1956–1961), a magisterial study of central Italian ballads. A. B. Graves, *Italo-Hispanic Ballad Relationships* (1986), provides useful parallels between Italian and Hispanic ballads.

Iberia (Spanish, Portuguese, Catalan, Judeo-Spanish)

There is indirect but incontrovertible evidence that ballads were already being composed and sung in Spain during the early 1300s. The first ballad text, "La gentil dama y el rústico pastor" (Noble Lady and Rustic Shepherd), in a mixture of Castilian and Catalan, dates from 1421, suggesting that the tradition, which originated in Castile, had by that date already reached the outer edges of the Hispanic linguistic domain. This impression is confirmed by three traditional ballads copied (or adapted) around 1470 by the Galician poet Juan Rodríguez del Padrón. Recent investigations by Encarnación Marín Padilla have brought to light other early manuscript texts dating from 1429 and 1448. Ballads began to be printed early in the 1500s, and until 1580 numerous traditional texts were selectively preserved, first in cheap broadsides and later in extensive ballad anthologies and guitar manuals. In the seventeenth and eighteenth centuries traditional ballads disappeared from view, but collecting from oral tradition began in the nineteenth century and has been systematically pursued since 1900. Today there is essentially no area of the Hispanic world that has not yielded some evidence of the pan-Hispanic tradition.

Unlike most European repertoires, the Hispanic *romancero* (ballad) derives directly from medieval epic. Though the earliest known texts are not concerned with epic themes, the first ballads undoubtedly originated as fragments of lengthy epic poems. Many epic-based ballads—reflecting both native Castilian and Old French narratives—are known from sixteenth-century printings and also from the modern tradition. Many events in medieval Spanish and Portuguese history are re-created in ballad form. Such balladic treatments usually reflect a direct knowledge of events rather than depending on any historiographic intermediary. Medieval interpretations of classical narratives likewise find their place in the early repertoire, as do ballads based on Arthurian matter and medieval romances. Though many ballads were locally composed, the major extra-Hispanic influence on the tradition was that of France, which contributed numerous text-types, some at a very early date. The Iberian tradition thus provides crucial evidence of the prehistory of Gallo-Romance balladry.

Three main subtraditions are present on the Iberian Peninsula: Portugal and Galicia, on the west (with important overseas extensions in the Atlantic islands and Brazil), the Castilian center (extending overseas to the Canary Islands, Spanish America, and the Sephardic Jewish communities of Morocco, the Balkans, and the Middle East), and Catalonia, on the east. The majority of Hispanic ballads are of postmedieval origin, but a substantial corpus of medieval narratives continues in circulation even today, not only on the peninsula but also, though to a lesser extent, in Spanish America and Brazil. In terms of medieval survivals, pride of place is taken by archaic lateral areas such as Spain's Northwest, the Portuguese province of Trás os Montes, the Atlantic islands (Azores, Madeira, Canaries), and the Judeo-Spanish communities.

See also: Hispanic Tradition

References and further reading: The Iberian tradition is now well supplied with type indices: A. Valenciano et al., *Romances tradicionais de Galicia: Catálogo exemplificado* (1998); D. Catalán et al., *Catálogo general del romancero* (1982–1988; abbreviated CGR); S. G. Armistead et al., *El romancero judeo-español en el Archivo Menéndez Pidal*, 3 vols. (1977, abbreviated CMP); and M. Costa Fontes, *Portuguese and Brazilian Balladry* (1997; abbreviated RPI). CGR, CMP, and RPI are bilingual, together with English. CGR and RPI access all subtraditions, as does CMP to a lesser degree. The basic, "canonical" collection is R. Menéndez Pidal and M. Goyri, *Romancero tradicional de las lenguas hispánicas (Español-portugués-catalán-sefardí)* (1957–1985). See also S. G. Armistead and J. H. Silverman, "El antiguo romancero sefardí: Citas de romances en himnarios hebreos (Siglos XVI–XIX)," *Nueva revista de filología hispánica* 30 (1981), and *Folk Literature of the Sephardic Jews*, 3 vols. (1971–1994; abbreviated FLSJ). G. Beutler, *Estudios sobre el romancero español en Colombia* (1977), is the best Spanish-American source. E. Marín Padilla, *Arcebispo de Çaragoça: Romance castellano … del año 1429* (1997), and M. Milá y Fontanals, *Romancerillo catalán* (1882), are useful; F. B. Wolf and C. Hofmann, *Primavera y flor de romances* (1856; rpt. 1945), though old, remains the handiest reference for the early texts.

Hungary

Lajos Vargyas, with great erudition and exhaustive documentation, has eloquently argued that many Hungarian ballads derive from early French prototypes brought to Hungary by medieval French-Walloon settlers. Vargyas's publications are central to our understanding of Hungarian balladry, but scholarship has not fully accepted his theory of its French origins. A different approach would not exclude the possibility of French influence but might put more stress on the Hungarian repertoire's complex interaction with neighboring traditions, reflecting the country's strategic location at the very heart of Eastern Europe. Ballad collecting in Hungary started very late; the first printed collection dates only from 1846 to 1848. The classic collection is Vargyas's *Hungarian Ballads and the European Ballad Tradition*, which assigns numbers to the major types. Using Vargyas together with Ninon Leader's *Hungarian Classical Ballads and Their Folklore*, readers with no knowledge of Hungarian can still attain a detailed knowledge of the tradition.

The Hungarian tradition shares a fine foundation sacrifice ballad, "Clement Mason," with the pan-Balkan tradition (Vargyas 2). Various text-types, to say nothing of many migratory motifs, are shared with other European traditions: "The Enticed Wife" (Vargyas 3), "The Dishonored Maiden" (Vargyas 10), "The Deceived Husband," and "The Soldier Girl" (Vargyas 80) correspond, in the first three cases, to Child's "Lady Isabel and the Elf-Knight" (4), "Lady Maisry" (65), and "Our Goodman" (274), while the venerable ancestry of all four ballads finds support in the sixteenth-century Spanish printings of "Rico Franco," "Conde Claros fraile," "Blancaniña," and "La doncella guerrera," though we must continue to wonder exactly when these narratives entered the Hungarian tradition. Especially significant for documenting earlier strata of Hungarian balladry are the archaic repertoires of such lateral communities as the Transylvania Székeleys and the Moldavian Csongos.

See also: Hungarian Tradition
References and further reading: See L. Vargyas, *Hungarian Ballads and the European Ballad Tradition*, 2 vols. (1983) and *Researches into the Mediaeval History of Folk Ballad* (1967). N. A. Leader, *Hungarian Classical Ballads and Their Folklore* (1967), stresses numerous parallels with English-Scottish tradition. See also H. Lüdeke et al., *Ungarische Balladen* (1926).

—Samuel G. Armistead

Baltic Tradition

The folkloric culture of medieval Livonia and Lithuania.

The southeast coast of the Baltic Sea was home to a number of peoples belonging to two cultural complexes: the Balts (speakers of languages in a conservative branch of the Indo-European language family, comprising Latvian, Lithuanian, and Prussian) and the Baltic Finns (speakers of a highly Indo-Europeanized branch of the Finno-Ugric language family, comprising Estonian, Finnish, Ingrian, Karelian, Livonian, Vepsian, and Votic). During the medieval period the majority of these peoples were forcibly consolidated into the realm of Livonia, ruled by the Teutonic Knights. Lithuanians, however, maintained their independence, rising to the status of empire during the thirteenth through the early fifteenth centuries, before finally succumbing to Polish domination. The medieval folk culture of the region was marked by the strong persistence of native traditions, overlaid by Christian, German, and Hanseatic influences.

The Livonian Rhymed Chronicle of the thirteenth century describes the peoples of the Baltic region thus: "All these pagans have most unusual customs. They dwell together of necessity, but they farm separately, scattered about through the forests. Their women are beautiful and wear exotic clothing. They ride in the ancient manner and their army is very strong whenever it is assembled." From such remarks, along with archaeological and later ethnographic evidence, it is possible to characterize early medieval Baltic life. Shifting slash-and-burn agriculture was the rule, supplemented by hunting and fishing. Loanwords for agricultural implements and many crops indicate that agriculture passed from the Balts to the Baltic Finns. Intermarriage among all the groups appears to have been prevalent. Women wore elaborate headdresses, breastplates, and jewelry, adopting styles developed elsewhere but modifying them to fit native tastes. Armies were assembled when needed, and hill forts were sometimes maintained for defense.

During the Viking Age, Baltic amber became a prime commodity throughout Europe and the Middle East. Viking traders from the island of Gotland in the West and from Novgorod in the East vied for control of the Baltic trade, but the various peoples of the region remained independent. Both Western and Eastern Christianity entered the region but failed to take root. Sporadic pirating of trading ships made the Baltic region uncertain ground for merchant interests.

In the twelfth century, however, German merchants from Lübeck entered the region, establishing a post among the Livonians (Livs) on the western Dvina River near the site of Riga. They profited from the regional cooperation of Saxon and Danish rulers and found the area lucrative. In the 1180s, soon after the creation of the settlement, the Augustinian priest Meinhard arrived to Christianize the populace. The subsequent Livonian crusade grew increasingly militaristic, spawning an order of German monastic knights, the Fratres Militae Christi, or Swordbrothers. These crusaders, recruited from Germany and Scandinavia, subdued one tribe after another, establishing fortresses at key defensive sites (e.g., Riga, Tallinn, Tartu, and Daugavpils), forcing native nobles into vassal status, pressing peasants into military service, and levying taxes to sustain their new institutions. The consolidated realm became known as Livonia. In the mid-thirteenth century the Swordbrothers merged with the larger Teutonic Knights, an order occupied in the conquest of Prussia.

In opposition to the Swordbrothers and Teutonic Knights, a coalition of Lithuanian tribes formed under the leadership of King Mindaugas. In 1260 Mindaugas abandoned the Christian faith—which he had accepted in the 1250s—and began to war actively against the German crusaders. The Lithuanians and closely related Samogitians damaged the German effort through frequent raiding. Lithuanian warriors pushed eastward as well, conquering Slavic cities abandoned by the Tartar retreat. The Lithuanian empire begun by Mindaugas was continued by a succession of worthy kings in the fourteenth century and eventually extended from the Baltic to the Black Sea. The empire fell in the early fifteenth century with the triumph of Poland and the nominal conversion of the Lithuanians to Christianity.

Following conversion, the entire Baltic region came to be dominated by German Hanseatic interests. The cities founded for defensive purposes became trading centers similar to those of northern Germany and Scandinavia. The peasant economy was greatly restructured to accord with the feudal system. The countryside continued to harbor a great many traditions, however, that predated contact and domination.

Pre-Christian Religions

The overtly mercantile nature of the Baltic crusades did little to endear common people to their new religion. Furthermore, although Pope Innocent II

(1130–1143) had urged the use of the Baltic vernaculars in prayer and preaching as early as 1138, nearly all of the region's clergy and services were German throughout the medieval period. The strong resistance to Christianity among the Lithuanians further bolstered the region's pre-Christian beliefs, so that the entire medieval period can be viewed as a negotiation between pre-Christian and Christian traditions.

Little is known of the religions of the Baltic Finns, although the beliefs of the Finns and Karelians further north were fairly well preserved. German and Polish chronicles provide glimpses of pre-Christian Prussian and Lithuanian religions. From these references it appears that the Balts possessed a religious system similar to that of other Indo-European peoples. In particular, the sources indicate a triad of male deities worshiped in conjunction with sacred oak groves at sites such as Romowe. A fierce god of the dead—associated with hanging, skulls, night rides, and fury and depicted as old, sometimes one-eyed, and green-bearded—was known by the various names Patollus, Pecullus, and Velinas. A thunder god—associated with perpetual fires and oracle priests and depicted as middle-aged and black-bearded—was known as Perkûnas. Finally, a youthful, beardless Potrimpos or Natrimpe was associated with agrarian fertility, good fortune, grain, milk, snakes, and a priestess class. Potrimpos merges with a wide range of "lower-order" deities associated with the earth, harvest, and fertility, including Zvempatis and Zvemyna, master and mistress of the earth. Many of these lower deities are male. References to a divine smith (Kalvelis), a woodland goddess, and deities associated with healing abound in late-medieval accounts of Lithuanian culture.

Although German conquest obliterated much of early Latvian (Lett) religion, we know of a supreme god, Dievs (or Debestêvs), and a thunder god, Perkuons. The sun and moon were viewed as husband and wife, and their daughters were said to play with the sons of the celestial deities. A goddess of birth and fate, Laima, is mentioned in many folksongs and was known among the Lithuanians as well. A variety of female lower-order dieties presided over water, fire, sea, and wind. Household spirits and the spirits of deceased relatives were venerated and feared among all the Balts and Baltic Finns.

Folksongs

In the Baltic region, native meters and genres of folksong persisted throughout the medieval period. A trochaic or trochaic-dactylic meter characterized Baltic-Finnic, Latvian, and Lithuanian songs, although each culture possessed its own devices and aesthetics. The Baltic-Finnic song tradition was strongly alliterative, and line-pair parallelism was a regular feature. The Latvian *daina* was terse (usually only two lines long) with some alliteration and much parallelism. The longer and more rhythmically variable Lithuanian *dainas* rarely relied on alliteration, rhymed occasionally, and possessed both elaborate parallelism and a nuanced use of diminutives.

Peasant life finds poignant expression in the folk music of the region, including songs concerning the life of orphans, wives, and shepherds. Ritual songs associated with weddings, harvest, birth, death, and holidays are plentiful and varied from village to village throughout the region. Courtship, too, was accompanied by singing, sometimes subdued and lyrical, other times bawdy and erotic. Although epics exist throughout the region, lyrical songs predominate; they were performed primarily by women. Traditional Baltic instruments include a small zither (Lithuanian *kankles*, Latvian *kokle*, Estonian *kannel*), panpipes, and various forms of wooden trumpets. The bagpipes were popular in the later Middle Ages, but the violin arrived relatively late.

Calendar Customs

Scholars disagree about the origin and age of Baltic calendar customs: some regard traditions connected with the agricultural year as pre-Christian, while others posit their introduction with Christianity. At any rate, during the Middle Ages festivities connected with sowing, the harvest, and the solar year were celebrated on the feast days of Christian saints. Important festivals were associated with St. George (spring planting), St. John's Eve (Midsummer), St. Anthony, a feast of the dead, Christmas, Easter, and others. Particularly striking were customs involving the creation of an idol or effigy, such as the Latvian Jumis or Estonian Metsik, Peko, or Tunn. Communal work was undertaken as a festival of its own, known in Latvian as *talka*, Estonian *talgud*. Such work parties combined heavy harvest labor with feasting, drinking, and dance.

See also: Finno-Ugric Tradition; Slavic Tradition, East
References and further reading: J. Smith and W. Urban provide a useful introduction and
historical overview of the Livonian conquest in *The Livonian Rhymed Chronicle* (1977),
quotation above from pages 5–6. J. Puhvel discusses Baltic mythology from an Indo-
Europeanist perspective in *Comparative Mythology* (1987). I. Paulson surveys Estonian
belief and custom in *The Old Estonian Folk Religion* (1871). A. Greimas provides a valuable
overview and semiotic analysis of Lithuanian folk religion in *Of Gods and Men* (1992).
Studies of specific types of Baltic folklore include M. Gimbutas, *Ancient Symbolism in
Lithuanian Folk Art* (1958), and F. Oinas, *Studies in Finnic Folklore* (1985). Another useful
collection of articles is E. Zygas and P. Voorheis, eds., *Folklorica* (1982). The range of
Baltic narrative genres may be sensed through L. Neuland, *Motif-Index of Latvian Folktales
and Legends* (1981). V. Vêis-Freibergs, ed., *Linguistics and Poetics of Latvian Folk Songs*
(1989), is an important collection of essays on Latvian and Lithuanian folksong.
—*Thomas A. DuBois*

Bear [*Ursus arctos arctos*]

The Eurasian brown bear, ranging from Spain to Siberia and as far south as India; eponym and heraldic charge, as at Bern, Switzerland, since at least 1224; trained to perform (motif K1728) and victimized in spectacles from Roman to modern times.

Bears were exported to the Roman Empire by the Germanic peoples, whose descendants preserved much ursine lore. In Norway and Denmark, Migration Age nobles were buried on bearskins, with bear claws or with clay models of bear claws. Claws have been recovered from Viking York, as has a bear's canine, partly pierced, from Norse Orkney (now a northern Scottish island). Ursiform ornament has a long history in Scandinavia, from Paleolithic petroglyphs through Neolithic clubs to brooches found on Gotland (an island east of Sweden) and on to the sword hilts and spear sockets of the Vendel period. Best known is a Torslunda die depicting a man flanked by two bear-like figures. These apparently whispering beasts parallel tales of the whispering bear (J1488).

The bear figures prominently in the folklore of Europe; in southern French tradition it is Ursus who seeks his shadow on Candlemas. Linking bear lore with St. Blaise, Emmanuel Le Roy Ladurie notes that "the bear's resounding fart of dehibernation celebrated the primordial rite of spring." *Roman de Renart* tells how Bruin lost his tail (AT 2). Icelandic sagas suggest totemic relationships between humans and bears: humans have bear fathers, mothers, and sons. This circumpolar theme may be reflected in Hallmund, who in *Grettir's Saga* lives in a cave under a glacier with his mysterious daughter. In Norway Grettir kills a bear, keeping its pelt and claws. He has been called a "bear hero," as have Beowulf, Bjarki, and others. Retold in *Hrolf's Saga*, the legend of Bjarki (Little Bear)— son of Björn (He-Bear) and Bera (She-Bear)—involves shapeshifting (G263.1.1), sorcery, bear marriage (B601.1), and breach of taboo (B635.1.1).

Germanic bear lore reflects lost ritual. The Eddic poem *Sigrdrifumal* prescribes carving runes *á bjarnar hrammi* (on a bear claw): fangs and claws were talismans. Sympathetic magic inspired ursiform design that gave bear power to

Warrior between two bears; from the sixth-century Torslunda dies. (Drawing by Karen Reynolds)

warriors—for example, the *berserkir* (bear shirts) were fanatical warriors dedicated to Odin, who worked themselves into battle rage. Saxo Grammaticus says men drank bear blood to attain ursine strength. According to Arent, initiation rites may even have pitted men against bears. Onomastic applications were common: like Björn, the name *Beowulf* (Wolf of the Bees) may be taken to mean "bear"; these terms presuppose names based on bruin's color or craving for honey. There are many such euphemisms—sweetfoot, wintersleeper, grandfather, forest king—coined for the one that wintered in the underworld, summered upon middle earth, and haunted heaven forever in the constellation called Great Bear by many besides the Romans (cf. Finnish *Otava*).

The Celts had a bear deity (A132.5) analogous to the Arcadian Kallisto. According to Rhys Carpenter, the Greeks also associated the bear with Zalmoxis, Odysseus's progenitor Arkeisios, and the oracle at Trophonios. Derivations from Celtic *airth* (including perhaps the name Arthur), Italic *ursus,* and Hellenic *arktos* reflect the Indo-European root word for bear, **rks*—a term long gone from Germanic (scholars have suggested that tribal hunting taboos on speaking the name of the bear led to the disappearance of the term). Place names like Björnhövda (Bear's Head) imply that the Swedes, like the Finns, had a bear cult. The Finno-Ugric bear hunt involved rich drama, with a "marriage" and feasting followed by the solemn burial of the reassembled skeleton—except for the skull, which was placed high in a tree. Totem and shamanic guardian, the bear was a natural fertility figure, too, reborn each spring along with the green shoots and summer birds. It was the most anthropomorphic animal of the North, hallowed by the rhythm of death and resurrection.

See also: Candlemas; Finno-Ugric Tradition

References and further reading: A. M. Arent relates bear heroes to archaeology in "The Heroic Pattern," in *Old Norse Literature and Mythology,* ed. E. C. Polomé (1969). S. O. Glosecki describes Germanic and circumpolar bear rites, artifacts, and beliefs in his *Shamanism and Old English Poetry* (1989). Veneration of the bear is treated in R. Carpenter's *Folktale, Fiction, and Saga in the Homeric Epics* (1946), B. Collinder's *The Lapps* (1949), and A. I. Hallowell's *Bear Ceremonialism in the Northern Hemisphere* (1926). The quotation above from E. Le Roy Ladurie is from *Carnival in Romans* (1980), page 99.

—*Stephen O. Glosecki*

Becket, Saint Thomas (c. 1120–1170)

Chancellor of England (1155–1162), archbishop of Canterbury (1162–1170), and the most extensively venerated English saint—famous since the twelfth century for his martyrdom at the hands of four knights in Canterbury Cathedral but even more celebrated in medieval times, almost from the moment of his death, for his afterlife as a miracle worker.

Although postmedieval legendry, seeking to identify Thomas Becket with the cultural underdogs of post-Conquest England, has sometimes portrayed him as Anglo-Saxon in descent, he was in fact of Norman parentage. Born in London as the city was becoming a major cultural center, Becket became known as London's saint almost as much as he was Canterbury's. His friend

William Fitzstephen, who wrote a *vita* (saint's life) of Thomas in the 1170s, prefaced his sacred biography with a description of London, for "St. Thomas has adorned both these cities, London by his rising and Canterbury by his setting."

Early Life

Biographers and scholars searching for the seeds of greatness in what is known of Thomas Becket's early life have been generally both puzzled and disappointed by the sketchiness of his education and his seeming lack of any clear aim or purpose. Although he was a bright, attractive youth, possessed of unusually keen senses and a wonderful memory (total recall, it is said), Thomas was an indifferent student who preferred field sports, such as hunting with hawks and hounds, to strict application to his studies. Nevertheless, it is known that he attended Merton, which served as a preparatory school, and after some years there entered one of the three principal schools of London, possibly St. Paul's. From the London grammar school, at age 16 or so, he went to Paris, where he would most likely have followed the arts curriculum, though there is evidence Thomas had not thoroughly mastered the subjects. The motivation for some of the changes in young Thomas's life is not clear, but certainly his father's financial misfortunes and then the deaths of both parents (it was his mother who had insisted on his studies and recognized his talents) affected his decisions. Forced to make his own living after his father fell on bad times, he was apprenticed as an accountant to a banker friend of his father's, Osbern Huitdeniers, and he also acted as clerk and auditor to the sheriffs of London. In these capacities he added a knowledge of the world of politics, diplomacy, and finance to what he already knew, through his father's contacts, of the interests and manners of the court circle.

As long as he was alive, Thomas's father, Gilbert Becket, was a prime agent in his son's advancement, so it is hard to know whether he arranged for the young man's introduction into the household of Theobald, archbishop of Canterbury, or whether this move was due to Thomas's desire for an ecclesiastical rather than an administrative career. Whatever the case, probably in the winter of 1143–1144 at age 25, Thomas joined the archbishop's household as a clerk. In this cathedral community, one of the most distinguished in the country, Thomas was doubtless groomed for an administrative post such as the archdeaconry, to which he was appointed in 1154 through Theobald's influence. But advancement followed hard upon advancement; only weeks later, also through Theobald's influence, Thomas was appointed chancellor to the new English king, Henry II. For both men, king and gifted, ambitious commoner, it was a fateful development. As was his nature (a trait that baffles some biographers), Thomas Becket gave to his new master his complete loyalty and his best efforts. The chancellorship gave Thomas the opportunity to indulge a taste for opulence and ostentation—lavish entertainments with gold and silver plate and exquisite foods, fine horses, a convoy of ships when he crossed the English Channel. The extent to which his intimate friendship with Henry II involved Thomas in debauchery is somewhat debatable; certainly the two rode together, hunted, hawked, and gamed together. Some biographers insist that

Thomas remained chaste in his private life and ate and drank in moderation. It is likewise suggested that during these years of achievement and success Thomas Becket was aware of trying to serve two masters, the king and the Church, the secular and the spiritual. That being the case, his proper allegiance was made manifest to him in 1162, when Henry II appointed him archbishop of Canterbury.

As Archbishop

No doubt the English king was convinced that he could control an archbishop as easily as he had controlled a chancellor. The king failed to understand—and the concept boggles the minds of some of Thomas's biographers—that Thomas Becket applied himself wholeheartedly and single-mindedly to whatever job he accepted without any residual sympathies or loyalties. From the time he was ordained a priest in order to serve as archbishop, Thomas was a churchman. Perhaps such had been his inclination from the early days of his mother's instruction, or perhaps his avid dedication to his duties was in part a matter of practical expedient. In any event, he brooked no intrusion on the Church's authority. For centuries in England, through a variety of political upheavals, the issue of the division between the functions and offices of the Church and royal power had been held somewhat in abeyance. Thomas's appointment came at a time when circumstances at last brought the issue to a head and when a group of men, all of them powerful and gifted but each of them seriously flawed, were brought together to engage in debate and combat: Thomas and Henry II, of course, as well as Pope Alexander III, Thomas's rival and archenemy Gilbert Foliot, and others. The confrontation came immediately. Thomas's rebuff of King Henry in the matter of clerical immunity led to Henry's presenting the Constitutions of Clarendon, a number of which were unacceptable not just to Thomas but to the Church hierarchy in Rome, and the ensuing bitter quarrel led to Thomas's escape from England and exile first in Rome and then in France. His exile lasted for six years, during which the quarrel continued through a complex web of emissaries and letters.

On January 19, 1170, the often indecisive Alexander III commanded that the English king and archbishop resolve their differences, with harsh penalties for both if they refused. Thomas returned to England amid scenes of rejoicing and omens of disaster. Rumors and a number of hostile incidents indicated that the archbishop was not safe on English soil. However, as his entourage made its way through the countryside, the streets and roadways were lined with cheering multitudes. It was a reception that neither Thomas nor Henry II could ignore. Henry had arranged to be out of the country, but there were those who were willing to act on his behalf. On Tuesday, December 29, 1170, four knights—Hugh of Moreville, William de Tracy, Reginald Fitz Urse, and Richard le Breton—murdered Thomas in the cathedral at Canterbury.

As Martyr and Saint

If the event had been staged to inspire public reaction and the immortality of the victim, it would not have been more effective. The church was full of people. The archbishop's courage in facing his assailants and his final words, "I accept death in the name of Jesus and his Church," were seen and heard by many. The murder was especially brutal and grisly; one knight sliced through the dying archbishop's skull while another scattered his brains across the stones. The night was stormy, with lightning and thunder. The monks who prepared the body for burial—in secret and without ceremony—discovered under Thomas's habit a hair shirt and drawers infested with vermin and concluded that his martyrdom by sword was more endurable than his self-inflicted, continuous martyrdom. Furthermore, more than any other moment of medieval history, the occasion was recorded by men of learning who could describe it in detail; four of the nine biographers who wrote about Thomas Becket were present at the martyrdom.

Thus, within hours of Thomas's death, his heroic afterlife began. Although for a short time the royal agents in Canterbury acted vigorously to prevent the murder having vexatious consequences, threatening monks and hampering pilgrims, they could not control the rapid spread of information or the burgeoning cult among the common people. In a matter of days reports and tales of signs

One of the thirteenth-century "miracle windows" in Canterbury Cathedral illustrating the posthumous acts of St. Thomas Becket: an apparition of St. Thomas hovers over the bed of the eldest son of Sir Jordan Fitz Eisulf. Because Sir Jordan has failed to keep his promise to make an offering at Becket's tomb, his son must die of plague. (Courtesy of Sonia Halliday and Laura Lushington)

and wonders began to pour in. Shortly after Whitsun, Robert de Broc's brother, William, was cured at Becket's tomb. Soon the cathedral, for a while left desolate and deserted, was changed into a kind of field-dressing station that was visited by a steady stream of the sick and indigent. The heart of the cult was the blood of the martyr, which at first the monks were hesitant to administer for both theological and practical reasons. Eventually they diluted the blood in wine or water or presented pilgrims with small patches of Thomas's blood-soaked garments. However, anything associated with the martyr—his cloak, scraps of the hair shirt, proximity to his tomb—was in time believed to have miraculous powers.

A monk named Benedict collected a series of oral testimonies concerning miracles experienced by those who prayed to St. Thomas; these are remarkable in the extent to which they record the experiences of the lower classes. In 1172 William of Canterbury, another monk, incorporated Benedict's together with his own collection, probably as part of a project to obtain the status of sainthood for Thomas, for the posthumous miracles known as *signa* (signs) were necessary evidence for canonization. These books may never have been presented in evidence, because Thomas was canonized speedily, within two years and two months of his death, on February 21, 1173. A year later, in July 1174, Henry crossed from Normandy to England in a tempest and did public penance at Canterbury, asking for pardon and being scourged by the whole community of monks. Louis VII, king of France, who had given Thomas sanctuary during his exile, paid a similar visit.

Fifty years after Becket's death his remains were removed from the crypt and reinterred in the newly completed Trinity Chapel on a raised portion of the ground floor of the cathedral. In subsequent centuries, so many pilgrims would visit this site that their feet wore down the stone steps leading up to the shrine. The new shrine was surrounded by the 12 tall "miracle windows," each depicting some of Thomas's miracles, and many closely following the tales earlier collected by Benedict and William. Much of the glass has been destroyed, but the surviving scenes are remarkable in depicting very few nobles but many common people. Quite clearly, the numerous lower-class pilgrims visiting the shrine could find echoes of their own status even within surroundings that were probably the most ornate and lavish they had ever experienced.

Some of the stories represented in the miracle windows present rather simple lessons in charity toward the lower classes. In the tale of Eilward of Westoning, a man who steals from his neighbors is blinded and mutilated by order of a magistrate. Thomas visits him in his bed and restores his sight. A group of pilgrims, moved by the miracle, give Eilward alms, which he promptly gives away to a beggar. The moral is clear: Thomas's mercy supersedes rough worldly justice; those who follow Thomas learn that generosity to the poor cancels crime and undoes punishment.

In other stories peasants are forgiven their faults and given redress for the inequities they suffer when they fail their lords. One of the glass stories traces the fortunes of Richard Sunieve, a herdsman who fell asleep while tending the horses of his lord. Awaking, he was stricken with leprosy, which can be read as punishment for failing to do the work of his master. Richard traveled to Thomas's

One of the thirteenth-century "miracle windows" in Canterbury Cathedral illustrating the posthumous acts of St. Thomas Becket: the story of Richard Sunieve, stricken by leprosy for falling asleep while minding his master's horses, and later cured by St. Thomas. (Courtesy of Sonia Halliday and Laura Lushington)

shrine and was healed. St. Thomas thus serves as a mediator who can be invoked to lessen the pains of the peasants. God and their masters may punish peasants who do not attend to the good of their lords, but Thomas, if not an equalizer, intervenes to clear the slate and spare them from disproportionate punishment.

If Thomas sometimes helps peasants avoid punishment, he also calls upon the lower orders to help him punish godless nobles. Perhaps the most striking instance of this is found in the complex tale of the Fitzeisulf windows. The nine panels recount an episode of the plague that kills Sir Jordan Fitzeisulf's nurse and threatens to kill his son. Water from St. Thomas's shrine cures the son, and Sir Jordan vows to pay a visit of thanks to the cathedral. When Fitzeisulf forgets to make the journey, the saint appears to a leprous crippled beggar, Gimp, and tells him to warn the family. Gimp delivers the warning from his sickbed, but Sir Jordan does not heed him. So Becket appears, like the avenging archangel Michael, hovering over the family with a sword drawn to deal out death. Most of the family and its servants fall ill; the oldest Fitzeisulf son dies; and Sir Jordan finally makes his too-long-delayed pilgrimage to pay homage to St. Thomas. This is probably the most revolutionary text of all. To punish a negligent noble, Thomas enlists the help of a leprous beggar. Gimp becomes the human voice of the saint, warning that a failure of generosity will lead to terrible vengeance.

It may be said that at a crucial time and under mostly accidental circumstances, Archbishop Thomas Becket died for the freedom of the spiritual authority of the Church and died proclaiming that he knew what he was doing and was willing to die for this cause. The reverberations of his death affected the course of history in a limited way and for a limited time. St. Thomas's influence as an ongoing source of folkloric materials of great richness and variety has been, however, much longer lasting.

See also: Blood; Pilgrimage; Saints, Cults of the

References and further reading: F. Barlow, *Thomas Becket* (1986), and D. Knowles, *Thomas Becket* (1970), stand out among the numerous biographies; see also Knowles's *The Episcopal Colleagues of Archbishop Thomas Becket* (1951). The folklife of Thomas Becket's London is vividly portrayed by his friend William Fitzstephen in *Norman London*, the prologue to Fitzstephen's *vita* of St. Thomas, excerpted and translated, with introductory essay by F. Stenton (1990). The miracles collected by the monks William of Canterbury and Benedict of Peterborough appear in volumes 1 and 2, respectively, of *Materials for the History of Thomas Becket, Archbishop of Canterbury*, ed. J. C. Robertson and J. B. Sheppard, Rolls Series (1875–1885). English-language accounts of Thomas's life after death are not as common as his biographies, but W. Urry, *Canterbury under the Angevin Kings* (1967), provides some documentation. The major study of the stained-glass representations of Becket's miracles is found in M. Caviness, *The Stained Glass of Canterbury Cathedral* (1977). More accessible depictions of the stained glass are found in Anonymous [E. Williams], *Notes on the Painted Glass in Canterbury Cathedral* (1897); B. Rackham, *The Stained Glass of Canterbury Cathedral* (1957); and S. Brown, *Stained Glass in Canterbury Cathedral* (1991).

—*Lee Winniford and Carl Lindahl*

Bede the Venerable (673–735)

Monastic theologian and historian of early England, whose works are rich sources of legends circulating in oral tradition.

Born in territory attached to the monastery of St. Peter and St. Paul—which had sites at both Wearmouth (now Monkwearmouth) and Jarrow in northern England—Bede was brought to the monastery at age seven and lived there for the rest of his life studying, teaching, and writing the many works that earned his reputation as the most distinguished scholar of his time.

Though much of his learning came from books, Bede also collected numerous legends from oral tradition, especially for his great *Ecclesiastical History of the English People* (731), which provides some memorable examples: that scrapings taken from an Irish manuscript and mixed with water was a cure for snakebite (1, 1); that St. Albans displayed power over a river before his martyrdom and that after his beheading the executioner's eyes popped out onto the ground (1, 7); that St. Germanus debated the Pelagian heretics before a crowd that finally judged him the victor when the saint defeated his opponents in a miracle contest (1, 17–18); that splinters from King (later St.) Oswald's cross, mixed in water, would cure sick humans and animals (3, 2); that so many people dug dirt from the spot where Oswald fell to mix with water for cures that they made a hole as deep as a man is tall (3, 9); that oil from the holy Aidan had power to calm the stormy sea (3, 15); that the same Aidan's prayers were responsible for averting the destruction by fire of the royal city of Bamburgh (3, 16); that the saintly Chad likewise had the power to calm storms (4, 3); that Imma's fetters kept falling off despite repeated efforts by his captors to chain him (4, 22); that Hilda's mother had a dream when the abbess was still an infant betokening, through a brightly shining necklace, the precious jewel that her daughter would later become for all Britain (4, 23); that St. Cuthbert's relics effected marvelous cures (4, 30–32); that the hermit Oethelwald had power to calm the stormy sea long enough for visitors to return from his island to the mainland (5, 1); that Bishop John chastised the abbess at Watton for bleeding a young nun on the fourth day of the moon (5, 3); that the hermit Dryhthelm related a terrifying, highly imaginative description of his traveling to the otherworld (5, 12); that when a dying man refused to confess his sins, demons inserted into different parts of his body sharp objects that, when they met, caused his death and dam-nation (5, 13); and that many people took soil from the spot where Hædde died, mixing it with water to cure illnesses in humans and cattle—and produc-ing a large hole in the ground by their digging (5, 18).

From Bede's accounts of the transmission of these legends it appears that Anglo-Saxon monastic communities were not so insulated as is often claimed. Such legends did not observe institutional boundaries; rather, they passed gen-erally from popular oral culture to the monasteries, circulated orally among and within various monastic communities, and often flowed from the monastery to popular culture. For example, in his *Vita Sancti Cuthberti* (Life of St. Cuthbert), Bede recounts an early miracle of Cuthbert's in which he saved monks from drowning (ch. 3). Toward the end of this account he describes how this legend was performed and circulated orally for generations among the local people before being related to Bede by a monk who heard the story in a live perfor-mance by a member of that folk community. While such legends did eventually get written down by a writer like Bede, they continued in oral tradition, some-times reappearing in later written versions as well.

In Alfred the Great's reign (871–899), Latin literacy had so far declined even among the clergy—according to Alfred's famous preface to the translation of Pope Gregory the Great's *Pastoral Care*—that a translation of Bede's history into Old English became a major event in Alfred's translation program. This late-ninth-century Old English Bede substantially reduces the scholarly appa-ratus and simplifies the style of the original for reading aloud to nonliterate audiences. As such, it is plausible to conceive of this version as a "re-oralizing" of the largely oral traditional legends written into Bede's Latin text, thus pro-viding a more complicated view of the relations between orality and literacy in early medieval contexts than has been recognized in much earlier scholarship.

See also: Cædmon; English Tradition: Anglo-Saxon Period; Monks; Nuns; Orality and Literacy

References and further reading: The standard edition of the *Historia ecclesiastica* is *Bede's Ecclesiastical History of the English People*, ed. B. Colgrave and R. A. B. Mynors (1969), with a translation by Colgrave. J. F. Webb has done a fine translation of Bede's *Life of St. Cuthbert* in *The Age of Bede*, rev. ed., ed. D. H. Farmer (1983). The best general account of Bede's social milieu, life, and works is G. H. Brown, *Bede the Venerable* (1987), which contains abundant references for further research. On oral legendry in Bede, see J. McNamara,

"Bede's Role in Circulating Legend in the *Historia ecclesiastica*," *Anglo-Saxon Studies in Archaeology and History* 7 (1994), and "Problems in Contextualizing Oral Circulation of Early Medieval Saints' Legends," in *Telling Tales: Medieval Narratives and the Folk Tradition*, ed. F. Canadé Sautman, D. Conchado, and G. C. Di Scipio (1998).

—John McNamara

Beheading Bargain

Episode (motif M221) in surviving Irish, French, and English medieval tales, in which a giant challenges the hero to exchange blows with an enormous axe, agreeing to receive the first blow.

At some later time, the hero must submit to a return blow if the giant survives. With a mighty stroke, the hero decapitates the giant, who rushes to retrieve his head. The giant gives the hero a stern warning not to shirk his half of the bargain. At the appointed time the hero remains true to his word, prepared to die. Stoically baring his neck for the axe, the hero receives a fearsome but innocuous stroke. After explaining that he has spared the hero's life because of his courage and fidelity, the giant reveals his true identity.

The earliest occurrence of "The Beheading Bargain" is in the eleventh-century *Fled Bricrend* (Bricriu's Feast). The hero Cú Chulainn proves himself worthy of the Champion's Portion by submitting twice to the return blow. The beheading game serves as a fitting test of chivalry for Arthur's knights, including Caradoc in the twelfth-century *Continuations* of Chrétien's *Perceval*, and Gawain in Paien de Maisière's twelfth-century *La mule sans frein* (The Mule without a Bridle) and Heinrich von dem Türlin's thirteenth-century *Diu Crône* (The Crown).

The fourteenth-century English romance *Sir Gawain and the Green Knight* contains the most famous example of the beheading game, interwoven with a temptation motif to present the ultimate test of the chivalric virtues represented by Gawain's pentangle. Beheading episodes also occur in several late-medieval English popular romances: *The Green Knight*, *Sir Gawain and the Carl of Carlisle*, and *The Turk and Gawain*.

See also: Gawain; *Sir Gawain and the Green Knight*
References and further reading: G. L. Kittredge, A *Study of* Sir Gawain and the Green Knight (1916), examines the beheading game and its analogs, including oral traditions worldwide. E. Brewer, Sir Gawain and the Green Knight: *Sources and Analogues*, 2nd ed. (1992), provides modern English translations of the medieval beheading game variants.

—Cathalin B. Folks

Beltane [Bealtaine, May Day]

In Ireland, the festival heralding the summer season.

Basic to the Celtic conception of time was the twofold division of the year into a winter period followed by a summer period. The summer part of the year began at Beltane, identified as May 1 in the Julian calendar. This twofold division of the year in Ireland is well attested in early and medieval literary texts in the Irish language, as is the further subdivision of winter and summer, giving four smaller seasons of three months each as the standard division of the year in Ireland.

The celebration of Beltane—in line with the celebration of the other major seasonal festivals in Ireland—commenced on the eve of the festival at sunset (and in modern oral tradition the preternatural power associated with this festival in particular was considered to be most potent between sunset on May Eve and midday on May Day). Thus, *Oíche Bhealtaine* (the night of May, May Eve) referred to the last day of April. The change of the calendar from the Old Style to the New Style around the mid-eighteenth century meant that 11 days were dropped from the reckoning, giving rise to such popular conceptions as New May Eve (*Oíche Bhealtaine úr*) on April 30, and New May Day (*Lá Bhealtaine úr*) on May 1, while May 11 became known as Old May Eve (*Oíche Shean Bhealtaine*) and May 12 as Old May Day (*Lá Shean Bhealtaine*). Thus, the period "between the two Mays" (*idir an dá Bhealtaine*), that is, between New May Eve and Old May Eve, was perceived as a hiatus during which certain farm activities, such as transferring stock to the mountain pastures, should be carried out. Hiring fairs, at which farmers took on farm servants and workers for the seasonal summer and autumn work, were held on May 11 and 12 in many places in Ireland, especially in Ulster. This also applied to some livestock fairs. The most important beliefs and customs connected with Beltane, however, transferred over time to New May Day, and this day was perceived as the appropriate time to observe the festival in order to avail oneself of its beneficent import and to avoid its potential dangers.

May Day inaugurates the summer season, when there is renewed life in the natural world, with trees in leaf, wildflowers in bloom, and a plentiful supply of fresh grass for the milk cows. It has strong agricultural and pastoral connotations, for it marked a new phase in the annual round of farming life and involved a considerable amount of reorganization on the farm, especially in relation to cattle.

It is also the bright half of the year, when the sun is high in the sky and when nature is favorable. These attributes of the season may be reflected in the festival's name, Beltane—which is also in Ireland the name of the first month of the summer season. The word, whose first element, *bel*, probably means "shining," "brilliant," or "favorable" and whose second, *teine*, means "fire," may be connected with the ancient Celtic god Belenus, possibly a solar deity. In modern folklore certain acts considered to involve magic were forbidden at sunset and sunrise, and the connection with fire, manifested in the lighting of bonfires, is an enduring aspect of the celebration of the festival.

The mythological significance of the festival of Beltane is attested in medieval literature, where it is claimed that it was on this festival that the Sons of Mil, the ancestors of the Gaels, landed in Ireland for the first time in the southwest of the country. They succeeded in wresting the sovereignty of Ireland from their predecessors, the Tuatha Dé Danann. Despite their defeat, however, the Tuatha Dé Danann deprived the Gaels of the basic foodstuffs—grain and milk— by means of magic, forcing the Gaels to come to terms with them.

The perception that milk cows and the milk yield could be adversely affected by magical acts continued to find expression in literature in Ireland during the medieval and later periods and also in the oral tradition. Milk magic is especially connected with the festival of Beltane, presumably because this feast signaled the commencement of the dairying season. The performance of milk magic is attributed to women especially, probably because they have traditionally been largely responsible for the care of the milk cows and the production and sale of dairy products. A persistent motif in narratives referring to the performance of milk magic is that some women could shapeshift, transforming themselves into hares in order to suck the milk from the cows lying in the fields. This is mentioned by Gerald of Wales (Giraldus Cambrensis) in his late-twelfth-century *Topography of Ireland* and by the English historian William Camden in his *Britannia* in the mid-sixteenth century, and it has remained a persistent element of the oral tradition in relation to Beltane in Ireland and in other parts of Europe.

A variety of verdure customs, concerned with protecting and promoting the milk yield and dairy produce, especially butter, and with welcoming the summer, are associated with the celebration of Beltane. Camden in his *Britannia* mentions the setting up of a green bough before the house in order to have an abundance of milk during the dairying season, and Sir Henry Pier's statement in his *Description of the County West-Meath* (1682) that a green bush placed before the house was strewn with yellow flowers undoubtedly strengthens its association with the production of milk and butter and with their protection and promotion. The May growths are intended to promote what they symbolize—the green leaves are representative of pasture and the yellow flowers are particularly associated with dairy produce. The erection before the house of a "May bush," with bunches of yellow flowers tied to its branches, is an enduring aspect of the celebration of Beltane, the festival of May, in parts of the eastern region of Ireland to the present day.

See also: Irish Tradition; Lugnasa; Samhain

References and further reading: For references to Beltane as a quarterly festival and the beginning of the summer season in legal, annalistic, and literary sources, see the *Contributions to a Dictionary of the Irish Language*, Fasciculus B (1975). P. Mac Cana, *Celtic Mythology* (1970), elucidates the mythological significance of Beltane and discusses the importance of milk as a basic foodstuff. For evidence of the importance of milk and milk products in the early Irish diet, see F. Kelly, *Early Irish Farming: A Study Based Mainly on the Law-Texts of the Seventh and Eighth Centuries AD*, Early Irish Law Series, no. 4 (1997); also A. T. Lucas, *Cattle in Ancient Ireland* (1989), and C. O'Rahilly, "The Bleeding of Living Cattle," *Celtica* 12 (1977). A. Rees and B. Rees discuss the paradoxical quality of Beltane's positive and negative aspects in *Celtic Heritage* (1961), and K. Danaher, *The Year in Ireland* (1972), discusses the perils of May Eve and customs practiced to avoid them. P. Lysaght distinguishes, maps, and discusses verdure customs involving May flowers, the May bough, and the May bush to protect dairy produce on May Eve and May Day in "Maytime Verdure Customs and Their Distribution in Ireland," *International Folklore Review* 8 (1991). On the role of symbolic boundaries for protecting dairy produce at Maytime, see P. Lysaght, "Bealtaine: Irish Maytime Customs and the Reaffirmation of Boundaries," in *Boundaries and Thresholds*, ed. H. Davidson (1993); and for the specific role of women, see her "Women, Milk, and Magic at the Boundary Festival of May," in *Milk and Milk Products from Medieval to Modern Times*, ed. P. Lysaght (1994).

—*Patricia Lysaght*

Beowulf

Anglo-Saxon heroic poem telling of fabulous events set in ancient Scandinavia.

The unique copy, written out by two scribes working about 1000 C.E., is found on folios 129a–198b of British Library MS Cotton Vitellius A.xv. There are no other medieval records of either the poem or its hero, but many of the characters and events to which the poet alludes in passing (such as Weland the Smith and Sigemund the Dragon-Slayer) are known in variant forms from other such early Germanic sources as the *Poetic Edda* and *Völsunga Saga*.

No other work of the early-medieval imagination provides such a detailed representation of Germanic society; no other puts the art of heroic poetry on such sustained display; no other provides such a wealth of information concerning the Anglo-Saxons' view of their legendary past. In language charged with ornamental epithets, the poet gives either sustained or glancing attention to such bedrock Germanic institutions as the feud, gift giving, cremation funerals, wergild, fosterage, exile, female exogamy, ritualistic drinking, the use of the harp, boasting, and flyting, as well as to the physical appearance of armaments, ships, and halls.

Theories of Date and Composition

While the first modern scholars to edit and translate *Beowulf* attributed it to a period as early as the Age of Migrations of the Germanic tribes, recent scholarship has dated the poem progressively closer to the date of the manuscript itself. Opinion is now divided between those who accept an eighth-century date of composition and those who favor the late ninth or tenth century, when a united Anglo-Scandinavian kingdom ruled by members of the West Saxon royal line was forming. Theories of monkish interpolation have generally been discarded, as has the old theory that the epic was stitched together from separate lays. Instead, most current scholars view the poem as a unified composition, the result of a gifted Christian poet's meditation about the remote pagan past.

No one knows how the poem was composed. Some scholars attribute it to a learned author who happened to write in the vernacular. Others see it as the work of a singer steeped in a traditional oral-formulaic technique, like epic songs recorded in the Balkans and Greece in recent times. The current tendency is to see the poem as in some sense oral-derived rather than as either a completely literary composition or the verbatim record of a normal oral performance. If the text came into being through the collaboration of a singer, a patron, and one or more scribes, like the poems attributed to Cædmon by Bede (*Historia ecclesiastica* 4, 24), then surely it was edited in the process of being written down, and its length and elaborate ornamentation may partly reflect the special conditions of an unusual process of textualization.

Folktale Analogs

Some scholars see the poem as closely indebted to Celtic tradition, particularly to the Old Irish tale known as "The Hand and the Child." In stories of this type, the hero wrenches off a long, demonic arm that reaches into a hall in an attempt to abduct a prince's newborn child. He then traces the wounded monster to a body of water and kills him. In its two-part action, its switch between a hall and a watery setting, and its lurid focus on a severed arm, the tale has much in common with the Grendel episode in *Beowulf*, and yet in the Old English poem there is no child or attempted kidnapping, nor does the arm appear as a threat in its own right. Among other motifs that have been held to show Celtic influence are the hero's swimming prowess, his battle rage, his use of a giant-wrought sword, and the choice of a mighty female creature as adversary. If such elements do derive from Celtic sources, whether via the folklore of a subjugated British population or via Ireland, then they have been assimilated to the Anglo-Saxon worldview while being adapted to a setting in the Germanic past.

The poem consists of two main episodes into which other materials are freely introduced, including historical and legendary digressions, retrospective speeches, and gnomic and elegiac passages. First Beowulf, a young Geatish warrior, vanquishes Grendel, a cannibalistic creature who for many years has terrorized the hall of Hrothgar, king of the Danes; then, after Grendel's mother avenges her son, Beowulf seeks her out and kills her in her underwater home (lines 1–2,199). After many years, now having become the aged king of the Geats, Beowulf dies in victorious combat against a huge firedrake (lines 2,200–3,182). While the plot of the dragon fight is too simple for this episode to be traced to a single source, the Grendel episode has been linked to a widely distributed European folktale known as the "Bear's Son" tale, or, more properly, "The Three Stolen Princesses" (AT 301). Like *Beowulf*, this international tale type features the adventures of a strong hero (sometimes with ursine attributes or parentage) who first puts one ogre into flight, then follows its tracks into a nether region where he dispatches a second, sometimes female, ogre. Similar story elements are found in the thirteenth-century *Grettir's Saga* and other Old Icelandic tales, and *Hrolfs Saga Kraka* includes a somewhat comic analog in its account of the monster-slayer Bödvar Bjarki, who is literally the son of a bear. It cannot be shown, however, that AT 301 existed during the Middle Ages in the same form as in recent tradition. Very likely both *Beowulf* and its Icelandic analogs represent a specialized northwest European reflex, set in a pseudo-historical context, of a very ancient two-part mythic-hero tale of a monster slaying.

Christian Influences

Although the poem is set in the pagan Continental homeland of the English peoples, nothing in it is inconsistent with Christian teachings. On the one occasion when the Danes offer sacrifice at a pagan shrine, the narrator vehemently condemns their error. Other scenes that contribute to what has been called the "pagan coloring" of the poem, such as the ship funeral at its start and the cremation burial at its end, are presented with such stately decorum as to elicit admiration for great kings and ceremonies rather than anxiety about theological doctrines. No pagan gods are mentioned by name. No word is breathed about such repugnant rites as human sacrifice, although divination is mentioned in passing and the dragon's treasure bears a curse. Beowulf, Hrothgar, and other main characters talk and act like pious monotheists, as if by their innate power of reason they are endowed with a knowledge of such matters as the Creation, Providence, Hell, and Doomsday. In addition, the narrator, who knows more than the characters do, informs us that Grendel is descended from Cain, that God sent Beowulf to the Danes as a savior, that the huge sword the hero finds in Grendel's lair was made by giants before the Flood, and that Beowulf's soul departs from his body at death "to seek out the judgment of the righteous." By such means the audience is assured that the heroes and kings of the ancient north, rather like the patriarchs of Old Testament times, acted out their fates in a world subject to God's will.

The Hero and the Monsters

At the center of the poem, lending the story such unity as it has, is the character of Beowulf himself. We are left wondering whether he has supernatural powers or is merely exceptionally strong. His maternal uncle, Hygelac, was renowned for his gigantic size, as is reported in the medieval Latin compendium known as the *Liber monstrorum* (Book of Monsters). His tribe, the Geats, while identifiable with the Gautar of southern Sweden, seems also to be linked through medieval pseudogeography with both the Jutes, whom Bede names as one of the founding tribes of England, and the Getae, an imaginary "proto-Germanic" tribe of the ancient north. True to both his tribal associations and his folktale affinities, Beowulf is described as not only the biggest of his band of warriors but also the strongest human being alive at that time, and he proves his might by wrenching the arm off a creature who is literally of gigantic stature. In addition, he can swim in the seas for days, fully armed in his mail coat, and he can survive underwater for longer than seems humanly possible. The poet makes it clear that God himself favors Beowulf, at least in his two first fights. On the other hand, nothing is said about Beowulf's having other than normal parentage, and the plot of the poem shows him to be mortal. Unlike heroes of the "Strong John" type, but much like the biblical patriarchs or the saints of the New Dispensation, Beowulf seems to win victory as much through his piety and fierce moral integrity as through his physical strength. He is larger than life; he is also, in his ultimate vulnerability, completely human.

A page from the sole surviving manuscript of Beowulf, *dating from the late tenth or early eleventh century. (British Museum, Cotton Vitellius A.xv.; North Wind Picture Archives)*

Like the hero, the monsters of *Beowulf* occupy an ambiguous realm between the natural and the supernatural. Grendel and his mother are not just cannibalistic ogres; they are literally devilish, and the eerie, icy pool in which they make their home is reminiscent of medieval theologians' descriptions of the mouth of hell. The dragon, while never described as demonic, is a figure for the devil in medieval typology outside of *Beowulf*, and some scholars have argued that he carries at least some of that typological weight in this poem as well. On the other hand, the Anglo-Saxons believed in the flesh-and-blood existence of dragons and cannibalistic giants, to judge from the place names built on the elements *thyrs* (monster) and *drake* (dragon) that dot the English landscape. Books of pseudoscience known to the English—in particular the collection known as *Marvels of the East* (a copy of which directly precedes *Beowulf* in the hand of the first scribe)—confirmed that such creatures existed in at least the exotic regions of the world, and a Wiltshire charter of 931 refers to a "Grendel's mere" in the vicinity of "Beowa's enclosure." The *Beowulf* poet's tale of the slaying of horrific monsters by a magnificent hero in ancient Scandinavia, however, probably reflects a myth-making tendency among the Anglo-Saxons more than it reflects their credulity about the world around them.

Theories of Mythic Origin

Sporadic scholarly attempts have been made to link the characters or events of the poem to ancient myths and religious practices. The temptation to read *Beowulf* as a reflex of ancient myth is strong, given that no similar literary work survives in northern Europe from such an early date, but specific links to myth and rite are hard to locate. Nineteenth-century interpretations of the poem as a kind of solar or nature myth are universally dismissed. Scyld Scefing, the founder of the Scylding dynasty of Danish kings, bears a name that translates roughly as "Defender" (from the Old English *scyld*, meaning "shield"), "son of Sheaf" (from Old English *scef* or *sceaf*, denoting "sheaf of grain"), and the poet's allusion to Scyld's mysterious arrival as a foundling links him to what appears to be an ancient fertility myth. But the *Beowulf* poet celebrates Scyld Scefing exclusively as a mighty warrior and father of kings. Herebeald, the elder brother of Beowulf's king Hygelac, bears a name that is reminiscent of Old Norse Baldr, but if the myth of Baldr's death provided some inspiration for the poet's account of Herebeald's death by arrow shot and his father Hrethel's inconsolable grief, then the parallel remains merely suggestive. Hrothgar's gold-adorned queen Wealhtheow may ultimately be related to the valkyrie figures of northern myth, at least in a broadly generic sense, but in the poem she functions simply as a gracious queen. Attempts to show an etymological link between her name and the valkyries involve special pleading. Vestiges of shamanism in the poem are equally tenuous. Somewhat like the shamans of northern lands, Beowulf travels "between worlds," as it were, as he descends to a nether region to kill Grendel's mother. But his descent is physical rather than mental; it involves no magic or drums; and its aim is the defense of a kingdom, not initiation or the curing of disease. The hero's name, Beowulf, or "Wolf of the Bees," to accept one etymology, may possibly be a euphemism for "Bear" (that is, a name that avoids using the bear's real name by calling the bear a honey eater, a "wolf of the bees"), and the poem might thus have some connection to a widespread ancient cult of the bear as totemic animal. If so, then the hero's nonhuman attributes have been almost wholly rationalized away.

Attempts have also been made to link the action of the poem's first episode to the Easter liturgy (the climax of the medieval liturgical year) and to the literature of baptism. From a Christian perspective, Beowulf could be thought of as descending, like Christ, into a nether region "to slay the ancient serpent," and the poem could take on aspects of an allegory of salvation. Such approaches have the virtue of explicating the poem in terms consistent with the actual functioning mythology of the Anglo-Saxons. They rightly call attention to the fight against Grendel's mother as the dramatic center of the poem and the site of extraordinary miracles. Still, they are based on arbitrary and predictable connections to a body of doctrine that lies outside the poem. While nothing can stop a devout Christian from interpreting the poem in typological or allegorical terms—for indeed, according to some medieval theological perspectives, the whole natural world and all of human history are open to interpretation through allegory—the poet gives no clear sign that a specific allegory is intended. Grendel is devilish, but he is not Satan. Beowulf is a great hero, but he is not Christ. In their pursuit of religious symbolism, Christological readings tend to slight the specific contours of the narrative and ignore the poet's sustained interest in the details of German legendry and the ethos of the heroic life.

Beowulf offers a mine of information bearing on Anglo-Saxon folklore, legendry, and popular belief. It also can easily become a minefield for critics intent on searching out elements that are thought to lie beneath its surface. Each such attempt has its interest, and from it something can be learned. At the same time, readers should not be distracted from seeing the poem in its literal narrative as a powerful story whose mood is darkened by Christian pessimism at the same time as its meaning is enriched by ethical concerns. Instead of looking for traces of ancient myth in the poem, current readers are increasingly approaching the poem as a myth; that is, as a work of major cultural synthesis in which the Anglo-Saxons addressed tensions concerning their national or cultural identity in the form of a story set in the ancient past: Are we ethically Christian or pagan, or in some sense both? Are we ethnically Saxons or Danes, or some fusion of the two? Is our cultural heritage to be sought out chiefly in the northern or the Mediterranean world? These are among the questions and controversies that a contemporary audience of Anglo-Saxons would have found posed, if not finally resolved, in the long, complex, and masterfully told story of the deeds of Beowulf, hero and king.

See also: Cædmon; Dragon; English Tradition: Anglo-Saxon Period; Epic; Funeral Customs and Burial Rites; Sutton Hoo

References and further reading: Most scholarly research about *Beowulf* takes as its starting point F. Klaeber, *Beowulf and the Fight at Finnsburg,* 3rd ed. (1950). Additional bibliography is to be found in D. K. Fry, Beowulf *and the Fight at Finnsburg: A Bibliography* (1969); D. D. Short, Beowulf *Scholarship: An Annotated Bibliography* (1980); and R. Hasenfratz, Beowulf *Scholarship: An Annotated Bibliography, 1979–1990* (1993). See also the articles in R. E. Bjork and J. D. Niles, eds., *A* Beowulf *Handbook* (1997). Texts and translations of many analogs are included in R. W. Chambers, Beowulf: *An Introduction,* 3rd ed., with a supplement by C. L. Wrenn (1959), and in G. N. Garmonsway, Beowulf *and Its Analogues* (1968). Articles reflecting different theories on dating the poem are collected in C. Chase, ed., *The Dating of* Beowulf (1981). J. D. Niles argues for the oral-derived character of the text and for the poem's place in tenth-century Anglo-Saxon culture, in Beowulf: *The Poem* *and Its Tradition* (1983) and in chs. 3–5 of *Homo Narrans: The Poetics and Anthropology of Oral Literature* (1999). Among studies of special interest to folklorists, G. Jones, *Kings, Beasts, and Heroes* (1972), offers an analysis of the poem with reference to both Celtic and Old Norse materials, as well as to folktale and heroic legend. A. M. Arent, "The Heroic Pattern: Old Germanic Helmets, *Beowulf*, and *Grettis saga*," in *Old Norse Literature and Mythology*, ed. E. C. Palomé (1969), gives a Jungian twist to the study of Beowulf as an example of *Heldenleben*. J. M. Stitt, Beowulf *and the Bear's Son* (1992), reviews the poem's relation to folktale and argues that AT 301, the poem, and its saga analogs are all rooted in an Indo-European dragon-slayer tradition-complex. Rather differently focused folkloric studies are C. Lindahl, "*Beowulf*, Old Law, Internalized Feud," and J. McNamara, "Legends of Breca and *Beowulf*," both in a special issue of *Southern Folklore* 53 (1996). M. Puhvel, Beowulf *and Celtic Tradition* (1979), reviews the case for Irish influence and adds new evidence in support of it. C. R. Davis provides a fresh examination of the poem within its Germanic context in Beowulf *and the Demise of Germanic Legend in England* (1996). S. B. Greenfield, "A Touch of the Monstrous in the Hero, or Beowulf Re-Marvellized," *English Studies* 63 (1982), argues that the hero's marvelous attributes are not merely the creation of modern critics. J. A. Leake, *The Geats of* Beowulf (1967), discusses medieval pseudogeography and links the Geats to the Getae. N. K. Chadwick, "The Monsters and Beowulf," in *The Anglo-Saxons*, ed. P. Clemoes (1959), reviews much relevant monster lore. H. Damico, Beowulf's *Wealhtheow and the Valkyrie Tradition* (1984), analyzes Hrothgar's queen and related female figures in the light of northern myths about shining goddesses. S. O. Glosecki, *Shamanism in Old English Poetry* (1989), sees a parallel to *Beowulf* in the infernal descent of shamanic initiates. Among the many authors who have written on the Christian elements in *Beowulf*, L. D. Benson, "The Pagan Coloring of *Beowulf*," in *Old English Poetry*, ed. R. P. Creed (1967), has made a strong case that the poet's thought world is essentially that of orthodox Christianity, with the addition of a few details meant to call up an image of pagan antiquity. A. Cabanis and M. B. McNamee explore the parallel between *Beowulf* and the Easter liturgy and argue for Christian allegory, respectively, in "*Beowulf* and the Liturgy" and "*Beowulf*: An Allegory of Salvation?," two articles reprinted in *An Anthology of* Beowulf *Criticism*, ed. L. E. Nicholson (1963).

—*John D. Niles*

Berserks

In Old Norse-Icelandic tradition, fierce warriors with animal-like characteristics who are impervious to wounds.

The first attestation appears to be in stanzas assigned by editors to *Haraldskvaedi*, a poem ordinarily attributed to a ninth-century Norwegian skald, Thorbjörn hornklofi, about whom little is known. The poem is an encomium to King Harold Hárfagri (Fairhair). In its reconstructed form the poem comprises, besides an introductory section, an account of the king's victory at the battle of Hafrsfjörd and a description of various members of his retinue: skalds, warriors, and jugglers. Among the warriors are berserks, "drinkers of blood, battle-bold men who go forth into the army." The next stanza is devoted to *úlfheðnar* (wolf skins), "who carry bloody shields into battle, who redden shields when they come into battle. . . . the king puts his trust only into bold men who hew into shields." Later, written narrative assigns to King Harold berserks called *úlfheðnar* who wore wolf skins and defended the prow of his ship (*Vatnsdæla saga*, ch. 9).

Elsewhere in the Sagas of Icelanders berserks sometimes show up as unruly challengers for a woman's hand (*Eyrbyggja Saga* and *Heidarviga Saga*), and the *fornaldarsögur* contain many similar scenes. In many cases the hero overcomes the berserk and himself wins the hand of the woman in an analog to folktales in which monsters threaten princesses and are rescued by heroes who slay the monster and marry the princess (see, e.g., AT 300, "The Dragon-Slayer" and related types). Often, however, berserks operate in groups, most often 12.

The *berserksgang* (going berserk) is known from *Ynglinga Saga*, the first saga in *Heimskringla*, the compilation of kings' sagas done by the Icelander Snorri Sturluson in the first half of the thirteenth century. In the early chapters of this saga Snorri attempts a euhemerization of the god Odin; that is, he presents Odin as a historical figure, a human king whom men later worshipped and thus elevated to the status of a deity. Among Odin's abilities was that of vitiating the strengths of his enemies, while at the same time, according to Snorri, "his men went without armor and were crazed like dogs or wolves, bit into their shields, were as strong as bears or bulls. They killed people, but neither fire nor iron affected them; that is called going berserk" (*Ynglinga Saga*, ch. 6). By stating that berserks go without armor, Snorri seems to understand the term *berserkr* as "bare shirt," but the parallel with the *úlfhe nar* renders more plausible the etymology "bear shirt." Certainly such an etymology accords with the animal characteristics Snorri associates with going berserk.

Theriomorphic (beast-form) warriors are known from Viking Age iconographic evidence, especially a sixth-century plate from Torslunda, Sweden, and accepting this etymology allows that evidence to be associated with the berserks. More generally, some scholars have seen in the crazed behavior and animal characteristics of the berserks, which are found in many Old Norse-Icelandic sources and in the *Gesta Danorum* (History of the Danes) of Saxo Grammaticus, the reflection of an ecstatic warrior cult of Odin. If the association is made with the etymology of Odin's name as deriving from an Indo-European form meaning "leader of the possessed," the phenomenon must be pushed back to well before the Viking Age, for the etymology is not transparent. Indeed, many scholars see the cult of the ecstatic warrior god as an ancient phenomenon inherited from the Indo-European ancestors of the Scandinavians.

See also: Scandinavian Mythology; Shapeshifting
References and further reading: Relatively recent articles in English include D. J. Beard, "The Berserkr in Icelandic Literature," in *Approaches to Oral Literature*, ed. R. Thelwall (1978), and B. Blaney, "The Berserk Suitor," *Scandinavian Studies* 54 (1982). The phenomenology of going berserk is treated by F. Grøn, *Berserksgangens vesen og årsaksforhold* (1929). On the ecstatic warrior cult, see B. Lincoln, *Priests, Warriors, and Cattle* (1981); the fundamental works are S. Wikander, *Der arische Männerbund* (1938); L. Weiser, *Altgermanische Jünglingsweihen und Männerbünde* (1927); and O. Höfler, *Kultische Geheimbünde der Germanen* (1934).

—John Lindow

Bestiality

Sexual contact between humans and animals.

The term usually refers to intercourse between humans and animals, but it may include other forms of sexual contact. Medieval texts both describe what may have been actual incidents and tell stories that seem to have derived from folk traditions, making it difficult to determine actual practices.

The early Christian medieval world inherited both texts and traditions that described human/animal intercourse. In the classical Greco-Roman texts, gods in the form of animals had intercourse with humans. For example, Zeus took the form of a bull to carry away Europa and the shape of a swan to seduce Leda. Classical "scientific" writings also told tales of bestial intercourse, probably drawing from folklore traditions. Aelian's *On the Characteristics of Animals* (c.170 C.E.) is full of tales that describe human relations with goats, horses, baboons, snakes, dogs, geese, and other animals. Pagan Germanic traditions also preserved tales of bestiality, whether between human and animal or between one human and another who took the shape of an animal. Many of the early myths refer to such liaisons, particularly favoring references to intercourse with horse gods and humans transforming into birds to have relations with people.

The Christian tradition did not accept bestial intercourse. During the early Middle Ages most of the references to bestiality were in the form of penitential manuals prohibiting the practice. Yet in some rare tales we can see the tension between old and new beliefs. For example, there is an Old Norse account of the conversion of a household by St. Olaf. Olaf encountered a pagan family worshipping a *völsi*, a preserved horse penis. Olaf fed the ritual item to the family dog, and the family was converted to Christian worship. This tale exemplifies the relationship between Christian and pagan tradition in which the former attempted to eradicate bestial eroticism in the latter.

Tales of bestial intercourse reappear and increase in frequency in Western European literature after the twelfth century. Gerald of Wales, who repeated much folk wisdom he acquired in his travels through Ireland and Wales, related a number of tales of bestiality. Gerald told of men who had intercourse with cows and of women with goats and a lion. He even recounted an incident of a man who passed a calf from his bowels after having been sodomized and impregnated by a bull. In his *Topography of Ireland,* he describes a ritual of kingship in which the man soon to be king has public intercourse with a white mare.

In the later Middle Ages churchmen became more concerned than they had been earlier with the presence of demons interacting with humans. As part of this preoccupation, tales of bestiality increasingly referred to intercourse with demons, the succubi and incubi that seemed ubiquitous. By the thirteenth century, the chronicler Caesarius of Heisterbach (who, like Gerald, delighted in retelling tales he had heard) reported so many stories of demons having intercourse with men and women that he claimed the practice was almost commonplace.

The evidence indicates that over time people in the Middle Ages changed their opinion about bestiality. Official culture, as expressed primarily in the secular and religious law codes, at first treated the practice as not serious, equating it with masturbation. By the thirteenth century, however, Thomas Aquinas ranked bestiality as the worst of the sexual sins, and the law codes recommended harsh penalties for the practice. Official culture's growing preoccupation with bestiality may have influenced chroniclers recording folktales about the practice, because only after the twelfth century do the sources show an increase in such stories as those of Gerald of Wales. However, it is impossible to tell whether the recounting of incidents of sexual contact with animals reflected a new pre-occupation simply on the part of members of official culture, who then chose to notice folktales that were already in circulation, or whether the new preoccupation permeated all of society, which then generated new tales of the practice. Nor is it possible to determine the relationship between the frequency of actual bestial intercourse and the growing popularity of stories about the practice.

In *The Beast Within*, Joyce Salisbury argues that the change in attitudes toward the practice of bestiality reflected a growing uncertainty about the separation of humans and animals. Preoccupation with and legislation against bestial intercourse thus expressed an attempt to secure the separation of species when that separation seemed endangered.

See also: Gerald of Wales; Olaf, Saint; Sexuality
References and further reading: Two works deal directly with this topic: M. Dekkers, *Dearest Pet* (1994), and J. Salisbury, *The Beast Within* (1994). In addition, one may locate primary and secondary source references in J. Salisbury, *Medieval Sexuality* (1990), an annotated bibliography. The best guides to ecclesiastical legislation against the practice are P. Payer, *Sex and the Penitentials* (1984), and J. Brundage, *Law, Sex, and Christian Society* (1987). Rich collections of bestiality tales may be found in Aelian, *On the Characteristics of Animals* (1959); Caesarius of Heisterbach, *Dialogue on Miracles*, 2 vols., trans. H. Scott and C. C. S. Bland (1929); and Gerald of Wales, *The Historical Works of Giraldus Cambrensis*, ed. T. Wright (1887). For an analysis of the *völsi* tale, see A. Heusler, "The Story of the Völsi, an Old Norse Anecdote of Conversion," in *Sex in the Middle Ages*, ed. J. Salisbury (1991).

—*Joyce E. Salisbury*

Bestiary

A book of imaginative and often moralized descriptions of various animals.

It would be unfair to suggest that the Bestiary is a compendium of what passed for natural history in the Middle Ages, or even that it is a handbook of the fauna, real and imagined, that inhabited the medieval world. Indeed, it is misguided of modern scholars to complain of the fantasies recorded about the various animals in these books as if their authors were particularly inept or even mendacious zoologists—it is anachronistic to see these books as handbooks of natural history, even moralized natural history. It was a matter of indifference to medieval clerics whether or not the habits ascribed to the various animals were actually true; what mattered was that these details could be read analogically as so many lessons in the Book of Nature promoting Christian virtues and discouraging vice. Modern scholars have too often, if for understandable reasons, been bedazzled by the Bestiary's illustrations at the expense of inquiring into its textual history.

The earliest extant illustrated Bestiary is the ninth-century Bern manuscript, but its style of illustration shows that it derives from a late-classical model of the fourth century or earlier. The text and illustrative cycle of the Bestiary as written in the central Middle Ages is essentially an English elaboration of a late-classical poem known as the *Physiologus*. Ron Baxter's analysis of the structure of the *Physiologus* reveals that its 36 chapters are divided into eight thematic groups, with the first chapter in each group referring to Christ and introducing the theme of the rest of the chapters in its group; the themes are Avoidance of Vice, the Jews and Gentiles, the Letter and the Spirit of the Law, Human Renunciation of the Devil, the Community of the Faithful, the Avoidance of the Devil's Snares by Turning to Christ, the Power of Christ in the Community of Saints, and Christ's Incarnation. Within groups the succession of animals can sometimes be shown to derive from some biblical prompt: in Group 3, for example, the hedgehog, in chapter 13, follows the siren and centaur, chapter 12, because all three creatures are mentioned in the verse from *Isaiah* quoted at the opening of chapter 12. The taxonomic principle of the *Physiologus* is shown to be fundamentally theological, based on the moralization to be drawn from each beast, so that even prescientific "commonsensical" categories such as birds, fish, and land animals find themselves jumbled together in any given grouping, to the despair of modern zoologically oriented scholars. Considering the overall structure of the work, the *Physiologus* is thus characterized as a treatise on virtue and vice.

On English soil this text evolved into the peculiarly English genre of the Bestiary. There are now known to be as many as 50 extant manuscripts of the work, and it has recently been suggested that the original English population of this popular work must have been somewhere in the order of 250–350 books. Detailed examination of library catalogs and other evidence proves conclusively that in medieval eyes these works were regarded principally as collections of exempla, handy for use in sermons, and, indeed, not all have illustrations. Careful analysis of the ownership of Bestiaries by the various religious orders shows a marked enthusiasm for them among the Cistercian monks, in whose sermons the creatures are frequently moralized.

Extant manuscripts are conventionally divided into four textual "families." Broadly speaking, First Family manuscripts follow the text of the *Physiologus* most closely; the Second Family, somewhat later, introduces materials from Isidore of Seville and others. The small Third Family uses different supplementary texts, especially the *Pantheologus* of Petrus Londiniensis; rearranges the animal groups of the Second Family; and opens with a discussion derived from Isidore of the so-called monstrous races. These literally marginal races, placed at the edges of *mappaemundi* (world maps), such as that from Hereford, are illustrated in some Bestiaries, such as the late-thirteenth-century York Bestiary. The Fourth Family is represented by only one manuscript, housed in Cambridge University Library and dated about 1425.

When in "The Nun's Priest's Tale" Chaucer compares Chanticleer's crowing to the singing of the "mermayde in the see," his appeal to authority is couched in the words "For Phisiologus seith" (7.3270f.), implying the poet's familiarity with the frequent introductory formula, "*Physiologus dicit,*" of the Latin manuscripts. Though it is clear that the popularity of the Bestiary was on the wane by the date of *The Canterbury Tales*, on the Continent, at least, Theobald's version of the *Physiologus* enjoyed a modest renaissance with the advent of printing, and at least a dozen early printed editions are known.

Some well-known Bestiary stories are in fact only found in the vernacular texts, such as the crocodile's tears in the Anglo-Norman French verse Bestiary

RIpes uocatur: quod sit animal pen
natum & quadrupes. hoc genus fera
rum in hyperboreis nascitur locis uel monti
b3. omni parte posteriori corporis leoni: aliſ
& facie aquilis simile. equis uehementer in
festum. nam & homines uisos discerpit.

Aſt animal quod dr elephanſ in quo
non eſt concupiſcencia coitus. Elephã

*Depiction of an elephant, displaying the arms of marcher lords on the shields and banner.
(Mid-thirteenth century; Oxford, Bodleian Library, MS Bodl. 764, fol. 12r)*

of Philippe de Thaon, dedicated to Henry I's queen and composed around 1135 (two of the three known manuscripts of which were written in England). More popular, surviving in more than 20 manuscripts, was the Anglo-Norman *Bestiaire Divin* of Guillaume le Clerc (c. 1210), some manuscripts of which were copied in England and most of which are illustrated. These Anglo-Norman Bestiaries constitute further important evidence for the great popularity of the work in England.

Of course, we must not necessarily infer Bestiary symbolism when confronted with Bestiary imagery, but the evidence of such outside the scriptorium is not without interest and, surely sometimes at least, not without symbolic import. One such case where we may be certain that the artist based his composition on a Bestiary manuscript is the archivolt of the mid-twelfth-century south doorway of the church at Alne, Yorkshire, which includes nine voussoirs (wedge-shaped stones in an arch) whose Bestiary origin are confirmed by their inscriptions.

Baxter has shown that the First Family Bestiary (still a preponderantly *Physiologus* text) was, like its parent, above all a work amenable to oral public performance, whereas the Second and Third Family manuscripts have moved into the study, for private consultation. The celebrated illustrations are also, he concludes, of little or no didactic value; their only value apart from decoration would be as a "finding aid" for a solitary reader looking for a particular chapter, and it is significant that even the earliest First Family manuscripts have already dropped the illustration of the moralizations that can still be seen in the illustrated Brussels *Physiologus*.

However, it is for its—to the modern eye—quirky illustrations and many of the commonplaces of medieval and early modern beliefs about the behavior of real and imagined animals that the Bestiary will be most often remembered. Whether or not it is the earliest source of some of the best-known stories and beliefs about animals, there is no doubt that it was one of the most influential, and several persisted into modern times or modern idiom, such as the statement that the bear literally "licks into shape" its cubs, or that the fox plays dead in order to pounce on unsuspecting carrion birds, the latter moralized thus: "The Devil has the same nature: with all those living according to the Flesh he feigns himself to be dead until he gets them in his gullet and punishes them."

Another remarkable case is that of the stag, which

> is called *cervus* from its habit of snuffling up the *cerastes* which are horned snakes. ... When they feel themselves to be weighed down by illness, they suck snakes from their holes with a snort of the nostrils and, having survived the danger of their venom, the stags are restored to health by a meal of them.

This passage not only typifies the absurd etymologizing (ultimately dependent on Isidore), but it is also typically moralized: "After snuffing up the Devil-snake, i.e., after the perpetration of sin, they run with confession to Our Lord Jesus Christ, who is the true fountain, and, drinking the precepts laid down by him, our Christians are renovated." It is typical, too, in that it presumably alludes to the biblical "panting hart" of Psalm 42 with its very similar moralization of a beast image. It is thus possible that the conjunction of the stag and snake sculpted on the Norman tympanum at Parwich (Derbyshire) is not wholly fortuitous; it might even be that the stag-and-snakes panel picked out in minute gold filigree work on the paten associated with the recently discovered ninth-century Derrynaflan chalice owes its origin to the same late-classical natural history source (but note that the story is also found in Pliny).

It seems likely that the person who carved the bird on a misericord at Denston had the Bestiary story in mind, for he has shown it clutching a pebble in its claw; should it fall asleep while on guard duty, the pebble will drop on its foot and wake it. The elephant allegedly had no joints in its knees and so was obliged to lean up against trees to rest; the hunter would saw almost through such supporter trees so that next time the elephant leaned against it, both would fall down, and the animal, unable to rise again, could be killed. The Bestiary method of capturing a unicorn is similarly unsporting: the unicorn is seduced—and the word does not seem inappropriate in the palpably suggestive context of this fantasy—into laying its horned head in the lap of a naked virgin, whereupon the hunter jumps out from behind a tree and spears it! This unlikely method of capture is frequently depicted, as on a misericord at Stratford-upon-Avon. Tiger cubs might be captured by dropping mirrors to confuse the pursuing tigress who, seeing her own reflection in the mirror, believes it to be her abducted cub.

The whale's appetite for small fish, lured by a sweet odor emitted from its mouth, was compared by the Bestiary to the devil's appetite for men: his attractions lure men of little faith to their destruction, as in the unintentionally humorous scene of the sailors whose ship comes to rest on the back of a whale where they make a campfire. From among the birds, we may single out for mention the eagle, which tests the fearless gaze of its young by obliging them to stare at the sun; those that avert their eyes are cast out. Whether original with the Bestiary or not, its stories and its illustrative tradition undoubtedly had a marked influence on late-medieval art and thought, from such an apparently frivolous image as that of the mermaid (originally appearing in the earliest Bestiaries as a siren of the bird-type but in later manuscripts depicted in the familiar fish-tailed form), to the far more theologically significant icon of the "Pelican in her piety," that is, pecking her own breast in order to feed her nestlings on the blood, a type of Christ's sacrifice for humankind.

See also: Griffin; Iconography; Mermaid; Unicorn

References and further reading: Much of the above depends on R. Baxter's important new book, *Bestiaries and Their Users in the Middle Ages* (1998). Baxter rightly takes to task much previous work, not least for having been preoccupied with the illustrations at the expense of the text, with the honorable exception of the great M. R. James in *The Bestiary* (1928). Baxter overlooks, however, important work done by W. B. Yapp, including, "Animals in Medieval Art: The Bayeux Tapestry as an Example," *Journal of Medieval History* 13 (1987), and "A New Look at English Bestiaries," *Medium Aevum* 54 (1985), in which he suggests a subdivision of Second Family manuscripts according to their illustrations; see also W. George and Y. B. Yapp, *The Naming of the Beasts: Natural History in the Medieval Bestiary* (1991). D. Hassig, *Medieval Bestiaries: Text, Image, Ideology* (1995), attractively represents the state of scholarship pre-Baxter. Still handy is T. H. White, *The Book of Beasts* (1954), for its translated text and reproductions of the line drawings from the twelfth-century manuscript, Cambridge University Library, Ii. 4. 26. For a typically encyclopedic treatment of one Bestiary bird, the pelican, and its symbolism, see C. Gerhardt, *Die Metamorphosen des Pelikans* (1979).

—Malcolm Jones

Black Death

Name given to the catastrophic plague pandemic in late-medieval Europe. The plague raged throughout Europe from 1347 through 1351.

The disease, spread by fleas, has three main forms: bubonic, septicemic, and pneumonic. The bubonic form is characterized by a gangrenous pustule at the site of the initial bite, followed by swelling of the lymph nodes. As the infection progresses, buboes (subcutaneous hemorrhages) appear. Ultimately the disease leads to neurological dysfunction and, in 50–60 percent of victims, death. The pneumonic form is far more deadly, with more than 90 percent of the victims dying. Pneumonic plague occurs mostly in colder climates. In the rarest form of the plague, the septicemic form, bacilli enter the bloodstream, causing a rash, and death follows within a day. The septicemic form is always fatal. The plague bacillus, *Yersinia pestis*, is carried by two types of fleas, *Xenopsylla cheopis* and *Pulex irritans*. The flea bites serve as a primary infection source. In the case of pneumonic plague, secondary infection, from human to human, occurs through bodily secretions, most notably saliva.

The Black Death appears to have sprung up in East Asia, although the plague is known to be native to numerous parts of the world, including Yunnan, China, central Asia, Iran, Libya, East Africa, and the Arabian Peninsula. Well-developed trade routes from East Asia to the Black Sea allowed for movement of goods both overland and by sea to transshipment points serving Europe. The plague reached the Crimean port of Caffa in 1345, spreading from there to the eastern ports of the Mediterranean Sea. In 1347 the plague reached Constantinople. From there it spread quickly to the European continent. The plague arrived in the Sicilian port of Messina in October 1347, and later that same year, the ports of Genoa and Marseilles. Thence it traveled west and north, reaching Paris in the spring of 1348. It skipped over the English Channel into southern England, traveled along the coast, and reached London in the autumn of 1348. In German-speaking lands it went on to both Switzerland and Austria, eventually following trade routes up through Basel, Frankfurt, Cologne, and Bremen.

Mortality rates for the plague were extraordinarily high. Even by conservative estimates, there is strong circumstantial evidence that close to one-quarter of the entire population of Europe died during the Black Death. For example, when the plague reached Holland the mortality was so high that all work on land reclamation along the Zuider Zee stopped. In Bremen, records from the period suggest a mortality rate of close to 50 percent. Some villages, certainly, were completely wiped out by the plague, but estimates of mortality for Europe suggesting close to 90 percent should be considered unlikely. Before the Black

Death the plague had reared its head in an earlier pandemic, commonly referred to as the Justinian plague, that ravaged southern Europe from 541 to 544. Later pandemics of the plague also continued to wreak havoc on Europe up through the early eighteenth century.

The extraordinary virulence of the plague, and the huge numbers of victims it claimed, profoundly affected the cultural expressions of many Europeans. The plague became the subject of legends, beliefs, ballads, paintings, and rituals, and it influenced literary works such as Boccaccio's *Decameron*. Recurring plague pandemics and epidemics in Europe ensured the continued relevance of many of these folkloric expressions, and legends concerning the plague could still be collected in the twentieth century.

In plague legends the disease is often portrayed in human form. One of the best-known personifications of the plague from central Europe is the Austrian *Pest Jungfrau* (Plague Maiden), who was said to fly over the land enveloped in a blue flame spreading disease and death in her wake. The celestial nature of the plague figure is also preserved in British tradition. These stories perhaps relate to the common belief that the plague was caused by the wrath of God and portended the end of the world. Other folk belief, reinforced by medieval medical conceptions of disease, maintained that the plague entered the body as a vapor. In postmedieval Scandinavian tradition, particularly from Sweden and Norway, the plague was represented as a traveling couple, often an old man and an old woman carrying a shovel and a broom: "When he [the plague] went forth with his shovel, some people were spared; but where she went forth with her broom, not even a mother's child was left alive."

In the fourteenth century there was very little knowledge of how diseases such as the plague spread. One thing people did know, however, was that the plague came from outside their communities. Numerous plague stories mention

The burial of victims of the Black Death, from a fourteenth-century Belgian manuscript. (Bibliothèque Royale, Brussels, MS 13076, fol. 24v)

ships drifting ashore with dead crews and subsequent outbreaks of the plague. Other traditions mention an unknown animal running through the village spreading the disease. In yet other traditions, wandering mendicants or witches are identified as the disease carrier.

Some of the best-known representations of the Black Death center around the phenomenon of the *danse macabre* (Dance of Death), although the first *danse macabre* was probably not held until August 1424 in Paris. The dance, led by a figure dressed as death, was intended to scare off diseases. Later historians have attempted to link the frenetic dancing associated with the plague to the neurological damage that the disease causes, suggesting that this choreomania was a physiological result of the disease.

The medieval population was generally unable to mount a significant defense against the onslaught of the disease. People felt, however, they had to do something to arrest or at least divert its spread. Fire was often seen as a preventive measure that would divert the plague vapors so they would not reach a village. Others maintained that the plague was unable to cross natural boundaries, such as streams or plowed fields. Numerous rituals sprang up that were intended to halt the plague's advance. Among the more colorful of these rituals is one from Eastern European tradition in which three naked virgins were forced to plow a furrow counterclockwise around the village. In other traditions, young children were buried alive to stop the plague. One of the better-known groups to develop during the time of the plague was the flagellants, a movement that started in Germany. The movement was closely related to the persecution of the Jews, whom some blamed for the plague, maintaining that Jews were poisoning wells and thereby causing the disease. The flagellant movement eventually dissolved into millenarianism and was condemned by the pope.

Numerous postmedieval stories concern the aftermath of the plague. The majority of these stories focus on the extraordinarily high mortality rate during the plague and tell of two lone survivors' subsequent repopulation of the area. Other stories mention the unpredictability of the plague, focusing on the randomness of its distribution in a region. Yet other stories mention the remarkable survival of individuals, often individuals who drove corpses to the cemetery for burial: "She had driven all the dead to the cemetery and had only one jade to drive them with, but she didn't get sick because she smoked a chalk pipe."

Although the plague is not at present a threat, a concern with the unimpeded spread of virulent, catastrophic disease continues to find expression in contemporary folklore. The AIDS epidemic and the emergence of other viral infectious agents, including hemorrhagic fevers such as the Ebola virus, are the subject of numerous contemporary legends and various folk beliefs.

See also: Funeral Customs and Burial Rites; *Memento mori*

References and further reading: One of the best critical accounts of the plague can be found in R. S. Gottfried, *The Black Death: Natural and Human Disaster in Medieval Europe* (1983). J. Nohl's early *The Black Death: A Chronicle of the Plague*, trans. C. H. Clarke (1926), is exhaustive and offers information on folkloric expressions associated with the Black Death. G. Marks offers a readable and engaging overview of the Black Death in *The Medieval Plague: The Black Death of the Middle Ages* (1971). A classic work is P. Ziegler, *The Black Death* (1969). Postmedieval legends concerning the Black Death have been exhaustively studied in both J. Lindow, "Personification and Narrative Structure in Scandinavian Plague Legends," *Arv* 29/30 (1973), and T. R. Tangherlini, "Ships, Fogs, and Traveling Pairs: Plague Legend Migration in Scandinavia," *Journal of American Folklore* 101 (1988).

—*Timothy R. Tangherlini*

Blasons Populaires

Generally known stereotypical statements directed against another ethnic, racial, social, professional, or religious group.

While *blason populaire* (signifying "conspicuous generalization") has become the international scholarly term for verbal stereotypes, it has gained no general acceptance, nor has the term *ethnophaulisms* (disparaging statements about any given group of people). The term *ethnic slurs* has become the generally accepted designation for such stereotypes in English. Blasons populaires, or ethnic slurs, are thus verbal statements that have as their topics the generalized characteristics of another group based on stereotypes, national character, ethnocentrism, xenophobia, misogyny, homophobia, prejudice, racism, and so on.

It is impossible to speak of blasons populaires in terms of one genre because they may appear in many forms: single word, phrase, proverb, riddle, joke, or even short narrative. Those that are merely a word usually are nicknames for another group, such as "Krauts" for Germans or "frog eaters" for the French. Examples of short stereotypical phrases are "to go Dutch treat" or "not to have a Chinaman's chance," and two stereotypical proverbs are "Beware of Greeks bearing gifts" and "The only good Indian is a dead Indian." In their longer forms these slurs usually play one ethnic or national group against the other, as in such epigrammatic characterizations as "The Pole is a thief; the Prussian, a traitor; the Bohemian, a heretic; and the Swabian, a chatterbox" or "The Russians act out of terror and compulsion, the Germans out of obedience, the Swiss because they want peace, the Poles in order to have free choice, the French for the sake of their king's glory, and the English for the love of freedom."

Ethnic slurs in the form of riddles are as popular as ethnic jokes—as, for example "What are the three shortest books in the world? *Italian War Heroes, Jewish Business Ethics*, and *Who's Who in Puerto Rico*." Stereotypical descriptions of outsiders are internationally disseminated, as might best be illustrated by the many traditional phrases alluding to venereal disease in which one nationality chooses a neighboring one to refer to this stigmatized disease: the "French disease" (by the English), the "Spanish disease" (by the Germans), the "Polish disease" (by the Russians), and so on.

Their form does not present a satisfactory basis for typing blasons populaires; rather, it is the function of these traditional insults or mockeries that binds them together as folk expressions. It has been noted in the scholarship on stereotypes that not all of them are necessarily malicious or evil. Stereotypes uttered as self-descriptions by a particular group are especially likely to be employed humorously or ironically. If there is such a thing as national character, then the "kernel of truth" argument would in fact hold that there is some slight validity to some stereotypes. Why would group members otherwise employ derogatory statements, expressed as invectives against them by others, to ridicule themselves? Nevertheless, stereotypes and verbal prejudices become immediately problematic socially and psychologically when directed as ethnic or racial slurs with evil intent toward the outside group. Usually those using such expressions are not aware that they are projecting their own fear, anxieties, and insecurities onto others by calling them names and making them the butts of their jokes.

The scholarly collection and study of blasons populaires went hand in hand with other major collecting projects during the nineteenth century. The two most significant collections of that time are Otto von Reinsberg-Düringsfeld's *Internationale Titulaturen* (1863) and Henri Gaidoz and Paul Sebillot's *Blason populaire de la France* (1884). They have been augmented by Abraham Roback's *Dictionary of International Slurs* (1944) and Hugh Rawson's *Wicked Words* (1989). These dictionaries include texts dating back to classical and medieval times, but many others and with more precise references are contained in the nine volumes of Hans Walther's *Proverbia sententiaeque latinitatis medii aevi* (1963–1986) and in the nine volumes of Samuel Singer's *Thesaurus proverbiorum medii aevi* (vol. 1, 1995). Vincent Stuckey Lean has also included numerous medieval English texts in the first volume of his *Collectanea* (1902–1904), as does Bartlett Jere Whiting in his *Proverbs, Sentences, and Proverbial Phrases from English Writings Mainly before 1500* (1968). For example, the last collection includes medieval expressions such as "Britons are boasters," "Englishmen are changeable," "Frenchmen sin in lechery, Englishmen in envy," "Scots are full of guile," and "The Welsh ever love treachery." This major collection also includes many proverbial invectives against women that reflect the misogynist's attitudes about medieval life: "Woman's words are but wind," "Women are the devil's mousetraps," and "Women can weep with one eye and laugh with the other." Wayland Hand collected numerous medieval slurs against people with red hair in his *Dictionary of Words and Idioms Associated with Judas Iscariot* (1942), and Carolyn Prager in her article, "'If I Be Devil'" (1987), has shown how the proverb "The Ethiopian cannot change his skin" (Jer. 13:23) has been employed as a biblical blason populaire in medieval and Renaissance literature. Yet many more such studies investigating the origin, history, and meaning of ethnic slurs are needed.

Much is known about medieval Latin blasons populaires, but very little systematic investigation has taken place about traditional insults in the vernacular languages of the Middle Ages. There are many in the literary works of such authors as Chrétien de Troyes, Geoffrey Chaucer, Hartmann von Aue, and others. Most of these texts are listed in Singer's multivolume collection of medieval proverbs. For example, under the keyword *Deutsch* (German), he lists 34 texts from various vernacular languages: "Germans are no real Christians and nobody's friends" (Latin); "The angriest people live in Germany" (French); "Nature took good care of us when it placed the Alps between us and the anger of the Germans" (Italian); "We Germans are wild, rough, and angry people" (German); "Germans don't want to do anything else but to drink" (Italian); "A Polish bridge, a Bohemian monk, a Swabian nun, an Austrian soldier, the piety of the Italians and the fasting of the Germans are not worth a bean" (Latin); "A German worries about the damage only after the deed" (German); and "In many ways Germans are beyond any rationality" (French). It is important to note from these examples that traditional insults can also be directed against one's own group. But for the most part ethnic slurs are spiteful invectives against the outsiders or foreigners seen as a collective group, generalizations that are quickly proven wrong when individual members of the ridiculed or aggressively insulted group do not behave in the manner described. Ethnic and racial slurs were ill conceived in classical and medieval times, and they continue to be dangerous verbal weapons today. The fact that many of them together with new invectives are in use to this day is ample proof that they need to be studied historically, comparatively, and critically in their social contexts. A better understanding of the meaning of blasons populaires will lead to a clearer appreciation of ethnic and racial tensions on the local and international level. Many of today's stereotypes and prejudices date back to medieval times, and their longevity is a clear indication of the task that still lies ahead to free the world of such preconceived and ill-founded notions.

See also: Jews, Stereotypes of; Proverbs

References and further reading: Many of the entries in W. Mieder's bibliography, *International Proverb Scholarship* (1982, 1990, 1993), deal with blasons populaires from around the world. O. von Reinsberg-Düringsfeld's *Internationale Titulaturen*, 2 vols. (1863), reappeared in 1992 edited by W. Mieder and with a bibliography. In addition to the already cited major collections of Gaidoz and Sébillot, Lean, Roback, Rawson, Singer, Walther, and Whiting, see R. M. Spears, *Slang and Euphemism* (1981), and the several smaller collections included in *Maledicta: The International Journal of Verbal Aggression* (1977–). The following books and essays are of particular interpretive significance: A. Taylor, "Blason Populaire," in A. Taylor, *The Proverb* (1931; rpt., ed. W. Mieder, 1985); J. Raymond, "Tensions in Proverbs: More Light on International Understanding," *Western Folklore* 15 (1956); H. Walther, "Scherz und Ernst in der Völker- und Stämme-Charakteristik mittellateinischer Verse," *Archiv für Kulturgeschichte* 41 (1959); J. Duijker and N. Fridja, *National Character and National Stereotypes* (1960); F. Oinas, "The Foreigner as Devil, Thistle, and Gadfly," *Proverbium*, no. 15 (1970); A. Paredes, "Proverbs and Ethnic Stereotypes," *Proverbium*, no. 15 (1970); M. Birnbaum, "On the Language of Prejudice," *Western Folklore* 30 (1971); H.-J. Schoeps, "Völkerpsychologie im Sprichwort," in his *Ungeflügelte Worte* (1971); A. Dundes, "Slurs International: Folk Comparisons of Ethnicity and National Character," *Southern Folklore Quarterly* 39 (1975); W. Mieder, "Proverbs in Nazi Germany: The Promulgation of Anti-Semitism and Stereotypes through Folklore," *Journal of American Folklore* 95 (1982); A.-M. Bautier, "Peuples, provinces, et villes dans la littérature proverbiale latine du moyen âge," in *Richesse du proverbe*, vol. 1, ed. F. Suard and C. Buridant (1984); A. Dundes, *Life Is Like a Chicken Coop Ladder: A Portrait of German Culture through Folklore* (1984); A. P. Orban, "Het spreekwoordelijke beeld van de 'rusticus,' de boer, in de middeleeuwen," in *Gewone mensen in de middeleeuwen*, ed. R. Stuip and C. Vellekoop (1987); C. Prager, "'If I Be Devil': English Renaissance Response to the Proverbial and Ecumenical Ethiopian," *Journal of Medieval and Renaissance Studies* 17 (1987); P. Grzybek, "Kulturelle Stereotype und stereotype Texte," in *Natürlichkeit der Sprache und der Kultur*, ed. W. Koch (1990); A. Iglesias, "El relato oral en la epoca clasica y en el folclore moderno: El caso del blasón popular," *Paremia*, no. 1 (1993); W. Eismann, "Nationales Stereotyp und sprachliches Klischee," in *Tendenzen der Phraseologieforschung*, ed. B. Sandig (1994); and W. Mieder, *The Politics of Proverbs: From Traditional Wisdom to Proverbial Stereotypes* (1997).

—Wolfgang Mieder

Blood

Bodily fluid of fundamental importance in medieval medicine and physiology, with uniquely ambiguous symbolic significance.

Medieval conceptions and uses of blood—including medical, religious, magical, anti-Semitic, courtly, and political ones—are characterized by their combination of opposites. For instance, blood can be both cleansing and contaminating, nourishing and inedible. Blood both reinforces and violates bodily boundaries, and it marks both exclusion and sameness in social groups.

The unique significance attributed to blood is perhaps most obvious in ideas of blood as a life force, ideas found not just in the Middle Ages but also in classical Greek, Roman, Egyptian, and biblical texts. Similar medieval constructions of blood as vital can be observed in the role of Christ's Eucharistic blood signifying his life (a development of classical blood sacrifices); in the medical preoccupation with stemming blood loss; and in magical rituals of bewitchment or of selling one's soul to the devil, where blood could represent the whole person. Traditionally, many scholars have regarded this association of blood with life as nearly universal, and they have explained it by assuming that many cultures establish a connection between blood loss and wounding or death and thus consider blood itself to contain the vanishing life and strength.

At all levels of medieval medicine, blood was commonly conceived of both as the cause of and the cure for many diseases. While learned medicine in the classical tradition had developed elaborate theories that imbalances of bodily fluids, as well as poisonous residues in the blood, were the cause of all illness, folk medicine often seems to have seen diseases quite literally as residing in the blood. Discharging it through bloodletting thus largely sufficed to maintain or regain health. Magical practices often complemented and overlapped with medical uses; the tenth-century Anglo-Saxon *Leechbook*, for instance, requires that the blood extracted to cure spider bites be subsequently applied to a green hazel stick and thrown away over a road.

Nevertheless, medieval medicine was also concerned with avoiding and controlling any spillage of the precious substance. Numerous charms to staunch bleeding in humans and animals survive in Latin and several vernacular languages from throughout the Middle Ages, often mixing pagan and Christian elements. Common types of such charms draw analogies between the stopping of the blood and the river Jordan or Christ's blood. Bloodletting was also subject to various regulations; it was recommended only on certain days of the lunar cycle and considered dangerous on others, as elaborate popular calendars specify.

Human and animal blood was even prescribed as a cure for many ailments, usually by being applied externally to the afflicted body part. Some manuscripts also recommend that magic spells be uttered simultaneously or even written in the blood itself. In literature and legend, the blood of innocent children or virgins could cure leprosy, a disease presented as a punishment for sinfully proud and lecherous behavior.

Menstrual blood, which combined the dangers of blood with those of feminine sexuality, was perceived as especially polluting and destructive. Learned texts claim that, among other things, it causes fruit to fall from trees and grain not to sprout, as well as rabies and a variation of the evil eye. A child conceived during menstruation could turn out to be not only red-haired but also leprous. On the other hand, according to physiological theory, menstrual blood sustained the fetus, and even milk was nothing but processed blood. Hildegard von Bingen (d. 1179) believed that a mere cloth stained with menstrual blood could protect against blows and fire.

The magical powers ascribed to blood go far beyond healing ones. It was the prime substance used by necromancers to conjure up demons. According to magical recipes, anointing one's eyes with bat's blood could improve night vision, while lion's blood protected against other animals. Bathing in dragon's blood also made the Nordic hero Sigurd's skin impenetrable. Penitentials and books of magic give ample evidence of blood being frequently used as a love potion (e.g., by mixing one's own blood into the beloved's food or drink to arouse her or his love). The widespread belief that a victim's corpse begins to bleed again in the presence of the murderer was even accepted as juridical proof in many late-medieval laws (the so-called bier right).

The Church generally saw blood as a pollutant, which was theologically justified by its association with bloodshed and sin, but nevertheless increasingly encouraged popular devotion to focus on blood, be it the blood of saints, martyrs, or Christ. Such holy blood worked miracles; stayed fresh for years; cured blindness, paralysis, and leprosy; restored severed limbs; and more. A famous example of a saint whose blood worked miracles is Thomas Becket (d. 1170); thousands of pilgrims went in search of healing to Canterbury. Saints' legends also tell of demons and blood being jointly forced out of the body of the possessed.

Christ's wounded body and blood became a similar focus of popular devotion in the late Middle Ages, in the form of his rediscovered relics from the crucifixion, images of the suffering Christ as Man of Sorrows, and blood collected by the Church from the wound in his side. Mystics describe themselves as drinking blood and milk from Christ's wounds (and the Virgin's breasts) to represent their compassion with him and the comfort and redemption received from his passion.

The blood of the Eucharist became another extremely popular object of devotion in the thirteenth century, as it was made the central rite of Christianity and the key image of Christ's salvation and spiritual nourishment. Eucharistic miracle stories and pictures told of hosts beginning to bleed or even turning into a bleeding body. This typically happened either to reward pious believers, when Jews tried to desecrate stolen hosts by stabbing or soiling them, or when Christians (usually women or heretics) doubted the actual presence of Christ's flesh and blood in the bread and wine (which was declared a dogma in 1215). One of the earliest of these stories tells of the Mass of St. Gregory, a seventh-century legend that became highly popular in the thirteenth century, in which the host turns into a bloody finger in order to convince a doubting woman of the real presence of Christ in the sacrament. Such miracles often initiated major pilgrimages (e.g., in Wilsnack in Germany from 1383).

Witches were associated with blood from the thirteenth century onward and were thought to abuse its powers in their potions (e.g., to cause impotence).

The late medieval idea of witches itself partly derives from classical and perhaps Germanic beliefs in blood-sucking women, as well as from fantasies about cults drinking and worshipping either menstrual blood or that of children (often born of incest). Roman writers were the first to accuse early Christians of such blood drinking in orgies of incest, sodomy, infanticide, and ritual cannibalism. Similar charges were repeated throughout the Middle Ages against several Christian splinter groups. Church and secular laws as well as penitentials frequently condemned but increasingly also shared and even cultivated the belief in such cannibalistic practices and their synthesis in the witch figure.

Jews were accused of and persecuted for similar bloody offenses. In addition to the traditional biblical allegation of having called Christ's blood upon them, Jews were linked with blood in other ways from the thirteenth century onward. At this time there appeared not only many bloody Eucharistic miracle tales but also charges of ritual murder of Christians (usually boys). This belief, the blood libel legend, led to accusations of murder in about 100 cases and perhaps more, mostly in Germany between the thirteenth and the sixteenth centuries; they persisted well into the twentieth century. While allegations of ritual murder go back to at least the case of William of Norwich (d. 1144), the first accusation that Jews had murdered Christians for their blood was probably in a case in the German town of Fulda in 1235, when 34 local Jews were killed as a consequence. The reasons cited for the supposed Jewish need for Christian blood vary, combining tales of cannibalism, crucifixion, ritual, and magic (e.g., blood was said to be required for the healing of hemorrhages or blindness, for circumcision, or for the preparation of unleavened bread). Jews and lepers were also said to have caused the Black Death in Aquitaine by poisoning wells with blood, among other substances.

This tendency of medieval people to think about blood in terms of contrast and opposition can be explained psychoanalytically by the ambiguous stance—comprising a mixture of rejection and desire—toward bodily emissions. It also fits anthropologist Mary Douglas's definition of a pollutant as something that resists neat categorization and is thus both considered dirty and to be avoided and yet given a place in a central ritual of the culture to incorporate its power. Moreover, Douglas sees much of the symbolic value of blood resulting from the analogy between the physical and the social body, where blood represents dangerous margins and transgressions of the social unit.

See also: Charms; Eucharist; Evil Eye; Jews, Stereotypes of; Medicine; Vampire; Witchcraft
References and further reading: Medieval ideas and folk beliefs about blood are not well
  researched. M. Douglas's *Purity and Danger* (1966) is the classic text about pollution,
  interpreting, for instance, the blood taboos of Brahmanic religions. M.-C. Pouchelle, *The
  Body and Surgery in the Middle Ages* (1990), includes a short chapter on the ambiguous and
  polluting status of blood in the Middle Ages. Medical beliefs about blood, especially about
  menstruation, are discussed by D. Jacquart and C. Thomasset, *Sexuality and Medicine in the
  Middle Ages* (1989). R. Kieckhefer's *Magic in the Middle Ages* (1989) and V. Flint's *The Rise
  of Magic in Early Medieval Europe* (1991) both describe several instances of the use of blood
  in magic, with Flint attributing somewhat more importance to it. M. Rubin examines
  Eucharistic devotion in *Corpus Christi* (1991). J. Russell's *Witchcraft in the Middle Ages*
  (1972) and N. Cohn's *Europe's Inner Demons* (1993) trace ideas of witchcraft in detail, as
  well as related beliefs about blood-sucking and cannibalism, through the centuries. One of

the most accurate overviews of the blood libel legend, though without much reference to blood, is provided by G. Langmuir's *Toward a Definition of Antisemitism* (1990). Other useful analyses of the legend can be found in the essays in A. Dundes, ed., *The Blood Libel Legend* (1991), and in R. Hsia, *The Myth of Ritual Murder* (1988), which deals primarily with sixteenth-century Germany. P. Camporesi's *Juice of Life* (1995) is an eclectic collection of popular, mainly Italian, beliefs about blood from the sixteenth to the eighteenth centuries. The relevant articles in H. Bächtold-Stäubli and E. Hoffmann-Krayer, eds., *Handwörterbuch des deutschen Aberglaubens* (1927–1942), though often uncritical and not specifically interested in medieval beliefs, collect a great deal of material from older scholarship.

—*Bettina Bildhauer*

Books of Hours

Devotional books designed for laypeople, deriving their name from the *Horae beatae Mariae Virginis* (Hours of the Blessed Virgin Mary) and the Marian office contained in them.

Although they were partially composed of liturgical texts contained in the Breviary, they are best known for their extraliturgical prayers, which were widely diffused in the late Middle Ages. From the thirteenth century onward books of hours tended to be physically small, but they often were lavishly decorated and illustrated. These illuminations came to include images of secular as well as religious import, so that in the famous fifteenth-century *Très riches heures* (Very Splendid Hours) and *Belles heures* (Beautiful Hours) of Jean, duke of Berry, there are remarkable pictures of both aristocratic and peasant activities, pictures that provide invaluable evidence about everyday life. Generally books of hours were extremely popular in the fourteenth and fifteenth centuries, especially in France and the Low Countries, and they appear to have survived in greater numbers than any other kind of medieval book.

The first such books had developed much earlier, in the great Carolingian abbeys, with the custom—later diffused through the influence of Cluny, a very famous abbey—of adding to the choral Office of Hours a number of supplementary prayers, such as the seven penitential psalms, litanies, offices of the dead and of the Virgin, and suffrages in honor of God and the saints. Such materials became the main elements of the books of hours, although they were characterized by a rich number of variants. Thus, by the twelfth century the book of hours was conceived of as a supplement inserted at the end of the Psalter (the Psalms of the Bible), sometimes at the end of the missal, or, more rarely, at the end of the Breviary. From the early thirteenth century onward, after its separation from the liturgical books and the introduction of new elements, it constituted an autonomous type of book. The widespread diffusion of the books of hours in the late Middle Ages can be explained as a consequence of new trends in spirituality that by emphasizing personal attitudes in the devotional life stimulated the utilization and circulation of religious objects for private purposes. From the fourteenth century onward, the patterns of pious life provided individuals, rather than just congregations, with a more intense contact with sacred texts, conceived of as means to guide the believer, through meditative reading, to the way of contemplation that came to be known as

Illumination for February, from the Très riches heures de Jean duc de Berry.
(Fol. 2v; Musée Condé; Giraudon/Art Resource, NY)

Illumination for August, from the Très riches heures de Jean duc de Berry.
(Fol. 8v; Musée Condé; Giraudon/Art Resource, NY)

devotio moderna—a form of "modern devotion" fostering very personal, even mystical, approaches to the sacred.

Books of hours were used not only by the educated aristocracy, which undoubtedly provided a model for sumptuous commissions, but also by the middle classes, who exerted an increasingly important role in the intellectual and spiritual life of the period. The popularity of books of hours in France and the Low Countries was a consequence both of the greater interest in the *devotio moderna* in these regions and of the key role played there by the educated middle classes.

In some cases the calendar, the litanies, or the local prayers reveal the destination of the manuscript by their relationship to specific cults. The insertion of special prayers could be owing to the donor's commission, and such insertions might include prayers designed to ask for or take away good or bad weather, to beseech the Virgin's and a special saint's intercession against illnesses and plagues, or to petition for a good death. From the fourteenth century onward Latin texts are often followed by vernacular prayers, especially those in honor of saints whose cults were widely popular, such as Catherine (against afflictions of the tongue), Christopher (against accidents while traveling), Margaret (invoked by pregnant women), and George (against skin diseases). Otherwise the donors could order the transcription of singular or adapted texts: specific references to the donor are often revealed in the litanies or in prayers relating to local contexts. Since they were relatively free from ecclesiastical control, the private use of books of hours stimulated the emergence of a wide range of texts whose decoration and illustration are among their most important elements. The humbler books are decorated by initials, marking the beginning of each text, and frames or borders, characterized on almost every page by vegetal patterns sometimes displaying animals. In the more sumptuous manuscripts, an illustrative cycle is added to the decorations.

The Marian cycle that became standard in the fourteenth century illustrates the office of the Virgin and includes the episodes of Christ's Birth and Childhood, from the Annunciation through the Coronation of the Virgin. Alternatively, the Marian office is sometimes illustrated as a Passion cycle, from the Betrayal through the Deposition, as in the *Hours of William de Brailes*. The penitential psalms could also be illustrated by episodes of David's life or, from the end of the fifteenth century onward, by scenes pertaining to Job. The Office of the Dead was more freely illustrated, sometimes by representing the funeral, the Encounter of the Living and the Dead, or the judgment of a single person, as in the *Rohan Book of Hours*. The calendar was usually illustrated with the labors of the months and the relative zodiacal signs. Portraits and hagiographic scenes often corresponded to the prayers of the saints, while the sections devoted to the Gospels usually displayed the Evangelists' images and sometimes also their symbols—the angel (or a man) for Matthew, the lion for Mark, the bull for Luke, and the eagle for John. The prayers to the Virgin, accompanied by an image of the Virgin and Child, sometimes displayed (in the most sumptuous exemplars) the portrait of the donor kneeling or being introduced to the Virgin by a holy intercessor. The ateliers that crafted books of hours, especially in great centers such as Paris or Bruges, often engaged in mass production by sharing the work of transcription and decoration or illustration among a number of specialized copyists and illuminators. The display of different techniques and styles reveals the variety of operations adopted in fashioning each manuscript. Since books of hours were usually destined for private use, some parts could be designed to accommodate the insertion of a coat of arms after the purchase of the manuscript.

Although their primary function was religious devotion, in the later Middle Ages books of hours eventually came to depict the social life of the secular world as well. For example, in the *Très riches heures* there is a sequence of illuminated pages accompanying the calendar for each month of the year. For the months of January, April, May, and August, scenes of aristocratic life show men and women in lavish dress feasting, riding, and courting in gestures reminiscent of romances. For the other months, however, we see ordinary farmworkers, both women and men, as they progress through the annual agricultural cycle. Thus, in February the firewood is being cut and the sheepfold tended in heavy snow, while a man and a woman inside raise their garments to warm their legs and feet before the fire, though the woman by the doorway raises her skirt more decorously. March finds the workers digging and plowing, still wrapped against the cold, but June pictures them lightly clad and barefoot for the warmer weather. Here the men cut green stalks with scythes, while one woman uses a pitchfork and another a rake to gather the stalks into piles. In July men harvest wheat with sickles in the background, while a couple shear sheep in the foreground. Dress has become increasingly informal for farmworkers, and some men are depicted here and in other warm months in nothing more than shirt and drawers. Although August foregrounds an outing of aristocrats, dressed in unseasonably warm attire, in the background are peasant men and women openly bathing nude in a pond while nearby workers appear not to notice (nor does the aristocratic party). September and October complete the scenes of working in the fields, while November depicts pig farming and December shows a grisly scene of hunting dogs tearing apart a boar. These depictions of ordinary secular life provide us with extraordinary views of the social life of the time.

In theory, the reading of books of hours corresponded to the official liturgical hours; however, their use in private homes and their illustrative programs suggest that they were definitely utilized in private devotions and in the late-medieval practice of meditation, as supported by the contemplation of images. Otherwise, the donors could read them in silence during the Eucharistic celebration. Although the most sumptuous books of hours constituted a minor part of the general production, they were thought of as precious objects to collect and exhibit.

See also: Iconography; Manuscript Marginalia

References and further reading: A fundamental source of information on the content and decoration of books of hours is V. Leroquais, *Les livres d'heures manuscrits de la Bibliothèque Nationale* (1927), with its 1943 Supplement. For a synthesis, see especially L. M. J. Delaissé, "The Importance of Books of Hours for the History of the Medieval Book," in *Gatherings in Honor of Dorothy E. Miner*, ed. O. E. McCracken, L. M. C. Randall, and R. H. Randall (1974). For production techniques, see J. D. Farouhar, *Creation and Imitation: The Work of a Fifteenth-Century Manuscript Illuminator* (1976), and M. O. Renger, "The Netherlandish Grisaille Miniatures: Some Unexplored Aspects," *Wallraf-Richartz-Jahrbuch* 44 (1983), as well as J. J. G. Alexander, *Medieval Illuminators and Their Methods of Work* (1992). For the commission and diffusion of the manuscript genre, see J. P. Harthan, *Books of Hours and Their Owners* (1977), and C. de Hamel's synthesis, *A History of Illuminated Manuscripts* (1986). For devotional aspects, see the essays included in *Pregare nel segreto: Libri d'Ore e testi di spiritualità nella tradizione cristiana*, ed. G. Cavallo (1994). For the connection of texts and illustrations in books of hours, see *Time Sanctified: The Book of Hours in Medieval Art and Life*, ed. R. S. Wieck (1988). A beautiful reproduction of pages from *The Très riches heures of Jean, Duke of Berry* has been edited by J. Longnon and R. Cazelles (1969).

—*Fabrizio Crivello*

Bowed Strings

String instruments that produce sound predominantly through the use of a bow.

The use of bowed strings is first recorded in surviving literature from the tenth century. No evidence exists prior to this date. Available sources indicate that bowing first appeared in central Asia. Several Byzantine illustrations from the tenth century show string instruments with extremely long bows. References in Arabic literature also appear in the tenth century, and bowed strings were first introduced into Europe in the eleventh century via Byzantium and Islamic Spain. Prior to the use of bows, rods for beating, rubbing, or plucking the strings were used.

The bow, from its early origins, had certain characteristics common to all its different manifestations: they were always convex, like an archer's drawn bow. The medieval bow stick was much weaker than its modern counterpart, so the hair was less firmly gripped. The hair was usually horsehair, strung on a shaft of elastic bamboo or wood that had been bent in an arc. The hair was affixed directly to the stick, not to an adjustable nut as in modern bows. This meant that no alterations on tension of the hairs were permitted.

By the eleventh century iconographic sources show a range from flat bows, hair almost touching the wood, to large strongly arched bows that are almost semicircular in shape and are held in the middle of the stick. There are only two varieties of bows tried during the experimental phase of the eleventh century. By the late-medieval period, uniform types of bows gradually appeared. They were 50 to 80 centimeters long and slightly curved. Performers were able to vary the tension on the hairs of the bow by holding the end of the bow as well as the end of the hair. Various types of nonadjustable nuts were added in the thirteenth century to keep the hair and stick apart on the flat bows.

Bows were held in the clenched fist until the fourteenth century, which made for greater pressure on the strings and a more powerful stroke but made a loose wrist and elasticity at the change of stroke difficult. By the late Middle Ages sources show the bow being held by the fingertips. Almost always, the instrument was held in the left hand and the bow in the right. When the instrument was held slanting upward or sideways from the body, the bow was held in an overhand grip, but if the instrument was supported on the knee (*a gamba*), the bow was held in an underhand grip.

The origins of bowed strings can be linked to the development of parallel organum and early forms of medieval polyphony. The bridge of the medieval fiddle meant sound could be produced from more than one string at a time: a drone effect could be created to accompany the melody. Further evolution of bowing technique developed the differentiation of angles in the bow's movement and the separate sounding of individual strings by the end of the medieval period.

Literature such as the chanson de geste and the romance is filled with references to stringed instruments played with bows, and such instruments were also used in public processions. Evidently class distinctions could be made regarding the perceived social standing of violin and viol players. According to Isabelle Cazeaux, members of the upper classes for a long time favored the viol, which was played by aristocrats, over the violin, which was played by professionals of a lower class.

See also: Folk Music and Folksong
References and further reading: Scholarly accounts include K. Schlesinger, *The Instruments of the Modern Orchestra and Early Records of the Precursors of the Violin Family* (1910); D. Boyden, *The History of Violin Playing from Its Origins to 1761* (1965); E. van der Straeten, *The History of the Violin* (1968); "Bow," in *New Grove Dictionary of Music and Musicians* (1995); L. Lockwood, *Music in Renaissance Ferrara, 1400–1505: The Creation of a Musical Center in the Fifteenth Century* (1984); I. Cazeaux, *French Music in the Fifteenth and Sixteenth Centuries* (1975); R. Strohm, *The Rise of European Music, 1380–1500* (1993); C. Page, *The Owl and the Nightingale: Musical Life and Ideas in France 1100–1300* (1990).

—*Bradford Lee Eden*

Boy Bishop, Feast of the

A liturgical feast of misrule and role reversal among the choirboys, held during the Christmas season on St. Nicholas's Day (December 6) or Holy Innocents' Day (December 28).

The earliest mention of the Feast of the Boy Bishop appears in manuscripts from the monastery of St. Gall in 911, when the German king Conrad I visited the monastery during the actual ceremony. The Winchester Troper of about 980 mentions this feast, along with the feasts of the deacons and priests, and all three feasts were commonly known as the Christmas *triduum*. Whereas the Feast of Fools became very popular in France, it was in England, with its rich tradition of boy choristers and alto choirs, that the Feast of the Boy Bishop had its greatest popularity.

Various locations celebrated this feast either on December 6, the feast day of St. Nicholas, the patron saint of children and scholars, or on December 28, the Feast of the Holy Innocents. By the eleventh century most Boy Bishop celebrations were on Holy Innocents' Day, since it had become the official feast day of students and choirboys, and also because it was closer to the dates of the other feasts of misrule, such as the Feast of Fools.

The boy bishop was chosen by his peers in the cathedral choir, the monastery school, or the grammar school. On Holy Innocents' Day the boys would rise up from their choir stalls during vespers, literally throwing the bishop and his colleagues out of their chairs, and install the chosen boy as their "bishop."

Vested in the clothing of a bishop, with miter and staff, he would preside over the ceremonies of the day, at some times and places reading serious sermons and at others participating in the reading of "farcical letters." The boy bishop paraded through the town or parish with his entourage, blessing the people and receiving gifts and alms. Later the alms collected would pay for a party of celebration.

Late-medieval records attest that this feast of misrule grew increasingly distasteful to the clergy and sometimes led to violence. The boys would often ruin church vestments and ornaments and would bully parishioners for money and gifts or vandalize their property. They also sang mocking songs—for example, a record from Hamburg, dated 1304, states that the schoolboys had agreed to refrain from "making rhymes, in Latin or in German, which would stain the reputation of anyone."

Because this and other feasts of misrule were perceived as threatening to the clergy, there was a strong movement in the Church from the thirteenth century onward to banish these feasts. On the Continent, in 1431 the Council of Basel restricted the Boy Bishop celebrations to some extent, although they were revived periodically as late as the eighteenth century. In England Henry VIII abolished the custom in 1512; it was revived by Queen Mary during her reign and was finally abolished permanently by Elizabeth I.

See also: Carnival; Christmas; Festivals and Celebrations; Fools, Feast of
References and further reading: E. K. Chambers, *The Mediaeval Stage*, vol. 1 (1903), is the source of the records quoted above, which are found on pages 340 and 351. Other information on the Boy Bishop is found in R. Hutton, *The Rise and Fall of Merry England* (1994), and F. X. Weiser, *Handbook of Christian Feasts and Customs* (1958).
—*Bradford Lee Eden*

Brigid, Saint (d. c. 525) [Saint Brighid]

A female saint who, along with St. Patrick and St. Columba, is viewed as one of the founders of Christian institutions in Ireland and is the subject of numerous, widely popular legends.

Little is known of St. Brigid except that she lived in the late fifth and early sixth centuries and that she founded a famous and powerful episcopal monastery in Kildare that included both women and men. This episcopal see soon came into competition with that of Armagh, whose prestige derived from its association with St. Patrick, for supremacy in the Christian Church of Ireland. Perhaps at least partly to enhance the claims of Kildare, legends of St. Brigid, and especially of her numerous miracles both during her life and after her death, were spread throughout the land. Her cult likewise took root abroad, and there were many churches dedicated to her not only throughout England and Wales but also on the Continent, churches founded by Irish monks. Though her fame circulated mainly in oral tradition, written versions of her life, originally in Latin and Old Irish, were translated into Old French, Middle English, and German, providing evidence of her growing popularity as a universal rather than merely local saint.

The earliest life of St. Brigid was composed in Latin by a monk named Cogitosus in the middle of the seventh century, about 100 years after her death. Although he mentions written sources, Cogitosus evidently depends mainly on popular oral tradition, which, as he says, preserves the wonders she performed "in the memories of the people." According to Cogitosus, St. Brigid was born to noble parents, though that claim may have been no more than a way of giving her elevated status to justify her prominence in the Irish Church. Traditions developing, or at least recorded, somewhat later make her parents more humble. In the ninth century her mother is described as the slave of a druid, and an eighth-century account in Irish has her mother carrying milk to the druid's house at sunrise when she goes into labor and gives birth to the future saint with one foot outside and one foot on the druid's doorstep. We may already see here the associations of St. Brigid with milk and the dairy, with the light and fire of the sun, and with her role in the transformation of pagan Ireland to Christian Ireland.

In the first legend related by Cogitosus, the young Brigid is sent to the dairy to churn butter, but her generous nature impels her "to obey God rather than men," and so she gives away the milk and butter to poor people passing by. Fearing her mother's anger, she then prays for divine help and by a miracle her full quota of butter appears, even more than that produced by her coworkers. According to at least one early life in Irish, when she later decides to become a nun, the bishop who presides over her taking the veil is so "intoxicated" by her holiness that by mistake he reads over her the text for consecrating a bishop, thus giving her a status that is unique among women saints—though other accounts merely indicate that she and the bishop become partners in overseeing the monastery she founds.

There are various tales about her multiplying food, causing a cow to produce an abundance of milk, and even turning bathwater into beer for thirsty lepers. Her most famous legends include her hanging a wet cloak on a sunbeam to dry; her saving the life of a man who mistakenly killed the king's performing fox by producing another, equally talented fox; and her saving a woman's virtue: the woman had been tricked by a man who, lusting after her, had entrusted a brooch to her, stolen it from her, thrown it into the sea, and demanded in payment that she sleep with him; but he was thwarted by the saint, who directed a fisherman to cut open a fish he had caught, and there the lost brooch was found. All of these wonders are related by Cogitosus as signs of St. Brigid's special power, though students of folklore will recognize in them many of the features found in widespread folktales.

Perhaps the best-known legend about St. Brigid comes from a tradition later than Cogitosus. It relates how she received land for her monastery from a chieftain in Kildare, who had refused to give her more land than she could cover with her cloak. When she spread it out on the ground, it miraculously increased in size, covering such a large area that the chieftain begged her to make it stop before he lost all his land.

As in saints' lives generally, narratives of St. Brigid not only include numerous miraculous cures during her life but also after her death, which was commonly understood as the proof of sainthood. As her cult developed, later accounts include even more wonders. For example, in the twelfth century Gerald of Wales, in his *Topography of Ireland*, describes "Brigid's Fire" at the site of her foundation in Kildare, tended by nuns and by the saint herself, surrounded by a hedge that no man may cross lest he suffer the saint's curse. Gerald goes on to tell of one man who crossed it who was driven mad and suffered a horrible death, and of another who put one foot over the hedge, whereupon his foot and leg perished and he remained a cripple the rest of his life.

This association of St. Brigid with fire appears to be connected to Cogitosus's placing the day of her death on February 1, which became her feast day in the Church and which coincides with the ancient festival of Imbolc, celebrating the beginning of spring and the return of the sun. Although it is still a matter of controversy among scholars, some argue that the saint is connected to the pre-Christian Celtic divinity also named Brigid, who was seen as a protector of her people and who was associated with the sun and light. In this view, legends of St. Brigid would have attributed to her some of the features of the earlier goddess, which would have enhanced the saint's reputation even though at the same time she is represented as distinctively Christian.

See also: Celtic Mythology; Irish Tradition; Patrick, Saint; Saints, Cults of the
References and further reading: Cogitosus's life of Brigid is translated in L. De Paor, *Saint Patrick's World* (1993), which also has useful historical background. For early Irish religious foundations generally, see L. Bitel, *Isle of the Saints: Monastic Settlement and Christian Community in Early Ireland* (1990). Narrative traditions are analyzed extensively in J. F. Nagy, *Conversing with Angels and Ancients: Literary Myths of Medieval Ireland* (1997). See also D. Ó hÓgáin, *Myth, Legend and Romance: An Encyclopedia of the Irish Folk Tradition* (1991), and D. A. Bray, *A List of Motifs in the Lives of the Early Irish Saints*, Folklore Fellows Communications 252 (1992).

—John McNamara

Brutus [Britus, Britto]

Legendary figure who, according to early histories, gave his name to Britain.

The quasi-learned traditions linking the origins of the Britons with Brutus are the Welsh expressions of the common European attempts to explain the origins of nations by reference either to the dispersion of the Trojans after the fall of their city or to the repopulating of the world by Noah's descendants after the Flood. These two accounts could, of course, be combined. The *Historia Brittonum* (History of the Britons, c. 830), attributed to Nennius, is the earliest witness and has three versions of the founding of Britain. In chapter 7, the island of Britain is named for Brutus, a Roman consul, probably derived from a notice in the chronicle of Eusebius-Jerome about the consul D. Junius Brutus (Callaicus) saying that "Brutus Hiberniam usque ad Occeanum subigit" [Brutus subjugated Ireland all the way to the Ocean]. This theme is not developed, and a more common explanation is found in chapter 17, a Welsh form of the "Frankish genealogy of nations" in which Brutus is the son of Hessitio, a descendant of Noah's son Japheth, and is one of four brothers—Francus, Romanus, Albanus, Britto—from whom are descended the Franks, Romans, Albans, and Britons.

But the origin tale that was generally adopted in the Welsh learned historical tradition was that in chapter 10. Here Brutus (Britto) is the son of Silvius, who was the son of Aeneas. The boy accidentally killed his father (as had been prophesied) and was driven from Italy. He and his followers came to the islands of the Tyrrhenian Sea but were driven from Greece because of the killing of Turnus by Aeneas. They came to Gaul, where Brutus founded the city of Tours, and then to Britain, which he and his followers settled. In chapter 18 the classical account is folded into biblical tradition as Brutus is described as a descendant of Japheth.

In his *Historia regum Brittaniae* (History of the Kings of Britain, c. 1138), Geoffrey of Monmouth closely followed the account in *Historia Brittonum*, chapter 10, but elaborated it greatly, bringing Brutus, after a number of adventures, to Albion, then inhabited by a few giants who were defeated by the new settlers. Geoffrey was inspired by the Frankish genealogy to create his own eponymous founders for the nations of Britain. He gave Brutus three sons who inherited the three parts of the island of Britain, Locrinus of England (*Lloegr* in Welsh), Albanactus of Scotland (*Alban* in Welsh), and Camber of Wales (*Cymru* in Welsh, *Cambria* in Latin). Geoffrey's account became the standard historical version of the settlement of Britain. The Welsh bards accepted this version, and in their eulogies to Welsh princes sometimes address them as the descendants of Aeneas. There are a few traces extant in medieval Welsh of native origin tales, but they are very fragmentary.

See also: Geoffrey of Monmouth; Nennius
References and further reading: J. Morris, *Nennius: British History and the Welsh Annals* (1980); J. D. Bruce, *The Evolution of Arthurian Romance*, vol. 2 (1928); P. C. Bartrum, A *Welsh Classical Dictionary* (1993).

—*Brynley F. Roberts*

Burgundian Cycle

Name traditionally attached to texts primarily in German and Scandinavian (but with texts and images all over the Western European medieval world) about the Völsungs and Niflungs/Nibelungen: Siegfried/Sigurd the Dragon-slayer, Brünhild/Brynhild, Kudrun, Günter/Gunnar, Hagen/Högni, and their loves and marriages, jealousies, battles, and final destruction.

The first recording of materials from the cycle is in the anonymous Latin epic *Waltharius* (ninth century), which is associated with the Carolingian court. There are also traces in Old English poetry. However, the principal manifestation is in the German epic *Nibelungenlied* (and its continuation, *Die Klage,* as well as other later texts) and in Scandinavia in the poems of the second half of the *Poetic Edda,* in *Völsunga Saga,* which summarizes these poems, and in *Thidrek's Saga.* The entry *Nibelungenlied* in this encyclopedia gives a detailed summary of the events of the cycle in German tradition, and here only a brief summary of the Scandinavian tradition will be offered, based on the poems of the second half of the *Poetic Edda.*

The story of Sigurd, carved in the portals of the wooden twelfth-century Hylestad Church, Setesdal, Norway. (Ove Holst/Universitetets Oldsaksamling)

The gods Odin, Hoenir, and Loki have killed Otr, the son of Hreidmar and brother of Regin and Fafnir, and must pay wergeld. Loki obtains gold from the dwarf Andvari, who curses the hoard. Fafnir kills Hreidmar and changes himself into a dragon to hoard the gold. Regin raises the boy Sigurd (*Reginsmal*). At Regin's behest, Sigurd kills the dragon but learns from birds—whose speech he can now understand, after accidentally swallowing the dragon's blood—that Regin is hostile to him. Sigurd kills Regin (*Fafnismal*). Riding up to a mountain, he awakens a sleeping woman, who says she is Sigrdrifa, a valkyrie put to sleep by Odin; she advises him about runes and other important matters (*Sigrdrifumal*). At this point the manuscript of the *Poetic Edda* is missing eight pages, which probably told about Sigurd's arrival at the court of Gjuki, oath of blood brotherhood with Gjuki's son Gunnar, marriage with Gjuki's daughter Kudrun, and wooing of Brynhild on Gunnar's behalf by taking on Gunnar's appearance and riding through flames. As the fragment of the next poem (the fragmentary *Sigurdarkvida*) begins, Kudrun has apparently told Brynhild of the betrayal, and Brynhild in turn has demanded Sigurd's death of Gunnar. Gunnar and his brother Högni arrange for Guttorm, a third brother, to kill Sigurd. The following poems take up the aftermath of this killing. Kudrun mourns Sigurd (*Gudrunarkvida* I). The next poem (*Sigurdarkvida in skamma* [The Short Lay of Sigurd]) tells the story up to this point once again.

Kudrun marries Atli (*Gudrunarkvida* II and III). She incites Atli to summon Gunnar and Högni and murder them, but thereafter she murders the children she bore Atli and Atli himself (*Atlakvida* and *Atlamal*; also *Oddrunargratr*). Kudrun marries Jonakr and incites her sons Hamdir and Sørli to avenge their sister Svanhild, who was killed by her husband Jörmunrekk (Ermanaric). On the journey they kill their half-brother Erp, and although they succeed in maiming Jörmunrekk, their attack ultimately fails because they are shorthanded without Erp (*Hamdismal*). So ends the Burgundian cycle in the *Poetic Edda*.

Each of these poems has its own history, and there are numerous repetitions and inconsistencies that a summary cannot suggest. Despite much scholarship on the subject, it is difficult to speak with any confidence of the forms of the individual poems, or of the legends behind them, before they were recorded in Iceland in the thirteenth century. The characters can be derived from actual historical figures of the Migration Age: Günter/Gunnar must be Gundicharius, last king of the Burgundians (whence the name of the cycle), and Etzil/Atil is Attila. Jörmunrekk is clearly Ermanaric. The Huns defeated the Burgundians in 437, though not under the leadership of Attila, and Attila died in bed in 453 with his Germanic bride, Hildico. Sigebert was the name of a Merovingian ruler who was married to the Visigothic princess Brunichildis (d. 613) and was murdered in 575 at the behest of his wife's brother. Because of this historical background and the rich recordings of the cycle in text and image in Germany and in Scandinavia, we know that there must have been extensive oral traditions and that the cycle belongs far more to heroic legend than to history.

See also: Attila and the Huns; Migrations, Age of, *Nibelungenlied*; Scandinavian Tradition
References and further reading: For translations of the Scandinavian texts see C. Larrington, trans., *The Poetic Edda* (1996), and J. L. Byock, trans., *The Saga of the Volsungs* (1990). A.

Heusler, *Nibelungensage und Nibelungenlied* (1920), remains the fundamental work on the relationship of the various texts; T. M. Andersson, *The Legend of Brynhild* (1980), is a more recent attempt in English. Nearly all the references and further reading suggested in the entry *Nibelungenlied* in this encyclopedia are also relevant and should be consulted.

—John Lindow

Burial Mounds [Barrows, lows, howes, *tumuli*]

Mounds of earth covering the bodies of prehistoric peoples (Roman and early medieval barrows are also common), with the corpses frequently interred within a megalithic chamber, which is often all that survives of the original denuded mound and thus regarded as a monument in its own right (portal or passage tomb, or cromlech).

Many of the picturesque names given to these monuments were not recorded until modern times, but there are also several that have impeccable medieval pedigrees and show something of the way in which medieval speculation accounted for their origin.

Mounds and Giants

Just as the Anglo-Saxons, when confronted by the massive walls of Roman Britain, concluded that such remains were *enta geweorc* (the work of giants), they naturally imagined that megalithic chamber-tombs must be so, too (see, e.g., *Beowulf*, line 2717). Thus, Giant's Grave is a common modern barrow name, sometimes the successor, presumably, of such Anglo-Saxon names as Thirshowe (from the Anglo-Saxon *thyrs* [giant], in *Beowulf*, line 1292), preserved in Trusey Hill (Barmston, in Yorkshire), which probably means "Giant's Howe," and the *entan hlewe* (Giant's Low) at Overton, Hampshire. In his *History of the Kings of Britain* (c. 1138), Geoffrey of Monmouth gives *chorea gigantum* (Giants' Dance) as the name for Stonehenge. In late-medieval Germany the term *hunegraber* (Huns' Graves) reflected a folk belief that the mounds were connected with the ancient Huns, who by this date were accorded gigantic stature. Similarly significantly, Rabelais, writing in 1532, makes his giant hero, Pantagruel, pick up a huge rock and plant it on top of four pillars in a field outside Poitiers for the local scholars to picnic on and inscribe their names, an allusion to the Pierre Levée dolmen. The same author took over medieval legends of a giant named Gargantua, who was also associated with megalithic construction.

Some burial mounds are named after individual legendary heroes who were clearly regarded as gigantic in stature. About 1540 the antiquary John Leland wrote, concerning the village of Barnby in Yorkshire: "The northe hille on top of it hath certen stones comunely caullid Waddes Grave, whom the people there say to have bene a gigant"; although the reference is apparently to a natural hill on or in which the giant hero Wade is supposedly buried, it is suggestive (note also the name Wade's Causeway, given to the nearby Roman road on Wheeldale Moor). The Germanic smith Weland (Wayland) gave his name to the barrow called Wayland's Smithy (Oxfordshire) as early as the Anglo-Saxon period, where it appears in a charter as *Welandes smiðe*. The several barrow names that seem to commemorate Germanic gods (i.e., the two Thunor's Lows,

Thor's Howe, the two Woden's Lows, and Woden's Barrow) were presumably not thought to be the burial place of these gods but, rather, perhaps were thought to be under their protection. The Wiltshire Woden's Low is now known as Adam's Grave, but if this is a deliberate Christianization of a pagan name, it would seem to be modern.

The *Mabinogi* tale of the burial of the severed head of the giant Bran in the Gwynfryn (White Mound) in London is an example of the motif of talismanic burial, in which the hero is usually (as in Irish sources) buried in a standing position and facing the direction of expected enemy attack. In his late-twelfth-century *De nugis curialium* (Courtier's Trifles), the gossipy Walter Map relates a tale about a group of three barrows or cairns in Breconshire, allegedly built over the severed right hands, left feet, and genitals of enemy soldiers slaughtered by Brychan and "each named after the part that lies in it"—this is apparently an onomastic legend (accounting for the names of the mounds).

In medieval and later Ireland, many a dolmen was given the name of Diarmaid and Grainne's Bed, on which these legendary lovers were said to have enjoyed each other during their year-and-a-day's elopement. Legendary heroes were also naturally felt to be buried in some barrows. For example, the tenth-century Welsh work *Englynion y Beddau* (On the Graves of Heroes) seems to make the cromlech at Dinorben hill fort (Denbighshire) the burial place of Hennin Henben. William of Malmesbury, writing around 1125, refers to the discovery of the grave (*sepulchrum et bustum*) of the Arthurian hero Walwen (Gawain) on the shore at Rhos (Pembrokeshire); as it is said to be 14 feet long, it may have constituted the inner chamber of a sea-eroded barrow. The ninth-century *History of the Britons*, attributed to Nennius, presents a list of *mirabilia* (wonders) found in Britain, including the immeasurable tumulus of Amr, who was killed by his father, King Arthur: it is sometimes 6, sometimes 9, 12, or 15

The burial mounds, or passage tombs, at Knowth, Ireland; circa 3000 B.C.E. (Photograph by John McNamara)

feet long, and it never has the same dimensions if measured twice in succession. The same text locates another sepulcher on top of Crug Mawr mountain (in Cardiganshire); it shifts its size to accommodate that of whoever lies down beside it and also conveys lifelong freedom from weariness to any traveler who kneels three times before it. In the late twelfth century Gerald of Wales added that weapons left beside the mound overnight would be found broken to pieces in the morning; thus, both these mounds certainly have peculiarities.

Otherworldly Properties of Mounds

Another important *Mabinogi* mound with distinctive properties of its own is that said to be just outside Arberth (in Pembrokeshire), not specifically stated to be a burial mound (though *gorsedd*, the term used to describe it, can bear this meaning in medieval Welsh). Its "peculiarity" (*cynneddf*) is that it rewards whoever dares sit upon it with either a blow or a wondrous sight. It is this mound from which Pwyll first sees Rhiannon and Pryderi sees the enchantment fall on Dyfed rendering it a wasteland, and on which Manawydan erects a small gallows. A very similar tradition is found in Old Norse literature, in which a king or seer sits on a burial mound (*haugr* in Old Norse, cognate with *howe*), the clear implication being that they receive inspiration from the interred.

It was only natural that barrows with their imposing portals should be seen as entrances to the otherworld, an especially common belief in early Ireland where the *síd* mounds were believed to be inhabited by an earlier race of divine beings known as the Tuatha Dé Danann (divine beings), whose womenfolk would sometimes lure heroes into the mound. Just as Pwyll's legendary court is located in close proximity to the *gorsedd* at Arberth, so the early Irish kings of Bregha, a branch of the Uí Neill dynasty, had their seat at or near the famous Knowth tumulus, which seems to imply that some of the numen felt to reside in such prehistoric monuments would thus be conferred on the successor court. Two passages in the twelfth-century *Book of Llandaff*, in which the Welsh king transfers land to the church while sitting or lying on the tomb of a former king— Morgan (d. 665), king of Glywysing, does so while lying on the tomb of his grandfather, Meurig—suggest a related and probably derivative rite, by then doubtless made acceptably Christian.

The same sort of transfer of power—poetic inspiration in this case—is recorded in an anecdote in the Icelandic *Flateyjarbók* (c. 1375). According to this account, a shepherd, Hallbjörn, who fell asleep on the burial mound of a poet named Thorleif (interestingly, a man "of great size"), was ever afterward able to compose poetry. Only in recent times has it been said that, should anyone sleep in his mound overnight, he would awake either a poet or an idiot. In a sixteenth-century Welsh tract on the "Names of Giants," by Sion Dafydd Rhys, the same story is told of anyone who will spend a night on the mountain *Cadair Idris* (Idris's Seat).

What may be a related attempt to mobilize the spirits of those interred in a barrow took place on the Sussex shore in 666: as Eddius Stephanus relates in his early-eighth-century *Life of Wilfred*, the saint's party was blown ashore, and prior to engaging the South Saxons in combat, they were ritually cursed by the pagan chief-priest as he was standing on a high mound. Barrows were frequently situated in such a manner as to look out to sea, as if guarding the land from seaborne invasion (cf. Beowulf's cliff-top barrow on the Geatish headland at Hronesness).

Sid-mounds were also regarded as repositories of fabulous treasure. In the eighth-century (?) Irish *Adventure of Art, Son of Conn*, the men of Connacht destroy a *sid* and bear away from it the crown of Brion, one of the Three Wonders of Ireland. The twelfth-century chronicler William of Newburgh tells of a man who witnessed a banquet within a tumulus (identified as Willy Howe at Thwing, Yorkshire); taking care not to drink from the goblet that was offered to him, he stole it and managed to evade pursuit. The vessel, according to William, ended up in the treasury of Henry II! William's contemporary, Gervase of Tilbury, tells an almost identical story (this time, however, located in Gloucestershire) of a golden cup stolen from "a hillock rising to the height of a man." The Yorkshire story suggests derivation from a Scandinavian source, where such tales are common: certain ancestral family "lucks" and talismans are said to have been acquired in similar ways. Bronze Age gold has, of course, been recovered from barrows and cairns in recent times.

Dragons and Mounds

A typically Germanic convention, also appearing in the Welsh tale *Peredur*, is that a barrow contains ancient treasure but is guarded by a dragon (cf. the Anglo-Saxon gnomic verse, "Dragon shall live in barrow, ancient, proud of his treasure"). Beowulf's death is brought about by just such an aggrieved dragon, at what is unmistakably described as a megalithic chamber-tomb. The twelfth-century Latin life of St. Modwenna records an incident of specters haunting Drakelow (Dragon Mound) in Derbyshire; a second life of this saint, written in Anglo-Norman in the thirteenth century, seems to show an awareness of the meaning of the place name, for in one episode concerning the mound shape-shifters assume the form of a dragon.

Evidence from Old Norse literature, indeed, suggests that the dead man in the mound himself was transformed into a dragon. A story from as early as 858 tells of a fiery dragon that issued from the tomb of the Frankish king Charles Martel (d. 741), blackening the tomb by fire as it left. In Old Norse sources (*Grettir's Saga*, among others), fire is said to issue from howes at night.

There are at least 15 medieval attestations of the place names linking words for "dragon" (drake, worm) with words for "mound" (how[e], low[e]), showing how widespread the belief was. Other names of the "Dragon-hoard" type—for example, Drakenhord at Garsington, Oxfordshire (c. 1230)—probably recall the successful outfacing of the barrow guardian and the recovery of precious grave goods. That these were often of gold is proved by the record of a treasure-trove inquiry held at Dunstable (in Bedfordshire) in 1290, from which we learn that a certain Matthew Tyler earlier in the century had become rich from the treasure he found in the Golden Lowe.

Not only were burial mounds opened by treasure hunters from the very earliest times, as recorded in Anglo-Saxon charter names meaning "Broken-barrow," "Burst-barrow," "Hollow-barrow," and "Idle-barrow" (i.e., "empty-barrow"), but royal licenses were also issued for this very purpose from at least

1237. In his *Chronicle*, Roger of Wendover records that one night in 1178, in St. Albans, the saint himself appeared to a man and miraculously led him to the sight of two *colliculi* (mounds) known as the Banner Hills (*Colles vexillorum*) at Redbourn, Hertfordshire, around which the local populace was accustomed to gather. The monks of the abbey dug into the barrows and were rewarded by finding the miracle-working bones of the martyr St. Amphibalus and nine others.

Mounds in Christian Traditions

Early Christianity clearly recognized the numinous nature of prehistoric burial mounds. One of the strategies it developed for coming to terms with their powerful hold on the popular imagination was occasionally to incorporate them within the church precincts, as at the famous Taplow barrow, which stands within the old churchyard; the former pagan royal site at Jelling in Denmark; Egloscrow (St. Issey, from Cornish *eglos* [church] and *crug* [barrow]); and Ludlow, where in 1199 three skeletons found in a barrow during the construction of the church were immediately identified as the bones of the saintly parents and uncle of the renowned Irish saint, Brendan (d. 577). Other strategies of assimilation were to build the church on top of the monument, as at Mont-Saint-Michel (in Carnac), La Hougue Bie (in Jersey), and Fimber (in Yorkshire) or to Christianize them in some other way: Lilla Howe, a round barrow at Fylingdales, Yorkshire, is still surmounted by a medieval stone cross attested from the early twelfth century; and a presumed late-medieval base crowns the Cleeve Hill barrow (in Worcestershire), as was formerly also the case at the Giant's Grave, the alleged burial place of the giant Tom Hickathrift, in Marshland St. James (in Norfolk). Ty Illtud (St. Illtud's House), a chamber-tomb at Llanhamlach, Wales, has one of its interior walls incised with crosses and other graffiti, including the date 1312.

That such a burial mound might really have been used by a saint is demonstrated by Felix's life of the early-eighth-century St. Guthlac: on a wooded island in the East Anglian fens there was "a mound (tumulus) built of clods of earth that greedy comers to the waste in former times had dug into and broken open, in the hope of finding wealth. On one side of the mound there seemed to be a sort of cistern, and in this Guthlac began to dwell after building a hut over it" (Felix, *Vita Guthlaci*, ch. 28). One of the Old English verses describes Guthlac's *beorg* (barrow) in more detail and states that it had formerly been occupied by the devils before Guthlac, too, broke into it, thus dispossessing them of it. Interestingly, he straightaway erected a cross and then dwelt in the barrow itself, before putting up additional shelter. The barrow is also several times referred to as his "seat" (*setl*; cf. the etymological sense of Welsh *gorsedd*, and note that Pwyll goes to Arberth mound "to sit"), which the demons are anxious to return to as the sole place in which they had been able to enjoy respite from their torment in hell.

An official record of 1261 shows that a band of murderous brigands used the chamber of a mound called Cuteslowe, hiding out *"in concavitate illius hoge"* [in the chamber of that "howe"], no doubt both taking advantage of such a "haunted" site, which must have helped protect their hideout from the curious, and then adding to its already sinister reputation. The local sheriff ordered it to be leveled to the ground.

The *Life of St. Cadoc*, written about 1100, includes an amusing account of the miraculous provision of grain during a period of famine in the saint's adopted home near Brecon in Wales. By means of a thread tied to its foot, Cadoc (also known as Cadog in Welsh) is able to follow a mouse to a certain tumulus, "under which there was a very beautiful subterranean house, built of old, and filled with clean wheat," which is taken to refer to the megalithic chamber within a tumulus. The bizarre scene, also featuring a mouse, that occurs in the *Mabinogi* tale of Manawydan, in which he erects a miniature gallows on the *gorsedd* at Arberth, from which he intends to hang the mouse he has caught devastating his crops, may well recall the medieval practice of erecting gallows on top of barrows. In 1425, for example, a new pair of gallows was erected in Luberlow field, Haughley (in Suffolk), presumably on the barrow itself, and one of the four Gally Hills barrows at Banstead (in Surrey) had a gallows on it in 1538. Gallows How (Galehoges, 1312) at Dunton (in Norfolk) was presumably the meeting place of the Gallow Hundred. Some of these barrows, at least, were reputed to be the abode of evil spirits, presumably of the interred. The poet of *Beowulf* speaks of *"scuccum ond scinnum"* [devils and evil spirits, line 939], which are said to haunt Heorot and which we may take to be the same kind of demons that threatened the tranquillity of Guthlac's barrow home. The names of these spirits survive in the names of the barrows at Scuckburgh (in Warwickshire) and Scuccanhlau (Horwood, Buckinghamshire), and possibly one at Skinburness, Cumbria (possibly derived from the Anglo-Saxon words *scinna*, "demon," and **burgaens*, "burial place"). Two Yorkshire barrows were named after an Old Norse word meaning "goblin" or "demon": Scratters and Scrathowes. In an Old English charm against a sudden stitch, the spirits that caused the pain are said to have been "loud as they rode over the low"—suggesting, incidentally, an alternative derivation to that usually advanced of the place name Ludlow. Certainly by the late-medieval period, at least, it was felt that these abodes of the ancient dead were appropriate sites on which to dispatch malefactors, whose spirits would be, as it were, in good company. In this connection, it is also worth remembering that Woden was the god of hanged men (cf. the Woden names above).

The Icelandic *Kormak's Saga* describes a sacrifice to the elves who dwell in a burial mound (cf. the thirteenth-century Yorkshire Alfhov, "Elf-howe"); their mound is smeared with the blood of a bull, and the bull's flesh is left for them to feast on. The purpose of this particular sacrifice is to gain the elves' help in healing wounds; other sagas indicate that the mound dwellers could also assist in childbirth. The belief that a barrow is haunted by the malevolent spirit of its occupant, who will attack anyone attempting to dig into the mound looking for treasure, is a commonplace of the Icelandic sagas, and the relatively late Christianization of Scandinavia has preserved tales of the vampire-like *draugr*, an animated corpse that inhabits mounds.

It has often been observed that the Old English element *low*, a common term for "barrow," is a frequent component of the names of places where people met to conduct the business of hundreds (administrative divisions of English counties); for example, the several "Moot-lows," which has led to the conclusion that these moots assembled on and around ancient tumuli. Of 12 such mounds excavated up to 1984, however, only one was positively identified as a prehistoric barrow: Culiford Tree Hundred, Dorset.

See also: *Beowulf;* Dragon; English Tradition: Anglo-Saxon Period; *Mabinogi;* Names, Place

References and further reading: Essential reading is L. Grinsell, *Folklore of Prehistoric Sites in Britain* (1976), though the majority of such folklore is only attested in postmedieval times. The antiquity of individual English tumuli may be traced in the relevant county volume of the *English Place Name Society's Survey.* Individual studies of particular aspects of the subject are H. R. E. Davidson's "The Hill of the Dragon," *Folklore* 61 (1950), and "The Custom of Sitting on a Howe," in *Road to Hel* (1943); both are highly recommended. See also C. Kerry, "St. Modwen and 'the Devill of Drakelowe,'" *Journal of the Derbeyshire Archaeological and Natural History Society* 17 (1895); L. K. Schook, "The Burial Mound in Guthlac A," *Modern Philology* 58 (1961); M. Gelling, "Further Thoughts on Pagan Place-Names," in *Otium et Negotium,* ed. F. Sandgren (1973); B. Dickens, "English Names and Old English Heathenism," *Essays and Studies* 19 (1934); D. J. Corner, "The Vita Cadoci and a Cotswold-Severn Chambered Cairn," *Bulletin of the Board of Celtic Studies* 32 (1985); and J. Lawson et al., *The Barrows of East Anglia* (1981), especially "The Place Name Evidence."
—*Malcolm Jones*

Cædmon (d. 680)

Often called "the first English poet," though it would be more correct to describe him as the first person recorded to have composed Christian poetry in English employing a poetic style and form traditional among pre-Christian Germanic peoples.

According to the legend preserved in Bede's *Ecclesiastical History of the English People* (731), Cædmon, whose name indicates he was a British Celt, was an illiterate farmworker of advanced age on an estate attached to the Anglo-Saxon monastery ruled by Abbess Hilda (d. 680) at Whitby. Though not himself a monk, Cædmon, like other laypersons connected to such foundations, participated in festivities of the larger monastic *familia,* which included beer drinking and passing a harp for each person to entertain the others with a song or poem. When the harp approached Cædmon, he fled the feast "for shame" because he did not know how to sing or compose verses. After returning to his own dwelling, he fell asleep among the cattle he was tending and dreamed that a man (perhaps an angel) appeared to him, miraculously bringing from God the gift of singing and composing poems, thus enabling him to produce the famous nine-line "Cædmon's Hymn." The next morning, Cædmon told his reeve (estate manager) about this miracle and was sent to Abbess Hilda, who marveled that he could not only perform that hymn but also compose new poems out of religious (mostly biblical) stories related to him by learned monks of the monastery. She then enlisted Cædmon as a full-fledged monk, and he continued to use his miraculous power to produce further Christian poems using traditional Germanic poetics. Because he composed poems in oral performances after ruminating on the holy texts read to him, and at least one of these poems survives because it was written down as "Cædmon's Hymn," the legend about his poetic gift provides an unusual opportunity for us to glimpse some of the relations between orality and literacy in an early-medieval context.

Bede does not designate Cædmon as a saint, though students of hagiography will recognize in his legend some familiar characteristics of the saints' lives that circulated widely in monastic and popular culture: Cædmon's unpromising youth, his dream vision, his gift of divine speech, his besting of his betters (the scholars who serve to write down his poems), and his ability to foresee the time of his own death. Though our only source for this legend is Bede, numerous manuscripts containing versions of "Cædmon's Hymn" survive as evidence of its wide circulation, and the conclusion of the legend in the Old English translation of Bede in Alfred the Great's time implies that the poem circulated in oral culture before being written down.

See also: Bede the Venerable; English Tradition: Anglo-Saxon Period; Orality and Literacy
References and further reading: B. Colgrave and R. A. B. Mynors have edited the Latin text of *Bede's Ecclesiastical History of the English People* (1969); the volume includes an English translation by Colgrave. The Alfredian translation into Old English has been edited and translated into modern English by T. Miller, *The Old English Version of Bede's* Ecclesiastical History of the English People (1890–1899; rpt. 1959, 1963). An excellent edition of "Cædmon's Hymn" with critical commentary may be found in J. C. Pope, ed., *Seven Old English Poems* (1981).

—John McNamara

Camlan

Arthur's last battle in Welsh legendry.

An entry in the *Annales Cambriae* (Annals of Wales), under the year 537, states: "Battle of Camlann in which Arthur and Medraut [Medrawd] fell." The site of the battle is unknown. In his *Historia regum Britanniae* (History of the Kings of Britain), Geoffrey of Monmouth locates it on the banks of the river Camel in Cornwall; another possible site, proposed by O. G. S. Crawford, is Camboglanna (Birdoswald), a Roman fort on Hadrian's Wall. However, Camlan, from *camboglanna* (crooked river bank) or *cambolanda* (curved enclosure), is not an uncommon Welsh place name, though none of the places so named appears to have popular Arthurian associations. The annals do not indicate that Arthur and Medrawd were leaders of opposing factions, but Welsh traditions ascribe the cause of the battle to the treachery of Medrawd and to discord at Arthur's court.

According to the Triads of the Island of Britain—allusions to Welsh legendary events, arranged in groups of three—Camlan was one of "the three futile battles of Britain," brought about by a quarrel between Queen Gwenhwyfar and Gwenhwyfach (Triad 84), and "one of the three harmful blows," struck by the latter on the former (Triad 53). Triad 54, which may have a similar context, refers to one of "the three unrestrained ravagings" when Medrawd dragged Gwenhwyfar from her throne and struck her. Geoffrey of Monmouth's account (c. 1138) of the abduction of Arthur's queen by Modred (the form he uses for Medrawd) and the subsequent final disastrous battle derives from the same tradition. The Welsh tale of *Rhonabwy's Dream* does not refer to Medrawd's assault on the queen, but here, too, Camlan is the result of plotting and mischief, as Iddawg Cordd Prydein confesses that he caused strife between Arthur and Medrawd by conveying twisted messages from the one to the other and that Camlan was thus "woven" from his actions. Another early Welsh tale, *Culhwch and Olwen*, refers to the nine who plotted Camlan. Other citations in the Triads and in poetry refer to the three, or seven, survivors of the battle.

The frequency of allusions in medieval Welsh literature and the diversity of the record suggest an active tradition about the battle of Camlan, and its core theme of treachery and internal rivalry leading to the loss of an ordered, harmonious world explains its impact on the popular imagination beyond its strictly

Arthurian context. Camlan was a furiously violent, as well as a disastrous, battle. This is the aspect emphasized by many medieval poets, especially Gruffudd ab yr Ynad Coch, who in his elegy to Llywelyn II (the last prince of Wales, killed in 1282) gives that event an apocalyptic significance, "like Camlan." The tradition of Camlan as a furious melee was long-lived, and the word *cadgamlan* (battle of Camlan) is found from the sixteenth century as a common noun for a confused, noisy rabble.

See also: Arthurian Lore; *Culhwch and Olwen;* Triads of the Island of Britain
References and further reading: See R. Bromwich, *Trioedd Ynys Prydein* (1978); P. C. Bartrum, A *Welsh Classical Dictionary* (1993); and O. G. S. Crawford, "Arthur and His Battles," *Antiquity* 9 (1935).

—*Brynley F. Roberts*

Candlemas

A feast traditionally celebrated on February 2, which formally marked the end of winter and the beginning of spring in parts of medieval Europe.

Also known as the Feast of the Purification of the Blessed Virgin Mary, Candlemas falls 40 days after Christmas, in imitation of the 40-day period of isolation that Hebrew law imposed upon mothers and their infants. If Christ was born on December 25, then Mary, with her newborn son, would be presented at the temple for purification on February 2.

In the Gospel of Luke a pious man named Simeon sees Jesus in the temple and, recognizing him as the Messiah, says that the infant will be "a light to lighten the Gentiles" (2:32). The early Church seized upon the symbolism of light and promoted the lighting and blessing of candles as an important fixture of this feast, hence its more popular name. The imagery of rebirth and renewal of light during the darkest time of the year, as well as the divine light of Christ appearing to banish the darkness of human sin, led to the ritual of a candlelit procession. The following morning, St. Blaise's Day (February 3), priests would use the burnt-out candles for a ceremony known as the "blessing of the throats": using two candles to make the sign of the cross on the throats of the parishioners, the priests would pronounce their benedictions.

In many regions Candlemas and St. Blaise's Day marked a turning point in the calendar, the beginning of the end of winter. In southern France and elsewhere in Europe, it was said that bears would emerge from hibernation on February 2; thus the Candlemas bear, not unlike the groundhog currently celebrated on February 2, was seen as a harbinger of spring. As the beginning of spring, Candlemas marked the beginning of the Carnival season in many parts of Europe. Candlemas also marked a transition in the rhythms of seasonal work. In England and elsewhere in northern Europe, Candlemas was the date on which cattle were driven off the newly plowed fields, which were fenced so that the work of sowing the seeds for the summer crops could begin.

The feast first appeared in Rome in the seventh century, but it appears to have developed in the Greek world in the fourth century. Surviving records have frequent references to the conflict in the British Isles between the feast of St. Brigid, held with great merrymaking on February 1 by those of Irish,

Hebridean, and Manx descent, and Candlemas, which the other Christians celebrated by fasting on the same day.

Due to its focus on the Blessed Virgin, Candlemas was banned from England during the sixteenth century.

See also: Brigid, Saint; Carnival
References and further reading: In *The Stations of the Sun* (1996) and *The Rise and Fall of Merry England* (1994), R. Hutton discusses the history of Candlemas celebrations in the British Isles. J. Kremer, *Celebrate Today* (1996); C. Gaignebet, *Le carnaval* (1974); and E. Le Roy Ladurie, *Carnival in Romans*, trans. M. Feeney (1980), discuss the relations between Candlemas, St. Blaise, and Carnival.

—*Bradford Lee Eden*

Cantar de mio Cid

Anonymous epic poem of 3,730 lines on the exploits of Rodrigo (or Ruy) Díaz de Vivar, a low-ranking noble who in the time of Alfonso VI, king of Castile and León, rose through his military talents to become the independent ruler of Valencia.

His epithet in the poem, *Cid,* is an Arabic word meaning "my lord." The poem concentrates on the Cid's campaigns in the valleys of the rivers Henares, Jalón, and Jiloca after he was exiled from Castile by Alfonso, relegating the capture of Valencia to a few lines. The second half is dominated by the story of the marriages of the Cid's daughters, Elvira and Sol, to the infantes de Carrión and the breakup of those unions occasioned by the infantes' criminal treatment of the two women in the oak wood of Corpes. In a magnificent court scene, the Cid obtains from his sons-in-law the return of gifts he has given them, including the swords Colada and Tizón. The two are challenged, along with their elder brother Ansur González, to fight judicial duels with the Cid's champions, who triumph. The poem ends with a celebration of the fact that all the kings of Spain are descended from its hero, an element important in dating the text to around the year 1200.

The portrayal of the Cid that emerges from the poem is one of an extremely capable warrior and military leader who acquires wealth through his martial talents and redistributes it to his retainers, his dependents, and King Alfonso as gifts, and who ultimately transforms the status he has achieved thereby into genealogical value when his daughters contract even more prestigious marriages with the infantes of Navarre and Aragon. Despite this majestic overall design, the poet includes many details of everyday life in his depiction, including the hero's belief in omens.

The *Cantar de mio Cid* survives in its poetic form in a single fourteenth-century manuscript whose first page is missing and that bears a colophon recording that a certain Per Abbat copied the text in 1207, no doubt a relict from an earlier stage of the manuscript tradition. Although the poem was once thought to have been composed around 1140, which would have been a little more than 40 years after the death of the historical Rodrigo Díaz de Vivar in July 1099, most scholars seem to agree, subsequent to the work of Antonio Ubieto Arteta, that the date is much closer to the date given in the colophon. The poem was incorporated into the vernacular prose chronicles that were initiated by King Alfonso the Wise, beginning in the second half of the thirteenth century; of those prose versions, the one found in the *Chronicle of Twenty Kings* is closest to the Per Abbat manuscript.

The meter of the *Cantar de mio Cid* is highly irregular, with lines varying from 10 to 20 syllables, and the most frequently occurring line, of 14 syllables, only attested in a little more than a quarter of the poem. The lines of each *tirada* (verse paragraph) are linked by a common assonance. The diction is formulaic, just under a third of the half lines consisting of repeated phrases. The text itself refers to its internal divisions as *cantares* (songs), and it was in all likelihood sung. That the irregularities of versification derive from the process through which it was taken down in writing rather than from compositional consider- ations is a possibility that I believe likely.

Much of the research devoted to the poem has concentrated on the rela- tionship between the occurrences it recounts and the events of Rodrigo's life, about which a fair amount is known for an eleventh-century figure. The poem clashes with recorded historical information in various ways. It combines the Cid's two exiles into one, changes the names of his daughters (María and Cristina in history), ascribes to them unhistorical marriages with the infantes de Carrión, and identifies them incorrectly at the end of the text as the queens of Navarre and Aragon. It fails to mention the hero's service under the Muslim king Mutamin of Saragossa in the period 1081–1085 and plays down his ties with Muslim al- lies, with the exception of King Abengalbón of Molina, represented as a good Moor. It also omits any mention of the fact that Rodrigo's wife Jimena was a cousin of Alfonso VI and was thus a woman of royal lineage, and of the fact that the king himself led an army against Valencia. Alvar Fáñez, the Cid's right- hand man in the poem, was in history an important military figure in his own right and could not have played the role the poet assigns to him. Bishop Jerónimo, in history the Cluniac Jérôme de Périgord, did not arrive in Valencia until 1097, three years after the Battle of Cuarte in which the poet has him take part. These and many other departures from the historical record make it clear that, con- trary to the theories of the renowned philologist and historian Ramón Menéndez Pidal, the poem has no special status as a documentary source.

A number of signs point to the poem's composition in a particular context, in my judgment for an audience of nobles and warriors connected with the milieu of Alfonso VIII of Castile near the end of the twelfth century. The focus on events occurring in the valley of the river Jalón raises the possibility of com- position in or near the monastery of Huerta, founded by Alfonso VIII in 1179. María Eugenia Lacarra has pointed out that two powerful Castilian clans of this period, the Laras and the Castros, were linked through genealogy with the prin- cipals of the poem—the Laras with the Cid, the Castros with his enemies. Alfonso VIII himself was descended from the hero. The vilification of the infantes de Carrión and their ally García Ordóñez could well derive from the poet's desire to flatter Alfonso VIII and the Laras, especially the Laras of Molina, by re- flected praise at the expense of the Castros. The poem's depiction of the pro- cesses of enrichment through the acquisition of plunder may have been meant to encourage Christian fighting men to engage in the struggle against the Moors in the perilous period between the Battle of Alarcos in 1095, disastrous for Alfonso VIII's side, and his decisive victory in the Battle of Las Navas de Tolosa in 1212.

One of the themes with which the poem concerns itself is the legitimacy of the Cid's birth. Whereas one would expect only two judicial duels in the climactic combat scene, a third battle matches the Cid's champion Muño Gustioz against Ansur González, brother of the infantes de Carrión, who has launched an obscurely worded and seemingly gratuitous insult at the Cid implying that he is the illegitimate son of a miller's wife. The motif of the Cid's illegitimacy is referred to clearly from the sixteenth century onward in the corpus of Spanish ballads devoted to him. Muño's victory in the single combat implies that the rumors of Rodrigo's illegitimacy are false, to the benefit of his descendants.

See also: Arabic-Islamic Tradition; Ballad; *Chanson de Roland*; Epic

References and further reading: The principal edition in English is C. Smith, ed., *Poema de mio Cid* (1972). The editions of I. Michael, *Poema de mio Cid* (1987), and A. Montaner, *Cantar de mio Cid* (1993), furnish extensive notes. Among good translations are W. S. Merwin, trans., *Poem of the Cid* (1975); L. B. Simpson, trans., *The Poem of the Cid* (1957); and R. Hamilton and J. Perry, trans., *The Poem of the Cid* (1984). A. U. Arteta, *El Cantar de mio Cid y algunos problemas históricos* (1973), found many features that are inexplicable if one dates the poem before the very early thirteenth century. E. de Chasca, *The Poem of the Cid* (1976), is a good general introduction. M. E. Lacarra, *El Poema de mio Cid: Realidad histórica e ideología* (1980), contains insights into the role of social context and law in the poem; R. Menéndez Pidal, *España del Cid* (1967), is the classic treatment of Rodrigo's role in eleventh-century Spanish history; C. Smith, *The Making of the Poema de mio Cid* (1983), posits an individual author, who would have conducted archival research in order to write the poem; B. Powell, *Epic and Chronicle* (1983), and D. G. Pattison, *From Legend to Chronicle: The Treatment of Epic Material in Alphonsine Historiography* (1983), evaluate the process of incorporating the epic into chronicles. G. G. Pérez traces the journeys mentioned in the poem in *Las rutas del Cid* (1988). J. Duggan, *The Cantar de mio Cid: Poetic Creation in Its Economic and Social Contexts* (1989), places the poem in the context of the medieval gift economy and evaluates it as a bearer of genealogical value. M. Harney focuses on kinship structures and social relations in *Kinship and Polity in the Poema de mio Cid* (1993).

—Joseph J. Duggan

Carnival

A festival created by medieval European Christians to mark the two or three days (sometimes extended to more than a week) that preceded Ash Wednesday, the beginning of Lenten abstinence.

The festival emerged slowly from the debris of Roman, Greek, Germanic, Slavic, and other ethnic celebrations of the end of winter and approach of spring. The Roman Lupercalia (celebrated on February 15) is documented for 495, which seems to be the latest mentioned of such celebrations, at least by official name. In the early 1140s Canon Benedict of St. Peter's at Rome described for the first time an organized ceremony taking place on Fat Tuesday (Mardi Gras). The pope rode ceremoniously with Roman secular nobility to Testaccio Hill, where a bear, young bulls, and a cock were killed. Benedict interprets the sacrifices as an orientation to Lent and hence to Easter: "so that we may henceforth live chastely and soberly in a testing of our souls, and merit reception of the body of the Lord on Easter."

A seasonal and ludic interpretation of the scene is just as possible as this liturgical one. Records show that Testaccio Hill was used for a bull-killing sport on Mardi Gras for the next 600 years. Equally relevant to the ambivalence of Carnival's meaning is the presence of the pope together with the prefect of the city, knights, and foot soldiers. Is Carnival "pagan" or "Christian"? It is both, just as it is secular and religious, solemn and playful by turns.

Humanists from the fifteenth century and many others since then have alleged undocumented continuities between Lupercalia, Saturnalia, Dionysia, and any number of other well-authenticated non-Christian practices by European ethnic groups. But the silence between 495 and 1140 remains, broken only by the emergence in the tenth century of family names and place names: *carnisprivium, carnelevare*. The word *carnival* means the end of meat eating. When the word is documented without any reference to ceremonies it is ambiguous, pointing as much to Lent as to the moment just before it, as Rabelais noticed in 1550 to the confusion of single-minded scholars ever since.

More plausible than the humanist idea of a hidden continuity from ancient times is the notion that Christian ideological dominance slowly but successfully dissolved all organized celebrations that possessed non-Christian ideas of spiritual force. By the eighth century Lenten ritual practices had become well codified. Between the eighth and twelfth centuries the old naturalistic religious practices, which certainly never ceased to exercise their hold on people's imaginations, reclustered at a number of points in the Christian liturgical calendar. Nowhere was this more true than on the days that then acquired the collective name to which Canon Benedict alludes matter-of-factly by describing *"de ludo Carnelevari"* [the Carnival game].

We possess only pinpoints of light about Carnival from 1140 until the early fourteenth century. Only 70 well-authenticated documents mentioning Carnival customs have been found for this period up to now; most are urban, but some are monastic and a few feudal-courtly. The number 70 does not count place names and personal names nor the use of the word as a means of dating feudal obligations. But it does include 15 references to the payment of a "Carnival hen" as a feudal obligation, even though such references may refer only to a practice of private conviviality rather than to any generally shared, public celebration.

From 1250 onward town evidence dominates the records, accounting for 90 percent of the total documented Carnival celebrations found in Europe west of Russia and north of the Balkans. The following sample periods illustrate the rapid increase in documentation now available to scholars in published studies: 1150–1175, 6 documents; 1250–1275, 15; 1350–1375, 35; 1450–1475, 101; and 1550–1575, 146. Before 1500 fewer than three dozen references to village carnivals in the indicated European area have been found; most of them record accidental crimes that occurred during Carnival or describe peasant behavior literarily in pejorative and satiric terms. Yet village practices were the basis for the Grimm-Mannhardt-Frazer idea of Carnival as a

The Combat of Carnival and Lent; *sixteenth-century oil painting on oak wood by Pieter Brueghel the Elder. (Ali Meyer/Corbis)*

repository of Indo-European myths and rituals that survived into the nineteenth century in "backward" villages. For ideological reasons as well as because of this scarce documentation, scholars since World War II have generally resisted the earlier tendency to attach the adjectives "age-old" and "customary" to every scrap of evidence about nonelite, popular, and especially "folk" behavior.

Carnival is the most fascinating of medieval festivities. This is not simply because Carnival took form on the edge of a Christian observance rather than beneath it, as in the case of Christmas or Saint John's. Quite apart from the festival's ambiguous ideological overtones, it is naturalistically ambivalent. Does it celebrate the end of winter or the beginning of spring? Young man Carnival (a character in literature from the 1220s onward) is exuberant, noisy, arrogant, and sexy, like spring, but he is also lazy, tyrannical, and fearful, like lingering, self-indulgent winter and like the hibernating bear, sacrificed at Rome in 1140 and still today a popular animal personification of the occasion. Old woman Lent may be ascetic but she is also energetic, enterprising, and forward-looking, like the new season. (The Viennese painting by Pieter Brueghel the Elder called *The Combat of Carnival and Lent* depicts the contrast comically, and in accord with a 300-year-long tradition.)

Carnival is ambivalent, looking forward and backward, toward spring and toward winter, and it is ambiguous, reminding humanity of both the ephemerality and the joyousness of sensuous pleasures. Hence it has proved extraordinarily prolific in modes of festive behavior. By 1500 one can divide European Carnival practices into five clusters, each of them with 20 to 30 modes of expression. Two of the five clusters are primarily concerned with food and three primarily with social organization. Modes and usages within the clusters exhibit the division and ambiguity characterizing the festival generally.

1. Most obviously, Carnival celebrates food consumption in unheeding excess, in total disregard for the future and for one's own body, mind, and intestines. Cakes and doughnuts, pretzels and pancakes, wine and beer, and every manner of beast and fowl, the fattier the better. These must be begged, borrowed, hunted, and stolen; offered to the lord by manorial custom; offered to the city council by public subsidy; given to the poor, to children, nuns, monks, soldiers, and to the family in picnics and banquets; paraded and smeared; and thrown away and thrown about. Most of these practices had serious, ritual forms as well as parodic, ironic, obscene forms.

2. No medieval person needed reminding that the reverse of food consumption is production. The year coming to an end in flagrant excess had simultaneously to be reborn. So the weather signs that moderns associate with New Year's Day, Groundhog Day, or the spring equinox were all consulted at one time and place or another during Carnival. Winter-versus-summer symbolic duels and fracases, usually ending in the victory of fertile, green-garbed summer, were frequent features of the holiday in Scandinavia and the eastern Alps. Greenery appeared on countless costumes. "Burying" winter/death/candlelight in the river or the earth would replenish the soil; bonfires, torches, and fireworks greeted the growing strength of sunlight. Besmearing a person with water or mud, hitching someone to plow or harrow or log, sowing the earth in the middle of town, cracking the trunks of fruit trees with whips and stocks to stimulate their sap—Mikhail Bakhtin's emphasis on the circular meaning of Carnival's inversionary character applies very well here: what goes down will come up.

3. The most prominent aspect of social organization feted in medieval Carnival was political-social hierarchy. Officials paraded or greeted the community at their residences or offices. The military displayed their power in parades and the elites their prowess, above all in jousting. But here, too, mockery and displacement were as evident as confirmation and celebration (not *more* so; in this respect Bakhtin's concept of Carnival errs). There was masking as kings and gods and clergy or conversely as peasants and beggars; indiscriminate public mixing, dancing, singing, and parading of high and low classes and even of women, married or unmarried (notorious in sixteenth-century Venice); and vindictive races pitting Jews and hunchbacks and prostitutes against each other (especially in sixteenth-century Rome). City hall was temporarily taken over; public proclamations condemned all manner of social and political excesses occurring during the previous year; all distinctions between the public and private were abolished; people ran in and out of houses and in and out of the city gates.

4. No less important to social organization than the hierarchies were the conventions separating human from nonhuman worlds. Medieval Europeans necessarily maintained an ambivalent understanding of the

conventions separating humanity, nature, and the invisible supernatural world. In this sphere, more than in the case of the preceding three clusters, official edicts condemning masking and costuming as sacrilegious or dangerous to public order produced the most documentation. Because material identifying the wild, demonic, foolish, monstrous, ghostly, and gigantic are more ambiguous in words than in gestures, iconographic evidence is of the essence here.

5.   Last but not least, conventions governing and contravening sexual boundaries were put into question; indeed what could be more pertinent to a winter-spring festival than reproductive relations? Male exhibitionism and male aggression against females were scarcely more in evidence than transvestitism, by women no less than by men. Simulating copulation, with all manner of verbal, visual, and gestural obscenities, was commonplace. But so were banquets, parades, and, in northern European areas, sledding parties to honor women. Carnival was a favored time for marriages because copulation was forbidden to good Christians during Lent. But Carnival was also a favorite time to perform charivaris, which ridiculed unseemly marriages by men or women.

All five clusters were celebrated by all social classes and both sexes, although of course individual usages were frequently very class-specific. The clusters were by turns elite, official, popular, and "folk" in character, and each of these kinds of cultural identity, chosen and combined by individuals no less than by occupational and economic groups (especially by the urban youth societies, which played central roles in organizing Carnival), borrowed from the others. In the status-conscious medieval and Renaissance framework of European society, Carnival was a time when people could cross social frontiers. It has been fruitfully studied from this perspective by Victor Turner and other anthropological scholars as a ritual process, on the model of Arnold van Gennep's rites of passage.

In the later fifteenth and sixteenth centuries the transgressive role of Carnival customs expanded its place in European culture at elite courtly and scholarly levels through humanist ideology. In the article Masking in this encyclopedia I have cited Dietrich Gresemund's exemplary expression of the new sense of the carnivalesque for those elites elsewhere. This more subjective and ultimately more subversive place of carnivalesque modes of thinking about the human condition is symbolized by the fact that personifications of the festival were presented by three of the most signal figures in European literature: Rabelais gave us Caresmeprenant (Fourth Book, 1552); Shakespeare, Sir John Falstaff (Henry IV, Part I, 1597, and The Merry Wives of Windsor, 1600); and Cervantes, Sancho Panza (Don Quixote, 1605).

This analysis has offered an overview oriented sociohistorically. But Carnival studies have always also been concerned with the problematics of representation. During the winter festival period between Christmas and Ash Wednesday, ecclesiastical and state authorities relaxed prohibitions on public theater; the winter season for drama was inspirationally as well as traditionally carnivalesque. Theatrical studies in the twentieth century moved beyond classicist and proscenium-arch prepossessions, inspired in the 1920s by surrealist-absurdist initiatives (e.g., Jean Duvignaud) and in the 1960s by semiotic-structuralist experiments (e.g., Richard Schechner), which in turn have engendered new academic fields like performance and communication studies that have strongly influenced the analysis of medieval Carnival. The observations about Carnival clusters above could be fruitfully supplemented by reformulation in performative, communicational, and representational terms. As indicated in the following bibliographical note, such reformulation has already been tried in many particular instances.

See also: Charivari; Festivals and Celebrations; Fool; Martinmas; Masking; Purim; Wild Man

References and further reading: Four independently developed initiatives have vivified Carnival studies in the last two generations. First was a greatly broadened conceptualization of the politico-moral implications of Carnival for medieval public culture in general, initiated in M. M. Bakhtin's *Rabelais and His World* (Russian 1955; English 1968) and carried forward by application to many other literary works of his concepts of grotesque realism and the circular and reversible embodiment of moral qualities in Carnival. Equally politico-moral, but theological rather than sociological, in orientation is the work of D. R. Moser and the richly documented doctoral thesis of W. Mezger, *Narrenidee und Fastnachtsbrauch* (1991). The second initiative has come from closer application of anthropological perspectives. In one direction, C. Gaignebet, *A plus hault sens: L'ésotérisme spirituel et charnel de Rabelais*, 2 vols. (1986), has refurbished Jacob Grimm's idea of Carnival as imbued with naturalistic mythology; like Bakhtin's book, Gaignebet surveys the whole period from later antiquity to the sixteenth century. A more eclectic application of anthropological theory is pursued in E. Le Roy Ladurie's *Carnival of Romans* (1980). Third, comparative studies have been rethought, this time within and across carefully traced regional boundaries during ample but delimited epochs, thus replacing the excessively local, excessively nationalistic, or excessively universalizing perspectives dominating Carnival scholarship until the 1950s. Hans Moser and his student Karl Kramer achieved the first renown in this direction (see Moser's collected studies in *Volksbräuche im geschichtlichen Wandel*, 1985), but the initial step toward regionalist comparativism, unequaled to this day, was taken much earlier by M. Arnaudov in his investigation at the beginning of the twentieth century of some 80 carnivals in Thracian, Macedonian, Greek, and Bulgarian villages, all adjacent to each other: "Kukeri i rusalii," *Sbornik za Narodni Umotrozeniya i narodpis* 34 (1920). The fourth new thrust, indicated in the last paragraph of the text above, has been to use semiotic, structural, and communicational modes of analysis to reveal the theatrical dimensions of Carnival. Cross-disciplinary methods have become indispensable; art history, theater studies, and literary history have joined hands with the traditional inquiries of cultural history, folklore, and anthropology in such a manner as to put in question the very boundaries of Carnival scholarship. Perhaps this subject-object still has some central qualities, but it would seem that there are scarcely any limits to its implications. See H. Pleij, *Het gilde van de blauwe Schuit, literatur, volkfeest, en burgermoraal* (1979); P. Vandenbroeck, *Over Wilden en Narren, Boeren en Bedelaars, Beeld van de Andere, Vertoog over het zelf* (1987); and S. Kinser, *Rabelais's Carnival* (1990), which addresses the ambiguities in references to Carnival. A few studies remain indispensable because of their easily accessible, wide-ranging, and careful documentation, even though their analytic approaches have been superseded: D. Wuttke, ed., *Fastnachtspiele des 15. und 16. Jahrhunderts* (1978), which contains a full bibliography concerning German Carnival plays through 1978; J. Caro Baroja, *El Carnaval* (1965); R. Bernheimer, *Wild Man in the Middle Ages* (1952); E. K. Chambers, *The Mediaeval Stage*, 2 vols. (1903); and B. Premoli, *Ludus Carnelevarii: Il Carnevale a Roma dal secolo XII al secolo XVI* (1981). The anthropological approaches of V. Turner (*The Ritual Process* [1969]) and A. van Gennep (*The Rites of Passage* [1960]) have been fruitfully applied to Carnival. The books listed under the articles on Festivals and Celebrations, Masking, and Wild Man are equally relevant to Carnival.

—*Samuel Kinser*

Carol

A festive combination of song and dance documented broadly throughout the late-medieval period.

The word *carol* finds its source in the Old French *carole*, which indicates both a ring dance and the song that accompanies it—apparently performed with great exuberance, for by the early fourteenth century, *carol* came to mean celebrating in general, as in 1308, when the mayor of London led a group that went caroling (*karolantes*) to the royal court to welcome Edward II upon his return to the city. Toward the end of the Middle Ages, however, the term became more restrictive, denoting only a type of song, usually sung on religious holidays.

As songs, carols are distinguished by their burden (chorus) and stanza structure. The short burden is sung at the beginning of the song and between each of the stanzas. The greater number of carols indicate the stanza as a solo part and the burden as group unison, but about one-quarter of the 474 carols preserved in English manuscripts indicate that sometimes both the stanzas and the burdens were noted for multiple voices.

The most frequent stanza form consists of four four-measure lines rhymed in *aaab*, with the final line serving as a refrain connecting to the burden, most often a couplet of four-measure lines rhymed in *bb*. For example, one of the famous Boar's Head carols, describing a festive meal in which the boar's head is the first course, begins with the burden,

Hey, Hey, Hey, Hey!
The borrys hede is armyd gay.

Then begins the first stanza, whose last line feeds back into the burden:

The boris hede in hond [hand] I bring
With garlond gay in porttoryng ["portering," or carrying]
I pray yow all witt me to synge,
Witt hay!

The subjects of surviving carols include not only the celebration of festivals, as in the example above, but also religious and moral counsel, satire, family life, politics, complaint, and love.

Another distinctive feature of the carol is its connection to the folk dances performed by both the peasantry and the aristocracy in the Middle Ages. The dance itself consisted of alternate periods of standing to count time and leftward (sunwise) motion in a ring or serpentine line. Most frequently the dancers would stand during the stanza and dance to the burden, but there are a few carols in which this sequence is reversed and the dance takes place during the stanza. The dance portion consisted most commonly of three steps to the left with accompanying arm motions, sometimes including sexually suggestive gestures. Male and female participants joined hands and followed the directions of the leader, who was usually the soloist of the stanzas.

Nearly all extant references to carols come from religious prohibitions and exempla that link the singing and dancing of carols to sacrilegious activities. In attempting to address cultural resistance against banning the popular secular songs, the Franciscans actively sought to retain well-known tunes, either altering their lyrics to discard lewd or secular subjects or attempting to interpret the words of the song in a religious vein. The carols, however, carried the added offense of being associated with non-Christian cultural practices. And because they were performed at holiday times, they attracted special condemnation from clerics promoting the pious observance of Christian feasts.

Between 600 and 1500 C.E. the Church formally banned the dancing of carols in church houses, on church grounds, and even in church neighborhoods more than 20 times; informally, numerous decrees, sermons, and exempla were written condemning the activity. In such texts as *Liber exemplorum ad usum praedicantium* (Book of Exempla for Use in Preaching) and Robert Mannyng's Middle English *Handlyng Synne* (1303), caroling at the wrong time or place attracts divine wrath. Mannyng, for example, states that anyone who practices caroling in churches or churchyards is in danger of committing sacrilege, especially at holiday times. He then tells a tale of 12 young men and women who congregated in a churchyard to carol on Christmas Eve. They disturb the priest as he is saying mass, and he curses the dancers, praying that they will be forced to dance for the entire following year. The prayer works, and the carolers are trapped in their motions for the next 12 months. While they danced, neither their hair nor their nails grew, they did not soil their clothes, and their complexions never changed. This legend, first situated in the German town of Kölbigk, was retold repeatedly in sermons from the eleventh century to the end of the Middle Ages.

In witchcraft trials of the sixteenth century and later, accused witches often confessed to caroling. The witches' carol was a perverse parody of the secular dance: instead of facing each other, the dancers faced outward from the ring, and in so doing moved "widdershins," or against the motion of the sun.

Nevertheless, caroling thoroughly permeated secular society from bottom to top, appearing in court dances at least as early as the twelfth century. In Wace's Anglo-Norman poem *Roman de Brut* (c. 1155), the women carol at Arthur's wedding, and the fourteenth-century Middle English romance *Sir Gawain and the Green Knight* depicts caroling, both the song and the dance, as a major part of the celebrations taking place in Arthur's hall during the Christmas season.

Most of the carols in existence today are found in fourteenth- and fifteenth-century manuscripts originating from religious houses. Because of their composition in this environment, most carols are anonymous, but it is known that John Audelay, a chaplain from Shropshire, penned 26 carols, and James Ryman, a Franciscan friar in Canterbury, penned more than 100. The most extensive collection of carols is the commonplace book of Richard Hill, which contains 78 carols on diverse subjects. The textuality of these carols is evidenced by their repetition among the late-medieval manuscripts, pointing to the genre's movement from oral folksong to its incorporation into religious uses.

Both religious and secular carols of the later Middle Ages served as entertainment at gatherings in monastic and secular halls. Five of every six of the preserved carols treat religious subjects such as moral counsel, the Nativity, and praises to the Virgin Mary, and most of the religious carols contain prominent

Latin phrasing, sometimes written specifically for the piece, sometimes borrowed from liturgical texts or from hymns of the Divine Office.

Carols that emphasize the secular side of such holidays as Christmas include a group celebrating the holly and the ivy, and indicating a festive game in which the men would portray themselves as holly and the women as ivy. The carol "In Praise of Holly" includes these lines:

> Her commys holly that is so gent [courteous],
> to pleasse all men is his intent. ...
>
> Whosoeuer ageynst holly do crye
> In a lepe [immediately] shall he hang full hye

Note that holly is depicted as male, and that the carol implies in a playfully threatening tone that some people may speak disparagingly of him. Similarly, in "In Praise of Ivy," ivy assumes a female identity, and also states that those who do not praise her adequately are in error:

> The most worthye she is in towne—
> He that seyth other [says otherwise] do amysse—
> And worthy to ber the crowne.

The reference to crown suggests that men impersonating holly and the women impersonating ivy are competing for a festive prize.

See also: Christmas; Dance; *Sir Gawain and the Green Knight*
References and further reading: R. L. Greene, *The Early English Carols* (1935; 2nd ed., 1977), presents an excellent overview of the genre, providing a detailed history replete with medieval references to caroling. Greene's "Carols," in *Manual of Writings in Middle English* (1980), focuses on the subjects of the carols. E. K. Chambers, *Early English Lyrics* (1966), also provides a good collection. See also Chambers, "The Carol and the Fifteenth-Century Lyric," in his *English Literature at the Close of the Fifteenth Century* (1945).
—*Sandra M. Salla*

Catherine of Alexandria, Saint (d. early fourth century) [Katherine]

One of the most popular saints of the Middle Ages; martyred at the beginning of the fourth century, the patron saint of Christian philosophers, women students, virgins, and wheelwrights.

Catherine's legend reached Western Europe in 1020 when Simeon of Treves, a monk of Rouen in Normandy, brought a relic (supposedly a knucklebone of the saint) back from Alexandria. In 1040 a monk at Rouen composed a long Latin account of Catherine's martyrdom. This account, known as the Vulgate version, served as the source for most later versions of Catherine's passion, including the highly influential one in Jacobus de Voragine's *Legenda aurea* (Golden Legend).

St. Catherine's veneration in England began when Robert, the abbot of Rouen monastery, became bishop of London in 1044. *Seinte Katerine*, the earliest Middle English version of her passion, served an instructional or devotional purpose for nuns in the West Midlands. Other tellings, such as the one in the *South English Legendary*, seem to have been intended for the enjoyment of the lay public. The most important English version is John Capgrave's fifteenth-century *Life of St. Katherine*, which includes the story of her early life and of her passion, both in greatly expanded form.

So far as all the versions agree, Catherine grows up in third-century Alexandria, the daughter of King Costus. Beautiful, chaste, serious, and highly educated, she has many suitors, but she wishes to remain a virgin and resists pressure to choose a husband. The Virgin Mary eventually summons Catherine to what is commonly called her Mystic Marriage, in which Catherine recognizes Christ as the perfect spouse she desires, and he gives her a ring. When she awakens from the vision the ring remains on her finger.

The story of her passion begins when Emperor Maxentius orders a sacrifice in honor of a heathen god and Catherine reproaches Maxentius for worshipping devils. Desiring to persuade her rather than kill her, he summons the 50 best rhetoricians in the realm to debate her. She defeats them all, and they confess themselves converted; the emperor orders them burnt. Maxentius then tries to tempt Catherine with promises of gold, power, and status, but to no effect. Infuriated, he has her stripped, beaten, and thrown into prison for 12 days without food. During this time an angel feeds her, and she converts the emperor's wife and his right-hand man, both of whom become martyrs. One of the emperor's minions then designs the "Catherine wheel": four wheels lined with spikes and saws, two moving in one direction, and two moving the other, so that anything put between them would be torn to shreds. Catherine, placed naked between the wheels, prays for God to show the gathered mob his power, and the wheel is smashed with such force that it kills 500 heathens. The emperor finally orders his men to behead her. Catherine, hearing her bridegroom calling, stretches out her neck for the axe. When her head is cut off, she bleeds milk instead of blood and angels carry her body to Sinai.

See also: Saints, Cults of the

References and further reading: See Jacobus de Voragine, *Legenda aurea*, trans. G. Ryan and H. Ripperger (1969). English-language versions of Catherine's life include J. Capgrave, *Life of St. Katherine of Alexandria*, Early English Text Society, Original Series 100 (1893); *Seinte Katerine*, ed. S. d'Ardenne and E. Dobson, Early English Text Society, Second Series 7 (1981); *The South-English Legendary*, ed. C. d'Evelyn and A. Mill, Early English Text Society 236 (1956); *St. Katherine of Alexandria: The Late Middle English Prose Legend in Southwell Minster MS 7*, ed. S. Nevanlinna and I. Taavitsainen (1993).

Helpful secondary works include E. J. Dobson's *Origins of Ancrene Wisse* (1976), which treats the context and probable authorship of *Seinte Katerine*. Two studies on hagiography and romance discuss the popularity of the Catherine legend and the use of romance techniques in Capgrave and the *South English Legendary*: D. Pearsall, "John Capgrave's *Life of St. Katherine* and Popular Romance Style," *Medievalia et Humanistica*, New Series 6 (1975), and S. Crane, *Insular Romance* (1986). Useful discussions of Capgrave's sources and influences appear in Pearsall's work just cited and in A. Kurvinen, "The Source of Capgrave's *Life of St. Katherine of Alexandria*," *Neuphilologische Mitteilungen* 61 (1960). Continuing Kurvinen's work, S. Nevanlinna and I. Taavitsainen, in the cited work, offer a convenient overview of the legend's development. See also J. A. McNamara, "A New Song: Celibate Women in the First Three Christian Centuries," *Women and History* 5 (1983).

—Leigh Smith

Cato's Distichs

A collection of sayings, known in schools as *Disticha* [or *Dicta*] *Catonis*, that was memorized in oral recitation by beginning Latin students all over Europe for a millennium and a half, ending around 1800.

Analogs to its sayings first appear in the third and fourth centuries C.E. A letter datable between 364 and 392 C.E. preserves the earliest reference to a compilation, with a quotation termed *illud Catonis*, "that saying of Cato's." Although this school text contains no specifically Christian concepts, it continued to constitute the most basic level of Christian education. Ignorance of Cato's distichs meant that a person had no schooling at all (e.g., the old carpenter John in Chaucer's "Miller's Tale," who "knew nat Catoun, for his wit was rude" [*Canterbury Tales*, l. 1.3227]).

A typical medieval schoolteacher might well have passed on a false belief by attributing the collection to one of two Romans both named Marcus Porcius Cato: Cato the Elder (234–149 B.C.E., also called Cato the Censor), praised by writers including Cicero for moral rectitude and oratorical skill; or his great-grandson Cato of Utica (95–46 B.C.E.), lionized by Lucan for stern opposition to Julius Caesar. Although no survey has yet been done of the massive distribution of *Disticha Catonis*, more frequent credit seems to have gone to Cato the Elder because of another collection of maxims (not extant) made for his son. As a third possibility, some medieval sources question individual authorship. A representative twelfth-century introduction describes each Cato, credits the elder, and then adds, "Others say that this book got its name, not from its author, but from the subject matter. For *catus* means 'wise.'"

Although the exact contents of course varied from manuscript to manuscript across the millennia, the structure of the collection remained quite stable. *Disticha Catonis* opens with an exhortation that "my very dear son" learn these precepts in order to shape his character. The first section, which some manuscripts label *parvus Cato* (little Cato) or *Cato minor*, consists of 50 to 60 short imperative sentences. In units of two words, usually, and never more than five, a student learns to respect public opinion, be clean, control anger, and so on. Memorized, the advice as well as the ability to understand Latin was meant to stay with the learner for life. Only a few sentences address concerns specific to children, such as "Win a parent over with patience." Many apply solely to adults, who are urged to love their spouses, teach their children, fear the magistrate, attend the tribunal, say little at a party, and otherwise behave in ways articulated during classical Roman times but still regarded as valid through the Middle Ages and beyond.

The second, much longer section of *Disticha Catonis* is sometimes entitled *magnus Cato* (great Cato) or *Cato major*. It is divided into four books, usually aligned with the cardinal virtues (Justice, Prudence, Fortitude, Temperance) even though no such shared themes are apparent to our postmedieval minds. Each of the four books lists several dozen pairs of metrical lines (i.e., distichs) in a verse form presumably easy to memorize: each first line in hexameter (six metrical feet), each second line one foot shorter. After internalizing this metrical pattern from *Disticha Catonis*, students' brains would develop the capacity to memorize longer works also in elegiac distichs, such as Ovid's love poetry, and then works in continuous hexameters, ultimately Virgil's entire *Aeneid*.

The memory-training distichs resemble in content the work's first section, as the advice proffered applies to both adults and children in both Christian and secular social contexts. Medieval educators remained untroubled by occasional anachronisms such as the hexameter "When you have bought slaves for your personal use," for that distich concludes unproblematically, "remember that they are human beings." In some manuscripts, commentary implies teachers' ingenuity at making fixed phrases from past tradition relevant to contemporary conditions. The very first hexameter line, for example, refers to certain songs about God as spirit—songs in the Judeo-Christian Bible, according to medieval commentators. One, having noted that Juvenal and Virgil both also mention divine spirit, even declares firmly that *carmina* understood as "Sacred Scriptures" is "the better reading and the author's intention." Not until Desiderius Erasmus's 1514 edition does divine spirit regain its Greco-Roman context (from *Aeneid* 6). Erasmus goes on to apply the verse to his own contemporary concerns: "And indeed, nowadays, the common run of Christians [i.e., Roman Catholics] worships God with certain bodily ceremonies, although the most pleasing worship is piety of soul [as among us proto-Protestants]."

Because of its unequaled longevity, *Disticha Catonis* can contribute in several ways to the study of medieval folklore. As discussed, it helps to demonstrate how fixed-phrase proverbs, and other verbal art passed on orally century after century, continue to generate immediate relevance for each new set of tradition bearers even across a major cultural upheaval like the onset of Christianity.

In addition, reference to the collection could enrich historical comparison of vernacular proverbs. Some manuscripts and many print editions (including four from William Caxton's press, 1475–1491, and one by Benjamin Franklin in 1735) provide vernacular analogs of each saying. Although presented as if translations, many diverge enough from the Latin that they probably preserve everyday proverbial speech. Except for I. A. Brunner's article cited below, which lists sources ripe for analysis in 17 European vernaculars, studies of this aspect are lacking. Richard Hazelton does supply potential examples. "*Sic ars deluditur arte*" [Thus art is tricked by art] concludes distich 26 of Book 1. Two Middle English translations of *Disticha Catonis* render this sentence "So gyle with gyle shal gyled be"; and the Reeve concludes his Canterbury tale, "A gylour shal hymself bigyled be" (*Canterbury Tales*, l. 1.4321). Presumably Chaucer did not examine those two translations. Possibly his primary-school teacher aided his and his classmates' memorization process by offering the same analog. Most likely, though, Chaucer knew from oral tradition the same proverb as did the two translators. Three sources thereby corroborate its active oral circulation.

Besides parallel texts of folkloric items, performance context occasionally appears in a medieval writer's adaptation of vernacular sayings directly related to *Disticha Catonis*. Again Chaucer provides an apt instance. In "The Nun's Priest's Tale" Pertelote dares to translate the first clause of a distich into the Middle English dialect that chickens speak: "Ne do no fors of dremes" (*Canterbury Tales*, l. 7.2941) for *Sompnia ne cures* (DC 2, 31). Her pretension to even the most basic learning is thoroughly trounced by her husband, the best-educated rooster in all of English literature.

Chanticleer, his creator Chaucer, and nearly everyone else whose thoughts are preserved in Europe for well over a thousand years had memorized *Disticha Catonis*. The compilation epitomizes "official culture," if one were to dichotomize in order to align "unofficial culture" with "folklore." Its ubiquity provides a solid point of reference, however, against which folklorists can test perceptions concerning the vast majority of both official and unofficial culture that has disappeared into thin air never to be heard again.

See also: Chaucer, Geoffrey; Proverbs
References and further reading: The standard edition of *Disticha Catonis* is that of M. Boas (1952), which has both text and apparatus in Latin. A text and facing-page translation appear in the Loeb volume *Minor Latin Poets*, ed. J. W. Duff and A. M. Duff (1934). For English translation (only) and overview, see I. Thomson and L. Perraud, *Ten Latin Schooltexts of the Later Middle Ages* (1990). For literary context see "Latin Poetry" in *The New Princeton Encyclopedia of Poetry and Poetics*, ed. A. Preminger and T. V. F. Brogan (1993). The standard edition of Chaucer is L. Benson, ed., *The Riverside Chaucer* (1987). The most significant studies remain two by R. Hazelton: "The Christianization of Cato," *Mediaeval Studies* 19 (1957), and "Cato and Chaucer," *Speculum* 35 (1960). Also see I. A. Brunner, "On Some of the Vernacular Translations of *Cato's Distichs*," in *Helen Adolf Festschrift*, ed. S. Z. Buehne, J. L. Hodge, and L. B. Pinto (1968). P. Roos, *Sentenza e proverbio nell'antichità e i Distici di Catone* (1984), following Erasmus's methodology, aligns parallel proverbs from classical Roman texts with current Italian ones. On proverb collections more broadly, see two items by B. Bowden: "Chaucer New Painted (1623)," *Oral Tradition* 10 (1995), and "A Modest Proposal, Relating Four Millennia of Proverb Collections to Chemistry within the Human Brain," *Journal of American Folklore* 109 (1996). On medieval pedagogy, see localized studies including P. Gehl, *A Moral Art* (1993), and W. J. F. Davies, *Teaching Reading in Early England* (1974). Histories of education must hereafter take into account the primacy of the mnemonic practices revealed by M. Carruthers, *The Book of Memory* (1990). Educational documents, including the introduction quoted above, are translated by A. J. Minnis and A. B. Scott with D. Wallace, *Medieval Literary Theory and Criticism* (1988).

—*Betsy Bowden*

Celtic Mythology

Narrative religious and belief traditions of pre-Christian Celts, now known largely through various medieval manuscripts in which the traditions have been Christianized, historicized, or fictionalized to reflect the values and tastes of later times, in which myths no longer functioned primarily as sacred narratives.

A wide variety of traditional beliefs, as well as some ancient mythical narratives, survived in the areas of Celtic Western Europe into the medieval period. The inhabitants of these areas were basically farmers, and as one might expect, they had strong and persistent mythical ideas concerning human dependence on the weather and the land and concerning the cyclic relationship between these. This is clear from echoes in the medieval Celtic literatures and to a lesser but not insignificant extent in the folklore of more recent times.

Early Irish literature often identifies the father deity, the Daghdha, with the sun—his name was derived from original Celtic *dago-dévos* (the good god), the term *dévos* being cognate with other Indo-European forms meaning "sky god." In Irish the sun was described as the "horseman" of the heavens, and emanations from the Daghdha are given appellations such as "herdsman" and "plowman." The mother goddess was identified with the land, responsible for the birth of young animals and for the growing of corn and fruit—she was known by many secondary names, but there are indications that her principal name was Danu, derived from that of an Indo-European river goddess. This combination of father deity and mother goddess, with its rich symbolism, can be seen behind many of the mythological narratives that are found in early Irish literature and also, in a less pronounced way, in the old literature of Wales.

It is often remarked that the Celts preserved no cosmological myths, but this may be true only in an overt sense. The Celtic tendency to put night before day and the winter half of the year before the summer half must be based on the movements of the sun, which accordingly was understood to give precedence to the dead ancestors over the living community. The ancestor cult that was so strong among the ancient Celts can thus be viewed as related to the movements of the sun, which sinks in the West, where the otherworld island was situated, and which passes through the underground realm of the dead during the night.

The progression from darkness to light would appear to have been rationalized among the prehistoric Celts into a dialectical relationship between the figures *Dhuosnos* (the dark one) and *Vindos* (the bright one). This emerges in medieval Irish and Welsh narratives in hints at contests (carried out in human, fairy, or animal form) between figures named Donn and Find in Irish narratives, or kindred characters in Welsh such as Arawn and Hafgan or Gwythyr and Gwynn. The ubiquitous Find or Finn (Fion, Fionn) in Irish tradition is a derivative of *Vindos*, while Donn (from *Dhuosnos*) was in persistent Irish lore a lord of the dead whose "house" was a solitary rock off the southwest coast.

The belief that the dead passed to an otherworld island in the West was held by the ancient Celts of the Continent as well as of Britain and Ireland. This realm became known by a variety of names, such as Tir na nog (the land of the young) or Ynys Avallach (the isle of apples), and ancient tradition that envisaged the Isle of Man in this way gave rise to lore concerning a great lord of that island, a magician called in Welsh Manawydan and in Irish Manannán. The idea of an otherworld island off the west coast survived not only in Gaelic areas but also in Welsh, Cornish, and Breton traditions of the Middle Ages. It was often elaborated into legends of a city on the coast or under a lake that had been submerged by a great catastrophe due to some human error or some rash act that brought about the anger of the elements or of God himself.

Early Irish and Welsh sources contain echoes of a mythical contest at a great rock in the western sea, an idea that must have sprung from similar archaic Celtic beliefs. This was developed—probably in the prehistoric period—by associating it with the far-flung plot of a primordial battle between two sets of deities. In its most elaborate form, in the early-medieval Irish text *Cath Maige Tuired*, a great battle is described between the divine Tuatha Dé Danann (people of the goddess Danu) and the sinister Fomorians (Fomoire) (underspirits, who had strong aquatic connections). Such development of mythic symbolism into historical legend is typical of how the detritus of ancient myth came to be treated in medieval lore. The Tuatha Dé Danann are described in the text as inhabitants of Ireland with their royal center at Tara, and the Fomorians as sea pirates who oppress them in a variety of ways. The cast of characters includes several Celtic deities, such the Daghdha himself, his consort the goddess Morrigan (Mor-Ríoghain, "phantom queen"), the smith god Goibhniu, and the polytechnic god Lug (Lugh).

Lug wins the battle for the Tuatha Dé Danann by slaying the Fomorian leader, Balar, who has a terrible eye that destroys all on which it looks. This Balar (from Celtic *Bolerios) dwells on the rocky island of Tory off the northwest coast, and perhaps of equal significance, he is also associated with Mizen Head, the extreme southwest point of Ireland. In fact, the extreme southwest area of Britain was anciently known as Bolerion, a cognate of his name. Balar's connections with both the scorching and the setting sun are therefore clear, and Lug may represent the sun in its more constructive role. Such a basic format was developed into a plot that had Lug as the prophesied son of Balar's daughter, a format that echoes a well-known mythic structure of the eastern Mediterranean region (such as accounts of Sargon, Cyrus, Moses, and Perseus). It seems likely that this plot had been borrowed in antiquity by the Continental Celts from the Greeks and attached to their deity Lugus, of whom Lug is the Irish development. Traces of it have also been argued for Lleu, the Welsh equivalent of the deity, who is described in the *Mabinogi* and other medieval Welsh sources. The plot was further used in medieval Irish accounts of the heroic

Portal tomb on the Burren, in the west of Ireland, built circa 3500 B.C.E. Such tombs and the mounds that often covered them are sometimes depicted as entryways to the otherworld in medieval Irish mythological traditions. (Photograph by Peter McNamara)

youth of Finn mac Cumaill, and in the Breton source that Marie de France used for her lay *Yonec*.

Other Celtic deities survived strongly in medieval lore, and in even more human forms. A noted example was the Celtic goddess *Rigantona* (exalted queen), cognate with the above-mentioned Irish Morrigan. In the *Mabinogi* she appears in the guise of Rhiannon, an otherworld woman riding on a large white horse that outstrips all her pursuers. Morrigan was in fact the original name of the otherworld lady known as Macha in the medieval Irish literature. As the goddess of Ulster kingship, she acquired the new name from that of the area that was the center of that kingdom—Macha meaning "plain" or "pasture." Macha was described as a great runner, and her most celebrated achievement was winning a race against horses. Such a *Rigantona*-personage, paralleling the ancestor deity in equine associations, must have been the same as the Continental Celtic goddess of horses known as Epona (exalted horse lady).

Medieval Irish literature relates that Macha warned her husband not to boast of her running skills, but he does so, leading to the tragic end of their union. This exemplifies the process by which suitable narratives were borrowed to underline the importance of mythical personages. The narrative plot here concerns an otherworld woman coming to live with an ordinary man and then leaving him after he breaks a prohibition she had put on him. This seems to have been a floating folklore plot in Western Europe in the early Middle Ages, for it appears later in French legends of Melusine. The floating motif easily attached itself to the goddess of Ulster kingship, as the marriage of the king to the land goddess was an ancient conceit in Celtic inauguration rites. The maintaining of kingship was of course a precarious business, and immemorial tradition had added many types of *gessa* (magical prohibitions) to the ordinary social pressures that a king had to endure.

Lofty personages were made the subjects of floating medieval plots in other contexts also. A popular story in early-medieval Ireland told of how the Daghdha was made to relinquish control of his dwelling in the prehistoric tumulus of Brugh na Bóinne (Newgrange in County Meath) to his son Aenghus. According to this, Aenghus got a loan of the dwelling "for a night and a day" and then kept it forever by claiming that all time is computed as night and day. There are several other ruses of the "tomorrow never comes" type described in Irish tradition, and clearly the plot has been borrowed here from popular lore. Again, however, it underlines the ancient mythic idea of son superseding father or by extension the ritual idea of a king gaining tenure of his realm from the ancestor deity. The name Aenghus meant "true vigor," and the process is again revealed in the name of a character in the Ulster cycle who also relinquishes a kingdom: Fergus mac Roig (or Ferghus mac Ro-éich, literally, "male vigor son of great horse"). The archaic basis of the ritual may further be exemplified by the pseudonym of Aenghus, Maccan Óg, which scholars regard as a development from the archaic Celtic youth deity Maponos, son of Matrona ("exalted mother" or "great mother"). Maponos appears in medieval Welsh sources as Mabon.

As in the case of narrative plots, the mythological personages themselves could gain popularity in comparatively mundane form. A clear instance is the smith god known in Irish as Goibhniu and in Welsh as Gofannon. His memory survived in a Christian context as a marvelous craftsman called Gobán Saer, and legends were told of how this Gobán built monasteries and round towers for saints throughout the length and breadth of Ireland. The images of Celtic deities, particularly Lug, have been deciphered by scholars in the cults of several early Irish saints, while the celebrated St. Brighid (Brigid) of the sixth century C.E. has attracted to her tradition much of the cult of her namesake, the Celtic goddess Brighid (the highest one), and accordingly was portrayed as a patroness of agriculture, of fertility, and of poetry. The cult of St. Brighid, in turn, exerted a large influence on the lore concerning other female saints, not only in Ireland but throughout much of the medieval Celtic world.

The goddess persona persisted into medieval Ireland in two ways: as a convention in the verses of poets, where goddesses were mentioned as consorts and protectresses of great kings and chieftains, and in ordinary folklore, where they were described as fairy queens ruling from palaces within several of the archaeological structures that dot the Irish countryside. One of the most famous of these ladies was Áine (the bright one), patroness of the Eoghanacht dynasty in Munster and later of the Norman family of Fitzgerald. Many folk legends tell of how she appeared from time to time to assist families in need. The patronage of the goddesses, indeed, developed through medieval tradition into one of the most celebrated of all spirits in Irish culture, the banshee (bean sí, meaning "woman of the tumulus," or "fairy woman"). She is heard to lament the death of a member of the old Gaelic race, thus showing her special connection with and affection for such a person. Another retention of goddess imagery is exemplified by lore of the Cailleach Bhéarra, an old hag who was said to have lived from time immemorial and was particularly associated in Ireland with farming and harvesting and in Scotland with the wilderness and forests.

Druidic lore did not survive in direct form from ancient Celtic belief, but the learned castes preserved into the Middle Ages and to more recent times much of the mystical and magical functions of their druidic predecessors. It is logical to relate to this context the prophetic and clairvoyant utterances of such figures as Finn and Mongán in Ireland and Myrddin and Taliesin in Wales, as well as the legends concerning the magical powers of many historical poets (resulting in particular from their satires). Aspects of druidic lore persisted in accounts of poets getting their inspiration from otherworld sources and (in a broader narrative context) in the frequent motif in heroic and romantic stories of entry to the otherworld while sleeping or in a trance or through biding at a tumulus. Adventures of this kind concerning Cú Chulainn and Finn in Ireland and Pwyll and Rhonabwy in Wales are the most celebrated, but such visits were a commonplace of the marvelous stories in medieval Celtic literature.

There were many accounts of pseudohistorical or historical ancient kings. The most celebrated of these was Arthur, who bore a Romanized Celtic name, and who probably was in origin a dux Britanniarum, a leader of native soldiers in the Britain of the fifth or sixth century C.E. Such leaders, with more or less conventional Roman military skills, tried to defend Britain against the Anglo-Saxon invaders after the imperial legions left. Early sources describe him as the head of a faithful body of warriors and winning several battles, and he was also claimed to have been a great hunter. From the eleventh century onward, the new Norman overlords of Britain expropriated his memory. Lore about him and his followers developed rapidly, and he came to be portrayed after the manner of a medieval feudal king with his Knights of the Round Table.

The most famous king in Irish medieval lore was Cormac mac Airt, whose origin is lost in remote antiquity but whose connection with the kingship of Tara was exploited by the Connachta or Uí Neill dynasty, predominant in Ireland from the fifth to the eleventh centuries C.E. Legends of Cormac depicted him as a great ancient king who was cared for by a wolf bitch as a child, who came to prominence at 30 years of age, and who delivered many wise counsels and judgments. As the model and claimed founder of Uí Neill kingship, he was thus being portrayed on the lines of the great founders whose fame was becoming known through biblical and classical learning: Romulus, Christ, and Solomon. Much of the regnal and historical lore of medieval Ireland in fact came from sources connected with the Uí Neill dynasty, but it contained within it archaic ritualistic and mythical notions such as the notion that the forces of nature take an active part in the reign of a king and determine his ultimate destiny.

A wide range of migratory motifs and legends circulated within the Celtic world of the Middle Ages. Some of these may have been part of local tradition from time immemorial—such as the cauldron possessed by a deity or magical being that was always full of food and that revived any dead warriors thrown into it. One of the best-known migratory legends had a "three-cornered" plot in which a young hero meets a tragic end through falling in love with a beautiful lady betrothed to a vengeful older man. This is the plot of the tragic stories of Deirdre and Naíse or Gráinne and Diarmaid in Ireland, and of Drystan and Essyllt (Tristan and Iseut) in Cornwall and Brittany. Other migratory motives that were well known in medieval Celtic lore concerned the workings of fate. Examples include the sacrifice of an innocent youth to use his blood in building a fortress, the botched attempt by a man to regain his wife from the fairy realm, the mysterious lake horse that brings great benefit to a farmer until it departs after being hit, and the prophesied death of an individual in an unlikely place or by unlikely means.

These motifs circulated orally, but others may have been spread mainly by literary borrowing. Examples of the latter include a ring being fortuitously recovered from the belly of a fish; a camp or fortress being captured by attackers who gain entry by concealing themselves in baskets or bags, the supernatural lapse of hundreds of years when a hero visits the otherworld, or the false accusation of an innocent young man by the wife of a powerful ruler. Motifs of this kind could be found in Greek and Latin writings, from which medieval Celtic writers borrowed them into their own works. When read out from these more homely sources, the motifs in turn passed into the oral lore of the ordinary people.

With the spread of the Roman Empire, and perhaps from an even earlier date, international tale types entered the cultural zones of the Celts. This process of plot borrowing was much accelerated in the medieval period through trade contacts with other countries; through the travels of clerics, pilgrims, and merchants; and also through the Viking settlements in many Celtic areas. Dozens of such international plots have been identified in medieval Welsh and

Irish literature, often being used in association with the names of mythical and historical characters from indigenous tradition. This was another aspect of the tendency to develop detritus of rituals and beliefs into romantic narratives, a process that modern scholars, from their different perspectives, might view as either a confusion of the earlier tradition or as a dramatic perpetuation of it.

One singular example of a very ancient folktale being embedded in early Irish tradition is the story of Mider and his love for Étaín. Both of these characters, as well as several others in the story, were mythical personages, and there are several echoes of ancient ritual and history involved. In the actual story, however, Mider loses Étaín and has to perform stupendous tasks to regain her— this and other motifs in the story possess relatives in AT 313, "The Girl as Helper in the Hero's Flight," one of the earliest and most far-flung international tale types known. It must have been connected with the ancient Irish traditional material sometime in the early centuries of the common era.

A celebrated story in the Welsh *Mabinogi* tells of a male child born to Rhiannon being stolen away by a giant. Rhiannon is accused of killing the baby. A foal is later stolen by the same giant, but the owner of the foal cuts off the giant's hand and manages to recover both baby and foal. Rhiannon and other characters belong to ancient Celtic tradition, but the plot of the story possesses strong parallels in AT 653 ("The Four Skillful Brothers"), AT 712, and other international narrative material. In fact, a similar use of some of the same material occurs in a later medieval Irish story in which Finn mac Cumaill recovers stolen children and puppies from a giant. Finn enlists the assistance of marvelous helpers in his task, a plot based on AT 653; and the related helper tale AT 513 ("The Helpers") is in fact the plot base for another celebrated *Mabinogi* story, that of *Culhwch and Olwen*.

Metamorphosis was a trait often associated with the deities of early Celtic myth, perhaps originating in druidic emphasis on such mystical faculties. By the medieval period it had become commonplace among Welsh and Irish writers when describing the great worthies of old, especially those who had divine names or divine attributes. It was claimed that they could take the forms of various animals and birds and could, when necessary, live for long periods in such forms. To underline and dramatize this belief, narrators made use of episodes and motifs well known elsewhere in international traditions, such as the final episode of the folktale "The Magician and His Pupil" (AT 325), in which two magicians take on various forms as they fight each other. Such tales of transformation influenced the contest of the bulls in the Ulster cycle and the Welsh story of Taliesin. One very popular tradition, frequently used by medieval storytellers in both Wales and Ireland, concerned the great age of particular animals, whose names were celebrated in tradition, and the task of seeking out these animals and comparing their ages. The two principal plots in question—AT 80A* ("Who Gets the Beehive") and AT 726 ("The Oldest on the Farm")—were very old in European lore, but their combination would appear to have been a particular development in the Celtic areas.

Of the many other international narrative plots utilized in medieval Celtic folklore, we may quote one example to show how such material could be at once simple in its structure and pervasive in its influence. This is the story of the king with ass's ears (AT 782), which was well known in classical sources (where the king is often said to be King Midas) and in other sources. A good deal of tradition centered on a king called March, reputed to have been the elderly lover of Essyllt and thus the rival of Drystan (these three characters are commonly known as Mark, Tristan, and Iseut in the Continental literature of the Middle Ages). The name was a corruption of the Latin one, Marcus, borne by a sixth-century local ruler in southwest Britain. It could, however, be interpreted as "horse" by speakers of Celtic. It was natural, then, for the ass's ears, transformed into horse's ears, to be attributed to him. The story was told in Wales, Cornwall, and Brittany that he concealed his ears, but his barber grew sick from keeping the secret and whispered it to a tree or to reeds. A musical instrument was made from the tree or the reeds, and when it was played it sang out the dreadful secret! This March was famous in tradition as a seafarer (*llynghessawc*), and thus the story traveled across the Irish Sea and became told of the ancient mythical Leinster king Labhraidh, who was also known as a seafarer (*loingseach*).

See also: Annwfn; Arthurian Lore; Fenian Cycle; Folktale; Gwynn ap Nudd; Irish Tradition; Myrddin; Myth; Taliesin

References and further reading: For mythical lore among the early Celts, see P. Mac Cana, *Celtic Mythology* (1970), and M. J. Green, *Dictionary of Celtic Myth and Legend* (1992). For the origin and development of myth and ritual in early Britain and Ireland, see A. Ross, *Pagan Celtic Britain* (1967), and D. Ó hÓgáin, *The Sacred Isle* (1999).

    Lore of mythical and early historical personages in Wales and Ireland, respectively, is described, citing full sources, in R. Bromwich, *Trioedd Ynys Prydain* (1961), and D. Ó hÓgáin, *Myth, Legend, and Romance* (1990).

    For magical attributes of poets, see D. Ó hÓgáin, "The Shamanic Image of the Irish Poet," in *That Other World*, ed. B. Stewart, vol. 1 (1998). For plots of folktales and migratory legends in medieval Welsh and Irish literature, see K. H. Jackson, *The International Popular Tale and Early Welsh Tradition* (1961), and D. Ó hÓgáin, *Myth, Legend, and Romance* (under tale headings Animal, Humorous, Religious, Romantic, Wonder), and "Migratory Legends in Medieval Irish Literature," *Béaloideas* 60/61 (1992).

—*Dáithí Ó hÓgáin*

Chanson de Geste

Medieval French epic legend.

    The chanson de geste (from the French *chanson*, "song," and *geste*, "action, exploit, history") is the medieval French epic legend, written in assonantal or rhymed verse. The earliest extant manuscript is of the *Song of Roland*, written around 1125–1150. Most extant chansons de geste were written down from the late twelfth to the early fourteenth centuries, and the genre remained popular for the duration of the Middle Ages, both in French and translated, and also through imitations in other languages. Most had nationalistic or military themes. Estimates of the number of chansons de geste extant range from 70 to 100, depending on the reasoning behind the estimate.

    The French epic tradition has been influential outside France, with works that borrow the form or the content of the chansons de geste appearing in

Western European countries into the early modern period. The *Song of Roland* is the most famous.

There are three major ways of classifying chansons de geste: by literary form, cycle, or main character. These forms of classification reveal a great deal about the epics themselves.

In terms of literary classification, the classic, but by no means universal, chanson de geste form is considered to be a *laisse* (irregular-length stanza) comprising decasyllabic lines, each with a caesura after the fourth or sixth syllable. A large number of the earlier chansons de geste use this form, with assonantal *laisses*. Later chansons de geste are more likely to have rhymed alexandrine (12-syllable) *laisses*. There were also prose redactions of the epics in the later Middle Ages.

The most common classification is by cycle. Chansons de geste were often linked in theme or dealt with episodes from a hero's life. A grouping of all the works on Charlemagne or on an epic hero is called a cycle. The earliest known cyclic classification was by thirteenth-century author Bertrand de Bar-sur-Aube. He defined three groupings: that of the kings of France, that of Doon de Mayence, and that of Garin de Monglane. The first refers to what is commonly called today the *cycle des rois*, or kings' cycle, in which Charlemagne is the chief figure. The second refers to the *cycle des Loherains*, or feuding barons' cycle, and the third features Guillaume d'Orange. More recent analysts have broken up the works differently, some adding a cycle concerning the First Crusade. The Crusade cycle, however, is seldom dealt with in the same context as other chansons de geste by modern scholars.

Classification by character refers to groupings of works based on the life of a single figure. While the date of writing may not follow the chronology of the epic hero's life, the order of the chansons de geste in the manuscripts invariably starts with the hero's youth, then moves to his early knighthood, then his major battles, followed by his death or retirement to a monastery. Not all heroes have all of these episodes, but the sequence is consistent across the genre. To enable a listener or reader to instantly identify important characters, they were often "marked" by distinguishing traits. Roland had his sword and his horn, whereas Guillaume d'Orange was known by his nose. Major epic heroes included Roland, Oliver, Raoul de Cambrai, Gerbert de Mes, Renaut de Montauban, William of Orange (Guillaume d'Orange), Ogier, and Godfrey of Bouillon.

While Roland is the best known today of the French epic heroes, William of Orange was considered one of the great heroes in the French Middle Ages. He has tentatively been identified with William of Toulouse by several scholars. His exploits were widely known even outside the French-speaking world—for example, he is mentioned in Dante's *Divine Comedy*, as was Godfrey of Bouillon, another great epic hero. The historical Godfrey was born around 1060 and was a key figure in the First Crusade; the legendary Godfrey was said to be the grandson of Elias, the Swan Knight. This gives the hero a mythic ancestry (compare the legend that named the fairy Melusine the ancestress of the French house of Lusignan). Godfrey is a key character in the Crusade cycle of chansons de geste.

Although the tales recounted in the chansons de geste were popular in the Middle Ages, few are well known today. Even the tale of the Swan Knight, made famous through Wagner's opera *Lohengrin*, significantly differs from its epic roots.

While the *Song of Roland* is deservedly famous, there are other epics that are close to it in stature, although very different in literary style. *Raoul de Cambrai*, for instance, is a brilliant treatment of the tragic consequences of injustice and unrelenting anger. The stories dealing with the Mez family build the looming threat of continuing vendettas into a violent series of mesmeric and haunting tales. Not all outstanding chansons de geste were serious: the *Pèlerinage de Charlemagne*, for instance, has brilliant comic sequences as Charles and his lords discover that France is not the center of the cultivated world.

No music has survived for a chanson de geste proper, although a small amount of music does survive for the satirical *Audigier*. Most scholars agree that chansons de geste demonstrate their oral and possibly musical origins through the retention of a large number of oral traits in the works, ranging from their form (division of the text into *laisses*, with a distinct narrative style linked to this, such as the appearance of *laisses similaires*, in which an episode of great importance is dwelled upon through incremental or varied repetition) to phrases that appear in texts (such as comments by the *jongleur* to the audience). Even as the genre became more "written and read" in the later Middle Ages, it retained this sense of being created for live performance.

Scholars are divided on the subject of authors and of the precise oral or written nature of the chanson de geste. One school holds that chansons de geste were written by individuals; another, that they are the product of the collective oral process. Modern scholars are tending toward the view that there may have been an oral or collective gestation period for many chansons de geste but that individual authors were more likely to have written down the extant versions. There are very few named authors for chansons de geste, and most of these are for later works. Interestingly, the *Song of Roland* has a possible named author. The final line names "Turoldus." The jury is still out on whether Turoldus was scribe, author, or performer.

Whether chansons de geste ranked in the Middle Ages as histories or as pure literature is also disputed. While not accounted histories by most modern historians and clearly thought of as works of literature by many modern medievalists, it is generally accepted that many works have a core of historical veracity. My work suggests that in the Middle Ages they were regarded as works of history, and internal evidence shows that they were written as a form of history, not simply as entertainment. Most scholarship on the chansons de geste is in French. While no work in English provides a complete introduction to the genre, several bibliographical guides and studies on specific aspects are useful.

See also: *Chanson de Roland*; Charlemagne; Epic; Feud; Swan Knight; William of Orange
References and further reading: The basic bibliographies in the field are L. Gautier, *Bibliographie des chansons de geste* (1897), and J. J. Duggan, *A Guide to Studies on the* Chanson de Roland (1976), with an update in S. Kay, *The Chansons de Geste in the Age of Romance* (1995). One of the best introductions, although dated, remains J. Crosland, *The*

Old French Epic (1951). For the student of French language and literature, A. Hindley and B. J. Levy, *The Old French Epic* (1983), provides a useful undergraduate-level introduction. A useful modern introduction to the genre on a more theoretical level can be found in Kay's book, while a work that places the chansons de geste in context with other French literary epics is W. Calin, *A Muse for Heroes* (1983). Good introductions to several cycles are W. Calin, *The Old French Epic of Revolt* (1962); D. A. Trotter, *Medieval French Literature and the Crusades (1100–1300)* (1988); J. M. Ferrante, *Guillaume d'Orange* (1974); and R. K. Bowman, *The Connection of the* Geste des Loherains *with other French Epics and Mediaeval Genres* (1940).

—Gillian S. Polack

Chanson de Roland [Song of Roland]

An epic poem that recounts the battle of Roncevaux, in which Roland, Emperor Charlemagne's sister's son and captain of the rearguard of his army, dies of the effort of blowing his elephant-tusk horn (olifant).

Roland sounds the horn to call his uncle and the rest of the Frankish force back across the Pyrenees into Spain when the rearguard is treacherously attacked by the Saracens under King Marsile. In the preceding battle, Roland's companion Oliver and ten other knights—who, along with Roland, are the leaders constituting the Twelve Peers—and all their followers had been killed. Charlemagne's efforts to capture Saragossa had been stymied, but he returns. Assisted by a miracle that stops the sun in the sky, he succeeds in pursuing the Saracens to the river Ebro, where most of them drown. He then defeats in single combat Baligant, the emperor of Islam, who has arrived to help his vassal Marsile. Charlemagne takes the city of Saragossa and completes his conquest of Spain in its entirety. Upon the army's return to Aix-la-Chapelle, Charlemagne tells Aude, Oliver's sister, who is betrothed to Roland, that the hero has died, upon which she falls dead herself rather than survive him. Roland's stepfather Ganelon, who plotted the ambush during his journey as envoy to Marsile's court and who nominated Roland to lead the rearguard, undergoes a trial at Aix-la-Chapelle in which the jury attempts to reconcile him with Charlemagne. In a subsequent ordeal by combat, his champion Pinabel is defeated by Roland's kinsman Thierry, and as a result Ganelon is executed by being torn apart by horses.

The *Song of Roland* belongs to the genre of the chansons de geste—epic songs that told the deeds of ancestral heroes. These works, ranging in length from 800 to more than 35,000 lines, were sung by itinerant performers, *jongleurs*, who typically accompanied themselves on a stringed instrument, the *vielle*. None of the music of the chansons de geste has been preserved except for that attached to a one-line parody of the genre found in Adam de la Halle's thirteenth-century *Jeu de Robin et de Marion* (Play of Robin and Marion). Over a hundred chansons de geste have been preserved from the Middle Ages. Like a number of older chansons de geste, the *Song of Roland* is based on a historical event, the defeat of Charlemagne's rearguard in a pass of the Pyrenees on August 15, 778. The main historical source for that event is the *Life of Charlemagne* written by one of the emperor's courtiers, Einhard, who lists a Roland, prefect of the March of Brittany, as one of those killed in the battle. Whether Roland was a historical personage is unresolved, however, as only one branch of the manuscripts of Einhard's *Life* mentions him.

The earliest of the seven texts and three fragments of the *Song of Roland* in Old French (the one found in manuscript Digby 23 of the Bodleian Library in Oxford, England; 4,002 lines) is composed in assonance. All but a handful of editions and all translations into modern English and French are based on this version, which was copied in England in the second quarter of the twelfth century and is the oldest manuscript of any chanson de geste. The other texts are in rhyme, with the exception of that found in the Venice 4 manuscript (thirteenth century), which is partly in assonance and partly in rhyme. Of the seven manuscripts, three were copied by Italian scribes, and the legend of Roland gave rise to a thriving tradition of derivative texts in Italy, including Boiardo's *Orlando innamorato* and Ariosto's *Orlando furioso*. The *Song of Roland* was translated or adapted in the Middle Ages into Norse, German, Welsh, Provençal, Spanish, Latin, English, and Dutch. Among its modern derivatives are Roland traditions in the Sicilian puppet theater, in the oral poetry and chapbooks of Brazil, and in Spanish and Faroese balladry.

The longest French version (late twelfth century, 8,397 lines) is found in the Venice 7 and Châteauroux manuscripts. Like the other versions in rhyme, this text adds a series of episodes that appear to satisfy the needs of a different audience from that of the Oxford manuscript. At the onset of those episodes God works two miracles to allow the Franks to distinguish the bodies of their fallen companions from those of the Saracens: the latter turn into hawthorn bushes, but hazel trees grow out of the mass graves dug for the Christians. Biers are constructed from these trees for the corpses of Roland, Oliver, and the archbishop Turpin. Their bodies, as well as those of the Twelve Peers, are taken to Saint-Jean-Pied-de-Port, whence Charlemagne sends messengers to summon Aude. At this point, Ganelon escapes from his captors and is pursued and taken. Aude and her uncle set out and during the journey she has a series of troubling dreams full of animal and vegetative symbolism. Both the priest who is called upon to interpret the dreams and Charlemagne himself, however, feign that nothing is amiss and that Aude is destined to marry Roland. The emperor initially purports to have lost his nephew to a Saracen princess, but finally he must tell her that Roland and her brother Oliver are dead. After spending time alone with the bodies of Roland and Oliver—whose voice is counterfeited by an angel—Aude confesses her sins and dies. She is buried with her two companions at Blaye. When the army overtakes Ganelon, he undergoes two trials by combat, the first against Gondelbof the Frisian, ending in another attempted escape; the second through his champion Pinabel who, as in the Oxford text, loses to Thierry. Ganelon confesses that he betrayed Roland and after a series of scenes in which the French barons vie in proposing the most gruesome punishment, he is torn apart by horses, again as in the texts in assonance. The French return to their homes, but Charlemagne remains behind. The greatly elaborated episode of Aude's death, the stasis of the final scene, the addition of the miracle scenes, Ganelon's twin escapes, and the debate over punishment change the nature of the *Song of Roland* by diluting its military character with effects of pathos and suspense. This transformation may correspond to the shift from an audience of warriors to one consisting of both men and women.

The early-twelfth-century historian William of Malmesbury mentions that a song about Roland was sung to the Norman army at the onset of the battle of Hastings (1066) so that the warriors might be inspired by the example of its hero. This reference is generally taken to refer to a version of the *Song of Roland* earlier than any now available to us. The Oxford version claims that Charlemagne had conquered England (ll. 372, 2332); had this been true, it would have provided a useful precedent for the Norman invaders. A persistent medieval legend ("Charlemagne's Sin"), to which the Oxford version may obliquely refer (ll. 2095–2098), holds that Roland was not only Charlemagne's nephew but also his son, born of an act of incest with his sister Gisele. God himself subsequently revealed this sin to the emperor's confessor, St. Giles, while the latter was saying mass. Branch 1 of the Old Norse *Karlamagnus Saga*, which summarizes a series of now lost chansons de geste and gives the story of Charlemagne and Roland up to the beginning of the *Song of Roland*, recounts this legend in detail. It also provides a motive for the enmity between Ganelon and Roland, telling how the young hero was seduced by Ganelon's second wife, Geluviz. The Provençal version makes open reference to Charlemagne's Sin, and it is also narrated clearly in the fourteenth-century epic *Tristan de Nanteuil*. The Charlemagne window in the cathedral of Chartres is dominated by the Mass of St. Giles. If one accepts that the legend of Charlemagne's Sin was known to the poet of the *Song of Roland*, the work may be interpreted as recounting Charlemagne's punishment for his sin by the death of his first-born son, the fruit of that sin. This interpretation has the additional attraction of explaining the location of the earthquake that takes place in the poem (ll. 1428–1429) in anticipation of Roland's demise: not in the Pyrenees where the battle is taking place but in the ancestral land of the Franks, which mourns the coming death of the offspring of the Frankish royal family.

The earliest indication that a *Song of Roland* was in existence comes from medieval documents dating to around the year 1000 that are witnessed by pairs of brothers named Roland and Oliver. Roland is not a very common name in the period, and Oliver is quite rare. Some of the Roland-Oliver brothers are twins. The linking of the two names in this period is seen as an anomaly, one that probably arose from the popularity of a version of the *Song of Roland*. Most Roland scholars accept this conclusion. A note found by Dámaso Alonso in a manuscript copied at the monastery of San Millan de la Cogolla in Spain, dated to the period 1065–1075, contains the summary of a *Song of Roland* that, to judge by the form of the proper names mentioned in it, was composed in Spanish. Some scholars believe on the basis of this "Nota Emilianense" and the onomastic evidence that a French version of the *Song of Roland* must have existed at least as early as the eleventh century. This evidence and arguments from a comparative study of oral-formulaic epic style have led me to conclude that the *Song of Roland* was composed and transmitted orally from a very early period up to the time it was committed to writing in a version close to that found in the Oxford manuscript.

The Oxford text ends with a line that is susceptible to a number of interpretations, the most probable being that the work that Turoldus writes is coming to an end. Some take this name as that of an author, some—as is more likely—as that of a scribe.

See also: Chanson de Geste; Charlemagne; Epic; French Tradition

References and further reading: J. Bédier, La Chanson de Roland (1923), edits the Oxford manuscript with a facing-page modern French translation, as does I. Short, La Chanson de Roland (1990). G. J. Brault, The Song of Roland: An Analytical Edition (1978), is lavishly annotated, interprets the poem in a Christian context, and provides a translation. Reliable translations into English are F. Goldin, The Song of Roland (1978); D. D. R. Owen, The Song of Roland (1972); and G. Burgess, The Song of Roland (1990). C. Hieatt, Karlamagnús Saga (1975–1980), translates in Branch 1 a medieval version of the legends leading up to the beginning of the poem. J. Duggan, A Guide to Studies on the Chanson de Roland (1976), places the bibliography in the context of scholarly problems. S. E. Farrier, The Medieval Charlemagne Legend: An Annotated Bibliography (1993), covers the Chanson de Roland and the other chansons de geste dealing with Charlemagne. A. B. Lord, The Singer of Tales (1960), was the first to link the poem to contemporary orally composed epics. J. Duggan, The Song of Roland (1973), studies the text as an orally composed poem. The poem's historical connections with the Normans are covered in D. Douglas, "The Song of Roland and the Norman Conquest of England," French Studies 14 (1960). The relationship between the poem and history is the subject of R. Menéndez Pidal, La Chanson de Roland et la tradition épique des Francs (1959), and P. Aebischer, Préhistoire et protohistoire du "Roland d'Oxford" (1972). R. Cook, The Sense of the Song of Roland (1987), is a personal interpretation. P. Haidu treats the text as a poem of violence in The Subject of Violence (1993).

—Joseph J. Duggan

Charivari

A medieval folk custom or ritual consisting of a noisy, masked demonstration, often performed at night, enacted to mortify some wrongdoer in the community, whose transgression was usually social rather than legal.

Both to protect their own identity and to further distress the victims, participants in this ritual of humiliation often concealed their identity by producing bestial noises and wearing animal masks, skins, and costumes or otherwise disguising themselves as animals. They performed raucous songs and made artificial racket by noisily banging pots and pans like drums, playing other makeshift "musical" instruments fashioned out of household implements, blowing whistles, and ringing bells outside the house of their victim. In the late Middle Ages charivari was an international phenomenon. Practices comparable to the French charivari (even in France, the spelling varied by region, including chalivali, calvali, chanavari, coribari) were called cencerrada in Spain, scampanate in Italy, and katzenmusik in Germany. In most cases the names for this ritual allude to this important aural element common in all cultures. The English version of charivari, "rough music," overlapped with similar local folk customs such as the "Skimmity" or "Skimmington," "Riding the Stang," and the "Stag Hunt."

The typical impetus for enacting this ritual was perceived marital disorder. In rural areas remarrying widows or widowers were the most frequent victims of charivari, especially if there was a gross disparity between the age of the bride and groom. The rationales for these youth-driven humiliations varied. Not only was the older partner removing a young person from the local pool of those eligible for marriage, but because remarriages were often conducted quietly and privately at night, the community was deprived of a daylong occasion for festivity and free food and drink. Both in rural and especially in urban centers, other common targets of charivaris were husbands who beat their wives or (more often) husbands who had been beaten by their wives, cuckolded husbands, adulterous wives, people who married foreigners or cultural outsiders, and various sexual transgressors or deviants. What all these offenses had in common was their inversion of the "natural" social order.

In the countryside the groups who enacted the charivaris, referred to as Abbeys of Misrule, were often comprised of disorderly local youths who identified themselves as the "abbots" of misrule in mockery of monastic and ecclesiastical rules. The masked, costumed modus operandi of the charivari was designed to divert attention away from the identity and status of these mock abbots. By this means the intended focus could be aimed at (and the onus suffered by) the designated victims, almost scapegoats—the socially transgressive, now shamed newlyweds, cuckolds, husband beaters, and so on. These organized groups secretly conspired to meet at night in costume and to process to the victim's house, yelling profanities, singing raucous songs, and sometimes carrying effigies of the victims. The following day the perpetrators of the charivari would act as if nothing had happened, but the victims had been forced to endure mortification in the community. The Church's official attitude to the charivari was disapproval. Strong opposition to the charivari was expressed in explicit interdictions against the custom at the 1329–1330 Council of Compiègne and the 1337 Synod of Avignon and continued to be registered in consistent ecclesiastical censure of the practice throughout the fourteenth and fifteenth centuries.

The first extensive medieval literary description of the charivari is found in the early-fourteenth-century *Roman de Fauvel*, a satirical allegory by Gervais du Bus, in which the title character, a donkey who represents disorder, attempts to marry Fortune. When she rejects his suit, he instead marries Vainglory. On the wedding night of this transgressively matched couple, Harlequin the clown and his bestially costumed followers mock the union by performing a *"chalivali"* with makeshift musical instruments. The manuscript of the *Roman de Fauvel* contains three illuminations that offer perhaps the most authentic period illustrations of medieval charivari. One depicts the disturbingly mismatched married couple, with the literally asinine Fauvel approaching the marriage bed of Vainglory, imaged as a human woman. Below this scene are two panels depicting the grotesquely masked and costumed charivari "musicians" who appear to be "serenading" the newlyweds derisively with their own version of rough music.

One of the most infamous incidents in the late-fourteenth-century reign of French King Charles VI, the so-called Bal des Ardents or "dance of the burning men" at a 1393 wedding reception hosted by the king, was interpreted by a royal chronicler, the Monk of St. Denis, as a charivari. Notwithstanding this arguable example (Jean Froissart and other chroniclers do not allude to charivari in

A charivari, as depicted in the early-fourteenth-century French Roman de Fauvel; *illustration by Gervais du Bus. (Paris, BN MS Fr. 146, fol. 36v)*

other accounts of the event), the charivari generally functioned as an ordered representation of disorder, a means by which the traditional community could express conscious or sublimated frustrations and anxieties, reaffirm social and cultural mores, defend local sexual standards, and release social tensions—all through the "safe" but inverted world of carnivalesque representation that the noise, disguises, and adoptions of animal personae permitted.

See also: Bal des Ardents; Dance
References and further reading: On the charivari in general, see M. Grinberg, "Charivaris au moyen âge et à la Renaissance: Condamnation des remariages ou rites d'inversion du

temps?" in *Le charivari*, ed. J. Le Goff and J.-C. Schmitt (1981), as well as other essays in this collection; E. P. Thompson, "'Rough Music': Le charivari anglais," *Annales* 27 (1972); V. Alford, "Rough Music or Charivari," *Folklore* 70 (1959); and N. Z. Davis, "The Reasons of Misrule," in her *Society and Culture in Early Modern France* (1975). On the charivari element of the *Roman de Fauvel*, see N. F. Regalado, "Masques réels dans le monde de l'imaginaire: Le rite et l'écrit dans le charivari du *Roman de Fauvel*, MS. B. N. FR. 146," *Masques et déguisements dans la littérature médiévale*, ed. M.-L. Ollier (1988).

—*Lorraine K. Stock*

Charlemagne (742–814) [Carolus Magnus, Charles the Great]

The most important monarch of the early Middle Ages.

He was born the son of Pepin III, also called Pepin the Short, and Bertrada on (probably) April 2, 742. With his brother Carloman, he succeeded his father in 768. At Carloman's death in 771 he became absolute ruler of the Frankish realm. In 800 Charlemagne was crowned emperor in Rome by Pope Leo III. He died on January 28, 814. Charlemagne was married four times, and from these marriages he had three sons and five daughters. In his lifetime he waged many wars, against the Langobards, Saxons, Avars, and Arabs, but he also maintained diplomatic relations with Byzantine emperors and with the ᶜAbbasid caliph Harun al-Rashid. He organized the Frankish realm in counties with a strong central administration and was actively involved in Church policy and education. His person and performance were so impressive that Charlemagne lived on after his death, sometimes even larger than life. This process of epic concentration, in which legendary acts are falsely ascribed to a person, can be followed in the extensive medieval literature on Charlemagne, which first appears in Latin within two decades of his death.

The first biography of Charlemagne, Einhard's *Vita Caroli* (c. 829–836), was modeled after Suetonius's *Lives of the Caesars*, especially the chapter on Augustus. Einhard (d. 840), who knew Charlemagne personally, presents him favorably but avoids the poetic exaggerations of later biographies, such as Notker the Stammerer's *De Carlo Magno* (884–887), written for Charles the Fat, Charlemagne's great-grandson. Notker mingles facts with legendary anecdotes relating, for example, how Charlemagne helped a monk who could not sing, and how he "measured with his sword" (decapitated) Norse children. The anecdotes in *De Carlo Magno* are mainly related to persons surrounding Charlemagne, and Notker uses them to convey his criticism of the secular clergy.

Three centuries after appearing in Latin accounts, Charlemagne himself emerges most fully as a folktale protagonist in vernacular literature. The youth of Charlemagne is the subject of the *Mainet* (Old French, twelfth century), which became popular throughout Europe. Here Charlemagne is the son of Pepin and Berte, but the circumstances of his conception are confusing: at that moment King Pepin does not know who his legitimate wife is. Young Charlemagne is threatened by his evil half brothers and flees to Spain, where he adopts the name Mainet and lives at the court of the Saracen king Galafre. On Galafre's behalf Charlemagne subdues the mighty Braiment, after which he has a love affair with the fair Galienne. Charlemagne is now recognized as the best knight in the world, worthy to wear King Pepin's crown. In some versions he then travels to Paris, where he vanquishes his half brothers and receives the crown. Other versions tell of an attack on him by Marsile and an episode in which Charlemagne relieves the besieged town of Rome. J. R. Mien sees at the core of the *Mainet* the archetypal story of a hero, a king's son who is fathered under unusual circumstances, only to be expelled from his own country. In a foreign land the hero must achieve glory by feats of arms to prove himself worthy of the crown. Though *Mainet* has no historical core, it is important that Charlemagne is represented as a worthy king, ennobled by tests of fortune and ruling in harmony and peace.

In *Karel ende Elegast* (Middle Dutch, twelfth–thirteenth centuries, with versions in German, Norse, and Danish), the folktale elements are even more obvious. As Charlemagne sleeps at Ingelheim, God orders him to go out stealing. Reluctantly he obeys, and in the dark woods he meets Elegast, a vassal he had banished. In a joust he vanquishes Elegast, who confesses to being a thief. Charlemagne then recognizes in him a possible help for his mission; presenting himself as the thief Adelbrecht, he proposes to rob king Charlemagne! Filled with indignation, Elegast refuses to do so and instead proposes to rob Eggeric, Charlemagne's wicked brother-in-law. En route to Eggeric's castle, Charlemagne-Adelbrecht takes hold of a coulter (a pointed or cutting implement), which he wants to use as a burglar's tool. Elegast is the first to sneak in, but a cock, whose language he understands by means of some magic herbs, warns him that the king is near the castle. He leaves the castle, but Charlemagne persuades him to go through with their plan. With a magic charm Elegast puts all the inhabitants of the castle to sleep and opens all locks. They gather many treasures and Charlemagne wants to go home. But Elegast wants to steal a precious saddle out of Eggeric's bedroom. There he overhears Eggeric tell his wife that he plans to murder Charlemagne. When Charlemagne's sister reacts with indignation, Eggeric strikes her in the face. Elegast catches her blood in his glove and subsequently informs Charlemagne about the conspiracy. The next day Charlemagne holds court and unmasks the conspirators. Elegast's glove proves Eggeric's guilt, but a trial by combat brings the ultimate decision: Elegast kills Eggeric. Elegast himself is rehabilitated and receives Eggeric's widow as his wife.

The nucleus of the story is formed by folktale traditions of the master thief (particularly AT 952, "The King and the Soldier," but see also AT 950, 951, 1525), combined with the motif of the disguised king who acts as an agent provocateur and discovers a conspiracy against himself (motif K1812.2). The use of magic herbs (to understand animal language) and incantations (to put people asleep and open doors) is well known from folktales, but Charlemagne's use of a coulter as a burglary tool can also be considered a folkloric element. The coulter was actually much used in burglary, to the extent that possessing one could be legally compromising. Because God is the initiator of Charlemagne's adventure, Charlemagne ends up as the just king, under protection of God. The combination of story elements that characterizes *Karel ende Elegast* remains common in many recently collected oral folktales. Modern scholarship has identified postmedieval folktales from Mongolia, Russia, Lithuania, Bohemia, and Poland possessing significant plot parallels to *Karel ende Elegast*. H. W. J. Kroes maintains that the Middle Dutch version represents the root tale from which the others were descended, but he does not explain their transmission history.

The *Pèlerinage de Charlemagne* (Pilgrimage of Charlemagne), a twelfth-century Anglo-Norman poem with Scandinavian versions, offers perhaps the most coherent example of a Charlemagne text with a folktale structure. Piqued by his wife's taunt that she knows a king greater than he, Charlemagne decides to find this king, Hugo the Strong of Constantinople. He tells his peers, however, that they are going on a pilgrimage to Jerusalem. When they arrive, they are mistaken for Christ and his apostles and receive many relics. After some time, Charlemagne remembers his original goal, and they set off for Constantinople. There the queen's words are justified: Charlemagne and his peers cut a poor figure amid the splendor of the Byzantine court. After being feasted, they make wild boasts, which Hugo learns of through a spy. He obliges them to carry out their boasts, which they do, but only with God's help. Thus Charlemagne's superiority over Hugo is affirmed, but not before he is humiliated: in the final test a flood occurs, which forces Hugo to capitulate but also threatens Charlemagne and his peers. In a procession, Charlemagne's superiority is expressed concretely: he is one foot three inches taller than Hugo. Then the company returns to France, Charlemagne distributes the relics from Jerusalem, and is reconciled with his queen.

In these medieval stories (as in many more) Charlemagne lives and acts like a folktale hero in a (more or less) folktale setting. He is put to the test, sometimes ridiculed, and sometimes mocked outright, but he always emerges as the great king, a better king than at the outset of the story. One should notice, however, that the magic elements surrounding the "folktale Charlemagne" are always subordinated to or even completely integrated into a Christian conception of him. Charlemagne is always represented as a monarch under the protection of God, ruling in a just and harmonious way. One might wonder whether it is notwithstanding this process of epic concentration or, on the contrary, thanks to it, that Charlemagne was canonized in 1165.

See also: Chanson de Geste; Folktale; Nine Worthies; Romance

References and further reading: A good bibliographical introduction is offered by S. E. Farrier, *The Medieval Charlemagne Legend: An Annotated Bibliography* (1993, Dutch materials treated by G. H. M. Claassens). A good general biography is D. A. Bullough, *The Age of Charlemagne* (1965; rpt. 1966, 1973), which pays a great deal of attention to the cultural aspects of Charlemagne's government. The Latin biographies are available in English in L. Thorpe, trans., *Einhard and Notker the Stammerer: Two Lives of Charlemagne* (1969). The most important version of the *Mainet* was edited by G. Paris in "Mainet: Fragments d'un chanson de geste du XIIe siècle," *Romania* 4 (1875). On the folkloric aspects of this text, see J. R. Mien, "Les structures de *Mainet*," in *Charlemagne et l'épopée romance: Actes du VIIe Congres International de la Société Rencesvals*, ed. M. Tyssens and C. Thiry (1978). *Karel ende Elegast* has been edited several times; I used G. Stellinga, *De ridderroman Karel ende Elegast*, 2nd ed. (1977). *Karel ende Elegast*'s folktale-like traits and its relations to postmedieval folktales are elaborately treated in M. Ramondt, *Karel ende Elegast oorspronkelijk Proeve van toegepaste sprookjeskunde* (1917), and H. W. J. Kroes, "*Karel ende Elegast* en de meesterdief-sprookjes," *Tijdschrift voor Nederlandse Taal- en Letterkunde* 69 (1952). The *Pèlerinage de Charlemagne* is edited and translated in G. S. Burgess and A. E. Cobby, eds. and trans., *The Pilgrimage of Charlemagne and Aucassin and Nicolette* (1988). The best introduction to the folkloric aspects of that text, in my view, is J. D. Niles, "On the Logic of *Le Pèlerinage de Charlemagne*," *Neuphilologische Mitteilungen* 81 (1980).

—*Geert H. M. Claassens*

Charms

Chants, songs, or poems used as incantations or words of power, found primarily in preventative or curative remedies for various afflictions.

The term *charm* refers specifically to the vocal portion of ritual performances designed to alter material conditions, either by bringing out hidden virtues in natural objects (animal, plant, or mineral) or by driving out invisible agencies (such as elves, demons). The use of such words relies on assumptions that medieval folk belief systems shared with scientific and religious traditions: the belief in the power of spoken words over physical objects and the belief in the existence of hidden or invisible powers contained in nature that could be invoked or controlled by humans who possess the knowledge of such words.

The Latin terms translated as "charm"—*carmen, cantio*, and *incantatio*—and the Anglo-Saxon *galdor* are rooted in the idea of singing or chanting rhythmically. Instructions with charms frequently specify that the words be sung. For example, for the "water-elf disease" the tenth-century *Leechbook* recommends singing this many times over a wound: "May the earth destroy you with all her might and main" (in Oswald Cockayne's *Leechdoms, Wortcunning, and Starcraft of Early England*, 3:lxiii).

The written samples we have of medieval charms clearly record a verbal performance and an oral tradition that is only partially preserved in and represented by their textual forms in surviving manuscripts. These verbal formulas were performance pieces, meant to be acted out with a set of ritual movements by a trained person for an audience anticipating a material result in the prevention or cure of illnesses or curses, change in weather, or improvement of productivity. The performance for catching a swarm of bees (Cockayne 1:385) involves throwing dirt and gravel in specific directions while commanding the bees: "Sit ye, my ladies, sink, sink ye to earth down; never be so wild, as to the wood to fly." Similarly, to ensure the birth of a healthy child, a pregnant woman steps over her husband in bed, saying, "Up I go, over thee I step, with quick child, not with a dying one, with one to be full born, not with a doomed one" (Cockayne 3:67).

Such words of power could be in any language, Germanic, Celtic, or classical, and the use of languages foreign to the speaker, such as Latin, Greek, or Hebrew, indicates the conservative character of such folklore and the power believed to be inherent in these ancient and noble traditions. Sometimes the results were gibberish; however, intelligibility of the words was not an issue for their effectiveness, since the power was innate in the words themselves.

Charms invoked power not only through language but also through narrative: telling a story about some past event (miracle or biblical story) worked by analogy. For example, to heal a wound the legend of the spear of Longinus that pierced the side of Christ was enacted through a combination of ritual actions and narrative.

Words of power were used to alter the nature of physical objects so that they became spiritually powerful. Amulets made of animal, plant, or mineral material were empowered by words spoken over them or written on them to ward off evil or prevent illness. Most common, however, was the use of words chanted over herbs as part of a ritual to bring out the effectiveness of the plant against a specific ailment. One fourteenth-century remedy for sorcery employs these words of adjuration: "In the name of Christ, amen. I conjure you, O herb, that I may conquer by Lord Peter ... by the moon and stars ... and may you conquer all my enemies, pontiffs and priests and all laymen and all women and all lawyers who are working against me ..." (in Kieckhefer, *Magic in the Middle Ages*, 84). Words of power used to drive out invisible agents (elves, for example) closely resemble exorcisms, many times using the same formulas, because spiritual and physical causes of illness were not separated.

Charms were the subject of condemnation by Christian reformers, who frequently perceived this practice as rooted in paganism and associated with the devil (e.g., in the Decretals of Burchard of Worms, early law codes of the Anglo-Saxons and others, and later treatises against magic). Nonetheless, because most of the charms that survive were written down by churchmen, they were partly "Christianized" and therefore had an ambivalent position in medieval practice. The use of Christian prayers, holy oil, and church property in some ways sanctified the rituals, although many strict reformers remained uneasy.

The extant charms are primarily located in mixed classical-Christian-Germanic medical texts, although some are found as marginalia in other manuscripts. This type of medicine assumed or demonstrated the existence of occult virtues contained in plants, animal parts, and minerals. Copies of classical texts such as the *Herbarium* attributed to Apuleius and the *Quadrupedipus de Medicine*, Germanic lists of herbs such as "The Nine Herbs Charm," and compendia such as the *Book of Secrets: Of the Virtues of Herbs, Stones, and Certain Beasts* of Albertus Magnus relied on these hidden virtues to rebalance the four humors propounded by classical medicine, sometimes through the use of charms.

Another medieval context for charms is Christian tradition, particularly found in the similarities between charms and the liturgy. Underlying both is the idea that words can change material objects, whether bread and wine or an herb created by God with hidden virtues. Sometimes the two modes were combined: remedies for enchanting herbs in the surviving monastically produced medical manuscripts frequently specify saying the mass or other liturgical prayers as the words of empowerment or in combination with nonliturgical words of power predating Christianity. The most famous instance is the Anglo-Saxon "Field Ceremonies"—a daylong event with charms that invoked both Mother Earth and Father God and required masses to be sung over sods of earth and samples of agricultural produce brought into the church.

These overlaps between written medicine, formal religion, and folk tradition, especially in the early medieval period (up to 1100), demonstrate that there were no strict divisions between spiritual cure and physical cure or between prayer as supplication and charm as manipulation. However, the intellectual climate of the twelfth century introduced distinctions between natural and supernatural, drawing a clearer line between science and religion, medicine and miracle. By the thirteenth century intellectual speculation was beginning to question how words could have effective value. Charms were left in an indeterminate position and came under greater condemnation, as did those who employed them.

Thus, in the central Middle Ages (after 1100) the growth of universities, literacy, and Church authority placed charms more and more in association with unacceptable practices such as heresy, magic, and witchcraft, as evidenced in Inquisition documents. Increasingly, people who possessed the knowledge of words of power and who did not have an official Church position were suspect. Charms became marginalized by this intellectual climate into the category of "popular," with overtones of ignorance and superstition, a bias that persists into twentieth-century scholarship. Nonetheless, their preservation in the Christian-dominated manuscript traditions as medicine or liturgy, condemned practice or intellectual speculation, provides a window into medieval folklore.

See also: English Tradition: Anglo-Saxon Period; Magic

References and further reading: Most of the surviving Anglo-Saxon charm texts are contained in the outdated but still useful three-volume set of O. Cockayne, *Leechdoms, Wortcunning, and Starcraft of Early England,* rev. ed. (1961). For other editions discussing classifications of charms, see G. Storms, *Anglo-Saxon Magic* (1948); F. Grendon, "The Anglo-Saxon Charms," *Journal of American Folklore* 22 (1909); and J. Grattan and C. Singer, eds., *Anglo-Saxon Magic and Medicine* (1952). For charms in the context of magic, see R. Kieckhefer's *Magic in the Middle Ages* (1989) and V. Flint's *The Rise of Magic in Early Medieval Europe* (1991). For charms as words of power, see S. O. Glosecki, *Shamanism in Old English Poetry* (1989), which links charms and poetry as having effective value. On the relationship of charms to Christianity, see K. Jolly, "Anglo-Saxon Charms in the Context of a Christian World View," *Journal of Medieval History* 11 (1985), and her *Popular Religion in Late Saxon England: Elf Charms in Context* (1996).

—Karen Louise Jolly

Chaucer, Geoffrey (1344?–1400)

English poet and courtier whose early work documents noble festive custom and whose *Canterbury Tales* constitutes one of the richest records of popular storytelling styles to have survived the Middle Ages.

Life and Courtly Context

Nearly 500 records signed by or mentioning Chaucer make his the best-documented life of any English medieval poet's, but it is noteworthy that not one of the records mentions Chaucer's poetry. To the official world, Chaucer is known first as the page of Countess Elizabeth, who was the wife of English prince Lionel (1357), then as a prisoner of war during Edward III's campaign against the French (1359–1360), and later as a member of the royal household (1367), ambassador for Edward III and Richard II (1366–1370, 1372–1373, 1377, 1378), controller of the London Customs (1374–1386), justice of the peace (1385–1390), member of Parliament (1386), clerk of the Works (1389–1391), and deputy forester (1391). Compared to the contemporary French royal court, the English court rewarded its poets informally; whatever their opinion of his poetry, Chaucer's patrons viewed him, formally, as a statesman and public official.

Chaucer's early poetry provides us teasing glimpses of the aristocratic folk-ways of late-medieval England, a world of festive pageantry in which members of a wealthy merchant class (Chaucer himself was the son of a rich London merchant) provided artistic backdrops for elaborate ritual. A suggestive record, dated April 23, 1374 (St. George's Day, a court holiday celebrating England's patron saint, during which little official business was conducted), granted Chaucer a gallon of wine a day for life; many scholars believe this to have been a reward for a festive poem. Most of Chaucer's early surviving poems were occasional pieces: the *Book of the Duchess* is apparently an elegy in honor of Blanche, the wife of John of Gaunt. The *Parlement of Foules* and *The Complaint of Mars* are the earliest surviving English poems to mention St. Valentine's Day, and they allude to the customary belief that birds chose their mates on this day, while sketching a picture of refined play in which men and women engaged in elaborate courtship rituals. The *Legend of Good Women* mentions two companies of people named Flowers and Leafs, each celebrating the particular virtues of the parts of the plant for which they are named. Reading Chaucer's poems in tandem with such anonymous contemporary works as *The Floure and the Leafe* and *The Assembly of Ladies*, we see his art adorning the pastimes of a noble "folk" who used elaborate, conventionalized, metaphorical "nature" games as part of their holiday celebrations. Real-life festive poetic performances such as the London Puy (popular in the thirteenth century and perhaps continuing into Chaucer's day) and the Parisian Cour Amoureuse (founded on St. Valentine's Day 1400) engaged noble and merchant-class men in song competitions; some of Chaucer's poems may well have been written for similar occasions.

The development of Chaucer's poetic and public careers shows him living in a time of transition during which the merchant and noble classes grew closer together. Unlike his contemporary John Gower—who composed in Latin, French, and English—Chaucer is the earliest known court poet to have written exclusively in English, the language of the great majority, which became during his lifetime the official language of Parliament. His commitment to the common tongue of England signifies the breadth of his association with his audiences, and after his death he was hailed by many poets as the man who "taught" English how to become a respectable poetic language. During and after Chaucer's life, knights, princes, and merchants often met together in London households to exchange verses, indicating the growth of a poetic movement well beyond the confines of the royal court.

Chaucer's allusions to traditional customs make him an important source for medieval English folk culture. If his early work documented noble pastimes, his later poetry—particularly *The Canterbury Tales*—is rife with accurate references to urban and village rituals and lifestyles. "The Cook's Tale" refers to a prisoner "led with revel to Newgate," thus alluding to the ceremonial procession humiliating criminals in fourteenth-century London. In "The Miller's Tale," John the Carpenter performs a ritual to protect his home from evil spirits. The Miller himself is described as a champion wrestler, also adept at breaking doors with his head, a pastime since recorded at many village fairs. The Wife of Bath refers to the Dunmowe Filch, a slab of bacon awarded to couples who survive a year and a day of wedded life without repenting their marriage; this is a reference to a village tradition later documented in many sources. Such allusions affirm not only that Chaucer was well acquainted with the folk cultures of artisans and villagers but also that his upper-class audience shared his knowledge. Although it was a highly stratified society, Chaucer's England was a place in which the highest and lowest social groups possessed great mutual familiarity.

The Canterbury Tales

Nowhere is the breadth of Chaucer's knowledge of both elite and folk artistry more apparent than in *The Canterbury Tales*, an ambitious work begun about 1387 and left unfinished at his death, which depicts a mixed social group—ranging from a knight and a prioress to a miller and a plowman (a social mix even broader than Chaucer's audience)—exchanging tales as they ride together on pilgrimage to England's most popular shrine, the tomb of St. Thomas Becket in Canterbury. The various tales borrow from the most-revered international literary figures of the time—Boccaccio, Dante, and Petrarch, for example—as well as from several popular English forms, including the tail-rhyme romance ("The Tale of Sir Thopas") and the Breton Lay ("The Franklin's Tale"), popular with nonnoble audiences in Chaucer's time. As Francis Lee Utley pointed out, nearly all of the tales possess extensive analogs in modern oral tradition. If folktales were defined exclusively by content, the *Tales* would rank among the greatest early folktale collections.

A close look at *The Canterbury Tales* reveals, however, that—considered apart from the storytelling frame in which Chaucer puts them—its various narratives are no more or less folktales than are most late-medieval literary productions. The poem represents a range of entertainment at least as broad as the diverse society of storytellers assembled by Chaucer: "The Knight's Tale" (borrowed from Boccaccio's *Teseida*) and "The Squire's Tale" (a fragmentary pastiche of "Oriental" romance motifs) reflect the tastes of contemporary gentility. A group of pious romances, including "The Clerk's Tale" (a close reworking of Petrarch's "Tale of Griselda") and "The Man of Law's Tale" (based, like Gower's "Tale of Constance," on an early-fourteenth-century Anglo-Norman chronicle) reflect the more sober tastes of upper-class patrons. Yet Chaucer is equally adept in portraying more popular styles. The poet has the Reeve speak in the regional dialect of Norfolk; the Parson mocks the "ruf, ram, ruf" style of Midlands alliterative poetry; and his own persona, the pilgrim Chaucer, delivers a parodic fragment of a romance, "The Tale of Sir Thopas," in the tail-rhyme style popular among nonnoble audiences in his time. Chaucer's allusions to Arthurian romance are true to the general social status of such stories in the fourteenth century: the Nun's Priest refers to Sir Lancelot in parodic context, and the Wife of Bath, a character of bourgeois background, tells the only Arthurian romance, reflecting the fact that such stories then enjoyed their greatest popularity among the less elevated segments of English society.

More suggestive than the tales themselves is the context into which the poet sets them. Unlike most medieval European frame tales, whose bracketing narratives often serve merely as excuses for authors to present a series of unrelated

Geoffrey Chaucer offers his Canterbury Tales *to readers (and listeners?); a fifteenth-century illumination. (British Library, MS Lansdowne 851, fol. 2)*

stories, *The Canterbury Tales* presents its narratives as extensions of the concerns and social standing of the storytellers. The tales are told as part of a storytelling contest similar in structure to documented fourteenth-century entertainments. In addition to providing a General Prologue that describes the occupation and personal quirks of each pilgrim, the poet supplies links that situate most of the tales in specific performance situations. The tales of the Miller and the Reeve, for example, are not only masterful comic poems but also pointed thrusts in a verbal dual between the two tellers, a duel that brings into play the traditional rivalry between reeves and millers, aspects of social criticism, personal slurs, and oral techniques of indirect insult. Adhering closely to the folklorist's premise that the meaning of a tale is inseparable from its function in context, *The Canterbury Tales* presents not only a rich sampling of the types of narrative popular in its time but also a vivid, extended lesson in why, how, and for whom such tales might be told.

Like nearly all accomplished medieval tale writers and modern oral folktale tellers, Chaucer did not generally create his stories out of whole cloth; rather, he re-created them from well-worn plots with which his audience was thoroughly familiar. The secret of his art, like that of any great oral artist, lay in making the familiar fresh—through nuances that first played upon and then surpassed the expectations of his audiences. By first examining other surviving variants of the individual *Canterbury Tales* likely to have been known by Chaucer's audience and then considering how Chaucer changes his tale to reflect the unique circumstances of the fictional teller and performance, folklorists find the pilgrim narrators strikingly similar to modern oral narrators in the way in which they personalize their public art. The best-told *Canterbury Tales* are both thoroughly traditional and brilliantly individualistic, each bearing the stamp of innumerable past tellings as well as the personal imprint of the teller.

A case in point is the Prioress and her tale: in the General Prologue the narrator introduces her as an extremely sensitive person, but one whose sensitivities seem so misplaced that some readers wonder if her cultivated innocence may in fact mask a kind of cruelty. She expresses her "conscience and tender heart" by weeping when she sees mice caught in traps and by feeding her "small hounds," yet she feeds them roast flesh and white bread, better food than the great majority of people ate in Chaucer's England. In the General Prologue Chaucer does not tell us what to think of the Prioress, but her tale—once one compares it to other similar tales known to the poet's audience—points to a distinct interpretation:

After exalting the mercy of the Virgin Mary, the Prioress tells of a pious schoolboy who walks daily through the Jewish ghetto while singing a song in honor of the Virgin. Satan enters the hearts of the Jews. They grow angry at the sound of the song and hire a thug, who cuts the boy's throat and flings his corpse in a latrine. The mother searches in vain for the boy until the Virgin in her mercy causes the child to sing even though he is dead, and his voice reveals his burial place. The local magistrate orders that all the Jews who knew of the murder be rounded up, torn apart by horses, and then hanged as well. The Prioress concludes by praising the mercy of the Virgin.

The tale teller exalts the child's innocence, but she also vividly recounts the torture of the Jews, thus combining naivete with a hint of cruelty. Indeed, in comparing "The Prioress's Tale" to 33 surviving medieval analogs, we find that there is something decidedly cruel about it. These tales, like the Prioress's, were told to exalt the mercy of the Virgin Mary and generally end with the Jews, witnessing the miracle of the boy singing while dead, converting to Christianity; in most versions, no one is executed in retaliation for the boy's death. In only one of the other surviving versions do the angry Christians mercilessly slaughter a whole company of Jews. "The Prioress's Tale," then, would probably have struck Chaucer's listeners as a brilliantly told tale, but one that is so disturbingly selective in its quality of mercy that mercy finally loses its meaning. The brilliant individual touches that Chaucer puts on this tale do not become clear to us until we, like Chaucer's first audience, immerse ourselves in the traditional tales and expectations from which "The Prioress's Tale" so stunningly departs in its final actions.

Chaucer's influence on subsequent elite literature has been exhaustively documented, but equally noteworthy is the affinity that his works possessed with fifteenth-century popular poetry. After his death he was imitated by many merchant-class and anonymous popular authors; this, and the number and distribution of manuscripts of Chaucer's own work, as well as the fact that his *Canterbury Tales* was the first major English poem printed in England (by William Caxton, in 1478), demonstrate the degree to which Chaucer had earned the status of a truly popular poet by the end of the fifteenth century. The anonymous *Tale of Beryn* provides a conclusion for *The Canterbury Tales* in which the pilgrims arrive at Canterbury Cathedral. Such popular romances as *The Sultan of Babylon* freely borrow from the language of the *Tales*. Comic poems such as *The Wedding of Sir Gawain and Dame Ragnell* and *The Squire of Low Degree* proliferated in the fifteenth century; these anonymous works bear some stylistic resemblance to Chaucer's playful verse. Some critics maintain that the fifteenth-century poems are examples of *gesunkenes kulturgut*, a process in which elite forms "trickle down" to the lower classes. At least as plausible, however, is the possibility that Chaucer's work was popular with the lower classes precisely because he employed the popular idioms of his own time, and did so with such talent that his poems were in essence popular poetry, imbued with folk values from the beginning. As late as the sixteenth century, the anonymous *Complaynt of Scotlande* states that Scottish shepherds told *The Canterbury Tales*, a reference suggesting that many of Chaucer's poems not only grew from but immediately reentered and long survived as part of living British storytelling traditions.

See also: Accused Queen; *Confessio amantis*; Folktale; Frame Tale; Loathly Lady; Trickster; Valentine's Day, Saint

References and further reading: *The Riverside Chaucer*, ed. L. D. Benson (1987), based on the Ellesmere manuscript, is the standard edition of Chaucer's works; *The Variorum Chaucer*, ed. P. Ruggiers et al. (1982–), is based on the Hengwrt manuscript. Invaluable biographical information is found in M. M. Crow and C. C. Olson, eds., *Chaucer Life-Records* (1966). Three biographies are S. Knight, *Geoffrey Chaucer* (1986); D. R. Howard, *Chaucer: His Life, His Works, His World* (1987); and D. Pearsall, *The Life of Geoffrey Chaucer* (1992), of which Knight's is the most useful for folkloric approaches. Chaucer's social milieu is well documented by P. Strohm, *Social Chaucer* (1989); R. F. Green, *Poets and Princepleasers* (1980), surveys poetic entertainments in English courts. L. Patterson, *Chaucer and the Subject of History* (1991), offers the fullest view of Chaucer's broader social context.

G. L. Kittredge, *Chaucer and His Poetry* (1915), pioneered the study of *The Canterbury Tales* as a demonstration of storytelling in which the tale reflects the philosophy of its teller. B. J. Whiting published a major study, *Chaucer's Use of Proverbs* (1934). W. A. Quinn, *Chaucer's Rehersynges: The Performability of the* Legend of Good Women (1994), summarizes many of the approaches to the possible oral performances of his work in courtly settings; other studies of the oral dimensions of Chaucer's poetry are R. Crosby, "Chaucer and the Custom of Oral Delivery," *Speculum* 13 (1938), and B. Bowden, *Chaucer Aloud: The Varieties of Textual Interpretation* (1987).

Some studies examining the relationships between Chaucer and folk culture include J. Ganim, *Chaucerian Theatricality* (1990); L. Kendrick, *Chaucerian Play* (1988); and C. Lindahl, "The Festive Form of *The Canterbury Tales*," *English Literary History* 52 (1985), which all focus on Chaucer's affinities with popular festive culture. C. Lindahl's *Earnest Games: Folkloric Patterns in* The Canterbury Tales (1987) correlates the tale telling of *The Canterbury Tales* with a medieval folk rhetoric in which stories are used as indirect insults.

F. L. Utley's "Some Implications of Chaucer's Folktales," *Laographia* 22 (1965), and "Boccaccio, Chaucer, and the International Popular Tale," *Western Folklore* 33 (1974), discuss, respectively, the modern folktale analogs and the fourteenth-century milieu of Chaucer's tales. C. Brown analyzes the medieval analogs of "The Prioress's Tale" in W. F. Bryan and G. Dempster, eds., *The Sources and Analogues of Chaucer's Canterbury Tales* (1941), which also presents analogs and analyses of the other tales. This encyclopedia contains discussions of several of Chaucer's other tales and their folktale counterparts: those of the Franklin (AT 976), Man of Law (AT 706), Merchant (AT 1423), Miller (AT 1361), and Wife of Bath (AT 406A). Consult the appendix "Index of Tale Types" to find discussions of these.

—Carl Lindahl

Childbirth

The birth process, with its associated beliefs, practices, and narratives.

Although much more information has come to us from the later Middle Ages than from the early-medieval period, scholars have been able to reconstruct some of the basic premises of Anglo-Saxon obstetrics. Both early- and later-medieval sources tell of predictions of sex, methods for handling a difficult delivery, and herbal remedies. Given the danger that childbirth posed to women throughout the Middle Ages, it is not surprising to find frequent reliance on magic objects, charms, and rituals. From the later medieval period (fourteenth–fifteenth centuries) come many detailed records of both folk medical practices and of systematized medicine at monasteries, hospitals, and universities. Manuscripts from this era describe birth positions, fetal development, and disposition of the afterbirth, as well as remedies for such ailments as puerperal fever, abscesses of the breast, and hemorrhage.

Goddesses of Birth

While only fragmentary evidence of goddess worship survives from the early-Christian era, it seems clear that veneration of mother goddesses affected birth rituals in the Middle Ages. Laima, a goddess of birth and fate, is one such deity of Lithuania. The Teutonic goddess Freyja, who protected love and fecundity, was labeled a witch by early Christians, who claimed that she strayed out at night like a female goat among a crowd of bucks—a slur similar to those made against accused witches. As Christianity gained strength, the Virgin Mary grew in prominence as a protectress of mothers and children; however, dangerous goddesses continued to worry some expectant mothers. One greatly feared goddess was Lilith, said to be the first wife of Adam, who had lost her own children. Charms to protect expectant mothers and their babies from the jealous Lilith and her children, the monstrous *lilim* or *lilin*, were common among medieval Jewish women.

Anglo-Saxon Obstetrics

Scholars have debated why there are so few Anglo-Saxon texts on the subject of childbirth. The main manuscripts are Bald's *Leechbook*, *Leechbook III*, and the *Lacnunga*. The first two, separate parts of the same manuscript—London, British Library, Royal 1 2.D.xvii—were written around the year 950 in Winchester. The manuscript from which they were copied dates from the reign of Alfred the Great (871–899). Unfortunately, all that remains of Bald's chapter on obstetrics is an outline of material now missing: remedies for infertility, hemorrhage, and uterine obstructions, as well as instructions for removing a dead child from the womb and predictions of the child's sex. *Leechbook III* is a shorter, simpler assortment of remedies, while the *Lacnunga* (British Library, Harley 585), from a somewhat later time than the *Leechbooks*, provides a good selection of charms. Most of the Old English texts were compiled by Oswald Cockayne in his *Leechdoms, Wortcunning, and Starcraft of Early England*.

One influential text included in Cockayne's collection is the *Herbarium*, attributed to Apuleius, which was written in Latin in the fifth or sixth century. It includes numerous remedies from Pliny's *Natural History*, written in the first century C.E. More than 50 manuscripts of the *Herbarium* from Anglo-Saxon times attest to the popularity of this sourcebook. The *Herbarium's* remedies include dried comfrey, added to wine, to stop excessive menstrual bleeding; 11 or 13 coriander seeds, held by a virgin against the laboring woman's left thigh, to hasten delivery; and fleabane, boiled in water and placed under a seated woman, to cleanse the womb.

Some scholars have asked whether early-medieval remedies for amenorrhea were actually meant to cause abortion; Anglo-Saxons used wild carrot, parsnip, brooklime, centaury, pennyroyal, and smallage for this purpose. However, Christine Fell has suggested that malnutrition and anemia were common enough to account for most cases of amenorrhea requiring treatment. Marilyn Deegan has attempted to analyze the active principles of Anglo-Saxon remedies, to assess their effects, and to ascertain the complaints for which the remedies were intended.

Certain charms from the *Lacnunga* are highly detailed and ritualistic. For example, a woman who wants to have milk to nurse her child is urged to take milk of a cow of one color into her mouth, then spit it into running water, swallow a mouthful of water, and recite a lengthy charm. A woman who has lost a child and hopes to nourish another is told to wrap dirt from her child's grave in black wool and sell it to a trader. The wording of these charms requires careful interpretation; M. L. Cameron suggests that translators should make no major emendations. While Cameron calls the *Lacnunga* "folk medicine at its lowest level," Deegan finds that many Anglo-Saxon remedies make good sense and that some are still prescribed by herbalists today. Treatments such as the use of fresh horse droppings to control bleeding are no longer common, but their efficacy within their historical period can still be examined.

Late-Medieval Practitioners

Most facilitators of medieval childbirth appear to have been wise women whose skills were recognized, though sometimes mistrusted, by their communities. The

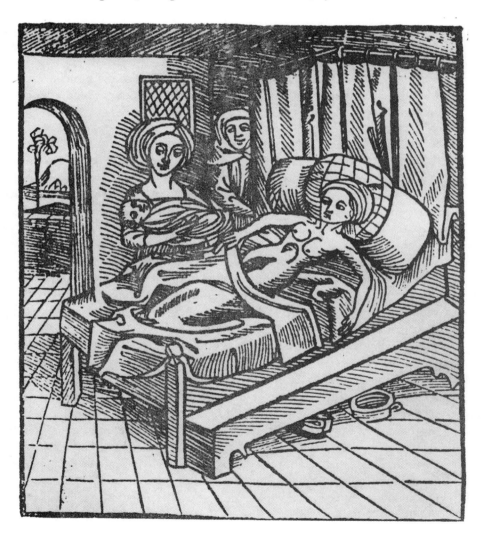

The birth of the anti-Christ, an often-depicted theme in medieval illustrations, which has given us much information about how medieval people viewed and administered Caesarian births. (Pseudo-Methodius, Opusculum divinarum revelationum, *New York, NYPL, Stuart *KB 1504)*

Malleus maleficarum (Hammer of Witches, c. 1486) tells of murderous midwives who, in harming mothers and their infants, proved themselves to be witches under the influence of Satan. These accounts of death-dealing midwives sound like local legends, but their authenticity is tainted by the book's intended use as a guide for witch-hunting. More neutral texts tell of both village wise women and more formally trained physicians who assisted with childbirth in the late-medieval period. One of the best-known spokespersons of medieval obstetrics is Trotula, eleventh-century Italian author of *De passionibus mulierum curandarum* (On the Sufferings of Women Patients). Whether Trotula was actually a woman and whether she wrote this treatise on women's diseases are controversial issues; however, it is known that female doctors practiced in Trotula's city, Salerno (during the Middle Ages, the University of Salerno was renowned for the teaching of medicine), in the fourteenth and fifteenth centuries. Both nuns and monks aided women giving birth, as noted in such manuscripts as Sloane 2463 (published as *The Medieval Woman's Guide to Health* by Beryl Rowland). While wise women continued to assist with childbirth through the late-medieval period, formally trained male and female physicians rose in prominence as the Renaissance approached.

Amulets, Predictions, and Guidebooks

The use of amulets was very common in the late Middle Ages. St. Hildegard von Bingen (twelfth century) wrote that pregnant women could protect themselves from evil spirits by holding the magic stone jasper in their hands; Trotula suggested that eagle stone (echinoids, that is, fossilized sea urchins), bound to a woman's thigh, would lessen the pains of birth. A snakeskin or hart-skin girdle was also favored as a talisman for making labor less painful.

Inherited from classical medicine, instructions for fertility tests stipulated that both the man and the woman should urinate upon wheat and bran; if the grain in one vessel became foul, the person who had urinated upon it was barren. Both Trotula and the writer of Sloane 2463 recommended ingesting the sex organs of a hare if one wanted to give birth to a male child. Once a pregnancy had advanced sufficiently, the child's gender could be predicted by the shape and position of the womb. Such predictions are still quite common today.

In contrast to early-medieval manuscripts, midwives' guidebooks of the fourteenth and fifteenth centuries go into considerable detail concerning unnatural birth positions, often with illustrations. These illustrations demonstrate some obstetrical sophistication, although the children in them do not generally resemble infants. Instructions on the removal of a dead child from the womb are sometimes accompanied by remedies, such as myrrh, rue, and dried beaver glands. Remedies for other ailments include such ingredients as herbs, fruits, minerals, animal parts, vinegar, and wine. Fumigation with a fat eel, burned alive, is recommended for curing bloody flux. A live turtledove, burned with its feathers and made into a powder with frankincense and sandragon, is a remedy suggested for a variety of ailments (Sloane 2463). In addition to mixtures and fumigations, the procedures of cupping and bleeding were favored in the late Middle Ages. Manuscripts such as the late-fifteenth-century *The Sekenesse of Wymmen* set a pattern for later, better-known guidebooks, including Thomas Raynalde's *The Byrth of Mankynde* (1552).

See also: Amulet and Talisman; Blood; Lilith; Medicine

References and further reading: M. L. Cameron's *Anglo-Saxon Medicine* (1993), quotation above from page 34, provides a thorough survey of obstetrical remedies from the Anglo-Saxon era. Other helpful sourcebooks are G. Storms, *Anglo-Saxon Magic* (1948), and H. J. de Vriend, *The Old English* Herbarium *and* Medicina in Quadrupedibus (1984). Many of the early texts are included in T. O. Cockayne's *Leechdoms, Wortcunning, and Starcraft of Early England*, 3 vols. (1864–1866). Innovative scholarship on medieval women's concerns includes C. Fell, *Women in Anglo-Saxon England* (1984), and M. Deegan and D. G. Scragg, eds., *Medicine in Early Medieval England* (1989). One of the most helpful books on late-medieval childbirth, for the general reader or the specialist, is B. Rowland's *Medieval Woman's Guide to Health* (1981). Another published guidebook for late-medieval midwives is M.-R. Hallaert, ed., *The Sekenesse of Wymmen* (1982). Regarding illustrations of birth positions, a detailed sourcebook is L. C. Mackinney's *Medical Illustrations in Medieval Manuscripts* (1965). Insight into women's roles in facilitating childbirth can be gained from J. Maubray's *The Female Physician* (1724) and R. M. Clay's *The Medieval Hospitals of England* (1909). E. A. Budge, *Amulets and Superstitions* (1930), contains valuable information about beliefs and practices related to medieval childbirth.

—*Elizabeth Tucker*

Chrétien de Troyes (fl. 1165–1191)

The greatest French practitioner of medieval romance and the author most influential in setting the themes and forms of the genre.

We know virtually nothing of Chrétien's life beyond the facts that he composed at least five romances and two lyric poems and that he wrote two of those romances under the patronage, respectively, of Countess Marie de Champagne (1138–1198) and Philippe d'Alsace, Count of Flanders (d. 1191). In all the works attributed to him with confidence, he shows himself to be an adept literary interpreter of the court culture of twelfth-century France; especially notable are his analyses of sentiments and his explorations of the potential conflicts between love and chivalry, between private pleasures and public duties.

The romances known to be by him all set their action in an Arthurian context and make Chrétien one of the most important popularizers of the legend of King Arthur and his knights. Those romances are *Erec et Enide* (Erec and Enide); *Cligés*; *Lancelot, ou Le chevalier de la charrette* (Lancelot, or The Knight of the Cart); *Yvain, ou Le chevalier au lion* (Yvain, or The Knight with the Lion); and the uncompleted *Perceval, ou Le conte du Graal* (Percival, or The Story of the Grail). The order given here appears to be the order of composition, though there is some evidence that Chrétien was working on *Lancelot* and *Yvain* at the same time.

Chrétien claims authorship also of some adaptations of Ovidian narratives and of a story of Iseut (Isolde) and Marc (and presumably of Tristan), but they have not survived. He may also be the author of a romance titled *Guillaume d'Angleterre* (William of England), a non-Arthurian composition attributed simply to a "Chrétien."

Chrétien de Troyes, the principal creator of medieval romance, is the first author to write of the love story of Lancelot and Guinevere—the former may be a character of his invention—and of the Grail; he is also the first to mention Camelot by name. More important, he allied love themes with an ideal of chivalric endeavor and, specifically, with the notion of a quest. That quest may be a search for the knight's lady or for another character, or it may be for an object. In his final, unfinished, romance (*Perceval*) it is for the Grail.

In the prologue to his first romance, *Erec et Enide*, Chrétien informs us with evident pride that he has drawn his story out of tales that others have regularly garbled. His is the story of a knight (Erec) who wins a bride and then, after their marriage, neglects his chivalric duties. This conflict between chivalric duty and personal inclination, or the potential conflict between chivalry and love, is a theme that Chrétien will develop in several of his romances. In this first one he works it out in a decidedly curious way: others begin to talk of Erec's failings, and Enide, hearing the talk, worries that she will be blamed. When she expresses her concern, Erec overhears her and immediately, without explanation, orders her to leave with him on a journey that will at the same time demonstrate his chivalric worth and test her love.

The second romance, *Cligés*, is written against the background of the Tristan and Iseut story, to which the narrator makes frequent reference. The love of Cligés for Fénice, the wife of his uncle, is reciprocated, but she refuses to duplicate the response of Iseut, whom she describes as having given her heart to one man but her body to two. The solution involves a potion, reflecting the one that bound Tristan and Iseut, but this potion makes Fénice appear to be dead and, until they are discovered by accident, provides an opportunity for Fénice and Cligés to indulge their love.

Lancelot, or The Knight of the Cart is undoubtedly Chrétien's most famous romance, introducing as it does the adulterous love of Lancelot for Queen Guinevere. Indeed, it was in regard to this romance that the term "courtly love" was coined in the nineteenth century. This composition treats the conflict of love and honor overtly and from a perspective unlike that of Chrétien's other romances. When Lancelot, seeking Guinevere, has an opportunity to find her by riding in a cart reserved for criminals, he hesitates for only an instant before concluding that his personal dishonor is nothing compared with his love for the queen. Later, however, she rejects him, not for having disgraced himself but for having hesitated to do so; he briefly put his honor before his devotion to her. He must later expiate this offense by publicly humiliating himself in a tourney.

Yvain, or The Knight with the Lion offers an inversion of the central theme of *Erec et Enide*. Unlike Erec, who neglects his chivalric duties to be with his wife, Yvain is intent on seeking adventure with his friend Gauvain (Gawain) and thus leaves his wife, Laudine, immediately after their marriage. He fails to return at the agreed time and thus loses her love. Accompanied by a grateful lion he had rescued (in an analog of the story of Androcles and the lion), he regains that love by repeatedly demonstrating a newfound sense of responsibility and unwavering devotion to others.

Chrétien's final romance, though uncompleted, was enormously influential: it introduced the Grail into world literature and made this object (which was a marvelous and holy vessel but not yet, in Chrétien, the chalice of the Last Supper) the focus of a quest. Perceval is an appealing character who evolves from a naive Welsh youth to a distinguished and devoted knight. The conflict in this romance turns on a fundamental incompatibility between Arthurian chivalry (at least as Perceval comes to understand it) and a religious ideal. When he first sees a striking procession that includes a display of a bleeding lance and a Grail, he chooses not to inquire about it, having been told that knights should avoid loquacity. He later learns that his silence cost him an opportunity to heal a maimed king and restore his barren land. Perceval eventually embarks on a quest for the Grail, but before the text breaks off Chrétien provides, amid parallel adventures by Gauvain, only a short sequence involving Perceval's spiritual renewal and an exposition of the Grail's meaning.

It was at one time assumed by many scholars that Chrétien drew heavily on Celtic sources—Welsh, Irish, or other—for his themes and motifs. Elaborate theories were offered to explain, for example, the Grail as an analog of a Celtic cauldron of plenty or a cornucopia and the Grail (or Fisher) King as a representation of Bran the Blessed, a Welsh hero or deity wounded with a poisoned lance. Numerous other characters and motifs have been traced to possible sources in Celtic legend. Most current scholars, without entirely denying the relationship of Celtic myth to Arthurian romance, view with skepticism the efforts to offer extensive and precise equivalences between Celtic myths and Arthurian tales. Analogs of a good many Arthurian motifs can also be located in Eastern or classical sources, and moreover it appears probable that stories incorporating material from many traditions were circulating freely, orally or in writing, at the time Chrétien set quill to vellum.

Whatever his sources, Chrétien de Troyes's central accomplishment involves the deft combination of preexisting motifs and stories with material of his own creation and the recasting of the resulting material into a form perfectly fitted to the court culture within which he was writing. Particularly at the court of Marie de Champagne (the daughter of Eleanor of Aquitaine), the literary arts were valued, and the relationships of chivalry to love and of ladies to knights must have been a favored topic of discussion. That is a contention supported by the fact that Chrétien's contemporary at the court, Andreas Capellanus, is the author of *De amore* (On Love), sometimes known as *The Art of Courtly Love*, a treatise that reflects court interest in the subject and even includes, if only tongue-in-cheek, a list of precise rules for lovers. Chrétien's own work is often ironic as well, but it is at the same time a serious effort to fashion an appropriate vehicle—the romance form—for the subtle and most often brilliant exposition of his themes. So successful was he that a good many writers of the following generation appear to have deliberately avoided Arthurian subjects, no doubt understanding that they could not favorably compete with the master on his own literary turf.

See also: Courtly Love; Geraint ab Erbin; Grail; Knight; Owain; Peredur, Son of Efrawg; Romance

References and further reading: Few medieval authors have received more scholarly attention than Chrétien de Troyes; the bibliography is vast. The standard introduction remains J. Frappier's *Chrétien de Troyes: L'homme et l'œuvre* (1957), trans. by R. Cormier as

Chrétien de Troyes: The Man and His Work (1982). To that should be added K. Uitti and M. Freeman, *Chrétien de Troyes Revisited* (1995).

R. S. Loomis's *Arthurian Tradition and Chrétien de Troyes* (1949) is one of the classical presentations of assumed Celtic sources for many of Chrétien's characters, themes, and motifs; however, many of Loomis's arguments are tortuous or highly speculative, and this volume is best considered simply as an important document in the history of scholarship. Many scholars would offer the same conclusions concerning other partisans of Celtic origins, such as H. Newstead in her *Bran the Blessed in Arthurian Romance* (1939). C. Luttrell's *The Creation of the First Arthurian Romance* (1974), a study of *Erec et Enide*, strongly attacks the notion that much of Chrétien's material had Celtic origins.

There exist several thematic studies of Chrétien's work: L. Topsfield's *Chrétien de Troyes: A Study of the Arthurian Romances* (1981) considers questions of chivalry and love; P. Noble studies the subjects indicated by his title, *Love and Marriage in Chrétien de Troyes* (1982); D. Maddox, in *The Arthurian Romances of Chrétien de Troyes: Once and Future Fictions* (1991), offers a fine analysis of the role of customs in Chrétien's romances; N. J. Lacy, in *The Craft of Chrétien de Troyes* (1980), examines the romancer's narrative voice and compositional methods.

—*Norris J. Lacy*

Christine de Pizan (c. 1364–c. 1430)

A Franco-Italian woman poet well known and highly regarded in her own day.

Although born in Venice, Christine de Pizan spent most of her childhood and all of her adult life primarily in Paris and then in the abbey at Poissy. She wrote exclusively in her adoptive tongue of Middle French. A prolific contemporary of Chaucer and near-contemporary of Dante, Petrarch, and Boccaccio (all Italian authors whom she admired and sought to emulate in her own writing), Christine completed 23 works between 1399 and 1429, various versions of which appear in over 200 manuscripts. Her subjects range from courtly love, chivalry, and warfare to history, the body politic, education, mythology, and philosophy. Her genres include the allegorical dream vision and courtly love lyric, the debate and romance, the universal history, and, especially later in her life, the didactic treatise. Her most popular work was a sumptuously illustrated mythographic prosimetrum (mixture of verse and prose), *L'epistre Othea la deesse, que elle envoya a Hector de Troye quant il estoit en l'aage de quinze ans* (The Letter of the Goddess Othea, Which She Sent to Hector of Troy When He Was Fifteen Years Old), written in 1400 and now extant in 43 of its original 48 manuscripts.

Although Christine herself was not a member of the nobility, she rose to prominence as a writer because of her ties with the royal court and her understanding of the French monarchy. In 1368–1369, at the age of five, Christine moved to the court of Charles V when her father, Tommaso de Benvenuto da Pizzano, was offered the position of court physician and astrologer. Educated by her father with books from the royal library, she was married at 15 (in 1380) to a royal secretary, Etienne du Castel, and gave birth to three children, one of whom died in infancy. Between 1386 and 1389, when she was in her early twenties, she lost both her husband and her father. Left with little in the way of an inheritance, Christine became involved in lengthy, unsuccessful lawsuits attempting to recover her father's property and thereby support her children, brothers, and mother. Finally she turned to copying and then to writing as a means of eking out a living. She quickly learned to cultivate the favor of royal patrons by means of her handsomely produced and illustrated books, copies of which she presented to various noblemen and women, domestic and foreign. Such was her fame that through her influence her son served as a page to the earl of Salisbury, Jean de Montecute, and later in the household of the Duke of Burgundy, and Henry IV invited her to England (an invitation she refused). Some of her works were translated into English, Portuguese, and Dutch and appeared in early printed editions in France and England. Information about her life is recorded in several of her own works, particularly *Cent ballades* (One Hundred Ballades; 1395–c. 1399), *Le livre de la mutacion de Fortune* (The Book of the Mutation of Fortune; 1404), *Le livre des fais et bonnes meurs du sage roy Charles V* (The Book of the Deeds and Good Character of the Wise King, Charles V; 1404), and *Lavision-Christine* (Christine's Vision; 1405). It should be noted that many of the dates of individual works can only be approximated.

Among Christine's most important works are those relating to courtly love, chivalry, and the female voice or perspective within the aristocratic milieu. Her first work was a series of courtly lyrics, *One Hundred Ballades*. Other courtly works include *L'epistre au Dieu d'Amours* (The Letter of the God of Love; 1399), *Le dit de la rose* (The Tale of the Rose; 1402); and *Le livre du Duc des Vrais Amants* (The Book of the Duke of True Lovers; c. 1403). Best known today are her reworking of her *Letter of Othea to Hector* as a feminized and mythological universal history of women, in the allegorical *Le livre de la Cité des Dames* (The Book of the City of Ladies; c. 1404–1405) and its sequel, *Le livre des Trois Vertus* (The Book of Three Virtues; 1404–1405), a courtesy book (that is, a manual teaching appropriate behavior) for women written during the same time span and dedicated to Marguerite of Burgundy, who married the French dauphin, Louis of Guienne. Structured according to the three estates, this book was known in early printings, as it is today, as *Le trésor de la Cité des Dames* (The Treasure [Treasury] of the City of Ladies).

After her first six years of writing, Christine began to shift her center of interest from the court to the structure of society; to the state and its political, civil, and martial concerns, national and international; and to morality and ethics, philosophy and education, and religious matters. Among her most significant such works are *Le livre du Chemin de Long Estude* (The Book of the Path of Long Study; 1402), *Le livre de la prod'hommie de l'homme* (The Book of the Integrity of Man, afterwards changed to *Le livre de prudence*, or The Book of Prudence; 1403–1406?), *Le livre du corps de policie* (The Book of the Body of Policy; 1405–1407?), and *Le livre de la paix* (The Book of Peace; 1412). Her most likely final work was *Le ditié de Jehanne d'Arc* (The Tale of Joan of Arc), dated July 31, 1429, a poem about Joan of Arc, whom she perceived as the incarnation of biblical heroic women such as Esther and Judith. This final poem was most likely written at the royal abbey of Poissy, where her daughter was a nun and where she had sought refuge during the civil wars in France in 1418.

In many of her works, Christine mirrors her own experience—with individual women, with the royal and legal courts of her day, and with customs and social life from all walks, but most particularly the aristocracy. For instance, in

The Book of the City of Ladies she counters the learned misogyny of Mattheolus in his Latin *Lamentations* by giving examples of virtuous and wise noble women she knows. In *The Book of Three Virtues* she describes, among many other aspects of contemporary culture, the careful housewife who checks throughout her house in the evening for candles left burning before she retires for the night and a merchant's wife's elaborate imitation of the queen's lying in. She informs much of *Le livre des fais d'armes et de chevalerie* (The Book of Feats of Arms and Chivalry; 1410) with her knowledge of contemporary knights and details about class structure and warfare.

Of particular folkloric interest is the *Letter of the God of Love*, as a satire on the *puys*, the courtly poetic contest popular in northern cities, especially among bourgeois poets. In addition, several of her poems appear at about the same time as the foundation in Paris of the *cour amoureuse*, or Court of Love, in imitation of early Provençal courts celebrating women: her Valentine poem, the *Tale of the Rose*, which takes place on St. Valentine's Day and invokes the support of lovers on their feast day, most especially parallels in date the foundation of Marshal Boucicaut's Order of the White Lady on the Green Shield; Virelay 10, "My Gentle Friend," from *One Hundred Ballades*, dramatizes the selection of a beloved on Valentine's Day; and her debate poem, the "Dit de Poissy" (Tale of Poissy; 1400), is framed by a Maying. In addition, *The Book of the Duke of True Lovers* details hunting, boating, and jousting ceremonies, most especially the garb and procedures of the jousters, the dress and location of spectators in their court, a feast at a Round Table, bathing in a pavilion, and other noble customs of country life.

See also: Courtly Love; Valentine's Day

References and further reading: Most helpful is the anthology of translations of and introductions to Christine's works edited by C. C. Willard, *The Writings of Christine de Pizan* (1994). Of the mushrooming bibliography about Christine, in addition to new editions and translations of her works, many of which still remain inaccessible, studies generally focus on her ironic literary and political feminism or on her indebtedness to other literary sources. See, for example, M. Brabant, ed., *Politics, Gender, and Genre: The Political Thought of Christine de Pizan* (1992); M. Quilligan, *The Allegory of Female Authority: Christine de Pizan's Cité des Dames* (1991); E. J. Richards et al., eds., *Reinterpreting Christine de Pizan* (1992); and M. Zimmermann and D. De Rentiis, ed., *The City of Scholars: New Approaches to Christine de Pizan* (1994). See also the annotated bibliographies about her work, A. J. Kennedy, *Christine de Pizan: A Bibliographical Guide* (1984); and E. Yenal, *Christine de Pisan: A Bibliography of Writings by Her and about Her* (1982; rpt. 1989).

Although little has been written per se on folklore in Christine, see the following for analyses of individual poems or topics of folkloric interest: on *The Letter of the God of Love* as a satire of the *puys*, C. C. Willard, "A New Look at Christine de Pizan's *Epistre au Dieu d'Amours*," in *Seconda miscellanea di studi e ricerche sul Quattrocento francese*, ed. F. Simone, J. Beck, and G. Mombello (1981). On the Court of Love in France and England as a fictional elaboration, with reference to Christine, see R. F. Green, "The Familia Regis and the Familia Cupidinis," in *English Court Culture in the Later Middle Ages*, ed. V. J. Scattergood and J. W. Sherborne (1983). On Saint Valentine as known to Oton de Graunson and Christine, among other writers, see H. F. Williams, "Saint Valentine in the *Champion des dames*," *Moyen Français* 17 (1985). On the Order of the Rose, in *Tale of the Rose*, see C. C. Willard, "Christine de Pizan and the Order of the Rose," in *Ideals of Women in the Works of Christine de Pizan*, ed. D. Bornstein (1981). On the courtesy book in this period (including and most especially Christine's) as a realistic assessment of the condition of women, see D. Bornstein, "Women's Public and Private Space in Some Medieval Courtesy Books," *Centerpoint* no. 11 (1980). On *Three Virtues* and its composition and illustrations, see the edition by C. C. Willard and M. P. Cosman and its introduction: *A Medieval Woman's Mirror of Honour: The Treasury of the City of Ladies* (1989). On the social practice and institution of chivalry as understood by Christine, see C. C. Willard, "Christine de Pizan on Chivalry," in *The Study of Chivalry: Resources and Approaches,* ed. H. Chickering and T. H. Seiler (1988).

—Jane Chance

Christmas

A Christian celebration of the birth of Jesus Christ, recorded in the Gospels of Matthew and Luke in the Bible, and whose name was first recorded in 1038 as *Cristes Maessan,* or Christ's Mass.

The New Testament does not provide the slightest indication of the date of Christ's birth. The first recorded date for Christmas is in the calendar of Philocalus in 354, where it is on December 25. From Rome this date appears to have spread to Antioch, Bethlehem, and Constantinople by the end of the fourth century. Both the initial choice of this date and the subsequent enthusiasm with which it was embraced can be accounted for if we examine its traditional pagan origins. From the third to the fourth centuries, December 25 was celebrated as the Birthday of the Sun in imperial Rome. Prior to this period the feast of the Saturnalia, honoring the god Saturn, had been celebrated by ancient pagan cultures on this date.

The Saturnalia was the most popular and lavishly celebrated feast in the Roman world. Moreover, many other cultures featured festivals at about the same time of year, which were known by a variety of names (e.g., winter solstice festivals or midwinter festivals). Apparently motivated by the fact that a major pagan festival was held near a date known from ancient times to be the shortest and darkest day of the year, early Christian leaders placed Christ's birth on this date, thus transforming this holiest of pagan days into one of the greatest of Christian feast days. The emotional and literary precedents inherent in this date were too obvious to be ignored—darkness to light, old order to new order, the junction of the divine and human. The acceptance of this date also guaranteed the quick conversion of pagans to the newly sponsored Christian religion because of the obvious analogies mentioned above. Placing the Nativity at the turning point of winter, therefore, gave Christmas a considerable symbolic potency.

In ancient Rome the Saturnalia was celebrated as a holiday: businesses closed, there was noisy rejoicing, and gambling in public was allowed. Presents were exchanged, especially candles and symbols of light. Some groups would elect a "king" to lead pranks and general merrymaking. Long before Roman times the solstice possessed ceremonial significance in northern Europe. In the prehistoric British Isles a number of megalithic and ceremonial monuments, such as New Grange in Ireland and Stonehenge in England, were built to identify the cardinal points of the sun, apparently for religious festivals that included the winter solstice. Early Irish and Welsh societies placed particular importance upon the power of midwinter mistletoe, a plant that was particularly sacred to their druid priests.

According to medieval legend, as recorded in the thirteenth-century *Legenda aurea* (The Golden Legend) by Jacobus de Voragine, the birth of Jesus took place 5,228 years after Adam, though Jacobus adds that the historian Eusebius of Caesarea reckons the figure at 5,199 years and others at 6,000. Jacobus continues with an account of Joseph and Mary traveling to Bethlehem, where, unable to find lodging, they set up a temporary shelter in a public passageway and "perhaps Joseph set up a manger for his ox and his ass, or as some think, peasants coming in to market were used to tying up their animals there and the crib was ready to hand." The Virgin Mary gave birth, without any pain, at midnight on the eve of Sunday and laid the baby in the manger on hay that "the ox and the ass had abstained from eating" and that was later brought to Rome by St. Helena. The midwife Zebel proclaimed Mary a virgin, but the second midwife, Salome, did not believe it, and when she touched the virgin to find out for herself, her hand instantly withered. But she was then instructed by an angel to touch the child, and her hand was restored. Various signs occurred in the heavens, such as the night turning into "the brightness of day," and at Rome the water from a fountain was changed into oil, which flowed into the Tiber and spread widely over the river.

The new Christian feast of the Nativity engendered an entire string of holy days around December 25. By the fourth century, the baptism of Christ by John the Baptist was celebrated on January 6. It came to be known by its Greek

Five masked dancers impersonating a donkey, monkey, buck, bull, and vulture. Similar costumes were often worn by Christmas mummers. (circa 1340; Oxford, Bodeian Library, MS Bodl. 264, fol. 181v)

name, Epiphany. By the fifth century, three other feasts had come to be celebrated immediately after the Nativity: the feast of the first Christian martyr, Stephen, on December 26; the feast for Christ's favorite disciple, John the Evangelist, on December 27; and the feast of the Holy Innocents slaughtered by Herod's soldiers, on December 28. In 567 C.E. the Council of Tours established that the time period between the feast of the Nativity and the Epiphany be celebrated as one festal cycle. The addition, in the eighth century, of the feast of Christ's circumcision (January 1) incorporated the ancient festive tradition of celebrating the New Year. Whereas the Eastern Christian lands placed more emphasis on the celebration of Easter, the celebration of the 12 days between Christmas and Epiphany became the major focus of the peoples in northern and central Europe. For the peasantry, this Christmas season marked their longest extended vacation, since during the Twelve Days they generally were exempt from work.

Danish invasions into England during the ninth century introduced the colloquial Scandinavian term "Yule" for Christmas, which explains its use in later medieval and Tudor England. Moreover, the Twelve Days became the major holiday celebration for England and northern Europe during the medieval period. Household accounts in England indicate that large festal entertainments were typical, including extravagant food centerpieces, such as the boar's head that is so well known through the Boar's Head carols. The wearing of festive masks and the presentation of short dramas were common in the English court. These "mummings," as they came to be called, became very popular by the fourteenth century, eventually growing into major theatrical productions. In British towns, mumming often caused problems, as the use of masks and disguises afforded excellent opportunities for crime.

The tradition of the wassail cup or bowl in England is also common during the Twelve Days' celebration. *Wassail* derives from the Old English phrase meaning "be of good health"; it was shouted as a toast by the cup bearer, who drank from the cup and kissed the next participant, who answered with "Drinkhail," and so on, through the gathering. By the fourteenth century the cup had been replaced by a bowl, and the wassail presentation had become an elaborate ceremony among the members of high society.

Feasting during the Twelve Days became increasingly intense throughout the medieval period. Songs and dances were often composed specifically for these festivities. By the end of the Middle Ages the term *carol*—earlier used to signify a dance accompanied by song, with no necessary religious significance—came to be used for songs and dances. Enormous examples of hospitality and generosity were shown toward commoners and the poor by the gentry and royalty during this time of year. It was expected that the gentry would open their houses for feasting and celebrating, and many landowners spent the Twelve Days celebrating in major metropolitan areas such as London and York in order to give alms to the needy and poor.

The religious establishment celebrated the Christmas season with as much revelry as did those in the secular environment. The traditions of role reversal and inverse hierarchy were ingrained in religious festivities. Gestures drawing on these traditions were often precipitated by the words in the Magnificat, one of the prayers from the Office of Vespers: "He hath put down the mighty from their seats, and exalted the humble and meek." In the twelfth and thirteenth centuries four feasts of inversion were celebrated during the Twelve Days: the feast of the deacons on St. Stephen's Day, December 26; the feast of the priests on St. John's Day, December 27; the feast of the choirboys, or the Feast of the Boy Bishop, on Holy Innocents' Day, December 28; and the feast of the subdeacons, or the Feast of Fools (Ass), usually held on New Year's Day.

These feasts of inversion were usually celebrated at cathedrals throughout Europe. While the Feast of Fools was observed with greater regularity in France, it was the Feast of the Boy Bishop that was the most popular in England because of the strong tradition of boys' choirs in cathedrals in England. All the feasts emphasized a reversal of authority in the ecclesiastical hierarchy: the bishop and other cathedral canons were literally thrown out of their posts by the lower clergy. While this tradition began as a festive and lighthearted reference to the biblical reading, by the thirteenth century it had taken on a life of its own as an occasion for intense parody, involving members of both the religious and secular communities in wild celebration.

Gambling, drinking, bawdy singing, and parodies of the liturgy were done openly and often without recrimination by the clergy, usually with the support of both the cathedral administration as well as the approval of the general public. The Boy Bishop and his entourage often held an expensive feast, supported by alms and gifts that the boys had collected during processions through the towns surrounding the cathedral precincts. Although many late-medieval ecclesiastics condemned these feasts, their popularity ensured their continuance until well into the seventeenth century.

See also: Boy Bishop, Feast of the; Fools, Feast of; Jesus Christ; New Year's; Virgin Mary
References and further reading: Medieval legends concerning Christmas may be found in J. de Voragine, *The Golden Legend: Readings on the Saints*, 2 vols., trans. W. G. Ryan (1993). Scholarly studies of Christmas lore and observances include J. Kremer, *Celebrate Today* (1996); E. C. Rodgers, *Discussions of Holidays in the Later Middle Ages* (1940); E. K. Chambers, *The Mediaeval Stage*, 2 vols. (1903); and three books by R. Hutton: *The Pagan Religions of the Ancient British Isles* (1991), *The Rise and Fall of Merry England* (1994), and *The Stations of the Sun* (1996).

—*Bradford Lee Eden*

Cockaigne, Land of [French *Cocagne*, German *Schlaraffenland*, Italian *Cuccagna*]

An imaginary land characterized by a paradisiacal inversion of life's harsh realities.

The Land of Cockaigne is a distinctly sensual paradise in which one is paid for sleeping, food and drink present themselves already prepared (a pig, for example, trots up ready-roasted, the carving knife already lodged in its side), and dwellings are built from food (roofs are thatched with pancakes), but the way there is sometimes extremely daunting (in the English poem one must wade seven years through pig shit up to one's chin).

The complex is certainly found in the classical literatures (Athenaeus, Lucian), and the burlesque Old Irish *Aislinge Meic Conglinne* (twelfth century) is an interesting early Celtic example. It is therefore suggestive that the earliest English literary source is an Anglo-Irish poem of the first quarter of the fourteenth century describing the "londe ihote [named] cokaygne," in which the topos is used satirically against the allegedly luxurious lifestyle of the monastic orders. Recently it has been suggested that the Irish abbey of Inislounaght (Island of Sweet Milk) is alluded to in the poem's "riuer of sweet milke."

There is then a considerable gap in the literary record until Hugh Plat's "Merrie tale of Master Mendax to his friend Credulus" from his *Pleasures of Poetrie* (London, 1572). The relevant section opens, "There is within Eutopia, / A house all tylde with tarte [tiled with tarts]," attesting to a quite unwarranted Elizabethan confusion with Thomas More's political vision. From the late sixteenth century onward the name Lubberland was to replace Cockaigne: the Christmas revels at St. John's College, Oxford, in 1607 were to have included an "Embassage from Lubberland."

English onomastic sources, however, attest to the existence of the topos almost as early as the mention (c. 1164) of an "abbot of Cockaigne" (*abbas Cucaniensis*) in the *Carmina Burana*. The name was applied to Cockaynes (Essex) in 1228, presumably implying a spot of great fertility, and a surname, William Cocaine, is found as early as 1193 in Warwickshire.

Although a place named Cuccagna is attested in Italy from 1142, Italian stories employing this name are not found before the fifteenth century. When the fabulous land appears in Boccaccio's *Decameron* (c. 1349–1351), it is named Bengodi and located in the Basque country.

In Germanic literature it appears incidentally in the fifteenth-century Easter plays with the comic character Mercator (e.g., that from Melk, in which it is called Leckant) and the tall tale *Vom Packofen*, where it is called Kuckormurre, the first syllable of which has doubtless been influenced by Latin *Cuccania*, but it is found a century earlier in the form Gugelmiure in the mid-fourteenth-century *Wachtelmaere*, which includes a fairly full description of the paradise. Unlike the English poem, the fifteenth-century Dutch *Cockaengen* appears to be directly dependent on the important thirteenth-century *Cocaigne*. Schluraffen Landt is the name of the country to which Brant's *Das Narrenschiff* (The Ship of Fools; 1494) is bound, but, oddly, this enormously influential work contains none of the traditional Cockaigne motifs such as occur in the derived *Spruch vom Schlauraffenlandt* (c. 1515), and—importantly for the later diffusion of the topos—Hans Sachs's *Schlauraffenlandt* of circa 1530, issued as a woodcut-illustrated broadsheet. It has only recently been noticed that the name that is now standard in German refers to the glutton's paradise as early as circa 1400 in Heinrich Wittenweiler's satire, *Ring*.

In medieval art the complex as a whole does not seem to be found. Even individual, constituent motifs are rare (e.g., the ready-roasted bird about to fly into the open mouth of the lobster-riding fool in the woodcut to chapter 57 of *Das Narrenschiff*). The earliest extant image of the entire Cockaigne topos is Erhard Schoen's woodcut to the Sachs poem, which includes the food house, the sausage fence, the man with open mouth waiting for a ready-roasted bird to fly into it, the ready-to-carve pig, the horse that shits baskets of eggs, and a Fountain of Youth (really an independent motif). The best-known image, however, is Pieter Brueghel the Elder's famous *Luilekkerland*, painted in 1567, after an engraving by Pieter Baltens.

See also: Iconography; World Turned Upside Down

References and further reading: V. Vaananen, "Le fablau de Cocagne," *Neuphilologische Mitteilungen* 48 (1947), provides a useful introduction to the theme and texts of the French and Dutch poems. E. M. Ackermann, *Das Schlarafferland in German Literature and Folksong* (1944), is a thorough general treatment with appended German texts. The October 1961 number of the French journal *Problèmes* (no. 77, *Utopia*) is very useful and well illustrated. Book-length treatments include G. Cocchiara, *Il paese di Cuccagna* (1956), and D. Richter, *Schlaraffenland: Geschichte einer populären Phantasie* (1984). The flavor of recent French scholarship, which many will find too speculative, may be had from G. Demerson, "Cocagne, utopie populaire?" *Revue Belge de Philologie* 59 (1981). P. L. Henry, "The Land of Cokaygne: Cultures in Contact in Medieval Ireland," *English Studies Today* 5 (1973), includes a glossed text of the Middle English poem and identifies the abbey as that of Inislounaght. Two recent papers that explore this and related genres are S. Westphal-Wihl, "Quodlibets: Introduction to a Middle High German Genre," in *Genres in Medieval Literature*, ed. H. Heinen and L. Henderson (1986), and L. O. Vasvari, "The Geography of Escape and Topsy-Turvy Literary Genres," in *Discovering New Worlds: Essays on Medieval Exploration and Imagination*, ed. S. D. Westrem (1991).

—Malcolm Jones

Confessio Amantis [The Lover's Confession]

A rhymed Middle English frame tale by John Gower (1325?–1408) that embeds many narratives with folkloric dimensions.

The *Confessio* contains 33,406 lines, with Latin prose commentaries beside the text and brief introductions to the sections in Latin verse. It was written around 1390 and exists in three versions. There are 48 manuscripts of the *Confessio*, attesting to the work's popularity. It was translated into Spanish and Portuguese (the first English work so translated) and printed by Caxton in 1483.

The *Confessio* is Gower's most famous work. It is not exclusively didactic, as are his earlier poems; instead, it was written "somwhat of lust, somwhat of lore"— that is, both for pleasure and for learning. The protagonist identifies himself as Amans (the Lover). He confesses his sins against love to Venus's priest Genius, and the latter teaches about the sins by telling tales in graceful language and verse form.

Gower is interested in the literary tradition of the "olde wyse." He has an image of a golden age when "Wrytinge was beloved evere / Of hem that weren vertuous." Many of his tales are based on Ovid's *Metamorphoses*, and others are based on biblical, classical, or medieval narratives. Gower's debt to literary sources and his moral purpose are what interest many recent scholars, who have provided a fresh view of Gower that accepts him on his own terms and praises his poetic excellence.

The folkloric roots of the *Confessio* have been comparatively little studied. It is a frame tale like Boccaccio's *Decameron* and Chaucer's *Canterbury Tales*, whose written form resonates with oral tradition going back to the Sanskrit *Panchatantra*. Both the frame tale of the teacher who illustrates moral lessons by stories and many of the stories themselves possess analogs in folk tradition. "The

Tale of Medea," for example, includes the motif of the girl as the hero's helper (tale type AT 313), present in both classical and medieval versions of the legend. Two tales of particular interest to folklorists are "The Tale of Apollinus" and "The Tale of Florent." "Apollinus" is a version of the tale *Apollonius of Tyre*, widely popular in the Middle Ages. The evidence suggests that "Florent" was drawn from a popular folktale (AT 406A). Its significant analogs, including Chaucer's "Wife of Bath's Tale," are found in Middle English romance. Searching for the answer to the question of what women most desire, Florent comes across "a lothly wommannysh figure" (motif D732, the Loathly Lady), who promises him the answer to the question if he agrees to marry her. He agrees, and she becomes a beautiful young woman. She had been under the spell of a wicked stepmother until she found a knight who would give her "sovereinte."

Also of interest to students of folklore is Gower's use of language, especially puns. Puns are part of the literate tradition, but they are also part of the oral tradition because they involve the play of sounds. For example, Middle English "beste" can mean both "best" and "beast," and Gower uses the pun to advantage in Book 1. He also uses puns to reinforce the originally oral-formulaic theme of the sea voyage in "The Tale of Apollinus."

See also: *Apollonius of Tyre*; Chaucer, Geoffrey; Folktale; Frame Tale; Loathly Lady
References and further reading: J. H. Fischer, *John Gower: Moral Philosopher and Friend of Chaucer* (1964), reexamines the relationship between Gower and Chaucer. P. J. Gallacher, *Love, the Word, and Mercury: A Reading of John Gower's* Confessio Amantis (1975), places Gower in a tradition that extends from the Greek philosophers to T. S. Eliot. R. F. Yeager, ed., *John Gower: Recent Readings* (1989), places Gower in the moral and literate tradition. In "What's in a Frame? The Textualization of Traditional Storytelling," *Oral Tradition* 10 (1995), B. Irwin discusses the tradition of the frame narrative and provides a reading context for the *Confessio*. In "Literary Artistry and the Oral-Formulaic Tradition: The Case of Gower's *Apollonius of Tyre*," in *Literary Artistry and the Oral-Formulaic Tradition*, ed. J. M. Foley (1987), A. H. Olsen discusses the oral-formulaic roots of the tale. In *"Between Ernest and Game": The Literary Artistry of the* Confessio Amantis (1990), she studies the language and puns of the *Confessio* to show its debt to native English poetic tradition.

—*Alexandra H. Olsen*

Courtly Love [French *Amour courtois*]

An elaborately formalized sexual relationship in which a knight worships his lady, enduring torment and performing great deeds in hopes of gaining her love; according to Joseph Bédier, essentially a "cult ... based, like Christian love, on the infinite disproportion of merit and desire, a necessary school of honor which ennobles the lover, ... a voluntary servitude ... that finds in suffering the dignity and the beauty of passion."

Courtly love strongly influenced medieval culture in at least two ways: first, as a major theme in lyric poetry and romance from the beginning of the twelfth century, and second, as a leading theme in such social games as tournaments and poetry contests. Some critics have argued that courtly love also effected a change in sentiments such as the world has seldom seen, transforming the nature of love for centuries to come.

The term itself dates back only to 1883, when Gaston Paris coined the phrase *amour courtois* to describe Lancelot's love for Guinevere in the romance *Lancelot* (c. 1177) by Chrétien de Troyes. Medieval literature employs a variety of terms for this kind of love. In Provençal the word is *cortezia* (courtliness), French texts use *fin amour* (refined love), in Latin the term is *amor honestus* (honorable, reputable love). In English *love* is used alone or with qualifiers, some less laudatory as those in other languages. Love *par amour* signifies passionate love, while *derne love* literally means "hidden love." This connotative difference is not surprising, considering that English writers tend to be less interested in love as a literary theme and less tolerant of extramarital amours than their French counterparts. According to Paris, courtly love combines secrecy (necessitated by an illicit relationship) with a quasi-religious devotion of the lover to his lady, a "kind of idolatry."

Literature

This specialized approach to love first appeared in the West about 1100 in the lyrics of troubadours, the poet-minstrels of southern France. While courtly ideals associated the poetic gift with noble birth, the best and most famous love poetry was written by talented professional minstrels. They assumed the personae of knights to satisfy their audiences' expectations and addressed their love poetry to real or fictional ladies. Troubadour poetry reverses medieval social reality by placing the lady above the knightly speaker, whom she dominates completely and often cruelly. He does not ask her love as an equal but prays that his abject devotion will earn her pity. For example, Peire Vidal (c. 1175–1215) hopes that "the submission and humble behaviors I use [will] move thy dear ruth thereto that it shall bring me to thy arms." C. S. Lewis points out the "feudalisation of love" in troubadour lyrics, where the lover vows service to his lady as a vassal would to his lord. Some actually address the lady as *midons*, which does not mean "my lady," but "my lord."

Some troubadours appear to have believed strongly in the ideal of courtly love, and through their efforts to live up to it they became subjects of legend themselves. For example, Vidal, whose poetry is quoted above, addressed certain lyrics to a lady whom he called La Loba (The She-Wolf). In her honor, one story goes, he had himself sewn into a wolf skin, which excited the attention of a shepherd's dogs; they chased and nearly killed him. La Loba watched, laughing, with her husband and afterward got medical attention for the injured poet. Another troubadour reportedly bought a gown, clapper, and bowl from a leper and waited for alms at his lady's door with the other beggars.

In the mid-twelfth century themes of courtly love began to appear in the romances, the narrative poetry of northern France. Some associate this development with Eleanor of Aquitaine, granddaughter of the first known troubadour, William IX of Aquitaine. When Eleanor moved north to marry Louis VII of France (1137), some claim she brought with her the courtiers and the tastes that would soon find their way into romance. Whatever the case, Chrétien de Troyes credits Eleanor's daughter, Marie de Champagne, with dictating the plot of his *Lancelot*, and Marie's court became the site where Andreas Capellanus set his treatise on love. Also, it was about the time that Eleanor took Henry II of

Lovers embrace in an early-fourteenth-century illustration from the Manesse Song Manuscript, Heidelberg. (Reproduced from Hans-Werner Goetz, Life in the Middle Ages: From the Seventh to the Thirteenth Century, *Notre Dame, 1993)*

England as her second husband (1155) that courtly love began to appear in such Anglo-Norman romances as the *Tristan* of Thomas of Britain.

Early critics viewed *Lancelot* and *Tristan* as the major expressions of courtly love in romance form. In many of the *Tristan* romances, the hero's love for Queen Iseut, though adulterous, is idealized and inspires him to great feats of arms. However, the story ends tragically because of the jealousy of her husband, King Mark. Most (if not all) of the authors present the love between Tristan and Iseut as noble because of its constancy. Tristan's love, though adulterous, is apparently justified by the devotion he demonstrates to his lady.

Chrétien de Troyes was the first to connect Guinevere with Lancelot, in the romance that served as the model for Paris's concept of courtly love. The relationship between Lancelot and Guinevere is adulterous but constant in its own terms. Lancelot's worship of the queen is such that he endures her cruelty and obeys her slightest wish. After he rescues her from a ruthless kidnapper, she refuses even to speak to him. She will not tell him why she is angry. In this romance, Lancelot is called "the knight of the cart" because he rides in a cart to reach Guinevere and rescue her. Because, states Chrétien, convicts were conveyed in carts to their place of execution, carts were shameful. Lancelot assumes that Guinevere is angry because he consented to ride in one, and he regards this reason as just. However, she is angry for the opposite reason: because he hesitated to get into the cart, knowing that he had no other way to reach her. When she finally reveals her reason, he regards it, too, as just. To Lancelot all the judgments of his deity are just. Paris's theory would not be controversial if applied only to this story.

However, the term *amour courtois* has been applied to a wide variety of literature, and scholars disagree on whether adultery is an essential part of it. Like Paris, C. S. Lewis considered adultery essential to the concept. In *The Allegory of Love* he considers courtly love an entirely new feeling, one of only three or four "real changes in human sentiment" ever recorded. Its characteristics are "Humility, Courtesy, Adultery, and the Religion of Love." The difficulty and secrecy of an illicit relationship create the agony and ecstasy that characterize *amour courtois*. On the other hand, E. Talbot Donaldson argues that adultery is not essential, noting that this theme receives only "perfunctory treatment" in Middle English romances and that English writers show little interest in it. Donaldson points out that Chaucer's *Troilus and Criseyde*, which Lewis treats at length, "concerns the love of a bachelor for a widow" and does not, therefore, fit Lewis's own definition. Peter Dronke regards adultery as only an incidental feature, arguing that the basic components of *amour courtois* are far from an original contribution of eleventh-century literature. Dronke accepts Bédier's "infinite disproportion of merit and desire" but believes that the lover's adoration of his lady is based on the "feeling that by loving such disproportion may be lessened, the infinite gulf bridged." In Dronke's view, this attempt to bridge the gulf produces the "divine," transcendent feelings that give courtly love its power to ennoble, as when the lover declares that his lady is worth all of Paradise to him, that he would willingly go to hell to be with her. Certainly, the lady's belonging to someone else is one way of envisioning a gulf that must be crossed, but it is far from the only one. Dronke observes that if this feeling is really what characterizes courtly love, then it dates back at least to ancient Egypt, where poetry from the second millennium B.C.E. compares the beloved to a goddess. Furthermore, the feeling is not confined to any particular class, as it appears in Byzantine folksongs of the twelfth century, far from the courtly culture of Provence.

The Social Game

The disagreement about what is essential to courtly love stems partly from debate over the meaning of a particular text: the *De amore* (On Love, c. 1190) by Andreas Capellanus, a contemporary of Chrétien and also attached to the court of Champagne. The *De amore* is a textbook on love. Perhaps written at the request of Marie de Champagne, it expounds a definition of love and rules for conducting an affair. Andreas presents numerous sample dialogues between men and women (usually of different classes) in which the man tries to convince the woman through dialectical argument that she ought to accept him as a lover. Andreas also reports various "Decisions in Love Cases" in which a court of noble ladies, including Marie de Champagne, hands down rulings in disputes over the proper conduct of lovers. In one of the dialogues the man and woman disagree on whether or not the woman's love for her husband is an excuse for not taking a lover. They submit the question to Marie, who declares that "love cannot exert its powers between two people who are married to each other." Therefore, says the countess, "no woman, even if she is married, can be crowned with the reward of the King of Love unless she is seen to be enlisted in the service of Love himself outside the bonds of wedlock." Such rulings are governed by a set of 31 laws, which Andreas dutifully lists. The first three are "Marriage is no real excuse for not loving," "He who is not jealous cannot love," and "No one can be bound by a double love."

C. S. Lewis, seeking a "professedly theoretical work" on the system that Chrétien showed through example, believed he had found it in the *De amore.* Lewis took it with absolute seriousness, as an authoritative guide to courtly love. From information such as the examples above, he naturally concluded that adultery was essential to love, as understood by the courtly culture of medieval France. But others have argued that Andreas intended his work to be humorous. D. W. Robertson Jr. does not believe that such a social system as we call "courtly love" ever existed. In his view, Andreas is satirizing "idolatrous passion" in the tradition of Ovid's *Ars amatoria,* which is structured so similarly to Andreas's treatise that it could have served as a model.

These perspectives are to some extent reconcilable. Given what we know about the "earnest games" (to use Carl Lindahl's phrase) that were played in medieval courts, Andreas could be referring to a real enough practice that was nevertheless not "real life." As Lindahl explains, there were occasions upon which poets would perform their best love poetry for ladies, who would judge it and select the winner. One such amorous society was the Cour Amoureuse (Court of Love, founded in Paris c. 1400), ruled by a Prince of Love—possibly analogous to Andreas's King of Love, who makes the rules for love affairs. Andreas's "Love Cases" could be referring to similar Love Debates, in which a Queen of Love presided over a mock court and participants would argue, as in a courtroom, how the rules of love should apply to particular cases. Then noble ladies would render decisions, much as Marie and her colleagues do in the *De amore*. As with any game that depends upon the creation of an alternate reality, the fun depends upon all the participants treating that reality with utmost seriousness. Therefore, Andreas's treatise may be understandable as a guide to being a successful courtier in such a Court of Love.

Questions of Social Reality

The controversy about the real meaning of courtly love in literature stems partly from controversy about its application to real life. C. S. Lewis and John J. Parry believe that what Parry calls "that strange social system" was taught and practiced in medieval courts throughout Western Europe. To Robertson the need to tremble in the presence of one's mistress and obey her every wish, no matter how cruel or arbitrary, seems "a terrible nuisance, and hardly the kind of thing that Henry II or Edward III would get involved in." Many have noted that it seems relentlessly, even joyfully, contrary to the rules of official culture, which was Christian and patriarchal. If courtly love was primarily a social game, much of its appeal surely stemmed from the relief it offered from the drab demands of reality, where marriages were made for commercial and political reasons and women were treated as bargaining chips.

The intensity with which some knights played their games argues that, for some at least, courtly love was a sort of social reality. For example, Jean sire de Boucicaut, also noted for his barefoot pilgrimages, founded an order for the protection of ladies. Captured while crusading and imprisoned in Damascus, Boucicaut and his fellow knights passed the time by composing poems focused on a question of love: does constancy in love or promiscuity bring greater pleasure? Once released (1389), Boucicaut and his fellow knights performed their love poetry in Avignon, with the brother of Pope Clement VII acting as master of the revels. This game touched their lives in many contexts, from prison to the papal palace.

Questions of Origin

Lewis asserts that courtly love "appeared quite suddenly at the end of the 11th century in Languedoc" for reasons that he does not claim to know. Investigations into Celtic, Byzantine, Arabic, and Ovidian influences have, according to Lewis, failed to explain the "new sentiment" that we find in Provençal love poetry. More recent scholars have disagreed, proposing a variety of sources. Dronke argues that courtly love poetry, with all the qualities that characterize it in eleventh-century France, has appeared in many times and places, including ancient Egypt and the Islamic world. Others have suggested that Christian Neoplatonism, which emphasizes the soul's longing to transcend carnality, influenced Provençal love poetry. Still others have argued that traditions of mysticism may have contributed the almost ascetic concern with unfulfilled desire that pervades the poetry. Possibly, as Theodore Silverstein has suggested, each of these operated to some degree on an unbroken tradition of quasi-religious love poetry dating back to the ancient world.

See also: Chrétien de Troyes; Knight; Minstrel; Tristan and Iseut; Valentine's Day, Saint
References and further reading: J. Bédier's characterization of courtly love appears in "Les
fêtes de mai et les commencements de la poésie lyrique au moyen âge," *Revue des deux
mondes*, May (1896), quotation above from page 172; G. Paris's classic formulation is
"Etudes sur les romans de la Table Ronde: Lancelot du Lac. II. *Le Conte de la Charrette*,"
Romania 12 (1883). Among many good studies of troubadour poetry is R. Briffault, *The
Troubadours* (1965). Andreas Capellanus's "treatise" is translated into English as *The Art of
Courtly Love*, ed. J. J. Parry (1941); Parry characterizes courtly love as a "strange social
system" on page 3 of his introduction. The classic English-language study of courtly love is
C. S. Lewis, *The Allegory of Love* (1936), quotations above from pages 2–6. For contrasting
views on the subject, see E. T. Donaldson, "The Myth of Courtly Love," in his *Speaking of
Chaucer* (1970), quotation above from page 156, and P. Dronke, *Medieval Latin and the
Rise of European Love-Lyric*, 2 vols. (1968), quotation above from page 4. The latter
gives a wide-ranging account of the origins of courtly love poetry. For several different
perspectives on courtly love, see F. X. Newman, ed., *The Meaning of Courtly Love* (1968),
which includes the cited essays by Robertson and Silverstein. C. Lindahl describes some
medieval courtly games in "The Festive Form of the *Canterbury Tales*," *English Literary
History* 52 (1985) and *Earnest Games: Folkloric Patterns in* The Canterbury Tales (1987),
which also discusses Boucicaut's *Cent ballades*. For a specific discussion of the role of
adultery in courtly romance, see P. McCracken, *The Romance of Adultery* (1998).

—*Leigh Smith*

Cross

Symbol commemorating the Crucifixion of Jesus, and more broadly, the Christian faith.

As the principal symbol of the dominant religion of medieval Europe, the cross pervaded European culture. Its form became incorporated into liturgical art, personal clothing, heraldry, cruciform architecture, and the lived religious experience of medieval Christians. Fitted with an image of a crucified Christ it became the crucifix, an object of progressively greater importance during the medieval era. The cross was pitted in narrative and art against symbols of all other major faiths, especially forms of pre-Christian worship, Judaism, and Islam.

Early Christian works, especially the epistles of St. Paul, stress the cross as a central aspect of Christian identity. It symbolized Christ's brutal sacrifice that had resulted in mankind's redemption and encapsulated the holiness to which each Christian was called. According to St. John Chrysostom (c. 347–407), the Holy Cross had risen to heaven along with the Savior and would play a key role in the Last Judgment. It was a conscious entity, capable of interceding on behalf of humans, much like Mary and the other saints. These concepts became central parts of the spiritual culture of the medieval era and are frequently depicted in religious art.

The gestural sign of the cross (*crux usualis*), one of the oldest forms of cross symbolism, emerged even prior to the legalization of the faith in the Roman Empire. Small gestural crosses gave way in the fifth century to a large cross traced across head, breast, and shoulders—usually with a formula designating the Trinity (Western tradition) or different aspects of the one God (Eastern tradition). In medieval Europe a gestured cross made large or small punctuated nearly every major act in life, from eating a meal to starting a trip to crowning a king. It was credited with warding off evil, bringing blessing, and even (when performed by a saintly individual) accomplishing miracles. In Odo of Cluny's tenth-century *Life of St. Gerald of Aurillac*, Gerald (c. 855–909) foils the trickery of an acrobat who is using demonic magic to accomplish his feats. Gerald makes the sign of the cross over the man, who is no longer able to jump as high as before. Writes Odo:

> And so it was manifest that this activity of the man's was the result of an incantation, which could no longer aid him, after the sign of the Cross, and that the power of Count Gerald was great, since the power of the enemy [i.e., the devil] had no force against his sign.

Soon thereafter Gerald uses the gesture to cure a woman who has been raving. He exorcises the demon inside her by making the sign of the cross over her; she vomits blood and matter and is cured.

Constantine and Helena

The rise of the Cross as an object of veneration owes much to Emperor Constantine (c. 280–337), his mother St. Helena (c. 250–c. 330), and the various chroniclers who transmitted or embroidered upon their experiences in later centuries. On the eve of the Battle of the Milvian Bridge in 312, Constantine was said to have seen a vision of the Cross in the sky accompanied by the inscription "In hoc signo vinces" [In this Sign you will conquer]. The pagan Constantine asked his advisers to explain the vision, and when he learned that the symbol represented Christ, he adopted the new religion for his own. With the new image inscribed on his men's banners and shields, Constantine won the battle and became the first Christian Roman emperor. His symbol, however, is not the usual perpendicular Roman cross but an X-shaped cross in saltire, one of many variations on the cross form common in the medieval period. Constantine's symbol developed into the chi-rho digraph (symbolic of the first two letters of the Greek word *Christos*) and was later reinvigorated as a symbol of the faith by Charlemagne (742–814).

Legends of St. Helena credited her with the discovery (termed the Invention) of the True Cross in Jerusalem, where it lay buried outside the city. According to legend, St. Helena compelled unwilling Jews to help in her search and eventually recognized the True Cross by its miraculous healing abilities. At Helena's bidding and Constantine's expense, basilicas were constructed in Jerusalem on the sites of the Resurrection and Calvary, and the latter became the home of the Cross relic from the time of its dedication in 325. Ritual kissing of this relic on Good Friday is reported by the Roman Aetheria (Sylvia) around 390, and the ritual became a part of the official office of the day throughout the Christian world during the medieval period. From the seventh century onward the anniversary of the dedication became a feast in the Roman calendar, celebrated on September 13 and 14, and known as the Exaltation of the Cross. Accounts of both Constantine's vision and St. Helena's Invention were immensely popular in the Middle Ages, and numerous Latin as well as vernacular versions survive, including the Anglo-Saxon poem *Elene* by Cynewulf.

The Vision of Constantine, from the Stavelot Triptych, enamel; Mosan, 1156–1158. (The Pierpont Morgan Library)

Constantine's miraculous vision was repeated a number of times afterward. Bishop St. Cyril (c. 315–c. 386) reported an apparition of the Cross over the city of Jerusalem in 351. King St. Oswald of Northumbria (605–642) reported seeing a vision of a Roman cross in 634, immediately prior to his battle against the pagan king Cadwallon of Wales. Erecting a wooden cross on the battlefield, Oswald won the battle and claimed his ancestral throne. His cross became an object of veneration in itself, and slivers from it were used in healing elixirs for centuries after. The erection of the cross announced the king's intent to Christianize his realm, an undertaking that was soon carried out by Irish missionaries. The cult of King St. Oswald became popular not only in England but in continental Europe as well.

Relics, Pendants, and Monuments

By the fourth century tiny fragments of the True Cross (many severed from the relic conserved in Jerusalem but others clearly from other pieces of wood) began to diffuse across the Christian world, finding places of honor in churches as well as in personal amulets. St. Cyril of Jerusalem and St. John Chrysostom mention this practice in fourth-century Jerusalem and Antioch, and fragments began to appear in Italy and Gaul during the fifth century. St. Venantius Fortunatus, a famed poet of his day, composed the hymn "Vexilla regis" (The Banner of the King) in honor of the translation of a fragment of the True Cross to Poitiers in the late sixth century. Popes and Eastern patriarchs alike honored royal guests to their courts through the gift of Cross relics: Patriarch George of Jerusalem presented one such fragment to Charlemagne in 799, Pope Marinus I awarded such a treasure to King Alfred of England in 883, and King Sigurd of Norway brought home a fragment from his expedition to the Holy Land (c. 1110). Kings and monastic leaders alike used presentations of fragments to mark important alliances. The churches and cathedrals endowed with relics of the True Cross often became important pilgrimage centers, as the faithful visited in hopes of miraculous cures. Wealthy patrons marked their gratitude through rich gifts and art, and reliquaries constructed to hold Cross fragments were often lavishly decorated. The twelfth-century Irish Cross of Cong, one of the finest pieces of Irish art known from the Middle Ages, was apparently created to hold a piece of the True Cross.

The rise of cross pendants is closely tied to the tradition of obtaining relics of the True Cross. Cross pendants begin to appear in graves often well in advance of the actual arrival of the faith in a given area, indicating that their owners viewed these items at first as merely valuable ornaments or perhaps as significant receptacles of magic power. Pendants vary in form from region to region during the Middle Ages, and certain motifs—such as the cross in saltire (St. Andrew's X-shaped cross) or the T-shaped Mediterranean tau cross—frequently represent Christianizations of prior pagan, often solar, symbols. The St. Andrew's cross motif occurs in Celtic areas such as Scotland and Gaul; a ringed Irish Cross developed in the eighth century, and crosses with arms of equal length became popular throughout the area of the Eastern Church. Crosses decorated with raised bumps or gems on the arms and center represented the Five Wounds of Christ in the Crucifixion, themselves an object of intense devotion in the Middle Ages. Heraldic reworkings of the cross motif led to designs including notched, flared, or crossed ends, each indicative of a different region or institution.

Christian theologians often treated pictorial art with suspicion, fearing a lapse into idolatry, and this recurrent fear led eventually to the violent iconoclastic controversies of the eighth and ninth centuries, particularly in the area of the Eastern Church, as well as in Gaul. The Roman Church never accepted the arguments of the iconoclasts, however, and in the Second General Council of Nicaea in 787, the use of objects such as crosses and icons was definitively endorsed. In the aftermath of this era, crosses became prescribed parts of the altar and other church sites.

Massive cross monuments of stone are central characteristics of Christianity in the British Isles of the eighth to twelfth centuries. These standing crosses decorated churches, churchyards, and crossroads, and they appear to have served as places of worship and preaching. They could also demonstrate the piety of wealthy patrons, who commissioned them in thanks for supernatural assistance

The Cross of Cong, Irish, fashioned from tubular gold and silver; twelfth century. (Erich Lessing/Art Resource, NY)

or in the memory of deceased relatives. The earliest such crosses were decorated only sparingly; during subsequent centuries, however, crosses became decorated with ornate inhabited vine-scroll (populated by tiny human and animal figures frolicking in or battling against the tendrils of the foliage) and eventually with carved depictions of biblical events or saints. In their latest development they became crucifixes, depicting a Christ in crucifixion.

The tradition spread with some modification to Scandinavia but is largely absent from the rest of Europe. It is certain that wooden crosses also existed in the British Isles, and some sort of standing-cross tradition may have existed on the European continent as well, where wood was more common. It is difficult to gauge the extent of wooden cross monuments and roadside shrines during the medieval period, however, because of the inevitable decay of such material over time.

Legends and Feasts

Medieval legendry teems with accounts of the Cross or cross symbols, their uses and abuses, and the miracles proceeding from them. These included the apocryphal Gospel of Nicodemus, which details the history of the tree that became the Cross and its relation to the fateful tree responsible for mankind's Fall in the Garden of Eden. The Anglo-Saxon poem known as *The Dream of the Rood* details a wondrous vision of the True Cross and the Cross's own eyewitness account of the Crucifixion. Saints' legends frequently tell of miracles attending the cross pendants of holy men and women after their deaths. In the widespread legend known as the *Flagellatio crucis* (Scourging of the Cross), Jewish persecutors attack a cross, only to find its insides filled with the miraculous healing blood and water of Christ's own body. In the Crusades the cross became a prime symbol of a warrior's acceptance of his holy mission and was emblazoned on shields, helmets, and banners. Some of the oldest flags of Europe reflect this cross symbolism, and many—as in the case of the Danish *Dannebrog* (a red field surrounding a cross of white)—were attributed to divine sources.

Given the centrality of the Cross to the Crusades, it is not surprising that the large relic of the True Cross in Jerusalem was seized by the Persians in 614. Its fate at the hands of Islamic tormentors was recounted in numerous legends until its return in 630. Its reinstallation on May 3 became celebrated as the Feast of the Invention from the eighth century onward, joining the Feast of the Exaltation (September 13–14) and the Good Friday devotions as the principal Cross-related feast days of the Western Church. In the Eastern Church, Cross feast days consisted of the third Sunday of Lent, Good Friday, the Feast of the Apparition in Jerusalem (May 7), and the Feast of the Adoration (August 1). All of these feasts attracted folk as well as liturgical expressions of devotion: for instance, a custom of burying crosses of wood or bread in farm fields on the Feast of the Invention (May 3) is attested in many parts of peasant Europe both in medieval and postmedieval sources.

The Image of Christ Crucified

Although poetry and pictorial art of the early Middle Ages depict a triumphant, heroic Christ on the Cross, the era of the Cistercian St. Bernard of Clairvaux (1090–1153) ushered in a more human, suffering image of the Savior. Crucifixes as well as devotional lyrics from this period stress the human pain of Christ and his mother and direct the faithful toward an intensely physical contemplation of the Crucifixion. This new mysticism spread widely throughout Europe, thanks in large part to the preaching of the Mendicant orders (Franciscans and Dominicans) of the thirteenth century. The Franciscan hymn "Stabat Mater gloriosa" (Stand, Glorious Mother), traditionally attributed to the Italian Franciscan friar Jacopone da Todi (d. 1306), illustrates this new emphasis. The hymn's speaker declares:

> Fac me plagis vulnerari
> Fac me cruce inebriari
> Et cruore Filii.
>
> [Let me suffer the injuries
> let me be overwhelmed by the Cross
> and the blood of the Son.]

The pained Christ and crucifix soon became the dominant image of the Cross or the Crucifixion in medieval Europe.

See also: Crusades; Jesus Christ; Relics
References and further reading: A. Frolow's detailed work *La relique de la vraie croix: Recherches sur le développement d'un culte* (1961) presents an exhaustive study of all physical relics of the True Cross from the medieval period, arranged historically and geographically. W. O. Stevens, *The Cross in the Life and Literature of the Anglo-Saxons* (1977), examines the literary and physical expressions of Cross devotion in England from the time of the first conversions. Quotations from Odo's *Life of St. Gerald of Aurillac*, chapters 31 and 32, are taken from the translation by G. Sitwell in *Soldiers of Christ: Saints and Saints' Lives from Late Antiquity and the Early Middle Ages*, ed. T. Noble and T. Head (1995). F. Tubach, *Index Exemplorum* (1969), provides an excellent starting point for the examination of Cross motifs in saints' legends and other texts of medieval religious folklore. D. L. Jeffrey's *The Early English Lyric and Franciscan Spirituality* (1975) focuses on the mystical interpretations of the Cross in thirteenth- and fourteenth-century England and their broader relations to European culture. T. A. DuBois, *Nordic Religions in the Viking Age* (1999), surveys the arrival of cross symbolism, monuments, and pendants in northern Europe during the ninth through thirteenth centuries.

—*Thomas A. DuBois*

Crusades

Wars waged by European Christian forces against Islam and other non-Christian religions and cultures, beginning in 1096 and continuing intermittently through the end of the Middle Ages, giving rise to legends and heroic poetry throughout Europe and creating channels for the folk traditions of the Middle East to influence Western culture.

Causes

Many factors combined to bring about the Crusades. The eleventh century witnessed a rejuvenation of the Christian Church, combined with a new religious spirituality affecting the masses. There were numerous pilgrimages to the Holy Land, and biblical learning and preaching dealt intensively with the holy sites in Palestine. Conflicts with the Islamic world intensified as the Muslim Seljuk Turks conquered Syria in 1055 and later attacked Anatolia (1072–1081). In 1071 the Turks defeated the Byzantine army in the battle of Mantzikert and captured Jerusalem from the Egyptian Fatimid caliphs in the same year. As

Byzantium was also threatened by Muslim forces, the Greek Orthodox Church and the Byzantine emperor, Alexius Comnenus (reigned 1081–1118), appealed for help from Christians in the West.

Pope Urban II, engaged in a vicious conflict with the German emperor Henry IV, sought help from the European knightly class and from Constantinople, using the conflict in the Middle East to rally troops for a crusade. His goal was to become the leader of a universal Church, uniting Eastern and Western Christianity under his rule. Elsewhere in Europe political and social chaos contended with visions of economic opportunism. In France a multitude of feudal conflicts had led to a form of anarchy and civil war—a disastrous situation that not only drove a vast number of French knights into exile but also caused multitudes of displaced peasants to flee the country. The Italian seaports, on the other hand, looked for military support to safely extend their eastern Mediterranean trade, which the Seljuks had interrupted.

Therefore, buoyed up by his personal ambitions and conscious of the need for remedies to the troubles in Europe, Pope Urban II appealed to European chivalry to take up arms against the infidels in the Holy Land and to recover it for the Christian faith. In preaching the Crusades, Urban drew upon traditional tales and stereotypes to create a mood of fervid animosity against the Muslims, establishing a pattern that other religious leaders would employ for several centuries. Addressing a large crowd in Clermont-Ferrand on November 27, 1095, the pope commented on reports from Constantinople that an evil people in the Persian Empire, bestial and godless, had conquered the Holy Land, killed and abducted people there, destroyed the Christian churches, circumcised the Christians, and tortured them in a horrible manner, raping women and disemboweling men.

The First Crusade and Godfrey of Bouillon

The first army of crusaders, made up of a hysterical mass of peasants and impoverished knights, immediately assembled and marched toward Anatolia. En route to their destination they attacked Jewish communities all over Germany and France. When this ragtag company of would-be soldiers eventually arrived in Anatolia, the Seljuks swiftly crushed them in the first battle (1096). A second Christian army arrived in Constantinople in 1097. It was led by Raymond of St. Gilles, Godfrey of Bouillon, Bohemond of Taranto, and others and included knights from all over Europe. They gained their first victory over the Seljuks at Antioch in 1098 and laid the foundations for making Antioch the center of the first crusader principality. In April 1099 they conquered the abandoned city of Ramlah, and in July they attacked and took Jerusalem. Consequently, the crusader Kingdom of Jerusalem was established under the rule of Godfrey of Bouillon, who died shortly after his victory and was succeeded by his brother Baldwin (reigned 1100–1118). Godfrey instantly became a Europe-wide hero. His stature grew throughout the twelfth and thirteenth centuries, as he was made the subject of heroic poetry. Legendry endowed him with a supernatural origin. A century after his death, French chansons de geste attributed to him a supernatural ancestry. In the poems Elioxe and Beatrix, Godfrey is the descendant of the Swan Knight, one of seven children born with silver chains around their necks.

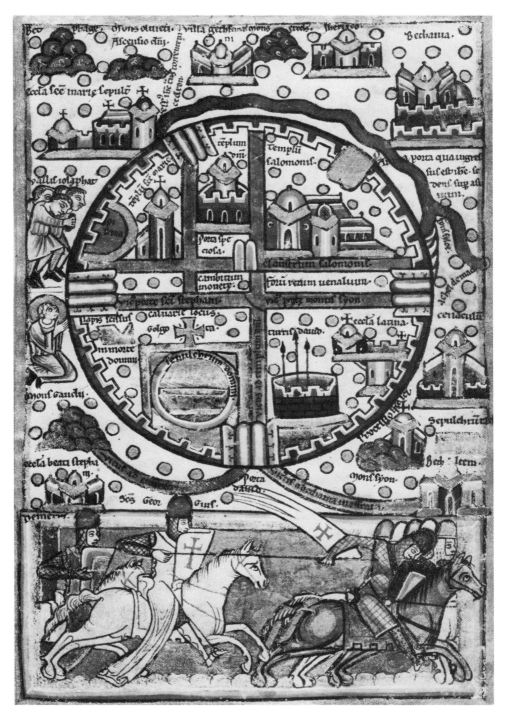

A crusader map of Jerusalem depicts St. George, on a white horse and in crusader dress, defeating a group of Muslims. (Koninklijk Institute, The Hague)

Six of the children have their chains removed and change into swans. The seventh retains his human form and becomes Godfrey's progenitor. In late-medieval tradition Godfrey became, along with King Arthur and Charlemagne, one of the Three Christian Worthies, a figure of enormous veneration.

Godfrey's Kingdom of Jerusalem did not enjoy the long-lasting glory of Godfrey himself. Conflicts between the Christian rulers and their opponents quickly weakened the kingdom. The Muslims also suffered setbacks, however, so the crusader states retained a weak hold over the Holy Land.

Twelfth- and Thirteenth-Century Campaigns

In the following two centuries many more crusades were organized. When the earldom of Edessa, north of the Syrian crusader states, was lost to the Muslims, the powerful Cistercian abbot St. Bernard of Clairvaux preached in favor of a new crusade. This Second Crusade began in 1144, under the leadership of the German emperor Conrad III and the French king Louis VII. Their goal was to conquer Damascus, but they never achieved it.

In 1187 Sultan Saladin (Salah ad-Din) defeated a Christian army at Hattin and then conquered Jerusalem, triggering the Third Crusade, which was conducted under the leadership of the German emperor Frederick I Barbarossa. When this great leader drowned in a river in Anatolia in 1189, the French king Philip II and the English king Richard the Lion-Heart assumed control of the crusaders. Richard proved to be an excellent strategist and a successful general; he conquered Cyprus and Acre and defeated Saladin, thereby liberating a long strip of the Mediterranean coast and providing Christian pilgrims with access to Jerusalem.

The Third Crusade inspired many legends and romances. Saladin, for example, became a major figure in European lore. The German poet Walther von der Vogelweide (fl. 1200–1220) praised Saladin's generosity in a poem, which the Viennese chronicler Jans Enenkel (late thirteenth century) expanded to a comprehensive song of praise of Saladin's generosity, tolerance, wisdom, and intelligence. Many Arabic poets also glorified Saladin in their works, and the sultan retained his legendary reputation throughout the centuries.

The Christian armies never again equaled the successes of the Third Crusade, and many of the subsequent expeditions were characterized by desperation. The Children's Crusade of 1212, inspired by a popular religious movement, drew upon the biblical concept that children possess greater innocence and godliness than adults. The crusade was made up of approximately 10,000 children, representing all social classes but coming principally from France and the Low Countries. Many died in shipwrecks, and others were sold into slavery, but many returned safely to their homes.

During the thirteenth century the Christians experienced some success—for example, in the Fifth Crusade (1228), when the German emperor Frederick II used diplomacy instead of warfare to regain Jerusalem, Bethlehem, and Nazareth peacefully from the Egyptian sultan al-Malik al-Kamil. Nevertheless, the Khwarizmians, an Iranian-Turkish people, reconquered Jerusalem in 1244, inciting the French king Louis IX to mount the Sixth Crusade (1248–1254), the last major European military effort to recapture and control the Holy Land. Louis was unsuccessful, and despite sporadic victories, Acre, the last Christian fortress in the Holy Land, fell to Islam in 1291.

The Failures of the Crusades

In the long run the Crusades failed because various national interests were constantly in conflict with one another. Byzantium only wanted help from Western Europe to defend its eastern borders; Venice, for economic reasons, was always in conflict with Byzantium; England and France could never agree on the ultimate objectives of the Crusades; and the German emperors and their followers continuously experienced religious and political conflicts with Rome.

Other problems were the religious and cultural differences between the Latin crusaders and the Greek Orthodox Church in Constantinople. Members of the Greek Orthodox Church observed rituals significantly different from those of the Western Church and espoused a relatively tolerant attitude toward other cultures and religions.

Despite their idealism and religious fervor, many of the crusaders behaved in a crudely barbaric fashion, lacked discipline, and earned the scorn of both Byzantines and the Muslims. The crusaders who settled in the new kingdoms, ruling over a large non-Western, non-Christian population, had no idea how to carry out their political functions. They seemed genuinely puzzled by the fact that among their subjects there were large groups of Eastern Christians, such as Greek Orthodox, "Syrians," and Jacobites. Although the Crusades had been organized in the name of God, the end result was a ruthless, brutal, and cruel form of imperialism based on a kind of medieval "apartheid" system, as the Christian lords lived in the cities, recognized no real obligations to their peasants, and exploited their lands.

Folkways and Cultural Exchanges

Distinct forms of dress separated the Muslims from the Christians. Although Christians made use of native textiles, they tailored their clothes in accordance with European fashions. The Christians greatly admired and used Eastern architecture for private housing, but not for religious and military constructions. The crusaders did, however, freely use and greatly enjoy the spices and perfumes of the East, which they exported in great quantities to Europe, exerting substantial impact on medieval lifestyles.

The public bathhouses of the East also impressed the crusaders, who established similar bathhouses in Europe. Christian warriors and Italian merchants took home with them new types of weapons, coats of arms, carpets, musical instruments, and paper. In addition, the crusaders copied their opponents' superior military technologies, including armor, siege engines, explosives, special techniques for combat on horseback, and fortification methods.

Perhaps the crusaders' greatest mistake lay in their failure to learn the native language, Arabic. By simply ignoring the culture of the people under their rule, the Christians missed the opportunity to establish a solid foundation for the continued existence of their kingdoms. Eventually their "apartheid" was to turn against them, and as a result of their indifference to the conquered peoples, they lost all the land they had previously conquered.

Some Christian and Arabic sources convey a slightly different picture. According to these accounts, a form of cohabitation was realized fairly soon. The Muslim chronicler Ibn Jubayr (1145–1217), who made a pilgrimage from Spain to Palestine, Syria, Baghdad, and Mecca at the end of the twelfth century, observed with great consternation that the two peoples coexisted rather peacefully and enjoyed the fruits of their work together. He saw both Christian and Muslim merchants carrying out their business peacefully, paying their taxes to their respective rulers, and ignoring the war. Surprisingly, he also reported that the Muslims in Acre were allowed to continue their religious services in their own mosque. Usama ibn Munquidh's *Chronicle* (1095–1188) describes a similar situation in Jerusalem, where the Knights Templar made sure that Christian zealots would not disturb Muslim religious services.

In contrast to this image of tolerance and peaceful coexistence, many Arabic accounts characterize the "Franks," as the crusaders were summarily called, as cruel, dishonest, treacherous, cowardly, and vengeful. These are, however, the same traits ascribed to the Muslims by Western chroniclers. A few of the Eastern chroniclers, such as Usama ibn Munquidh, praised the crusaders for their bravery, heroism, virtues, and strength. Baha' ad-Din ibn Shaddad (1145–1234) portrayed Richard the Lion-Heart as a man of good judgment, great courage, swift and resolute decisions, and as a highly esteemed leader of his people. Interestingly, some Western sources reflect the dual portrait of Richard by depicting him both as a hero and as a monster. The fourteenth-century English romance *Richard* describes the king as superlatively courageous, but it also characterizes him as serving and eating the heads of Saracens at banquets.

There may have been occasional friendships between Muslims and crusaders, as Usama ibn Munquidh and Gamal ad-Din ibn Wasil (1207–1298) report. Overall, however, the Arabs cared as little for learning about the Europeans as the Europeans cared for learning about them. Both cultures tended to dismiss the other as worthless and primitive.

At least one particularly astonishing example of intercultural communication did take place. St. Francis of Assisi, traveling with the Sixth Crusade in 1219, obtained an audience with the Egyptian sultan al-Malik al-Kamil in order to preach to him. Although the sultan listened to Francis, gave him gifts, and provided him with safe passage, this contact led to no lasting peace.

The Crusades led to some positive effects. For a long time, the Crusades inspired European chivalry with new idealism and provided the knightly class with a specific goal. These military enterprises also brought together many people from many different nations and opened their minds to cultures in other parts of the world. However, the long-term consequences of the Crusades for the West were generally negative, as the high cost of foreign warfare impoverished the aristocracy. The population of Europe was depleted, and the Church lost much of its stature after successive defeats. Nevertheless, the Crusades played a major role in opening routes for major cultural and commercial contacts between East and West.

See also: Arabic-Islamic Tradition; Foreign Races; Hispanic Tradition; Richard the Lion-Heart; Swan Knight

References and further reading: A seminal historical study of the Crusades is J. A. Brundage's *The Crusades* (1962). J. Prawer presents a powerful argument that the Crusades were the medieval equivalent to modern-day imperialism in his *The Latin Kingdom of Jerusalem* (1972). H. Prutz published an insightful and learned cultural history of the Crusades, *Kulturgeschichte der Kreuzzüge*, 5 vols. (1964), which should be read in conjunction with S. Runciman's *History of the Crusades* (1951–1954). A. Maalouf discusses the Islamic perspectives in *The Crusades through Arab Eyes* (1984), F. Gabrieli examines *The Arab Historians of the Crusades* (1985), and in Usama ibn Munquidh's autobiographical account, *An Arab-Syrian Gentleman and Warrior in the Period of the Crusades* (1987), we hear a contemporary voice from the twelfth century. V. P. Goos and C. V. Bornstein edited an excellent collection of articles in *Exchanges between East and West during the Period of the Crusades* (1986). A. Khattab offers a fascinating though somewhat superficial reading of Arabic sources from the time of the Crusades in *Das Bild der Franken in der arabischen Literatur des Mittelalters: Ein Beitrag zum Dialog über die Kreuzzüge* (1989). One of the aims of my article is to correct the impression that there was no positive interaction between the two cultures during the crusading period.

—Albrecht Classen

Cuckold

The husband whose wife has sex with another man; a traditional figure of fun, whose humiliation—in societies that regard the wife as firmly under the husband's control, especially in sexual matters—is the mainspring of countless fabliaux and other comic works; more rarely, a rejected lover.

Iconographically, the "attribute" par excellence of the cuckolded husband is his horn or horns. A misericord in Rotherham church carved in 1483 depicts a man in a close-fitting hood from which horns emerge: this image may well have been intended to represent a cuckold. In Germany and England—certainly in vernacular literature—the evidence for this convention is relatively late, however. The first English citations unequivocally linked to cuckold imagery are from the fifteenth-century works of the English poet John Lydgate (c. 1370–c. 1450).

Nevertheless, British Latin authors do evidence a familiarity with the cuckold's horns as early as about 1200, in one of the fables of Walter of England, but more significantly, in Geoffrey of Monmouth's *Vita Merlini* (Life of Merlin; c. 1150). In this work Merlin is portrayed as a Wild Man who, mounted on a stag, comes riding up to the house of his former mistress. He finds her enjoying the night of her wedding to his rival, and in a fit of jealous rage Merlin tears off the stag's antlers and hurls them at the couple.

Continental literature features references to the horns of the rejected lover, for example, in a late-twelfth-century poem by the troubadour Bernart de Ventadour. There is reason to believe that the convention evolved in the Middle Ages in regions where Romance languages were spoken. The earliest reference, however, is the expression, "to wear the horned hat," which appears in Artemidorus's Latin dreambook of c. 200 C.E. and later appears in the Provençal poetry of twelfth-century troubadours Guilhem de Bergueda (*"porta cofa cornuda"*) and Marcabru (*"porta capel cornut"*). Compare this expression with the punishment meted out to a fourteenth-century Italian who pimped for his wife (thus by definition cuckolding himself) and was subsequently forced to wear a two-horned cap.

A late-fifteenth-century Florentine engraving satirizing cuckolds goes by the title *I Re de Becchi* (King of the Goats); in this scene, the horns are clearly those of the goat, but a reference to "brow-antlers" by the English poet John Skelton (c. 1460–1529) is late evidence that the stag was often seen as the source of the cuckold's "horns." In fact, a mid-thirteenth-century account by Boncompagno da Signa records that almost any horned animal might figure in this convention, noting that Italian women referred to the deceived husbands as goats, bulls, and stags, as well as cuckoos (*cuculi;* singular *cuculus*). In addition, the women used various jocular phrases involving words beginning with the syllables *cucu,* such as *cucurbita* (gourd), alluding, of course, to the word *cuculus,* which had already acquired the sense "cuckold" by this time. A remarkable miniature in a French manuscript of Gratian's Decretals, circa 1300, depicts a priest marrying a couple while a nobleman looks on. From the groom's temples rise two four-tined antlers; the implication is clearly that he has already been cuckolded by the onlooker.

It is not possible to say whether the various medieval nicknames involving the element *horn* allude to this convention, since horns were common instruments and trophies, but potential English candidates include Panhorn (1251) and, more obliquely perhaps, Bukenheved (Buck's Head; 1301; cf. a stage direction in a *Merry Wives of Windsor* quarto: "Enter sir John [Falstaff] with a Buck's head upon him") and Herteheued (Hart's Head; 1332). There can be no doubt about Uluric Cucuold from Suffolk (c. 1087), and little about the Parisians Guille and Guillaume le Cornu (1292). The well-known two-finger "horned hand" gesture is found in such early works of art as ancient Etruscan and Pompeiian wall paintings; however, such early notices of the gesture are rare. Moreover, even in these wall paintings, the context is not necessarily one suggestive of adultery, although it is often assumed that the positioning of the fingers symbolizes the horns of the cuckold.

A miniature of an antlered man from a French manuscript of Gratian's Decretals, circa 1300. (Paris, BN MS Lat. 3898, fol. 397)

The term *cuckold* is usually accepted as deriving from the bird name cuckoo, despite semantic difficulties (for it is not the cuckoo that raises the offspring of others, but they hers). Rightly or wrongly, the connection was certainly made by medieval people. The cuckoo was the cuckold's bird long before Shakespeare. Chaucer's "Knight's Tale," for example, describes Jalousye with "a cukkow sittynge on his hand," and Chaucer's contemporary, the Scotsman Thomas Clanvowe, in his poem on the bird, writes that among lovers, "it was a comune tale, / That it were good to here the nightingale / Rather than the lewde cukkow singe." Jean de Condé (c. 1325) says of the cuckoo, "Ce fu li kuqus de pute aire / Ki a maint home a dit grant lait" [It was the cuckoo, of foul kin, / Who spoke great evil to many men]. In his *Fulgens and Lucrece* (c. 1497), Henry Medwall appears to record an interesting, clearly related folk belief: "Men say amonge / He that throwyth stone or stycke / At such a byrde he is lycke [likely] / To synge that byrdes songe."

The hood seems also to have been part of the folklore of the cuckold (cf. the expression "wered a cukwold hoode" in the fifteenth-century manuscript of *Ipomadon*) for which the coincidence of Latin *cucullus* (hood) with *cuculus* (cuckoo) may bear some responsibility. Pieter Brueghel the Elder's famous *Netherlandish Proverbs* painting of 1559 is also known as *The Blue Hood* (a phrase attested from the late fourteenth century), from the central image, which shows a young wife pulling a hooded cape over her husband's head, clearly symbolizing her intention to hoodwink or deceive him. This particular iconographic motif can certainly be traced back to a late-fifteenth-century wooden carving by a Flemish craftsman in Toledo cathedral, but from at least the late fourteenth century, English sources also record various "hood" expressions in a cuckoldry context. Consider, for example, that in this phrase from Lydgate, "With such a metyerde she hathe shape him an hoode," "metyerde" (literally, "measuring-rod") puns on the combination of "meat" and "yard" to signify a penis.

In a glossary of circa 1440 the word *cockney* (coken + ey = cock's egg) is defined as *cornutus* (cuckold, literally "horned") and probably already has this sense in Chaucer's "Reeve's Tale." The German name for the cuckold, *Hahnrei*, might also seem to be composed of *hahn* (cock) and *ei* (egg), but the second element is *-rei*, explained as meaning "castrated," so that the word means "castrated cock," that is, capon. The word *capon* is itself similarly used to mean "eunuch" in thirteenth-century English, and a most interesting early-fifteenth-century gloss on the Latin word *gallinacius* reads "*homo debilis* [weak man], a malkyn [otherwise a nickname for a promiscuous young woman] & a *capoun*." This is of particular interest, as Konrad Gesner, in his *Vogelbuch* (Bird Book) of 1557), records that one method of contemporary caponization was to excise the cock's testicles, comb, and one of its spurs, grafting the spur in place of the comb, where it continued to grow, resembling a small horn. This grafting of a "horn," it is suggested, then served as a sign by which to identify the caponized birds.

The cuckold is naturally assimilated to the "hen-pecked" husband or effeminate man. The *hennetaster* (hen groper), a type of the effeminate man, is depicted circa 1500 in stallwork at Emmerich, Kempen, and Aarschot. The earliest English reference (contemporary with his appearing in Brueghel's *Netherlandish Proverbs*) is Dame Chat's insulting insinuation that Hodge came "creeping into my pens, / And there was caught within my house groping among my hens" (*Gammer Gurton's Needle*, c. 1563). It is notable how so many of these terms concerning dominant and subservient sexual roles revolve around the barnyard relations of the cock and hen.

A late but interesting instance of the public ridicule of cuckolds is recorded in Henry Machyn's diary for May 15, 1562: "The same day was set up at the Cuckold Haven a great May-pole by butchers and fisher-men, full of horns; and they made great cheer." That derisive horns were a constituent of the mocking rituals known as charivaris, when aimed at cuckolds, may be gathered from early descriptions and depictions (e.g., Joris Hoefnagel's drawing of 1569). The apprentices of a goldsmith insulted their master by "making a horned head upon his dore sett betwene the lettres of his name and other lyke villanyes" in London in 1558. Throughout the Elizabethan era, court records make frequent allusion to the setting up of horns at the doors of houses where the husband was believed to be a cuckold. An especially elaborate instance occurred in Wiltshire in 1616, when a buck's horn stuck with a wisp of hay and "a picture of a woman's privities" was used.

See also: Charivari; Fabliau
References and further reading: See H. Dünger, "Hörner aufsetzen und Hahnrei," *Germania* 29 (1884); P. Falk, "Le couvre-chef comme symbole du mari trompé: Étude sur trois mots galloromans (galea, cuppa, cucutium)," *Studia Neophilologica* 33 (1961), which is essential reading; and R. B. Graber and G. C. Richter, "The Capon Theory of the Cuckold's Horns: Confirmation or Conjecture," *Journal of American Folklore* 100 (1987). Also suggestive is S. S. Smith, "Game in Myn Hood: The Traditions of a Comic Proverb," *Studies in Iconography* 9 (1984). The entry "cocu" in P. Guiraud, *Dictionnaire des étymologies obscures* (1982), should be read with some caution. Interesting, for the immediately postmedieval period, is D. Bruster, "The Horn of Plenty: Cuckoldry and Capital in the Drama of the Age of Shakespeare," *Studies in English Literature* 39 (1990). L. Röhrich's magisterial *Lexikon der sprichwörtlichen Redensarten*, 2nd rev. ed. (1991), is, as ever, invaluable; see its entries on Hahnrei and Horn.

—Malcolm Jones

Culhwch and Olwen [Culhwch ac Olwen]

Welsh prose tale, extant in two fourteenth-century manuscripts, probably composed in its present form somewhere in southwest Wales in the last decades of the eleventh century.

Culhwch and Olwen shares its plot with an internationally distributed folktale known as "Six Go through the Whole World" (AT 513A), in which the hero gathers a number of companions, each possessing some remarkable skill or extraordinary power, and sets out to find and win a giant's daughter as his bride. Her father sets a series of difficult tasks, which the hero accomplishes with the essential aid of his companions. In *Culhwch and Olwen* the core plot is greatly elaborated by incorporating a number of other story elements and Celtic legends into its narrative and, most strikingly, by placing the entire story into the framework of Arthurian legend, so that King Arthur and his warrior band perform for Culhwch the difficult tasks required to win Olwen, the daughter of the giant Ysbaddaden. The earliest developed picture in European literature of an established Arthurian court is seen in this work.

Another distinctive departure from the traditional oral tale in *Culhwch and Olwen* occurs in two extended catalogs that interrupt the narrative, first when Culhwch appears at Arthur's court to ask for help in his quest and then when Ysbaddaden specifies the tasks required to win his daughter. Invoking the aid of Arthur, his cousin, in the name of Arthur's court, Culhwch proceeds to name all the men and women who belong to that court. In that extensive list of names, many with epithets and allusions to marvelous exploits attached to them, we hear the echoes of a world of traditional story lost to us—of Teithi Hen, whose kingdom was inundated by the sea, of Hueil, son of Caw, who never submitted to a lord's hand and who stabbed his sister's son, and of many others. In the other catalog, the three tasks demanded of the suitor in the traditional tale are expanded by Ysbaddaden to a list of 40 *anoethau* (wonders, things difficult to obtain), which Culhwch and the Arthurian band must accomplish. The fulfilling of each task is a potential tale, but we actually hear the stories of only ten and brief references to the completion of a few others. Here, especially, we see drawn into the story motifs and tales known elsewhere in Celtic tradition and international folk narrative, such as the "unending battle" motif (A162.1.0.1), a tale of progressively older animals aiding in a quest (B124.1; B841.l; F571.2; H1235), and the ancient and widespread story of grateful ants who perform the task of sorting seeds (B365.2.1; B481.l; H1091.1).

The language of *Culhwch and Olwen* is consciously archaic, but the narrative style is energetic and richly varied, in turn heroic, comic, lyrical, boisterous, and learned. The stirring climax of the story is the hunt of a great boar, named Twrch Trwyth, an epic chase across the landscapes of Ireland, Wales, and Cornwall. Two descriptive set pieces, one describing Culhwch and the other Olwen, seem to depend on oral delivery for their full effect. They are early examples of Welsh *araitheu* (rhetorics), rhythmical and alliterative passages of extravagant prose analogous to the "runs" in Irish oral storytelling, and are perhaps the clearest examples of the many strong suggestions of performance running through *Culhwch and Olwen*. It is generally believed, however, that this tale is a literary composition, the product of an unknown author, and not a transcribed example of the art of the *cyfarwydd*, the Welsh oral storyteller. Side by side with the folktale elements and the performance style are the formal structuring, internal cross-references, allusive language, and ironic voice of literary composition. *Culhwch and Olwen* appears to be one of those interesting medieval works that is a mimesis of traditional style by an individual author, blending oral and written ways of telling a story.

See also: Arthurian Lore; Folktale; *Mabinogi*; Welsh Tradition

References and further reading: *Culhwch and Olwen*, an edition of the text by R. Bromwich and D. S. Evans (1992), has a very full introduction. Translations include G. Jones and T. Jones, trans., *The Mabinogion* (1949), and P. K. Ford, trans., *The Mabinogi and Other Medieval Welsh Tales* (1977). Folklore material is discussed in K. H. Jackson, *The International Popular Tale and Early Welsh Tradition* (1961); G. Jones, *Kings, Beasts, and Heroes* (1972), moves from folklore to literary analysis; B. F. Roberts, "Culhwch ac Olwen, the Triads, Saints' Lives," in *The Arthur of the Welsh*, ed. R. Bromwich, A. O. H. Jarman, and B. F. Roberts (1991), is a brief but valuable introduction; J. N. Radner, "Interpreting Irony in Medieval Celtic Narrative: The Case of Culhwch ac Olwen," *Cambridge Medieval*

Celtic Studies 16 (1988), is an informed critical study; and S. Knight, *Arthurian Literature and Society* (1986), contains an extensive study of the social meanings of *Culhwch and Olwen*.

—*Andrew Welsh*

Dance

The performance of a succession of rhythmic and controlled or patterned bodily movements, usually within a predetermined framework of time and space, and often to music.

Such a generic definition is admittedly inadequate for "dance" in its broadest sense. There is a tendency for such definitions to be too exclusive or too all-inclusive; for instance, emphasizing bodily movement, in an attempt to evoke a concrete image, disregards other dimensions of the activity. George S. Emmerson states that "dance draws energy from something deep in the human spirit or psyche and shares the mystical powers of all the arts, music, poetry, and sculpture in particular. It is a vehicle of ecstasy, liberating the body from the mind, the body's mass from gravity, and inspiring with ritualistic power." Thus, dancing is physical action, but action that has meaning, generally on multiple levels of consciousness, and invites interaction and evokes response. The use of rhythm, gesture, and movement as a means of externalizing feelings and conveying messages appears to be one of the basic human needs. Its origins, therefore, are lost somewhere in humankind's prehistory, which fact in itself makes definition and interpretation difficult.

Evidence of Medieval Dancing Practices

The key words for dance used by the early Church fathers in the early Middle Ages were *saltare*, *ballare*, and *choreare*. *Saltario*, or pantomime, was representative dance by professional performers. From this word came the dance term *saltarello*. *Ballare* was the most general term used for dance in the Middle Ages, while *choreare* became associated with group dancing in circle or line patterns. *Danzare* (and later, *dancier*, *danser*, and *tantzen*) did not appear in the vocabulary until the late Middle Ages. Proper names for specific dances began to appear in the twelfth century: *estample*, *trotto*, *cazzole*, *carole*, *reien*, *hovetantz*; German peasants danced *hoppaldei*, *firlefanz*, and *ridewanz*. The *carole*, a circle dance, became the form most often described by medieval poets. It was the ancestor of the *branle* and the *farandole*. Sometimes it was contracted into a closed circle and was accompanied by musical forms like the virelai, rondeau, and ballade. The more formal *danse* referred to couples or groups of three people and was usually mentioned in relation to nobility. These formal dances eventually led to the Burgundian *basse danse*, the Italian *bassadanza*, and the early modern *pavan*.

We lack concrete evidence for the prehistories of both music and dance, although mythic tales of their origins abound in almost every culture. While there was a change in the style, technique, and development of dance during the Middle Ages, it is difficult to provide more than the barest description of the whole period. The reason is the absence of primary dance sources. Most dance information must be gathered from iconographic sources, literary references, and musical evidence. Ironically, a significant portion of the limited concrete information available about dance in the medieval period comes not from the folk who engaged in dancing for whatever reason but from entities opposed to and critical of the practice, representing generally the medieval Christian Church. When Christianity replaced the so-called pagan belief systems of Europe, worship of the new deity was superimposed on the old cults, and through the influence of tolerant churchmen such as Pope Gregory the Great—who directed the Christianization of England beginning in 597—ancient religious

An open-air peasant dance; German copperplate engraving by Daniel Hopfer, circa 1500. (Reproduced from Werner Rösener, Peasants in the Middle Ages, *Urbana and London, 1992)*

practices were perpetuated in a new guise. Although devout ecclesiastics never came to terms with practices such as dancing, playing, and masquerading, the people of Europe were deeply attached to their ancient customs and heedless of their pagan implications. The two great cultural divisions of northern Europe—Celtic and Germanic—celebrated such festivals as Samhain (November 1), the beginning of the winter feast; Beltane (May 1), the beginning of the summer feast; and Lugnasa (August 1), the harvest feast. The Church superimposed its own festivals over these, with the result that in the winter celebrations extended from All Souls' Day to Twelfth Night, in the summer from Palm Sunday through May Day and Whitsun (Pentecost), and the harvest feast, Michaelmas (September 29), which took place all over Europe, might likewise involve protracted periods of festivity. While dancing was not a part of official Christian ritual, it retained its festive function despite ecclesiastical opposition. For instance, though the May Day festivities differed from place to place and from century to century, during the Middle Ages the aristocracy generally engaged in such martial activities as archery, minstrels performed, and villagers danced, often around and in the churchyard and sometimes in the church itself. Bishops throughout the Middle Ages denounced the use of the church and churchyard for secular pursuits, but with little effect. In 1210 Jacques de Vitry declared that the "woman who leadeth the dance [may] be said to have the devil's bell on her." A thirteenth-century statute of the Diocese of Aberdeen decrees that neither "choree" (from the Greek, indicating song and dance) nor "turpes et inhonesti ludi" be permitted in the church or churchyard. Even Robert Mannyng's use, in *Handlyng Synne* (1303), of the widely known legend of the sacrilegious dancers of Kölbigk implies a warning against the excesses of dance that interfere with the services of the church.

In addition to edicts from the Church and ecclesiastical commentaries, historical and literary references, paintings, manuscript illuminations, and carvings offer piecemeal information about medieval dance. As early as circa 98 C.E., Tacitus in his *Germania* commented on a dance of the Germans, performed by "naked youths ... among swords and spears," perhaps a pyrrhic dance or rhythmical weapon drill of the sort used by special groups such as the trade guilds during the medieval period. The author of the fourteenth-century English romance *Sir Gawain and the Green Knight* describes a carol, or song and dance combination, performed at Christmas. Chaucer, especially in the *Legend of Good Women* (c. 1385) and portions of *The Canterbury Tales* (c. 1387–1400), and Gower in *Confessio Amantis* (c. 1390) refer to ring dances performed mostly by the lower classes. In the fourteenth-century *Stanzaic Life of Christ* the word *ring* is used to indicate a closed round dance, and in the fifteenth-century rhymed ecclesiastical calendar (presumably by John Lydgate), a whole company of saints is depicted as dancing a joyous carol or ring dance. Carols, or ring dances, figure repeatedly in French romances of the medieval period, such as *Le roman de la rose*, *Guillaume de Dole*, and *Le roman de la violette*.

Dancing Patterns

European folk dances combine the elements of pattern, steps, and sometimes costume. Common patterns are the circle or ring, the chain, and the processional;

more complicated patterns developed in some countries. The simplest and perhaps earliest form, the closed circle, is found everywhere in postmedieval Europe. In its most elemental state—examples of which are the Yugoslav, Romanian, and Bulgarian Kolos and Horas and the Breton Bondes—the dancers are equal and sex is immaterial because all must join in; often there is no progression, or at most a gradual movement to left or right; the dancers hold each other's hands, wrists, shoulders, elbows, or belts and face the center. In the more complex ring dances, such as the Celtic Sellenger's Round and Circassian Circle and Russian and Yugoslav dances like the Moonshine and Neda Grivny, the dancers move in and out of the circle, and though maintaining contact with each other during most passages, they open out to perform individual movements. Many of the dances associated with work, such as the Armenian Carpetweaving Dance and the Hebridean Weaving Lilt, utilize this more complicated circle pattern, with the individual movements representing the motions of the particular labor involved. In the Middle Ages the trade guilds, which had to teach their apprentices the secrets of their craft, made several of these dances their particular property. The dances of the guilds were pyrrhic in nature, that is, they were rhythmic drills employing the tools of the particular craft.

The many morris dances and the point-and-hilt sword dances also employ the circle or ring and are sometimes confused with each other. These dances are ritualistic rather than communal or social and are performed either by professional dancers or by amateurs representing a particular brotherhood, organization, or guild. In the morris dance, six morris men carry sticks or handkerchiefs and are dressed in ritual costume, with bright-colored ribbons, flowers, and greenery as well as a pad of bells on each leg. Unlike the sword dances, the morris—as known in postmedieval times—is a step dance with highly developed foot, hand, and body movements. It is danced in the spring, usually during Whitsun week. The dance may have got its name from the custom of blackening the faces of the dancers so that they looked like Moors or Moresco—hence morris. The point-and-hilt sword dance, sometimes confused with the morris, was performed primarily during the Christmas season and was familiar in all European countries during the late-medieval period. In this dance the participants are linked together in a circle joined by swords held hilt and point; they dance to a drum or fiddle through a series of evolutions, ending with swords in a locked formation about the neck of one of the dancers. In the fifteenth century and later, certain dramatic personages became a part of festival celebrations and were incorporated in the morris dance—Robin Hood, Little John, Friar Tuck, and others. Consequently, also associated with the morris dance and the sword dance are guisers and grotesques, fundamentally of two kinds: those wearing the skin or tail of some animal and those masquerading in the dress of the opposite sex, usually men dressed as women.

Some of the more social or communal ring dances involve forming double circles, often an inner circle of men and an outer circle of women.

Interestingly, the carol or carole, generally described as a circle or ring dance, also contains elements of the chain. The word *carol* occurs in extant British literature about 1300 in the *Cursor Mundi* in the exact sense of the Old French *carole*, meaning a ring dance in which the singers-dancers themselves sing the governing music. Throughout the medieval period the carol enjoyed enormous vogue as a pastime, figuring repeatedly in the medieval French romances already mentioned and in other medieval literature. It consisted of a chain, open or closed, of male and female dancers moving to the accompaniment of the voice or instruments. The movement was usually three steps in measure to the left, followed by marking time in place. Though the dancers joined hands, the clasp had to be broken for the frequent gestures. It was the duty of the leader not only to direct the proceedings but to sing the song to which the carol was being danced, and during the singing the ring moved to the left. The company of dancers would then stand in place while they responded to the leader's stanza with the refrain, or burden, of the song. The popular dance inspired the legend of the cursed carolers recounted in the Middle English *Handlyng Synne* of Robert Mannyng, among other sources. The legend tells of a group of boisterous dancers of Kölbigk who, for disturbing mass, were condemned to continue their round for a year without stopping.

Many Scandinavian and German dances open with the processional or promenade, another common pattern. Modern England retains two such processionals, the Helston Furry Dance and the Abbots Bromley Horned Dance, the latter of which dates back at least to the seventeenth century. The whole community took part in these processionals, dancing in and out of the houses and through the town, sweeping everything with branches of May or green broom and sometimes being led by a hobbyhorse or other animal. The Irish Rinnce Fada is also of this form and was probably familiar during the medieval period, though the first literary description of it is given in James Boswick's *Who Are the Irish?* in connection with a visit by James II to Ireland in the seventeenth century. In this dance, three leaders were followed by a line of dancers in couples joined by holding white clothes or handkerchiefs. Certain of these dances involved a single file of men and one of women and are akin to the popular couple dances that became the principal feature of many Scandinavian, Teutonic, and Alpine traditions. The more complicated patterns involving circle and longways dances developed from the early court and social dances, and many of these innovations were not available to medieval dancers, particularly the lower classes. The actual steps of these figured dances were often simple, but different ways of holding a partner or of changing places were introduced: Inside Hands Joined, Two Hands Hold, Cross Hands Hold, Arming, Double Ring Grasp, and others.

Emotional and Social Dimensions

It is impossible to know with any certainty what emotional, intellectual, social, and spiritual dimensions the various folk dances possessed for medieval dancers. It is very likely that some of the dances retained remnants of their pre-Christian association with magic and supernatural ritual; for instance, ecstatic dances, associated with the fear of death, gave rise to the *Danse macabre* (Dance of Death). This dance madness was associated with the plague and other diseases. Certainly, there were dances that were used in connection with Christian festivals and activities—dances such as the carol, depending on the contents of the dance song, and the war-like dances of the trade guilds in conjunction with morality plays. The medieval Church steadfastly imposed strong restrictions against the use of dance in the liturgy, but this did not curtail its popularity in secular society. From a political and social standpoint, dance provided a means of communication and interchange between different nations and cultures and for a time at least between the privileged and lower classes. The dances of Scotland were transmitted to France, for instance, and the dances of France were influential in England. Likewise the dances of the peasants were appropriated by the courts, where they were changed by the nobility, and these changes were often then adopted by the lower classes. However, during the medieval period a countermovement was already under way, and dance became a vehicle for exhibiting and defining class distinctions (the dances of the elite prioritized rigid posture, impassive countenances, emotional containment or withdrawal, and graceful movement while the dances of the lower classes invited spontaneity, vigorous action, rudeness, and awkwardness) and for training the privileged in the qualities that set them apart as superior and excluded the poor. The basse dances (which flourished from about 1350 to 1550) and the pavaynes (from 1450 to the middle of the seventeenth century) were slow, dignified, stately dances with intricate steps better suited to hall and castle than to the village green and peasant revelry. The introduction of dance masters and the self-conscious practice of dance as an art form peculiar to the socially elite created an ever-widening gap between how dances were performed by the rich and the poor and what the dances meant for the performers. The dances appropriated and modified by the court elite thus differed significantly from the lower-class dances in nature and function.

See also: Ballad; Carol; Hungarian Tradition; Sword Dance

References and further reading: See M. Clarke, *The History of Dance* (1981); G. S. Emmerson, *A Social History of Scottish Dance: Ane Celestial Recreatioun* (1972); R. L. Greene, ed., *The Early English Carols* (1977); S. Howard, *The Politics of Courtly Dancing in Early Modern England* (1998); J. Lawson, *European Folk Dance: Its National and Musical Characteristics* (1970); C. Page, *The Owl and the Nightingale: Musical Life and Ideas in France, 1100–1300* (1989); C. L. Sharp, *The Dance: An Historical Survey of Dancing in Europe* (1924); "Dance," in *New Grove Dictionary of Music and Musicians*, vol. 5 (1995).

—*Bradford Lee Eden and Lee Winniford*

Dance of Death [French *Danse macabre*, German *Totentanz*]

A late-medieval topos apparently owing its popularity to a series of paintings of 30 men led off by skeletal apparitions of themselves.

Accompanied by verses, these paintings were done on the walls of the Cimitière des Saints Innocents (Cemetery of the Holy Innocents) in Paris in 1424–1425 and recorded in Guy Marchant's illustrated book, printed in Paris in 1485. The earliest surviving printed versions of the *Danse*, however, are blockbooks depicting both males and females issued with German texts in 1465 and about 1480.

Very shortly after the appearance of the text from the Cimitière des Saints Innocents, the poet John Lydgate translated it into English, and this accompanied copies of the paintings made on the cloister walls of Old St. Paul's in Lon-

A German depiction of the Dance of Death involving a usurer, a mayor, and a landowner. (Foto Marburg/Art Resource, NY)

don soon after 1430, hence its English vernacular name, "the dance of Paul's." Other early derivatives were the paintings at Basel (c. 1440), Ker-Maria, Brittany (c. 1460), Lübeck (1463), and Berlin (1484) and a *Danse* sculpted in snow in Arras in 1434. Processional and dramatized *Danses* are also attested—one performed before the duke of Burgundy in Bruges in 1449, another in Besançon Cathedral four years later, and in England, in St. Edmund's Church, Salisbury; even one in the church at Caudebec in 1393, a generation *before* the Innocents murals. Kenneth Varty has recently noted that an altarpiece painted for the Abbey of St. Omer in 1458 by Simon Marmion includes a view of a Benedictine cloister painted with the *Danse*. A *horae* (book of hours) that he illuminated in the late 1470s (now in the Victoria and Albert Museum) includes marginal figures of a skeletal Death seizing, for instance, a fashionably dressed young woman, the immediate precursor of the *Danse*-derived images found in the earliest Parisian *horae*.

English cycles include the murals formerly in the Guild Chapel at Stratford-on-Avon (c. 1500) and the late-fifteenth-century misericords of Coventry Cathedral (destroyed in World War II), but the best extant complete example of the theme is a series of carvings on the roof ribs of the mid-fifteenth-century chapel at Roslin in Scotland, based on French models. It has also only recently been pointed out that verses on a rudimentary *Dance of Death* (independent of Lydgate's) are found in the earliest London editions of the *Kalender of Shepherdes* (1506, c. 1510, and later) along with a few woodcuts first used in Marchant's late-fifteenth-century *Danse macabre* editions. The Dance series proper appeared as border decorations in Parisian printed *horae* from the 1490s on, but it was not until 1521, apparently, that they appear as a sort of appendix to a Parisian *horae* printed for the English market accompanied by the Lydgate verses.

Some impression of early-sixteenth-century England's familiarity with the paintings of the *Danse macabre* is suggested by the thirty-third *demaunde* in the earliest printed English riddle-book, Wynkyn de Worde's *Demaundes Joyous* of 1511: "Wherefore be there not as many women conteyned in the daunce of poules as there be men?"—"Bycause a women is so ferefull of herte that she had leuer [rather] daunce amonge quycke [living] folke than deed!" Although not found in the extant late-fifteenth-century French incunabula from which roughly half of the other *demaundes* were taken, the same *demaunde* does occur in a manuscript text of about 1470: "Pourquoy en la danse macabree ne dansent nulles femmes mais ung mort et ung homme vif?" "Pour tant que les femmes n'ont cure de danser aveuc les mors mais tres bein aveuc les vifs!" The obscene pun on *vits* (penises) is lost, of course, in the literal English translation.

See also: Black Death; Funeral Customs and Burial Rites; *Memento Mori*
References and further reading: See R. Helm, *Skelett- und Todesdarstellungen bis zum Auftreten der Totentänze* (1928); S. Kozaky, *Geschichte der Totentänze* (1936); E. C. Williams, "The Dance of Death in Painting and Sculpture in the Middle Ages," *Journal of the British Archaeological Association* (1937); J. M. Clark, *The Dance of Death* (1950); A. Tenenti, *La vie et la mort à travers l'art du XVe siècle* (1952); S. Cosacchi, *Makabertanz der Totentanz in Kunst, Poesie, und Brauchtum des Mittelalters* (1965); K. Mayer-Baer, *The Music of the Spheres and the Dance of Death* (1970); J. Saugnieux, *Les danses macabres de France et d'Espagne* (1971); H. Rosenfeld, *Der mittlelalterliche Totentanz* (1974); J. Wirth, *La jeune fille et la mort* (1979); R. Hammerstein, *Tanz und Musik des Todes: Die mittelalterlichen Totentänze und ihr Nachleben* (1980). Two exhibition catalogs are useful: *Europe in Torment 1450–1550* (Brown University and Museum of Art, 1974) and *Images of Love and Death in Late Medieval and Renaissance Art* (University of Michigan Museum of Art, 1975). A most useful collection of texts and illustrations is G. Kaiser, *Der tanzende Tod* (1983). See also J. Delumeau, "Du mépris du monde aux danses macabres," in his *Le péché et la peur* (1983). A. Breeze, "The Dance of Death," *Cambridge Medieval Celtic Studies* 13 (1987), surveys the English and introduces much new Welsh evidence.

—Malcolm Jones

Dante Alighieri (1265–1321)

The greatest Italian poet, whose works, particularly *La divina commedia* (The Divine Comedy, 1308–1321), draw extensively upon the folk traditions of his time.

Dante titled his masterpiece simply the *Commedia*; only much later, in the sixteenth century, did readers christen it "Divine." In choosing the term *commedia* (from two Greek words, meaning "rustic song"), the poet was following classical literary tradition of casting comedy in language less elevated and more accessible than that of tragedy. Dante, intending his work to be accessible to all his compatriots, wrote it in Italian rather than in Latin. The *Commedia* describes a journey through the three otherworlds of Catholic doctrine: *Inferno* (Hell), *Purgatorio* (Purgatory), and *Paradiso* (Paradise).

Dante's earlier Italian works—such as *La vita nuova* (The New Life, c. 1292–1294), *Il convivio* (The Banquet, c. 1304–1308), and the *Rime* (Rhymes, 1293–c. 1310)—serve as introductions to the *Commedia*. Several of his Latin works, especially *De monarchia* (On Monarchy, c. 1310–1317) and *De vulgari eloquentia* (On the Eloquence of the Vernacular, or Common, Language—i. e., Italian, as opposed to Latin, c. 1304–1305), add to an understanding of the *Commedia*. In all these writings of lofty content and erudition, there is always a certain presence of popular traditions and folkways, especially in the vernacular works and above all in the *Commedia*. Popular and learned traditions enjoy a parallel development in Dante's work. The former does not diminish the latter; on the contrary, it enhances and enlightens the text. Dante intended the *Commedia* as an exemplary poem in the vernacular, in imitation of its most immediate model, Virgil's *Aeneid*, as well as Homer's *Iliad* and *Odyssey*. He also employs folklore abundantly as a reflection of his world and times, thus enriching his work with concrete realism and imagination. The author is the perfect example of an intellectual who creates a symbiosis of erudite and popular culture to portray his world in colorful and dramatic ways. As Dante himself said, this is "the sacred poem to which heaven and earth have so set hands" (*Par.* 25:1–2).

Dante's Documentation of Folk Traditions

Numerous folk traditions appear in the *Commedia*. Life-cycle customs include calling out the name of the Virgin Mary upon giving birth (*Purg.* 20:19–21; *Par.* 17:34–37), betrothal and wedding traditions (*Purg.* 5:130–136, 24:43; *Par.* 10:140–141, 15:104, 25:105), and death and burial rites (*Purg.* 3:112–132, 33:35–36). In referring to the *ninna-nanna* (lullaby, *Purg.* 23:111) and a child's

Italian artist Domenico di Michelino shows Dante Alighieri, center, as part of a depiction of The Divine Comedy. (*Dante and His Poem, 1465; Florence Cathedral; Art Resource, NY*)

toy, *il paleo* (spinning top, *Par.* 18:41–42; see also *Aeneid* 7, 378), Dante draws upon lore surrounding children. He also refers to feasts, festivals, tournaments, and races (*Inf.* 15:121–124, 22:1–12; *Purg.* 28:36; *Par.* 16:40–43), as well as proverbs and sayings (*Inf.* 15:95–96, 18:66, 22:14–15, 23:142–144; 28:107; *Purg.* 16:113, 22:149, 33:97; *Par.* 16:58–59, 18:52–53, 22:16). The *Convivio* features the proverb "Una rondine non fa primavera" [One swallow does not make a spring].

Dante also depicts traditional beliefs, clothing customs, dances and songs, legends and tales, fables, gestures, astrology and numerology, and metaphors and metaphorical language. His keen observations of daily life, combined with his purpose of portraying a realistic society, account for the richness and precision of his descriptions of popular customs and his use of diverse—and appropriately employed—linguistic registers (some drawn from traditions of the grotesque and low comedy), as in the cantos of the barrators and the devils (*Inf.* 21 and 22).

In his early work *The New Life* Dante describes the wedding custom (14:1–15) in which the bride's young female friends attend a banquet at the groom's house. The young men present initiate the custom of *corteggiamento, donneare*, courting the young women. Traditionally, the groom's banquet lasted three days and then moved to the bride's house, where it could last for several more. *The New Life* also depicts *corrottos* (chs. 8 and 22), funeral laments, performed by women and men in different groups.

Use of Numerological and Calendar Traditions

In *The New Life* Dante also describes his obsessive love for Beatrice, who would later appear in the *Commedia* (*Purg.* 30) as the poet's guide to Paradise. Significantly, Beatrice first appeared to Dante on the calendar feast of Calendimaggio (May Day) 1274, when he was almost nine and she was entering her ninth year. She died on June 19, 1290. Nine would become Beatrice's symbolic number. Nine comprises three 3's, thus evoking the Christian Trinity. Dante also draws upon the learned lore of the Syrian, Latin, and Arabic calendars (*Vita nova* ch. 29) to lend significance to the number 9; he identifies the death of Beatrice with the numbers 9 and 10, the latter being the perfect number. Indeed, numerology and astrology (which in the Middle Ages was equivalent to astronomy) are very much part of Dante's intellectual tradition and play an important role in his art, as demonstrated by the structure and form of the *Commedia*. The *Commedia* comprises 100 cantos composed in three-line stanzas, subdivided into four groups—1 + 33 + 33 + 33—one canto for the prologue and 33 each for the three realms, a structure based on the trinitarian 1 and 3. Symbolic numbers also structure each of the three realms: the ten circles of the *Inferno*—whose eighth circle contains ten pouches encasing the sins of fraud; *Purgatorio*, with its seven terraces, its Ante-Purgatory, and the Earthly Paradise; and the ten spheres of the *Paradiso*. There are several strategic places in which numerology plays an important role, as in the appearance of the three beasts encountered by Dante as he begins his journey: the *Lonza* (leopard), *Leone* (lion), and *Lupa* (she-wolf). The three L's represent the evil trinity (Lucifer); in canto 34 Lucifer will appear as a three-headed monster, described as "the Emperor of this dolorous kingdom." In *Paradiso*, the Heaven of the Sun (cantos 10–12) possesses two groups, with 12 figures in each, bearing a direct correspondence with the 12 signs of the zodiac, the 12 tribes of Israel, and the 12 apostles.

Dante structures the chronology of the *Commedia* in close correspondence with the Christian calendar. He begins his journey on the evening of Holy Thursday, April 7, 1300, as he becomes lost in the forest. On Saturday night, the traveler emerges from hell, having spent 24 hours there. By crossing the equator into the Southern Hemisphere, he finds himself on the shore of purgatory at the dawn of Easter Sunday, April 10. He enters Paradise on the Wednesday after Easter at noon, and the journey ends seven days later, when on the evening of Thursday, April 14, the *viator* (wayfarer) enjoys the final vision of Paradise. Dante's journey, then, coincides ritually to Christ's death and resurrection.

La vita nova and the *Commedia* also register religious customs and popular piety: Dante sees Beatrice in church probably on the Feast of the Visitation (May 31), when *laudes* for the Virgin Mary were sung (*Vita nova* ch. 5); later, as Dante laments Beatrice's death, he describes pilgrims on the way to Rome to see the famous Veronica's veil. In chapter 40 the narrator offers a definition and classification of pilgrims and pilgrimages, naming those who go to Jerusalem *palmieri* (bearers of palms), those who go to Rome, *romei,* and those who go to Santiago de Compostela in Galicia *peregrini* (pilgrims). The terminology is determined by the pilgrim's insignia: two crossed keys, symbolic of St. Peter, for the *romei*; two crossed palms from Jericho for the *palmieri*; two crossed walking canes for those going to the shrine at Santiago and a shell for them on their way back. In a previous chapter the narrator tells us that Love appeared to him like a pilgrim dressed humbly, "without pomp" (*Vita nova* ch. 9), mirroring the medieval image of the pilgrim as *homo viator* (man the wayfarer), one who journeys for the expiation of sins. Dante himself is a pilgrim in the *Commedia*, as he is reminded in *Purgatorio* 13:96.

Dream and Color Symbolism

Dreams (*Vita nova* chs. 3 and 13), oneiric (dream) literature, and oneiromancy (divination through dreams) play a significant role in *La vita nova*, predicting such future events as Beatrice's death (ch. 23). Dreams are also vital and meaningful components of *The Divine Comedy*. In *Purgatorio* 9, the pilgrim Dante dreams that a golden-winged eagle has flown him to the sphere of fire; dreaming that he and the eagle are burning, he awakes. In canto 19 he dreams of a *femmina balba,* a stammering, pale, cross-eyed, club-footed woman, who transforms into a beauty and tells him in a song that she is the siren who confounds mariners like Ulysses. She turns out to be the symbol of incontinence or the sins of the flesh, and her ventral stench awakens the pilgrim. In canto 27 (91–109), the poet, having reached Earthly Paradise, dreams of Leah and Rachel, who traditionally represent, respectively, the active and the contemplative life. All three oneiric visions occur just before dawn—a time at which, according to medieval traditions, the most truly prophetic dreams occur.

Another element present in both *La vita nova* and *The Divine Comedy* is the symbolism of colors, often represented through clothing customs. Beatrice first appears to the narrator dressed in red, a color of the highest dignity, and wearing a belt stylish in Dante's time. The second time she appears dressed in white, a color worn by both angels and brides. The *cinta*, or belt, was a customary part of dress codes for both sexes in Dante's time. In *Paradiso* 14 we learn through Dante's predecessor Cacciaguida (c. 1091–1147) that Florentine women wore highly prized belts adorned with precious metals and stones. Indeed, the cantos of Cacciaguida (15–18) are a mine of information regarding popular traditions, as, here, Cacciaguida is reminiscing about the Florence of old. In canto 15 there are references to both male and female dress codes (100–102). When Beatrice reappears in *Purgatorio* 30, she wears the colors of the three theological virtues: a white veil crowned with olive boughs, a green cape, and a red dress. Other examples of dress traditions occur in *Purgatorio* 23, which calls the shameless Florentine women less chaste than the women of Barbagia, a wild region of Sardinia (94–96), and *Purgatorio* 8 and 24, which describe the band or veil that distinguished married women or widows.

Inferno 21 and 22 treat magicians, astrologers, necromancers, and diviners from such ancient seers as Tiresias and Calchas to relatively recent figures legendary in Dante's time: Guido Bonatti of Forlì, who practiced in the court of Frederick II; Asdente, a poor cobbler of Parma; or the renowned Michael Scot, who enjoyed a great reputation as a sorcerer and prophet at the court of Frederick II. All have their heads twisted backward and shed tears of anguish, because of the law of *contrapasso*, punishment that fits the crime, that Dante applies in his *Inferno*. This particular canto is rich in an atmosphere of magic, evoking witches and witchcraft (20:121–130), even mentioning "the man on the moon," which in Italian folklore is Cain carrying a bundle of thorns: "See the wretched women who left the needle, the spool and the spindle, and became fortune tellers: they wrought spells with herbs and with images. But now come, for already Cain with his thorns holds the confines of both the hemispheres, and touches the waves below Seville; and already last night the moon was round" (Singleton translation). It is well known that witches congregate under a full moon and that traditionally one should not begin anything new under a full moon.

There are devils whose names are derived directly from popular beliefs and early theatrical representations. These devils are assigned to hook, massacre, and quarter the lawyers. Malebranche (Evil Claws) leads the others, whose names indicate their popular origin: Malacoda (Evil Tail), Scarmiglione (Rougher Up), Alichino (Bent on Wings?—the French Hallequin, a predecessor from popular farce of the Arlecchino of the commedia dell'arte), Calcabrina (Frost Trampler), Cagnazzo (Doggish, or Bad Dog), Barbariccia (Curly Beard), Libicocco (from two winds "libeccio" and "scirocco," thus Blaster), Draghignazzo (Dragonish, or Bad Dragon), Ciriatto (Hoggish), Graffiacane (Dog Scratcher), Rubicante (Rabid Red). Dante also relates the beliefs about the devil traditional in his time, for example, that the bodies of those who betray guests are seized by the devil while still alive on earth, as their souls lie in hell (*Inf.* 33:121–126).

There are games such as chess (*Purg.* 28:93) and a dicing game called *zara* (*Purg.* 6:1–3), and dances such as the *ridda* (*Inf.* 7:24) and *tresca* (*Inf.* 14:40; *Purg.* 10:65). There are references to dolphins who warn sailors of approaching inclement weather (*Inf.* 22:18), the swallow's appearance in January as a false sign of spring (*Purg.* 13:123), boar hunting (*Inf.* 13:113), and falcons and falconry (*Inf.* 17:127–129, 22:130; *Purg.* 19:64; *Par.* 18:45, 19:34). Traditional gestures occur: A usurer sticks out his tongue out as a sign of mockery (*Inf.* 17:74–75), and a thief turned into a serpent spits as a sign of scorn or disdain (*Inf.* 25:136–138).

At the end of *Purgatorio* there appears a tableau that evokes the urban festivities of Dante's time: a cart representing the Church, pulled by a griffin (Christ), leads a procession of many figures representing the Old and New Testaments, imitating the form of medieval pageants.

Two examples epitomize Dante's proximity to popular culture. First, at the end of *Purgatorio* Beatrice says *"che vendetta di Dio non teme suppe"* [that God's vengeance fears no soups (that is, hindrances)], referring to those who are to be blamed for the corruption of the Church and who should expect imminent punishment (*Purg.* 33:36). This refers to the popular belief, probably of Greek origin, that a murderer who consumed a wine soup within nine days of the homicide, either on the body or on the tomb of the victim, would be safe from the relatives' revenge. For this reason the family of the deceased would guard the body for as many days. Dante's expression is equivalent to an Italian proverb saying that God does not pay on the Sabbath, "Dio non paga il sabato," meaning that his vengeance can occur at any time. In his study of popular tradition in *The Divine Comedy*, Giuseppe Pitrè has shown that this tradition was widespread throughout Europe.

The second example alludes to the custom of throwing stones on the unburied body of a slain enemy, thus creating a stone burial. It is part of a well-known ancient custom in which stone throwing signifies sympathy or respect. This same passage also records the practice of burying excommunicated people or heretics outside the church grounds and the symbolism of unlit candles, in which burials are conducted *"sine luce et cruce"* [without light and cross]. In this passage King Manfred of Sicily narrates his own burial, while telling Dante how he died, saved by his last-minute repentance, unbeknownst to the pope, who had excommunicated him.

Popular tradition finds its way into all of Dante's works in varying degrees, of course, but always as an integral part of the whole and essential to the vision of the author. Along the way in Dante's poem one encounters so many references to folkloric tradition that Benedetto Croce labeled Dante "a poet of his people." In other words, Dante's poem should be considered a national poem, as Jacob Grimm viewed national epics—as works belonging to a whole people and not to a specific author.

See also: *Decameron*; Dreams and Dream Poetry; Hell; Italian Tradition; Purgatory

References and further reading: Dante Alighieri, *The Divine Comedy*, 3 vols., ed. and trans. C. S. Singleton (1970–1975), contains the Italian text with facing English translations accompanied by detailed commentary. See also P. Antonetti, *La vita quotidiana a Firenze al tempi di Dante*, trans. G. Capiero (1986); two works by G. B. Bronzini, "Tradizioni popolari," in *Enciclopedia Dantesca*, 6 vols., ed. U. Bosco et al. (1970–1976), and "Prospetto critico delle tradizioni popolari dantesche," in *Studi filologici letterari e storici in memoria di Guido Favati*, ed. G. Varanini and P. Pinagli (1977); G. Crocioni, *Le tradizioni popolari nella letteratura italiana* (1965); G. Cocchiara, "Folklore e letteratura," *Scuola e cultura* 6 (1963); G. C. Di Scipio, "St. Paul and Popular Traditions," in *Telling Tales: Medieval Narrative and the Folk Tradition*, ed. F. Canadé Sautman, D. Conchado, and

G. C. Di Scipio (1998); E. Ernault, "Une formule magique chez Dante," *Melusine* 5 (1989); A. Falassi, *Italian Folklore: An Annotated Bibliography* (1985); C. Naselli, "Aggiunte alle tradizioni popolari nella *Divina Commedia* raccolte dal Pitrè," in *Atti del Convegno di studi su Dante e la Magna Curia* (1967); A. Graf, *Miti, leggende e superstizioni nel medio evo*, 2 vols. (1925); J. B. Halloway, "The *Vita nuova*: Paradigms of Pilgrimage," *Dante Studies* 103 (1985); three works by G. Pitrè, "Le tradizioni popolari nella *Divina commedia*," rpt. in *Nuovi quaderni del meridione* 3, no. 9 (1965), and *Archivio delle tradizioni popolari* 4 (1885) and 6 (1887); J.-C. Schmidt, *Medioevo superstizioso*, trans. M. Garin (1992); C. Speroni, "Folklore in the *Divine Comedy*," in *A Dante Profile, 1265– 1965*, ed. F. Schettino (1967); three works by P. Toschi, *Le origini del teatro italiano* (1955), "Tradizioni popolari nella *Divina commedia*,' *Rassegna trimestrale di cultura dell'Istituto Tecnico di Lanciano* 3 (1965), and *Invito al folklore italiano* (1963).

—*Giuseppe C. Di Scipio*

David, Saint (d. c. 589) [Dewi Sant]

Sixth-century monk and missionary, patron saint of Wales.

David's feast day, commemorating his death, is March 1. Tradition credits him with founding 12 monasteries, including Glastonbury, before he settled in his own religious foundation in Vallis Rosina (Glyn Rhosyn) or Mynyw, the eventual St. Davids in southwestern Wales. We have no contemporary reports of his life, though Irish annals note his death, and the Irish *Catalogue of Saints* (c. 730) and *Martyrology of Oengus* (c. 800) also refer to him, but traditions about him were recorded in a number of Latin *vitae*, mainly deriving from Rhigyfarch's *Vita Dauidis* (c. 1095). A Welsh life, the *Buchedd Dewi*, closely related to a twelfth-century Latin text, was compiled about 1346, and Gerald of Wales composed *Vita Sancti Davidis* about 1194. David also appears in the legends of other saints (including that of St. Paul de Leon, c. 884). Poets of the twelfth to fifteenth centuries (most notably Gwynfardd Brycheiniog, Iolo Goch, Ieuan ap Rhydderch, Dafydd Llwyd o Fathafarn, Lewis Glyn Cothi, and Rhisiart ap Rhys) also recorded traditions about David.

Many of the motifs in the traditions about David are common to the Welsh saints, fitting the heroic biographical pattern (in religious form), but appear in specific forms that are also distinctively David's. For example, his conception and birth are accompanied by miracles: his birth was prophesied 30 years in advance (to his father Sant, a king, who raped the virgin Non when he met her on the road); St. Patrick and St. Gildas gave way before him; from the time of conception he (and his mother) ate only bread and water (and sometimes cress), perhaps contributing to his epithet *Dyfrwr* or *Aquaticus* (Waterman); at his baptism he healed a blind *wynepclawr* (flat-face). Though many saints work wonders with water, only David depoisoned and heated the waters of Bath, giving them their healing properties. Like most of the saints, David came into conflict with a secular power, in his case the prince Boya, but the form of the conflict is unusual: threatened by David's increasing authority (demonstrated by the smoke from his fire covering the land), Boya and his wife send first armed men and then naked women against David and his followers, and Boya's wife, in a last wicked step before madness, kills her stepdaughter. David prevails, and in the end Boya is killed and his tower destroyed by a fire from heaven.

When or how David came to be considered the patron saint of Wales is unknown. The tenth-century *Armes Prydein* prophesies that David's banner will lead the united Celtic forces and calls on him to lead the warriors against the Saxon intruders, sentiments echoed over the centuries by other prophetic poems invoking his name. We have later evidence of the political struggles for his supremacy, both as the leading saint in Wales and as archbishop of a see having equal status to that of Canterbury. Rhigyfarch, while drawing on local traditions about David, was also responding to ongoing disputes between the dioceses of St. Davids and Llandaff, represented by St. Cadog. In David's *vitae*, the simplest statement of his supremacy is in the Synod of Brefi, which was convened to select an archbishop through a contest in preaching. David did not attend, but after none of the contenders could make themselves heard even by the closest audience, messengers were sent for him. As David preached the ground rose under him (forming the hill on which the church of Llanddewibrefi now stands), and he could be heard clearly by everyone even at a great distance. According to tradition, David's right to his position was also established while he was on pilgrimage with St. Teilo and St. Padarn to Jerusalem, where the patriarch of that city consecrated him archbishop or, in an alternate tradition (possibly owing to the narrators' need to align the Welsh Church with Rome), while on pilgrimage to Rome, where he was raised to the archiepiscopate. David's archiepiscopacy was further guaranteed in tradition when St. Dyfrig, archbishop of Caerleon, passed his mantle to David, who transferred it to his own city Mynyw. This tradition was influenced by Geoffrey of Monmouth, who apparently introduced the Caerleon element, and was used by Gerald of Wales in his own twelfth-century attempts to have the metropolitan status of St. Davids recognized by the pope in Rome.

The importance of St. David and his church is apparent, moreover, in the way other saints are measured against him, either as associates or as competitors (*Vita Cadoci* repeatedly stresses Cadog's superiority over David), in the 53 churches and 32 wells dedicated to him, and in the medieval mathematics of pilgrimages (two journeys to St. Davids equal one to Rome, and three equal one to Jerusalem). In the early twelfth century, David was recognized as a saint by Pope Calixtus II, unlike all the other Welsh saints who acquired their titles from their roles as hermits and ecclesiastics, which was the meaning of the word *sant* (*sanctus*) in the early Middle Ages. Allusions to David in medieval poetry show that the audience could be expected to know many traditions about him, including some not recorded in the various *vitae*. The poetry also shows him associated with the prophetic tradition.

Although his religious role was affected by the Protestant Reformation, David has remained a national figure—one whose Church could be used to vie with Canterbury, one who represents Welsh spiritual independence from the period before influences of the Roman Church, and one who can be honored by even the most secular as an early Welsh leader and symbol of Wales.

See also: Geoffrey of Monmouth; Gerald of Wales; Saints, Cults of the; Welsh Tradition
References and further reading: Rhigyfarch's *Life of St. David*, ed. J. W. James (1967), a
    twelfth-century manuscript (BL MS Cotton Nero E.i), is thought to be closest to the Latin

original; *Vitae sanctorum Britanniae et genealogiae*, ed. A. W. Wade Evans (1944), presents an edition of the twelfth-century manuscript (BL MS Cotton Vespasian A.xiv) that has the most additional material, particularly local traditions from west and southeast Wales. *The Welsh Life of St David*, ed. D. Simon Evans (1988), presents the Welsh manuscript (Jesus College, MS 119). See also G. Williams, *Religion, Language, and Nationality in Wales* (1979), and E. R. Henken, *Traditions of the Welsh Saints* (1987).

—*Elissa R. Henken*

Decameron

One of the most important frame tale collections of the Middle Ages, in which ten young people, having fled Florence to escape the Black Death, pass time during their exile by telling stories, each a tale a day for ten days, for a total of 100 tales.

The author, Giovanni Boccaccio (1313–1375), was born in Certaldo, near Florence—surroundings that provided the stage for the 100 tales told in his *Decameron* (c. 1349–1351) by seven well-bred young ladies and three young men. The tale tellers' number (the perfect number 10) and names conceal symbolic meanings: Neiphile, for example, means "new in love" and Dioneo "a new lustful god," Venus being the daughter of Dione by Jupiter. As the author's mouthpiece, Dioneo is the most daring storyteller among the ten and has the freedom to choose any topic, while the others must stick to the theme of the day.

The *Decameron*, "an epic of the merchant class," describing people from all walks of life, is rich with folkloric traditions, containing, for example, folk beliefs from fourteenth-century Tuscany, where the action unfolds. Though the storytellers are from the elite class, they show familiarity with folkways from both oral and literary traditions, from both the countryside and the city. This is also due to the author's own inclination, his studies, and his practical worldly experience, especially in the 1320s at the court of King Robert of Sicily. Boccaccio trained to be a banker in Naples and came in contact with merchants, sailors, adventurers, and people of various social classes, as is attested in the *novella* (tale; plural *novelle*) of Andreuccio of Perugia (2, 5), a horse trader whose misadventures and final fortune are re-created in an atmosphere of complete realism depicting the places and people of Naples. In his tales Boccaccio alludes to cults of false relics and false saints (2, 1; 3, 10; 6, 10), prophetic dreams (4, 5; 7, 10), powders, plants (4, 7), and specters and phantasms (3, 8). He also treats many of the most important legendary figures known in fourteenth-century Italy, some of whom were known throughout Europe and some of whom were celebrated principally in his native Tuscany: for example, Saladin (Salah ad-Din, 1138–1193), whose legendary munificence earned him a place in Dante's Limbo (*Inf.* 4:129) (1, 3 and 10, 9); the sultan of Babylon (2, 7); Ghino di Tacco, a famous thief (10, 2); and Calandrino, a legendary fool and object of pranks by the notorious painters Bruno and Buffalmacco (8, 6; 9, 5). There are contemporary figures, such as Cangrande della Scala, the famous Ghibelline lord of Verona (1, 7), to whom Dante dedicated *Paradiso*; Ciacco, a notoriously witty glutton of Florence (9, 8), known also to Dante (*Inferno* 6); and many other colorful personages. The text also includes songs, dances, and the playing of musical instruments such as the lute (at the end of Day 1) as a part of the daily routine of entertainment, along with the narration of stories often derived from oral tradition.

Folklore has therefore a tremendous role in Boccaccio's work, where it represents the sum of a cultural era; this is especially true of the *Decameron*, which represents the bourgeois society of fourteenth-century Italy and was supposedly written primarily for women of that class.

From the very beginning, through the description of the plague that provides the frame of the work, the reader is alerted to the customs of this society and how they are altered by a calamitous epidemic that afflicted Italy and Europe in 1347–1351. Boccaccio, perhaps in jest, attributes the plague either to the "works of the stars" or to divine punishment for human iniquity. As a result of the Florentine outbreak of 1348, the most common societal practices, such as wakes, burials, and religious rites for the dead, were all suspended; instead, hundreds of bodies were thrown in common graves as if they were merchandise on a ship. There were those who engaged in eating, singing, and drinking excessively, believing that this would ward off the plague, and those who decided to lead a moderate or even Spartan life in order to fight off the disease. Others, following vernacular medical practices, would go around the city with flowers in their hands, carrying odorous herbs or spices, believing thus to escape the plague. Yet others abandoned the city and their property. In this fashion laws and customs totally disintegrated, not only in the city but also in the *contado*, the countryside, where animals roamed as they pleased, even returning home at night as if they were rational beings, ironically doing what humans did not do in these circumstances. Boccaccio tells all this with a sense of wonderment,

Two scenes from Boccaccio's Decameron, *depicted in a 1492 woodcut. (National Museum of Ireland; North Wind Picture Archives)*

of play, rather than in a dramatic tone. The introduction, however, is very important because it sets the stage for the entire work, so that the tales told by the ten narrators are in a sense a reconstruction of this same society with the customs and beliefs that had dominated normal everyday life, as well as an echo of an ideal multifaceted life.

Popular Beliefs

Another important characteristic of the *Decameron* is the oral nature of many of the *novelle* dealing with personages who peopled the city-state of Florence and other cities and the merchants whose business took them throughout the Mediterranean, France, Flanders, and elsewhere. The very first *novella*, in fact, tells the story of one Ser Cepparello of Prato who has gone to Burgundy, charged with collecting money owed to Musciatto Franzesi, a Florentine merchant. Ser Cepparello is a wicked, immoral being who through a false confession on his deathbed ends up being declared a saint: the people readily believe his confessor's near-beatification of Cepparello and contrast his life to their sinful ways. The tale parodies the superficial, customary way in which saints were sometimes created, and it also presents references to folk customs, portraying the ready acceptance of relics, miracles, and newly created saints in popular religion.

The same popular religious practices are shown in the boisterous *novella* of Frate Cipolla (Brother Onion), in which the author reaches a height of comic inventiveness when describing Cipolla's ability to convince the common folk of the existence of false relics while at the same time collecting their money and saving his own skin. The central characters of this *novella* (6, 10) are really the people of Certaldo, Boccaccio's hometown (a town famous for its onions, says its native-born narrator). The townspeople, whose faith and devotion must rely on something concrete and tangible, are easily duped into accepting Brother Cipolla's claim that he possesses a feather from the wings of the Angel Gabriel or the coals with which St. Lawrence was roasted in martyrdom. Boccaccio has Brother Cipolla speak of the many relics shown to him by the most reverend patriarch of Jerusalem, whom he names Nonmiblasmete Sevoipiace (Don't-blame-me If-you-please), including the finger of the Holy Spirit and a lock of hair of the seraphim who appeared to St. Francis.

Another major theme in Boccaccio is the belief in ghosts, apparitions, and other supernatural phenomena, as in the *novella* of Nastagio degli Onesti (5, 8). Nastagio, rejected by his beloved, wanders in the woods. There he sees a terrifying vision of a woman hunted down by dogs followed by a knight threatening to kill her as punishment for her unwillingness to return his love. The knight catches up with the woman, kills her, and throws her heart to the dogs. Then the woman comes back to "life" as if she had never been injured. Nastagio learns from the spectral knight that the woman's murder is reenacted in the same spot every Friday morning, and he invites his beloved to that spot. She witnesses the same vision and is driven by fear to accept Nastagio as her husband.

Magic and Incantations

Day 7 of the *Decameron* is devoted to stories based on the tricks women play on their husbands either for self-preservation or out of erotic passion, a theme common in medieval popular traditions. In the first tale, Gianni Otterighi is led to believe by his wife that the person tapping on the door is a werewolf; she knows quite well that it is her lover, and she convinces Gianni to exorcise the werewolf with an incantation filled with sexual innuendo. She then orders her husband to spit, an act that according to contemporary folk belief is effective in incantations.

Tale 7, 3 also contains incantations, as well as the custom of *comparatico*, which prohibits sexual union between a godfather and his *comare* (the mother of his godchild) on the ground that it is incestuous (see also 7, 10), a rule that Brother Rinaldo easily ignores. The use of wax images as votive offerings is also recorded here. Popular religion is present in 7, 2, a tale derived from Apuleius (*Metamorphoses* 9, 5–7), and in the "Lover in the Cask" (the fabliau "Du Cuvier"), in which the husband goes home because it is the feast of St. Galeone (the Calendar of Saints, in which every day is a holiday, is a frequent narrative device) just as Peronella, his wife, is receiving her lover. An incantation appears in *novella* 7, 9, in which Lydia makes love to Pyrrhus in a tree and persuades her husband, who witnesses the event, that what he saw with his eyes was a deception caused by the enchanted tree; this is a classic fabliau plot with Eastern sources (AT 1423, "The Enchanted Pear Tree"), also reworked by Chaucer in "The Merchant's Tale." Supernatural elements and the return from the dead are the subject of the last tale of Day 7, in which Tingoccio returns from purgatory to inform his friend Meuccio about conditions in the otherworld. Meuccio learns that there is no special punishment for violating the custom of *comparatico*, that is, for making love to the mother of one's godchild. The incantation element is also found in the *novella* of Donno Gianni (9, 10), who makes his *compare* Pietro believe that by casting a spell he can turn a mare into a fair young maid and vice versa. As the priest proceeds to do this to Gemmata, the fool's wife, by attaching his "tail" (member) to her, Pietro protests and the spell is broken.

Another tale of magic and incantations is that of Diadora and Messer Ansaldo (10, 5), an analog to Chaucer's "Franklin's Tale." Exemplary for the presence of magical beliefs, as well as for allusions to Sabbats, witches, and the cult of Diana, is the *novella* of the tricksters Bruno and Buffalmacco and the prank they play on Master Simone, telling him that their jovial mood and good luck are due to their "going on course," which means "to meet with the witches" (8, 9). Such details demonstrate Boccaccio's familiarity with lore about witches.

Though Boccaccio may seem to ridicule magical practices, he is also a product of an age in which they were part of life and admired by intellectuals, such as Dante and himself. There is a legend, perhaps born from these tales of magic, concerning Boccaccio himself: according to legend, Boccaccio's tomb was demolished and his ashes thrown to the wind. As a necromancer he had a devil that would periodically transport him to Naples to visit his beloved Maria D'Aquino and return him to Certaldo within two hours. On his last flight, hearing the Ave Maria sung at vespers, he gave thanks to God, and the devil dropped him near Certaldo, where he died. There is another popular belief that Boccaccio had the devil build a hill near Certaldo in one night with a bushel of dirt. Then Boccaccio requested a crystal bridge connecting his castle to the hill. The devil found this impossible and instead strangled him the night before the bridge was to be built.

Perhaps the young Boccaccio, author of the *Decameron*, ridiculed and spurned such beliefs, but the older one did not, as can be seen in such later works as *Commento* and the *Corbaccio*. Boccaccio remains constant in his admiration for intelligence, reason, and wit, but also in his wish to represent the nature of medieval people, with all their fears, customs, and beliefs—and that is what he did in narrating these 100 tales, or as he says, "stories or fables or parables or histories or whatever you choose to call them."

See also: Chaucer, Geoffrey; Italian Tradition; *Novella*

References and further reading: See V. Branca's introduction and notes to G. Boccaccio, *Decameron* (1985); F. Canadé Sautman, *La religion du quotidien: Rites et croyance populaire de la fin du moyen âge* (1995); F. Capozzi, "Food and Food Images in the *Decameron*," *Canadian Journal of Italian Studies* 10, no. 34 (1987); M. P. Giardini, *Tradizioni popolari nel* Decameron (1965); C. Gaignebet and J. D. Lajoux, *Art profane et religion populaire au moyen âge* (1985); A. Graf, *Miti, leggende e superstizioni del Medioevo*, vol 2 (1893); M. Marcus, "Cross-Fertilizations: Folklore and Literature in *Decameron* 4, 5," *Italica* 66 (1989). O. Bacchi, *Burle e arti magiche di Giovanni Boccaccio* (1904), and G. Pitrè and S. Salomone-Marino, *Archivio per lo studio delle tradizioni popolari* 12 (1893), present the legendary traditions of Boccaccio as necromancer. See also D. P. Rotunda, *Motif-Index of the Italian Novella* (1942), and J.-C. Schmitt, *Medioevo Superstizioso* (1992).

—*Giuseppe C. Di Scipio*

Doghead [Latin *Cynocephalus*]

Legendary creature with a human body and canine head.

First adequately recorded by the geographer Ctesias (fl. c. 400 B.C.E.) as one of the many "monstrous races" inhabiting India, the *cynocephali* were said to have dogs' heads and to "not use articulate speech, but bark like dogs"; like the other most picturesque "races," the dogheads were assured currency in medieval thought and literature by the dissemination of the so-called *Marvels of the East* text and the associated *Romance of Alexander*, in which the conqueror encounters (and destroys) many of the same monsters. In the mid-twelfth century, a cleric named Ratramnus even wrote an *Epistola de Cynocephalis*.

In art, representations are found as early as the middle of the ninth century: A mid-ninth-century ivory panel carved at Tours depicts the *cynocephalus*—though it receives no specific mention in the Bible—as part of the hierarchy of creatures made on the sixth day; the creature appears in a list below Adam and Eve, of course, but being semihuman, above the register of the brute beasts. As expected, they appear in illustrated manuscripts of the texts mentioned above. They also appear as one of the marginal creatures at the edge of the world on the Hereford *mappamundi* (world map), though curiously, they are here labeled "Gigantes" (giants). This is probably part of the same rationale that gave St. Christopher, traditionally said to be of giant stature, a dog's head in the iconographic schemes that attempt to depict the entire creation, as on the tympanum of the Romanesque church at Vézelay and in the thirteenth-century rose window of the cathedral at Lausanne. From the thirteenth century onward with the inclusion of the "monstrous races" in some bestiaries, they were moralized as representing quarrelsome people and slanderers on account of their inarticulate barking.

A cynocephalus butcher shop, depicted in a woodcut from Lorenz Fries, Uslegung der Carta Marina, *printed at Strassburg in 1527. (New York Public Library, Rare Books Division)*

Perhaps some remnant of the *cynocephalus* tradition lies behind more modern "black dog" legends in which a spectral dog is really a demon in canine form, but as early as 1450 a proclamation against Jack Cade's Rebellion issued by Henry VI accused Cade, among other things, of having "rered up the Devell in semblance of a blak dogge" in his room at Dartford.

See also: Bestiary; Foreign Races; Giants
References and further reading: See J.-P. Migne, *Patrologia Latina,* vol. 121 (Ratramnus, *Epistola de Cynocephalis*); P. Saintyves, "St. Christophe successeur d'Anubis, d'Hermes, et d'Heracles," *Revue anthropologique* 45 (1935); W. Klinger, "Hundsköpfige Gestalten in der antiken und neuzeitlichen Überlieferung," *Bulletin international de l'Académie Polonaise des sciences* (1936); R. Wittköwer, "Marvels-of-the-East," *Journal of the Warburg and Courtauld Institutes* 5 (1942); V. Newall, "The Dog-Headed Saint Christopher," in *Folklore on Two Continents,* ed. N. Burlakoff and C. Lindahl (1981); J. B. Friedman, "The-Marvels-of-the-East Tradition in Anglo-Saxon Art," in *Sources of Anglo-Saxon Culture,* ed. P. E. Szarmach (1986); D. G. White, *Myths of the Dogman* (1991).

—Malcolm Jones

Dragon

A fabulous creature usually described in medieval narratives as a serpent of great size, with wings and a tail, two or four feet, sharp talons, and (often) impenetrable scales and fiery breath.

The dragon figures m̄ost prominently in medieval narratives as an opponent or assailant of human heroes, who typically vanquish the monster. The origins of the dragon are to be found in creation stories and other myths that feature a chthonic monster—that is, a beast born from the earth or living underground. In the ancient Middle East the dragon is associated with life-giving waters; in early-medieval northwest Europe the world-encircling Midgard Serpent (*Midgardsormr*) demarcates between primeval chaos and the inhabited world. In narrative terms, the dragon of medieval folklore exists principally as a monstrous serpent, acting as a vicious opponent of human saints, warriors, and heroes of popular culture. The slaying of a dragon is a desideratum in the careers of many heroic and chivalric figures in medieval literature; though most dragons' human opponents are male, some females—especially female Christian saints—also play a role as slayers or tamers of dragons.

Narratives of the dragon-slayer have been regarded by Joseph Fontenrose and Calvert Watkins as fundamental expressions of an underlying theme in Western mythology—the theme of heroic combat—and Vladimir Propp treated the structure of the folktale version of this myth as basic to the narrative structure of all European märchen, or wonder tales. Motifs associated with the figure of the dragon are indexed as B11, dragon. under the general heading of Mythical Animals. The most important narratives are indexed as tale type AT 300, "The Dragon-Slayer," a plot closely related to AT 301, "The Three Stolen Princesses," some variants of which—notably, in *Beowulf*—include a dragon as one of the monstrous adversaries faced by the hero.

Whereas the etymology of the other Indo-European words for snakes, adders, and other similar creatures derives from their length or means of locomotion, the word *dragon* (Old English *draca*, Middle English *drake*, Old Norse *dreki*, Old High German *trahho*, deriving from Latin *draco*. Greek *drakon*) has been associated with the Indo-European root *derk*, "see," and this is assumed to refer to the dragon's glittering eyes or its sharpness of sight. This may explain the origin of the motif, attested frequently in Hellenic, Italic, and Germanic dragon lore, whereby the dragon functions as the sharp-sighted guardian of something of value, normally a golden object or hoard of objects. The hoard-guarding dragon is commonplace in Germanic folklore, and dragon-slayers' fights with dragons are often part of an attempt to seize the monster's treasure.

Classical Dragon Lore

Sources of medieval dragon lore are to be found in its classical antecedents, where dragons were treated both as supernatural creatures of legend and mythology and as subspecies of the serpentine order. In the classical cosmographies and natural histories of Aelian, Solinus, Pliny, and others, dragons are said to inhabit the known—albeit usually remote—locations in the natural world. They appear frequently in bestiaries and encyclopedic, geographic, and travel literature and also as characters in Greek and Roman fables. Giant worms and winged snakes are described in Herodotus's *Historiae* and in the descriptions of India by Ctesias and Megasthenes (fifth and fourth centuries B.C.E.). Dragons proper are described in numerous works, including Pliny's *Natural History*, Lucan's *Pharsalia*, Isidore of Seville's *Etymologies*, *The Wonders of the East*, Brunetto Latini's *Li livres dou tresor*, Pierre Bersuire's *Ovidius moralizatus*, *Mandeville's Travels*, and Guillaume du Bartas's *Devine Weekes and Works*.

Bestiaries compiled by Gervase of Tilbury, Guillaume le Clerc, Pierre de Beauvais, and Richard de Fournival all contain a section on the dragon; the Old English *Wonders of the East* includes a description of 50-foot-long dragons, and the *Liber monstrorum* (Book of Monsters) includes a description of a giant serpent.

Elaborate narratives of dragons and dragon-slayers in classical mythology include the stories of Jason, Cadmus, Perseus, Hercules, and Apollo; biblical material paralleled in ancient Middle Eastern mythology contributed significantly to the popularity of the dragon in the learned Latin culture of medieval ecclesiastical literature. Texts in all these genres were known throughout Europe in the Middle Ages, and, translated into most of the European vernacular languages, they contributed significantly to the medieval figure of the dragon appearing in folklore and popular literature. Indeed, one of the vexed questions in the study of medieval dragon lore is that of the relationship between learned, classical, and sacred traditions—which were mediated to medieval European culture through written sources—and indigenous, vernacular traditions emerging through oral transmission. The diversity both of the sources of dragon motifs and of the genres, themes, and linguistic and national traditions within which these motifs were elaborated in the Middle Ages has led Lutz Röhrich to conclude that no single unifying formulation can possibly summarize medieval folklore related to the dragon. As a figure of folklore, then, the medieval dragon should be regarded as an amalgamation of indigenous Germanic and Celtic motifs with Christian biblical theological symbolism laid on a foundation of Middle Eastern, Anatolian, and Illyrian cosmogonic and mythographic concepts.

Christian Dragon Lore

The dragon's importance as a medieval popular motif derives in no small part from biblical associations of the dragon with the arch-figure of diabolical evil in the Christian tradition. By a series of mistranslations, three Hebrew words for sea and land monsters hostile to God or the people of God were rendered into various Greek terms by the translators of the Greek Bible and later into Latin by St. Jerome, with the result that medieval readers and hearers of the Bible, particularly of the Psalms and the prophets, interpreted the dragon as a symbol of pride. A fourth term, the Hebrew word for "jackal," was mistranslated as "dragon," and this error is the origin of the long tradition, culminating in the medieval bestiaries, in which the dragon appears as an allegorical symbol for the sin of pride and thus for the original author of pride, Satan. This error lies behind the repeated designation of the "desert wastelands of foreign enemies" as the habitation of dragons in medieval literature, standing for the desolation resulting from a people's wandering from God. The Authorized version of the Bible contains 20 readings of Hebrew words as "dragon."

Dragons appear frequently in medieval saints' lives, the earliest popular narrative genre in the Western European tradition. By the end of the Middle Ages well over 100 saints had been credited with critical encounters with diabolical foes manifest in the form of a dragon or monstrous serpent, including such influential figures as St. Perpetua, St. Anthony of Egypt, St. Margaret of

Antioch, St. Gregory, St. Martin of Tours—and of course St. George. Although many such saints were venerated in local, relatively isolated cults (e.g., in Cornwall, Ireland, and Scotland), a significant number are canonical saints with genuinely international reputations and associated paraphernalia—visual, ritual, votive, and literary—indicating the widespread influence of the dragon as a figure of popular belief not only within the culture of ecclesiastical learning but also in the lay population. Among them, St. Martha seems to have been quite popular in early-medieval Provence, where a body of legend and Rogation-tide (i.e., the three days before Ascension Day) ritual surrounding the saint survived into the twentieth century in the form of an annual procession in which the vanquished monster was displayed amid celebration.

By far the most famous dragon-slaying saint is George of Cappadocia, whose rescue of a condemned maiden was translated again and again in late-medieval literature largely as a result of the immensely popular thirteenth-century *Legenda aurea* (The Golden Legend) of Jacobus de Voragine. George's adventure against the dragon, set in Libya, is a relatively late (probably late-eleventh- or early-twelfth-century) addition to the martyr's legend. Scholars have not determined precisely how the episode of the dragon became attached to the martyr, but it would appear that St. George's legend was amalgamated either with the figure of the dragon-slayer from medieval romance or with the figure of Perseus, whose seaside rescue of Andromeda bears an unmistakable resemblance to George's rescue of the doomed maiden from the dragon.

Germanic and Celtic Dragon Lore

The richest vein of medieval dragon lore is to be found in the epic/heroic and romance traditions that flourished in northwest Europe in the Germanic languages, where the legendary figure of Sigurd/Siegfried is regarded as the most renowned of the dragon-slayers. The earliest reference to this legend appears in Old English, in a digression early in *Beowulf*, whose date has been placed by scholars anywhere from the eighth to the tenth century: the hero—himself a dragon-slayer in his final adventure—is compared favorably with Sigurd's father, Sigemund, said by the poet to be the supreme hero of the north. Later literary accounts ascribe the dragon adventure to the more famous son, whose unsurpassed reputation for heroic valor is echoed in *Völsunga Saga*. A different version of the story is extant in *Thidrek's Saga*, which contains Continental Germanic legend and folklore of a provenance almost as early as that of *Beowulf*. A large number of poetic allusions to Sigurd, slayer of the dragon Fafnir, in Old Norse skaldic verse attests to widespread familiarity with the legend, as do a similar number of runic and monumental stone and wood carvings from medieval Scandinavia and the British Isles. Besides Sigurd and Beowulf in the Old Norse and Old English traditions, dragon-slayers and associated dragon lore may be found in scores of Old Norse prose and poetic narratives in addition to those mentioned above, especially the *Poetic Edda* and the *Prose Edda* of Snorri Sturluson. The Latin narratives in Saxo Grammaticus's *Gesta Danorum* give accounts of the dragon fights of Frotho, Fridlevus, and Harold Hardraada. The last of these, the Norwegian King Harold, is associated with dragons in several episodes not included by Snorri Sturluson in the *Heimskringla*—including the

Icelandic tale of "Thorstein the Over-Curious" and two adventures of Prince Harold in Byzantium.

Dragons appear under Vortigern's castle in the works of Geoffrey of Monmouth and Gervase of Tilbury, in the work attributed to Nennius, in Ranulf Higden's *Polychronicon*, and in the *Roman de Brut* as well as in the *Alliterative Morte Arthure* and Malory's *Morte Darthur*, where Lancelot, Tristram (Tristan), and Yvain all are described as dragon-slayers. King Arthur's dream of the airborne battle between a dragon and a boar is interpreted by "a wise philosopher" as representing the conflict between Arthur's Welsh forces and "some tyrant." Other dragon-slayers in medieval English romance include Beves of Hampton, Guy of Warwick, Sir Torrent of Portyngale, Sir Degaré, Tom á Lincolne, Sir Eglamour of Artois, and the Knight of Curtesy as well as St. George, whose sacred legend was revised repeatedly along the generic lines of medieval romance. Dragons appear in all major vernacular manifestations of the Tristan legend. In *Sir Gawain and the Green Knight*, the eponymous hero fights "with wyrmes" [against dragons] among the other malevolent beings set to waylay him in his journey through Logres (line 720).

The motif indexes typically catalog various elements of dragon lore under several main headings, including the origin, form, habitat, and habits of dragons. As to form, dragons appear generally as serpentine creatures of immense size, capable of swallowing human beings and large animals whole. Their origins are seldom described, though several Old Norse sagas refer to broods of young dragons reminiscent of the offspring of nesting birds. The dragon is generally described as a large serpent with two wings, two clawed feet, and a lashing tail. The dragon in the legend of St. Martha is a composite of physiognomic

Lancelot kills a dragon, from William Copland's 1557 edition of Le Morte Darthur. *(British Library)*

features of bird, bear, fish, ox, lion, and viper. The medieval encyclopedic tradition (represented, e.g., in Isidore of Seville's *Etymologies*) ascribes the dragon's main offensive strength to its tail; in other sources, however, either poisonous or fiery breath constitutes the monster's main offensive weapon. For defense the dragon relies on its horny or scaly hide; in some instances its imperviousness to iron weapons is attributed to supernatural or magical power. In a number of instances, including the Sigurd texts and episodes in *Gull-Thorir's Saga*, *Ector's Saga*, and *Ragnar's Saga*, the dragon is a human who has been transformed into monstrous shape either through greed or through a curse placed upon the treasure that the dragon possesses. This feature seems to suggest the influence of Old Norse folklore concerning the *draugar* or *haugbúar*—otherworldly human revenants appearing sometimes as the inhabitants of grave mounds in repose with priceless burial goods.

Dragons as Guardians of Treasure

The motif of the dragon guarding treasure is found in ancient Greek mythology and classical Latin legend, and it seems to be central to the Germanic folklore concerning the creature: Fafnir, the dragon slain by Sigurd, is the greedy possessor of a cursed treasure seized by Loki, Hœnir, and Odin from the hoard of the dwarf Andvari; so also is the dragon slain by Beowulf—Sigurd's counterpart among the legendary northern heroes. Fafnir, Sigurd's draconian enemy, is motivated by greed to murder his father and take the treasure his father had extorted from Loki for the murder of Fafnir's brother Otr. The treasure is cursed by its original owner, and whoever comes to possess it dies violently—until the Nibelungs cast it into the Rhine forever.

Beowulf's treasure also seems to have this same sort of curse on it. Even though he possesses it only briefly, it seems to have something to do with his death and with the decline of his people the Geats (who wisely bury most of it and burn some of it on Beowulf's pyre). An Anglo-Saxon proverb from the Old English poetic Cotton Maxims says "the dragon shall [be] on the mound, old, exultant in treasure," and a similar gnomic passage in *Beowulf* repeats the observation; a marginal gloss in a fifteenth-century codex of Icelandic law says "Just as the dragon loves the gold, so does the greedy love ill-gotten gain." Treasure-guarding dragons appear twice in *Ector's Saga*, and in the fourteenth-century *Konrad's Saga* the hero undertakes a quest to an otherworldly castle filled with treasure-guarding dragons in order to acquire jewels as part of a bride-price.

Combat with Dragons

Motivations for the hero's fight with a dragon are various, deriving from characteristic attributes and habits ascribed to dragons themselves. Friedrich Panzer divides these into two broad categories: fights with dragons to relieve a people or nation from the dragons' attacks; fights to acquire treasure. The dragon episode at the end of *Beowulf* represents a combination of these two motifs. Dragonslayers achieve their goal through a variety of methods and instruments. In the St. George legend the episode is typically depicted in iconography with the saint impaling the monster with a lance or spear through its mouth; in the

Sigurd narratives and in stone and wood pictographs throughout Scandinavia and the British Isles the hero—sometimes instructed by Odin—digs a trench in the dragon's path and from this position stabs the dragon's underbelly with a sword. Elsewhere in Germanic legend the dragon is impervious to weapons except for a special spot on the underside of its torso; this is the point of entry where Wiglaf's ancient, giant-made sword penetrates the dragon in *Beowulf*. A number of Old Norse sagas identify a vulnerable spot on the left wing or along the spinal ridge.

In the Middle English *Sir Degaré*, the hero beats the monster to pieces with a wooden club. In Icelandic hagiography, Bishop Gudmund sprinkles holy water on a dragon/sea monster, which then bursts into 12 pieces and washes ashore. In later Icelandic popular romance, heroes and their helpers engage in elaborate machinations to reach dragons in their remote places of habitation. Rewards for slaying dragons often include not only treasure but also a bride and possession of part of an afflicted kingdom. The Welsh narrative *Owain*, the Old French *Yvain*, and the Old Icelandic *Iven's Saga* share an episode in which the hero slays a dragon that has a lion gripped in its claws and the coils of its tail. Afterward the lion becomes a sort of mascot and traveling companion of the hero, accompanying him on subsequent adventures. In Old Icelandic this story found its way from *Iven's Saga* into several other sagas as well. While most medieval heroes slay the dragons they encounter, the saints of medieval hagiography frequently banish the monster to deserts or wastelands. Jacques Le Goff regards this as the narrative expression of ritual cleansing of a pagan geographical site for Christian occupation. Paul Sorrell applies this insight to *Beowulf*.

In *Thidrek's Saga* the king is captured by a dragon, flown to the dragon's nest deep in a remote forest, dropped among the dragon's brood, dismembered, and eaten. Beowulf is successful only with the help of his retainer Wiglaf and is himself mortally wounded. Dragon-slayers protect themselves from dragons' fire and poison by various means, including sable-lined cloaks, shields covered with ox hide, and tar-soaked fur breeches; in *Ector's Saga*, Fenacius receives a magical ointment from a cave-dwelling dwarf, which protects him from injury. The swords with which heroes slay dragons are sometimes legendary or magical swords; the one with which Wiglaf delivers the strategic blow in *Beowulf* is an *ealdsweord eotonisc* (giant-made ancient sword), required to penetrate the monster's otherwise impervious scales.

The great body of traditional lore and legend surrounding dragons waned at the end of the Middle Ages even as the figure of St. George the dragon-slayer came to be an extremely popular embodiment of Renaissance chivalric and aristocratic ideals. Ulisse Aldrovandi's *Serpentum et draconum historiae libri duo* (Two Books on the History of Serpents and Dragons, 1640), though post-medieval, is the last great compendium of popular and learned lore passed down through the Middle Ages.

See also: *Beowulf*; Bestiary; George, Saint; Scandinavian Tradition
References and further reading: Bibliographic material related to the study of dragons in medieval folklore includes several important indexes: in addition to S. Thompson's *Motif-Index* (1955–1958), G. Bordman's *Motif-Index of the English Metrical Romances*, Folklore

Fellows Communications 190 (1963); I. M. Boberg's *Motif-Index of Early Icelandic Literature* (1968); and T. P. Cross's *Motif-Index of Early Irish Literature* (1952) all treat dragon motifs. J. F. Campbell's *The Celtic Dragon Myth* (1911) ascribes medieval origins to a folktale gathered in Scotland in the nineteenth century, making useful connections with the Old Irish narrative of *Bricriu's Feast*. V. Propp's theories on the structure and theory of folktales are found in *The Morphology of the Folktale* (1968) and *Theory and History of the Folktale* (1984). Two comprehensive studies, though old, are still useful: E. Ingersoll, *Dragons and Dragon Lore* (1928), and G. E. Smith, *The Evolution of the Dragon* (1919). Another classic study is F. Panzer, *Studien zur germanische Sagengeschichte*, vol. 1: *Beowulf* (1910). See also J. Evans, "The Dragon," in *Mythical and Fabulous Creatures: A Source Book and Research Guide*, ed. M. South (1987). Much better is J. Fontenrose, *Python: A Study of Delphic Myth and Its Origins* (1959), which is comprehensive and indispensable. C. Watkins, *How to Kill a Dragon in Indo-European* (1995), examines the Indo-European deep-linguistic structure of the poetic formula of dragon-slaying and is highly specialized. L. C. Kordecki, "Traditions and Developments of the Medieval English Dragon," Ph.D. diss., University of Toronto (1980), gives the best overview of antecedents in the encyclopedias, bestiaries, and travel literature and developments in medieval English literature, but unfortunately it remains unpublished. A. Orchard, *Pride and Prodigies* (1995), gives insights into medieval monster lore, including the dragon in *Beowulf*, the *Liber monstrorum*, and related texts. E. S. Hartland, *The Legend of Perseus: A Study of Tradition in Story, Custom, and Belief*, 3 vols. (1894–1896; rpt. 1973), is important for the Perseus/Andromeda legend and connections to the St. George material. J. Lionarons's *The Germanic Dragon* (1998) is brief and brilliant. Sacred traditions contributing to the dragon in hagiography are treated in Paul Sorrell, "The approach to the Dragon-fight in *Beowulf*," *Paragon* 12 (1994) and N. K. Kiessling, "Antecedents of the medieval Dragon in Sacred History," *Journal of Biblical Literature* 89 (1970). J. Day, *God's Conflict with the Dragon and the Sea* (1988), develops the ancient Semitic traditions contributing to Medieval Christian dragon lore. Hagiography and hagiographic imagery associating various saints with dragon opposition may be gathered from A. Maury, *Croyances et légendes du moyen âge* (1896; rpt. 1974), and C. Cahier, *Charactéristiques des saints dans l' art populaire*, 2 vols. (1867; rpt., 1966, 1981) and C. Rauer, *Beowulf and the Dragon* (2000). Specific details of the St. Martha legend, including both medieval manifestations and modern survivals, are developed in L. Dumont, *La tarasque*, 2nd ed. (1987). St. George has been discussed widely in scholarly and popular studies, including J. E. Matzke, "Contributions to the History of the Legend of St. George," *Publications of the Modern Language Association* 17 (1902), 18 (1903), and 19 (1904), and J. B. Aufhauser, *Das Drachenwunder des Heiligen Georg* (1911). B. Meyers, "St. George and the Dragon," Ph.D. diss., New York University (1933), provides useful material on medieval pictorial representations of the legend. The motif of taking the dragon's tongue as a trophy is examined by S. Eisner in *The Tristan Legend* (1969), and the motif of the treasure-hoarding dragon is the subject of several important studies, including, for classical antecedents, M. P. Nilsson, "The Dragon on the Treasure," *American Journal of Philology* 68 (1947).

—*Jonathan Evans*

Drama

A performance genre that in the Middle Ages included popular mystery cycles and morality plays, both drawing heavily on traditional character types and comic rituals.

Earlier scholars of medieval drama tended to perpetuate a rather simple evolutionary model of development, according to which a simple speech in the Easter matins liturgy marked the birth of the genre. In the tenth century church performances began to elaborate upon the words spoken by the angel in Christ's tomb: "*Quem quaeritis?*" [Whom do you seek?]. From these elaborations, more complex liturgical dramas evolved and eventually passed into the vernaculars, yielding the great Mystery Cycles and Passion, and saints plays of the fifteenth and sixteenth centuries. Like its biological equivalent, this evolutionary model has been replaced by one of greater complexity and more discontinuity. Instead of a smooth line of upward development, we now recognize a pattern of radical bursts of activity followed by periods of relative inactivity. We must also give far more attention to various secular (i.e., nonclerical) influences, obscure though they tend to be, upon the growth and development of medieval sacred drama and eventually the Renaissance professional stage.

Foundations of Profane Drama

One must begin with the fall of the Roman Empire and the end of a vast "entertainment industry" that had penetrated to every corner of the empire. Numerous theaters, amphitheaters, and circuses existed even in frontier regions such as Britain. What happened to the myriad personnel of this entertainment industry in the so-called Dark Ages? It is quite likely that a substantial proportion of these performers continued their trade in some fashion in the new barbarian regimes and created future generations of entertainers. We have a thin but constant stream of references to *mimi, ioculari,* and *histriones* for the early Middle Ages, a good number of these gathered by E. K. Chambers in his magisterial *The Mediæval Stage* (1903) and by Allardyce Nicoll in *Masks, Mimes, and Miracles* (1931).

These predominantly clerical records are, of course, of a negative sort, and we can also find a constant theme in later exemplum literature of saintly opposition to popular entertainers. How these shadowy professional entertainers related to the bards, minstrels, and jesters of the indigenous Celtic, Germanic, and Slavic traditions is a matter of almost total speculation, but some interaction, some coalescence there must have been. Attempts to prove the existence of fully developed theater (ritual dramas of combat or wooing, the antics of "sacred clowns," etc.) for the pagan cultures of Europe have not been very convincing. Yet the clerical record also reveals the persistence of uproarious animal masquerades (particularly horse, stag, and bull), especially during the midwinter season, which may well be pagan survivals. (The well-known illuminations for the *Roman de Fauvel* show a range of such animal masks in performance.)

Even if we cannot point to very much in the way of pagan Celtic or Germanic performance directly influencing the dramatic traditions of early-medieval Europe, it is quite clear that by the tenth century—that is, when the dramatic molecule of the *Quem quaeritis* trope was supposedly re-creating drama all over again out of nothing—there was a considerable body of popular theater (if not of scripted dramatic texts) that began almost at once to interact with the so-called liturgical drama. In this fusion we can perhaps detect two separate if intertwined types of profane dramatic activity: (1) that bearing the earmarks of professional itinerant players, and (2) that rising more directly from community needs and a communal theatrical/mimetic impulse geared to the yearly cycle and not dependent on professional performers. Thus, there existed a "professional" and a "folk" popular theater, both of which interacted with and influenced the sacred drama of the Church and later that of lay organizations.

We must also bear in mind, however, the existence of certain universals of popular theater and physical comedy, based on deprivation (especially hunger), pain, and physical or symbolic humiliation; these can crop up in just about any context, including the sacred. After all, the Christian liturgy itself (particularly the Magnificat verse "He has put down the mighty from their thrones, and has raised high the lowly" [Luke 1:52]) gave rise to such quasi-dramatic, *monde renversé* events as the Feast of the Ass or Feast of Fools in certain French cathedrals. If we examine the play texts of Hrosvitha (c. 1000), the Saxon nun who produced edifying "dramatic" works for her convent of Gandersheim, we notice not only the literary influence of Terence but also certain elements of low comedy. In *Dulcitius*, for example, the evil governor on his way to violate his female Christian prisoners winds up befuddled in the kitchen, hugging and kissing the sooty pots and pans, and presenting a ridiculous spectacle to his own astonished guards. Some 400 years later in one of the earliest vernacular farces, the Dutch *sotternien* (sot play) entitled *Die Buskenblaser* (The Boxblower), a dumb peasant, returning from the sale of his cow, is tricked by a mountebank into trading his silver for a magic box that will restore his wife's desire for him. He must blow into the box, which is full of powdered charcoal, and he thus renders himself a sooty "devil" when he believes he has become irresistibly handsome. There is no need to speculate on influence here, from Hrosvitha's book Latin to the vernacular Dutch, as we are clearly dealing with a kind of "universal grammar" of the laughable. Sooting up, moreover, remains one of the most available disguises (as well as a threat to spectators) for folk masqueraders of all sorts up to the present time. Its associations with the demonic, anarchic, or the sexually "dirty" are what we might call archetypal.

"Professional" Influences

The influence of professionals may be detected quite early on in the liturgical drama. We have the curious example of the Mercator episode in that most central and sacred of the sacred dramas, the Easter play. On the slim basis of Mark 16:1 ("When the Sabbath was over Mary Magdalene, Mary the Mother of James, and Salome bought aromatic oils so that they could come and anoint him [Jesus]"), an unguent seller entered the Latin liturgical drama. By the fourteenth century, in the German Easter plays, the figure had acquired a brace of servants and a wife, and his dramatic action had evolved into a virtually independent farce. The Mercator scene, for example, takes up at least 40 percent of the Easter play from Innsbruck (c. 1390), and it has little thematic justification for so dominating the sacred story (unlike the Mak episode in the Wakefield Master's *Second Shepherd's Play*, for example). This irrepressible mountebank scene, moreover, must surely have reflected something of mercantile performances in real life. In other words, theater and life were already influencing each other through the figure of the itinerant "professional."

Mercator and his servant Rubin in the Easter play are paralleled by a similar pair in the earliest recorded vernacular farce, *Le garcon et l'aveugle* (The Boy and the Blind Man) of late-thirteenth-century France. The physical demands of this piece are minimal, and its story line is absolutely basic—the victimization of the testy blind man by the cheeky servant. It probably represents part of the repertory of an itinerant, nuclear acting company: the *histrion* and his boy apprentice. By the late fifteenth century, we can be certain of full acting companies responsible for such pieces as the famous English morality play *Mankind* (c. 1470). Scholars of early English drama have often remarked on the seriously competing aspects of moral teaching and popular entertainment in this work. A strong vein of decidedly low comedy centers upon the three outrageously costumed vices, New Guise, Nowadays, and Nought, who stage what appears to be a mock bear-baiting-*cum*-dance, then a scatological Christmas carol involving audience participation, and finally a collection from the audience before bringing on the final "thrill" of the performance, the appearance of the devil Titivillus himself. With these obvious "crowd-pleasing" shenanigans, the play was evidently the property of a wandering company of five or six professional actors. Scholars have pointed out that the demanding roles of Mercy and Titivillus could well have been doubled by the lead actor of the troupe. In the Elizabethan play *Sir Thomas More* (c. 1595) we have a scene reflecting this earlier practice. A small troupe of Moral Interlude players, "four men and a boy" (for all the female roles), present themselves and their repertory to the chancellor. A similar scene, of course, occurs in Shakespeare's *Hamlet*, but there the company has a decidedly Renaissance repertory.

"Folk" and Communal Influences

Shakespeare's other famous play-within-a-play is also our touchstone for early amateur theatricals. Although Pyramus and Thisbe is a tragic Renaissance theme, the "rude mechanicals" who perform the story in *A Midsummer's Night Dream* reflect something of medieval practice, although the naivete of their representation no doubt reflects the later professional theater man's sense of easy superiority. Medieval Latin liturgical drama (monastic or ecclesiastic) reached its peak of development in the late twelfth century, but only in a relatively limited area, and it can be argued that it represented an evolutionary dead end. The thirteenth century is relatively bare of dramatic texts, but when a vibrant literary theater reemerges in the fourteenth century it is in the new vernaculars and for the most part in the hands of the laity. Various organs of urban lay power became the producing agents for this second wave of medieval drama. Craft guilds were crucial in the development of the extended cycles of mystery plays in the English cities of York, Chester, Coventry, and elsewhere, whereas lay religious confraternities were more often responsible for theater production on the Continent. Both infused into religious drama artisanal and bourgeois values and interests, including substantial elements of low comedy and folk material. Comic figures, partly based on realistic observation, partly on venerable types of the folktale, are found throughout the sacred vernacular plays. The Wakefield Cain, a foul-mouthed, miserly, malcontented plowman, acquires a lovable wacky servant, Garcio; in a sense, the play gives us the two faces of the Trickster figure. Other contemporary workmen bitch and moan for grotesque effect, for example, the clumsy, incompetent carpenter-soldiers of the York Crucifixion. Shrewish women are everywhere, from Noah's wife, who exchanges blows with her husband, to the Chester alewife hauled off to hell in the Last Judgment for her short measures, to the blacksmith's wife in a Parisian Passion play who, in order not to lose a sale, takes it upon herself to forge the nails of the Crucifixion. Even saints could be handled popularly (and ambiguously). St. Joseph, almost always portrayed as a *senex* (old man) in the medieval period, might rant and rave like the cuckolded husband of a fabliau, or, as in the German tradition, he might behave like a doddering fool, blowing on the fire and stirring up porridge for Baby Jesus or rinsing out his diapers.

Marginal types are also common. A whole tavern full of thieves and gamblers is vividly presented in Jean Bodel's *Jeu de Saint Nicholas* (c. 1200). Mak in the Wakefield Master's *Second Shepherd's Play* with his larcenous nocturnal lurkings, his wolf-skin clothing and magic spells, together with his fecund "dirty bride," Gill, represents a kind of residual pagan of the medieval hinterlands. On the other end of the spectrum, lordly figures—Herod, Pharaoh, and Pilate particularly—pushed tyrannical language to near-absurd extremes and approached the intensity of the *diableries*, the comic performance of the devils themselves. These latter were immensely popular, with their roaring, obscene speech, "rough music," acrobatics, pyrotechnics, and periodic assaults upon the audience. They were prime examples of the "threat-deflated" model of the laughable and were no doubt related to and perhaps influenced by archaic rural performances of the winter season, which featured the intrusions of anarchic, ugly, masked figures, whether these were imagined as the "old gods" demonized or more purely biblical figures of evil. Extensive *diableries* were characteristic of many French and German religious dramas, whether appropriate or not to the action. Generally, however, the comic figures and episodes in the vernacular religious drama were subsumed in the larger purpose of presenting sacred history. They might be used for sophisticated iconographic play (for example, Mak's stolen lamb in the cradle parodies the *Agnus Dei*), or to make a wry theological point vis-à-vis unredeemed humankind (for example, Noah's wife, dragged kicking and screaming into the safety of the Ark), or simply as negative exempla in more generalized moral teaching.

While this comic leavening was rising in the vernacular sacred drama, purely secular plays were, not surprisingly, also developing, and under similar circumstances. Paralleling the lay religious confraternities were a variety of secular organizations, often related to them, that turned out seasonal and other occasional entertainments such as greetings to noble visitors. A remarkable body of early plays emerged from the Confrérie des Jongleurs et des Bourgeois d'Arras. One of these, Adam de la Halle's *Jeu de la feuillée* (Play of the Leafy Bower, c. 1280) was evidently a Maytide entertainment in which a cross section of Arras townspeople, including the author himself, set up a bower to entertain the Queen of the Fairies. Morgan le Fay and her entourage duly arrive and interact with the mortals. A raving idiot also weaves in and out of the scene, supplying a different kind of entertainment. The play is an intriguing intersection of bourgeois lifeways, aristocratic romance, and rural folklore.

Secular drama was more frequently found indoors, however, during the winter or "festival" half of the year (roughly November to March). The societies of French law clerks, the Basoche, were responsible for many of the classic early farces (and particularly that masterpiece of legal double-dealing, *Pierre Pathelin*), all probably entertainments for holidays in term time. Such organizations also spawned actual fool societies, such as Les Enfants sans Souci, which developed not only parades of motley antics but also a type of very topical satirical review called the *sottie*. Similar developments occurred in the Low Countries, leading to a wide variety of dramatic forms there—farces, romances, moralities, even experiments with the play-within-the-play—and the development of important performance-oriented literary guilds, the Chambers of Rhetoric.

Drama at Christmastime was particularly popular in cathedral schools and the later colleges and universities, as were such parodic ceremonies as that of the Boy Bishop, which arose from the feast of the patron of children, St. Nicholas (December 6) or the Feast of the Holy Innocents (December 28). A late example of such school drama embodying the mock-king motif is *The Christmas Prince* staged at St. John's College, Oxford, in 1607.

Carnival was another, relatively late focus for communal theater. The French were fond of *sermons joyeux* praising mock saints based on festival foods—Saint Jambon (Ham), Saint Andouille (Chitterling), Saint Oignon (Onion), and so on. The Italian tradition had dramatized Combats of Carnival and Lent, for example, the fifteenth-century *Rappresentazione et Festa di Carnasciale et della Quaresima*. Several German cities evolved their own bodies of Carnival drama, Nuremberg being the most prolific among them. Members of the prestigious Nuremberg Meistersinger guild, such as Hans Rosenplüt or Hans Folz, would also toss off crude sketches *(Fastnachtspiele)* for the Carnival season. Apart from the occasional literary themes essayed, these dramatic efforts directly reflected the festival process itself. Overindulgence and uproarious behavior were the subject matter, with the dramatic situations typically involving diagnoses by quack doctors, mock trials, or ridiculous competitions. The plays were dominated by the figure of the violent, stupid, and gluttonous *Bauer* (peasant), a favorite festival disguise of the urban-dwellers. In the following century Hans Sachs attempted to tame the often wittily obscene and scatological *Fastnachtspiele* in the interests of the new Reformation. His *Das Narrenschneiden* (Fool Surgery) of 1536 delivers a serious sermon on the seven deadly sins, who are imagined, however, as embryonic Fools, a kind of worm infestation, in the bloated belly of a Carnivalist. The Fools (evidently little puppets) are removed in a slapstick surgical operation by a traditionally extravagant quack doctor and his cheeky servant. The piece thus exemplifies the tensions between moral teaching and untrammeled festival entertainment in the theatrical life of the early modern city.

It is harder to trace the forms of popular theater in the medieval countryside, given the limitations and fragmentary nature of the evidence. Pieter Brueghel the Elder's painting *The Combat of Carnival and Lent* (1559) is set in a Flemish village and is a major piece of visual evidence in this area. The central figures of Carnival and Lent and their burlesque combat may be more fantasy than strict reportage, but the surrounding figures evidently accurately reflect the masking and theatrical practice of the folk. We notice bag and other improvised masks, false noses made of hollowed-out tubers, the wearing of food items (waffles) and cooking utensils, and "rough music" on gridirons and rummel pots (rummel is a mixture of grains). On the peripheries of the crowded canvas one notices actual play scenes. One is a procession of a Warrior, an Emperor, and a shaggy Wild Man, identified as the story of Orson and Valentine, which also shows a collection being taken up among the spectators. Another scene, identified as "The Marriage of Mopsus and Nissa" or "The Dirty Bride," features a pair of grotesque lovers and a very makeshift "set," evidently the shelter in which they consummate their love. Other scenes of rural folk performance can be found in other Brueghel works, particularly his *Kermis* (church anniversary) scenes. *The Fair at Hoboken* engraving shows a small booth stage on barrel tops for a cuckolding farce performance, and *The Fair of St. George's Day* (i.e., April 23) shows an enactment of the dragon-slaying, with the smallish monster built on a kind of wheelbarrow.

England provides an example of actual folk-play texts in the Robin Hood plays performed as part of parish fund-raising May games in the early sixteenth century. These were directly derived from the medieval Robin Hood ballads, evidently through the new medium of print. They involved few impersonations, but they featured large set combat scenes and morris dances. Despite extravagant claims for the antiquity of the English mummers' play, another combat-based sketch performed as a perambulation at Christmastime, its origins cannot be pushed back much beyond this first age of popular print culture.

Keeping the Brueghel scenes in mind, it should be clear that rural folk drama and the more sophisticated artistic expressions of the urban centers were not mutually exclusive; rather, they influenced each other constantly. The countryside was not remote from the medieval town, either in physical distance or in outlook. The *Romance of Valentine and Orson* could "devolve" into a village play at holiday time. But conversely, the figure of the Wild Man in the romance might well have been influenced by earlier folk enactments. In that quintessentially urban farce *Pierre Pathelin,* with its drapers and law courts and fast-talking shyster hero, the last word is given to a smelly shepherd who turns the tables on the trickster by resorting to his "natural" language, the baa-ing of a sheep.

Folk material, or more narrowly the popular character type and the grotesque comic situation, passed into the religious drama of Europe in large doses through many conduits over the centuries. At the same time, and under the same impulses, a profane drama flourished and gradually became professionalized. Both streams merged (as in the *Mankind* example) and helped create the glories of the professional Renaissance stage. The religious drama, in turn, was taken up by the folk when it faded in the centers of power in the Early Modern period, and it remains today one of the living legacies of the Middle Ages. From the Mexican *Pastores* (Shepherds' play) to the Tyrolean *Nicholausspiele* (St. Nicholas play), an essentially medieval drama lives, as it has always done, with its complement of Wild Men, demons, tricksters, dolts, and capering fools. Even in urban America one can find the phenomenon. The Hungarian neighborhood church of St. Stephen in Toledo, Ohio, annually stages a Bethlehem play on Christmas Eve in which an axe-wielding, fur-clad monster also raises his ugly voice in the sanctuary but is ultimately brought tamely to the crib of the Christ Child.

See also: Carnival; Festivals and Celebrations; Fool; George, Saint; Robin Hood
References and further reading: The classic study of medieval drama and its social contexts is E. K. Chambers, *The Mediaeval Stage*, 2 vols. (1903; rpt. 1978). This should now be

supplemented with more-recent scholarship treating specific aspects of this broad field, including R. Axton, *European Drama of the Early Middle Ages* (1974); E. Catholy, *Fastnachtspiel* (1966); G. Frank, *The Medieval French Drama* (1954); H. G. Harvey, *The Theatre of the Basoche: The Contribution of the Law Societies to French Mediaeval Comedy* (1941); J. Heers, *Fêtes de fous et Carnavals* (1983); A. Nicholl, *Masks, Mimes, and Miracles: Studies in the Popular Theatre* (1931); E. Simon, ed., *The Theatre of Medieval Europe: New Research in Early Drama* (1991); M. Twycross, ed., *Festive Drama* (1996); and D. Wiles, *The Early Plays of Robin Hood* (1981).

Among the attempts to reconstruct a pagan theater are B. Phillpotts, *The Elder Edda and Ancient Scandinavian Drama* (1920), and a recent examination of the same field, T. Gunnell, *The Origins of Drama in Scandinavia* (1995). On the mumming plays, see A. Brody, *The English Mummers and Their Plays: Traces of an Ancient Mystery,* 1969.

—Martin Walsh

Dreams and Dream Poetry

Often interpreted in the Middle Ages as supernatural messages or as forecasts of future events; frequently represented in poetry, or even as a poetic form in its own right, throughout medieval literature.

According to modern psychology, dreams arise from the unconscious and have reference to the dreamer's past. Medieval thinkers knew of such dreams, but these were only one kind in a hierarchy of dream types, and not a particularly valuable one at that. The dreams that were valued in the Middle Ages were those believed to come from supernatural sources and to have reference to future events. There were some who were skeptical of divination by means of dreams on philosophical grounds, but most medieval thinkers who mistrusted dreams did so because they believed the supernatural source of dreams to be the devil far more often than God. The interpretation of dreams was also a cornerstone of medieval medicine, and the value that was placed on the phenomenon of dreaming at the time is reflected in the frequency and importance of dreams in medieval literature as a whole.

Sources

Medieval Christian attitudes toward dreaming have roots in several sources, including the Bible, Greco-Roman antiquity, and Celtic and Germanic cultures—as well as influences from beyond Europe itself. The notions inherited from these sources were contradictory, and medieval speculation on dreams is characterized by an attempt to reconcile them.

Dreams are an important aspect of biblical narrative, in which they are portrayed as the sacred breaking into the profane realm, as a major means by which God talks to or makes his will known to his people. The majority of references to dreams and dreaming in the Bible are positive, but there are also passages critical of dream interpretation, particularly in those books traditionally called Wisdom literature. Medieval exegetes struggled to reconcile the examples of Daniel and Joseph with specific prohibitions and condemnations of dreams, such as that in Lev. 19:26.

Dream interpretation, or oneirology, was such a highly valued art in the Greco-Roman world that the Church, especially in the early-medieval period, tended to regard it as a pagan trait and was suspicious of the practice. Dream incubation, or sleeping in a temple to induce dream visions, was condemned, but the practice continued through the Middle Ages at the shrines of saints. Moreover, much pagan philosophical speculation about dreams remained important, and the classification of dream types in general use in the Roman Empire was held throughout much of the Middle Ages. Antique oneirology reached its acme and was crystallized in the writings of Artemidorus (second century C.E.) and the Neoplatonic Macrobius (c. 360–422), which were of crucial importance in medieval dream theory. Artemidorus was known only indirectly, so much of the practical and theoretical material in his *Oneirocritica*, a manual of dream interpretation, may not have been known, but the symbols found in this book form the ultimate source of medieval dreambooks such as the *Somniale Danielis* (Dreambook of Daniel), though in a vastly simplified alphabetical listing. Macrobius's *Commentary on the Dream of Scipio* was the most important work on dreams known and used in the Middle Ages, and in it can be found the authoritative fivefold classification of dreams used through the period: the *somnium* (symbolic dream), the prophetic *visio* (vision), the *oraculum* (oracular dream), the *insomnium* (nightmare), and the *visum* (apparition). Apparitions and nightmares were not deemed worthy of notice, but the other three kinds of dreams were believed capable of foretelling the future. Oracles and visions do this directly, but enigmatic or symbolic dreams require interpretation.

Early Christian Transformations

According to Jacques Le Goff, there are two crucial periods in the formation of medieval Christian dream theory—the second through seventh centuries, and then again in the twelfth—and only after the first period were Celtic and Germanic influences felt. Of the two influences at play in the earlier period, the classical seems to have been stronger than the biblical. Angels appeared in biblical dreams, but there were no demons or dead people, and these are very common elements of many recorded early-Christian dreams. Furthermore, Christian dreams were used to interpret the future, whereas biblical ones served only to put the dreamer in contact with God. In oneirology, as in many other areas of thought, the Church Fathers simply put a Christian cloak on pagan philosophy. By the time of Pope Gregory the Great (540–614), however, there is evidence of a belief not present in pagan philosophy, that of a general correspondence between the truth value and the source of a dream. Gregory warns that only saints can tell if a dream is sent by God or by demons. This important development in Christian dream theory was a moral one. It was now necessary to know not just whether a dream was true or false but whether it was a revelation or a temptation. Earlier thinkers, including Augustine, had held that individuals were not morally responsible for the content of their dreams, but this had changed by the time of Isidore of Seville (c. 560–636), who believed demons had God's permission to drag dreamers through the terrors of hell, both to punish and to test them. Irish penitential manuals of the seventh century also indicate that from this time on dreamers were held culpable for the sexuality of their dreams.

In sum, Christian thinkers' faith in dreams tended to weaken in the early Middle Ages. Part of the establishment of the Church in the fourth through the seventh centuries was an attempt to turn Christians away from their dreams. Dreams were mistrusted because of a developing notion of demons actively tempting the sleeper; because of their links to heresy, individuality, and sexuality; and because of a strengthening theological notion that divination was wrong even if possible, as the future belongs only to God. By decree of Pope Gregory II (reigned 715–731), dream interpreters were to be avoided. Such decrees were common in the time and realm of Charlemagne (reigned 771–814).

Official condemnation notwithstanding, dream theory developed, and dreambooks and interpreters circulated unabated. While theologians had to reconcile contradictory attitudes toward dreams and thus sometimes mistrusted them, there is no evidence that the common people shared their doubts. In fact, dream narratives in both hagiography and historical works such as those of Bede and Gregory of Tours multiply and become more detailed as time goes on. In Bede's *Ecclesiastical History of the English People* (731), one of the most famous early medieval accounts of a dream vision relates the story of Cædmon, a farmworker attached to St. Hilda's famous monastery at Whitby. One day he flees the company of those who share in singing tales out of embarrassment over his inadequacy, but later that night he is visited by an angelic figure who teaches him to sing of God's creation. The next day, Abbess Hilda and her learned monks marvel at Cædmon's newfound ability to turn biblical narratives into traditional Old English poetry, and Bede records the event as a miracle.

The Twelfth Century and Beyond

Dream theory underwent no fundamental changes or developments until the twelfth century. The fullest treatment of medieval dream theory at this time, before it underwent substantial changes, is found in Book 2 of the *Policraticus* of John of Salisbury (c. 1115–1180). John clearly finds himself in a dilemma over what to believe about the phenomenon of dreams and the issue of their interpretation. He knows the dream to be both a psychological and a physiological phenomenon, but more than either of these, it can sometimes be an experience by which the human soul can access the realm of the divine and gain knowledge about the future. The problem is one of certainty. On the one hand, Christ is known to work through *somnia*, or dreams, yet on the other hand, the attempt to interpret the symbols found therein is not only vain but wrong without Christ's own illumination. In her *Causae et curae*, Hildegard von Bingen (1098–1179) ascribes greater moral significance to dreaming than others had done, as she correlates the dreamer's moral status directly with the quality of the dream, stating that both God and the devil evaluate the moral fitness of a dreamer's thoughts.

The main twelfth-century development was the increasing availability and prestige of Aristotelian philosophical and medical works. The integration of Aristotelian thought on dreams with Christianity was a difficult task, as Aristotle said that dreams had no divine significance and the Church said that they did. The notions that dreams are a natural medical phenomenon and that they are realms of interaction with the divine are fraught with potential conflict. In the Middle Ages, though there may have been a few theologians who argued for one extreme or the other, the majority of thinkers managed to find a middle path according to which dreams could have natural causes and at the same time be the realm of supernatural influences.

The new teachings brought on increased interest in the physiology of the "lower" kinds of dreams and their relation to bodily health, and the net result was an overall increase in interest in dreams, as those thought insignificant before were now held to have as much meaning as those that had been believed powerful all along. Medieval doctors came to hold that dreams were expressions of the condition of the "virtues" that regulate the functions of the body and that any disturbance in the normal balance existing in a healthy person among the bodily humors was reflected in dream images. All humans contained the four "humors"—the sanguine, which produced an optimistic, perhaps a foolishly optimistic, outlook; the choleric, which made for hot tempers; the melancholic, characterized by introspection, even depression; and the phlegmatic, with its tendency toward withdrawal and inaction. This general theory influenced thought on dreams in two ways. First, there was a general correspondence between the seasons and the most common type of dream: sanguine in spring, choleric in summer, melancholic in fall, and phlegmatic in winter. Second, people of a certain humor or temperament were believed to dream in a certain way.

Another important development in dream theory was the increasing importance of astrology in the central Middle Ages. The connection with oneiromancy and astrology is the cornerstone of *De prognosticatione sompniorum* (Forecasting through Dreams, c. 1330), attributed to Guillelmo de Aragonia, in which the most salient feature of dream interpretation is found to be in the stars.

Despite all the schemes of categorization and hierarchization, at no point in the Middle Ages is there any clear distinction between dreams and visions. In his *De probatione spirituum* (The Examination of Spirits, 1415), Johanes Gerson writes that many who in good faith have regarded themselves as vi-

A demon visits a woman in her dream; twelfth-century illustration from Herrad of Landsberg's Garden of Delights. *(Reproduced from Gérard Cames,* Allégories et symboles dans l'Hortus deliciarum, *Leiden, 1971)*

sionaries have really only seen dream images. A millennium earlier, the early Christian martyr Perpetua recorded a whole series of narrative visions in her diary, but only at the end did she mention that she awoke, indicating for the first time that she had been asleep during all that preceded. Many other Christian visions may have been received and recorded without knowledge or indication of awakening.

A number of recent studies have suggested that it is possible to know how and about what medieval people really dreamed. Medieval writings are peppered with personal dream narratives accompanied by background circumstances, and autobiographies proliferated in the twelfth century. The most prominent examples of this are the autobiographical *Monodiae* of Guibert de Nogent (c. 1115) and the *Opusculum de conversione sua* (Little Book of His Conversion) of Hermann of Cologne, a twelfth-century convert from Judaism to Christianity.

Dreambooks

Medieval dream interpretation was founded upon analogical thinking. The language of dreams is a symbolic language, and the popularity of dreams in the Middle Ages is due to the fact that they were a normal expression, a part of the cycle of medieval symbolic thought. The most common way of interpreting dreams was through use of "dreambooks." Physiological dreambooks, such as that of Hans Lobenzweig (thirteenth century), were used by doctors and reflected medical teachings. They were a later development and did not challenge the popularity of symbolic dreambooks, which remained far more numerous throughout the medieval period and which can be classed into three other kinds of dreambooks according to the way they assign meanings to symbol. All three faced some official prohibition but were openly and commonly used throughout the Middle Ages.

The first kind was the "dream alphabet" or "chancebook," an alphabetical list of possible dream interpretations that used only the fact that a dream had occurred and had nothing at all to do with the content of the dream. To use it, one would pray, open the psalter, and compare the first letter seen with the list in the dream alphabet. The most common chancebook was known as the *Somniale Joseph* (Manual on Dreams Associated with Joseph), which is found in both Latin and in many vernacular languages. The second kind of dreambook was the "dreamlunar." As with the chancebooks, the interpretation of dreams by means of the dreamlunars had nothing to do with the specific content of any given dream. Rather, all dreams on a given night have the exact same meaning, which is assigned by the dreamlunar on the basis of the phases of the moon. It is the date of the night that determines the meaning, not the dream itself. This kind of dreambook is found only in Latin, and its circulation was more limited than the other kinds of dreambooks. The "interpretation of dreams" by means of these two kinds of books was really nothing of the sort; rather, the occasion of a dream was used as an excuse for practicing divination.

The lists of interpretations of dream symbols found in a third kind of dreambook, or "dreambooks proper," are keyed to the images of specific dreams. Symbols in these dreambooks proper were grouped according to class. The order was alphabetical in Latin, but this was usually lost in vernacular translations. These books were meant as an aid to the universal and quotidian experience of dreaming. They have prefaces indicating the importance of such factors as individual station and disposition, time of year, time of night, and so on in the interpretation of dreams, but in the works themselves they ignore this complexity and give only one interpretation per symbol. These books are all indebted to Artemidorus's *Oneirocritica* (Judgment of Dreams). Works in this category include Pascalis Romanus's *Liber thesaurus occultus* (Treasury of the Occult, 1165), Arnald of Villanova's *Expositiones visionum* (Explanations of Visions), and the Byzantine/Arabic Achmet's *Oneirocritica* (Judgment of Dreams; Latin translation c. 1170).

However, the dreambook known as the *Somniale Danielis* (attributed to the biblical Daniel) was without a doubt the most important and famous work of this type in the Middle Ages. It was also the most widely circulated medieval dreambook, with hundreds of extant manuscripts dating from the ninth to the fifteenth centuries. These are found in Latin as well as in translations into many vernaculars. Indeed, the *Somniale Danielis* had such a wide circulation that it seems safe to assume that its dream topoi, or commonplaces, were general property in medieval civilization. Stephen Fischer, the scholar who has done the most work on it, considers it to be the medievalist's primary source for understanding the significance of dream topoi.

Dream Poetry

The interpretation of medieval literary dreams is not always given with their depiction, and so their meaning can be missed by modern readers. Contextualization and knowledge of medieval Christian imagery may sometimes reveal the meaning of a symbol, but when they do not, dreambooks such as the *Somniale Danielis* may be valuable aids to interpretation. However, not all medieval literary dreams draw their symbols from Christian imagery, and Celtic and Germanic dream lore also appears throughout much medieval literature. While the old sagas of the North often contained rich and complex dreams, as in *Gisli's Saga*, they did not consist entirely of dreams. The old northern and the Christian dream symbolism may, however, be joined, as in the Anglo-Saxon poem *The Dream of the Rood*, which provides striking imagery of Christ's cross in the language of Germanic heroic poetry.

This poem is an example of dream poetry, a whole genre of allegorical literature in which narrative material is structured as a dream or is presented as having occurred in a dream. The genre can be found throughout the Middle Ages, but it flourished most in the twelfth to fourteenth centuries and is generally acknowledged to have reached its acme in Middle English literature. Not surprisingly, much of this poetry is religious. Thus, specifically Christian imagery may be found in the fourteenth-century *Pearl*, in which a grieving father has a dream vision of his dead daughter in the heavenly Jerusalem, described in images that clearly derive from biblical and patristic tradition. Even so, the late-medieval dream vision can, as in the earlier *Dream of the Rood*, combine the religious and the secular in such a work as the fourteenth-century *Piers Plowman*, which depicts the dreamer searching for spiritual truth while passing through a world that provides vivid images of the society of the time.

Dream poetry, however, also depicted many nonreligious visions, and from the thirteenth century onward it dealt frequently with themes of quite earthly love. The single most important work of the form is the *Roman de la rose* of Jean de Meun and Guillaume de Lorris, with its focus on the God of Love and on inner emotions of the dreamer, named only the Lover, who in a garden impetuously approaches the Rose, the object of his desire, is rebuffed, and must go through a long education in the rules and art of love before finally achieving his quest. This work was immensely popular during the later Middle Ages and was the model for much subsequent medieval French dream poetry, such as Deguileville's *Pèlerinage de la vie humaine*, Froissart's *Paradys d'amours*, and Machaut's *Dit dou Lyon*. Chaucer translated at least part of the *Roman de la rose* into Middle English, and his own dream poetry was also directly indebted to it. His *Book of the Duchesse*, *House of Fame*, *Parlement of Foules*, and *Legend of Good Women* are among the most masterful dream poems written in England, and largely through his influence the form proliferated and was still popular in the sixteenth century.

See also: English Tradition: Anglo-Saxon Period; French Tradition; Medicine
References and further reading: Translations of the medieval sources given here are readily available. Scholarly studies include S. Fischer, *The Complete Medieval Dreambook* (1982); L. T. Martin, *Somniale Danielis* (1981); and W. Schmitt, "Das Traumbuch des Hans Lobenzweig," *Archiv für Kulturgeschichte* 48 (1966). The single most important work on understanding dreams in the Middle Ages is T. Gregory, ed., *I sogni nel Medioevo* (1985), which contains a dozen essays in Italian, German, and French on as many different aspects of dreams in medieval thought and literature. A. Bagliani and G. Stabile, eds., *Träume im Mittelalter* (1989), treats the depiction of dreams in plastic arts. M. R. Wittmer-Butsch, *Zur Bedeutung von Schlaf und Traum in Mittelalter* (1990), is the best work on the actual dreams of individuals in the Middle Ages. Important general overviews include J. Le Goff, *The Medieval Imagination*, trans. A. Goldhammer (1988); L. M. Bitel, "In visu noctis," in *History of Religions* (1991); W. C. Curry, *Chaucer and the Medieval Sciences* (1960); M. Kelsey, *God, Dreams, and Revelation* (1974); S. F. Kruger, *Dreaming in the Middle Ages* (1992); K. L. Lynch, *The High Medieval Dream Vision* (1988); and R. E. V. Stuip and C. Vellekoop, *Visionen* (1986). S. Fischer, *Dreams in the Middle High German Epic* (1978), is an examination of literature via the *Somniale Danielis*. Books that treat dream symbols in medieval thought include D. Buschinger and A. Crepin, *Les quatre éléments dans la culture médiévale* (1938); J. Chydenius, *The Theory of Medieval Symbolism* (1960); J. Duchaussoy, *Le bestiare divin, ou la symbolique des animaux* (1958); H. F. Dunbar, *Symbolism in Medieval Thought* (1929); M. Eliade, *Images and Symbols* (1961); M. Kearny, *Role of Swine Symbolism in Medieval Culture* (1991); and M. South, *Mythical and Fabulous Creatures* (1988).

—*Alexander Argüelles*

Druids

Priestly class among the ancient Celtic peoples.

As the priests of the pagan Celts, the druids evidently ceased to exist in Gaul after the conquest by Caesar in 58–57 B.C.E., and in Roman Britain after the defeat by Suetonius Paulinus of their rebellion on Anglesey in 61 C.E. It is uncertain how long they continued in Ireland and lowland Scotland, since written history begins in these areas only after conversion to Christianity from the fifth century onward. Nonetheless, it is safe to assume that during the Middle

Ages the druid proper was by and large a figure of legend rather than a living reality. What is known about druids from medieval times comes almost solely through the medium of writings by Christian monks, who had a vested interest in portraying them as the defeated opposition, and certainly as figures of the past.

The druids of the free Celtic era were organized in colleges of three possibly overlapping classes: the *druides*, who were in charge of justice and the observation of ritual as well as being the counselors of kings; the *vates* or *ovates*, who were prophets; and the *bardoi* or bards, in charge of the preservation of history and lore through the medium of poetry and story. After the demise of the druidic institution, it seems probable that the bards continued to operate in a secular forum as poets and storytellers, and if the ethnographic observations of medieval and early modern researchers are correct, they assimilated the prophetic role of the *ovates* as well. The druids' function as both priests and regal advisers was taken over by the priests of the Christian Church. The judicial function was partly taken over by practitioners of canon law, but the *brehon* judges in Ireland may have preserved the remnants of druidic precepts in their administration of secular law (known as *brehon* law, which circulated in oral tradition until first written down by direction of St. Patrick in the fifth century). Classical commentators noted that druids were skilled in natural science and medicine, although it is unclear which of the three classes was in charge of these disciplines.

The first representations of druids in medieval Celtic literature come in the early Irish saints' lives. The druidic antagonists of Irish saints usually engage in magical contests with the holy men and women, illustrating that the pyrotechnics of their false religion are inferior to the simple power of the saint's faith in the true God. For instance, Luccet Mael, adviser to the pagan king Lóegaire, can create a huge snowfall by his magic, but only St. Patrick can cause the snow to melt away. St. Brigid, in most accounts, is the daughter of a druid's slave girl, and one of the first signs of her Christian holiness occurs when she finds she can no longer eat the food of the druid's household; she must be fed only from the milk of a pure, Christian cow.

In the medieval Irish tales set in the pre-Christian past, representations of druids going about their daily lives compare well with the depictions found in the Greco-Roman writings. Cathbad the druid, a major figure in the Ulster cycle of tales, is a counselor to kings, an educator of youth, and a prophet. However, in contrast to Caesar's statement that druids were exempt from military service, Cathbad is also the leader of one of the *fianna*, or warrior bands. The druid Mug Ruith, Slave of the Wheel, is depicted as one-eyed or blind, clad in a bird-skin cloak, and driving a gleaming metal chariot. He engages another druid, Ciodruadh, in aerial battle. Other druids in the sagas are healers, shapeshifters, dream interpreters, stargazers, and magicians.

In the tales of *The Destruction of Da Derga's Hostel* and *The Love-Sickness of Cú Chulainn*, druids are depicted engaging in a kind of prophesy called the *tarbfeis*, or bull feast. A white bull was sacrificed and skinned and a broth made of the flesh. One druid would drink the broth and go to sleep on the skin, watched over by four other druids. In his sleep he was supposed to dream of the appearance of the next king. Martin Martin, in his *Description of the Western Islands of*

Scotland (1716), tells of a similar practice still being carried out in the late seventeenth century, and the elaborate *Dream of Rhonabwy* may be a fourteenth-century Welsh literary reflex of the same ritual.

In these stories about the conversion of Ireland to Christianity, the druid appears in order to show how Christianity surpasses paganism. The druids themselves are depicted as knowing through their prophetic powers that their time is over. In the story of the death of the king Conchobor mac Nessa, the son of Cathbad the druid, the king is incapacitated when an enemy hurls the calcified brain of the warrior Mes Gegra so that it lodges in Conchobor's skull. Druid doctors tell him that he must live quietly, without excitement, without drinking, without having sex. Conchobor lives like this for seven years, until one day there is an earthquake. His druids inform him that this is because, off in Palestine, the Son of God—who coincidentally shares Conchobor's birthday—is being crucified. Conchobor springs to his feet in a passion and dies as the embedded brain ball explodes from his head, baptizing Conchobor in a gush of his own blood. This, we are told, is how Conchobor became one of two men in Ireland to believe in Christ before the coming of Patrick. Conchobor only acquires the requisite knowledge through the skills of his druids, but his baptism is accomplished through the expulsion of a literally concrete symbol of the pagan Celtic way of life, which was, as the classical ethnographers noted, marked by the practice of head-hunting.

What survived of Druidism after its defeat by Romans and Christians, then, is found in the narrative, legal, and medical lore of the medieval Irish and Welsh and in the less abundant material in Cornish, Scots, and Breton. However, since the poets, storytellers, lawyers, and doctors—not to mention monks—of medieval Wales and Ireland did not live frozen in a time capsule like Merlin in his Crystal Palace, we cannot assume that the medieval Celtic literatures present a shattered jewel of pagan thought that merely needs to be reassembled into wholeness. Particularly in Ireland, the druid became, in medieval times, an active folkloric figure whose narrative deeds and symbolism provided a dynamic forum in which the medieval Irish might explore the relationship between their pagan past and Christian present.

See also: Irish Tradition

References and further reading: The major classical texts referring to druids are collected in N. K. Chadwick, *The Druids* (1966); T. D. Kendrick, *The Druids: A Study in Keltic Prehistory* (1927; rpt. 1966); and J. J. Tierney, "The Celtic Ethnography of Posidonius," *Proceedings of the Royal Irish Academy* 60 (1960). The standard work on druids through the ages is S. Piggott, *The Druids* (1975), while P. B. Ellis, *The Druids* (1994), and L. E. Jones, *Druids, Shamans, Priests: Metaphors of Celtic Paganism* (1997), are somewhat more speculative. The major medieval tales featuring druidic characters may be found in T. P. Cross and C. Slover, *Ancient Irish Tales* (1969). J. E. C. Williams, *The Court Poet in Medieval Ireland* (1971), covers the cultural environment of the druids' poetic descendants. J. F. Nagy, *The Wisdom of the Outlaw: The Boyhood Deeds of Finn in Gaelic Narrative Tradition* (1985), discusses the function of druids in medieval texts; see also his *Conversing with Angels and Ancients: Literary Myths of Medieval Ireland* (1997). K. McCone, *Pagan Past and Christian Present in Irish History* (1991), considers the symbolism of the figure of the druid in the medieval revision of its pagan past.

—*Leslie Ellen Jones*

Drums and Percussion

Instruments played by shaking or striking either a membrane or a plate, bar of wood, metal, or other hard material.

Percussion may be divided into instruments that produce a definite pitch (kettledrums, celestas) and those that do not. Instruments that produce sound from tightly stretched membranes are called membranophones; these include all manner of drums and the kazoo. Instruments that produce their sound from the substance of the instrument itself, such as cymbals, gongs, bells, and rattles, are called idiophones.

Membranophones can be subdivided into struck drums, plucked drums, friction drums, and singing membranes. Struck drums include timpani, tambourines, rattle drums, and side drums. Plucked drums feature a string knotted below the center of the membrane; vibrations are transmitted to the membrane when the string is plucked. Friction drums vibrate by means of a stick, the hand, or a cord. Singing membranes, like the kazoo, vibrate when the musician speaks or sings into them.

Idiophones can be subdivided into instruments that are plucked, blown, or struck or that vibrate by friction. Plucked idiophones are represented by the Jew's harp, musical boxes, and the African *sansas*. Struck idiophones can be sounded directly (cymbals, gongs, clappers, bells, and castanets) or indirectly (rattles, scraped sticks, and tubes). Blown idiophones take the form of plaques or sticks (*Aeolsklavier*). Finally, friction idiophones are instruments like the nail violin, the glass harmonica, and the nail piano.

The best-known member of the membranophone family is the drum. Drums can be sounded in three ways: as percussion instruments, when they are struck with the bare hands or with beaters; as friction instruments, when the membrane is rubbed by a stick or cord in contact with it; or as plucked instruments, when a string knotted below the membrane is plucked and its vibrations are transferred to the membrane. The Western world has focused on the percussion aspect of drums. Drums can be classified according to body shape: bowl-shaped, like kettledrums; tubular, as in barrel-shaped, hourglass-shaped, conical or goblet-shaped, cylindrical, and double-conical bodies; and frame drums. Tubular drums can be further subdivided into double skins, single skins that are closed, and single skins that are open-ended. The membrane on these tubular bodies may be laced, nailed, glued, or attached by a combination of these methods to the body of the drum.

The history of humankind is closely related to the rise and development of percussion instruments. Drums, as well as concussion sticks and rattles, were probably among the earliest instruments. Our knowledge of prehistoric instruments, traced back over 30,000 years, is based on three sources: archaeological evidence, pictorial representations, and when we encounter historical records, literary references. Early humans apparently used their bodies as percussion instruments by stamping on the ground, slapping parts of the body, clapping the hands, and beating upon the throat. These techniques were then transferred to various implements of bone, pottery, stone, and metal—as supported by archaeological evidence. The Old Testament of the Bible records these efforts: "because thou hast clapped thine hands, and stamped with the feet, and rejoiced in heart …" (Ezek. 25:6).

Two women play percussion as the Children of Israel celebrate their crossing of the Red Sea; from a twelfth-century illustration in Herrad of Landsberg's Garden of Delights. *(Reproduced from Gérard Cames,* Allégories et symboles dans l'Hortus deliciarum, Leiden, 1971)*

Early percussion instruments were also used in the sacred and ritual realms, and they were believed endowed with magical and sacred powers themselves. Often aligned with the dance, the drum has been and still is an indispensable element in tribal religious rituals. Sumerian sculptures dated 2500 B.C.E. portray a form of bass drum almost as big as the player. Eastern legends suggest that the drum came from central Asia into China around 3500 B.C.E. Early warriors in Celtic cultures are recorded as striking or pounding on their shields to intimidate their enemies and to coordinate rhythmically the precise moment to attack.

The use of percussion instruments in the Middle Ages is well recorded in the religious artwork of this period, especially in sculpture and painting, such as the manuscript illuminations in the late medieval *Belles heures* and *Très riches heures* made for Jean, duke of Berry. Although few actual instruments survive, it is assumed that secular cultures in the medieval period accompanied their rituals and music with percussion. The illuminated manuscripts, religious sculptures, literary references, and drawings and paintings of the medieval period record a wealth of percussive instruments. The Arabic world introduced many of these into European culture via the Crusades: the bass drum, the large and small naker, the cymbal, the sistra, the tabor, the triangle, the tambourine, and the castanets. In the West most percussion instruments were used for three main purposes: military signals and encouragement, dance, and religious ceremonies.

Percussion was an essential component of many medieval festive practices, notably the charivari, sometimes called "rough music," a ritual mounted by young men to ridicule mismatched couples—for example, older men married to younger women—on their wedding nights. Often masked and in costume, the men would sound their drums and other instruments loudly to keep the couple awake. A famous illustration from the French *Roman de Fauvel* (1314–1316) depicts five musicians among the 15 revelers, all using beaters to sound drums or cymbals.

The drum was an especially popular instrument in the medieval period. The earliest known side drum is the medieval tabor, which first appears in thirteenth-century art as a rope-tensioned side drum with a snare or snares, beaten with either one or two sticks. Other percussive instruments that began their development in the Middle Ages are chime bells and the xylophone.

See also: Books of Hours; Charivari; Dance; Folk Music and Folksong
References and further reading: For relevant scholarship, see J. Blades and J. Montagu, *Early Percussion Instruments from the Middle Ages to the Baroque* (1976); J. Blades, *Percussion Instruments and Their History* (1974); and "Drum," in *New Groves Dictionary of Music and Musicians*, vol. 5 (1995). For the illustration from the *Roman de Fauvel*, depicting a festive use of percussion, see the entry Charivari in this encyclopedia.

—*Bradford Lee Eden*

Dwarfs

A supernatural race of master artisans who serve as donor figures to the gods in Scandinavian mythology and as donors or servants to knights and heroes in Old French, Middle High German, and medieval Scandinavian chivalric and heroic literature.

Scandinavian mythological sources depict *dvergar* (dwarfs) as an all-male race of supernatural beings, residing in cliffs and stones, created asexually from the bones and blood of giants. Though in most instances dwarfs appear to be quite separate from other mythical races, Snorri Sturluson, in his thirteenth-century mythological manual, the *Prose Edda*, conflates dwarfs and "black elves," a subcategory of beings that appears only in his writings.

In the grand dichotomy of the mythology, dwarfs are aligned with giants in opposition to gods and humans. Nevertheless, their most important role in Scandinavian sources is that of donors to the two latter races. Dwarfs are said to have created the most powerful weapons and prized possessions of the gods. They are reluctant donors, however, and the gods generally obtain the goods through deceit, threats, or bribery.

Some Eddic poems, recorded in the thirteenth century, attribute occult knowledge to dwarfs, yet they seem rather gullible and are always shortchanged when dealing with the gods. However, dwarfs can get the better of humans; consider King Sveigdir, who, according to Snorri Sturluson's thirteenth-century *Ynglinga Saga* (Saga of the Ynglings, ch. 12), was lured into a stone by a dwarf, never to emerge again.

While dwarfs hardly figure in the Norse family sagas at all, they abound in the more fantastic, heroic genres of the *fornaldarsögur* (sagas of antiquity) and the *riddarasögur* (sagas of knights). However, in these sagas the dwarfs usually appear as servants to knights and heroes and do not present a threat to their masters. Dwarfs of this bent are also encountered in some Scandinavian ballads. They are cognate with their kinsmen in medieval romances from the European continent, the German dwarfs and French *nains*.

Dwarfs frequently appear in Middle High German literature, particularly in the cycle of Dietrich von Bern, preserved in the thirteenth-century *Heldenbuch* (Book of Heroes) and in other romances. The earliest reference to a *nanus* (dwarf) is from an eleventh-century fragment, but most are encountered in works from the twelfth to fourteenth centuries. As in Scandinavian sources, they are master artisans, unsurpassed in the art of forging weapons. They are said to be small and are often dressed according to chivalric fashion. Female dwarfs are attested, but their importance is negligible.

The role that dwarfs fill in Middle High German literature is most often that of the knight's sidekick or servant. In this they closely resemble the *nains* of the Old French romances. Though the *nains* are often uglier and more conniving than their German cousins, they, too, are sharp dressers of diminutive size. More consistently than German dwarfs, the *nains* are always cast as servants to knights, and they habitually accompany them in their adventures.

Most of the scholarly literature on dwarfs centers on questions of origins. In 1906 Fritz Wohlgemuth hypothesized that the *nains* were modeled on historical court dwarfs. August Lötjens, in a work from 1911, refuted this literal-historical explanation, citing a lack of evidence for the existence of court dwarfs, and suggested that the dependence of French romances on Celtic folklore might provide a better context in which to seek the origin of the *nains*—a view echoed by Vernon Harward in 1958, in his book on dwarfs in Arthurian romance. As to the dwarfs of Middle High German literature, Lötjens is of the opinion that they are literary hybrids of the chivalric *nains* and the more earthy dwarfs of Germanic folk tradition.

In a book on medieval dwarfs and elves in Europe, Claude Lecouteux claims that dwarfs are closely related to the dead, a hypothesis previously argued in the Scandinavian context by Chester Gould in 1929. Lecouteux also refers to the theories of Georges Dumézil about the tripartite system of Indo-European mythologies and suggests that dwarfs should be seen as third-function (i.e., fertility) beings, since they work the riches of the earth through their metalwork.

In a number of works from the 1970s and 1980s Lotte Motz proposed another theory of the origin of dwarfs: that dwarfs harken back to an Indo-European class of artisans, preserved as a faded memory in folklore and also in the Greek Hephaestus (blacksmith of the gods). According to Motz, the main characteristics of this class are craftsmanship and physical deformity, and she claims that its historical achievements may be observed in the megalithic stone structures of Europe.

Though Motz, like many before her, is confident that the dwarfs of medieval literature derive immediately from contemporary folk belief and legend tradition, there is good reason to think otherwise. The *nains* of chivalric romance are a clearly defined, formulaic literary type, perpetuated through literary borrowings. They bear a much closer resemblance to helper figures in fairy tales than to supernaturals from legend tradition. Although the dwarfs of Middle High German tradition are more diverse, they too usually function as helpers or donors. In an article from 1924 on Scandinavian dwarfs, Helmut de Boor made a similar claim when he contrasted elves and dwarfs, arguing that the former belong to legend and belief whereas the latter inhabit the enchanted world of the fairy tale. Elves, he notes, appear in historical works and the more realistic family sagas, but dwarfs are mostly confined to more fanciful genres, such as the *fornaldarsögur*, on the one hand and to learned, speculative reworkings of folk tradition, like the Eddic poems and Snorri's *Prose Edda*, on the other.

Nonetheless, de Boor acknowledges a trace of folk legend tradition in two motifs associated with Scandinavian dwarfs, namely, their supernatural craftsmanship and their living quarters in stones. Scandinavian place names like Dvergaberg (Dwarf-Rock) and Dvergasteinn (Dwarf-Stone) lend support to the latter, as does the Sveigdir episode cited above, which has countless analogs in more recent folk legends of stone dwellers. It may be added that in this respect dwarfs are hard to tell from other nature beings of folk tradition, such as elves and fairies, and by the time of the folklore collections of the nineteenth century dwarfs are interchangeable with these beings in a number of supernatural legends from northern Europe.

See also: Eddic Poetry; *Fornaldarsögur;* Scandinavian Mythology; Snorri Sturluson's *Edda*
References and further reading: Important scholarship includes H. de Boor, "Der Zwerg in Skandinavien," in *Festschrift Eugen Mogk* (1924); C. Gould, "Dwarf-Names," *Publications of the Modern Language Association* 44 (1929); V. Harward, *The Dwarfs of Arthurian Romance and Celtic Tradition* (1958); C. Lecouteux, *Les nains et les elfes au moyen âge* (1988); A. Lötjens, *Der Zwerg in der deutschen Heldendichtung des Mittelalters* (1911); L. Motz, "The Chanter at the Door," *Mankind Quarterly* 22 (1982), "The Craftsman in the Mound," *Folklore* 88 (1977), *The Wise One of the Mountain* (1983), and "Of Elves and Dwarves," *Arv* 29–30 (1973–1974); F. Wohlgemuth, *Riesen und Zwerge in der altfranzösischen erzählenden Dichtung* (1906). A classic study of northern European mythology is G. Dumézil, *Gods of the Ancient Northmen*, trans. J. Lindow et al. (1973).

—*Valdimar Tr. Hafstein*

Eddic Poetry

The mythological and heroic poetry of medieval Scandinavia.

These poems concern themselves with three main topics: mythology, particularly the exploits of the gods and their relationship with other groups such as giants; ethics and codes of behavior; and the heroic North. One can divide the Eddic corpus into three groups. There are 29 main Eddic poems found in the primary manuscript, and a thirtieth, *Baldrs draumar* (Baldr's Dreams), is often added to this central corpus. Most Eddic compilations include other poems as well in what is known as the "Eddic Appendix," such as the *Rigsthula, Hyndluljod, Hlödskvida,* and *Grottasöngr.* Finally, a group of poems and stanzas taken from the *fornaldarsögur* (legendary sagas) is called the Eddica Minora.

The primary manuscript for the Eddic poetry, containing the main 29 poems, is the *Codex Regius.* Codicological evidence suggests a date of 1270 for the composition of this work. This manuscript, discovered by Bishop Brynjolf Sveinsson in 1643, was originally attributed to Saemund Sigfusson, thus explaining the frequently confusing allusions to both the *Poetic Edda* and Saemund's *Edda* for the Eddic poems. This attribution has been abandoned. The *Poetic Edda,* or *Elder Edda* as it is also known, is distinct from *Snorra Edda,* or the *Prose Edda* as it is known in English. This latter text, written by Snorri Sturluson in the early part of the thirteenth century, includes an elaboration of many of the myths found in the *Poetic Edda.* Indeed, there has been considerable debate concerning the relationship between Snorri's work and possible earlier written Eddic poems.

A general logic governs the placement of the poems in the *Codex Regius* manuscript. Poems in the first section recount stories about the gods, the Aesir. The work is introduced by the *Voluspa* (Sibyl's Prophecy), which chronicles the fate of the gods, detailing the events at the end of the world. Next follow three poems about the god Odin, a poem about the god Frey, and then five poems about the god Thor. The second large section of the manuscript deals with the heroic lays of Sigurd, and these poems generally follow a chronological pattern. They are joined together by short prose interludes.

The word *edda* used to describe these poems is actually borrowed from the title of Snorri's work. The origins of the word are somewhat obscure, and several etymologies have been suggested. Some contend that the word derives from *óðr,* meaning "poetry" and by extension "poetics." Another suggestion is the word *Oddi*, the name of a farm and literary center where Snorri received some education. And yet a third suggestion is *edda*, a word meaning "great-grand-mother." The myths would then be stories of a great-grandmother. A final suggestion is the derivation from the Latin *edere*, "to produce," much like the derivation of *kredda* (creed) from *credere*, "to believe."

There are four main meters of the Eddic poems. The most common of these is *fornyrðislag*, or "old way meter." In this meter each stanza consists of eight half lines (four long lines) of four or five syllables each. The stanzas, in turn, are broken into two equal units of four half lines, the *helmingar* (singular *helmingr*), each of which forms a syntactic unit expressing a complete idea. The first half line of each long line has one or two syllables referred to as the *studlar*, or supports, followed by a single alliterating syllable that generally falls on the first stressed syllable of the second half line. This syllable is known as the *höfuðstafr*, or main pillar. Alliteration occurs either in consonants with like consonants or any vowel with any other vowel. The stanzaic form of the *Edda* contrasts notably with the stichic forms in early Indo-European and Germanic verse, such as the *Hildebrandslied* (Lay of Hildebrand) or *Beowulf*. The earliest Eddic poems have varying stanza lengths, possibly marking the transition from stichic forms to stanzaic forms. The *ljóðaháttr*, or song meter, is also stanzaic but consists of stanzas of six lines. Each *helming* consists of two half lines, followed by a full line that alliterates with itself. The *galdralag* is a variation on *ljóðaháttr* and is associated with magic. It includes a repetition of the long line in each *helmingr*, often incorporating a variation of that line. The final, and least frequent, of the Eddic meters is *málaháttr*, or speech meter. Generally similar to the *fornyrðislag*, it has a longer half line. While scholars often try to make clear distinctions between Eddic verse and skaldic verse, it is not clear that such a distinction was made by medieval Scandinavians. In general, however, Eddic poems tend to have a more distinct narrative component, do not follow the strict rules of syllable counting that characterize the skaldic forms, and make far less use of kennings—metaphors forged from compounding words (e.g., "whale-road" for the tempestuous sea).

There has been significant debate surrounding the composition and transmission of the Eddic poems. Since they are considered to be of considerable value in the study of pre-Christian Scandinavia, a great deal of effort has been expended on determining the oral roots of the poetry. The Parry-Lord model of oral-formulaic composition had significant influence on the theorizing of these oral origins for the Eddic corpus in the pagan period. Because of the lack of significant variants of many of the Eddic poems, much of this type of investigation has been inconclusive. It appears that, rather than showing the significant variation characteristic of oral epic forms, such as those studied by Albert Lord and Milman Parry, the Eddic poems had a rather stable form and were quite likely learned and performed from memory, with little if any formulaic recomposition.

See also: Burgundian Cycle; *Fornaldarsögur*; Scandinavian Mythology; Snorri Sturluson's *Edda*

References and further reading: Major scholarship on the subject includes R. J. Glendinning and H. Bessason, eds., *Edda: A Collection of Essays* (1983); J. Harris, "Eddic Poetry," in *Old Norse-Icelandic Literature: A Critical Guide*, ed. C. J. Clover and J. Lindow (1985); A.

Heusler, *Codex Regius of the Elder Edda* (1937); L. M. Hollander, *The Poetic Edda, with Introduction and Explanatory Notes* (1962); R. Kellogg, "A Concordance to the Elder Edda," Ph.D. diss., Harvard University (1958); H. Kuhn, *Edda: Die Lieder des Codex Regius nebst verwandten Denkmälern*, 5th ed., ed. G. Neckel (1983); J. Lindow, *Scandinavian Mythology: An Annotated Bibliography* (1988); M. C. Ross, *Prolonged Echoes: Old Norse Myths in Medieval Northern Society*, vol. 1: *The Myths* (1994); P. Terry, *Poems of the Vikings: The Elder Edda* (1969).

—*Timothy R. Tangherlini*

English Tradition: Anglo-Saxon Period

The folkloric culture of the English before the Norman invasion of 1066.

Historical Context

Anglo-Saxon folk culture has its origins among the Continental Germanic peoples of northern Europe, but its specifically English tradition begins with their migration to Britain. Historians now think this migration may have begun as early as the fourth century, though an older tradition has it that the Angles, Saxons, and Jutes came to this former Roman province in 449. Soon afterward the migration inspired myths of origin that persisted throughout the Anglo-Saxon period in lore and literature. The pagan Anglo-Saxons eventually over-ran England (from *Engla-lond*, "land of the Angles"), wiping away most of Roman Christianity until they were converted by missionaries coming separately from Ireland and from the Continent. As related by the historian Bede writing in 731, the conversion of Anglo-Saxon England was for the most part slow, un-even, halting, and even at times reversed. Gradually, however, churches were consecrated throughout the land, and great monasteries were founded, monas-teries that became some of the most important centers of learning in Europe. Consequently, Anglo-Saxon culture became an increasingly diverse mixture of the older lore and customs of the North combined, at least among the educated, with the Latin culture from the South consisting mainly of classical and Chris-tian writings.

This early English culture was disrupted in 793 when the Vikings began raiding, and later invading, throughout the British Isles. Their advance was eventually halted by the military victories of Alfred the Great (849–899), who then labored to restore the high level of learning that England had enjoyed before these invasions. And even though Viking raids resumed in the late tenth and early eleventh centuries, the periods of peaceful relations were sufficient for an Anglo-Scandinavian culture to develop in the North. The conversion of the Vikings to Christianity encouraged their assimilation, and by the time of the Norman Conquest (1066) there was little to distinguish between English and Scandinavian elements at the level of folk culture.

Social Context

Even with persistent warfare, the essential ordering and rhythms of the pre-dominantly rural society remained fairly constant, as indicated by comparison of early settlement and landholding patterns established by archaeological research with those found, often centuries later, in the great Domesday Book survey of 1086. Dwellings were not large compared to those of the later Middle Ages. Surviving foundations of an apparently typical longhouse measure twenty-four to twenty-seven meters in length by about five meters in width, while many smaller houses measure around eight and a half meters by five and a half meters, as found on small farms or in villages of 50 to 150 inhabitants. Compared to such modest structures, the Old English poem *The Ruin* expresses awe at the "race of giants" that Anglo-Saxons believed must originally have erected the old (Roman) stone structures—or even more ancient Neolithic monuments—that they sometimes encountered in their midst. Besides kings and a few powerful nobles, most of the population consisted of free farmers, each of whom had a holding, called a "hide," deemed sufficient to feed an average family, though the size of the holding would vary from region to region according to the quality of the land. As the population grew, farming tended to shift from three-field to two-field rotation, which diminished the productivity of the soil. Their diet, primarily grains, was supplemented by dairy products and some meat, mostly from sheep, whose wool also became a major product for export, particularly toward the end of the period. Women and men shared in agricultural labor, and although grave goods for women include objects associated with spinning, weaving, and household economy, there does not seem to have been as clear a line between the "women's sphere" and the "men's sphere" as appeared at a later time. Indeed, laws and wills show that women had considerable status and legal rights alongside men, and the literature of northern Europe abounds with powerful female figures. Evidence from paleopathology indicates that hard work in the fields contributed to widespread osteoarthritis, along with numerous injuries, especially to the ankles and feet. Although precise figures on life expectancy are unavailable, and would in any event vary according to local conditions, life was precarious for members of all classes. Infant and early childhood mor-

The megalithic circle known as "The Merry Maidens," located in Cornwall, England, is characteristic of Neolithic constructions the Anglo-Saxons thought were "the work of giants." (Second millennium B.C.E., photograph by Dianne Sudduth)

tality were high: Excavations at Thetford show that 87.5 percent of child deaths had occurred by age 6, though that figure seems high compared with other sites. Research in some areas suggests a 50 percent mortality rate by age 30, rising to about 90 percent by age 50. Life expectancy for the average person would therefore have been in the early thirties, with a slightly lower figure for women than men because of the dangers of childbirth. The very few persons recorded as reaching their seventies or beyond were typically from the upper nobility or clergy, who probably enjoyed the healthiest diet and hygiene. Yet even with some stratification of society, no sharp division between folk and elite culture existed among the Anglo-Saxons, so that even their "sophisticated" art and literature were permeated by folkloric patterns and materials.

From these social conditions emerged the traditional worldview of the Anglo-Saxons. As elsewhere in the literature of the North, Old English poems stressed the power of fate, or *wyrd*, as the "most powerful of forces" (*Maxims II*: 5). The individual's identity was so inextricably tied to that of the group that the greatest terror was to be isolated from community (as in the poem *The Wanderer*), and the bonds of loyalty between lord and retainer could not be broken without the greatest dishonor (as in the heroic poem *The Battle of Maldon*). The very shortness and uncertainty of life implied that the greatest virtue lay not so much in living a long and prosperous life as in living and, if need be, dying so as to live on in communal memory with honor (as throughout *Beowulf*). Wealth was valuable to the extent that it was shared, thereby strengthening communal bonds, and the ending of *Beowulf* sings of the uselessness of riches amassed but unshared.

Sources for Anglo-Saxon Folklore

Though Anglo-Saxon folklore generally circulated orally, most of it comes to us in texts written by the literate fraction of the population, whose education took place either in or under the influence of the monasteries. Yet in many cases the traditional folk culture and the newer Christian (and to some extent classical) learning became so intertwined that for us to try to separate these elements analytically would distort the mental and social world that the Anglo-Saxons themselves experienced.

A case in point is the great scholar Bede's work on computing the calendar, *De temporum ratione* (725). After discussing the Hebrew, Egyptian, Roman, and Greek systems, he writes a chapter on the Anglo-Saxon year, which began on December 25 and consisted of 12 lunar months: (1) Giuli, or "Yule"; (2) Solmonath, for offering cakes; (3) Hrethmonath, for the goddess Hretha; (4) Eosturmonath, for the goddess Eostre; (5) Thrimilchi, when cows are milked three times a day; (6 and 7) Litha, possibly for the moon or for the "calm time"; (8) Weodmonath, month of the weeds; (9) Halegmonath, month of holy offerings; (10) Winterfyllith, first full moon of winter; (11) Blotmonath, month of slaughter or sacrifice; (12) a repetition of Giuli, apparently the beginning of "Yule," leading again to December 25, which was known as Modranect, or "Night of the Mothers." Bede goes on to offer a prayer of thanks to Christ for being delivered from these "vain" matters, but he nevertheless has provided us with invaluable evidence of one aspect of the popular culture of his time.

Other works comfortably mix folklore with bookish learning. *The Exeter Book,* which contains some of the most sophisticated Old English poetry, also contains numerous riddles to tease the wits with images of such commonplace objects as horns, fish, cuckoos, beer, and bows—alongside riddles about a book and a pen and fingers. Only someone familiar with the village market could have a fair chance at "A One-Eyed Seller of Garlic," and only someone who had long observed the creatures of the woods could solve "A Badger." Yet these riddles survive only because monks took great delight in collecting and preserving such folklore at the same desks where they carried out the more "serious" tasks of writing and transcribing commentaries on the Psalms and the Gospels.

So also with the many charms that fill the leechbooks, or medical manuals, together with other lore about illnesses, injuries, and their treatments. These manuals often combine information from classical works on medicine with incantations "For a Sudden Stitch," "Against Wens," or even "Against a Dwarf" (apparently one who causes disease). Charms were often filled with references to pre-Christian beliefs and rituals associated with ancient folk medicine, and it seems remarkable that monastic scribes copied them even into the margins of such a Christian classic as Bede's *Ecclesiastical History* (e.g., in a manuscript now at Corpus Christi College, Cambridge). In "The Nine Herbs Charm" a passage in which Woden used plants to cure snakebite and defend human habitation against poison is immediately followed by a passage in which Christ is credited with creating thyme and fennel, endowing them with great power, and giving them to aid poor and rich alike, all while he hung on the cross. Some charms offer power over nature, as in "For a Swarm of Bees." "Land Remedy" promises to cure fields that failed to produce or had been harmed by sorcery or witchcraft. It combines the Christian power of chanting in Latin the Benedicite, the Magnificat, and the Pater Noster with boring a hole in the beam of the plow and inserting incense, fennel, holy soap, and salt and placing the seed to be planted on the body of the plow, all the while chanting an incantation to "Erce, Erce, Erce, mother of earth." Then, while making the first furrow, the plowman is to chant "Hail to thee, Earth, mother of men! Be fruitful in God's embrace, Filled with food for the use of men." It may seem curious to us that medical manuals dealt with nonphysical causes of disorders in humans or in nature, but it was evidently extremely important for Anglo-Saxons to protect themselves by charms, potions, and the like against sorcery and witchcraft. When witchcraft or sorcery was discovered, terrible punishment could be exacted, as is recorded in a tenth-century document declaring that a widow and her son must forfeit their land for driving an iron pin into the image of a man. The woman was then denounced as a witch and drowned at London Bridge, and her son was made an outlaw.

Perhaps less ominous but equally mysterious are the diagnoses in Bald's *Leechbook,* a collection of medical lore, for disorders resulting from "elfshot," though the book also offers more straightforward cures for everything from poisonous spider bites to potions "for a man who is over-virile" or "for a man who is not virile enough." We may also infer from this work and *Lacnunga* that their frequent references to dysentery, toothache, and various forms of bleeding suggest that these were of particular concern at the time. Yet the distance from

The remains of Whitby Abbey, site of the Synod of Whitby in 664. The poet Cædmon became a member of the community during the time St. Hilda was serving as abbess. See the entries on Bede the Venerable and Cædmon. (Photograph by John McNamara)

practical advice on such matters to something approaching folk magic was never very great. *Lacnunga* elsewhere recommends that a woman trying to avoid a miscarriage should first step three times over the grave of a dead man while reciting a certain incantation, and next she should step over her (live) husband's body in bed while reciting, "Up I go, I step over you, with a live child, not a dying one, with a child to be fully born, not with a doomed one." Those who think that there was a sharp division between elite culture and folklore in Anglo-Saxon England would do well to consider that such prescriptions were commonplace in learned works at the time.

Another area for research is the complex body of law through which the Anglo-Saxons sought to define themselves as a people. Of the legal codes that survive, Aethelberht's Laws (c. 602–603) is by far the oldest. It not only lists prohibitions against various actions, along with fines appropriate for the violations, but it also provides an elaborate system of compensations—payments that must be made to an offended party for injuries to different parts of the body or for sexual violations against a spouse or servant. Each payment is measured according to the severity of the injury, so that cutting off someone's thumb requires a higher compensation than removing a little finger, and wounding a man's sexual "branch" so badly that it is ineffective demands a recompense three times his wergeld, or the amount of compensation due for taking his life. The laws give us insight into social practices and values, and despite the impression that acts of violence were commonplace, these laws actually stress the ways people attempted to settle conflicts peaceably once they had arisen.

Still other sources for folklore are the penitentials, manuals listing and defining the penances for various sins requiring confession to a priest. Penitentials offer us a vivid view of folk culture, at least as presented by the ecclesiastical writers who filled them with an amazing host of sins, defining their seriousness relative to one another and the penance to be meted out for each offense. Both the penitential of the great Archbishop Theodore and the penitential ascribed by Albers to Bede list numerous forbidden sexual practices—from adultery and fornication to various homosexual activities and even "unnatural intercourse" between a married couple "from behind." Ejaculating semen in another's mouth is "the worst of evils," far worse than incest between parent and child or brother and sister. Yet beyond this clerical fascination with sexuality there are numerous references to folk practices that threatened the official Church. There are specific prohibitions against sacrificing to demons, engaging in auguries or divinations, consulting omens from birds or dreams, conjuring up storms (presumably against enemies), and "seeking out any trick of the magicians." (Compare the horror at *hel-runan*, those who know or can "read" the mysterious runes of hell, in *Beowulf* 163.) Also intriguing are the injunctions against any woman who "puts her daughter upon a roof or in an oven for cure of a fever," a man "who causes grains to be burned where a man has died, for the health of the living and of the house," or a woman who mixes her husband's (or lover's?) semen in food to increase his ardor for her.

Yet another source of folklore is the large body of saints' lives from this period. Saints' lives naturally had the full endorsement of the official Church, but they are also filled with folkloric elements and suggest a point at which ecclesiastical and popular beliefs could mingle freely. Consider Ælfric's *Life of St. Edmund*, the Christian king of East Anglia slain by "heathen" Vikings in 869. Within a quarter of a century his cult was flourishing and he was widely revered as a martyr-saint whose passion and death became the subject of traditional legend, first as popular oral narrative and then in a Latin account by Abbo of Fleury, followed by Ælfric's Old English adaptation of Abbo. Ælfric's version generally follows the generic conventions of hagiography, yet it derives its main interest and memorability from strong folkloric elements: the king's body pierced by so many Viking javelins that it resembled a hedgehog with bristles sticking out in all directions; the decapitated head protected in the deep woods by a wolf that despite its hunger would not eat of it; the head calling out directions to the folk searching for it; the uncorrupted flesh and miraculous cure of Edmund's neck wound even after having been buried for a long time; his corpse continuing to grow hair and fingernails so that a widow had to trim them every year; the dead saint's power to freeze in their various positions the would-be grave robbers of his tomb until they could be apprehended and punished the next morning; and of course the conventional note that numerous miracles—especially cures—occurred at his burial site. Ælfric comments at the end of his story that the saint's miracles preserved "in the speech of common folk" were far more numerous than he could write down in his book. The presence of these elements in the work of such a scholarly monastic writer suggests the extent to which folk culture permeated the mental world of the monastery.

Such evidence demands that we not only recognize the enormous importance of Latin learning in Anglo-Saxon monastic communities, but also that we accord equal importance to the fact that these communities were not sealed off from the larger social world. Monasteries not only recruited members from the surrounding folk culture but also incorporated many folkloric elements in their own oral lore, which provided material for many of their writings. After the Vikings sacked Lindisfarne in 793, a monastic author noted in the *Anglo-Saxon Chronicle* that this catastrophe had been forecast by various portents, including the "fiery dragons" that "were seen flying in the air" (cf. *Beowulf*).

See also: Bede the Venerable; *Beowulf*; Cædmon; Charms; German Tradition; Medicine; Oral Theory; Scandinavian Tradition; Sutton Hoo

References and further reading: Although the classic history is still F. M. Stenton, *Anglo-Saxon England*, 3rd ed. (1971), a very thorough and well-illustrated recent history is J. Campbell, *The Anglo-Saxons* (1982). N. Howe addresses popular lore about the migration in *Migration and Mythmaking in Anglo-Saxon England* (1989). A folkloric analysis of legend and history in Bede is J. McNamara, "Bede's Role in Circulating Oral Legends in the *Historia ecclesiastica*," *Anglo-Saxon Studies in Archaeology and History* 7 (1994). C. Fell, *Women in Anglo-Saxon England* (1984), provides a social history of women. S. Rubin, *Medieval English Medicine*, AD 500–1300 (1974), is standard for medicine, paleopathology, and mortality rates; see also M. L. Cameron, *Anglo-Saxon Medicine* (1993). S. B. Greenfield and D. G. Calder, *A New Critical History of Old English Literature* (1986), gives excellent literary history. G. R. Owen's *Rites and Religions of the Anglo-Saxons* (1981) is an excellent survey of pre-Christian and Christian beliefs and practices. H. Mayr-Hartung, *The Coming of Christianity to Anglo-Saxon England*, 3rd ed. (1991), is a standard overview. On leechbooks and charms, see G. Storms, *Anglo-Saxon Magic* (1948), and V. Flint, *The Rise of Magic in Early Medieval Europe* (1991). For penitentials the standard source is J. McNeill and H. Gamer, *Medieval Handbooks of Penance* (1938), and for saints' lives the essays in P. E. Szarmach, ed., *Holy Men and Holy Women: Old English Prose Saints' Lives and Their Contexts* (1996), provide a good sampling of recent research. Specifically folkloric approaches may be found in F. Canadé Sautman, D. Conchado, and G. C. Di Scipio, eds., *Telling Tales: Medieval Narratives and the Folk Tradition* (1998). K. Crossley-Holland, *The Anglo-Saxon World* (1982), translates many of the materials included in this article.

—John McNamara

English Tradition: Middle English Period

The folkloric culture of England following the Norman invasion of 1066.

Conquest

The line traditionally drawn between the Old and Middle English eras is 1066, the date of the Norman invasion. Yet there was a long, slow period of transition during which the native English culture absorbed that of the Norman conquerors and transformed itself in the process. The most obvious changes occurred at the top. Though Anglo-Saxon government had become increasingly organized from the time of Alfred, England was largely a culture of chieftains and family-centered communities before the Normans imposed their strongly centralized government. More than 4,000 Anglo-Saxon thanes had served Harold Godwinson in 1066. After William the Conqueror defeated Harold, the thanes' roles at the top of a tighter power structure were filled by fewer than 200 Norman barons.

The move away from familial communities and toward centralized government would take centuries to complete, but from the beginning it caused major changes in upper-class pastimes. Old English heroic verse, enjoyed by a now decimated aristocracy, disappeared from writing, replaced by French chansons de geste. The most famous of the new French poems celebrated Charlemagne's nephew, Roland. Chronicles report that during the Battle of Hastings the Norman minstrel Taillefer rallied the invading troops by singing a version of Roland's story. Although some question these accounts, they demonstrate that Roland was well known to twelfth-century Anglo-Normans.

Because the Anglo-Saxons lost control of most of the centers of education and means of preserving writing, we do not know much about the legendry of the losers. Yet chronicles and other sources mention English heroes who battled the Normans. The most celebrated resister was Earl Hereward the Wake. According to the *Book of Ely*, peasants were still singing songs in praise of Hereward a century after his revolt. Hereward's legends trace the fortunes of Anglo-Saxon warrior culture. Accounts of the young hero in *Gesta Herewardi* present a figure resembling Beowulf who fights a Cornish giant and a magical bear. Stories set after the conquest depict Hereward as an outlaw like Robin Hood, living among commoners. Young Hereward is an aristocratic warrior hero; the adult is a guerrilla. The popularity of Hereward's stories in East Anglia was no accident, for in this region the Norman administration was forcing free people into bondage.

See also: *Chanson de Roland;* Folklore; Outlaw

References and further reading: The most accessible account of Hereward is M. Keen, *The Outlaws of Medieval Legend,* 2nd ed. (1977). On Taillefer, see J. Southworth, *The English Medieval Minstrel* (1989).

Farming and Housing

Political changes in England were swift and momentous, but country life proceeded by slow turns. The open-field system of agriculture, allowing crop rotation, preceded the Normans, but importations soon after the Norman invasion such as the leather harness for horses enabled each peasant to plow more land and the land to sustain a denser population. There were two agricultural regions in medieval England, corresponding with the two major topographical patterns. The west and north were relatively heavily wooded and sparsely populated. Here, as in Celtic Scotland and Wales, agriculture, herding, and hunting combined to create a subsistence economy for noncentralized tribal societies. Central England, however, was flat and not heavily forested—well suited for the new farming technology.

As the villages grew, so did the distances between the rural lords and the local peasantry. In Old English architecture most dwellings had been similar in design: although structures varied in size and quality with the status of the occupants, the wood-framed longhouse had served the earls, the peasants, and the farm animals alike. Now the Norman barons, more powerful than their Old English predecessors, began to occupy stone castles, creating obvious and visible distances between the classes. Castle dwellers attained a degree of privacy unheard of in earlier society. Such twelfth-century romances as Thomas of Britain's *Tristan* made much of this newfound sense of privacy, as heroes and heroines began to cultivate fantasies of secret lives. Isolation from one's lord and fellow warriors had been one of the greatest curses of Old English poetry, but for Tristan and other romance heroes such separation is desirable, as long as the hero can share his privacy with his lady.

See also: Courtly Love; Plow and Plowing; Tristan and Iseut
References and further reading: For details on housing, see N. Pounds, *Hearth and Home* (1989). For issues of privacy, see G. Duby and P. Ariès, *A History of Private Life*, vol. 2 (1988).

Rural Seasonal Customs and Ceremonies

Daily life was driven by seasonal change. Both lower-class and upper-class celebrations were firmly rooted in the agricultural calendar, and both retained aspects of "natural religion," beliefs in supernatural links between society and nature retained from Anglo-Saxon times. Some traditions (such as folk celebrations of All Hallows' Eve) incorporated elements of Celtic ritual, reflecting the combining of Celtic and Anglo-Saxon traditions that had occurred in the monasteries centuries before. The peasant's work year is neatly summarized in this fifteenth-century poem:

Januar	By this fire I warme my handes;
Februar	And with my spade I delfe [dig] my landes.
Marche	Here I sette my thinge to springe;
Aprile	And here I heer the fowles [birds] synge.
Maii	I am light [happy] as birde in bow [bough];
Junii	And I weede my corne well ynow.
Julii	With my sythe [scythe] my mede [meadow] I mowe;
Auguste	And here I shere [shear] my corne full lowe.
September	With my flail I erne my bred;
October	And here I sowe my whete so rede.
November	At Martynesmasse I kille my swine;
December	And at Cristesmasse I drynke redde wyne.

Work dominates the year. Recreation is mentioned for only those four months—December, January, April, May—when peasants were granted vacations of a week or more by their lords. The greatest amount of social ritual took place when the least work was required: the colder months, otherwise intolerably dark and dull. After the harvests were gathered and the grain tallied, villagers determined how many animals could be sustained by their grain. The remaining stock was slaughtered, and many animals were consumed in the autumn feasts, which combined extravagance and necessity. Because summer work had left little time for socializing, the cold months featured intensive visiting and courtship, during which neighbors reasserted communal bonds and began new families. Winter celebrations began after Michaelmas (September 29), the traditional date of the final harvest. November 1, the new year of Celtic tradition, and Martinmas (November 11) marked the beginning of winter, as communities gathered for slaughtering, feasting, and courtship. The next great holidays fell on Christmas (December 25) and the following Twelve Days, ending at Epiphany (January 6). These Christian celebrations were marked with feasts, gifts, and processions, as people normally separated by their work would travel to neighbors' homes. Peasants were expected to provide their lords with additional holiday food, but they were usually released from labor during the Twelve Days. Winter ended with the candlelight procession of Candlemas (February 2) and the wild games of Shrove Tuesday, when the last of the meat set aside for winter was consumed and the fasts of Lent began.

Another work break occurred at Easter, when lords granted peasants a week off. Easter week ended with Hocktide, which probably featured courting games. May Day (May 1), based on the Celtic holiday Beltane, was another lovers' day: young men and women gathered greenery, paired off, and spent the evening in the woods. Rogation, a men's festival, occurred on the days preceding Ascension Day (40 days after Easter). Led by a priest, men went "ganging"—walking the borders of their villages and initiating boys by throwing them into the creeks and against the trees that marked those boundaries. The ritual stressed community solidarity, male bonding, and prayer for the fertility of the fields. The final spring festivals fell during the week of Pentecost, when again peasants were released from labor, and the processions and plays of Corpus Christi (the Thursday following Pentecost, which fell 50 days after Easter) were enacted.

Because summer work was so demanding, little ceremonial took place then, but one important feast was St. John's Day (June 24), or Midsummer, marking the summer solstice. Peasants tended fires through the night, and young men leaped over the fires, presumably to assure virility, certainly to impress watching women.

See also: Festivals and Celebrations; Harvest Festivals and Rituals

References and further reading: The poem on the seasons, titled "The Months," is quoted from *The Oxford Book of English Medieval Verse*, ed. C. Sisam and K. Sisam (1970). G. H. Homans, *English Villagers of the Thirteenth Century* (1941), and B. A. Hanawalt, *The Ties That Bound* (1986), discuss the rural calendar. S. Justice, *Writing and Rebellion: England in 1381* (1993), analyzes the festivals of Corpus Christi and the beating of the bounds.

Urban Celebrations

From the twelfth century forward, with the rise of the merchant class, urban celebrations took on increasing importance. Towns grew as rural people arrived to take on craft work and as merchants from the Continent swelled the ranks of wealthy commoners. The most successful merchant families imitated the nobility, sometimes adopting aristocratic dress and heraldic arms. Craftspeople in effect created a middle world that drew some of its traditions from the peasantry and some from the nobility.

Urban and noble ceremonial constituted a sometimes refined borrowing of the agricultural calendar. During the major seasonal festivities, nature "visited" the city. In a twelfth-century description of Christmas in London, William Fitzstephen reported that houses and churches were filled with holly, ivy, bay, and other evergreens. Rural holiday processions were echoed by city mummings. In 1377, 130 mummers visited Richard II, played dice with him, and gave gifts to his court. Not all mummings were so staid; numerous London ordinances forbade masks and rioting during the Twelve Days.

Like the peasants at Rogation, urban groups possessed rituals of community definition; like city life in general, these tended to be specialized and factional in comparison to the rural. Norwich observed the day of England's patron, St. George (April 23), by sending the entire hierarchy of the town on a procession to the country, where an actor playing George slew a mock dragon. Corpus Christi celebrations included torchlight parades representing the city's hierarchy; a group's place in the parade was so important that guildsmen fought violently for choice positions.

Londoners observed at least ten annual processions, most including stops at the church of Thomas Becket, the most popular English saint, and with visits to the graves of Thomas's parents. Among the most elaborate noble ceremonies were celebrations of love. The poetry of Geoffrey Chaucer provides the earliest mention of St. Valentine's Day (February 14) as a time when men and women paired off. Chaucer and other court poets also mention lovers' games in May; these rituals seem to have differed from the rural customs mainly in their lavishness. Merchants imitated noble courtship patterns in such festivals as the London Puy, a song competition founded in the thirteenth century for the celebration of love.

See also: Becket, Saint Thomas; Valentine's Day, Saint
References and further reading: S. Thrupp, *The Merchant Class of Medieval London* (1948), records urban lifestyles; E. K. Chambers, *The Mediaeval Stage*, 2 vols. (1903), supplies copious evidence on mummings and folk drama; D. W. Robertson Jr., *Chaucer's London* (1968), describes urban ceremonials.

Romance and Folktale

In the process of colonization the Normans capitalized on ethnic conflicts in Britain. In order to conquer Wales the Normans befriended elements of the Welsh aristocracy. Neither the Romans nor the Saxons had conquered Wales, but the Normans came much closer, largely by intermarrying with Celts, settling Bretons and Flemings from across the English Channel, and playing upon the Welsh hatred of the English. The new aristocracy developed a mythology that served as a charter for their conquest. Histories and romances combined French aristocratic values with elements of Celtic folk tradition. Stories of King Arthur, long popular with the Welsh and Bretons, were reworked and made part of an elite history. About 1138 Geoffrey of Monmouth, drawing upon British literary and oral tradition and his own imagination, completed his *History of the Kings of Britain*, which inspired writers to tell Arthur's stories in Latin, French, and ultimately English. From their earliest appearance in the mid-twelfth century, romances based on Celtic legend resembled postmedieval märchen in content and form. Beginning in a courtly world of kings and queens, the stories proceeded to relate supernatural encounters. An otherworldly visitor (such as the bird-knight in Marie de France's *Yonec*), or a journey into an enchanted woods (as in Chaucer's "Wife of Bath's Tale" and the Middle English *Sir Launfal* and *Sir Orfeo*), would bring the everyday and the otherworldly face to face. As do most märchen, many romances told the story of a single young hero, beginning with a series of initiatory tests and ending with that figure's coming of age or marriage: the Middle English *Sir Degaré* and *Perceval of Galles* demonstrate this pattern.

Overlapping the supernatural romances was a group of feudal tales celebrating legendary heroes: *King Horn, Havelok the Dane, Guy of Warwick,* and *Beves of Hampton* exist in both Anglo-Norman and English versions. They tell of young men whose valor gains them kingdoms and royal wives. Unlike the Celtic-inspired tales, these works build upon English and Anglo-Scandinavian heroic legendry, and they also possess their share of marvels: Guy of Warwick, for example, battles giants, a dragon, and an impressive bovine, the Dun Cow.

Like the postmedieval oral tales to which they are clearly related, romances varied according to the status of the groups that shared them. The Anglo-Norman *Romance of Horn* extols kingship and the male world of knighthood; Marie's *Yonec,* written at nearly the same time, presents women's negative response to the male world and introduces a supernatural lover who saves an oppressed woman from her cruel lord. *Guy of Warwick,* perhaps the most popular Middle English romance, introduces a common hero, a steward's son, whose deeds

"Arthur's" Round Table, fashioned in the thirteenth or fourteenth century, perhaps for Edward I of England, and now on display at Winchester Castle. (British Tourist Authority)

elevate him and make an earl's daughter his wife. Elite romance celebrates hierarchy; popular romance, more directly related to the modern folktale, presents a compensation fantasy in which the lowly find power.

The deeds of romances—even the supernatural romances—were presented as true, sometimes with corroborating evidence. Although contemporary critics tend to dismiss such truth claims as mere conventions, the complex interaction between romance and historical legendry cannot be overlooked. In 1191 monks at Glastonbury claimed they had found the grave of Arthur, while for centuries, others claimed that Arthur lay asleep in a cave. As late as 1485, in his introduction to Malory's *Morte Darthur*, William Caxton states that seeing such relics as Gawain's skull and Cradok's mantle convinced him that the tales of Arthur were true.

Whether or not we believe that medieval listeners believed these tales, there is no doubt that the romances presented models for society to emulate. Around 1300, an English king, perhaps Edward I, had a Round Table built; like English kings before and since, he played the role of Arthur. Guy of Warwick's battle with the dragon became the subject for sermons on courage. By the end of the fifteenth century knighthood was essentially dead as a military phenomenon, but it continued to thrive in aristocratic play.

See also: Arthur; Fairy Lover; Geoffrey of Monmouth; Guy of Warwick; Havelok; Loathly Lady; Marie de France; Romance; Welsh Tradition

References and further reading: W. R. J. Barron, *English Medieval Romance* (1987), and S. Crane, *Insular Romance* (1986), discuss English and Anglo-Norman romance. V. B. Richmond, *Guy of Warwick* (1994), presents a thorough study of the development of this most popular English hero. N. M. Bradbury, *Writing Aloud* (1998), examines the oral and popular dimensions of such Middle English romances as *Gamelyn* and *Havelok*.

Religious Lore

Religious lore took on new shapes as society changed. Parish guilds, created as congregants banded together for mutual security and recreation, participated in pilgrimages, processions, and annual feasts that embraced music, gaming, and speech making. In urban centers such as York, Beverley, and Chester, craft guilds combined their talents to stage Corpus Christi cycles, enacting in as many as 40 different plays the important scenes of Christian history. Such works as the Wakefield Master's *Second Shepherd's Play* borrowed from folktale to create an energetic blend of popular culture and religious doctrine. The *Second Shepherd's Play* utilizes a humorous narrative ("Mak and the Sheep," AT 1525M) widespread in medieval and postmedieval tradition—in which a man who has stolen a sheep disguises it as a baby in order to escape arrest and punishment—and turns it into a comic echo of the birth of Christ, the biblical event celebrated in this drama.

Folktale and Christian doctrine also met in the pulpit. From the twelfth century onward sermon collections were filled with popular narratives adapted to moral and religious purposes. Such legends as "The Spider in the Hairdo" were localized and used to warn parishioners of the consequences of ungodly

Sow playing the harp; misericord supporter, Beverley Minster, Yorkshire, 1520. (Photograph by Malcolm Jones)

behavior: an Oxfordshire woman took so long to adorn her hair each Sunday that she began arriving later and later at church. One week she entered church just as the mass was ending, and the devil, disguised as an enormous spider, descended upon her head and would not leave until a priest administered communion to the woman.

The popularity of exempla is attested in verse treatments like Robert Mannyng's *Handlyng Synne* (1303), which provides a wealth of belief narratives, such as the tale of the couple that became stuck together while having sex on holy ground; only the prayers of monks could separate them. Also popular were Middle English saints' lives, which reinforced Christian values through heroic models rather than through the scare tactics of the exempla. Late-medieval England saw the rise of pilgrims' processions, especially to the shrine of St. Thomas Becket in Canterbury. Murdered by servants of his king in 1170, Thomas became the center of a popular cult. Visits to his shrine were supposed to cure all manner of physical and spiritual ills. As the Middle Ages wore to a close, the pilgrimage to the shrine of the Virgin of Walsingham eventually superseded the Canterbury pilgrimage in popularity.

The great cathedrals present concrete proof of the blendings and tensions of elite and folk cultures. At Canterbury folklore was enlisted to support official fund-raising efforts through stained glass panels depicting popular legends of people saved by St. Thomas or punished for failing to honor him. Throughout England, misericords, the carved undersides of bishops' seats, depicted folk themes. As the bishop promoted the official order, the carvings beneath his buttocks challenged that order, presenting a world turned upside down in which mice hanged cats, carts pulled horses, and wives beat their husbands.

See also: Becket, Saint Thomas; Carol; Drama; Folktale; Misericords; World Turned Upside Down

References and further reading: The social details attending the presentation of mystery cycles are published in the REED (Records of Early English Drama) series (1980–). On the folktale analogs of the *Second Shepherd's Play*, see B. J. Whiting, "An Antecedent of the Mak Story," *Speculum* 7 (1932). G. R. Owst, *Literature and Pulpit in Medieval England* (1933), presents many folk exempla, including the tale of the devil-spider; D. Weinstein and R. M. Bell, *Saints and Society* (1982), discusses the special nature of late-medieval saints' lives; V. Turner and E. Turner, *Image and Pilgrimage in Christian Culture* (1978), discusses English medieval pilgrimage. G. M. Gibson, *The Theater of Devotion* (1989), treats popular piety and drama, as well as the cult of the Virgin of Walsingham.

—Carl Lindahl

Epic

Long narrative poem dealing with legendary or mythic events in a particular culture.

Epics are often archaic or elevated in style and deal with important social and cultural themes. They usually concern themselves with the exploits of a culturally significant hero such as the Germanic Beowulf, the ancient Greek Achilles, or the medieval French Roland. The term *epic* is used to characterize both written works, such as Virgil's *Aeneid*, and orally composed (or orally derived) works, such as the Old English *Beowulf*, Old French *Chanson de Roland*, or the ancient Greek *Iliad* and *Odyssey*. Many traditional epics are the product of so-called heroic societies, characterized by a warrior nobility and a class of professional court poets whose task it was to record and celebrate the deeds of the aristocrats. The term is often used loosely to refer to any lengthy narrative with a pretentious or historical theme.

The origins of epic lie in the oral preservation of history, legend, and myth in preliterate cultures. Remarkably, the earliest extensive written material in many cultures is not the first fumbling steps of a new art form but a major literary masterpiece in a complex verbal form; not the stirrings of a new medium but the fully formed flower of an ancient one. For example, we find the Homeric epics and Hesiod's *Theogony* being written down in the eighth century B.C.E. in Greece, the Sumerian *Gilgamesh* epic around 2000 B.C.E. in Mesopotamia, the Sanskrit epic *The Mahabharata* around 300 B.C.E. in India, and the Old English *Beowulf* perhaps as early as 800 C.E. The length and complexity of these early epics, the fact that once they are written down they tend to become frozen in form, and the fact that they are not followed immediately in their own cultures by similar works in writing all indicate that the written texts that survive represent the partial record of a fully developed oral genre from the long ages before writing.

Early Epic

Although epic is found in many places in the world, our knowledge of traditional epic in Europe begins with the *Iliad* and the *Odyssey,* attributed to the legendary ancient Greek poet Homer. The Homeric poems as we have them in writing were probably finally composed in the eighth century B.C.E., but they are set 400 years earlier during the time of the Trojan War. The poems are a product of oral tradition, composed by means of traditional formulas and themes and expressing the values of a warrior aristocracy. As with other oral compositions, epics would have been recomposed during performance, making each performance unique but nevertheless fully consonant with the entire tradition. An interesting feature of the Homeric poems is that they depict their own performance. In the *Iliad* Odysseus leads a deputation to placate the angry hero Achilles and finds him in his tent, playing the lyre and singing "the famous deeds of heroes" (*Iliad* 9.189).

The Homeric epics provide a model for the preservation and transmission of other epic traditions. The epic tales themselves are the product of long development by professional oral singers in an aristocratic setting. Some time after the introduction of writing as a technology in the culture, one or more oral performances are reduced to written form by some means (dictation, writing by a trained singer) or committed to memory in fixed form. Widespread use of written texts and the passing of the social class that supported the oral poets leads to the canonization and written preservation of certain important epic texts, which then become cultural icons and literary models. Once fixed in substantially their present form, sections of the Homeric poems were presented publicly by performers called *rhapsodes* (stitchers) who memorized the texts. Homer is constantly reproduced and quoted in post-fifth-century B.C.E. Greek literature and served as the model for Virgil's first-century B.C.E. Latin literary epic, the *Aeneid*. Some similar process explains the genesis of ancient epics such as *The Mahabharata* and medieval epics such as the *Chanson de Roland* (Song of Roland). The terms *traditional epic* and *literary epic* are useful designations for the two varieties of text described above, with the term *literary epic* reserved for those works clearly composed in writing.

The origin of epic seems to have been in highly stratified cultures with a need to preserve historical, genealogical, and mythical information about the important families. Although the story patterns themselves are often focused on incidents of small historical scope, the broad reach of the overall tradition can be seen both in embedded tales and in the knowledge presupposed of the audience. Homer's *Iliad*, for instance, is concerned with the particular moment in the long siege of Troy by the Achaeans at which the premier Greek hero, Achilles, refuses to leave his tent to fight the Trojans because of a dispute with Agamemnon, the leader of the expedition. While neither the death of Achilles nor the fall of Troy is recounted in the *Iliad* itself, knowledge of both is presupposed by the narrative. The story also recounts within it many incidents from the legendary history of Greece and many mythological stories concerning the Olympian gods and their interactions with men. The story of the blinding of Lycurgus, for instance, is recounted in Book 6. History, genealogy, and myth come together in traditional epic. Agamemnon and his brother Menalaus, the Achaean leaders, and Priam, the king of Troy, all are descended from the chief god, Zeus.

So long as epic is produced in an oral environment it lives in a constant state of revision. It must always be intelligible to its immediate audience, so it evolves linguistically and descriptively. But it must also retain its narrative power, so it keeps its important characters, story patterns, and key type scenes. For example, the Achaean heroes in the *Iliad* and *Odyssey* fight with round hoplite shields that did not come into use in Greece until centuries after the events depicted in the epics. The so-called catalog of ships in Book 3 of the *Iliad*, on the other hand, seems to preserve a list of chieftains and their forces that was established much earlier in the tradition than the version that survives to us. Likewise, the ninth-century Irish prosimetric epic *Táin Bó Cúailnge* (Cattle Raid of Cooley) depicts a chariot-using heroic culture of around the year 1, thus preserving well into the Christian era descriptive remnants of a physical culture that probably never existed in Ireland at all. The Celts used war chariots on the Continent and in Britain, but archaeology has uncovered no evidence of their use in Ireland.

It is a characteristic of traditional epics that they tend to be reduced to writing in the last stages of the cultures that value them and to disappear as a genre soon after. This is not to say, however, that the important cultural information contained in them is dissipated. The story material in epic is often shared with other oral and written genres: legend, folktale, onomastics. It can, in fact, be said that epic is in constant dialogue with other forms of recording important cultural information. Rhŷs Carpenter has pointed out the strong resemblance between the plot of the *Odyssey* and that of the folktale often referred to as "The Bear's Son" (AT 301, "The Three Stolen Princesses"). It has been suggested that the story patterns of epics among the Indo-European language group preserve within the framework of legendary history the early myths of these peoples. In particular, Georges Dumézil has postulated a tripartite structure for Indo-European myth (consisting of levels that he designates Sovereignty, War, and Fertility) that reveals itself in epic as standard plot elements, such as a war between the Fertility figures on one side and the Sovereignty and War figures on the other, an example being the war between the Vanir and the Aesir in Norse myth. Dumézil's theories have produced lively controversy among scholars, but the fact remains that many of the motifs he points to—such as the initiatory battle between the culture hero and a triple adversary found in Germanic, Celtic, Roman, and Indic narratives—are deeply embedded in a large number of epic and mythic traditions in the Indo-European world.

European Epic

In Europe, the Germanic, Romance, Celtic, Greek, and Slavic traditions have all left epic texts. Some of these texts are fragmentary, some are literary reworkings of traditional material, some are in prose or mixed prose and verse, and some verge on the folkloric rather than epic, but all can be identified as deriving directly from traditional epic. In Germanic, the earliest materials are in Old English: *Beowulf* and the fragmentary *Finn*, *Waldhere*, and *The Battle of Maldon*, all of which take place in a world of common Germanic tribal interactions involving Geats, Burgundians, Goths, and other Germanic tribes and groups. Evidence that epic composition was a living tradition into the Middle Ages is provided by the Continental Germanic epic fragments *Dietrich von Bern* and the *Hildebrandslied*, which were apparently composed sometime in the ninth century and which tell of the exploits of Theodoric the Great, the Ostrogothic king of Italy from 493 to 526.

Old French epic is represented by a large number of chansons de geste (literally, "songs of exploits"), most notable among them the twelfth-century *Chan-*

son de Roland (Song of Roland), which tells of the heroic death of Charlemagne's nephew, Roland, at the eighth-century battle of Roncevaux and Charlemagne's revenge on the Moors of Spain for Roland's killing. Other poems in this genre deal with the legendary Guillaume d'Orange and with the wars of a group of powerful barons, such as Raoul de Cambrai. Of the same period is the Spanish *Cantar de mio Cid* (Song of My Cid), recounting the eleventh-century deeds of Rodrigo Díaz de Vivar, called El Cid (My Lord), who became a heroic figure in the struggle to reconquer Spain from the ruling Muslims. These Romance-language narrative poems almost certainly have a variety of compositional histories, but the earliest of them, particularly *Roland* and *Cid*, show very strong evidence of having emerged from an oral milieu.

Celtic epic tradition consists of a body of tales, mainly in prose and in the language of the ninth century, concerning the heroes of the five legendary provinces of Ireland in a hypothetical heroic age around the year 1. The primary set of heroic tales is the so-called Ulster cycle. Although these tales are in prose, many of them share story patterns with other Indo-European epic; the *Táin Bó Cúailnge* with the *Iliad*, for example, or the *Aided Oenfer Aife* (The Death of Aife's Only Son) with the *Hildebrandslied* and the Iranian legend of Sohrab and Rustam, in which a heroic figure unknowingly kills his own son who is under an injunction never to reveal his name. Medieval reflexes of epic material are found in the twelfth-century Russian poem *Prince Igor*, which may have been composed orally or in careful imitation of oral style, and the Byzantine Greek narratives about Digenis Akritas, which though found only in written form and in post-fourteenth-century manuscripts shows signs of reflecting a recent oral tra-

Eleventh-century illustration of Spanish Christian warriors outfitted to fight the Saracens. (From Comentarios al Apocalipsis, *Biblioteca Nacional, Madrid; reproduced from Elizabeth Hallam,* Chronicles of the Crusades, *New York, 1989)*

dition. Many of the motifs and story patterns that characterize traditional heroic epics are later found in other literary forms, such as medieval romances (the English *King Horn*, for example), story collections (Chaucer's "Wife of Bath's Tale"), local legends, and folktales.

The *Aeneid*

Because of the prestige of Virgil, the *Aeneid* is the literary epic that had the most influence on the medieval world. Not just the property of the learned, Virgil's work resurfaces in romance, such as the Old French *Roman d'Aeneas*, and in many references in popular culture. The Homeric epics were primarily known in the Middle Ages through two late-antique Latin paraphrases attributed to Dares Phrygius and Dictys Cretensis. The *Aeneid* has often been seen as a model even for what has been described above as traditional epic, but as the *Aeneid* itself is carefully modeled on Homer's works, the question of influence on overall structure and heroic tone in any particular work cannot in principle ever be settled. Additionally, since traditional material passed in and out of various media and various genres, modern distinctions between "literary" and "popular" or "learned" and "folk" often make little sense in periods before the introduction of uniform mass printing. The real era of the European literary epic is the Renaissance, which saw the composition of long narrative poems such as Edmund Spenser's *Faerie Queene*, John Milton's *Paradise Lost*, and Ludovico Ariosto's *Orlando furioso* (Roland's Madness).

See also: *Beowulf; Cantar de mio Cid;* Chanson de Geste; *Chanson de Roland;* Oral Theory; Ulster Cycle

References and further reading: J. Foley, *Oral-Formulaic Theory and Research: An Introduction and Annotated Bibliography* (1985), contains a very large number of references to works specifically concerned with epic. For medieval Norse material, see C. Clover and J. Lindow, *Old Norse-Icelandic Literature: A Critical Guide* (1985). The magisterial *The Growth of Literature* (1932; rpt. 1986) of H. M. Chadwick and N. K. Chadwick is of primary importance for traditional epic. A. Lord's *The Singer of Tales* (1960) and *The Singer Resumes the Tale* (1995), the latter ed. M. Lord, and A. Parry, ed., *The Making of Homeric Verse: The Collected Papers of Milman Parry* (1987), are the clearest statements of the history and theory of oral-traditional epic composition. The most extensive study of the Indo-European poetic background of oral-traditional epic is C. Watkins, *How to Kill a Dragon* (1995). Other general studies include C. Whitman, *Homer and the Heroic Tradition* (1958), G. Nagy, *Greek Mythology and Poetics* (1990), and *The Best of the Achaeans: Concepts of the Hero in Archaic Greek Poetry* (1979). R. Carpenter, *Folktale, Fiction, and Saga in the Homeric Epics* (1946), points to a variety of similarities and interconnections between folk and epic material. A collection of essays on a variety of medieval traditions is J. Duggan, ed., *Oral Literature: Seven Essays* (1975). T. Andersson, *Early Epic Scenery: Homer, Virgil, and the Medieval Legacy* (1976), is an uncompromising argument for the direct influence of literary epic on medieval genres and stands in opposition to J. Foley, *Traditional Oral Epic: The* Odyssey, Beowulf, *and the Serbo-Croatian Return Song* (1990). J. Harris, "*Beowulf* in Literary History," *Pacific Coast Philology* 16 (1981), and J. Niles, Beowulf: *The Poem and Its Tradition* (1983), are good starting places for Old English epic. For Old French and other Romance-language epics, see J. Duggan, *The Song of Roland: Formulaic Style and Poetic Craft* (1973), and for medieval Spanish, T. Montgomery, *Medieval Spanish Epic: Mythic Roots and Ritual Language* (1998). For the proposed mythic background of Indo-European epic, see G. Dumézil, *Mythe et epopée*, 4th ed. (1986).

—*Daniel F. Melia*

Eucharist

Both an object and a ritual, enfolded within the sacrament that was raised above all others in the central Middle Ages, circa 1200.

The Eucharist was the ritual of remembrance of Christ's sacrifice as presaged and offered by Jesus to the Apostles at the Last Supper and celebrated in a variety of forms by early Christians. Throughout the twelfth century its significance and the details of the procedures attached to it became increasingly clarified and codified by theologians and canonists. During the celebration of the Mass, the words of consecration were pronounced by the priest at the altar over an unleavened wheaten disc of bread (the Eucharistic host, the Eucharist) and a chalice of wine; these words in turn summoned Christ as his body became present in the bread and wine. The nature of this "presence" was the subject of heated debate in the central Middle Ages, but it was strongly formulated in 1215 as being a substantial presence—a real one, in the sense that the bread and wine had been transformed into Christ's flesh and blood through the operation of "transubstantiation" at the pronouncement of the priest's words, the very words that Christ had enunciated at the Last Supper. The wheaten disc of bread thus became Christ's body, the real historical body of the Passion, even as the external appearance of bread (and wine) remained on the altar. This statement dictated highly ritualized treatments of the host-Christ and also prompted a barrage of investigation into the consequences of the theological claims about it: Was Christ there flesh and blood? Did he exist on the altar and in heaven simultaneously? Could even a sinful priest effect the transformation of transubstantiation? Believers were encouraged to participate in the Eucharistic Christ by receiving the Eucharistic host at communion at least once a year, as the final stage of an annual self-examination, following confession and penance. Following the pastoral rulings of the Fourth Lateran Council of 1215, communion became the annual touchstone of Christian virtue, of membership in the community of the Church, and of social acceptability. Monks and nuns were allowed to take communion more frequently, and priests could celebrate it daily and twice on Christmas Day.

The enormous power attributed to the simple wheaten disc that was the host gave rise to problems related to the manner of its handling and containment. It was to be contained in precious metal vessels and locked away in the church; it was to be put into transparent containers for occasional viewing by the populace; it was to be carried out of the church in procession only with the utmost care and decorum, held by the priest and accompanied by a retinue of clerical servers and adoring believers. The very marking out of the Eucharist and its space evoked desires to increase the frequency of occasion for gazing at it. In response, Church authorities from the Middle Ages and later inveighed against too frequent display of the Eucharist or too frequent reception of communion by lay people. The world of exemplary religious tales known as exempla, which reflect popular understandings and widespread practice, repeatedly dramatized the many ways in which laypeople attempted to appropriate the host to themselves for private use. Most often this was achieved by taking the host out of the mouth after communion, and less frequently through theft from a church.

A layperson may have procured the host for use in the pursuit of health, love, or prosperity. One of the most famous tales of the period is that of the woman who sprinkled her beehive with crumbs of the host to encourage the bees' productivity, only to find that her bees had erected a waxen altar and adored the Eucharist on it. Another common tale had the host used in the pursuit of love as a wife held it in her mouth while kissing her husband in the hope of rekindling his affection. When employed in magic, the useful Eucharist could also effect harm: poison could be concocted with the host as an important ingredient, like that which the Jews were claimed to have prepared for the poisoning of the wells in 1321 and 1348.

Eucharistic ideas and practices offered scope for the development of a wide range of related beliefs. Groups that came to be considered dissenting, aberrant, or heretical (e.g., the Lollards, Cathars, and female Beguines of northern Europe) often developed critiques of Eucharistic lore. As a central symbol of Christian orthodoxy, the Eucharist became a focus for fantasies of abuse and labeling of difference. Thus, in the later Middle Ages, marginal groups, especially the Jews, were accused of desecrating the host. Such accusations often inspired violent mob actions. In the anti-Semitic narratives, which are to be found both in guidebooks for preaching and in chronicle reports of rumors and actions of communities, the Eucharist is said to have been tested or abused by Jews and to have reacted potently: by turning into a crucifix, into flesh, or into a wounded child (Christ).

See also: Blood; Jews, Stereotypes of

References and further reading: Folklorists would be advised to begin with the more recent works on the Eucharist, which tend to integrate social and cultural concerns, rather than to begin with theological considerations. A helpful introduction to the theologies of the Middle Ages is G. Macy, *The Theologies of the Eucharist in the Early Scholastic Period* (1985). For popular ideas about and practices revolving around the Eucharist, see M. Rubin, *Corpus Christi: The Eucharist in Late Medieval Culture*, chs. 2 and 5 (1991); for a still helpful treatment of a variety of uses in magic, see "Die Eucharistie als Zaubermittel im Mittelalter," *Archiv für Kirchengeschichte* 20 (1930); for some of the tales associating Jews with the Eucharist, see M. Rubin, *Gentile Tales: The Narrative Assault on Late-Medieval Jews*, ch. 2 (1998). On the claims of dissenting groups against Eucharistic lore through tale and vernacular lore, see A. Hudson, *The Premature Reformation* (1988), and C. W. Bynum's description of the elaborate practices and traditions developed by and around religious women: *Holy Feast and Holy Fast: The Religious Significance of Food for Medieval Women* (1987).

—Miri Rubin

Eulenspiegel

German trickster figure whose pranks were first published circa 1510, in a form recently discovered to have been codified by Hermann Bote of Brunswick.

It seems certain, however, that the anecdotes that Bote recorded had circulated in oral tradition since about 1400. Eulenspiegel's name, conveyed in early woodcuts by a rebus of an owl (*Eule*) and mirror (*Spiegel*) that he holds aloft

An early-sixteenth-century German representation of Eulenspiegel; note the owl and the mirror from which his name is derived. (North Wind Picture Archives)

(hence the c. 1519 English translation as *Howleglass*), seems actually to be composed of *ulen* (to clean) and *Spiegel* (in hunter's terminology, an animal's rump). The name is thus originally a scatological joke at the hearer's expense, meaning something like "Wipe my arse," a fitting sobriquet for a figure with such a pronounced penchant for scatology.

Even as a child, riding behind his father on the same horse, he deliberately exposed his bare bottom to passersby, who were duly scandalized. His first recorded exploit as a young man derives from a characteristic linguistic perversion of a task commanded by his lord: he was always to defecate on any hemp (*Henep*) he might find growing by the wayside, in order to fertilize this valuable plant from which the ropes that hang thieves were made. He pretends to have become confused and treats the mustard (*Senep*) he brings up to the lord's table in the same manner as he treats the hemp. This behavior is curiously reminiscent of an actual incident that took place during the early days of the Swiss Reformation: upon his arrival in Zug in 1523, a mustard dealer was told that all his mustard came from Zurich and that *hette der Zwingli darin geschissen* (Zwingli had shat in it); here we see the Swiss Protestant leader Huldrych Zwingli (1484–1531) portrayed as Eulenspiegel.

Eulenspiegel even obtains rewards by eating his own excrement, and in this manner succeeds in outdoing the king of Poland's court jester. On another occasion, by substituting his own excrement for that of a constipated child, Eulenspiegel earns the thanks of the child's mother. He tricks a cobbler into thinking that frozen excrement is tallow, drives away his employer with a particularly noxious fart, and introduces a pile of his excrement into a tavern, thereby driving out the company. He defecates in a bathhouse, pretending that he had thought it was a latrine; he imitates an innkeeper's small children, relieving himself in the middle of the floor, and tricks another innkeeper's wife into sitting on hot ashes with a bare bottom; he soils his bed in another inn and claims a priest did it (this last episode is perhaps the subject sculpted on a corbel in the staircase tower of the Hotel de Ville in Noyon). He "moons" a messenger, and so on. Even on his deathbed, the arch-trickster contrives to fool the avaricious priest who comes to hear his confession, causing him to thrust his hand into a pot full of excrement covered with a layer of coins! It is noticeable, however, that Eulenspiegel's scatological pranks are directed against aristocrats, priests, burghers, and tradesmen, but never against the lowliest stratum of society, to which he himself belongs.

There seems to be little iconography that can be indisputably linked to Eulenspiegel before the first woodcut-illustrated editions of the early sixteenth century. However, one such presumed reference is that of a wooden carving in the shape of his rebus (i.e., an owl holding a mirror) at Kempen (1493).

See also: Fool; Scatology; Trickster

References and further reading: See W. Mieder, "'Eulenspiegel macht seine Mitbürger durch Schaden klug' Sprichwörtliches im *Dil Ulenspiegel* von 1515," *Eulenspiegel-Jahrbuch* 29 (1989); *Till Eulenspiegel: His Adventures*, trans. P. Oppenheimer (1995); R. Pfefferkorn, *Ausstellung Till Eulenspiegel: Einst und jetzt* (1983); P. Rusterholz, "Till Eulenspiegel als Sprachkritiker," *Wirkendes Wort* 27 (1977); W. Wunderlich, *Till Eulenspiegel* (1984).

—*Malcolm Jones*

Evil Eye

The ability to inflict death, disease, or destruction by a glance.

Belief in the evil eye is widespread throughout Christian, Jewish, and Islamic cultures and shows remarkable similarities of detail wherever and whenever it occurs. This belief is also ancient; it is found in Sumerian and Egyptian texts and throughout the Greco-Roman world. In the folk belief of recent centuries, it is strongest in countries bordering the Mediterranean, whether Christian or Islamic, and it also exists in Ireland and Gaelic Scotland, though not quite so intensely. More sporadic allusions occur in the folklore of virtually every European country. The evil eye is regarded as a natural, inborn power, unlike witchcraft or sorcery, but there are divergent traditions as to whether it is under the control of its possessor. Sometimes it is spoken of as a force deliberately projected in a spirit of envious malice; sometimes, as something automatic and unconscious.

The actual term *evil eye*, together with its equivalents in other languages (Italian *malocchio*, French *mauvais oeil*, German *böser Blick*), derives ultimately from biblical references to envy and malice: "Is thine eye evil because I am good?" (Matt. 20:15); Christ's listing of "an evil eye" among sins that "come from within" (Mark 7:22–23); and "Eat not the bread of him that hath an evil eye" (Prov. 23:6–7). In southern Italy, the power is commonly called *jettatura*, alluding to its being "cast" upon the victim. A learned Latin-based term, found in several languages, was *fascination*. In more colloquial English, from the Middle Ages to recent rural dialects, the concept was conveyed through a verb: people said their children, or their cattle, had been "overlooked." This was Shakespeare's usage: "Vile worm, thou wast o'erlook'd even in thy birth" (*Merry Wives of Windsor* 5.5.87).

By medieval criteria, belief in the evil eye was not a superstition, for its existence was a theory endorsed by the best authorities: not only Scripture but also many respected writers of antiquity. In his influential *Natural History* (7,2) Pliny says that among the Triballi and Illyni there are enchanters who can kill anyone they stare at, especially if the look is an angry one. They can be recognized because they have a double pupil in one eye. Cicero likewise held that the glance of any woman who has a double pupil is harmful. Moreover, medieval science held that vision was an active power, in which eyes emitted rays; the evil eye could therefore be a natural force, not a magical one, as the lawyer Bartolo of Saxoferrato pointed out in the 1330s. Thomas Aquinas refers casually to old women who harm children by looking at them. Francis Bacon, in his essay "Of Envy," says love and envy are passions that can "fascinate or bewitch" and that envy is accompanied by "an ejaculation or irradiation of the eye" that becomes a harmful "stroke or percussion" to the person envied.

There is such similarity between classical sources and recent folklore about the nature and effects of the evil eye, and even what amulets, words, and gestures to use against it, that one can safely assume continuity of tradition across the centuries. The beliefs and practices of an Italian in Dante's time can hardly have been very different from those of a Roman in Pompeii or a Neapolitan of the nineteenth century when these latter have so much in common. This is fortunate, since direct evidence from the Middle Ages is curiously scarce—much scarcer than in either the preceding or the later periods. In some Italian paintings of the fourteenth and fifteenth centuries, the infant Jesus is depicted wearing coral beads, probably because, as Reginald Scot says, "The corall preserveth such as beare it from fascination or bewitching, and in this respect they are hanged about children's necks" (*Discoverie of Witchcraft*, 1584: 13, 6). Similarly, many lead badges from Flanders, France, and England, dating from around 1400, are blatantly sexual and may be meant to avert the evil eye, as were Roman phallic amulets.

Allusions in medieval literature are few but striking. Irish mythological texts tell of the giant Balar (also Balor) Birug-derc (Piercing-Eyed), whose eye is kept covered by a metal lid except on the battlefield; once opened, it destroys whole armies by its poison. In Icelandic sagas there are several mentions of wizards or witches whose glance could blunt weapons, drive men mad, cause any living creature to drop dead, and "make the land turn over" so that nothing ever grew there again. Before killing such a wizard, it was necessary to put a bag over his head to guard against the power of his dying glance. As these literary sources are concerned with heroism, possessors of the evil eye are then defeated in combat, not thwarted by amulets.

See also: Amulet and Talisman; Phallic Imagery; Witchcraft; Wizard
References and further reading: The main discussions are F. T. Elworthy, *The Evil Eye* (1895); S. Seligman, *Der böse Blick* (1910); and A. Dundes, ed., *The Evil Eye: A Casebook* (1981), but their focus is either on antiquity or on recent folklore. There is a relevant chapter in G. Schleusner-Eichholz, *Das Auge im Mittelalter* (1985). For the lead badges, see M. Jones, "Secular Badges," in *Heilig en profaan: 1000 laat-middeleuwse insinges uit de collectie J. H. E. van Beuningen*, ed. E. van Beuningen and A. M. Koldeweij (1993).

—*Jacqueline Simpson*

Exemplum [Pl. exempla]

A story told to illustrate a moral lesson.

Stories with morals have been told since ancient times, from Aesop's fables in ancient Greece, through the long traditions of fables and animal tales with morals in the Middle Ages, and even beyond into modern times. However, the most distinctive form of the medieval exemplum is found in sermons preached to popular audiences, though the term has sometimes been used more loosely in modern literary studies to designate exemplary stories in general.

In preaching aimed at lay audiences, exempla functioned to bridge the gap between a more or less theologically educated clergy and the popular religion of ordinary people, and therefore many exempla either came from or became widespread in the folklore of town and country alike. In the early Middle Ages, exempla for sermons tended not to be available in highly schematized form. There are numerous accounts of exempla in the preaching of St. Patrick, St. Cuthbert, and St. Boniface, all of whom traveled widely to bring their message to the common people. In Bede's *Ecclesiastical History of the English People* (731) there are numerous stories related as exempla—such as the blacksmith monk who dies unrepentant and is carried by devils to hell—with the observation that the circulation of such stories has confirmed many in the faith and brought them to amend their lives. While Bede does not always describe the precise way these stories circulate in oral tradition, it is clear they are functioning as exempla whether they are presented in sermons or in more informal storytelling events. Evidence of more formal presentation of exempla in sermons is available, however, as indicated by the Anglo-Saxon *Blickling Homilies* (c. 970), which, like the contemporary homilies of Ælfric, were composed in the language spoken by ordinary people. Here, in the Blickling sermon for Easter, we have an account of Christ's triumphant Harrowing of Hell, based on the popular apocryphal fourth-century Gospel of Nicodemus, complete with Christ loosing Adam from his bonds but leaving Eve still bound, and being persuaded by Eve to release her as well by reminding him that, however remotely, she is the mother of his mother. Like most exempla set in hell, the story is filled with vivid and terrifying images of punishments that await unrepentant sinners. In the sermon for Michaelmas, the Blickling homilist recounts a vision of St. Paul, who was

> gazing towards the northern part of this world, where all waters pass below, and saw there above the water a certain gray stone. And to the north of the stone there had grown very frosty groves; and there were dark mists; and beneath the stone was the dwelling place of water-monsters and evil spirits. And he saw that on the cliff many black souls bound by their hands were hanging in the icy groves; and the devils in the shape of water-monsters were clutching at them, just like ravenous wolves. And the water under the cliff below was black; and between the cliff and the water was about twelve miles. And when the twigs broke, the souls which hung on the twigs dropped below and the water-monsters seized them. These were the souls of those who had sinned wickedly here in the world, and would not turn from it before their life's end. But now let us earnestly beseech St. Michael to lead our souls into bliss, where they may rejoice in eternity without end. Amen.

Here the Anglo-Saxon preacher invokes the horrors of the frozen North for the damned, and scholars have often noted the similarity between this description and the mere in *Beowulf*, showing the kind of link that could exist between the sermon exemplum and heroic poetry in popular culture of the time.

During the twelfth and thirteenth centuries the Church became increasingly anxious about heresies spreading among the laity, so various efforts were undertaken to ensure the orthodoxy of lay Christianity. Thus, in 1215 the Fourth Lateran Council legislated annual participation in the sacraments of penance and communion for everyone, and this promoted the spread of penitential manuals among priests hearing confessions or preaching against the sins described in them. In 1235 Robert Grosseteste, bishop of London, required clergy in his diocese to preach sermons specifically in English on the seven deadly sins, the Creed, the sacraments, and similar subjects. In 1281 John Peckham, archbishop of Canterbury, in the Constitutions of Lambeth extended the list for required preaching in English to include 14 articles of faith, the Ten Commandments, the seven sacraments, and so forth.

Since many of the clergy were unprepared for this new requirement, numerous manuals on preaching began to appear in the thirteenth century, complete with compilations of numerous exempla to be used in sermons. For example, Jacques de Vitry (c. 1170–1240) produced *Sermones vulgares* (Popular Sermons), a collection of model sermons filled with exempla drawn from literature and from personal experience, which did much to popularize their use in preaching. Some manuals were organized around lists of virtues and vices arranged alphabetically, as in the *Summa predicantium* (Compendium for Preach-

A woman leaves the altar with a demon riding the tail of her cloak; fifteenth-century German woodcut. (Dover Pictorial Archive Series)

ers) by John of Bromyard (d. 1352), which contained numerous stories to illustrate the moral lessons. Still others could be organized around a particular theme common in preaching. A well-known example would be Chaucer's "Monk's Tale," which presents a long series of stories, all of which exemplify the fall of the mighty and the theme of mutability, guiding the audience to look beyond the transient glories of this world to the eternal ones of the next.

Of particular interest were the founding and flourishing of the new preaching orders, especially the Franciscans and the Dominicans, in the thirteenth century. They were specifically trained for popular preaching, and they seem in some cases to have outshone the local clergy in their ability to attract popular audiences, along with the donations that went with such popularity. These friars spiced their sermons with fables and animal tales as well as with more conventional fare. They brought many of these out of the Latin classroom, where they had been used in textbooks for monastic students, and gave them wide circulation in popular culture. In turn, these friars also drew upon much folkloric material already circulating in oral tradition, as the research of Frederic Tubach suggests.

In 1312 the Council of Vienne gave Dominicans and Franciscans license to take their preaching out of the churches and into the streets (*in plateis communibus*). In addition, they directed the hierarchy and parish priests not to criticize them for this activity. Nevertheless, criticism of the friars did spread, as the case of Chaucer's Friar suggests, and in Florence one critic noted that after the popular Bernardino of Siena had finished his sermon and left, the people, no longer inspired by his preaching, "like snails in flight that had drawn in their horns . . . [now] shot them out again as soon as the danger was over," giving themselves over to "cards, dice, false hair, rouge pots, and . . . even to chess boards."

Popular sermon exempla ranged from the fearful to the humorous. In one, a bishop hears from a recently dead hermit that of the 30,000 people who died that day, only he and St. Bernard went to heaven, while three went to purgatory, and all the rest went to hell. In another, a con man offers to ornament a king's palace with paintings, telling him that no one who is a cuckold, a bastard, or a traitor will be able to see them. When the king and his entourage come to see the paintings, they all exclaim their pleasure at the art even though they do not see anything. Finally, of course, one knight among the court has the courage to point out that there are no paintings on the walls. But perhaps the most famous exemplum of them all is Chaucer's "Pardoner's Tale," in which three drunken revelers set out to kill Death in the midst of a plague, but ironically they all meet their own deaths through their greed. In Chaucer's fourteenth-century *Canterbury Tales*, this exemplum is itself ironic in that it is presented in a sermon directed against greed by the very pilgrim who uses his skills as a popular preacher to fulfill his own greed.

See also: Animal Tale; Chaucer, Geoffrey; Fable; Folklore; Judah the Pious
References and further reading: The classic studies of the subject are still G. R. Owst's *Literature and Pulpit in Medieval England*, 2nd ed. (1961) and his *Preaching in Medieval England* (1926). For a vast catalog of folkloric elements, see F. C. Tubach, *Index Exemplorum: A Handbook of Medieval Religious Tales* (1969). This should now be supplemented by the studies based on Tubach in J. Berlioz and M. A. Polo de Beaulieu, eds., *Les exempla médiévaux* (1992). Translations of some of the *Blickling Homilies* may be found in M. Swanton, *Anglo-Saxon Prose* (1975; rev. 1993). For Chaucer, the standard edition is *The Riverside Chaucer*, ed. Larry Benson (1987).

—*John McNamara*

Fable

A short narrative, often but not always with animal characters, to which memorable bits of wisdom, often proverbs or moral lessons, are appended.

The Western fable tradition traces its origin back to Aesop, a Greek living in the sixth century B.C.E., though it is likely that at least some of his fables circulated orally much earlier. Aesop himself appears not to have written them down, but very ancient tradition claims that the form in which they were eventually put in writing is faithful to the way Aesop himself told them. Little is known of this Aesop; legend has it that he was a clever slave, but that may simply be a way of explaining why his fables often favor underdogs. In any event, Aesopic fables became very popular in antiquity, eventually becoming a part of the Roman curriculum for teaching grammar and rhetoric in the schools, as recommended by Quintilian and Priscian.

Broadly speaking, the history of the fable in the European Middle Ages is the history of two fable collections: the first-century Latin prose and verse versions of Phaedrus and the fourth-century Latin prose translations of Babrius's earlier Greek collection. Both collections included fables that circulated in both written and oral traditions, but neither was associated with its original author: the Phaedrus collection traveled under the name of Aesop, Romulus (after a fourth-century popularization with that name), and others; part of Babrius's collection came through the Middle Ages under the name of the fourth- or early-fifth-century Latin translator Avianus. Both collections eliminated some of the fables in their sources—Romulus contains about half of the Phaedrus material and Avianus about one-third to one-fourth of Babrius—and together they constituted the essential corpus of Aesopica through the Middle Ages. To this must be added some of the Indian fable tradition that arrived in the West during the thirteenth century along with Arabic-Persian fables encountered by Europeans during the Crusades. Fables in Greek appear not to have been known in the West, though they continued to flourish in Byzantium.

The Avianus collection retained its integrity throughout the Middle Ages, and it was used as a standard textbook for young Latin students to the thirteenth century. The Romulus collection underwent a much more complicated history, producing different versions of individual fables as well as different versions of the collection itself. Even so, the Romulus tradition gradually replaced Avianus in the schools during the later Middle Ages, largely through the success of the twelfth-century collection by one "Gualterus Anglicus" (Walter of England, the same person called by German scholars the "Anonymous Neveleti," the name of a seventeenth-century editor of the work). Also in the twelfth century, but without any direct connection with Walter, Marie de France produced the first vernacular collection (in French). The first 40 of her 103 fables are from a branch of Romulus and thus go back to classical antiquity, but her remaining 63 appear to come from other sources, including folk tradition, and some may very well be original with her. Later, in the fifteenth century, the Scottish poet Robert Henryson wrote his famous *Moral Fables*, which were based partly on the Romulus version of Walter but also contained much new material.

Only at the very end of the Middle Ages did the romance of the *Vita Aesopi* (Life of Aesop), with its ten or so fables, arrive in Western Europe. The first Latin versions arrived in Italy perhaps as early as the end of the fourteenth century, and its first vernacular translation (into French) seems to have been Heinrich Steinhöwel's *Esopus* (1476–1477). Though typical of medieval Aesopica, *Esopus* also marks the beginning of the new humanistic collections, which would swell the number of fabular motifs from the medieval corpus of roughly 125 to well over 500. Steinhöwel's work was immensely popular and served as the basis for the famous English translation by William Caxton in 1484.

There are several features that contribute to the popularity of fables. Typically they are short, develop characters and action rapidly, and come to conclusions that often involve paradoxical twists of plot. They often use animals as characters, though they also may use humans (about one-third of Marie de France's fables include humans), and they are thus similar in some respects to the animal tale, such as that found in the famous Reynard cycle (discussed in the entry Animal Tale in this encyclopedia). But perhaps the main feature that distinguishes the fable from other narrative forms is the pithy statement of folk wisdom, often amusing, appended to the story as its "moral" or, in the later Middle Ages, the elaborate allegorical exegesis of the story that precedes it.

Take, for example, the fable that appears first in the works of Walter of England, Marie de France, and Robert Henryson. In Walter this is "De gallo et lapide" (The Cock and the Gem), a simple story told in 10 lines about a rooster digging for food, uncovering a precious jewel, rejecting the jewel because he cannot eat it, and therefore described as foolish at the end. What is remarkable is the 35-line allegorical interpretation that follows, in which the rooster becomes a figure for foolish persons who reject the grace of the Holy Spirit. Walter goes on to cite such authorities as Cicero and Seneca in a discussion that shifts attention away from the fable and focuses entirely on the commentary for its own sake. In Marie's version, "Del cok e de la gemme," she relates the same basic story but with a simple 4-line conclusion, noting that for some men and women, "The worst they seize; the best, despise." Henryson lengthens the fable itself, stressing the plight of the poor who need food rather than beautiful things. Yet in the moral commentary he shifts to blaming the rooster for being more concerned with worldly than spiritual needs. Even so, he does not abandon the fable itself in the manner of Walter.

Fables of Aesop, the frontispiece to Caxton's late-fifteenth-century edition. (Woodcut)

There are, of course, more complex and interesting fables. For example, in some of Marie's fables that are not part of the Romulus tradition, she produces something very close to fabliaux. In "Del vilein ki vit un autre od sa femme" (The Peasant Who Saw Another with His Wife), a peasant actually sees his wife in bed with another man. When he confronts her, she makes him gaze upon his own image in a vat of water, noting that what he sees there is not the reality it appears to be, and concluding therefore that seeing is not believing. The gullible husband agrees and apologizes to his wife for accusing her of infidelity. Marie's "moral" is very simple, stressing the importance of using one's common sense.

More typical of the medieval fable is Henryson's "The Wolf and the Wether." The fable begins with a shepherd's loss of his sheepdog, which causes terrible fear and lamentation. We hear in the shepherd's words that this man of the country, whose livelihood is now threatened by the loss of his dog, not only fears the prospect of becoming a penniless beggar in the town but is genuinely touched by the loss of his "darling deid." Touched in turn by this lament, the wether replies with proverbial wisdom, enjoining him not to grieve. The wether then proposes the deception of putting the dog's hide on himself, and in his new guise he simulates the dog's ability to chase off enemies with great success. Thus, when a wolf snatches one of the sheep and the chase ensues, Henryson describes the wolf fleeing what he thinks is the dog, letting out "his taill on lenth," ignoring the dangers of "busk" and "boig" in his panic to escape. Inevitably, the wether-dog's pelt is stripped off by his mad pursuit of the wolf through the briars. In the final exchange between the wolf and the wether, we have vivid details of the wolf's humiliation at having befouled himself ("schot behind") three times through fear in the chase. The exposed wether tries to pass it all off as a game, but the wolf seizes him by the neck and kills him. It is worth noting that Henryson expands the exchange beyond earlier versions, thus heightening the comic, if rather brutal, realism of his narrative.

But then comes the "moral." As the *moralitas* would have it, the wether deserves his fate because through pride he presumed beyond his proper station. However, if we look back at the fable itself, it would appear that while the wether does exceed his proper sphere, he does so not by pretending to be a dog, nor by presuming to wear the dog's hide, nor even by chasing the wolf. His mistake lies in pursuing the wolf beyond the limits of his responsibility, beyond his agreement with the shepherd, and certainly beyond what is necessary to protect the sheep. It is in carrying out his mad pursuit that he forces the wolf to befoul himself out of fear no less than three times. Clearly the wolf punishes the wether for humiliating him, not for presuming above his station. None of this appears in the *moralitas*, of course, and it is easy to see how the details of the wolf befouling himself—a common motif in folk humor—could resist the control of an "official" interpretation.

See also: Animal Tale; Marie de France
References and further reading: Gualterus Anglicus may be found in A. E. Wright, ed., *The Fables of "Walter of England"* (1997), which contains an excellent account of the Latin fable tradition. Marie de France, *Fables*, ed. and trans. H. Spiegel (1987), has the original

French with facing-page English translations. The standard text for Henryson is D. Fox, ed., *The Poems of Robert Henryson* (1981). These all contain extensive discussions, notes, and bibliographies. But even more comprehensive is P. Carnes, ed., *Fable Scholarship: An Annotated Bibliography* (1985), to be followed by *Fable Scholarship II* (forthcoming, 2000).

—*Pack Carnes and John McNamara*

Fabliau [Pl. fabliaux]

A distinctive type of short tale, centering on a trick or deception, that usually leads to, although occasionally it thwarts, a misdeed.

Fabliaux are comical—often darkly or ironically so—and normally feature bawdy, scatological, or criminal activities, often in combination. They are a significant feature of the medieval literature of several Western European vernaculars.

The term *fabliau* is French, a diminutive of *fable*, and derives from northeast France, where it appears as a dialectal form in Picard in the twelfth to fourteenth centuries. Of at least 127 fabliaux known in French literature of this period, a high proportion are set in this region, and several of these explicitly label themselves fabliaux, as in the first line of "Le prestre qui ot mere a force" (The Priest Who Had a Mother Forced upon Him): "Icil fableau ce est la voire" [This fabliau is the truth]. Although Old French literature offers the greatest range of fabliaux, they were also strongly represented in Middle English, Middle High German, Middle Dutch, and medieval Italian.

Fabliaux often share characteristics with the exempla, to the extent that the same tales sharing the same plot appear in both genres. Exempla are also short narrative tales; they were used to demonstrate or emphasize a moral argument or an accepted truism and were intended to be affective and didactic, to guide the audience toward morally virtuous behavior. Fabliaux are not lacking in morality—indeed, many of them end emphatically with a moral pronouncement—but they are considerably more tolerant of immoral conduct, both within the narrative (such as adultery between two characters) and in the form of telling the stories (as, for example, when Chaucer's Miller drunkenly upsets the prescribed social order to tell his fabliau in *The Canterbury Tales*). The relaxed attitude of the fabliaux to immorality is apparent in their use of marked language, either through the blunt use of crude or improper terms or through the use of euphemisms that clearly signify a vulgar action or object. This is particularly noticeable in fabliaux with a sexual theme. Exempla, however, uphold conventional propriety in every respect.

The apparent knowingness of the fabliaux—implicit in their carefully crafted plots—suggested to Joseph Bédier, among others, that their social and cultural origins lay with the bourgeoisie and that they should be viewed as the literary expression of that particular social class. The informal style, colloquial speech, and urban settings that are common to many fabliaux can be seen as supporting this theory. However, Per Nykrog suggested, rather, that fabliaux represent the antithesis of romance, a subtle parody that only an aristocratic audience would have recognized and appreciated. More recently, John Hines has argued that the focus of such speculation is misplaced and that a more pertinent focus is on the tone and content of the fabliaux. Many authors of fabliaux drew attention to themselves in their texts, and the most common persona adopted was that of the *jongleur* (the typecast figure of an itinerant minstrel), who has many parallels with the narrative figure of the clerk (student). Both of these figures are presented as being able to obtain all of their needs and desires (food, sex, etc.) by using their wits, and indeed they appear to delight in doing so, outwitting figures from every social stratum from peasant to knight. The most famous fabliau writer in Middle English, Chaucer, provides useful examples of this sort of tone in his "Miller's Tale" and "Reeve's Tale" in *The Canterbury Tales*. In both of these tales clerks outwit artisans. They are juxtaposed with "The Knight's Tale" (a romance) and are deliberately introduced as "cherles tales" (tales told by lower-class men), yet the sophistication and erudition displayed in the tales seems to preclude such lowly and uneducated origins. Such a focus on wit, combined with the connections between fabliaux and the medieval satirical tradition (as discussed by Peter Dronke), suggests that locating the fabliau in a wide-ranging scholarly milieu is more productive than trying to precisely define its exact source and intended audience.

Although putting forward the Miller's and Reeve's narratives as "cherles tales" is a device for Chaucer to suggest that conventional propriety and morality may be bypassed here and that he cannot be held responsible as author, fabliaux are neither immoral nor amoral. Many fabliaux end with an explicit moral, although the exaggerated and absurd nature of many fabliaux means that a conventional moral can seem inadequate, if not facetious. The actual moral message of a fabliau is more likely to be found in poetic justice, in a down-to-earth aside that balances the excesses of the narrative, or in the implicit warning found in the consequences of foolish or unlawful conduct—that is, as part of the narrative itself rather than in the conventional moral that is appended.

Although the term *fabliau* derives from Old French and the majority of extant examples of the genre is French, there is some evidence (adduced in the work of Jan de Vries and John Hines) that their original derivation was more widely rooted and that French authors (particularly in the Picard region) were probably involved in mutual exchange of material with the Middle Dutch authors of fabliaux, which were known in their native language as *boerden* (sg. *boerde*). There is also some evidence of similarly

Chaucer's Miller, a famous fictional fabliau narrator; adapted from an illustration in the early-fifteenth-century Ellesmere manuscript of The Canterbury Tales. *(North Wind Picture Archives)*

Chaucer's Reeve, the Miller's storytelling rival; adapted from an illustration in the early-fifteenth-century Ellesmere manuscript of The Canterbury Tales. *(North Wind Picture Archives)*

close relationships among European fabliaux. However, France remains the center of fabliau production, and many of the early French fabliaux name their authors; Jean Bodel and Rutebeuf are among the best known. The willingness of the authors of these narratives to name themselves suggests that despite their typical content and language, the tales would probably have been regarded as socially acceptable and valid literature—one only has to look at the fabliaux from such well-known and respected authors as Chaucer and Boccaccio (whose narratives in the *Decameron* are, interestingly, told by a mixed-gender group of aristocrats) to see that this was clearly the case by the later Middle Ages.

The acceptability of the genre is further demonstrated by the fact of its survival and circulation in the postmedieval period. In the early sixteenth century jestbooks (collections of amusing prose narratives) began to be compiled, often featuring narratives that are recognizable as fabliaux. Interestingly, however (as the first English translation of Boccaccio's *Decameron* was not available until 1620), the primary source for these was Boccaccio rather than Chaucer. The postmedieval fabliau tradition flourished most extensively in the form of ballads, many of which feature the sexual, scatological, or criminal behavior associated with the fabliau and draw either on literary material from Chaucer, Boccaccio, and early French fabliaux or on more localized traditions.

Undoubtedly the fabliaux are closely allied to the oral traditions of medieval and postmedieval Europe. This relationship, suggested by the fictional storytellers of the *Decameron* and *The Canterbury Tales*, is demonstrated by Boccaccio and other medieval novella writers such as Sercambi who often name their oral sources and make it clear that the plots and storytelling contexts themselves were distributed through a wide social range, embracing the merchant classes, artisans, and peasants. The social breadth of the fabliau is also indicated by the huge number and variety of surviving texts. For example, Chaucer's "Friar's Tale," a narrative that like many others can function either as an exemplum or a fabliau, exists in well over 60 late-medieval versions, in Latin as well as German and English and several other vernaculars, and persists in later oral tradition as "With His Whole Heart" (AT 1186), vastly popular in twentieth-century Europe. The written medieval fabliaux demonstrate the same fluidity of plot and style found in later oral storytelling contexts, in which the narrator freely reshapes the received traditional material to fit his or her personal rhetorical stance and the tastes and expectations of the audience.

See also: Chaucer, Geoffrey; *Decameron*; Folktale; *Novella*; Trickster; *Unibos*
References and further reading: For editions and translations of French fabliaux, see A. de Montaiglon and G. Raynaud, *Recueil général et complet des fabliaux* (1872–1890); W. Noomen and N. van den Boogaard, eds., *Nouveau recueil complet des fabliaux* (1982–); and R. Eichmann and J. DuVal, eds. and trans., *The French Fabliau* (1985). For English fabliaux, see *The Riverside Chaucer*, ed. L. D. Benson (1988), and for Italian fabliaux, see C. H. McWilliam, trans., *Decameron* (1972). For general studies, see J. Bédier, *Les fabliaux: Etudes de littérature et d'histoire littéraire du moyen âge* (1893); P. Nykrog, *Les fabliaux: Etude d'histoire littéraire et de stylistique mediévale* (1957); J. Rychner, *Contribution à l'étude des fabliaux: Variants, remaniements, dégradations*, 2 vols. (1960); P. Dronke, "The Rise of the Medieval Fabliau: Latin and Vernacular Evidence," *Romanische Forschungen* 85 (1973); T. D. Cooke and B. L. Honeycutt, eds., *The Humor of the Fabliaux: A Collection of Critical Essays* (1974); T. D. Cooke, *The Old French and Chaucerian Fabliaux: A Study of Their Comic Climax* (1978); M.-T. Lorcin, *Façons de sentir et de penser: Les fabliaux français* (1979); P. Ménard, *Les fabliaux: Contes à rire du moyen âge* (1983); C. Muscatine, *The Old French Fabliaux* (1986); M. J. S. Schenk, *The Fabliaux: Tales of Wit and Deception* (1987); and J. Hines, *The Fabliau in English* (1993). For studies of Chaucer's fabliaux, see J. Richardson, *Blameth Nat Me: A Study of Imagery in Chaucer's Fabliaux* (1970); D. Brewer, "The Fabliaux," in *Companion to Chaucer Studies*, ed. B. Rowland (1979); and R. E. Hertog, *Chaucer's Fabliaux as Analogues* (1991). On the close relationship between fabliaux and exempla, see S. Wenzel, "The Joyous Art of Preaching; or, The Preacher and the Fabliau," *Anglia* 97 (1979).

On the relationships between fabliaux and oral traditions, see F. L. Utley, "Chaucer, Boccaccio, and the International Popular Tale," *Western Folklore* 33 (1974); C. Lindahl, *Earnest Games: Folkloric Patterns in* The Canterbury Tales (1987); and L. Röhrich, *Erzählungen des späten Mittelalters*, vol. 2 (1967), which documents the breadth of medieval fabliaux with specific reference to "The Friar's Tale."

—Nicola Chatten

Fairies

Supernatural beings of medieval legendry and romance who maintain their own realm, sometimes venturing into the human world or drawing mortals into theirs.

Some classes of supernatural beings belong to the realm of mainstream religion: gods, angels, demons, devils. Other classes belong to the secular realm of the supernatural, and these may conveniently be termed *fairies*, although every language and culture area has its own names for these beings. Yet while fairies represent the secular supernatural, both scholarship and various folk traditions suggest that many fairies are descended from pagan deities.

Fairies and Witches

While fairies are the secular complement to the angels and demons of the religious sphere, fairies can also be seen as the supernatural complement to the witches of the mundane realms. As several scholars of early modern witch beliefs have pointed out, fairies and witches are both blamed for causing sudden and otherwise inexplicable illnesses in humans and animals (a stroke was originally a fairy stroke) or changes in the weather (whirlwinds are troops of fairies passing by), for affecting the fertility of fields and livestock, and for having a particular interest in human children, whom they may kidnap or otherwise harm. Both fairies and witches are believed to be predominantly female, and congruent with their association with matters of fertility, many stories deal with the consequences of a man marrying a woman who turns out to be a fairy (positive) or a witch (negative). In some cases in early modern Europe it appears that human women may have formed groups that were believed to mirror in the mundane realm the groups of trooping fairies believed to inhabit the supernatural realm. These trooping fairies are headed by a figure known as Herodias, Herodiana, Perhta, or Holda, suggesting a continuity with classical and northern goddess figures. Fleeting references in medieval texts, such as Regino von Prüm's tenth-century *De ecclesiasticis disciplinis* and Burchard of Worms's eleventh-century Decretals, to groups of deluded women who followed "Diana" suggest that this belief may also have existed in the Middle Ages.

Fairies are believed to inhabit liminal zones: in the wilderness they are encountered in the parts of the forest where people go to pick berries or gather firewood; in the domestic realm they live in barns and outbuildings or enter the house at night when humans sleep. Many fairies are found living in or near water: wells, lakes, fountains, streams, or the ocean. Other fairies are found in mountains or dwelling within the "hollow hills" that often are Neolithic burial mounds. Thus, fairies belong not to places that are completely shut off from human access but to places that are incompletely incorporated into the mundane world, places where animals or fish (sources of food) dwell, places where humans no longer dwell, places where humans venture to collect goods (such as berries and firewood) that are not cultivated but found by the bounty of nature.

Names and Traits of Fairies

The names of fairies vary from locale to locale. Perhaps the most famous are the Irish Tuatha Dé Danann (Tribes of the Goddess Danu) or people of the *sidh*, or fairy mound. In Wales they are the Tylwyth Teg (the Fair Tribe) or Plant Rhys Ddwfn (Children of Rhys the Deep). English fairies have more names that can be listed in one breath: boggarts, brownies, greenies, pixies, knockers, lobs, hobs, and lubberkins. The French call them *fées*, the Bretons *Korrigans*. In Sicily there are the *donas de fuera* (ladies from outside). In the Balkans the main word is *vila*; in Russia *rusalka*; in Greece the classical *nereid*, originally a water sprite, has expanded to cover all fairy-like beings.

Many of the names of fairies are euphemistic, often translating merely as "they." Other euphemisms mean things like "the Gentry," "the Fair Ones," "the Good Ones," "the Mothers." Tomás Ó Cathasaigh has pointed out that in Irish, *sidh* is the term used to name both "dwellings of the fairies" and "peace." He proposes that the name for the otherworld and those who live there is a reflection of the state encountered there, for the land of the Irish fairies is preeminently a land of peace and plenty. Good relations with the otherworld on the part of the king extend this state to the mundane world. Likewise, the Welsh Tylwyth Teg may be "fair" in the sense of "beautiful" or "light-skinned and blonde," but *teg* also has the sense of "fairness, justice," qualities that are believed to mark the otherworld and its inhabitants. At the same time, names of fairies often refer to "fairness" in the sense of whiteness, and whiteness and luminescence are typically associated with the alternate reality of the otherworld.

The fairy realms are also marked by temporal distortions. An hour with the fairies is a century at home. Many mortal heroes, such as the Irish Oisín, tarry with fairy women only to discover, when their homesickness grows too much to bear, that they themselves have become the stuff of legend. Either eating mortal food or setting foot on mortal soil returns them from eternity to chronology, and their bodies crumble to the dust that they should have become.

Fairies are shapeshifters. In Celtic traditions their most common guise is as water birds: Caer, the love of the god Oengus, spends alternate years as a swan or as a maiden; Mider and Étain become swans as they escape the mortal Eochaid; the father of king Conaire Mór appears as a bird but takes off his bird skin and assumes the shape of a man to sleep with Mes Buachalla; and his "people" are birds who ride on the waves of the sea. Water birds, like fairies, are multivalent creatures since they can live on land, air, and water. But fairies also take the forms of deer, bulls, wolves, dogs, eels, worms, or even flies.

Fairies, then, are preeminently Other. They are tiny or huge, compared with humans. They are primarily female, when seen through the eyes of a male-dominated society. They live in all the places where humans go but do not stay and are most active at the times when humans are asleep or in a liminal state (giving birth, about to be married, intoxicated). Yet they also look like humans, can mate with humans and produce viable offspring, and live socially under a monarchy. They enjoy food and drink and music, nice clothes and jewels, and value gold as highly as any human. They are both more and less, both seen and unseen, both canny and uncanny.

Most material collected on fairies dates from the early modern period. Medieval sources are patchy at best, but every element of modern fairy lore seems to make at least a cursory appearance in the medieval period. There are references to the Wild Hunt as early as the *Anglo-Saxon Chronicle* in 1127, a troop of unhallowed souls led howling through the night sky by the fairy king (Gwynn ap Nudd, Odin, Herla, Wild Edric). The great French romances of the twelfth century draw upon fairy beliefs for literary ends but probably do not tell us as much about folk belief as they do about elite concerns. Fairy women in the romances can be seen as anima figures, initiating the hero into his proper place in society. They may also be seen as "shattered jewels" of former goddesses, classical or Celtic.

Fairy Women

Many of these medieval fairy women are ancestor figures. Melusine, half woman, half snake, whose legend predates the fourteenth century, was the progenetrix of the French house of Lusignan and was said to appear to announce the death of each lord until the castle itself was destroyed. The Lady of Llyn-y-Fan-Fach in Wales was the mother of the famed Meddygyon Myddfai, a family of physicians who claimed to have learned their healing skills from their fairy ancestress in the twelfth century. Both Melusine and the Lady were typical fairy brides, who married a mortal under certain conditions that he must not break under

The fairy Melusine takes on the traits of a serpent and flies from her locked chamber; from a fifteenth-century French woodcut. (Dover Pictorial Archive Series)

pain of losing her. Inevitably the conditions are broken (Melusine is seen in her snaky form, the Lady is struck three times without cause), and the fairy must return to her otherworldly habitation. Nonetheless, the fairy bride still visits those she left behind her, to announce a death or to teach her children, becoming a medium of communication between the supernatural and the mundane worlds. A similar fairy bride is the woman Macha in the Irish story of the "Debility of the Ulsterman," a precursory tale to the epic *Táin Bó Cúailnge* (Cattle Raid of Cooley). Here the taboo is against her husband speaking of her; when he boasts of her swiftness before the king of Ulster she is forced to run a race against the king's fleetest horses even though she is heavily pregnant. She wins the race but dies giving birth to twins and puts a curse on the Ulstermen: in their times of greatest need they will be afflicted with pangs of childbirth for nine days. This Macha is perhaps closest to an identifiable goddess, for Macha is also a name of one of the three forms of the Irish war goddess, the Morrigan. It should be noted that all these tales of fairy brides are marked by a state of "either/or": Melusine is both woman *and* snake and gives birth to deformed children; the Lady of Llyn-y-Fan-Fach is won through an offering of bread that is neither raw *nor* cooked; and Macha curses men to feel the pains of women in labor, placing them in a status between genders.

Fairy Realms

The land of the fairies is often represented as being within or under the earth. The Tuatha Dé Danann are closely associated with the fairy mounds of Ireland, and whereas stories set in the earliest days locate gods in the mounds—Oengus with Brugh na Boyne, Mider with Brí Léith—later stories call the mounds' inhabitants fairies. The fourteenth-century romance of *Sir Orfeo* represents the fairies who have kidnapped Queen Meroudys as living within the earth in a fair country reached through a cave. Gerald of Wales, in his *Itinerarium Cambriae* (based on a journey through Wales in 1188), tells the story of Elidyr, a priest who as a young man was met by two small men who took him underground to a wealthy country where the sun never shone but the people were beautiful and fair—both blonde and just. They worshipped nothing but the truth. Elidyr traveled happily back and forth between his land and the fairies' until his mother incited him to steal some gold for her. He tried to make off with a golden ball but was caught in the act, chased out of fairyland, lost the ball in his escape, and was never able to find his way back. The green children, said to have appeared during King Stephen's reign and recorded in the chronicles of Ralph of Coggeshall and William of Newburgh, claimed to have come from a subterranean land where there was no direct light and the people were all of a light green color. The boy and girl, who were found in a pit in Suffolk, lost their greenness over time. Like the fairies met by Elidyr, the green children seemed to be vegetarians, living only on beans. Elidyr's fairies spoke a language like Greek, and the green children initially spoke an unintelligible tongue. The boy eventually died, but the girl lived and learned English and was able to tell their story.

Though the green girl claimed that her native land was called "St. Martin's Land" and its inhabitants were Christians, as a general rule fairies are not believed to subscribe to the Christian faith. Chaucer, in "The Wife of Bath's Tale,"

depicts the fairies as being driven out of their haunts by the prayers and inces-
sant blessings of itinerant priests. Indeed, from the earliest mentions of fairies,
they are always already on their way out, whether driven by ethnic invasion in
the legendary history of Ireland, religion in the medieval and early modern
ages, or technology in the industrial and postindustrial eras. But they have never
disappeared altogether.

See also: Annwfn; Celtic Mythology; Fairy Lover; Gerald of Wales; Map, Walter; Maxen
    Wledig; Wild Hunt
References and further reading: The literature of fairyland is extensive and of widely varying
    quality. T. Keightley, *Fairy Mythology* (1880), and K. M. Briggs, *The Encyclopedia of Fairies*
    (1976), are still two of the best overview collections of European fairy beliefs from the
    Middle Ages to the twentieth century. T. P. Cross and C. H. Slover, *Ancient Irish Tales*
    (1936; rpt. 1981), collects many stories relating to the Tuatha Dé Danann, and J. Rhŷs,
    Celtic Folklore, Welsh and Manx, 2 vols. (1901), collects nineteenth-century Welsh fairy
    lore and traces its medieval roots. W. Y. Evans-Wentz, *The Fairy Faith in Celtic Countries*
    (1911), compares medieval and modern fairy beliefs and contains a great deal of raw
    material. H. Patch, *The Otherworld in Medieval Literature* (1950), is a good summary guide
    to the representation of the fairy realms in medieval elite culture.
        Much work has been done since the mid-1980s on the interrelationship between witch
    and fairy beliefs in early modern Europe, work that can be of relevance to beliefs in the
    preceding age, most notably, C. Ginzburg, *Ecstasies: Deciphering the Witches' Sabbath* (1991), B.
    Ankarloo and G. Henningsen, eds., *Early Modern Witchcraft: Centres and Peripheries* (1993),
    and especially É. Pócs, *Fairies and Witches at the Boundary of Southeastern and Central Europe*
    (1989). P. Narváez, ed., *The Good People: New Fairy Lore Essays* (1991), offers studies of
    contemporary fairy belief that can be useful in understanding medieval lore.
        K. L. Jolly, *Popular Religion in Anglo-Saxon England: Elf Charms in Context* (1996), and
    V. I. J. Flint, *The Rise of Magic in Early Medieval Europe* (1991), are useful and enlightening
    in contextualizing fairy beliefs in the medieval period. L. Harf-Lancer, *Les fées au moyen
    âge: Morgane et Mélusine, la naissance des fées* (1984), traces the interaction of myth and
    folklore in the development of the literary fairies of French romance, and F. Clier-
    Columbani, *La fée Mélusine au moyen âge: Images, mythes, et symboles* (1991), provides a
    rare look at the visual representation of fairies in medieval illumination.
                                                                —*Leslie Ellen Jones*

Fairy Lover

A supernatural figure of medieval legend and romance, who engages a mortal in
sex, love, or marriage (motifs F300–F305).

Occasionally the male fairy is a rapist—like the fairy knight in *Sir Degaré*
(English, fourteenth century), who forces himself upon a king's daughter when
he finds her alone in the woods—or an abductor, like the king of Faerie (the
fairy realm) in *Sir Orfeo* (English, fourteenth century), who seizes Orfeo's wife
as she sleeps beneath a tree and spirits her off to his otherworld. Occasionally
the female fairy is at least at first the unwilling target of a mortal man's advances, as in *Thomas of Erceldoune* (Scottish, fifteenth century). But most often, in the romances at least, a strong mutual attraction binds mortal and fairy.

Many fairy-lover tales feature a command or taboo that the mortal must
obey in order to preserve his or her relationship with the fairy. The greater
number of taboos entail secrecy and involve the speech of the mortal (motif

C400). In Marie de France's twelfth-century poem *Lanval* the hero is forbidden to speak of his fairy mistress to King Arthur's court; Wild Edric, central figure of a twelfth-century British legend, must promise never to reproach his fairy wife because of her sisters; and Thomas of Erceldoune is forbidden to talk to the inhabitants of Elfland save for the Fairy Queen (C715.1). Other conditions imposed by otherworldly lovers include time or place taboos, such as Melusine's restriction on her husband never to visit her on Saturday, and conduct taboos, such as the restraint on the mortal husband in Walter Map's "The Fairy of Fan y Fach," who is forbidden to strike his fairy bride with a bridle. Other types of tests and restrictions also appear in the fairy-lover tales. For example, Sir Orfeo wins back his wife from the Fairy King by impressing the king with his harp-playing skills.

The fairies of the fairy-lover tales generally take one of two forms. They are either fairy nobility (such as a fairy king or queen) or they appear at times to be part animal or monster and part human. Tales involving a fairy king or queen center on the abduction (whether voluntary or involuntary) of a mortal, who generally possesses some extraordinary quality. The abductees tend to be nobles— for example, the wife of Sir Orfeo—or bards who excel at their craft, as in *Thomas of Erceldoune*. When the fairy is part monster or animal, the mortal lover is also often noble—for example, the king who marries the monstrous Melusine (French tales call her half serpent; Norman versions call her half dragon).

Except in Irish tradition, where male fairies abound, female fairies significantly outnumber males in surviving medieval texts, romances in particular. This may offer some explanation of the generalized gendering of fairies as female in the Middle Ages, as in the Arthurian legends' classifications of Morgan le Fay as "fairy" and Merlin as "demon." Even the Wife of Bath, in the introduction to her tale in which she laments the disappearance of the fairies of King Arthur's day, distinguishes the fey "elf queen" from the masculine-gendered "incubus."

Also revealed in the fairy-lover variants is the apparent belief that the contact between a fairy and mortal may produce children (F305, offspring of fairy and mortal). Belief in the generation of "fey blood" in mortals led a number of families, such as the Lusignans of Poitou and the Meddygyon Myddfai of Wales, to claim fairy ancestresses for their line. Most notable and far-reaching is the tale of Melusine, the grande dame of the house of Lusignan:

> King Elinas of Albany (Scotland), after the death of his wife, found refuge in hunting alone. One day, he approached a fountain where he found a woman named Pressia singing. He at once fell in love with her, and she consented to marry him on the condition that he never visit her at the time of her lying-in. Later, she gave birth to triplet girls, Melusine, Melior, and Palatina, and the king, forgetting his promise, rushed to her side, where he found his wife bathing the babies. The moment she realized he was there, she snatched up the daughters and vanished. Taking refuge at Cephalonia, the Hidden Island, Pressia showed Albany to her children every day, explaining that had their father kept his word they would be happy there together. The triplets swore revenge, and led by Melusine, they enclosed King Elinas's holdings. Pressia was displeased and punished Melusine by

turning her into a serpent from the waist down. The infliction would periodically plague her until she could find a man who would marry her under the condition of never seeing her on a Saturday. Raymond of Poitou agreed to marry her under these conditions, and the couple fell deeply in love. With her fairy wealth, Raymond built the Castle of Lusignan. The couple had a joyful marriage. Their children, however, were always deformed at birth. Raymond's cousin suggested to him that Melusine had another lover, whom she met on Saturdays when he was forbidden to see her. To prove or disprove her loyalty, Raymond hid behind the arras the following Saturday, only to see Melusine emerging from her bath with the body of a serpent. He decided that he would keep his knowledge a secret. When Melusine tried to comfort her husband after one of their children set fire to the Abbey of Melliers, however, Raymond reproached her: "Get out of my sight, you pernicious snake! You have contaminated my children!" Melusine fainted. When she recovered she cursed the lords of Lusignan to hear her wailing voice before their deaths, and she disappeared through a window.

This tale, the *Chronique de Mélusine*, composed by Jean d'Arras at the end of the fourteenth century, features not only sexual contact between a mortal and a fairy but also the fairy's half-human, half-animal form and the common taboo pattern. Jean ends his tale with reports of recent sightings of Melusine, who reappears whenever the Lusignan's castle is about to change hands.

The fairy Melusine; from a fifteenth-century French woodcut. (Dover Pictorial Archive Series)

Mélusine was preceded by many similarly structured legends dating back to the twelfth century, although the earlier tales tended to give the "fairy" a demonic character. For example, "Long-Toothed Henno" in Walter Map's *De nugis curialium* tells of Henno's marriage to a beautiful young stranger he has found on the coast of Normandy. The couple have several children and live in happiness until Henno's mother notices that the mysterious bride avoids holy water and does not take communion. Henno spies on her and sees her in the form of a dragon. He then joins forces with a priest, and the two sprinkle her with holy water, which causes her to disappear shrieking.

In both romance and legend a love relationship with a fairy could bring special powers to a mortal. When Thomas of Erceldoune must depart from Faerie, his fairy lover endows him with the gift of prophecy. The prophecies ascribed to Thomas, like the prophecies of Merlin (also inspired by the love of a fairy), discuss the political and social climate of the British Isles and were upheld as inspired revelations of the future throughout and beyond the Middle Ages.

See also: Fairies; Map, Walter; Romance

References and further reading: See F. Clier-Columbani, *La fée Mélusine au moyen âge: Images, mythes, et symboles* (1991); J. Le Goff, "Melusina: Mother and Pioneer," in *Time, Work, and Culture in the Middle Ages*, trans. A. Goldhammer (1980); L. Harf-Lancer, *Les fées au moyen âge: Morgane et Mélusine, la naissance des fées* (1984); K. M. Briggs, *The Encyclopedia of Fairies* (1976), and *The Fairies in Tradition and Literature* (1967); L. A. Paton, *Studies in the Fairy Mythology of Arthurian Romance* (1960); T. Keightley, *Fairy Mythology* (1880); and J. M. Burnham, "A Study of Thomas of Erceldoune," *Publications of the Modern Language Association* 23 (1908).

—*Sandra M. Salla*

Fenian Cycle [Fianna Cycle]

Stories of Finn (Fion, Fionn) mac Cumaill and his Fianna warriors, extremely popular in Ireland, Scotland, and the Isle of Man during the Middle Ages and later.

The cycle has its roots in antiquity. The name *Finn* (written *Find* in medieval literature) is the modern form of the ancient Celtic name *Vindos* (The Bright One), and the character known to tradition seems to have developed from a general Celtic cult of a bright deity reflecting wisdom. The cult further appears to have been part of the druidic lore that centered on the Boyne River in prehistory. The warrior band called Fianna, on the other hand, derives from early young men's groups of hunter-warriors, groups that were common in Celtic culture as in the early history of many other peoples.

The words *Finn* and *Fianna* are not etymologically related, and it is therefore necessary to explain how Finn in tradition came to be the leader of such a band. There is no real evidence that such a connection existed in archaic Celtic lore. It is significant that Finn occurs in the earliest literary sources (beginning in the sixth century C.E.) in a distinctly Leinster context, and it has therefore been suggested that the loss of the Boyne valley by the Leinstermen caused them to use the seer cult of Finn as a spur to their young warriors to attempt to regain that rich and fertile territory. This would have caused the personage Finn to be intimately linked to Fianna lore in the Leinster of that period. It is significant that tradition always claims that Finn's headquarters was on the Hill of Allen in County Kildare, which was probably a sacred site of the pre-Christian Leinstermen. The sources show, nevertheless, that by the eighth and ninth centuries stories of Finn and his Fianna had already spread to other parts of Ireland, and we may surmise that accounts were reaching Scotland and the Isle of Man by that time also. There are also traces of Finn in medieval Welsh literature, which in several cases exhibits early Leinster influence.

Finn is at all stages of tradition as much a seer as a warrior, and he has a distinctive way to gain knowledge of past, present, and future: by placing his thumb in his mouth and chewing it. This, and the perpetual theme of youth in the lore concerning him, may have their origins in ancient druidic lore of a child deity. The Fianna focus of the lore is also clear, however, from the early stories, in which he features as a typical youth, frequently engaging in armed combat with other young men, especially concerning women. As the lore gained impetus from repeated oral telling, particular companions became the highlighted members of his troop: these included the swift runner Caoilte, the handsome young warrior Diarmaid, and Finn's son Oisín. The twelfth century was a watershed in the development of this lore, for at that time biographies of Finn were assembled and a whole new format was given to the corpus of the lore.

The accounts of Finn's youth record that he was born after his father Cumall was killed in battle, that as a boy he had to be reared in the wilderness for fear of his father's enemies, that he obtained wisdom by accidentally gaining the first taste of the Boyne salmon, and that he regained his father's position of leader of the Fianna of Ireland by saving the royal citadel of Tara from a ferocious fire-breathing phantom. When he ascended to the position of leadership, he was reconciled to Goll mac Morna, the incumbent leader who had slain Cumall. Goll proved to be a brave and honorable colleague to Finn, but the fact that he had killed Finn's father was a continuing source of insecurity within the Fianna. Storytellers exploited this dramatic tension to the full, describing many savage outbreaks of fighting between the two and their supporters.

The new format for the lore came from a long and varied text entitled *Acallam na Senórach* (Dialogue of the Ancients, or Conversation of the Old Men). This used the popular medieval theme of pagan worthies being posthumously baptized by Christian saints, but in this case Oisín and Caoilte were described as survivors after all the rest of the Fianna had died. They met the missionary St. Patrick and brought him on journeys throughout Ireland, describing the deeds performed at the different sites by Finn and his warriors of old. The text used much earlier material but did not hesitate to invent where necessary, and it thereby gave impetus to the growing fashion of composing new Fianna narratives. Nature poetry had already become a staple of Fianna lore, reflecting the fact that Finn and his companions often lived in the wilderness, and in the twelfth century this poetic impulse was developed into the composition of narrative lays consisting of loosely rhymed quatrains. These lays were usually couched in terms of the debate between Patrick and Oisin, and they told of great single combats, hunts, and adventures of the Fianna abroad as well as in Ireland. The composition of Fianna lays continued all through the later Middle Ages and down to recent times. They were chanted and frequently passed into oral tradition. They were particularly popular in Scotland, where they were in greater demand than even the prose stories.

It is remarkable how certain basic themes are continually reworked within the Fenian cycle. Such themes as the conflict between youth and age; the restoration of ladies, children, or even warriors abducted by human enemies or by supernatural beings; and the personal conflicts between members of the Fianna were played upon by storytellers with a great range of variety and with elaborate background detail. Tales of massive battles fought by the Fianna against foreign invaders owe much to the Viking wars of the Middle Ages, while accounts of Finn's adventures in love were indebted to late-medieval accounts in other languages of Arthur and Charlemagne.

Certain stories, however, were transmitted through the centuries in comparatively stable form. The story of Finn's betrothal to Grainne and of her love for the younger Diarmaid was being told as early as the eighth century C.E. and continued to be popular throughout the whole Gaelic world, as medieval storytellers made much of the tragic death of Diarmaid brought about by Finn's rather uncharacteristic jealousy and lust for vengeance. Another story, which appears to have been current from the tenth or eleventh century, is allegorical and is thought to have influenced (through Viking contacts) the medieval Norse myth of Thor's visit to the dwelling of Utgarda-Loki. We are told that Finn and some of his men once visited a strange house, where they failed to control a vicious ram and where a beautiful young lady refused Finn's advances. The ram could only be subdued by a doddering old man who lived there, and it was later explained to Finn that the ram was the world, the old man was time, and the beautiful maiden was youth.

The cycle was enriched in the Middle Ages by several plots borrowed from international folktales. Whereas the story of how Finn gained wisdom from the Boyne salmon belonged to ancient lore of seer-craft, the actual plot—which has him unwittingly getting the first taste of the salmon intended for another person—closely parallels episodes of AT 673 (an international plot concerning the eating of a white serpent). Most influential was a series of international plots concerning marvelous helpers (AT 513, AT 570, and AT 653). These plots must have been attracted to Finn by accounts of his companion Caoilte, who was a stupendous runner. The helpers, portrayed as members of the Fianna or as visitors to the celebrated troop, assist Finn in such matters as gaining a wife, winning his freedom from captivity, or recovering babies stolen away by a giant.

The ultimate origins of the Finn persona in druidic practices exerted its influence on stories of him at all stages. One early source describes him as having a multicolored cloak enabling him to change his shape at will, and others tell of his visits to tumuli, cairns, and underground caverns in which he either gains special information or overcomes monstrous beings. From the thirteenth century onward such traditions developed, through combination with accounts of great battles won by the Fianna, into stories of how Finn and his companions had to attack and destroy sinister dwellings where some of their people had been enticed to a feast and then made captive. Folklore further rationalized this by claiming that the Fianna, though confined to hell as war-like pagans, conquered the devils and fought their way to freedom from that terrible place!

In later centuries folk traditions portrayed Finn as a vanquisher of giants, and many hills and rocks in the landscape are associated with him and his adventures. The scope and diversity of the lore has led to his being regarded as a mirror of human character, and this is echoed by many folk saws that refer to his experiences and behavior. The influence of the cycle on modern international culture is for the most part due to the sensational but inaccurate prose-poems composed in English in the late eighteenth century by James Macpherson.

See also: Celtic Mythology; Folktale; Irish Tradition; Ulster Cycle
References and further reading: A comprehensive account of the Fenian cycle and its development, with full sources, is in D. Ó hÓgáin, *Fionn mac Cumhaill: Images of the Gaelic Hero* (1988). For the medieval biography of Finn and related data, see J. F. Nagy, *The Wisdom of the Outlaw: The Boyhood Deeds of Finn in Gaelic Narrative Tradition* (1985). See also J. MacKillop, *Fionn mac Cumhaill: Celtic Myth in English Literature* (1986).
—Dáithí Ó hÓgáin

Festivals and Celebrations

Events, feasts, rituals, and performances enacted annually for religious purposes and to mark the rhythms of seasonal agricultural work.

The Two Calendars

The annual celebrations of the medieval laity were determined by two interlocking but by no means identical calendars, the liturgical calendar of the Church and the pre-Christian calendars of the agricultural year. When Christianity became the official religion of the Roman Empire in the fourth century it was in a position to either eliminate altogether or modify and Christianize the major Roman festivals. A most conspicuous example is the Saturnalia (December 25–31), which was absorbed into celebrations of events surrounding Christ's Nativity, along with the Kalends of January (New Years' Day), to become by medieval times the Twelve Days stretching from December 25 to January 6.

With the fall of the Roman Empire it was in the Church's interest, in its gradual conversion of Celtic and Germanic Europe, to translate important aboriginal calendar dates into Christian terms as well. Pope Gregory the Great, in a famous letter to Mellitus of Canterbury, as recorded in Bede's *Historia ecclesiastica*, outlines such a policy of appropriation and transmutation. It would be a mistake, however, to view this Christianization of the pagan calendar as a straightforward process, the product of a continuous, rational campaign. Rather, we should speak of an evolving rapprochement of the two calendars, liturgical and traditional, over the early-medieval centuries, resulting in a rich mix of festival practice wherein one might occasionally glimpse a less-than-thorough Christianization of the pagan underlay.

Such nineteenth-century German mythographers as Wilhelm Mannhardt and Jacob Grimm, early-twentieth-century British folklorists of the Cambridge

School, and followers of James G. Frazer, author of *The Golden Bough* (1890), were all too ready to find fully intact "pagan survivals" in medieval and Early Modern annual celebrations. More recent titles, such as *Saints, Successors of the Gods* (1932), by Paul Saint-Yves, betray an almost romantic attachment to the idea of an undying paganism. Today, however, only the most uncritical New Age enthusiast can subscribe to the theory of a vibrant, coherent paganism existing in the Middle Ages in opposition to the "official culture" of the Church and the landlords. The reality is far more complex and elusive, resisting such easy generalizations.

Our model for European popular belief of the early Middle Ages should be the hybrid and eclectic Christianity readily observable in the indigenous populations of Mexico or Peru. There one cannot speak of "Aztec," "Mayan," or "Inca" survivals as absolutes, within an essentially baroque Christianity, but merely as components of a new, "third-term" spirituality.

Recent scholars of late antiquity/early Christianity, such as Peter Brown, have restored to a certain extent, and on a firmer historical basis, the Church's role as creative transformer of European culture rather than as simply the exterminator of pagan practices and outlook. The cult of the martyrs, for example, expanded the festival calendar without any necessary reference to the year cycle. Paulinus of Nola gives a vivid account of a fifth-century "secular" festival achieved within such a religious commemoration, that of his patron saint, Felix, whose *dies natalis*, or "birth into a higher life" (i.e., date of death) was celebrated on January 14:

> They now in great numbers keep vigil and prolong their joy throughout the night, dispelling sleep with joy and darkness with torchlight. I only wish they would channel this joy in sober prayer, and not introduce their winecups within the holy thresholds. . . . I none the less believe that such merriment . . . is pardonable because . . . their naivety is unconscious of the extent of their guilt, and their sins arise from devotion for they wrongly believe that saints are delighted to have their tombs doused with reeking wine. (Poem 27)

It might not be an exaggeration to say that the most conspicuous festival of the calendar year for the average medieval agriculturalist was the parish anniversary, or *kermis*. Again, this did not necessarily have any connection with the year cycle, being simply the feast day of the patron saint to whom the parish church was dedicated. It should be pointed out, though, that the majority of these took place in mild weather, taking advantage of a saint's multiple feast days for optimum community participation. Martin of Tours, for example, who was buried on November 11, also had a convenient summer feast day—July 4— that commemorated the translation of his relics. Moreover, some medieval saints of minimal historicity, such as George and Nicholas, could develop genuinely mythic dimensions without, it would seem, any "source" in a pagan pantheon. Their festivals—April 23 and December 6, respectively—often featured secular enactments, thus expanding the festival calendar. Even such a festival as Corpus Christi (Thursday after Trinity Sunday), established by the Church as late as 1311 for theological purposes, could be easily absorbed by the populace. It became the occasion for one of the most vibrant expressions of vernacular culture, the Corpus Christi pageant cycles.

The Two Halves of the Year

Though it is important to emphasize the historical as opposed to the seasonal nature of many Christian feasts, it is nevertheless also true that the Church's calendar responded at a fairly deep level to the year cycle. Advent, symbolizing the benighted era of the Old Law, took place at a time of dying back into the earth. Christ's Nativity was coterminous with the sun beginning to regain its strength after the winter solstice. Christ's death and resurrection paralleled the season of germination and flowering, and so on. Certain conspicuous saints, moreover, appear to occupy positions of importance on the year wheel—John the Baptist (June 24) at midsummer, Michael the Archangel (September 29) near the autumnal equinox, and so on. The Irish St. Brigid's multiple parallels with the ancient Celtic fire festival of February 1 seem more than just coincidental, and All Saints' Day and All Souls' Day (November 1 and 2) occupy the place of Samhain, the Celtic new year and feast of the dead. Europe's pagan past, then, certainly cannot be dismissed entirely from the equation, however difficult it might be to prove "survival" in specific instances.

The Church year, moreover, breaks into two large segments in roughly the same way the agricultural year does. After Pentecost or Whitsun (40 days after Easter) the liturgical year no longer paralleled the career of Christ on earth. The 23 Sundays after Pentecost, a period relieved by very few major feast days, corresponded to the months of intensive labor in the agricultural year, when major secular festival activity was likewise minimal. We can thus speak, in gross terms, of two half years, the "working" half and the "holiday" half. This distinction has recently been developed by French scholars, such as Claude Gaignebet and François Laroque. Within the interweaving of the two calendars we can perceive, then, areas of tension (not the same as outright opposition between "popular" and "elite") between the Church's concerns and those of the country folk.

The harvest season heralded the beginning of the holiday half of the year. A "harvest home" would feature a church service of thanksgiving, but often in tandem with archaic rituals of weaving anthropomorphic and other figures (corn dollies) from the final sheaves or felling the last sheaf by means of thrown sickles. With the grain processed and stored or brewed, and later, in November, with the herds culled, the animals slaughtered, and their meat preserved, the work of the year was over. It was a time then for feasting and particularly for recognizing the obligations of masters to men in view of their control of the winter food supply and shelter. In later medieval centuries the late autumn was the principal turnover period for hired agricultural labor and involved many such welcome or farewell feasts. This period of plenty, however, soon had to accommodate the penitential season of Advent in preparation for Christmas, as well as the more general phenomenon of the dying of the year. Special commemoration of the dead, with consequent close proximity of ghosts and wraiths, only partially ameliorated by the Church's feasts of All Saints' and All Souls', perhaps retained a sense of the dangerous threshold represented by the

A peasant festival, painted in the sixteenth century by Pieter Brueghel the Elder. (Corbis/
Archivo Iconografico, S.A.)

pre-Christian Celtic and Germanic new years. Our Halloween is a dim survival
of this period.

The conjunction of the Nativity with the winter solstice and such pagan
midwinter festival periods as the Germanic Yule produced a very complex pattern of celebrations. Folkloric activity certainly flourished within the Christian
mythos, from Francis of Assisi's first crèche at Greccio to the German cradle-
rocking ceremonies and Epiphany star-singers. But also within the Yuletide season of feasting, storytelling, and gambling, masquerades could take on a decidedly
non-Christian character. Repeated early Church prohibitions, evidently unsuccessful, against animal-masking (stags and bulls particularly) at the New Year
have been conveniently collected by E. K. Chambers in his *The Mediaeval Stage*.
Wild Men and other menacing grotesques were popular in later medieval Yuletide assemblies. The late-medieval development in German-speaking areas of a
Ruprecht figure—a devilish figure dressed in black—as shadow to the gift-giv-
ing, child-oriented St. Nicholas epitomizes the dichotomies of the Season of
Peace. The piquant "sport" of King Arthur's Christmas was, we might recall,
the beheading game of a gigantic Green Knight.

The Twelve Days of the Christmas–New Year–Epiphany season, moreover,
developed pronounced "rituals of inversion" for which we may legitimately use
the Bakhtinian adjective *carnivalesque*. These cannot be solely accounted for
by reference back to the Roman Saturnalia festivities in which masters and

slaves switched places. They appear rather to be sui generis, developing even within the walls of the Church itself in the famous *festa asinorum* (Feast of the Ass) or *festa stultorum* (Feast of Fools), which were in the hands of the minor clerics, especially in some French cathedral hierarchies. A less raucous but seemingly related phenomenon is the Boy Bishop ceremony in which youth and innocence invert with age and experience for a good stretch of the Christmas season, beginning either on St. Nicholas's Day or on Holy Innocents' Day (December 28). A late-medieval, bourgeois example of the type was the "King of the Bean" ceremony on Twelfth Night (January 5–6). Inverted kingdoms continued to be part of medieval school and university celebrations, with their "Christmas Princes," and so on.

Rituals of inversion reached their most intense expression in the span of three or more days known as Carnival or *Fastnacht* preceding the penitential season of Lent. Since Lent was calculated back 40 days from the movable feast of Easter (which was in turn calculated by the lunar Hebrew calendar), Carnival had no specific dates but nevertheless clearly represented an end-of-winter celebration. At the same time, however, the withered, deprived figure of Lent, a personification almost of "back winter," always triumphed over the bloated King Carnival in the mock combats so typical of the festival. Rather late in development compared to other medieval festivals, Carnival grew to be the most conspicuous and influential manifestation of European popular culture in the period. No doubt the improvement of agricultural technology partially accounts for the development of this festival of "conspicuous consumption" at a time, in earlier centuries, when winter supplies would have been at a point of near exhaustion. It may also have expressed, indirectly to be sure, some of the accumulating spiritual tensions that would result in the Reformation. In any case, the influence of Carnival upon early modern culture is undeniable, and it remains the principal focus of contemporary scholars of popular culture. The precise *meaning* of Carnival, however, remains very much in contention between the "pagans," who follow Mikhail Bakhtin's antiestablishment bent, and the "Christians," exemplified by Dietz-Rüdiger Moser, who find it a relatively unambiguous expression of an essential Christian culture. In such a widespread and complex phenomenon, no doubt both points of view need to be creatively synthesized.

Eastertide, by contrast, is rather anticlimactic from the popular cultural point of view. The season's playful festival release from the pressures of Lent was certainly not comparable to Carnival. Nevertheless, the period is rich in festival activity involving fertility and renewal of the growing earth, quite apart from Easter-egg ceremonies, relatively late arrivals from the East. Plow processions had begun as early as the end of the Twelve Days of Christmas, and agriculturally oriented ceremonies and sports naturally dominate the spring months of March, April, and May. With the opening up of travel routes after winter we get events like the beating of the (parish) bounds, various "ridings" and local pilgrimages, and mass gatherings on hilltops. Maytide was conspicuously celebrated by the landed aristocracy in outdoor fetes with boating and music, dancing about the first violet of the spring, and various forms of dalliance, all celebrated by the great secular poets of the Romance and Germanic languages, the troubadours and minnesingers. Dalliance was also practiced on the commoners' level, with Lords and Ladies of the May and various nocturnal woodland jaunts. Rustic sports, often with a combat motif, were also a conspicuous feature of outdoor celebrations: enactments of Robin Hood and St. George and the dragon, water jousts, and so on. The creatures of the "third way" between heaven and hell, the fairies, satyrs, and so on, were also more benevolent in this season than their rough counterparts of the late autumn and winter impersonations. Adam de la Halle's late-thirteenth-century play *Jeu de la feuillée* shows an easy mingling of the fairy bands with the good burghers of Arras in their May bower.

With the great midsummer bonfires of St. John's Day (June 24), this "green" phase of the festival half year may be said to come to an end. The months of July, August, September, and October are clearly given over to the "working" half year with very few festivals of note, apart from the locally determined *kermis* celebrations, as mentioned above. In their toil, medieval agriculturalists could look forward again to a rather crowded procession of saints, Wild Men, infant saviors, were-animals, fools, cannibals, and fairies as festival "objectifications" of their complex and often conflicted worldview.

See also: Candlemas; Carnival; Christmas; Harvest Festivals and Rituals; Midsummer; Peasants

References and further reading: Major sources for this article include M. Bakhtin, *Rabelais and His World*, trans. H. Iswolsky (1965); E. K. Chambers, *The Mediaeval Stage*, 2 vols. (1903; rpt. 1978); M. Collins and V. Davis, *A Medieval Book of Seasons* (1992); C. Gaignebet, *Le carneval* (1974); C. Gaignebet and J.-D. Lajoux, *Art profane et religion populaire au moyen âge* (1985); T. Gaster, *New Year: Its History, Customs, and Superstitions* (1955); R. Hutton, *The Rise and Fall of Merry England: The Ritual Year, 1400–1700* (1994), and *The Stations of the Sun: A History of the Ritual Year in Britain* (1996); F. Laroque, *Shakespeare's Festive World*, trans. J. Lloyd (1991); C. A. Miles, *Christmas Customs and Traditions: Their History and Significance* (1912; rpt. 1976); D.-R. Moser, "Narren-Prinzen-Jesuiten," *Zeitschrift für Volkskunde* 77 (1981); and A. Tille, *Yule and Christmas: Their Place in the Germanic Year* (1899).

—Martin W. Walsh

Feud

A process of disputation and settlement between conflicting parties in societies characterized by strong kinship ties, little central political control, and lack of policing institutions.

Feuds have occurred in many past and present cultures across the world and were common in medieval societies, where their presence is acknowledged in early law codes and chronicles as well as commemorated in epic and saga.

In most systems, plaintiffs and their kinship group are responsible for publicly identifying a crime or dishonor that has been committed against them. The wronged individual and his or her supporters are expected to gain revenge in the form of public seizure of property, the acknowledged killing of the person claimed to be a criminal or one of the criminal's close kin, or settlement from the criminal and the criminal's kin (often a payment in currency or other practical resources). Both the participants in the feud and the larger community view violent retaliations as lawful retribution. Indeed, feuding helps maintain social order by instilling fear of revenge in would-be aggressors. This process tends to function *within* an autonomous political group (such as a tribe or feudal kingdom); conflicts *between* tribes or kingdoms, on the other hand, usually involve larger-scale destruction and are more properly termed warfare.

In feud, revenge and counterrevenge alternate. Both sides keep score of the casualties so that revenge or compensation can be planned to "balance" each casualty according to the severity of the affront. Revenge is often done by ambush. Victims may be the perpetrators of crimes or close kin of the perpetrators, as long as the social status of the victim is generally sufficient to pay for the severity of the affront being requited. Revenge and counterrevenge can be extended through many years, although casualties in the conflict are usually low, seldom exceeding 20 or 30 people. Prosecutors are not expected to gain more revenge (i.e., to kill more people) than socially acceptable norms require.

However, violence may be avoided, or existing violence ended, by paying compensation to the kin of the victim for deaths incurred in the feud. Third-party mediators often broker such settlements. Although the conflicting parties may never be satisfied with the terms, and the feud may be reawakened, settlements bring about a welcome if sometimes temporary peace.

Medieval Iceland

In the decentralized society of medieval Iceland, feuding throve as a mechanism for regulating conflicts. Evidence of the feud has been preserved in manuscripts of law codes and traditional literary art. Certain sagas, particularly *Njal's Saga* and such later works as *The Saga of the Sturlungs*, are noted for portraying feuding patterns. These stories form the primary record of the Icelandic feud, with the laws setting the limits of action pertaining to feuds. The view of feuding that the sagas offer compares remarkably well with feuds observed ethnographically throughout the world, justifying the use of the sagas as evidence for the practice.

Icelandic society used sophisticated laws and hierarchies of Things, periodic assemblies convened by chiefs and their followers. At the Things, individuals were responsible for acting as their own prosecutors, declaring crimes perpetrated against themselves and rallying kinship support to form a "critical mass" of witnesses and evidence of group resolve. The assembly judged the legitimacy of claims and set the penalty. Serious crimes usually called for full outlawry: the criminal lost all social status, property, and legal rights and could be killed by anyone. Yet the feud was the only enforcement mechanism, a self-help of the plaintiff legally sanctioned by the community at the Things. Some conflicts brought successfully to court could result in less serious judgments; in lesser outlawry, a person was subject to exile for some number of years but was free to return afterward.

Central to prosecuting the feud was the gathering of supporters from among kin, chieftains, and clients to ensure that opponents would not gain unfair advantage during judgments or "win" cases by force of arms. The reciprocal support of chiefs and their clients was the primary social background of feuds, although chiefs often profited by receiving a share of the compensation they had helped clients obtain. Indeed, powerful people manipulated feuding to enhance their own wealth and status. Although direct participation in the legal process was restricted to free males, women and others of relatively low status could participate through "goading": a ritual verbal performance that shamed a potential (free male) prosecutor into taking responsibility for vengeance.

For a variety of reasons, one or both of the parties involved in the feud might want to settle the conflict through compensation. Indeed, Miller contends that the primary goal of the whole process was not blood taking but peacemaking. Neutral third parties might try to intervene. Local people, fearing the long-term disruption of a feud, were motivated to attempt arbitration. Arbitrated settlements tended to be more satisfactory than legal judgments, since the defendant might not cooperate in accepting judgments deemed too harsh, or the plaintiff might not be satisfied in a judgment, and both could resort again to violence. But arbitration could offer terms at least somewhat agreeable to both parties. Settlement did not guarantee a lasting peace, but it could make violence dormant for some time. This peacemaking feature of feud predated the coming of Christianity, but the new religion did create a class of people—its clergy—with a firm drive toward peacemaking. Thus, Christianity became part of the established feud process.

Old Norse Eddic Poems

The Old Norse Eddic poems recounting Scandinavian legends and myth incorporate feuding as a general rather than a detailed frame for certain episodes. *The Lay of Regin* is a good example. The Norse gods Odin, Hoenir, and Loki kill an otter for a meal but discover afterward that it is Otr, a shapeshifting dwarf. Otr's family, Hreidmar the father and Regin and Fafnir the brothers, demand compensation for the accidental murder: the gods are to stuff the otter's skin and cover it with gold. Loki steals this gold (the fabled Rhine Gold) from another dwarf. When the skin is finally covered, Hreidmar notes that one whisker is left uncovered, and Odin covers this with the last and most precious remaining treasure, a magical gold ring that reproduces itself. Loki complains that the value of the compensation has been great. This portion of the poem models a feud process that is quickly channeled into negotiated settlement. However, too harsh a demand for compensation could mar the peacemaking process of a feud, as Hreidmar's demand seems to do. Certainly the value of the wergeld causes much trouble in this tale cycle. Fafnir kills his father, steals the Rhine Gold, and turns into a dragon to guard it. In *The Lay of Fafnir*, Regin persuades the hero Sigurd to slay Fafnir to win back the treasure. Yet Regin decides that he must now kill Sigurd to avenge the murder of his brother even though Regin himself had goaded Sigurd to the deed! Here, the starkly legalistic outlook of the feud suggests the legal tangles this institution might create in reality.

Anglo-Saxon Culture

Though sources of English law do not clarify the practice, Anglo-Saxon culture was also marked by feud. The familiar institution of compensation (wergeld) is obvious in seventh-century law codes. These codes directed that wergeld be paid to the kin of the victim in a killing, rated according to the status of the victim, and laid out an elaborate inventory of compensations for lesser injuries. Even some eighth-century religious texts—penitentials, or manuals used by priests for assessing penances due to sins—recognized feud: if the murderer had paid compensation, then less penance for the killing was required.

In England, however, the size of the group that paid and received compensation is not clear. The kin group seems to have included parents-in-law and a sister's husband, as well as foster kin, all of which widened the kinship group bilaterally (a person could trace kinship through both parents). This broad definition of kinship caused complications. A person could be related (by kinship or political relationship) to two opposing groups engaged in a feud and so be torn between different loyalties.

Some evidence suggests that legislation attempted to restrict the target of retribution to the killer rather than other family members. Alfred's laws limited the liability of the kin if they disowned the murderer. Other legislation allowed a lord and his client to aid each other in feuds, but this aid was not to embroil the kin of either person. In these restrictions we are probably seeing the feud institution decaying slowly under political centralization.

The feud process in the Anglo-Saxon tradition is evidenced in historical documents, in both Latin and Old English. The *Anglo-Saxon Chronicle* and Bede's *Ecclesiastical History of the English People* record some historical cases. A tragic and tantalizing treatment of a feud is related in the story of Finnsburh, sung in Old English narrative poetry in an episode in *Beowulf* and in the *Finnsburh Fragment*. Even though the story is preserved incompletely, we can see in it the typical features of a feud: the Danish princess Hildeburh is married to the Frisian king Finn, presumably in the traditional role as "peace-weaver" to form an alliance between the two peoples. Her brother Hnæf, king of the Danes, and other Danes are killed in a fight while they are their guests. Hnæf's successor Hengest reaches a settlement with Finn but, unable to sail home in winter, is forced to stay with the hated Frisians. The son of one of the Danes slain with Hnæf lays his father's sword in Hengest's lap, obliging him to break the peace and seek revenge. In the ensuing fight, Finn is killed, and his queen is returned to her people.

Irish Feuding Traditions

In Ireland, legal manuscripts set forth the responsibility of the kin group for both the crimes and the debts of its members, which forms the background social paradigm necessary for feud. (Note, however, that other kinds of killings, such as those during battle or of thieves caught stealing, were legal and entailed no fines.) Reparations to wronged parties were made by the kin group comprising the male descendants from a great-grandfather. If payment was not prompt, the plaintiff could exercise "distraint" against the offending kin group, wherein an individual acting before witnesses formally seizes the property of an offender or the offender's kin after sufficient warning has been given. In the case of a killing, the culprit was expected to pay a "body fine" to the kin group of the victim, who shared the payment in amounts depending on their distance of relation to the victim. The fine was set according to the status, or "honor price," of the victim, of which the lord took a third when he had assisted in mediation. If the body fine was not given, the victim's kin group was expected to initiate a feud. The culprit could be captured and held until payment was made. Failing payment, the culprit could be sold into slavery or executed. The killing of the culprit was considered legal. Assisting in the feud were clients (followers) of a lord, who were not necessarily kin, and a lord could assist his clients in their own feud.

Ireland's medieval saga literature reflects in a general way some of these laws and the cross-cultural pattern of feuding. Deaths of heroes and insults against them result in deadly vengeance against offenders. Vengeance rather than compensation is indeed the focus of these tales. A good example is the tale of the death of the hero of one of the story cycles, Cú Chulainn.

Two major factors lead to Cú Chulainn's death. First is his feuding relationship with Cú Roi: in the story *Bricriu's Feast*, Cú Roi humiliates Cú Chulainn and the men of Ulster. In *The Death of Cú Roi*, Cú Chulainn exacts revenge. In *The Death of Cú Chulainn*, Cú Roi's son, Lugaid, seeks revenge. The second factor is the ambush set by Medb, a female chieftain of Connacht, angry because Cú Chulainn's prowess causes her to fail in her great cattle raid against Ulster. Cú Chulainn has slain many enemies in his career, so there is no lack of victims' kinsmen to attack him. He fights and dies against great odds, and then the counterrevenge begins. Conall Cernach, the hero's foster brother, hunts down the men who ambushed Cú Chulainn and takes all of their heads in a methodical reciprocation for Cú Chulainn's ambush. Other examples of stories structured by feud patterns are from the mythological cycle *The Fate of the Sons of Tuirenn* and *The Destruction of Da Derga's Hostel*. The relation between war and feud in medieval Irish saga is not clear, though. Whereas the laws differentiate between deaths in war and feud, the sagas are not clear on this point, as is shown in Medb's culling of avengers from the kin of those Cú Chulainn killed in war.

Welsh Feuding Traditions

Welsh traditions governing feuds are outlined in early-medieval law texts and in later legal documents pertaining to the relations of the Welsh and the English. In the Welsh system, the kin group assumed responsibility for the payment of fines on the behalf of one of their own who had committed a murder. The kin group also received and distributed among themselves compensation received if one of their own was a victim. The local lord took a one-third share of the compensation for his help in mediation. In later times, when English-style law was used in Wales, feud compensation was still part of the legal system (although not in England). The old concepts of kin responsibility in crime were intermixed with the English jury system of judgment as late as the sixteenth century.

Features of the feud appear in several of the medieval Welsh stories, with the fullest manifestation in the *Mabinogi* story *Branwen, Daughter of Llyr*. Matholwch, king of Ireland, wishes to ally himself with Bendigeidfran, son of Llyr and king of Britain, by marrying his sister, Branwen. Her other brother, Efnisien, is so enraged that his opinion was not asked that he insults Matholwch by mutilating his horses. Bendigeidfran sends mediators to offer reparation. Matholwch and his men evaluate the reparation and consider whether to seek more. They decide that the amount offered is fair and that to seek more would be shameful. However, to Bendigeidfran, Matholwch seems heavy hearted, so he offers further reparation in the form of a magical cauldron that revives slain warriors. Unfortunately, once home the Irish begin murmuring about the insult endured by Matholwch. He permits his people to gain vengeance by mistreating Branwen. Her kin hear of the insult and invade Ireland. The Irish offer compensation but later ambush the Britons, and a great battle ensues. The original instigator of the conflict, Efnisien, sees that the Irish have the advantage of the life-giving cauldron, so he sacrifices himself by climbing within and bursting it, but not before he has killed the son born of Branwen and Matholwch. The result is a severe victory: all the Irish people are killed, and only seven Britons escape.

Branwen contains a feud structure. At first the group tries to avoid a feud by immediately moving to compensation. Additionally, the concern over the economics and honor of reparation shown by the Irishmen's analysis of Bendigeidfran's compensation compares well with the balancing of public honor, traditional legal expectations, and personal gain in feuding societies. The feud is reawakened in Ireland, where Branwen's mistreatment and the invasion by the Britons reflect an exchange of vengeance. Finally, the tale makes a sophisticated literary comment on the complexities and realities of this institution, since even the "winners" of the feud do not end with an agreeable victory.

Continental Europe

Feuding was performed throughout medieval continental Europe. Evidence is preserved in administrative documents, chronicles, and traditional literature. In some cases, the literary depiction of feud is diffused, perhaps reflecting the slow decay of the ideology of the institution ahead of its actual decay of use. For example, in the *Nibelungenlied*, feud seems hardly distinguishable from personal vendetta, and in the *Cantar de mio Cid* personal vengeance is replaced by loyalty to a feudal lord and the feudal court in the settlement of disputes. But in other cases, both in literature and in lived practice, the feud is alive and well. The practice is excellently documented in medieval France, from its early instances in the Migration Age chiefdoms to its late occurrences in the feudal political systems.

The Franks of the Merovingian dynasty (fifth century to mid-eighth century) brought their Germanic traditions of feuding to a region already acclimated to Roman law, which held only the criminal responsible for the crime, not his kin. The Church was inclined against the feud, yet it often found itself acting as part of the feud process in the function of arbitrator. Thus, the Franks melded into Gaulish culture in a variety of ways that created a complex legal context.

Evidence from the early Merovingian period comes from historical chronicles and saints' lives. Gregory of Tours's (d. 594) *History of the Franks* relates much of the evidence from the early Merovingian period, with later records coming from the chronicler Fredegar (d. c. 660). The basic patterns of feuding appear in these works: groups in disagreement who are distant enough to come into bloody conflict but related enough to engage in feud rather than open warfare; revenge for crimes committed; trickery to gain revenge; and occasional settlements.

Typical of feuding societies, the Merovingians lacked centrally organized states and policing institutions. The feud process of revenge and settlement remained "right" in Merovingian eyes. Neither Church nor king in general questioned the right of a kin group to seek vengeance for crimes or insulted honor, although in some individual cases we see attempts to restrict feud under royal or ecclesiastical authority. Kings sometimes intervened in feuds as fee-collecting arbitrators. Some evidence suggests that liability in feud was being narrowed by laws restricting punishment to the criminal.

Feud continued under the Carolingian dynasty (mid-eighth century to late tenth century). Charlemagne tried to limit feuding under royal prerogative, yet the practice survived far into the French medieval period. Strong family ties in addition to the feudal lord-client relationships ensured the group involvement in conflict and settlement that characterizes feuding. Later, Norman dukes and eventually the Capetian rulers were able to limit feuds, but the restriction only lessened feuding among the peasant classes; nobles still engaged in the practice.

Such chansons de geste as *Raoul de Cambrai* emphasize the detailed social workings of disputes. Raoul has been dealt injustice in his inheritance by the kin of his vassal; he retaliates but is eventually killed by his vassal. His family continues the feud and prefers vengeance over settlement, whereas Raoul's slayer and his kin desire settlement. An abbot mediates the conflict and warns that Raoul's kin will earn condemnation if they do not accept settlement. On the slayer's side, his sin will be pardoned if he and his family reconcile with Raoul's family by making a ritual submission to them (proffering of swords). The process of feud as well as complexities of loyalty are realistically portrayed in this story.

Although feuding permeated medieval society, as it has in many other times and places, it did not survive in full expression as centralized polities developed. Increasing social stratification—involving differential access to military technology—permitted the use of force by a small number of elites against a large number of people. Such systems lessen the effect of kinship solidarity and local communal oversight on the performance and negotiation of conflicts.

See also: Chanson de Geste; English Tradition: Anglo-Saxon Period; Irish Tradition; Law; Outlaw; Sagas of Icelanders

References and further reading: Anthropological and general studies of feud include C. Boehm, *Blood Revenge* (1984), which used fieldwork and archival records of feud in Montenegro as a starting point for wide-ranging discussion and theorizing. Other important cross-cultural studies include M. Gluckman, *Politics, Law, and Ritual in Tribal Society* (1967), and K. Otterbein, *Feuding and Warfare* (1994). Discussions of Frankish feud include J. M. Wallace-Hadrill, *The Long-Haired Kings* (1962), which focuses on feuds before the ninth century, and S. D. White, "Feuding and Peace-Making in the Touraine around the Year 1100," *Traditio* 42 (1986). For Anglo-Saxon England, see J. Hill, *The Cultural World in Beowulf* (1995), and for Wales, R. R. Davies, "The Survival of the Bloodfeud in Medieval Wales," *History* 54 (1969), which discusses aspects of the feud that changed under influence of the English jural system. The most extensive study of Icelandic feud as reflected in both law and literature is W. I. Miller, *Bloodtaking and Peacemaking: Feud, Law, and Society in Saga Iceland* (1990). Miller's "Choosing the Avenger," *Law and History Review* 1 (1983), discusses the traditional customs used to provoke vengeance in Iceland; see also J. L. Byock, *Feud in the Icelandic Saga* (1982). F. Kelly, *A Guide to Early Irish Law* (1988), provides an overview of the medieval Irish laws concerning family privilege and responsibility, kinship relations, and prosecution and punishments for crimes. See also R. P. M. Lehmann, "Death and Vengeance in the Ulster Cycle," *Zeitschrift für celtische Philologie* 43 (1989).

—*Wade Tarzia*

Finnic Song

A native song tradition found among the Baltic-Finnic peoples of northern Europe.

Songs composed in an alliterative trochaic tetrameter (i.e., four two-syllable feet, with the stress on the first syllable of each) are widespread in the Baltic-Finnic region and are shared by Finns, Karelians, Ingrians, Vepsians, Votes, and Estonians. These songs were sung either solo or in groups, generally without instrumental accompaniment, and they declined in popularity with the introduction of the rhymed ballad and other imports of central European art music in the seventeenth century. The greatest challenge to any discussion of medieval Finnic song lies in the paucity of early references to the tradition and the lateness of extant collections. The earliest references to songs in a Finnic language date from the sixteenth century, with more extensive documentation occurring only later. The Lutheran reformers Mikael Agricola (who cataloged Finnish and Karelian gods in 1551) and (in a record dated 1582) Jaakko Finno disapproved strenuously of such songs, which they associated with peasant Finland and Karelia. Agricola charged that they preserved pagan memories that should be expunged from Christian Finland, and cited singing associated with spring planting in particular. Finno stated that native songs were used for a variety of purposes, including entertainment, celebration, and satire. He found them shameful and laughable and called for the development of a Finnish Psalter that would replace the indigenous genre in performance and popularity. Since we know that neither Finnish-language hymns nor the European rhymed ballad had become established in Finland at this point, we may conjecture that these sixteenth-century diatribes refer to songs in trochaic tetrameter.

The tradition survived into the nineteenth century in more remote areas of Finland, Karelia, and Estonia. The songs are differentiated from the typical idioms of nineteenth-century peasants by their archaic diction and grammar, which have been used to ascertain the age and origin of particular songs. Musicological analysis of collected melodies points to the medieval character of the tradition as well. Much of our understanding of the medieval tradition is thus based on postmedieval data and on an appreciation of the relative conservatism of the Baltic-Finnic region in terms of language and culture. Agricola's mention of the use of native songs in ritual is reinforced by the court records of seventeenth-century Finnish witchcraft trials. These documents indicate the widespread use of chanted incantations (Finnish *loitsut*) in healing and propitiation. Songs of various types were performed at sowing, reaping, and slaughtering and to stanch blood, drive away snakes, protect cattle, and so on. Women performed lament songs at the graves of deceased family members, a tradition that survived the medieval period among Karelians, Ingrians, Vepsians, and Setu-Estonians. Elaborate wedding songs encoded communal wisdom regarding marital relations, expressed the sorrows of leave-taking, and lamented the hard life of a bride and daughter-in-law. Narrative songs focus on the magic and bravery of cultural heroes (especially shaman singers), the adventures of rebellious youths, the plight of orphans and serfs, and the occurrence of momentous historical events. Songs recounting the lives of Catholic saints (e.g., Finland's English-born missionary St. Henrik or the universally popular St. Catherine) abound as well, clearly predating the introduction of Lutheranism into the region in the sixteenth century. The extant evidence indicates that there was a lively and important song tradition in the past, one drawing on a native aesthetic system but incorporating thematic and stylistic influences from the rest of Europe as well.

See also: Baltic Tradition; Finno-Ugric Tradition
References and further reading: General overviews of the epic and lyric song traditions of the Finnic peoples include M. Kuusi, K. Bosley, and M. Branch, *Finnish Folk Poetry: Epic* (1977), and L. Honko, S. Timonen, and M. Branch, *The Great Bear* (1993). F. Oinas's *Studies in Finnic Folklore* (1985) provides useful discussions of some of the mythological figures that occur in the songs. A. Siikala and S. Vakimo, eds., *Songs beyond the* Kalevala (1994), is a useful collection of essays on the tradition, with discussion of its origins, antiquity, and form.

—*Thomas A. DuBois*

Finno-Ugric Tradition

The folkloric culture of the Sámi (Lapps), Finns, Karelians, Estonians, and related peoples of the Baltic region.

Speakers of Finno-Ugric languages were well established in northeastern Europe by the Middle Ages. Occupying a vast area from central Scandinavia to the White Sea and south to the Volga, these peoples formed a wedge between the expanding settlements of Scandinavians, Slavs, Balts, and Tartars. They figure in medieval texts first as unrepentant heathens and later as subjugated tribes. Although Cheremis, Permian, and Mordvin peoples all figure in medieval sources, this entry focuses on Sámi and Baltic Finns (i.e., those Finno-Ugric peoples best attested during the medieval period).

The Sámi (Lapps) of Scandinavia and Finland lived by hunting and fishing, supplemented with small-scale sheep or reindeer herding. Life revolved around the *siida*, a collective organization of extended families residing on common lands. Families tended to migrate seasonally, sometimes congregating in a single place for winter. Clothing was made of wood, leather, fur, and birch bark.

Many Sámi legends center on outside threats to the *siida*. Accounts of marauding demons, the *Chudit*, and their defeat and legends of a vengeful creature named Staalo probably reflect early-medieval contacts with non-Sámi traders and Vikings.

The Baltic Finns (Finns, Karelians, Estonians, Ingrians, Vepsians, Votes, and Livonians) practiced shifting agriculture along the coasts of the Baltic, Lake Peipus, and Lake Ladoga. Typical crops included barley, rye, roots, flax, and hemp. Hunting supplemented the diet. No kingship system existed, but tribes banded together in times of war and maintained hill fortresses in some regions.

The ancient house was conical, made of logs inclined inward toward a central ridgepole. Rectangular log homes became the norm by the early-medieval period. During the twelfth and thirteenth centuries a Swedish-derived house type replaced the earlier Slavic cabin in western Finland and Estonia. The sauna played an essential role in both practical and ritual life.

Both the Sámi and the Baltic Finns possessed epic songs that related myths and detailed the adventures of heroes. A regular meter and alliteration stabilized texts over generations. During the Viking Age and later, songs of seagoing heroes, wanderlust, and sexual exploits arise in the genre as well. After Christianization the genre became adapted to European ballad themes and peasant pastimes. A west Finnish song details the martyrdom of the English missionary St. Henrik; an Orthodox Karelian song cycle relates the life of Christ. Lyric songs concerning the plight of orphans, daughters-in-law, and shepherds voice protest. Courtship and game songs abound as well. Advice songs codify traditional wisdom with regard to weddings. The formal features of balladry (e.g., rhyme and refrains) were not adopted until the seventeenth century. Most church music, many dances, and the violin were also postmedieval arrivals.

Pre-Christian Religion

Evidence from folksongs, combined with mentions of vanquished deities in medieval chronicles, Mikael Agricola's catalog of Finnish and Karelian gods (1551), Lutheran accounts of Sámi religion, and insights from comparative Finno-Ugric mythology shed light on the gods, cosmology, and rituals of these peoples.

In general, Finnic peoples worshipped a variety of celestial deities, most of them male, including a thunder god (e.g., Sámi Dierpmis, Finnish Ukko) and a god of the sky (e.g., Sámi Radien, Finnish Ilmarinen). In addition, people worshipped "lower-order" deities, most of them female, associated with water, forest, and home. Proper appeasement of these spirits guaranteed health and prosperity. Generalizations are difficult, however, since many gods seem to have been particular to a single community and others go by multiple names. In many cases it is unclear whether the object worshipped is a natural entity itself (e.g., the sun) or a personified deity. The Finno-Ugric practice of naming demons after the supreme deities of neighboring peoples adds further confusion.

The cosmos was formed of the earth, a celestial realm, and often multiple underworlds inhabited by deities, demons, and the dead. Dead relatives were buried in groves, and their spirits were venerated as sources of help and guidance. Women's lamentations formed part of Ingrian and Karelian funerals and may have occurred elsewhere as well. Ritual sacrifices of livestock and bears were common to all Finno-Ugric peoples, as were beliefs in various forms of losing one's soul or of the soul's traveling. Among agrarian populations planting and harvest rituals ensured good fortune.

Shamans (Finno-Ugric *nojta, Finnish noita, Estonian noid, Sámi noaide) played important roles. Through drumming, song, or intense physical activity they induced a death-like trance, during which their soul, freed, could wander the cosmos to discover valuable information (e.g., the origin of a disease) or retrieve a lost soul. Shamans also served as cult leaders, overseeing sacrifices at sacred places and prophesying. Such activities earned the Sámi and Baltic Finns a reputation for sorcery among their Scandinavian neighbors. Adventures of shaman heroes, such as the Finnish Lemminkäinen and Väinämöinen, were preserved in folksongs. Hundreds of incantations relating the origins of iron, fire, rickets, snakes, and so on survived Christianization.

From Contact to Conquest

Sources such as Ohthere's report to the English king Alfred (892) indicate early Scandinavian trading ties with both Sámi and Finns. Finnic grave finds from the period indicate familiarity with trading centers such as Birka and with worshippers of both Thor and Christ.

As the Viking Age subsided, Finnic peoples were drawn into wider political unions. During the 1140s western Finns—the Häme people—became allied with the Swedish crown, while Karelians allied themselves with the Novgorod Empire. These alliances led to the Swedish crusade against Finland in the 1150s. Real Christianization was aided by the arrival of the Dominican Order in 1249. Dominican monasteries and convents became important channels for the spread of European saints' legends and exempla and were instrumental in recording native Finnish herbal lore.

After a series of Swedish crusades, the Karelians were finally converted to the Eastern rite through mass baptisms imposed by Duke Jaroslav of Novgorod in 1227. A thirteenth-century birch-bark text contains a Karelian prayer to *Jumala* (God), also called *Bou* (from Russian *Bog,* "God") and associated with *jumalannuoli* (God's arrow)—apparently a thunderbolt. This text reflects the syncretic nature of postconversion Christianity. By the Peace of Päkinäsaari in 1323, however, Karelia was firmly established as an Orthodox realm. Monasteries such as the one at Vellamo spread the traditions of the Orthodox church and the "northern style" of icon painting—characterized by bright colors and folk elements—developed among Slavs and Finnic Christians of the region.

Parts of western Estonia were Christianized by the Danes in 1218. Christianity came to the rest of Estonia through the efforts of the crusading Fratres Militae Christi, or Swordbrothers, an order of German monastic knights who built castles at Tallinn (Reval) and Tartu (Dorpat). The Swordbrothers depended on taxation of the subjugated for their survival and bent the Finnic peoples of Estonia into feudal serfdom.

That the Sámi were spared such ruthless conquest during the Middle Ages probably stems from their location and willingness to comply with outside demands for trade and taxes.

With Christianity came a host of folk traditions, including etiological legends—belief tales explaining the origins of natural features, animals, and personal and places names—as well as saints' legends, witch lore, and saints'-day festivals. Their celebrations contained elements typical of Europe in general, but unique customs existed as well, some of which may reflect earlier beliefs and practices.

See also: Baltic Tradition; Shamanism

References and further reading: For Sámi culture, K. Nickul's *The Lappish Nation* (1977) provides a useful overview of traditional ways of life and linguistic variation. For a discussion of Sámi worldview and religion prior to Christianization, two useful collections of articles exist: L. Bäckman and Å. Hultkranz, eds., *Saami Pre-Christian Religion* (1985), and T. Ahlbäck, ed., *Saami Religion* (1987). For a catalog of Sámi märchen and legend types, see J. Qvigstad, *Lappische Märchen and Sagenvarianten* (1925). Parallels to the Sámi legend of the demon warriors are classified under legend number 8000 in R. T. Christiansen, *The Migratory Legends* (1958).

In the area of Baltic-Finnic tradition, M. Kuusi, K. Bosley, and M. Branch provide a useful overview of ancient folksong in *Finnish Folk Poetry: Epic* (1977). F. J. Oinas's collection of articles, *Studies in Finnic Folklore* (1985), also provides valuable insights. Baltic-Finnic pre-Christian religion is explored in a Finno-Ugric context in M. Hoppál and J. Pentikäinen, eds., *Uralic Mythology and Folklore* (1989); the religion's Nordic context is explored in T. Ahlbäck, ed., *Old Norse and Finnish Religions and Cultic Place-Names* (1990). A. Nenola-Kallio examines lament songs of various types in *Studies in Ingrian Laments* (1982).

—*Thomas A. DuBois*

Flyting [Fliting]

An exchange of vituperation or ad hominem verbal abuse.

Descending from the Old English *flit* (strife, contention) and *flitan* (to dispute, quarrel), the word *flyting* entered into the dialect of Middle Scots popular culture, where it designated abusive speech or quarreling that sometimes culminated in legal action. Scottish court poets of the fifteenth and sixteenth centuries used "flyting" as a generic term for their poetic duels, of which *The Flyting of Dunbar and Kennedy* and *Polwart and Montgomerie Flyting* are outstanding examples. Featuring flamboyant hyperbole, verbal pyrotechnics, and vitriol not untempered by a sense of the comic, these poetic exchanges stand at the head of an enduring Scottish tradition and are responsible for the currency of the word "flyting" as a general designation for verbal duels of this kind.

The term has also been applied by scholars to an assortment of quarrels in early Germanic literature. The flyting between Beowulf and Unferth in the Old English epic *Beowulf* features heroic adversaries in the hospitable setting of a mead hall, whereas the flyting between Byrhtnoth and the Vikings in *The Battle of Maldon* pits enemies about to commence battle. Flytings in Icelandic saga, such as that between Skarphedin and Flosi (and others) at the Althing in *Njal's Saga*, belong to the feuding process around which the legal institutions of medieval Iceland were in large part built. More extravagant are the quarrels between the gods in the *Poetic Edda*, such as the squaring off between Thor and Odin in *Harbardsljod* or between Loki and the other gods and goddesses in the Lokasenna; or again, in early Celtic literature, as in the seriatim contests between Cet mac Matach of Connacht and the men of Ulster in *Scéla Mucce Meic Dathó* (The Tale of Mac Dathó's Pig). Nomenclatures vary: Old Irish provides the word *comram*, while some scholars prefer the indigenous terms *senna* and *mannjafnaðr* in discussions of Norse literature. Whether "flyting" will win acceptance as an inclusive, cross-cultural rubric remains to be seen. In any event, the generic and historical relations between flyting and other medieval debate forms, such as the *débat* or *tenso*, still need elucidation.

Other works of medieval literature, such as the Middle High German *Wartburgkrieg*, the Middle English *The Owl and the Nightingale*, and pairs of tales in Chaucer's *Canterbury Tales* (such as "The Miller's Tale" and "The Reeve's Tales"), might productively be characterized as flytings. Similarities have further been noted between medieval flytings and the verbal dueling practices that flourished in the literatures and civilizations of the ancient Greeks, Chinese, Indians, Turks, Mayans, and others. Of contemporary relevance is the practice of "playing the dozens" among inner-city African Americans or the highly formalized poetic dueling still cultivated in the Arab world and recently transmitted through the airwaves between Saudi and Iraqi adversaries during the Iraq war of 1991.

In this heterogeneous mass of material, several fundamental definitions and distinctions can be offered. Despite its untamed appearance, flyting represents a contest mode whose rules, though usually unstated and shaped by local practice and convention, are known to the participants. As with most games, flyting as an originally oral activity (even when represented in written texts) typically transpires before witnesses and often contains mechanisms for self-evaluation, that is, for the determination of who has won and lost. What differentiates flyting from other forms of disputation, such as intellectual debate, is its personal orientation: flyting insults and boasts are targeted at the flyters themselves or at other persons (such as ancestors or kinsfolk) with whom their reputations are intertwined.

A flyting can be linked to some performance, usually martial or athletic, that is itself external to the verbal disputation, or it can be self-contained and self-fulfilling. Into the former category fall most flytings of the "heroic" type, in which warrior boasts or insults are intended to carry a contractual and predictive value on an upcoming heroic test. The dispute between Beowulf and Unferth is resolved not in words but in deeds, as Beowulf proves his heroic mettle in hand-to-hand combat with Grendel. In this way the Beowulf-Unferth flyting represents just one stage in a larger contesting process. By contrast, the "ludic" flyting—that is, one in which poetic proficiency and wit under pressure are cultivated and prized—of Dunbar and Kennedy proposes no material test by which the quarrel can be adjudicated; rather, it consummates itself as verbal display. "Heroic" flyters in combat situations, on the other hand, assign greater value to manly prowess, to whose demonstration the flyting is an elaborate preliminary.

See also: *Beowulf*; Chaucer, Geoffrey; Scottish Tradition

References and further reading: *Homo Ludens* (1955), J. Huizinga's classic discussion of play in human culture, includes extensive cross-cultural comparison of flyting-type dialogic forms. Incorporating evolutionary perspectives, W. Ong, *Fighting for Life* (1981), studies agonistic and contest patterns exhibited in disputation and other cultural activities. The Germanic and Scottish flyting traditions, respectively, are reviewed in C. Clover, "The Germanic Context of the Unferth Episode," *Speculum* 55 (1980), and P. Bawcutt, "The Art of Flyting," *Scottish Literary Journal* 10, no. 2 (1983). C. Lindahl's *Earnest Games: Folkloric Patterns in* The Canterbury Tales (1987) provides a folkloric and sociological study of verbal duels in Chaucer's *Canterbury Tales*. Concentrating on ancient Greek and medieval English but ranging to other cultural traditions, W. Parks, *Verbal Dueling in Heroic Narrative* (1990), investigates heroic flyting and its generic interrelations with other verbal contest forms.

—*Ward Parks*

Folk Music and Folksong

The traditional, unofficial performance of instrumental music and song, learned outside of elite institutions and passed on from person to person, through imitation and observation generally without the aid of written musical notation, and employed for entertainments that are not formally sanctioned—such as work songs, dance music, and lovers' serenades.

Ethnomusicology

The study of folk music is called ethnomusicology. This field has a long and respected history, which has only recently been recognized and accepted into the academic mainstream. Known as comparative musicology before 1950, it is an interdisciplinary field that combines both musicology (the study of all aspects of music in a scholarly manner) and anthropology (the study of humans and their culture, especially cultures outside the investigator's own background). Ethnomusicology involves both fieldwork and desk or laboratory work. Fieldwork entails going out to the source to make sound recordings and observations of the music in the culture, and those materials are analyzed and described in the desk work. These two activities were done by separate individuals in previous decades, but current ethnomusicologists combine the two activities and display both technical competence in the field and scholarly acumen in the academic environment.

Theories of Origin

There is no shortage of theories about the origins of folk music, some arising within traditional cultures, others in the speculations of social scientists. Music and dance probably developed simultaneously once the basic needs of food, shelter, and security were satisfied for early humans. According to the mythological traditions of various cultures, music came to humanity through the intervention of a god, such as Apollo, or through a single human being, such as the biblical Yuval. Mythological explanations of the origins of music often articulate a specific power or event as the catalyst. According to a number of psychological and social theories, the expression of music is fundamental to the human species, and its creation may even mark the beginnings of human culture. The interconnecting development of speech and musical sound was postulated by such early German folklorists as Johann Gottfried von Herder (1744–1803) and Jacob and Wilhelm Grimm (fl. 1810–1860). In any event, music was probably of paramount importance in early peoples' development of speech, community, and culture.

Classifications

The classification of folk music has also undergone an interesting history. By its very nature as "unofficial culture," folk music defies the kinds of classification scholars employ for other kinds of music. The first attempts at classification focused on song texts; melodies received relatively little attention. Melodic classification began in the nineteenth century but was difficult before the advent of sound-recording devices. As collections of folk music grew larger, so too did the need for easy access to large collections and for the opportunity to interpret

"Svmer is icumen in" [Spring Has Come], one of the most famous Middle English lyrics; words and music were written down circa 1240–1310. (British Museum, MS Harley 978, fol. 11b; North Wind Picture Archives)

relationships between melodies in collections. Therefore, tune families and melodic similarities began to be examined. Finally, the classification of musical instruments into family-like groupings assisted in the examination of instrument evolution and relatedness between cultures.

The world is usually divided into two areas in the study of folk music. Europe, sub-Saharan Africa, and the Americas are generally regarded as one study group, and the Asian, Pacific, Indic, and Russian cultures are regarded as another. These divisions do not mean there are no cross-cultural associations or sharings in folk music melodies; it merely makes the study of their developments easier, given the interrelationships within the two divisions.

Oral Tradition

Most folk music has an oral tradition, having been handed down through generations of the community by word of mouth. People learn to play instruments by watching and imitating, and they learn songs and melodies by hearing and repetition. In a musical culture based on written scores, music is printed, read, and recorded for perpetuity. In most folk culture, music is sung, remembered, and taught by one generation to the next. In folk communities this oral method often results in gradual changes over time in the melodic shape and presentation of the musical repertoire because of the changing needs and desires of the community. Some of the more fascinating ethnomusicological studies have involved the systematic cataloging of melodic variants and word changes in one particular folksong over time.

The process of composition in folk music can also take a variety of forms. New music may be created by individuals, and past composers may develop almost mythic status in the community. It can be the result of group creativity: the community may gather and together either create or re-create melodies and songs. And sometimes it can be created or re-created by a small group of leaders in conjunction with the community.

Cultural Associations

Folk music is often closely associated with a culture, a nation, or a people. In some cultures the words for "folk music" and "national music" are synonymous. Although no culture can claim a body of music as solely its own, it is often held that some distinctive and essential qualities of a culture find their way into music and become identified with it. This nationalistic view of folk music was especially strong in the folk music scholarship of the late nineteenth and early twentieth centuries because of the rise of nation-states in Europe. Unfortunately, this nationalism in music has sometimes been used to promote racist and aggressive policies toward other nations (for example, in Nazi Germany in the 1940s and the Soviet Union in the 1950s). Nevertheless, general characteristics of musical intervals and rhythms, the instruments used, and poetic and language inflections often uniquely identify a song or musical composition as national. And, of course, if people accept a song or composition as their own, it becomes a part of the culture no matter what process was involved in its creation. In fact, many late-nineteenth-century European composers inserted folk tunes, melodies, and songs into their "classical" music in order to incite or encourage nationalistic tendencies in their countrymen (Richard Wagner for Germany and Edward McDowell for the United States, for example).

The processes of canon formation in folk music are varied. Popularity, importance of the text over the music and vice versa, and versions of tunes that develop through generations or between cultures are but a few of the variables that contribute to the development of folk music canons within cultures. There are, however, three types of canon-formation activities that have been identified and help to distinguish change in folk music traditions. The first type of canon is the small-group canon. It is found in many social settings but especially in close-knit groups. Here folk music is a shared activity; many members know the group's shared repertory. Oral transmission usually predominates, and there may be little change in the musical repertory over time. The second type of canon is the mediated canon. This type of folk music cuts across and is determined by several communities, who combine characteristics and social patterns together into a shared repertory that enlivens the contributing communities and often affects other communities in close proximity. The third type of canon is the imagined canon, which combines seemingly disparate elements into a bricolage-type assemblage. The community involved in this type of activity is in itself disparate and tries to combine its characteristics into an assemblage of elements that it determines as its identity and defining symbol. It is a conscious effort; one example is the creation of an Israeli national folk music by Russian immigrants in the early twentieth century.

Styles

In addition to the cultural context of folk music, ethnomusicologists also study its musical "grammar" or "vocabulary." One of the defining characteristics of the musical style of folk music is a singing/speaking style. Spoken and sung inflections combine and interweave through tone color, texture, vocal tension and the use of vibrato or tremolo, nasality, and ornamentation (such as grace notes and trills) to distinguish one culture's repertoire from another's. Form is another dimension of definition; it involves tempo, repetition, sectionalization of phrases, and melodic and pitch variations. Whether music is polyphonic (containing many lines of music at once), monophonic (one line of music), or homophonic (a melody supported by chords) also helps to distinguish one folk music from another. The place of instruments often assists in the identification and classification of musical differences between cultures: do they accompany vocal expression or play in solo situations only, or are they perhaps not used at all? Rhythm, tempo, melodic scales and intervals, microtones—all combine to define a culture's musical identity. In fact, identification of a culture's use of certain musical scales, such as pentatonic (five-note), tritonic (three-note), tetratonic (four-note), hexatonic (six-note), or heptatonic (seven-note), is often the first step in ethnomusicological research.

European folk music of the medieval period is characterized both by a single corpus of musical style and by a group of separate musical styles. Although researchers know very little about the history of European folk music prior to the fifteenth century, determining the versions and variations of particular folksongs through the centuries has helped to document cultural and ethnic similarities. The most characteristic trait of European folk music is its strophic structure. In this type of music a tune with several lines of melody is repeated several times, each time with different words. Folk poetry is usually arranged into units of two, three, four, or more lines, commonly called stanzas or strophes. Often the words tell a story as well, so that the repetition of music fits well into the word focus.

Scales

The musical scale structure of European folk music exhibits great variety, but most tend to use intervals that fit into the diatonic system. This scale system, which can be heard by playing contiguous white keys on the piano, is a series of major and minor second intervals. An examination of a few representative song collections shows that the most common intervals in European folk music are major seconds and minor thirds. During the Middle Ages most music fit into what became known as the eight Church modes. The Dorian, Phrygian, Lydian, and Mixolydian modes, along with other modes, may or may not have influenced medieval secular music, but they are important nonetheless. In any case, seven-tone scales, with their modal arrangements, are a hallmark of European folk music.

Most European folk music can be classified as isometric; that is, a single meter predominates throughout the song. Much of the poetic structure determined the metric character of the music. The use of complex meter also assists in the identification of regional and ethnic folk music differences. For instance, the regular alteration of 3/8, 4/8, and 5/8 measures is a characteristic of certain eastern European folksongs.

Singing style, that is, use of the voice, facial expressions and movements, and types of tone color, is another distinguishing feature of European folk music. Vocal parameters include the degree of tension, raspiness, and nasality in the voice; group vocal blend; the use of ornamentation and accentuation; and pitch level.

Song Types

Ethnomusicological research has also been able to identify particular song types found in medieval European folk music. Narrative song appears in two main types: epics and ballads. In fact, epics constitute one of the most important folksong types in European music, perhaps more than in any other world culture. Surviving medieval ballads tend to date from the closing years of the period (for example, from the fifteenth century in England). Some of these songs show evidence of a circular motion, passing from folk sources into the specialized repertories of court minstrels and *jongleurs* and then moving back into the oral repertories of folk communities. Whereas epics are long and complex, involving several events tied together by a central theme, ballads usually tell one story or theme succinctly and in strophic form.

Among nonnarrative songs, love songs flourished in medieval European folk music. Ceremonial songs, especially in sacred music, appear in many varieties throughout European cultures. Songs for rites of passage, as well as songs marking the passing of seasons and equinoxes, are prolific in both pre-Christian and Christian European musical traditions. Songs sung during or about agricultural functions also survive in many cultures. Humorous songs take many forms, including children's songs, ballads, and work songs. Finally, dance music is not uniquely European, but it is one of the important folk music genres throughout the West. Two main types predominate: an older, relatively simple form involved in rituals and ceremonies and a later form that was more social and musically complex. Mimetic dances (those that represent feelings, persons, actions, animals, and events in dance) are as common in medieval European culture as in other folk cultures.

Instruments

Finally, musical instruments are important in the medieval European folk tradition, as is instrumental music. While the instruments vary in size, design, and type, they can be divided into four categories in European folk cultures: (1) simple instruments like flutes and rattles; (2) instruments brought to Europe from non-European cultures, for example, the Middle East and Africa; (3) instruments developed in the European folk cultures themselves, such as the bowed lyre and the Dolle (fiddle made from a wooden shoe in northwestern Germany); and (4) instruments used in urban musical culture that were then taken over by the folk cultures and changed—including the bass viol, the clarinet, the violin, the guitar, and the hurdy-gurdy.

Musical Lore

Literary evidence of medieval folk music, including lore about folk music, is abundant. There are numerous examples in Old and Middle Irish sagas and

A fourteenth-century French portrayal of a group of musicians. (Chrétien Legouais, Ovide Moralise. MS 1044, fol. 103v; Giraudon/Art Resource, NY)

poems, such as the reference in *The Tale of Mac Dathó's Pig* to the women and their daughters singing every night "Fer Loga Is My Darling" at Emuin Machae; an apparent reference to women keening at a grave in *The Wooing of Étain*; and the famous statement in *The Exile of the Sons of Uisliu* that "the singing of the sons of Uisliu was very melodious: every cow that heard it gave two thirds more milk, and every man who heard it grew peaceful and sated with music." Anglo-Saxon culture is likewise filled with musical lore, including references to the *scop*, or public singer, in *Beowulf* and *Deor's Lament*; Bede's story of Cædmon's embarrassment when the harp approached him during an evening of communal singing; and Alcuin's famous letter to the monks of Lindisfarne (in 797) that it was unseemly for them to be singing old heroic lays when they could be singing God's praises.

A memorable example of another kind of traditional music would be the performance of the Miller in Chaucer's *Canterbury Tales* (c. 1387–1400), who plays his bagpipes to accompany the pilgrims' journey to the shrine of St. Thomas Becket. Here we may assume that the Miller has learned his skill (along with the scurrilous songs he is noted for singing) through informal, traditional means in his village, but it is notable that his music entertains a mixed group, including members of the aristocracy as well as the Cook and the Plowman.

See also: Ballad; Carol; Dance; Folklore; Harp; Lute; Minstrel
References and further reading: Scholarly studies include W. Danckert, *Das europäische Volkslied* (1970); M. Karpeles, *Folksong in Europe* (1956); B. Nettl, *Folk and Traditional Music of the Western Continents* (1973); and P. Bohlman, *The Study of Folk Music in the Modern World* (1988).

—*Bradford Lee Eden*

Folklore

The traditional, unofficial culture of communities (folk groups); the academic discipline that studies such culture.

When British antiquarian William John Thoms coined the term *folklore* in 1846 he was seeking a new name for "popular antiquities": the customs, beliefs, stories, and artifacts shared by the old-fashioned and poorer segments of society as part of their communal legacy.

To early scholars folklore was first and foremost an *item*: a proverb, riddle, song, tale, dance, custom, ritual, design, tool, or building. Items of folklore were assumed to be of great antiquity, passed down from generation to generation with little change. A second trait that early definitions focused on was folklore's strong association with certain *groups*: ethnic (for example, the Germanic Jutes who settled southeast England or the Basques of the Pyrenees, both culturally distinct from surrounding populations), religious (the southern French villagers who formed the folk cult of St. Guinefort; or Irish monks, who established a lifestyle distinctly different from monks trained by the Roman Church), regional (Scandinavia, where numerous north Germanic tribes shared many cultural traits derived from social interaction and common geographical conditions), occupational (blacksmiths, friars, minstrels), social (the upper aristocracy of northern France, or the peasants of the same region), or national (English or French, though the concept of nationhood did not become a major cultural force until the late Middle Ages).

More recently folklorists have stressed a third trait: folklore is a community-based *process*, most often involving word-of-mouth and face-to-face communication in close-knit groups, through which people express and negotiate their shared understandings, values, beliefs, and concerns. Folklore is constantly changing to reflect the changing circumstances of those who share it. Thus, contemporary folklorists reject the old assumption that lore is a fossil, passed on unaltered for generations. In any vital folk group, old traditions are continually remade in response to current conditions.

Today's folklorists also view folklore as the unofficial culture of *any group*, not just the poor or old-fashioned. No matter what their social background, such groups as families share beliefs, attitudes, gestures, and behaviors—as well as such material traditions as food preparation and crafts—that they create and reshape as unofficial expressions of group identity.

The process of folklore is both conservative and dynamic. Because such folk performers as storytellers must meet the expectations of a live audience, they present their hearers with familiar, time-tested plots, themes, and styles, ensuring that each performance owes much to the norms established by past performers and audiences. Yet because no two storytelling sessions are identical, each performance is also new and unique, reflecting the concerns of its immediate context as well as the special artistry of its teller.

Thus, to know the folkloric meaning of a tale, for example, nothing is more important than, first, knowing the community that shares it and, second, experiencing (not merely witnessing) the actual performance: the moment at which the "item" comes to life, both as the personal expression of the teller and the shared experience of the group. For this reason fieldwork—the intensive immersion in a community, through which the folklorist gets to know and share its daily life, not just its performative moments—is the single most important requirement of contemporary folklore studies. Without such firsthand experience, anything—no matter how thoughtful or how long considered—that a folklorist says about a community is guesswork. (Even with such experience, the best efforts of the most dedicated and sensitive fieldworker still cannot do justice to the complex realities of even the smallest community, but that is a limitation that anyone who studies human groups, from any perspective, must live with.)

Today's specialists in medieval folklore are denied the most important experience a folklorist must have: every single member of every community from which they may wish to learn has been dead for many centuries. There are no performances to witness, no one to listen to or watch. We have only a fraction of the material remains of these communities, and those remains heavily favor the official culture of the most powerful and wealthy. Hundreds of medieval cathedrals still stand today, but the average peasant's house stood for no more than 30 years. Thousands of papal bulls and royal edicts survive, but not one oral performance of a folktale. For most of the Middle Ages, writing—the only medium through which we can know the words of medieval people—was reserved for a relatively small and specialized segment of the population comprising principally those trained and indoctrinated in official Christian culture.

Recovering the Contexts of Medieval Folklore

Fortunately, because the folkloric process is the day-to-day, unofficial, community basis on which most other culture is based, its influence on society is pervasive. Folklore does not exist simply in oral documents; it also permeates many written sources, even within the universities, monasteries, and palaces of the Middle Ages. And occasionally even the frozen text of a dusty document will display something of the vividness of a live performance. In the late twelfth century an anonymous monk in Cambridgeshire took the time to write a satire on the people of the neighboring shire of Norfolk, a poem in Latin, the *Descriptio norfolciensium* (Description of the Norfolkers). Anything but an official document, the *Descriptio* presents a series of numskull jokes that stereotype the Norfolker as an irredeemable idiot. This manuscript represents some of the earliest occurrences of jokes still widely told today—for example, one about a Norfolker who felt so sorry that his horse had a heavy load to bear that he shouldered the load himself—and then mounted the horse, so that it would have to carry him as well (AT 1242A, "Carrying Part of the Load").

We have some complete copies of this priceless expression of regional folk rivalry. But even more impressive is a partial copy of the same poem, written by a monk from Norfolk. Up to a point, the monk dutifully copies these diatribes

This misericord presents a folly popular in numskull jokes from the Middle Ages to the present: to spare his horse, a man shoulders the horse's load himself—but rides the horse, so that it will have to carry him as well; fifteenth century, La Guerche de Bretagne, France. (Photograph by Elaine Block)

against his own shire, but then he can take it no longer, breaks off the tale, and launches into his own performance, blasting the author of the *Descriptio* and singing the praises of Norfolk. It is possible that this response was composed at the very moment it was written down, just as a folktale is re-created anew during an oral artist's performance. The Norfolk monk may have been alone, writing silently as he composed it, or he may have spoken it as he wrote, in the company of other monks who urged him on and otherwise contributed to the performance. (Or—perhaps more likely—the performance was shaped not by the creator of either text but by the audience, a Norfolk copyist who had both complete works in front of him and who grew so angry reading the *Descriptio* that he refused to write down any more of it and proceeded immediately to copy the response. Yet even this more prosaic explanation would demonstrate the audience's enormous power in folk tradition, the power either to sustain a performer's work for generations or to consign it to oblivion.) We will never know exactly how this text came to be. The performance preserved on paper remains just a shadow of an actual folk performance, but it is nevertheless a particularly rich and deep one.

Much more often, however, medieval records of folk performance offer one sort or another of negative evidence. For example, the great majority of the copious records of the famous medieval Feast of Fools celebration are either sets of rules ordering that certain playful activities not be performed (thereby giving us good reason to think that they were indeed performed, and in defiance of the authorities) or pronouncements banning the festival altogether. Only rarely do we get an eyewitness account of an actual performance, and in not one case is the festival described by someone who approves of it.

Folkloric Studies and Sourcebooks

Because the contexts essential to understanding medieval folklore are most often fragmentary, folklorists must be resourceful, eclectic, and rigorous. They must collect as much information as they can find and use it carefully to reconstruct as fully as possible the lifestyles and value systems of past societies. Historians of unofficial culture, some identifying themselves as folklorists and some not, have marshaled diverse written records and archaeological evidence to supplement or substitute for oral traditions. In *Montaillou: The Promised Land of Error* (1978) Emmanuel Le Roy Ladurie artfully rereads testimony from the trials of accused heretics and finds beneath the official veneer of these documents a wealth of evidence from which he is able to describe the home life, social relationships, sexual practices, funeral customs, and folk religion of a thirteenth-century French village. In *Medieval Popular Culture* (1988) Aron Gurevich sifts through saints' lives, penitential manuals, clerical tracts, and other Latin sources to find evidence of a folk culture (possessing unique conceptions of time, symbolism, morality, and the afterlife) alive in the midst of elite clerical culture. In *Medieval Marriage: Two Models from Twelfth-Century France* (1978) Georges Duby examines annulment proceedings, clerical tracts on marriage, family histories of noble houses, and archaeological records to reconstruct the attitudes and customs surrounding sex, marriage, gender roles, and family values shared by the upper aristocracy of northern France. In *Earnest Games: Folkloric Patterns in* The Canterbury Tales (1987) Carl Lindahl employs slander

records, courtesy books (that is, a manual teaching appropriate behavior), coro-
ners' rolls, and Chaucer's poetry to reconstruct folk techniques of indirect insult
employed in fourteenth-century England.

As a rule, it is far easier to recover a broad social context for a medieval
song or tale than to situate an actual performance. To get a sense of the style,
content, and meaning of any one poorly described festive enactment or written
approximation of a folktale, it is especially important to look at as many related
examples as possible. Items of folklore are available to medievalists in many
extensive collections. E. K. Chambers's *The Mediaeval Stage* (1903)—though
outdated as a theoretical statement—remains useful as a compendium of records
related to minstrel performances, mummings, interludes, Feast of Fools enactments, and other medieval rituals and entertainments. Lütz Röhrich's *Erzählungen
des späten Mittelalters* (Tales of the Late Middle Ages, 2 vols., 1962) brings together late-medieval folktales from Latin and vernacular prose and verse
and sets them alongside oral tales collected centuries later from peasant
narrators, allowing readers to learn something of the continuities and differences between these two vastly different cultural contexts. Roger Vaultier's
Folklore pendant la Guerre de Cent Ans (Folklore during the Hundred Years'
War; 1965) presents a catalog of pilgrimage activities, seasonal festivals,
and rites of passage mentioned in certain French legal documents. Though
it presents many unsupported theories, Claude Gaignebet's and Jean-Domi-
nique Lajoux's *Art profane et religion populaire au moyen âge* (Secular Art and
Folk Religion in the Middle Ages; 1985) is a virtual encyclopedia of the
secular beliefs, tales, gestures, and customs represented in visual form in
French sculptures and carvings.

Although any one of these records, taken alone, may reveal little about the
meaning of a folkloric performance in its original context, we can nonetheless
learn much by viewing the records together, creating a multitextual context,
allowing us to discover what is especially important or unique about any given
text by learning how it differs from the others. Medievalists can best benefit
from such sources by first considering some of the leading premises, methods,
and tools developed by folklorists.

Patterns and Variations

Because folklore tends to combine stable, long-lived patterns with the needs
and nuances of its immediate context, such forms as folktales present an excellent medium for studying intercultural variation as well as change over time.
For example, certain British stories of outlaw heroes spanned a period of centuries, during which time they told of the Anglo-Saxon resister Hereward (eleventh century), the Scottish rebel William Wallace (thirteenth century), and
the legendary yeoman Robin Hood (fourteenth century or earlier). The plot of
one of the tales told about Hereward in the twelfth century is also found in
fifteenth-century tales of Wallace and Robin Hood: the hero befriends a lowly
potter, borrows his clothes, and uses this disguise to infiltrate enemy territory,
where he embarrasses his chief enemy (William the Conqueror, for Hereward;
Edward I of England, for Wallace; and the Sheriff of Nottingham, for Robin
Hood).

The traits shared by all three groups of stories allow us to say something about the nature and function of medieval English outlaw legends in general. In all cases the stories arose in the midst of domestic unrest, and the outlaw hero emerged to represent the values of groups alienated from and threatened by the dominant power structure. By aiding the oppressed at the expense of the oppressors, the outlaw hero represents a rejection of the dominant culture and the assertion of the moral superiority of the underdog.

Yet, more specifically, the differences between the outlaw heroes reveal something of the social climate in which each emerged. Hereward is an Anglo-Saxon earl allied with Anglo-Saxons of lower social standing against the Norman occupation. His stories show the English side of an ethnic conflict and a rejection of the values of the new French-speaking rulers. William Wallace plays a similar role for Scottish patriots resentful of English rule, as the hero and his poor followers continually outsmart and embarrass the numerically superior English. Robin Hood unites yeomen and dispossessed nobles against Church leaders and corrupt members of the upper aristocracy, thus revealing the common concerns of minor landowners and tradespeople threatened by the entrenched interests of the most powerful landlords and lawmakers.

As similar as these groups of outlaw legends are, each can be located in a different general social context, a context that is "truer" than the events of the story. Hereward and Wallace were flesh-and-blood outlaws; Robin Hood probably was not. The specific legends just discussed almost certainly do not represent actual events. Like so much folklore, these tales are older than the events portrayed; their truth lies in the ways in which they are molded to reflect the concerns of the tellers.

Medievalists using tales to document social contexts should know as many intercultural versions of a tale as possible. That knowledge will help them discover what is unique to the region, period, group, or individual performer under study. Such international catalogs as Antti Aarne's and Stith Thompson's *The Types of the Folktale* (1961) and Thompson's *Motif-Index of Folk-Literature* (6 vols., 1955–1958) help researchers find variants of internationally distributed narrative plots. Although both indexes incorporate a great deal of pre- and postmedieval folklore, they are invaluable tools for the study of the traditions of the Middle Ages.

Other indexes present exclusively medieval material, although these tend to be limited to one specific genre or culture. Among the most important for their respective areas are Gerald M. Bordman, *Motif-Index of the Middle English Metrical Romances* (1963); Tom Peate Cross, *Motif-Index of Ancient Irish Literature* (1952); D. P. Rotunda, *Motif-Index of the Italian Novella* (1942); and F. C. Tubach, *Index Exemplorum* (1969), a catalog of 5,400 late-medieval exempla (tales told for moral purposes) circulating in clerical communities throughout late-medieval Europe.

Close Comparative Studies

In comparative folklore studies, the more similar two items of lore, the more significant the differences between them. For example, any item of folklore will possess at least three kinds of style: generic, cultural, and individual. In order to identify significant differences in the cultural styles of two different groups or periods, one must first minimize the generic and individual variables of the texts under study.

To illustrate: different forms, or genres, of folklore are told for various purposes and according to differing rules (their "generic styles"). The exemplum, for instance, is a moral tale—sometimes fictional, sometimes believed to be true—told most often by religious specialists to reinforce moral and spiritual precepts. The belief legend, on the other hand, is a narrative or a debate that tests the limits of belief. The contents of exempla and legends overlap considerably, and the two forms often blend together, yet they tend to differ significantly in function and style. In the second half of the thirteenth century, in the north of England, an Anglo-Norman author composed *Manuel des pechiez* (Manual of Sins), a collection of exempla, each of which concludes with a moral illustrating appropriate Christian behavior. The tales of the *Manuel* are told as true, but the truths that it intends to illustrate are moral and doctrinal truths. On the other hand, in his *Journey through Wales* and *Description of Wales*, Gerald of Wales (c. 1146–1223) relates many belief legends concerning strange events that defy orthodox explanation. We learn from Gerald that such tales actually circulated among his Welsh contemporaries, who told them to illustrate their notions of ways in which the supernatural was manifested in their lives. Although the received Christian doctrine of Gerald's time denied that humans had the power to foretell the future, Gerald told legends about Welshmen with prophetic powers and attempted to reconcile these stories with official Church precepts. Gerald's stories and explanations tell us much about the overlaps, differences, and conflicts between Welsh folk belief and Christian orthodoxy in the twelfth century.

Both the *Manuel des pechiez* and Gerald's stories are valuable sources of medieval folklore, but to compare them with the intent of finding differences between twelfth-century Welsh and fourteenth-century English folk beliefs is to compare apples and oranges: the *Manuel*'s exempla are framed and presented as spiritual truths, while Gerald's legends are actual records of orally circulating legends that show us much about how the people of twelfth-century Wales used stories to express and negotiate their concerns about the nature of their world and the supernatural forces believed to inhabit it. These generic differences are too great to allow significant cultural distinctions. Robert Darnton's *The Great Cat Massacre and Other Episodes in French Cultural History* (1984) commits a similar error in trying to reveal differences between French and English folk cultures through a comparison of French märchen and English nursery rhymes.

Yet by comparing two more-similar texts, a folklorist can learn a great deal. In 1303, about 40 years after the *Manuel des pechiez* appeared, the Englishman Robert Mannyng wrote *Handlyng Synne*, a direct translation of the *Manuel* yet at the same time an entirely new work, which addresses a lower-class English-speaking audience rather than the elite French-speaking community of the same district, for whom the author of the *Manuel* wrote. Here are two texts from the same area, between which we can establish a direct connection, and the contrasts between them are very striking. Yet in comparing just two texts it is important to ask if the differences between the two represent something more general than the individual stylistic differences between the two authors.

Mannyng relates many tales not told in his original; in many cases he states that he has heard them told in his community. In other cases he translates tales from other sources, such as the famous legend of the "cursed dancers" (motif C94.1.1). This tale, which first emerged in eleventh-century Germany, tells of a raucous group of young people who one Christmas violated the sacred space of a churchyard and became stuck together, forced to dance incessantly for the following year. Mannyng expressly writes *Handlyng Synne* to appeal to "lewde" (unlearned) speakers of English, especially for those who love listening to tales while at play, feasting, and drinking ale. Thus, when Mannyng changes his Anglo-Norman source material in certain ways, we have reason to think he may be doing so not merely to express his individual style but, more important, to accommodate a different audience from the *Manuel's*, a lower-class audience. We might thus conclude his version reflects the oral styles current among this group in his time. A close look at his changes supports this interpretation. To give just one example: Mannyng's Latin sources clearly indicate that the events related in the legend of the cursed dancers took place in Germany. But Mannyng first says this tale is as true "as the gospel" and then goes on to situate it "in this land, in England." The truth that Mannyng imparts by changing the locale is definitely not a literal truth (indeed, literally, Mannyng could be charged with lying) but an important "social truth" for legend tellers, who in medieval times, as today, intensify their stories by localizing them, making them more immediate, as if to say, "not only did this event happen, but it happened here, and it could happen to you." Localization is a widespread generic marker through which members of a legend-telling community express the idea that the story "belongs to us, and is about us."

Read against each other, the *Manuel des pechiez* and *Handlyng Synne* do indeed tell us much about medieval oral traditions, but even so, it is important to note that they *still* do not tell us about the differences between the beliefs of upper-class Normans and those of lower-class English people in northern England in the later Middle Ages, because the works accent different types of belief, in two different generic styles.

Again, finding the real cultural differences embedded in diverse folkloric texts requires researchers to take into close account variations of genre, plot, theme, context, and function and to recognize that the most telling differences are likely to emerge from comparisons of those texts that are most similar (here is where such works as *The Types of the Folktale* are particularly valuable). Moreover, in efforts to use folklore to characterize general cultural trends, it is important to compare as many such texts as possible because every storyteller has an individual style. Cultural style becomes apparent only after one has examined the shared traits of many different tellers from the same group.

Historical Fact and Social Truth

Folklore combines two types of truth: actual historical fact and "social truth." Both types are valuable for different purposes, but they are often difficult to distinguish. For example, William Camden's *Britannia* (1586) records an oral tradition about a giant named Jul Laber buried in a mound in southern England. Camden noted that the mound stood near a battle site from Julius Caesar's invasion of Britain and deduced that it was the burial place of the Roman tribune Laberius Durus, killed in Caesar's invasion. If so, a tenacious oral tradition helped preserve the name of the tribune for more than 1,600 years. Yet this "actual fact" was combined with the social fact that the tribune had been converted to a giant, adapted to an English folk tradition of ascribing ancient Celtic and Roman ruins to giants—thus expressing a social truth important for the tellers of these tales, and for folklorists as well.

Distinguishing social truth also requires consulting as many sources of as many different kinds as possible. For example, there are five separate medieval accounts relating that the Norman jester, Taillefer, entertained the troops of William the Conqueror during their battle against the English at Hastings (1066). Only the two latest of the five accounts, beginning with William of Malmesbury's (1125), claim that Taillefer sang the *Chanson de Roland* (Song of Roland) to inspire William's army. The late date of these accounts leads us to believe that Taillefer probably did not sing the *Chanson* at Hastings, but the claims that he did may tell us something significant about the social truth of twelfth-century English aristocrats: their adoption of the *Chanson de Roland* demonstrates their continued identification with mainland French aristocratic culture long after their initial occupation of England.

Folklore as a Reflection of Its Tellers and Its Time

Folklore—though a strong indicator of the teller's worldview—may provide a very skewed version of someone else's reality. For example, legends told during the fourteenth and fifteenth centuries and summarized in such documents as the *Malleus maleficarum* (Hammer of Witches, c. 1486) claim to describe the actual practices of witches, but they are in large part retellings of older stories once used by monks to stereotype Jews and heretics. These stories tell us little about the folk practices of accused witches, but they reveal much about the fears and folk beliefs of the accusers. Again, only a thorough knowledge of earlier and international legends about witches can help separate the claims of the inquisitors from the reality of the accused. Studies like Carlo Ginzburg's *Night Battles* (1983) apply such knowledge to transcripts from Italian witchcraft trials to peel away the outsiders' lore and to recover important information about the actual practice of folk magic and religion buried in surviving records.

As ancient as much folklore appears, the fact that it changes over time makes it a much better indicator of the present than of the past. Folklore collected in one era will not necessarily reveal the beliefs of an earlier time. This last point deserves special stress, as some of the greatest early folklore studies are based on the premise that current folklore can explain the worldviews of long-dead peoples. Jacob Grimm's *Teutonic Mythology* (1835), for instance, presents a wealth of medieval and postmedieval stories, rhymes, and customs, from which he attempts to reconstruct ancient Germanic religion. Grimm's study remains extremely valuable because it brings together so many important sources for the study of medieval Germanic folklore. Yet twentieth-century folklorists do not share Grimm's conviction that a nineteenth-century folktale can reveal much about medieval folk belief. To the contrary, the great value of folklore lies in its living, changing qualities—the ways in which it adapts received traditions to new conditions, becoming in the process both the personal expression of the individual performer and the communal property of those who share those traditions.

See also: Folktale; Legend; Motif; Myth

References and further reading: The only comprehensive history of folklore studies is G. Cocchiara, *History of Folklore in Europe* (1981). P. Burke's *Popular Culture in Early Modern Europe* (1978) provides a valuable survey of the social forces that led to the formation of folklore studies in Europe. General introductions to recent theories and methods of folklore research include D. Ben-Amos, *Folklore Genres* (1976); R. M. Dorson, ed., *Folklore and Folklife* (1972) and *A Handbook of American Folklore* (1986); R. Georges and M. O. Jones, *Folkloristics* (1995); B. Toelken, *The Dynamics of Folklore*, 2nd ed. (1996).

For model studies based on intensive fieldwork, see L. Dégh, *Folktales and Society*, 2nd ed. (1989) and *Narratives in Society: A Performer-Centered Study of Narration* (1995), as well as H. Glassie, *Passing the Time in Ballymenone* (1982). For a general introduction to some methods of fieldwork, see B. Jackson, *Fieldwork* (1987); for ethical and representational issues in fieldwork, see C. Lindahl, "The Power of Being Outnumbered," *Louisiana Folklore Miscellany* 12 (1997).

There is no comprehensive textbook on medieval folklore, but among the more relevant recent studies are P. Boglioni, ed., *La culture populaire au moyen âge* (1979); A. Gurevich, *Medieval Popular Culture* (1988); S. L. Kaplan, ed., *Understanding Popular Culture*; and J. Le Goff, *Time, Work, and Culture in the Middle Ages* (1980) and *The Medieval Imagination* (1988). Also valuable is the journal *Medieval Folklore* (1991–).

For the five different accounts of the Battle of Hastings, see J. Southworth, *The English Medieval Minstrel* (1989). The importance of distinguishing individual, generic, and cultural styles is discussed in J. Ball, "Style in the Folktale," *Folklore* 65 (1954).

—Carl Lindahl

Folktale

An oral prose narrative shared by a traditional community, relatively stable in plot but varied at each telling to suit the artistic and rhetorical purposes of the teller, as well as the tastes and expectations of the immediate audience.

Some scholars use the term *folktale* very generally and literally, to designate any tale shared orally in folk communities. More commonly, however, folklorists use the term for works of oral fiction told to entertain or educate, thus separating them from *legends*, tales in which belief is a major factor and which are usually told as true, even if their truth is often debated.

This characterization of folktale presents two major difficulties to students of medieval folklore. First, as oral performance is a defining trait of the folktale, and as we cannot say for sure that any surviving written versions are verbatim transcriptions of oral performances, we could easily conclude that there are no medieval folktales available to us. There is plenty of evidence that oral storytelling was rife in the Middle Ages, but most of it is negative evidence. The pious authors of saints' lives tended to trivialize folktales, and they did not repeat them. Felix, the author of a Latin *Life of St. Guthlac* (eighth century), says of the saint, "He did not imitate the chattering nonsense of matrons, nor the vain fables of the common people, nor the stupid whining of the country folk"—a strong suggestion that there is a vital storytelling tradition in early-medieval England, but the author's scorn for the contents of these stories prevents him from telling any. More rarely, writers intimate that they enjoy oral tales: Alvar of Cordova, a twelfth-century Spanish Christian, laments the fact that his country is under the control of the Arabs, then adds "and yet we are delighted by a thousand of their verses and tales"—but note that even this satisfied listener did not retell the Arabs' stories. So we are left with certain knowledge of the importance of oral narrative in medieval Europe but great uncertainty about what the tales were or how and why they were told.

The second problem has to do with fiction. If we choose to define folktales not simply as narratives but particularly as fictional narratives, we must establish that such tales were considered fictional by the *medieval* narrators and their listeners. We seldom get such precise information. For example, in the passage cited earlier from the *Life of St. Guthlac* the author considers the country tales to be "vain fables," but it is altogether possible that the folk themselves believe them true even if the writer does not. Folklorists may—and often do—identify a medieval narrative as a folktale simply because it shares its plot with well-known oral fictions from more recent times. A classic märchen such as "Red Riding Hood" (AT 333), considered an entertaining fiction by modern readers familiar with the literary versions of Charles Perrault (1697) and the Grimm brothers (1812), may appear in a medieval manuscript, but the fact that the medieval tale resembles the modern is no guarantee that it was performed as fiction in the Middle Ages. Indeed, the earliest surviving version of "Red Riding Hood," in Latin in the eleventh century, seems to have been told as a true story. The German author, Egbert of Liège, introduces it as follows: "What I have to relate, the country folk can tell along with me, and it is not such a wonder to believe the truth."

Consider the plot of one of the most popular tales in European tradition, known and endlessly repeated from ancient Greece to twentieth-century Scotland: a monster terrorizes a kingdom, demanding an annual tribute of virgins, chosen by lot, to fulfill his lust and hunger. One year the lot falls to the king's daughter, and the desperate king offers her in marriage to anyone who will slay the monster. A hero appears, kills the monster, and then cuts out its tongue. An impostor, intent on marrying the princess and inheriting the kingdom, finds the dead monster, cuts off its head and presents it to the king, and is about to marry the princess when the hero suddenly reappears to produce the tongue and prove that he is the rightful husband of the princess.

This plot, known to folklorists as "The Dragon-Slayer" (AT 300), appears, fully or partially, in Greek myth (the story of Perseus), medieval saints' lives (including the story of St. George and the dragon) and romances (for example, the *Tristan* of Gottfried von Strassburg), as well as postmedieval märchen—for example, as the tale of the "Two Brothers" in the Grimms' *Kinder- und Hausmärchen* (Children's and Household Tales), better known as the *Grimms' Fairy Tales*. This simple plot runs a long generic gamut, from classical myth to medieval Christian legend and adult entertainment to bedtime stories for twentieth-century children. Many medieval and postmedieval narrators have

The legend of St. George and the Dragon was the most popular medieval version of the plot identified by folklorists as AT 300, "The Dragon-Slayer." (Dotted print, upper Rhine, 1460; Bettmann/Corbis)

presented the tale of St. George as a true story, but few if any listeners believe the Grimms' version of the same plot to be a factual account. Thus, plot outline and content alone simply cannot establish whether a surviving medieval tale is a work of fiction.

With no extant medieval oral tales and precious few written ones that we can clearly identify as fiction, today's students of medieval folklore must ask themselves what we *do* have to work with. The answer is not disappointing.

First, there is the fact that even the most sophisticated medieval writers lived in a world in which oral entertainment was the norm. Because they heard tales both told and read aloud, they tended (to use Nancy Bradbury's phrase) to *write* aloud: rather than slavishly imitating their sources, they often rewrote the tales much as an oral artist would retell them, changing details and emphasizing styles suitable not only to their own tastes but to the audience that would hear the tale performed aloud. For example, the fourteenth-century English poets Geoffrey Chaucer and John Gower both wrote versions of a story known to folklorists as "The Maiden without Hands" (AT 706). The two men both wrote in medieval London, for members of the court of Richard II (reigned 1377–1399). Both, unquestionably, drew upon the same source, Nicholas Trivet's *Anglo-Norman Chronicle*, written nearly a century earlier for Richard's royal ancestors. The two men's stories—Chaucer's "Man of Law's Tale" and Gower's "Tale of Constance"—resemble each other more than either resembles Trivet's. Trivet told his story as history; Chaucer and Gower told theirs more as exempla, stories shaped to fit a moral purpose. That Chaucer's and Gower's versions are so similar no doubt has much to do with the fact that they lived at the same time and in the same place and shared the same courtly audience. Yet Chaucer's and Gower's versions, though much alike, are in many ways radically different.

The supremely educated Chaucer and Gower, two of the most respected artists and thinkers of their time, have this in common with the tellers of oral folktales: both believe that *familiar stories are always the best*, that the art of storytelling lies not in surprise, surface variation, or superfluous innovation but in retelling a well-known story so well that an audience thoroughly familiar with its contents will still respond with excitement, experiencing it as if for the first time.

Another way in which Chaucer and Gower resemble oral folktale tellers is in the social breadth of their sources. In addition to their retellings of "The Maiden without Hands," both tell versions of the tale of the Loathly Lady (AT 406A, "The Defeated King Regains the Throne"). Whereas they drew their separate versions of the former from a royal chronicle, it is much more likely that they derived their versions of the Loathly Lady tale from oral traditions. Here the differences between Chaucer's and Gower's versions are intense. Their common plot rests on the question "What do women most desire?" In both tales a male protagonist must forfeit his life unless he can answer this question. In both, a Loathly Lady, an abominably ugly woman, supplies the correct answer—that women desire sovereignty in love (in Gower's tale) or unqualified sovereignty (in Chaucer's)—but the monstrous woman demands compensation for sharing her secret: the knight must marry her.

Gower presents a gentrified version of the story, with a supremely chivalrous knight as hero. Sir Florent kills a rival in fair combat and then is sentenced to his quest by the villainous mother of the slain knight. The Loathly Lady provides Florent with the answers he needs—that women desire sovereignty in love—and on their wedding night she transforms herself into a beautiful woman. Gower's story asserts that women who rule in love are beautiful and good, but women who attempt to rule in other respects—as did the villainous mother of the slain knight—are morally ugly. Gower uses the story of what women most desire to convey a predictable message of male social dominance.

Chaucer's Loathly Lady tale is told to an entirely different purpose. He places his version in the mouth of his fictional character, the Wife of Bath, an outspoken advocate of female dominance. In her tale the knight is a rapist, a

The Wife of Bath, Chaucer's famous fictional storyteller; adapted from an illustration in the early-fifteenth-century Ellesmere manuscript of The Canterbury Tales. *(North Wind Picture Archives)*

criminal so unheroic that the Wife does not even deign to give him a name. King Arthur condemns the knight to death, but Guinevere and the ladies of Arthur's court intervene to teach the knight a valuable lesson rather than to kill him (the narrator's way of pointing out the greater mercy and wisdom of female rule). On their wedding night, after the Loathly Lady has saved and married the rapist, she delivers a long lecture to the effect that nobility is not a birthright but must be earned. She then asks the knight if he would rather have her be ugly but faithful to him or beautiful and unfaithful. The knight puts the decision in her hands, and when granted sovereignty, the Loathly Lady becomes beautiful at all times and rules over the knight in happiness and harmony.

In this amazing performance Chaucer makes his tale suitable for the nonnoble Wife of Bath by rejecting courtly storytelling styles and values. He presents instead a popular romance in which women turn the male-dominated world upside down and establish a better one.

Chaucer is an acute practitioner of lower-class storytelling styles. His "Wife of Bath's Tale" is in some ways remarkably similar to another version of AT 406A, *The Wedding of Sir Gawain and Dame Ragnell,* a popular romance of the mid-fifteenth century. Here, Sir Gawain is the hero, and by showing himself braver and truer to his word than the cowardly King Arthur, he saves the king. Gawain's "reward" for bravery is to marry the Loathly Lady, but folktale justice prevails when she transforms into a beautiful woman. It is the heroine who provides the rewards that Gawain truly deserves, and she effectively supplants King Arthur as a fair and rightful ruler.

Thus, surviving written tales do tell us something about medieval storytelling. Though deprived of the voices of medieval narrators, we still have the means of comparing their plots and styles to illumine aspects of the artistry and worldviews of the long-dead tellers and their listeners.

See also: Accused Queen; Dragon; George, Saint; Legend; Loathly Lady

References and further reading: The best general overview on the themes and contents of medieval and postmedieval folktales remains S. Thompson, *The Folktale* (1946). Many medieval descriptions of oral storytelling are collected in J. Bolte and G. Polívka, *Anmerkungen zu den Kinder- und Hausmärchen der Brüder Grimm,* vol. 4 (1929), which is the source of the Latin quotations translated above. On "Red Riding Hood," see J. M. Ziolkowski, "A Fairy Tale from before Fairy Tales: Egbert of Liège's 'De puella a lupellis seruata' and the Medieval Background of 'Little Red Riding Hood,'" *Speculum* 67 (1992), which, despite some quirky notions concerning oral tradition, offers an excellent refutation to the psychoanalytic readings presented by A. Dundes in his *Little Red Riding Hood: A Folklore Casebook* (1990). On differences between Chaucer's "Man of Law's Tale" and Gower's "Tale of Constance," see N. D. Isaacs, "Constance in Fourteenth-Century England," *Neuphilologische Mitteilungen* 59 (1958), and E. A. Block, "Originality, Controlling Purpose, and Craftsmanship in Chaucer's Man of Law's Tale," *Publications of the Modern Language Association* 68 (1953). For comparisons of the Loathly Lady romances, see C. Lindahl, "The Aural Undertones of Late Medieval Romance," in *Oral Tradition in the Middle Ages,* ed. W. F. H. Nicolaisen (1995). See also N. M. Bradbury, *Writing Aloud: Storytelling in Late Medieval England* (1998).

Comparative Studies

Since the early nineteenth century, when the Grimm brothers pioneered the study of folktales, scholars have been intrigued by a pervasive paradox in traditional narrative: how a given plot can be simultaneously so stable and so fluid. For all their differences, oral tales current in traditional cultures throughout Europe, the Middle East, and India resemble each other remarkably. Folklorists, assuming that these widespread tales were ultimately related, devised means of classifying their plots for comparative study. One of their basic assumptions— that a plot as varied and complex as the "Dragon-Slayer" or "Red Riding Hood" would not have been independently invented but instead spread orally from teller to teller over long periods of time—is broadly supported by today's folkloric research. The more complex the plot of a tale, the more likely that the different versions share a common history and were passed on in chain-like fashion from teller to teller (although the chains are many and tangled).

Building on the assumption that all the tales of a shared plot had an ultimate oral source, folklorists further reasoned that if they amassed enough variants of a single plot, grouping the oral versions by the language in which they were told and the written versions by date, they would discover the tale's original form (urform), age, and place of origin. Investigators sharing these assumptions and methods came to be identified as the Historic-Geographic School, or the Finnish School, because the Finns Kaarle Krohn and Antti Aarne were instrumental in its development. They used the term *Märchentyp*, "tale type," to designate plots with significant international distribution. In 1910 Aarne published the first numbered catalog of such plots, *Verzeichnis der Märchentypen* (Catalog of Tale Types), which the American folklorist Stith Thompson expanded in two English editions, renaming it the *Types of the Folktale* (1928, 1961).

Using the methods and cataloging principles outlined above, folklorists began assembling versions of a given tale type and attempting to reconstruct its life history. Kurt Ranke, for example, examined more than 800 variants related to the Grimms' tale of "The Two Brothers" (AT 303), which incorporates the "Dragon-Slayer" tale type. Ranke concluded that the ultimate source of the complex tale was medieval France and that its plot has preserved a remarkable continuity in oral storytelling communities without significant influence from written versions.

Scholars now generally discredit some of the premises of the Historic-Geographic method. First, many early folklorists assumed that the tales were primarily oral and evolved independently of written versions. In their view, the medieval stories that survive in writing would be considered more or less incidental to the history of the tales. Yet from the 1920s onward Albert Wesselski and others have demonstrated that written and oral tales interacted and influenced each other significantly in the Middle Ages, a finding fully supported by twentieth-century field research by Linda Dégh and others, who observed that even illiterate narrators readily seize upon written tales read aloud to them and work such writings into their repertories, though of course they recast such narratives to suit their personal aesthetics and the tastes of their audiences.

A second objection to the Historic-Geographic School has to do with its assumption that we can establish, even approximately, the date, place, and form of origin of a given tale. Close observations of living oral traditions work against this proposition. Individual narrators are often so creative in adapting new tales that even one retelling can make certain unpredicted changes, disguising the shape of the received tale. Thousands, even millions of retellings, such as medieval tales experienced, would probably disguise the original beyond recognition or recovery. Similarly, individual communities often possess such distinctive tastes and expectations that they will demand a tale be told their way from the beginning, or they will simply refuse to listen to it again.

Swedish folklorist Carl von Sydow was among the first to reject the assumptions of the Finnish School, but he argued that their catalogs and methods were still valuable because even if they could not reveal the urform of a given tale, they could reveal much about the oikotype, literally the "home type," of a tale—a distinct form adopted to the aesthetics and values of a given culture or community. Building on von Sydow's ideas, recent folklorists have shown that significant shifts of style and structure occur as a plot shifts from culture to culture, genre to genre, or class to class. Thus, one may view Gower's and Chaucer's versions of the Loathly Lady tale as expressions of two social oikotypes, the aristocratic and popular versions of the same basic plot.

See also: Folklore; Motif

References and further reading: K. Krohn outlines the standard Finnish School method in *Die folkloristische Arbeitsmethode* (1926), translated by R. Welsh as *Folklore Methodology* (1972). R. A. Georges and M. O. Jones, in *Folkloristics: An Introduction*, chs. 4 and 5 (1995), discuss recent variations and applications of the method. On "The Two Brothers" and the "Dragon-Slayer," see K. Ranke, *Die Zwei Brüder* (1934). A. Wesselski's most important work is *Versuch einer Theorie des Märchens* (1929); see also C. von Sydow's *Selected Papers on Folklore* (1948). The most thorough and insightful study of oral storytelling traditions in twentieth-century Europe is L. Dégh, *Folktales and Society*, 2nd ed. (1989).

The Types of the Folktale

There are three broad subdivisions of oral prose fiction: AT 1–299, Animal Tales (treated in a separate article of that title in this encyclopedia); AT 300–1199, Ordinary Folktales; AT 1200 and above, Jokes and Anecdotes.

Ordinary Folktales are far from ordinary in content: they generally concern objects such as cloaks that render the wearer invisible, supernatural beings such as dragons, witches, and talking animals; wondrous events such as transformations of humans into animals; and extraordinary landscapes containing glass mountains, trees that stretch to the stars, rotating palaces, and so on. Such tales are generally identified as "fairy tales" by nonfolklorists because the literary adaptations of their plots—by Charles Perrault, Madame de Beaumont, and Hans Christian Andersen—are generally known by that name. But folklorists identify the oral versions as märchen (German for "little story"), or sometimes magic tales (*Zaubermärchen*) or wonder tales.

Most often the märchen focuses on a single protagonist, a boy or girl, who becomes separated from his or her family and becomes an adult through a series of adventures involving wanderings through otherworldly landscapes and encounters with supernatural beings. Such popular postmedieval tales as the "Dragon-Slayer," "Jack and the Beanstalk" (AT 328), and "Beauty and the Beast" (AT 425C) follow this general form. In many oral traditions still active in the late twentieth century, from Eastern Europe to the U.S. Appalachians, such folktales are still told with a distinctly medieval frame of reference: The hero is a knight, the heroine a princess, and combats are conducted by "champions" in armor, bearing swords.

The medieval narratives that have most in common with these recent oral tales are romances, appearing first in rhymed form in France in the second half of the twelfth century and spreading to Germany, England, Italy, and other cultures through the following century. Innumerable romances follow the general sketch given above, and a substantial number have exact analogs or major parallels in recent oral traditions: to name a few, the Middle Dutch *Torec* (cognate with AT 301, "The Three Stolen Princesses"), Chaucer's "Wife of Bath's Tale" (AT 406A, "Defeated King Regains the Throne"), the French *Yonec* (AT 432, "The Prince as Bird"), the French *Eloixe* and the Middle English *Chevelere assigne* (AT 451, "The Maiden Who Seeks Her Brothers"), the German *Rittertreue* and the English *Sir Amadas* (AT 505–508, "The Grateful Dead"), Latin and French versions of Amicus and Amelius (AT 516, "The Faithful Servant"), and the French *Belle Helene* and the English *Emare* (AT 706, "The Maiden without Hands").

Postmedieval märchen are generally identified by their formulaic frames, verbal cues at the tale's beginning, to alert the listener that the story to follow will be fanciful (for example, the English "Once upon a time …"), and end, to close the tale with a similar marker (such as "They lived happily ever after"). The closing formula often playfully suggests that the story just told may be true: "They are still alive today; this is all, and tomorrow you can have them call" or "And that is all there is to the story. Take it, or, if you don't believe it, leave it."

Medieval tales resembling märchen sometimes possess similar but briefer opening formulas: Middle English "whilom" and Latin "*quondam*" (both meaning "once") or the slightly more elaborate "*Ein man sprach ze sinem wibe …*" [A man said to his wife …], used by the thirteenth-century poet Der Stricker to begin most of his rhymed tales about marital situations. Some medieval tales play more intensively with the frame. For example, the Old Icelandic *fornaldarsaga* (saga of former times) the *Saga of Hrolf Gautreksson* ends with a formula evocative of those in modern tradition: "I think you shouldn't find fault with the story unless you can improve on it. But whether it's true or not, let those enjoy the story who can, while those who can't had better look for some other amusement."

In addition to the princesses, kings, and knights common to both medieval romance and modern märchen, the two forms also share a number of villains: giants and dragons, for example, are as easily found in romance as in märchen. Fairies abound in both medieval and modern versions, playing more varied roles: they may be lovers, villains, or helpers.

In addition to tales of magic, Ordinary Folktales embrace two other categories. In Religious Tales (AT 750–849) supernatural aid comes from figures such as Christ or St. Peter rather than from fairies, and supernatural adversaries tend to be demons rather than giants. These oral tales greatly resemble medieval exempla, and it is indeed in exempla collections that we tend to find their medieval predecessors. In the widespread modern versions of "The Wishes" (AT 750A), Christ and St. Peter walk the earth, dispensing three wishes to a pious peasant, who uses them well, and three more to a foolish one, who uses the first two poorly and must then use the third to undo the others. Medieval predecessors of this tale often include only half of the modern plot: pious exemplum literature tends to focus on the three good wishes granted the pious man, while medieval fables and jokes often develop the plot of the three foolish wishes, which are sometimes the "gifts" of a demon rather than God. A variant of the latter occurs in "Del vilein e del folet" (The Peasant and the Goblin), a rhymed tale told by Marie de France in her *Fables* (no. 57, twelfth century): a goblin visits a peasant and gives him three wishes; the peasant gives two to his wife and keeps one, a secret, to himself. They come upon a cooked sheep with its marrow bones dripping fat. The wife craves to eat the fat but can't get hold of it, so she wishes that her husband would have a giant bird's beak so that he could get it for her. As soon as he realizes that he has been deformed through his wife's wishes, the husband uses his only wish to regain his human face. The tale ends with the third wish still unused, but Marie seems to imply that with only one wish remaining, and that in the hands of the foolish wife, the couple's future does not look good.

A third category of Ordinary Folktale is the Novella, a tale in which the magic elements of the märchen are generally missing or at least subdued. Thompson groups a good many novellas together as romantic tales; they concern themselves with situations of courtship, marriage, and love. One variation on the courtship theme is "King Thrushbeard" (AT 900), known from a thirteenth-century German poem and in other medieval texts ranging from Iceland (*Clarus's Saga*, fourteenth century) to Italy (where several versions appear). The plot concerns a haughty princess who humiliates a noble suitor; she is punished by having to marry or live with a wretched beggar or tramp. The beggar turns the tables on her by making her do degrading work until she is humbled. The beggar ultimately turns out to be the suitor (or his ally) in disguise, and the tale ends with the reconciliation and marriage of the princess and the suitor.

Many of the oral tales now known as novellas appeared first as medieval Italian *novelle* (singular *novella*, a term that in Italy referred not only to realistic tales but to legends and märchen as well). These short prose fictions began to appear in collections at the end of the thirteenth century, and in the fourteenth they gave rise to such masterful frame tales as Boccaccio's *Decameron* and Sercambi's *Novelle*. Whereas the rhymed romances of northern Europe most strongly suggest the imagery and magical atmosphere of today's oral märchen, the Italian *novelle* are the medieval tales that best evoke the oral prose styles found in today's more realistic oral fictions.

Typical of the Italian *novella* are acts of romantic deception and its inverse, steadfast love, both of which are combined in "Which Was the Noblest Act?" (AT 976), a plot rendered into writing twice by Boccaccio (in *Il Filocolo* and the *Decameron*) and once by Chaucer (in "The Franklin's Tale"). A suitor pressures a married woman to become his lover. To put him off, she says that she will sleep with him if he can perform an act that she believes impossible—such as creating a garden in the midst of winter *(Filocolo)* or making the rocks disappear from the Breton seacoast ("The Franklin's Tale"). With the help of a magician, to whom he has promised an enormous payment, the would-be lover actually accomplishes the impossible (or creates the illusion that he has). The wife resists her suitor, but her husband, discovering that she has made a promise, tells her that she must keep her word. Upon hearing of the husband's nobility, the suitor releases the wife from her promise, and when the magician hears of the suitor's nobility, he in turn refuses payment for the magic he has performed. The tale ends as the narrator asks the audience which of the characters was noblest. In Chaucer's tale no answer is given—listeners, or readers, must decide for themselves. In Boccaccio's *Filocolo*, the Lady Fiammeta delivers a judgment, finding the husband the most noble because he made no promises or bargains, yet enjoined his wife to keep hers even at the cost of his own honor.

In addition to being a *novella*, "Which Was the Noblest Act?" is also what folklorists call a dilemma tale, a story that ends with a riddle-like question that the audience must solve. Like the version of "Which Was the Noblest Act?" presented by Boccaccio in *Il Filocolo*, many medieval dilemma tales took the form of "questions of love," tales that posed romantic problems, leading to audience debates and judgments concerning the relative merits of the fictional lovers and their actions. Dilemma tales have enjoyed enormous popularity in Arabic-Islamic traditions from the Middle Ages to the present, and it is reasonable to assume that Islamic influences lie behind the dilemma tales that influenced both storytelling traditions and courtly love games in Europe from the twelfth century onward.

See also: *Amicus et Amelius; Fornaldarsögur;* Frame Tale; Marie de France; *Novella; Seven Sages, The;* Swan Knight

References and further reading: One of the best general introductions to medieval analogs of the magic tale is J. Berlioz et al., *Formes médiévaux du conte populaire* (1992). A good stylistic study of the literary forms of the märchen is M. Lüthi, *The Fairy Tale as Art Form and Portrait of Man* (1986). The best overall study of märchen is B. Holbek, *Interpretation of Fairy Tales* (1986). The closing formulas of modern oral märchen are quoted from L. Dégh, *Hungarian Folktales: The Art of Zsuzsanna Palkó* (1995); see *Hrolf Gautreksson: A Viking Romance,* trans. H. Pálsson and P. Edwards (1972), for the medieval example. On "The Wishes," see L. Röhrich, *Erzählungen des späten Mittelalters,* vol. 1 (1962); on the dilemma tale, see W. Bascom, *The African Dilemma Tale* (1975).

Jokes and Anecdotes

In this catchall category can be found a host of tales, some of them quite realistic, many obviously humorous in intent. Some, such as *Unibos* (AT 1535) and "The Master Thief" (AT 1525), exist in lengthy and complex medieval forms, but most are short fictions. Their brevity made them extraordinarily popular for use in sermons and fables, where they could summarize moral points briefly and entertainingly, as well as in the tale collections that became increasingly popular in the later centuries of the Middle Ages.

These tales generally involve trickery, concentrating on extremes of cleverness (AT 1525–1629) and stupidity (AT 1200–1349, 1675–1724), often ridiculing religious orders (AT 1725–1829) or other groups or professions (AT 1850–1874).

Typical of such short narratives is "With His Whole Heart" (AT 1186), told in diverse ways by various tellers to ridicule the greed of either lawyers, judges, bailiffs, knights, or peasants. In one fifteenth-century Swiss version, appearing in a Latin exemplum collection, a lawyer makes a pact with the devil, who has assumed a human form. They will travel together, each taking what is freely offered him, and see who gets the most. They pass a poor man trying to drive a troublesome pig. When the pauper screams at the pig, "Devil take you!" the lawyer turns to the devil and tells him to take the animal. But the devil responds that the pig wasn't really offered "from the heart." Next the travelers pass a mother berating her child: "Devil take you!" But again the devil does not take the offering, because the woman was merely speaking in anger and her words did not come from the heart. Finally, the devil and lawyer enter a town, and the lawyer is surrounded by villagers screaming, "Devil take you!" Because the villagers meant what they said with their whole hearts, the devil drags the lawyer off to hell.

This tale appears in dozens of versions. Though the writer of the above version claimed it was true and presented it as a legend, the tale most often appeared as an exemplum or as a joke. In Chaucer's "Friar's Tale," the most famous example of this plot, the Friar shapes the story as a narrative weapon to ridicule the person and profession of his enemy, the Summoner.

A substantial number of the jokes and anecdotes about married couples (AT 1350–1439) concern adultery and other sexual exploits, and they find many medieval examples in the Old French fabliaux (twelfth and thirteenth centuries) and the Italian novelle. Typical is "The Enchanted Pear Tree" (AT 1423), versions of which appear in thirteenth-century Latin verse fables, Boccaccio's Decameron, and Chaucer's Canterbury Tales ("The Merchant's Tale"). The following version of the plot appears in the anonymous Novellino (c. 1280), the oldest surviving collection of Italian prose tales: a blind man, deeply jealous of his beautiful wife, holds her near at hand. Another man, smitten by the wife's beauty, begins courting her with silent gestures in the presence of her husband. The woman concocts a plan to have sex with her suitor. He climbs into a pear tree and waits for her, she tells her husband that she has an overwhelming desire for pears, and the husband helps her into the tree. As he stands at its base, with his arms around the trunk to keep his wife from wandering off, she connects with her lover. They zestfully enjoy their long-deferred pleasure, shaking the boughs of the tree, which rain pears on the head of the husband. Christ and St. Peter look on at the scene. Peter is outraged and asks Christ to restore sight to the man so that he can see what his wife is doing. Christ replies that as soon as the husband's sight is restored, the wife will find a way to escape the consequences of her actions. When Christ allows him to see again, the husband yells angrily at his wife, but she answers immediately, "If I had not done thus with him, you would never have seen the light"—a true statement. The tale concludes with a terse moral: "And thus you see how faithful women are, and how quickly they can find an excuse."

This short tale, brief as a fable, illustrates a major difficulty in classifying folktales. If we analyze folktales according to both plot and content, as the *Types of the Folktale* does, we soon discover that individual narrators are far too flexible and creative to observe such arbitrary boundaries. Marie's "The Peasant and the Goblin" (summarized in the previous section) is classified as a religious tale, but no representatives of Christian religion appear in her narrative, nor is a religious moral drawn. The Italian *novella* just summarized features Christ and St. Peter, and—at least in terms of its content—it is more worthy than Marie's narrative to be classified as a religious tale. However, Chaucer's version of the pear tree story places the Greek gods Pluto and Proserpine in the roles of Christ and Saint Peter and would not therefore be classified as a religious tale.

Every folktale follows some sort of generic conventions, but those conventions vary widely from group to group, place to place, time to time. Moreover, every folktale possesses a cultural style adapted to the values of the audience that enjoys it. And every well-told folktale is largely shaped by the individual style of the narrator—a fact as demonstrable for oral artists as for writers—giving rise to a variety of styles as numerous as there are great narrators, a variety that could never be captured by any catalog that folklorists could devise.

Much more knowledge of oral folktales is available from the end of the medieval period than from its beginnings. There are still no verbatim oral folktales from these later times, but there is some remarkable documentation of the sorts of stories told by common folk. The *Complaynt of Scotlande* (1547) presents a catalog of the tales told by Scottish shepherds in the first half of the sixteenth century. More than 40 specific titles appear. These poorer members of the social order are decidedly tale-rich. Some of their tales come from classical mythology: "the tale where Perseus saved Andromeda from the cruel monster," "the tale where Hercules slew the serpent Hydra that had vii heads," "the tale where Jupiter transformed his dear love Io into a cow." Some derive from the literary masterpieces and popular romances of the late Middle Ages: "the tales of Canterbury," "Lancelot du lac," "Bevis of Southamtoun." Others suggest (indeed, bear the same titles as) the oral folktales told in Scotland up to the present day: "the tale of the red etin [giant] with three heads," "the tale of the three-footed dog of Norway," and "the tale of giants that eat quick men." The world of the medieval folktale continually blurs the boundaries of oral artistry and literature, Christian religion and classical myth, realism and fantasy, belief and love of fabulation.

See also: Exemplum; Fabliau; Trickster; *Unibos*
References and further reading: A. Taylor, "The Devil and the Advocate," *Publications of the Modern Language Association* 36 (1921), presents a comparative study of AT 1186 ("With His Whole Heart"). L. Röhrich, *Erzählungen des späten Mittelalters*, vol. 2 (1967), presents 18 versions of the tale, half medieval and half modern, along with extensive notes on all

versions and their major interrelationships. See also A. Taylor, "The Friar's Tale," in *Sources and Analogues of Chaucer's* Canterbury Tales, ed. W. F. Bryan and G. Dempster (1941), which is also an excellent source for analogs to the tales of the Franklin (AT 976) and the Merchant (AT 1423). One of the best texts for illustrating the stylistic and generic range of medieval jokes and anecdotes is L. D. Benson and T. M. Andersson, *The Literary Context of Chaucer's Fabliaux* (1975), which presents 35 analogs of Chaucer's tales, including those of the Friar, Merchant, Franklin, Miller (AT 1361, "The Flood"), Reeve (AT 1363, "The Cradle"), and Shipman (AT 1420C, "The Lover's Gift Regained").

—*Carl Lindahl*

Foodways

Traditional styles of food preparation and use.

What food a family (or other group, such as a monastery) ate in medieval Europe depended on a number of factors: principally religion, income, and social level; whether they lived in the country or the city; and whether their region was southern—that is, near the Mediterranean—or northern. But in general the diet was not basically very different from today's—or at least yesterday's. Bread of one sort or another, whether hearth-baked "cakes" or loaves purchased from a baker or baked in a manor house, was the staff of life everywhere. It was washed down preferably with wine in the South and by those who could afford it in the North, and otherwise with ale or, in some areas, cider or other mildly alcoholic fruit-based drinks. Milk was an alternative for those who kept cows, but it was of dubious quality in the cities, and water was a last (and sometimes unhealthy) resort.

With the bread, at least for the main meals of the day (dinner and supper), went meat, fish, eggs, cheese, or legumes such as fava beans (listed in descending order of prestige and price); they were often accompanied by such vegetables as onions, leeks, and cabbage or by salads in the summer. Pasta was popular in Italy and was sometimes served in England. Rice was grown around the Mediterranean, and during the later centuries it was imported as a luxury in the North. But pasta was not served with tomato sauce, and the available vegetables did not include peppers, both tomatoes and peppers being among the New World imports that were later to transform eating habits in Europe and elsewhere.

Regional and Seasonal Cuisine

Regional differences in food choices were similar to those found today. Pork was, of course, forbidden to Jews and to Muslims—who had a considerable impact on the culinary habits of the parts of Spain and Italy they inhabited in the early Middle Ages. For example, it was they who introduced carrots and spinach to the Western world. Olive oil was central to the cooking of southern Europe, and butter was widely used in Scandinavia and the Low Countries. Elsewhere, animal fats such as lard were more used than either butter or olive oil. Walnut oil was a possible alternative on days when animal products were forbidden, which meant *all* of Lent, including Sundays. Thus, eggs, butter, and cheese were forbidden during this period, although they were permissible on ordinary "fast days." We may well doubt, however, that the peasants whose normal diet depended on eggs and dairy products (such as the poor widow of Chaucer's "Nun's Priest's Tale") took this Lenten prohibition seriously: the hens' best laying season would often have coincided with Lent.

There were a great many fast days for Christians, who were the vast majority of the population. In monastic communities, often only the very young or the infirm were allowed to eat meat. While the fasts decreed by the Church for the general population varied somewhat over the approximately ten centuries of the Middle Ages, typically Wednesday, Friday, and Saturday were meatless every week; to these were added the "vigils" before various feast days. For example, the English household of Dame Alice de Bryene, from which we are fortunate to have a record of all purchases for the kitchen for a full year, abstained from meat on Thursday, October 27, 1412, because it was the Vigil of St. Simon and St. Jude, and on six other days of the year that would ordinarily have been "meat" days but that in that year were the vigils of feasts.

Dame Alice's household also fasted on the three Rogation days preceding the Ascension Day feast, but they did not observe a fast resembling that of Lent during Advent, the pre-Christmas season beginning four Sundays before Christmas. At some other times and places, Advent was also a continuous fast. Even without a rigorous four-week fast before Christmas, obviously meatless days generally amounted to considerably more than half of the year. We might envy the fish-day diets of those who lived near the sea: Dame Alice's household and guests were frequently fed Dover sole, shrimps, and oysters, among other fresh fish. But most people had good reason to get very tired of the dried salt cod known as stockfish and an endless parade of smoked ("red") and pickled ("white") herring.

The most common method of cooking was boiling in a pot. Thus, the majority of medieval dishes for which we have recipes are "pottages," usually soups or stews. But a well-equipped kitchen would also have had frying pans, often used for cooking fresh fish, and a spit for roasting. Ovens were built into the walls of the kitchens of greater houses, but most residents of towns and cities did not have ovens, even in a prosperous household. Instead, they took their pies or other food requiring baking to a cookshop or to a community baker. Alternatively, they could buy pastries of various sorts, especially pieces of meat or poultry enclosed in a leaf of pastry and known as pasties, from a cookshop or a specialized pasty maker.

Throughout the period and all over Europe the peasantry subsisted primarily on pottages made from what could be grown in their kitchen gardens, plus whatever fish, game, or meat from domestic fowls or animals they could spare, and, of course, coarse bread and dairy products. What is still known in English pubs as plowman's lunch—bread and cheese with (usually) pickled onions—is pretty close to what a medieval plowman got to eat, except that no peasant would have had the white bread generally supplied by pubs today. Dame Alice's steward records a quantity of cheese for "certain laborers" in his 1419 account book, and he frequently records a number of loaves of "black" bread distributed to outdoor workers. Of course, a plowman in the Mediterranean area would have been likely to supplement his bread and cheese with olives rather than onions.

Servants roasting poultry, as depicted on the eleventh-century French Bayeux Tapestry. (Gianni Dagli Orti/Corbis)

Recipes

A few culinary recipes can be found in early-medical texts, and there are accounts of food served on various occasions in many works of literature, but most of these are of the later period. It is probable that food gets less attention in works of the early Middle Ages because it was so basic as not to seem of special interest. The bulk of the recipes that have survived are from the later centuries, that is, from the late thirteenth century through the fifteenth. And they are all from upper-class or clerical households, naturally enough, since only such establishments would have had a literate clerk to write out recipes. But that does not mean they do not contain recipes that would have been thoroughly familiar to much humbler people.

Many recipe collections begin with basic vegetable pottages, which were no doubt what everyone had been eating for centuries and which the peasantry still relied on, such as stewed cabbage with onions or leeks and dried beans, with or without bacon. Pieter Brueghel the Elder's sixteenth-century paintings of peasant festivities show peasants eating bowls of what seems to be either a thick pea soup or the wheat porridge known as frumenty. There are also recipes for these dishes in collections emanating from such distinguished households as that of Richard II (reigned 1377–1399). Later in such recipe collections we often find directions for roasting a variety of meats and poultry; there would be nothing very new about this, either. We can see similar roasts (as well as bowls of pottage) in one of the dining scenes on the Bayeux Tapestry (c. 1100).

But most of the recipes found in medieval culinary collections are far from being peasant fare. By the late thirteenth century a new and more sophisticated cuisine, ultimately of Middle Eastern origin, had spread across Western Europe, and truly luxurious cooking had become a mark of prestige. The most obvious feature of this cuisine was the use of imported (and thus expensive) spices. Dame Alice paid 25s. 1d. a pound for pepper in 1419—more than 25 times the price of a *bushel* of mustard seed, 12d. Pepper and cumin seem to have been the only widely used imported spices in the early Middle Ages, but by the fourteenth century cinnamon, ginger, nutmeg, mace, and a number of other spices (some of which, such as cubebs, are rare today) were widely used in sauces and in pottages with a base of meat, poultry, or fish.

Spices and Food Preservation

Spices were used partly *because* they were expensive—the twentieth century did not invent conspicuous consumption—but also because they were supposed to have medicinal benefits and, probably most important, to make the food more interesting. Many people think that spices were used to cover up the "off" flavors of none-too-fresh meats. That this was not the case should be obvious, when we consider that refrigeration was not invented until a number of centuries after Western cooks had largely relegated most spices to sweet dishes, retaining only pepper as a common seasoning for meats and fish. Any meat or fish that had to be kept for longer than it would stay fresh was preserved by salting or smoking: ham, bacon, smoked sausages, dried cod, and pickled herring were eaten in most parts of Europe, and in areas where beef was a common food it was apt to appear as corned beef.

But there must have been cool storage areas where cooked food could be safely stored for a day or more. One of the reasons for the popularity of jellied dishes was that they were regarded as a safe way to keep fish or meat from spoiling for a number of days; many of the directions for such dishes tell us to keep them in a cool place. On some days, Dame Alice's provisions seem to have been especially generous for no particular reason. For example, "one quarter of bacon, one lamb, one heron, seven geese, eggs" to serve 20 people at dinner and 8 at supper. But almost invariably, the following day shows so little provided that the kitchen must have been depending on leftovers, some of them probably presented as entirely different dishes, since many medieval recipes call for already-cooked meats.

Another new feature of medieval haute cuisine was a love of food colorings. The most ubiquitous was saffron, which gave many a dish a golden color. But there were also red food dyes, such as "sanders," and blue ones. These, however, were not used as frequently as was ground parsley or other green herbs, to give a "gaudy green" color, and blood, to give a deep, almost black, shade of brown. Some of the fancier dishes were parti-colored: one side of a pudding-like dish might be dyed pink or yellow and the other side left white. Pure white was also regarded with favor: one of the internationally famous dishes of the period was *blancmanger* (white food), which usually got its white base from the use of rice (another food introduced by Muslims in the Mediterranean area).

One very important ingredient in this style of cooking was almond milk. It was used instead of cow's milk as a basis for many sauces and thickened pottages, especially during Lent, when milk was forbidden, but also by preference in a great many dishes even on "meat" days. No doubt this was partly because town dwellers could not trust the freshness of the milk, but since almonds were expensive, at least in the North, it was also no doubt a prestige ingredient like spices. And anyone who has tasted dishes made with almond milk knows that it has an interesting flavor of its own.

The almonds to make this "milk" were ground in a mortar. The mortar and pestle were in constant use in a sophisticated medieval kitchen. For example, meat and fish, usually cooked, were turned into various specialties, including one named for the mortar itself, *mortreux* in English, *mortereul* in French, *morterol* in Catalan, and so forth. Spices, herbs, and many other things were also ground in mortars. No professional cook could conceivably have done without one.

One more important "new" ingredient introduced from the East was sugar. It was thought to be especially good for sick people and sickly children, but it was not the only sweetener in wide use in the late Middle Ages. Honey, produced domestically, was cheaper. Dried fruits were also much used, especially in England, where some of the later collections seem to call for at least two of figs, dates, or raisins in one recipe after another. But sugar was considered to be a spice and was usually used in small quantities, like salt, except when it was sprinkled over fritters or made into sugar candies. The dishes intended to be really sweet generally specify "a large quantity" of sugar; we can infer that sparing use was otherwise the rule.

Feasting

Those who have seen some of the menus for great historical feasts—for such occasions as coronations, royal weddings, and the installations of bishops—may have been surprised (or appalled) at the length of these menus. Many of them run to three courses, in each one of which there may be as many as 20 different dishes. Spicy pottages have their place in this array, but the majority of dishes listed are usually plain roasts and simpler dishes. Few vegetables appear on feast menus; they were so commonplace they simply were not treats worthy of a formal occasion. And it must be remembered that these were very special occasions. Most people had far less to choose from (if they had any choice at all) as a general rule, even in well-to-do households.

Still, a fair proportion of the population must have been able to partake of a pretty lavish "feast" on occasion: on Sunday, January 1, 1413, 160 people were recorded as being present for dinner at Dame Alice's manor, including a harper, servants, tenants, "and other strangers." It would be nice to know what the kitchen did with the 12 gallons of milk purchased for that occasion. That would have made an enormous amount of junket, sweet tart filling, or other special dishes requiring a very skilled cook, such as "larded milk," a savory custard containing bacon. But this lavish feast menu does not mean that the humbler members of such a gathering got their choice of the swans, geese, capons, rabbits, mutton, beef, veal, and pork: two swans would not have gone very far among 160 diners.

Invariably the choicest foods were served to the head of the household and to honored guests of high rank. Nevertheless, almost everyone must have had a share of the white bread, of which the supply for the day was 314 loaves. This was 82 more than had been baked and used in the entire preceding month. That would probably have been in itself a treat for most of the lower-ranking "guests." Presumably, those low-ranking guests, however, were not so naive as to think they could toss bones around, and generally behave as Hollywood would have us think people acted in this period. Medieval standards for table manners and associated rituals for serving food were in fact a lot stricter than are accepted manners today.

See also: Wine
References and further reading: For extensive, generally reliable information about food in medieval Europe, see T. Scully's *The Art of Cookery in the Middle Ages* (1995) and *Histoire de l'alimentation*, ed. J.-L. Flandrin and M. Montanari (1996). An illustrated and readable account of English food and cooking is P. W. Hammond's *Food and Feast in Medieval England* (1993), and for the Mediterranean area (along with recipes) there is B. Santich's *The Original Mediterranean Cuisine* (1995). *The Household Book of Dame Alice de Bryene*, trans. M. K. Dale, 2nd ed. (1984), is the only such account book with full details about how many were served and who the guests were, but there are many others in C. M. Woolgar's *Household Accounts from Medieval England*, 2 vols. (1992–1993). An account of bourgeois housekeeping, kitchen gardening, shopping, and entertaining, along with many recipes and some contemporary menus, is in the fourteenth-century *Menagier de Paris*, ed. G. E. Brereton and J. M. Ferrier (1981). A recent study, largely based on the *Menagier*, is N. Crossley-Holland's *Living and Dining in Medieval Paris* (1996). Representative collections of English recipes, with selected menus, are in T. Austin's *Two Fifteenth-Century Cookery-Books* (1888; rpt. 1964), and *Curye on Inglysch*, ed. C. B. Hieatt and S. Butler (1985); the latter gives bibliographic references to a number of important culinary collections from elsewhere in Europe. B. Laurioux's "Le 'Registre de cuisine' de Jean de Bockenheim," *Mélanges de l'école française de Rome* 100 (1988), gives recipes from a fifteenth-century papal kitchen with notes on what to serve visitors of various nationalities, as well as such disparate groups as prostitutes and Lollards. For matters of table etiquette, proper ways of serving at the table, and so on, see F. J. Furnivall, ed., *The Babees Book* (1868; rpt. 1969); this prints only English sources, but these are very similar to what was written on these subjects elsewhere, by clerics (such as Hugh of St. Victor) as well as secular writers.
—Constance B. Hieatt

Fool

Not only one of the most important cultural figures of the late Middle Ages but also perhaps the most interesting, a paradoxical figure who at his most servile merely uses empty, puerile buffoonery to entertain the society that patronizes him, but who at his most heroic challenges the very assumptions on which that society is founded.

The fool vacillates between simpleton and satirist, between Vice and "fool for Christ's sake," between whipping boy and scourge; he is both the problem and the commentary on that problem—all these are encompassed in the term *fool*. He is especially a key figure in any understanding of the transitional period between the end of the Middle Ages and the beginning of the early modern era; this is nowhere better demonstrated than in the Germanic region, where Sebastian Brant's *Das Narrenschiff* (The Ship of Fools), published in Basel in 1494, rapidly became a Europe-wide best-seller. It was translated into Latin, the lingua franca of scholarship, in 1497 and into the various vernaculars in the years following (two English translations appeared in 1509), inspiring various imitative ships-of-fools, such as the English *Cock Lorelles Bote* (1518). It is important to note that Brant's innumerable oceangoing fools—*"stultorum infinitus est numerus"* [the number of fools is infinite], from the Latin Vulgate Bible, Eccles. 1:15, is a favorite quotation in folly literature—are not funny men (despite the caps and bells given to them by the illustrator) but a company of Vices, and they are sailing to perdition.

The Iconography of the Fool

The particular *insipiens* (fool) to whom we owe much of our knowledge of fool iconography is the one who, in the opening words of both Psalm 52 (Authorized Version 53) and Psalm 13 (Authorized Version 14), "hath said in his heart, 'There is no God.'" From the early thirteenth century on, the illuminated "D" of the opening of the psalm (*"Dixit insipiens"* [The fool said]) becomes a circular frame displaying the atheistic fool, often disputing with King David, reputed author of the Psalms, so that in later manuscripts he is visualized very much as David's court jester.

Sometimes he is completely naked, a madman who has thrown off his clothes in his frenzy, and he carries only a club for his protection and perhaps he chews on a stone. (Interesting evidence that nudity played a part in real-life fooling

"Classic" court fool—with parti-colored costume, knee bells, ass-eared hood, marotte, and foxtail stick—stands before King David; from a fifteenth-century English Psalter. (Oxford, Bodleian Library, Laud. Lat. 114, fol. 71)

comes from the Wardrobe Accounts of Edward I, which record a payment made to Bernard the Fool and 54 of his companions, who came before the king at Pontoise near Paris, "naked and with dancing revelry," c. 1300.) The simple stick type of club was perhaps a staff allowed the fool, for his own protection as much as anything else in an age that exposed many unfortunates, "natural" as opposed to "artificial" fools, to public humiliation. In the *Prose Tristan*, for example, the hero, having lost his reason, having become a real fool, takes a shepherd's cudgel to fend off those who torment him. The fool's club is perhaps also implicit in the matronymic of Edward II's court fool, Robert, who is named in the royal accounts for 1310–1311 as the son of one Dulcia Withastaf (With-a-Staff).

By the late thirteenth century the club had been transformed into the familiar fool's-head-on-a-stick, or *marotte* (bauble), which is sometimes made to deliver the fool's speeches, as in a Dutch play of circa 1500, in which the fool repeatedly punches his marotte whenever it criticizes abuses committed by the clergy and the better-off burghers, thus ostensibly dissociating himself from the criticisms of these powerful groups voiced by the marotte.

Other types of marotte are also represented: the bladder-on-a-stick, for example, and the sometimes distinctly phalli-form padded leather cosh. A phallic marotte is carried by the preacher of the *Sermon joyeux* [parody sermon] *de Saint Velu*, a burlesque phallic saint. In addition to exhibiting to his congregation the "tomb" of the martyred St. Velu (Hairy), in the shape of a *brayette* (codpiece), the sermon's editor suggests that at the sermon's climax, the fool-preacher held aloft the pseudosaint himself, in the form of a phallic marotte. In his *Traité contre les masques* (1608), Jean Savaron recorded that in Clermont during the year-end festivals, young men, masked and disguised as fools, ran through the streets armed with clubs "in the form of codpieces stuffed with straw or padding, striking men and women." Another widely represented aspect of fool phallicism is the suggestive use he makes of the bagpipe.

An important non-Psalter court fool appears in one of the mid-thirteenth-century English Apocalypse manuscripts: he is partially nude and his perhaps crippled legs parody Domitian's *attitude royale*, as his phalli-form marotte similarly parallels the emperor's scepter. Two other features of this careful image deserve consideration, for this fool is tonsured and has his fingers in his mouth.

A homily "Against Contention," intended for preaching throughout the churches of Henry VIII's realm in 1547, includes the question "Shall I stand still, like a goose or a fool, with my finger in my mouth?" This quotation significantly combines all three of the elements that go to make up a misericord in Beverly Minster, carved in 1520—the fool, the goose, and the finger in the mouth—and constitutes valuable proof that the misericord's goose "supporters" are not merely whimsical, decorative additions (the goose has been a proverbially foolish bird since circa 1500, at least). The finger in the mouth gesture perhaps originally betokened the drooling nature of the fool, the village idiot, rather than the "artificial" fool or jester.

Fools' heads seem either to have been completely shaved—"lette the madde persons hed be shauen ones a moneth," recommends Andrew Boorde's *Dyetary of Helth* (1542)—or to have been shaved in some special manner. Double and triple tonsures are commonly illustrated. In the late Middle English romance *Ipomadon* the hero disguises himself as a fool by having a barber shave his head in an "indented" pattern, and "half his chin" shaved as well.

Another distinctive fool attribute, his attire, classically includes the ass-eared hood and the cock's comb (English coxcomb, "fool"): while the former is certainly in evidence by 1350, the latter seems not to have made its appearance for another century. The ass had long been associated with foolishness, of course, but where did the notion of adorning the fool's head with the comb or head and neck of a cockerel come from? One of the common features of descriptions of the classical fool is the insistence that—when not shaved completely bald—he wore his hair in some distinctive manner. St. Augustine, writing around 400 C.E., referred to the *"excordes cirrati"* [crested fools] of the late Roman Empire, a description seemingly applicable to the Greek "laughter maker" who entertained Lucian's Philosophers' Banquet some three centuries earlier: his head was shaved except for a few hairs that stood up straight on his crown. A sixth-century B.C.E. vase painting shows two actors masked as cockerels with crests and wattles. Allardyce Nicoll claimed that "all through the course of the mimic drama [the cockerel-type] held its popularity, and it is not fanciful to see in the cockscomb of the medieval fool the remnants of this character."

Court Fools

Although more archival research remains to be done on real-life fools, much of significance has already been uncovered, including the names of household fools—such as the "John Goose, my lord of York's fole," recorded in the Privy Purse Expenses of Henry VII's queen, Elizabeth of York (1465–1503), or the early "Tom-fool," whose funeral expenses are recorded in the Durham Cathedral Accounts in 1365.

The saintly fourteenth-century Fra Jacopone da Todi, "the Fool of God," "in a fervour of spirit and on fire with disdain for the world," it is said, "took off all his clothes, then taking a pack-saddle put it on his back, set a bit in his mouth, and went about on all fours just as though he were an ass." A similar—but involuntary—humiliation seems to have delighted Tudor monarchs. The accounts detailing court entertainments during the reign of Henry VII reveal that one of the king's favorite jests was to dress the fool as a horse, with shoes, saddles, and bridles provided for by the royal Privy Purse. Both Jacopone and Henry's court fool perhaps ultimately owed their equine capers to one of the rites of inversion that made up the extraordinary Feast of Fools. Writing circa 1289, the French theologian, Guillaume Peraldus, attacked the nakedness of both clerical and lay revelers, referring significantly to the cleric who clothed his horse in scarlet and himself with his horse's blanket.

The hobbyhorse is another of the fool's attributes seen in Psalter illuminations and elsewhere. The Wardrobe Accounts of 1334–1335 for the court of Edward III interestingly mention "xiiij hobbihorses pro ludo Regis." The Christmas revels in which these hobbyhorses may have been used in a mock joust, in 1347–1348, mention a similar number of "viseres" and "crestes" as part of the entertainers' festive costume, including a set of the latter in the form of up-ended legs wearing shoes. An interesting parallel is the arms of the Foljambe family, displayed on an alabaster panel of the 1370s, which includes a helmet with just such a crest, a *folle jambe* (crazy leg), the leg being "mad" or "foolish" because, in classic *monde renversé* fashion, it springs from the head! Similarly, in a *Proverbes en rimes* manuscript of circa 1500, the illustrated proverb depicts a fool with marotte in one hand wearing only one shoe; the other he holds on his head with his free hand!

Fools' Dress

The fool depicted in the woodcut to the Venetian Malermi Bible printed in 1490 (the *insipiens* of Psalm 52 again) wears only one shoe. At the same point in a mid-fourteenth-century Scandinavian Bible, the fool is also so shod. Indeed, as early as 1209 a goliard (composer of satirical poetry in Latin) named Durianus—who styled himself "long favoured with the fools' dementia, bishop and archpriest of the wandering scholars of Austria, Styria, and Bavaria"—composed a parody in which he describes how all the members of that "sect," "impelled by sheer simplicity and sluggish folly," wander about "with one bare foot."

German and Welsh medieval legal codes, among others, prescribe the cutting short of a garment as a punishment for certain crimes, and this may parallel the characteristic short tunic often worn by the fool. In her spiritual autobiography the English mystic Margery Kempe states that while en route to the Holy Land on her pilgrimage of 1413, she so irritated her traveling companions in the neighborhood of Konstanz that "they cut her gown so short that it only came a little below her knee, and made her put on a piece of white canvas like

Fool, depicted with ass's ears and belled hood; stall-elbow, Manchester Cathedral, England, circa 1506. (Photograph by Malcolm Jones)

a sackcloth apron, so that she would be taken for a fool." In Wolfram von Eschenbach's romance *Parzival* (c. 1210), the hero's mother uses sackcloth to make him a disguise of *toren kleit* (fool's clothes). Similarly, it seems that Margery's German tormentors were deliberately intent on making a fool of her, but she was doubtless not entirely unhappy to find herself made "a fool for Christ's sake."

Nothing in the costume of the fool is accidental. Everything is symbolic of his folly, of his derangement, including the familiar "motley": the checkered, tattered, or diagonally opposed colors of his tunic, especially the yellow and green, which Michel Pastoureau has termed the "colors of disorder." It is a red and blue check, however, that covers a most interesting entertainer in the famous Luttrell Psalter; the same pattern appears on the bishop's miter that the fool wears. Precisely contemporary, the Durham Cathedral Accounts for 1338–1339 record the purchase of four ells of checked "burel" (*burelli scacciati*) for clothing Thome Fole.

A most important portrait of a jester, containing several common iconographic features, is attributed to Quentin Massys (c. 1515). The figure is physically deformed (hunchbacked), has an abnormally long nose (phallic symbol), wears a hood through which ass's ears poke (and on top of which are the head and neck of a cockerel), and has a scalloped edge to his short tunic, which is kept in place by a belt hung with bells, and he shoulders a marotte that terminates in a grinning armless fool who has pulled down his trousers, exposing his bare bottom to the viewer. But still the picture is not exhausted. The fool himself places his finger on his lips and says, mysteriously, *Mondeken toe* (Mouth shut)! Werner Mezger was the first to note that the apparent bulge visible in his forehead alludes to another well-known motif, the "stone of folly." The burlesque operation in which this "stone," held to be the cause of all the foolishness in the fool's head, is surgically removed was illustrated by Hieronymus Bosch and Pieter Brueghel the Elder, among others.

An important aspect of fool iconography is his commentary function; if the man depicted is not designated a fool by the placing of an ass-eared hood on his head, then his folly is often quite literally pointed to by an accompanying fool.

Proverbial follies are many and various, and sometimes their representation in medieval art demonstrates a strange kinship between the fool and the saint, the "fool for God," who can, indeed, achieve the impossible. When the late-medieval "foles of Gotam" (later, ironically, the "Wise Men of Gotham") attempt to prolong the spring by "penning the cuckoo" (cf. the many English fields that recall this folly with the names "Cuckoo Pen" and "Cuckoo Bush"), it simply flies above the fence they have hastily erected around the bush on which it has alighted.

In late-medieval art the fool is ubiquitous, not just in the graphic arts but in every conceivable applied or decorative art. He appears on ornamental garden fountains, public town fountains, bronze candelabra, wooden towel rails, jewels, and the finials and feet of precious vessels.

It is important to emphasize that the fool and fool literature are Europe-wide phenomena; they reach their climax around 1500, in the wake of Brant's *Das Narrenschiff*, with Erasmus's *Praise of Folly* (c. 1511) and Thomas Murner's two books of the following year with their important woodcut illustrations. In France, the land of *sociétés joyeuses* (fool societies) such as the Infanterie Dijonnaise or the Parisian Les Enfants sans Souci, there is an explosion of fool literature throughout the fifteenth century, with farces and *sermons joyeux*, and contemporary Germany had the *Fastnachtspiele* (Carnival plays). In England, Lydgate's *Order of Fools*, cataloging 63 types of fools, predates *Das Narrenschiff*, which to some extent it anticipates, as does the Scots poem "The Foly of Fulys," and French lists from the early fourteenth century, which catalog 32 types of fools.

See also: Carnival; Fools, Feast of; Masking; Names, Personal; Trickster
References and further reading: Recently there has been a tremendous upsurge of interest in the figure of the fool, and we are fortunate that he has attracted the attention of scholars of the caliber of Werner Mezger in Germany and Philippe Menard in France. See Mezger's fundamental *Narrenidee und Fastnachtsbrauch: Studien zum Fortleben des Mittelalters in der europäischen Festkultur* (1991) and Menard's "Les fous dans la société médiévale: Le témoignage de la littérature au XIIe et au XIII siècle," *Romania* 98 (1977). A. Gross, *"La Folie": Wahnsinn und Narrheit im spätmittelalterlichen Text und Bild* (1990), is also of considerable interest. S. Billington's *A Social History of the Fool* (1984) builds on E. Welsford's classic *The Fool* (1935) and is useful but restricted mainly to the English fool. P. Vandenbroeck's published exhibition catalog, *Beeld van de andere, vertoog over het zelf: Over wilden en narren, boeren en bedelaars* (1987), is superb and considers in particular the relationship between the various marginal figures of his title. M. Lever, *Le sceptre et la marotte* (1983), is somewhat slight but very readable. The long tradition discussed by J. Saward in his *Perfect Fools* (1980) is also treated more briefly by A. Y. Syrkin, "On the Behavior of the 'Fool for Christ's Sake,'" *History of Religions* 22 (1982). L. Hotson's unjustly neglected *Shakespeare's Motley* (1952), though concentrating on the Elizabethan fool, is most informative concerning fool costume and attributes in the immediately postmedieval era. The quotation above from A. Nicoll is from *Mask, Mimes, and Miracles* (1931), page 32.

—Malcolm Jones

Fools, Feast of

A festival of misrule and role reversal among the clergy, usually held during the Christmas season (most commonly on New Year's Day) and famous as an occasion for celebration and wild parody among the population at large.

The earliest accounts of the feast, emerging at the end of the twelfth century, refer to it as the "feast of the subdeacons." During the celebration, members of the lower clergy in cathedral chapters would switch places with their superiors and take control of cathedral functions. The practice of turning a lowly person into a "king for a day" or "lord of misrule" was extremely common in medieval celebrations of the Christmas season. Writing circa 1180, Joannes Belethus, a Parisian theologian, mentions four such role-reversal festivals held "after Christmas": "those of the deacons, priests, and choir-children [later known as the Feast of the Boy Bishop], and finally that of the sub-deacons, which we call the Feast of Fools."

All of these celebrations possessed a degree of official support from the Church, which generally marked holidays with a certain measure of festive equality, in which lowly people would temporarily and playfully assume roles of power.

Yet from the earliest allusions to the Feast of Fools, it is clear that Church officials wished to limit the powers of the subdeacons, at the same time that the subdeacons were clearly pushing to extend those powers. The first extensive record bears witness to this conflict: it is a document, dated 1199, in which Eudes de Sully, bishop of Paris, attempts to reform the festival as practiced in the Cathedral of Notre Dame. Eudes give us an idea of the Church's view of how the festival should ideally be performed: the subdeacon chosen as ruler for a day would receive the *baculus*, or baton, normally used by the choir director to lead the singing, and he would lead part or all of the divine service for the day, including verses from the biblical passage "He has put down the mighty from their seats and exalted them of low degree" (Luke 1:52)—words referring to God's exaltation of the Virgin Mary but obviously important to the lower clergy because it gave them a script for temporarily unseating their superiors. Near or at the end of the service, the *baculus* was to be passed back to the director.

Eudes's document, however, makes it abundantly clear that the activities of the day went far beyond the minor symbolic revolution that the bishop had in mind. His letter implies that the subdeacons sang "He has overthrown the mighty" repeatedly and with particular zeal and pulled the higher clergy from their customary seats, seating themselves in their places. Further references indicate that the festival not only had spread beyond its prescribed limits in the church but had spilled into the streets. Eudes states that there was to be no masking, no songs, and no processions accompanying the mock leader to the cathedral or back to his home.

Eudes's attempts at reform met with only temporary success at best, for during the following decades a host of further orders and prohibitions appeared, attempting to rein in a festival that had clearly taken on a life of its own. In 1212 a French national church council directed the clergy to abstain from the feast, and in 1234 a decretal from the pope himself banned masking and performances in churches during the Christmas season. After this date the references to the feast multiply: nearly every account is negative, and many are attempts to ban it. About 1400 the Paris theologian Jean-Charlier de Gerson—who found the festival filled with cursing and "almost idolatrous" activities, "more execrable" than the excesses of taverns—despaired that only an order from the king of France could stop it. In 1438 Charles VII issued just such a decree, but the Feast of Fools persisted nonetheless, surviving well into the seventeenth century in some places before it was fully suppressed.

The richest records, from the thirteenth and fourteenth centuries, indicate that the festival was most popular in northern France, but it was also celebrated extensively in Germany and was further recorded in Bohemia, Italy, and England. Although the Feast of Fools may have been at one time specifically the property of the subdeacons, the canons and other secular clergy were in charge of most of the events for which we have records; more important, the feast possessed an enormous appeal for the public at large and no doubt drew upon certain folk customs associated with winter revelry. The celebration assumed the character of a major spectacle—a citywide New Year's party—both within and without the walls of the church.

Inside the church a full-scale religious parody developed, as the lower clergy burned old shoe leather or even dung instead of incense, played dice on the altar, jangled the bells of their fools' costumes, and dressed their leader in full ecclesiastical regalia—though sometimes the fool bishop wore the bishop's holy trousers on his head. In the streets there were massive costumed processions, in which some of the clergy wore their garments inside out or traded clothes with townspeople, dressed up as women, wore grotesque masks, and even paraded nude, sometimes whipping each other.

Much of the festivity centered upon the actions and ritual mockery of the ruling fool himself. Depending on the location, the ruler for a day was known variously as the "lord," "king," "prelate," "bishop," "archbishop," or even "pope" of fools. Sometimes he was ceremonially shaved in front of the church before the service began, a spectacle that occurred as part of the public feast in Sens in 1494. In other ceremonies he pronounced benedictions and passed out mock indulgences.

Central to many enactments was the celebration of the ass, or donkey. The image of the ass emerged in two major and overlapping manifestations: first, as the beast that carried the Virgin Mary and her newborn son on their flight from Jerusalem and, second, as the emblematic animal of the fool, for fools wore ass's ears as part of the costuming and were generally associated with the ass. Indeed, the Bishop of Fools would sometimes ride a donkey. A French manuscript of circa 1280 shows him making the gesture of blessing while riding backward on a donkey. The reformer Jan Hus described a Feast of Fools in which he had himself participated in late-fourteenth-century Prague: a "bishop" had been chosen and seated backward on a she-ass, being led like that into mass, whereupon the animal had brayed and even polluted the very altar itself. In some places the clergy and congregation would bray like asses during the performance of the parody service.

Although the Feast of Fools did not survive into modern times, it currently persists in popular imagination as one of the defining images of medieval culture through such fictional treatments as Victor Hugo's novel *Notre Dame de Paris*—adapted in drama, film, and cartoons as *The Hunchback of Notre Dame*—and in such influential scholarly studies as Harvey Cox's *Feast of Fools* and Mikhail Bakhtin's *Rabelais and His World*, which, respectively, view the feast as a master symbol of religious playfulness and as the ultimate expression of folk creativity.

See also: Boy Bishop, Feast of the; Carnival; Christmas; Fool; Masking; New Year's

References and further reading: After a century, E. K. Chambers, *The Mediaeval Stage*, 2 vols. (1903), remains the best single source on the celebration of the Feast of Fools, although his theories of its development are out of date; Chambers is the source for all of the quotations that appear in this article. Two much later books by R. Hutton, *The Rise and Fall of Merry England* (1994) and *The Stations of the Sun* (1996), present more recent perspectives. Despite its title, H. Cox's *The Feast of Fools* (1969) contains little concrete medieval material, but M. M. Bakhtin's *Rabelais and His World*, trans. H. Iswolsky (1968), offers significant information on the Feast of Fools as well as medieval enactments of Carnival and other related winter festivals. Specific information on the fool, including his role in the Feast of Fools, is found in the entry Fool in this encyclopedia, written by Malcolm Jones, who contributed the discussion on fools to this entry.

—*Bradford Lee Eden and Malcolm Jones*

Foreign Races

Unknown, little-known, and sometimes imaginary peoples beyond the borders of the Christian world.

Xenophobia and curiosity led medieval Europeans to react to these strangers in various and sometimes contradictory ways. In the early part of the Middle Ages, encounters with strangers were generally hostile, as the Huns threatened the European heartland in the fourth and fifth centuries C.E. and were finally defeated during an attempt to invade Gaul in 451. In the ninth century the Magyars (ancestors of the modern Hungarians) attacked the West and were only defeated in 955, near Augsburg, after the Germans had established a new force of horsemen equipped with chivalric armcr.

The next major contact with non-Europeans occurred during the age of the Crusades (beginning in 1096), when huge Christian armies went to the eastern Mediterranean to liberate the Holy Land from the Arabs. Although some of the Crusades were simple military enterprises, many European knights found themselves not only settling in Palestine at the end of some of these conflicts but also establishing surprisingly close relationships with their Muslim neighbors.

Although his birth and rank placed him well above the knightly class, Holy Roman Emperor Frederick II (1194–1250) shared these knights' affinity for Saracen culture. Perhaps it is not surprising that Frederick, who also preferred his residences in his southern lands in Sicily to his northern estates in the area of present-day Germany, enjoyed great familiarity with the Arabic world. His enthusiasm for the lands of the Crusades was such that his nonmilitary crusade to the Holy Land (1228–1229) quickly took on the trappings and pomp of a state visit.

Perhaps because of Frederick II's extreme fascination with "infidel" territories—a fascination that might have been considered unseemly in a Christian ruler—or perhaps for other reasons, the pope excommunicated him in 1228. In spite of the pope's protests, Frederick also established a Saracen colony at Lucera in southern Italy, and he further enraged the pontiff by refusing to try to forcefully convert the Muslim inhabitants to Christianity.

In a few cases such contacts led to early forms of tolerant behavior and thinking. In most other cases, however, they led to rejection and stereotyping, not because of a dearth of information but because many Europeans were stubbornly certain that Christianity was superior to Islam and all other religions. Nevertheless, we need to distinguish between personal concepts about foreign races, as they have been expressed in literary works, for example, and theoretical discussions about races, such as those found in religious texts and theological treatises. Both in the Old Testament and in the writings of the Church Fathers there are statements indicating that God has the power to create many races, miracles, and phenomena.

The vast majority of medieval people knew nothing at all concrete about foreign races, and they viewed them with great suspicion and fear—an uneasiness best represented by the many images of grotesque monsters carved into capitals and by the strange beings portrayed on maps of the world. In most cases

Foreign races, as depicted in Konrad von Megenberg, Book of Nature; *Augsburg, Germany, 1475. (Dover Pictorial Archive Series)*

"monsters" have to stand in for "foreign races," as the classical Greek tradition, established by Ctesias (fl. c. 400 B.C.E.), a court physician in Persia, and reemphasized by Pliny the Elder (23–79 C.E.), had a profound impact on medieval people. Alexander the Great's experience in India became a highly influential source of material for medieval writers, and it preconditioned their minds about foreign races in that part of the world. In *The City of God* St. Augustine (354–430) wrote of "monstrous races" as proof of God's providential power and as an indicator of how little Christians actually know about the universe. In his important work *Etymologiae* the Spanish scholar Isidore of Seville (c. 560–636) shows that he is fully convinced of the existence of monsters, and he lists all their characteristics in detail. But these arguments all clearly represent theoretical speculation and mirror popular beliefs. The first real contacts with foreign races occurred when Europeans traveled to the East. The pilgrim Egeria was the first to write about her experiences on her travels (sometime between the fourth and the sixth centuries); however, she paid little attention to things non-Christian.

It was not until the fourteenth century that travel accounts would actually pay attention to native populations. During her tour of the Holy Land the English mystic Margery Kempe (c. 1373–c. 1440) experienced bad treatment and indifference from her fellow pilgrims, but a friendly and beautiful Saracen man helped her climb up the mountain where Christ had fasted. One of the earliest German travel accounts—a 1336 work by Ludolf von Sudheim—indicates, however, that these pilgrims were like modern travelers, accompanied and guided by Franciscan friars who blocked their view of foreigners and foreign culture and directed their attention toward the holy sites.

One of the most important testimonies about foreign races was that of the Venetian merchant and traveler Marco Polo (1254–1324), who undertook a major trip as far as China (1271–1295) and returned with a book filled with highly exotic but—to a certain extent—accurate information about foreign races. Because his contemporaries did not believe his account, the book was called *Il milione* (Millions of Lies). By contrast, John Mandeville, who composed an entirely fictional travel report (c. 1356)—one in which the monstrous and the miraculous play a much greater role—appealed to his audience and met with resounding success, probably because during this time contacts with the East had been cut back dramatically and any fanciful account could easily claim to present authoritative information. The more medieval Europeans knew about foreign races, and the less threatening the latter appeared to them, the more likely it was that Europeans acknowledged their common humanity, even though the foreigners might practice a different religion.

Sir Jean de Joinville (1225–1317), who composed a comprehensive crusade chronicle, indicated that to his mind the caliph of Baghdad had the same rank as the pope. In this way Joinville was insinuating that neither Christianity nor medieval Europe was the only force in this world. Fulcher of Chartres (d. 1127), who had stayed in the Holy Land after the First Crusade, writes that all the Occidentals living in the East had adapted so well to the new world that they almost could be considered natives; this is a remarkable statement about ethnic acculturation.

The most impressive observation about foreign races can be found in Wolfram von Eschenbach's *Willehalm* (c. 1218–1220), wherein Giburg, the formerly
heathen wife of the protagonist, appeals to the court council not to forget that
despite their different religious beliefs, the enemies besieging their castle are part of
God's creation and should paradoxically be treated kindly, even in the middle of
deadly combat: "Spare the creatures of God's Hand!" Furthermore, she points out
that all Christians were once heathens and that they should have pity on their
adversaries in battle, because Christ also forgave those who killed him. At the
end of the story the Christians win a resounding victory over the Saracens, but
Willehalm acknowledges their worthiness as warriors and helps them prepare
their dead for burial, thus honoring the human quality of his opponents and
accepting them as members of this universe. Although Wolfram did not succeed in changing the prevailing medieval attitudes about foreign races, he was a
remarkable observer and a deeply humanistic thinker for his time.

In this respect we can also refer to many of the Byzantine verse romances,
such as the Middle High German *Herzog Ernst* (1180–1220), in which the protagonist spends a long time among foreign races, whom he treats like any other
people. These people, in turn, acknowledge him for his chivalric virtues. They
are clearly depicted as monsters, but in evaluating them this does not matter at
all; instead what counts are their character and inner nobility. The Old French
romance *Aucassin et Nicolette* presents a prince who is in love with a Saracen
slave girl, although his parents object to this mésalliance. Despite the profound
racial conflict, the lovers overcome all difficulties, eventually marry, and rule
over their inherited lands. The most famous marriage between a Christian and
a person from a different race can be found in Wolfram von Eschenbach's *Parzival*
(c. 1205–1210). In this romance Gahmuret marries the black queen, Belakane.
Their child, Feirefiz, although checkered black and white, emerges as an admi-
rable figure who is the absolute ruler of the entire world of Asia. He arrives at
Arthur's court at the moment when his brother Parzival is about to embark on
the adventure of bringing back the Grail.

In later centuries European travelers began to make explorations farther
and farther into the unknown East. Odoric of Pordenone went to Asia from
1314 to 1330, and Niccolò de Conti went as far as Indonesia. Bertrandon de la
Brocquière, who visited the Holy Land (1432–1433), expressed great admiration for the civility of the Turks. Others, however, sharply criticized them and
portrayed them as monstrous and cruel. This ambivalence was characteristic of
medieval attitudes, inasmuch as foreigners were perceived either as evil or as
part of God's creation, depending on the function they were assumed to occupy
within each specific context. It would be problematic to charge the European
peoples of the Middle Ages with outright racism in the modern sense of the
word. On the other hand, it does seem appropriate to credit some people from
that time period with having tolerant opinions regarding foreign races. There
were many contacts with foreign peoples, and some of these contacts were of
quite a positive nature.

See also: Crusades; Giants; *Mandeville's Travels*; Travel Literature; Wolfram von Eschenbach
References and further reading: R. W. Southern composed the seminal study on *Western
Views of Islam in the Middle Ages* (1991), but W. M. Watt expanded on this analysis in his

Muslim-Christian Encounters (1991). The extent to which the crusaders went through a profound acculturation process in Palestine is discussed in the papers collected in V. P. Goss, ed., *The Meeting of Two Worlds* (1986). J. V. Tolan has edited a volume of essays, *Medieval Christian Perceptions of Islam* (1996), in which many new elements of the interaction between Europeans and foreign races are discussed. One of the best historical investigations of medieval European travel literature seems to be M. B. Campbell's *The Witness and Her World* (1988), though she concentrates only on the major accounts. J. Critchley, in *Marco Polo* (1992), deals primarily with Marco Polo but also refers to some of the most amazing European travelers who explored the East and Southeast Asia. The best survey of contacts between medieval Europeans and East Asians is F. E. Reichert, *Begegnung mit China* (1992). The confrontation with foreign races was often expressed in terms of the monster tradition and the imagery of the "Wild Man," as R. Berheimer outlined in *Wild Men in the Middle Ages: A Study in Art, Sentiment, and Demonology* (1952).

—Albrecht Classen

Fornaldarsögur [Sagas of Antiquity]

Icelandic prose narratives, also known as mythical-heroic sagas, based on traditional heroic themes, whose numerous fabulous episodes and motifs result in an atmosphere of unreality.

Several subcategories of *fornaldarsögur* exist: the Adventure Tales and the Heroic Legends, corresponding roughly to comic and tragic modes within the genre. Some scholars have suggested a third group, Viking Sagas. The Adventure Tales are characterized by similarities of structure and personae to the folktale and by their generally happy conclusions. Courtship and quests play a major role, as in the *Saga of Hrolf Gautreksson*, which tells the story of four different wooing expeditions, the first undertaken by Hrolf's father, and the next three by Hrolf himself, his brother, and his blood brother. Hrolf defeats a woman warrior, "King Thorberg," in battle and marries her. He then accompanies his brother to Russia in a bride quest that involves blinding a one-eyed giant (AT 1137, *Polyphemus*, a narrative episode known as early as the *Odyssey* and still persisting in the oral traditions of northern and Eastern Europe). The final wooing takes Hrolf and his blood brother to Ireland, and among the companions' adventures en route is an encounter with a lion, which they kill through trickery.

The Heroic Legends, which usually end tragically, include the *Saga of the Völsungs*, part of which is rooted in a complex web of oral traditions concerning the fifth-century struggle pitting the Germanic Burgundian culture against Attila and the Huns. Atli (Attila) appears late in the saga, when he marries Kudrun. Greedy for the treasure possessed by Kudrun's brother, Gunnar, Atli invites him to a feast, but then takes Gunnar prisoner and demands the treasure. When Gunnar refuses to reveal its location, Atli has him bound and thrown into a snake pit, where the hero plays the harp with his toes until killed by snake venom. Kudrun avenges her brother's death by killing her own children and feeding them to her husband Atli. She then kills Atli and sets fire to his hall.

The extant *fornaldarsögur* date mainly from the Icelandic fourteenth and fifteenth centuries, but the traditions on which they are based are generally well attested from earlier periods. In addition to their heavy reliance on tradition, that is, on native mythological, folkloric, and literary goods, the *fornaldar-*

Gunnar playing the harp with his toes as serpents writhe around him; from a twelfth-century wooden carving. (Drawing by Stephen O. Glosecki)

sögur also show the influence of foreign literary texts. The *fornaldarsögur* differ qualitatively from the more realistic saga genres, a difference exemplified by their alternatively comic and mystifying use of the supernatural (e.g., talking animals, pagan theophanies, supernatural beings) versus the often dramatic treatment of the supernatural (e.g., premonitions) in other saga genres.

The *fornaldarsögur* enjoyed great popularity and are preserved in numerous manuscripts (including some post-Reformation manuscripts), and their subject matter also finds expression in the ballad traditions of the Faroes, Norway, Sweden, and Denmark and in the Icelandic metrical romances *(rímur)*. The sagas are set in periods before the colonization of Iceland, but though the world they conjure and the traditions on which they are based are archaic, the written *fornaldarsögur* themselves are among the most recent innovations of saga literature. There is evidence (e.g., *Thorgils saga ok Haflida, Sturlu saga*) that *fornaldarsögur* were recited orally, but of such performances we know little of substance. And despite the fact that the heroes and villains of the tales are commonly Norwegians, Danes, and Swedes, the *fornaldarsögur* are a decidedly Icelandic genre, although many of the *fornaldarsögur* traditions are well attested in such non-Icelandic works as the *Gesta Danorum* of Saxo Grammaticus.

The flourishing of the *fornaldarsögur* in the postclassical saga period suggests a revitalization in Icelandic literature and culture, but many modern critics have assumed that the "artless" (and otherwise negatively described) *fornaldarsögur* may thereby be dismissed as escapist (i.e., the Verfall Theory). Although these narratives undoubtedly served as diversions, I have argued that their function in late-medieval Icelandic literature and society was multifaceted. In a period of national distress and cultural retrogression, the *fornaldarsögur* represented a conduit to a glorious heroic past and thus fulfilled an important cultural and psychological function in addition to their value as robust entertainment. The *fornaldarsögur* heroes are often linked in the sagas' genealogies to Icelandic families, and prominent Icelanders would certainly have been well served by the valorization of their legendary ancestors' exploits. The impulse for the Icelanders to prove that they, too, like their more-established Nordic neighbors, had connections to the Scandinavian Heroic Age must have been powerful. One manuscript of the *Landnamabok* (Book of Settlements) suggests just such a motivation: "But we can better answer the criticism of foreigners when they accuse us of coming from slaves or rogues, if we know for certain the truth about our ancestry" (*Melabók*, ch. 335).

Modern critical reactions to the *fornaldarsögur* have been quite negative overall: If they are judged by the aesthetic standards largely appropriate to the realistic saga genres, the *fornaldarsögur* can hardly escape critical condemnation, given the affection they evince for recurrent tale types (e.g., AT 1187, "Meleager": permission to live as long as candle lasts); well-worn motifs (such as D1056, magic shirt); and stock characters (such as the "ash lad" or *kolbítr* [coal biter] figure who, like Cinderella, derives his name from the fact that he spends his time sitting in the ashes of the hearth). As the important relationships between the *fornaldarsögur*, folklore, and Nordic literary consciousness are explored and as the *fornaldarsögur* are perceived as the means by which medieval Icelanders themselves looked back at the Heroic Age, the *fornaldarsögur* will take a more highly regarded place in discussions of Icelandic literary and cultural history.

See also: *Riddarasögur*; Sagas of Icelanders; Scandinavian Tradition

References and further reading: The most recent collective edition is G. Jónsson, ed., *Fornaldarsögur Nordurlanda* (1954). *Islandica* 5 (1912) and 26 (1937) are especially helpful bibliographic tools. Secondary literature includes P. Buchholz, *Vorzeitkunde* (1980); P. Hallberg, "Some Aspects of the *Fornaldarsögur* as a Corpus," *Arkiv för nordisk filologi* 97 (1982); M. Kalinke, "Norse Romance," in *Old Norse-Icelandic Literature*, ed. C. J. Clover and J. Lindow (1985); K. Liestøl, *Den norrœne arven*, with an English summary (1970); S. A. Mitchell, *Heroic Sagas and Ballads* (1991); S. A. Mitchell, "Fornaldarsögur," in *Medieval Scandinavia*, ed. P. Pulsiano and K. Wolf (1993); H. Pálsson, "Early Icelandic Imaginative Literature," in *Medieval Narrative*, ed. H. Bekker-Nielsen (1979) and "Fornaldarsögur," in *Dictionary of the Middle Ages* (1985); H. Pálsson and P. Edwards, *Legendary Fiction in Medieval Iceland* (1971); H. Reuschel, *Untersuchungen über Stoff und Stil der Fornaldarsaga* (1933); R. Righter-Gould, "The Fornaldar Sögur Northurlanda: A Structural Analysis," *Scandinavian Studies* 52 (1980); and M. Schlauch, *Romance in Iceland* (1934).

—*Stephen A. Mitchell*

Fossils

Mineralized remains—such as bones, teeth, and shells—of extinct life-forms, which in prescientific cultures are objects of mystery and believed to possess special properties.

Throughout Europe fossil remains of prehistoric reptiles, marine creatures, and Ice Age mammals (mammoths, rhinoceroses, saber-toothed tigers, cave bears) are exposed by natural weathering or by human actions. Among ordinary folk and learned "experts" alike, such marvels demanded explanation: in the Middle Ages fossils were identified as games of nature, objects from outer space, divinely formed stones, evidence of the biblical Flood, and the remains of giants, monsters, or people of ancient history or myth. Fossils were collected for luck, magic, and medicine; they were stolen, traded, made into jewelry, enshrined, or exhibited as valuable curiosities; some were revered as sacred relics.

Marine fossils are common in Europe, and they generated many folk beliefs; their colloquial names reflect perceived resemblances and associations with local saints. For example, bean-shaped Nummulites gave rise to legends of lentils left behind by ancient people. "Devil's toenails," fossil oysters with a distorted shape, were believed to alleviate arthritic pain. Cylindrical belemnites (fossil cuttlefish), known as lynx stones, thunderbolts, or devil's fingers, were thought to ward off evil or to cure those struck by lightning, bewitched, or suffering eye problems. Bead-like crinoids were called "St. Cuthbert's beads" or "fairy money" in England and "St. Boniface's pennies" in Germany. Crinoids were often strung into rosaries.

Because of what looked like claw marks on echinoids (fossilized sea urchins), they were called eagle stones; to others, they resembled "fairy loaves." They were alleged to cure seasickness and to protect from lightning and witchcraft. Great magical powers were attributed to an echinoid called *ovum anguinium* (eel egg), thought to be tossed in the air by snakes. A fifteenth-century woodcut shows a man capturing such a fossil as it is ejected by a tangle of serpents; this charm would ensure victory in war and other disputes. Crusaders returned from Judea with numerous echinoids, known as Jew stones, whose resemblance to a bladder led to the idea that they cured kidney ailments.

Fossil shark teeth, taken for petrified serpents' tongues, were named *glossopetrae* (tongue stones) or St. Paul's tongues and were worn as amulets to neutralize poisons. Beginning in the fifteenth century it was fashionable to suspend an array of sharks' teeth on a gilded and bejeweled tree-shaped rack, called a *languier* or *Natternzungenbaum*, on one's dining table ready for dipping into wine. *Languiers* were also hung over babies' cots for protection. Magical "toadstones" (button-like teeth of Jurassic rays) were thought to be jewels formed in the heads of toads; from the fourteenth century onward they were set in rings and lockets. A woodcut of 1497 shows a man removing a stone from a toad.

St. Hilda (614–680) was credited with petrifying snakes around Whitby, England, into ammonites, distinctively coiled mollusk shells also found in continental Europe. There were various folk explanations for why these "snake stones" were headless, and amulet dealers often carved snakes' heads on the polished ammonites. In several regions of southern Europe hoof-shaped cross sections of fossil mussels in bedrock were said to be the petrified tracks of ancient cattle or horses. Amber, fossilized tree resin from the Baltic Sea, was used as a remedy for sore throat, blindness, miscarriage, nosebleed, and the pains of teething.

The remains of large extinct vertebrates inspired legends of giants and monsters; for example, an area in France where huge Tertiary elephant skeletons came to light was known as the Field of Giants. Strange bones found in wells and caves were alleged to be those of a basilisk, a fabulous medieval monster. In 1250 a chronicler wrote that the bones of a giant named Heymo were kept in the monastery at Wilten, Austria. Heymo had reportedly slain a dragon and donated its treasure to the monks, who later commissioned a statue of Heymo based on giant bones found nearby. In the fourteenth century the monastery also displayed the dragon's tongue, actually the rostrum of a swordfish. Also in the fourteenth century Boccaccio announced the discovery of a classical Cyclops, based on a colossal skeleton in a cave in Sicily. In about 1335 quarrymen near Klagenfurt, Austria, unearthed the skull of a "dragon," which was depicted on the city's coat of arms. The skull, later identified as that of an Ice Age woolly rhinoceros, was the model for the famous dragon statue still in the town square.

In 1443 workmen building St. Stephen's Church in Vienna excavated a giant thigh bone, which was later identified as that of a mammoth. It was inscribed with the motto of Friedrich III (who was described as a "giant" by his contemporaries) and kept at the cathedral as a relic of St. Christopher until the eighteenth century (by tradition St. Christopher was a giant).

It has been suggested that medieval tales of dragons lurking in caves were based on discoveries of the huge, fearsome skeletons of cave bears, which are abundant in caverns of the Alps and Carpathians. The bones of extinct mammoths, saber-toothed tigers, reptiles, and pterosaurs may also have influenced the image of the European dragon.

Although fossils were objects of superstition in the Middle Ages, some individuals tried to understand their real origins. In 1282 an Italian naturalist, Ristoro d'Arezzo, rejected the current notion that fossils were created by cosmic rays and wrote that fish bones and shells on mountains proved that the peaks were once "overwhelmed by the Flood." Two centuries later, in about 1484, Leonardo da Vinci examined countless marine fossils in northern Italy and concluded that the land had long ago been inundated. When the wa-

Removal of a toadstone; from a German woodcut, 1497. (National Museum of Wales)

ter receded, decaying fish left hollows in the mud that were later filled with other, new mud, "preserving the exact forms of the creatures embedded in the older mud."

See also: Dragon; Giants; Griffin

References and further reading: The most comprehensive surveys of beliefs about fossils are by K. Oakley, in "Folklore of Fossils, Parts I and II," *Antiquity* 39 (1965), and *Decorative and Symbolic Uses of Vertebrate Fossils* (1975), which has illustrations of *languiers* and toadstone rings. M. Bassett, "Formed Stones, Folklore, and Fossils," *National Museum of Wales Geology Series* 1 (1982), gathers and illustrates a wealth of mostly English fossil lore; his documented examples, however, are postmedieval. W. Stephens, *Giants in Those Days* (1989), discusses medieval and Renaissance giantologies, mentioning some discoveries of large bones. E. Buffetaut, a paleontologist, discusses some famous medieval fossil discoveries in chapter 1 of his *Short History of Vertebrate Paleontology* (1987). E. Thenius, *Fossils and the Life of the Past* (1973), discusses examples of marine fossils that inspired medieval folklore, but without documentation or dates.

—Adrienne Mayor

Frame Tale

A fictional narrative composed primarily for the purpose of presenting the other narratives that it surrounds.

A frame tale depicts a series of stories whose narrators are characters in the frame. While frame tales vary considerably in length and complexity, each provides a context for reading, listening to, and interpreting the interior tales. A frame tale derives its own meaning largely from what it contains and does not stand independently from the tales enclosed within it. The interpolated tales can appear independently, however, or in a different frame with a different connotation.

Frame tales have also been called *novellae*, boxing tales, or stories within stories. The genre appears to have been an Eastern invention, most likely originating in India, where it can be traced back at least three millennia. By the tenth century it had reached the Middle East, and by the twelfth, Europe. The frame tale gained the height of its popularity in Europe in the fourteenth century but faded in most areas in the early modern period.

Some of the best-known and most studied frame tales appear here in the approximate order of their creation. It is impossible to date the origin of many of these works or the longevity of many others. For example, estimates of the date of origin of the *Panchatantra*, generally accepted as the earliest surviving frame tale, vary by 700 years and more. Other frame tales had different periods of influence in the East and West. For example, the famed *Thousand and One Nights* has exerted a continuous influence in the East from about 800, but it had a relatively slight effect on Western narrative traditions until after 1300, when its influence became substantial. After the Sanskrit *Panchatantra*, there appeared the *Book of Sindibad* (c. 800), which spawned many versions in the East and found its way to the West in the form of *The Seven Sages of Rome*, in which seven wise men tell stories to dissuade a king from executing his own son. Then followed the Arabic *Alf Layla wa-Layla* (Thousand and One Nights), in which

Shahrazad narrates a story each night so that her tyrannical husband will not kill her as he has all his former wives; *Kalila wa-Dimna*, an Arabic version of the *Panchatantra*, in which two jackals trade stories about ethics and behavior; Petrus Alfonsi's *Disciplina clericalis* (twelfth century); the Persian *Tuti-Nameh* (c. 1300), the story of a parrot who tells stories night after night to keep his mistress from an adulterous rendezvous; Juan Manuel's *Conde Lucanor* (1335), in which Patronio, a counselor, answers the count's questions, illuminating each with an exemplum; Boccaccio's *Decameron* (c. 1349–1351), the story of seven young women and three young men who flee to the country to escape the plague and entertain each other with stories of love and lust; John Gower's *Confessio Amantis* (The Lover's Confession, c. 1387–1393), in which Genius tells tales illustrating the seven deadly sins; Chaucer's *Canterbury Tales*, which depicts a variety of characters, of varied classes, on a pilgrimage to Canterbury during which they compete to tell the most edifying and entertaining tale; and Marguerite de Navarre's *Heptameron* (first printed edition, 1558), similar to the *Decameron* but with fewer narrators, who are apparently based on Marguerite's own acquaintances. Certain wisdom books, or "mirrors for princes," may also be included in a broad definition of the frame tale.

The frame tale covers a spectrum from the primarily diverting to the primarily didactic. The structures also vary from loose to tight, a tight structure being one where the frame tale strictly limits the type of story that can be interpolated in any given position. The *Thousand and One Nights*, for example, has a loose frame because Shahrazad can theoretically tell any kind of story as long as it is entertaining. Gower's *Confessio Amantis*, on the other hand, links its stories tightly to their contexts. When Genius is presenting a lesson on pride, he tells tales in which this emotion is highlighted. This type of structure also allows for irony in texts such as Juan Ruiz's *Libro de buen amor* (1330, 1343), in which a character presents a lesson and then tells a story that contradicts it.

Most of the earlier frame tales are of anonymous authorship and probably descend from an oral storytelling tradition. Later texts, particularly in the European tradition, have named authors, but they still appear to draw heavily on both oral traditions and earlier frame tale texts. Different frame tales may have interpolated tales in common. For example, tales in Boccaccio's or Chaucer's works may have made earlier appearances in the *Thousand and One Nights* or *The Seven Sages of Rome*. Stories in common among frame tales have led some to conclude that medieval authors read earlier texts. That frame tales both in oral and written form worked as conduits transmitting tales across linguistic and cultural boundaries seems certain; however, it has been difficult to determine which frame tale a particular author might have read or heard.

The frame tale depicts the oral storytelling tradition and works as a bridge between oral and literate narrative. Along with exempla collections that do not have frames, framed collections present traditional tales to a literate audience. An audience is written into the frame tale, allowing an author or compiler to guide the reader's interpretation. Different frame tales thereby contain different narrator/audience dynamics. Some have a sole narrator for the interpolated tales, indicative of storytelling by teachers and parents; others have several narrators, thus leading to an agonistic environment characteristic of public storytelling. A frame tale is thus a self-reflexive form, a story about storytelling in all its variety.

See also: Chaucer, Geoffrey; *Confessio Amantis*; *Decameron*; Folktale; *Novella*; *Seven Sages, The*; *Thousand and One Nights*

References and further reading: One must look to sources on individual frame tales, for there are no comprehensive studies of the form. R. J. Clements and J. Gibaldi, *Anatomy of the Novella: The European Tale Collection from Boccaccio to Cervantes* (1977), traces European developments. L. Arathoon, *Chaucer and the Craft of Fiction* (1986); W. F. Bryan and G. Dempster, *Sources and Analogues of Chaucer's* Canterbury Tales (1941); and K. Gittes, *Framing* The Canterbury Tales (1991), deal with Chaucer's contribution. J. Potter, *Five Frames for the* Decameron: *Communication and Social Systems in the Cornice* (1982), applies Erving Goffman's theories to the frame tale. M. Gerhardt, *The Art of Story-Telling: A Literary Study of the* Thousand and One Nights (1963), and D. Pinault, *Story-Telling Techniques in the* Arabian Nights (1992), contain the best discussions of structure in the Arabic tradition.

—*Bonnie D. Irwin*

French Tradition

The folkloric culture of France.

History and Context

At Charlemagne's death in 814 the empire of the Franks covered not only present-day France but also Germanic lands north to Hamburg, including the Netherlands, and east to Regensburg and Salzburg; its southern borders stretched down the Italian peninsula and across the northern quarter of Spain. However, by the time of the First Crusade (1096–1099) the kingdom of France had been considerably pared down, extending to the north only to Flanders, and to the east to an axis from Champagne down the Rhone valley to Arles. Burgundy contained, along with most of its present territory, the region of Besançon and part of Provence. By 1494 France's borders had not stretched much: they now extended to the tip of Lombardy but still fell just short of Metz and did not include Franche-Comté or Savoy.

The fluctuations of the French kingdom's borders during the Middle Ages pose specific problems in understanding French history: today, in referring to "French" history, customs, or folklore, we could easily be speaking of something found in an area that was part of a separate kingdom at a given time in medieval history. Thus, there are considerable differences between the political history of France and its cultural history, which is defined by language, commercial intercourse, family and vassalic ties, and social interaction based on common natural borders.

At the dawn of the Middle Ages, Gaul (as France was called during the Roman period) was already a mix of religious and customary traditions. Roman feasts, calendar systems, popular beliefs, and rituals added a layer of folk religion to the Celtic substratum, and a third layer, Christian traditions, followed. Some Roman ceremonial complexes became important components of later folk culture, such as the rituals of winter solstice, or aspects of Fevralia present in the February Carnival.

During the great invasions that followed the withdrawal of Roman forces in the fifth century, numerous Germanic tribes brought with them a new input of mores, customs, and beliefs. Around 526 the territory of France was crisscrossed by Barbarian invasions. The Franks, from north of Cologne, migrated along a northeast-to-southwest axis, through Tournai, Paris, Orléans, and Bordeaux. The Burgundians traveled south from around Mainz to their future territory down the Rhone valley. Visigoths covered the southernmost areas, from Toulouse to the old Roman Narbonensis (later Narbonnaise) and Provence. The Vandals swept across the eastern plains, parallel to the Frankish axis but stretching further down, to Toulouse, and the famous Huns reached Paris and Troyes.

The cultural history of these invasions remains incompletely understood, and their impact is very difficult to determine. Fragments of symbolic iconography point to a spreading of solar cults across Europe during this period. The last wave of Germanic invaders left linguistic traces: the dialect of today's Normandy bears the imprint of the marauding Viking armies that invaded northern France in the ninth century and eventually, in 911 under Rollo (known in Denmark as Hrolf the Walker), became the rulers of Normandy. The northmen's incursions were not, however, limited to Normandy. They also set upon the entire Atlantic coast, from Nantes to Bordeaux and the Pyrenees, and along the Mediterranean, upon the regions of Narbonne and Provence.

Although the Muslim invasions were pushed back at the dramatic encounter of Poitiers in 732, small groups were said to have remained in France. Some were settled as populations of prisoners, for instance in the silver-mining region of Largentière (Ardèche). Chronicles tell of Saracen strongholds controlling the Alps as late as 927. In fact, Muslim garrisons did not evacuate from Grenoble until 965 and from Provence until 973. Some Saracens, according to local oral traditions, settled even in northern villages, dubbed "Saracen" in the region, such as the little town of Uchizy, near Mâcon.

Miracles of the French Monarchy

Several legends arguing for the divine origins of French kingship began during the time of these invasions with the conversion of the Frankish king Clovis to Christianity in the late fifth century. However, some of the legends did not come into being until considerably later than this, and all of them changed during the course of the Middle Ages, reaching their final form by the end of the fifteenth century.

Perhaps the most famous is the legend of the Holy Phial, which says that on the day when Clovis was baptized the priest responsible for bringing the sacred oil was delayed by the crowd and did not arrive at the proper time. However, a dove came down from heaven bearing a small phial of the necessary oil, which was used for the ceremony. The phial was preserved at the Abbey of St.-Rémi and used for the anointing of the kings of France from 869 forward. No matter how many kings were anointed, the container never ran dry. The miracle of the dove and the oil was interpreted as giving divine sanction to the French monarchy. The practice of anointing French kings, which began with Clovis and became de rigueur in the ninth century, also explains the sacerdotal powers that

Illumination showing the baptism of Clovis, from the fifteenth-century Great Chronicles of France. *(Corbis/Archivo Iconografico, S.A.)*

kings of France enjoyed in addition to secular powers throughout the Middle Ages and beyond.

The legend of the fleur-de-lis also centers on Clovis, though it dates only from the fourteenth century. Before Clovis's conversion to Christianity he married Clotilda, a Christian who tried in vain for many years to convert him. Queen Clotilda made a habit of visiting a holy hermit, and she prayed with him shortly before an important battle that Clovis was expected to lose. After they prayed, an angel appeared bearing an escutcheon with armorial bearings in the form of golden fleurs-de-lis on an azure background. The angel told the holy man that if Clovis wore this coat of arms in place of his usual crescent, he would win the battle. Queen Clotilda quickly contrived to have the crescents removed from all of Clovis's equipment and replaced by fleurs-de-lis. When Clovis called for his armor, he was astonished to find the "wrong" coat of arms on it and sent it back for another. Of course, the next suit of armor also bore the fleur-de-lis. Four times Clovis sent his armor back, and four times he was brought armor with the new pattern. Finally, having graver concerns than the appearance of his armor, Clovis wore the fleur-de-lis into battle and won a miraculous victory at the battle of Montjoie. When Clotilda afterward revealed the subterfuge, Clovis finally became a Christian.

The legend of the oriflamme inevitably came to focus on Clovis as well because of his role in the other two miracles. In this one, the emperor of Constantinople dreamed that he saw a knight holding a flaming lance standing by his bedside. An angel then told him that this knight would free Constantinople from the Saracens. In earlier versions the knight turns out to be Charlemagne, but in a later form he becomes Clovis. The flaming lance is the oriflamme, the red standard of the Capetian kings.

Beginning in the eleventh century with Philip I, French kings were believed to have healing powers, another powerful claim to divine sanction of their rule. Scrofula, an inflammation of the lymph nodes, was a very common disease in the Middle Ages, owing largely to unsanitary living conditions. Scrofula produces sores and swellings about the face and can be badly disfiguring, but it is hardly ever fatal and often goes away on its own. The kings of France claimed to be able to heal this disease, which came to be called the king's evil, by ritually touching the sores. As scrofula often does vanish as suddenly as it comes, numerous "cures" were recorded, and the French government kept careful records of them. Philip I and his successors would touch for scrofula in elaborate, very public rituals, to which sufferers would flock in hopes of a miracle. As Marc Bloch observes in his classic study of sacred monarchy, French kings must have gained great prestige from this healing touch, because in the twelfth century their English rivals began also to touch for scrofula. In the thirteenth century St. Louis (Louis IX) expanded the ritual, adding certain holy words to the traditional sign of the cross. He taught these words to his grandson, Philip the Fair, who despite being far from saintly also spoke them when he touched for scrofula. Another indication of the hold of this ritual on popular imagination is that it continued long past the Middle Ages, into the nineteenth century.

The Folk Calendar

Folk time is increasingly recognized as an all-encompassing worldview that translates daily experience onto a sacred plane. Arnold van Gennep's approach to French folklore has provided a temporal framework of specific calendar cycles throughout the year that proves useful for the study of medieval French folklore. Van Gennep's delineation of "minicycles" completes the year, extending past the vast cycles of Christmas, Carnival, and Easter to embrace, for instance, the late-fall festival, St. Martin's Carnival (November 11), and such end-of-summer celebrations as the feasts of St. Margaret (July 20), Mary Magdalen (July 22), St. Anne (July 26), and St. Sixtus (August 6).

Folk calendar symbolism emerges in the dramatization of crucial calendar moments, acted out, for instance, through recitations of the Combat between Sir Carnival and Lady Lent or, as is frequent in France, a gaunt, irascible male figure named Caresprenant (Lent). In these combats, each side mobilizes vast quantities of foodstuffs, raw, still alive and kicking, as well as prepared, to engage in a mock battle that ends—nonrealistically—with the victory of the infinitely more popular Carnival. The medieval poetic tradition of the *débats* between seasons (summer against winter) or months (April against May) can be seen as another expression of ritualized calendar behaviors.

Local traditions exemplify the link between crucial calendar points and nature lore, in forms often maintained by modern French folklore. For instance, Gervase of Tilbury tells us of a walnut tree in Barjols, near Arles, that does not regain its leaves in spring but remains fallow and bare until the feast of St. John the Baptist (June 24), when it suddenly "celebrates" the Precursor's birth and is covered with leaves and fruits. He also recounts the tradition of a deadly battle waged for eight days around the feast of St. John the Baptist by armies of gigantic horned scarabs in the two towers of the castle of Remoulins, near Uzes, a version of the tradition, common in France, of a supernatural battle of animals (usually cats or birds).

Folk Rituals and Beliefs

In France, as elsewhere in Western Europe, many folk beliefs centered on the popular saints of a particular locality. After the Virgin Mary in a variety of guises (such as Notre Dame des Neiges), the most venerated were the Baptist, St. John the Evangelist, Mary Magdalen, Margaret, Anne, Catherine, Blaise, Nicholas, George, and Christopher. However, every region and even subregion had its focal saint, whose cult attracted a wide range of ceremonial behavior, hagiographical tradition, and folk belief: Martin around Limoges, Yves and Anne in Brittany, the child Foix around Conques. Outstanding in Provence were Mary Magdalen and the local cult of the "Three Marys." Curiously, sometime in the twelfth century in Corbeny, St. Marcoul became associated with the healing of the king's evil. The monks of Corbeny duly began selling small bottles of water sanctified by having Marcoul's relics immersed in it. Sufferers would then purchase this water and use it for washing their sores. Some would even drink it. The perceived power of saints' relics was so great that some holy people were assaulted on their deathbeds by crowds of believers; such was the fate of the Joachimite Beguine Douceline of Digne, whose clothing and body were torn to pieces.

Facetious folklore also created its own imaginary saints who people the folk theater, the fabliaux, and popular sayings: St. Caquette, patron of talkative women, and the obscene or profane saints Couillebault (Boldball), Jambon (Ham), and Andouille (Chitterling), to name a few.

Localized folk worship easily crossed the line into heresy. For example, in the thirteenth century the Dominican friar Stephen of Bourbon was appalled to learn that the people of the Dombes, near his convent at Lyons, worshipped a greyhound, whom they called St. Guinefort. According to the local legend, this "Holy Greyhound" had saved an infant from a snake. The child's guardians, however, killed the dog, mistaking the snake's blood on the dog's muzzle for the child's blood and assuming the dog had hurt the child. Afterward, realizing their mistake and overcome with remorse, the lord and lady placed the dog in a well, filled the well with stones, and planted trees around it. Apparently the local peasants treated the Holy Greyhound as a martyr, praying to him in times of sickness or need.

Women with sick children would bring offerings to the well and perform various rituals that provide a fine illustration of the melding of Christian traditions with local pagan practices. After passing the naked infants between the trees nine times, they would hang their swaddling clothes on the surrounding bushes and place the babies at the feet of the trees. They would then ask the fauns of the forest to take back their sick children and leave the mothers their own children, whom they said the fauns had taken away. They left the children lying on straw, with burning candles on either side of their heads. Naturally, the straw often caught fire, and many of the babies burned to death. As soon as Stephen discovered this ritual, he outlawed it and had the dog disinterred. He also had the trees chopped down and burned along with the remains of the dog. However, local belief in the Holy Greyhound and his healing powers did not die out so easily; it continued for several centuries longer, as Jean-Claude Schmitt shows in his folkloric study of St. Guinefort.

A larger and more influential heresy was that of the Albigenses, or Cathars, which sprang up in parts of the Southwest, in particular around Foix. The Dominican Order of friars was founded to combat this heresy, more by argument than by physical means. However, in 1209 Pope Innocent III declared a crusade against them, and the northern armies crushed them brutally, as in Béziers, where the entire population, Catholic and heretic, was put to the sword. "Kill them all; God will know His own," the papal envoy was reported to have said. This grisly victory was followed by a process of religious reconquest, with Inquisitors pressing local populations to reveal the extent and manner of their contamination by heretical practices and beliefs.

Such was the task of Jacques Fournier, who centered his inquiry on Montaillou, a small village whose inhabitants were intensely concerned with salvation and a spirituality that resembled Manichaeism in its conception of the universe as divided between equal and opposing forces of good and evil. The elite of this sect, the *parfaits* (perfect ones), sought to imitate the Twelve Apostles as far as possible, and they met high standards of poverty and chastity—apparently higher than the officials of the established Church. They were also very learned and skilled in disputation. In order to meet their adversaries on an equal footing, St. Dominic's order also had to become well educated and to eschew personal property.

Fournier was a thorough and conscientious Inquisitor. His records of the villagers' testimony are so detailed that Emmanuel Le Roy Ladurie, a twentieth-century historian, was able to use them to conduct a thorough analysis of village life: hearth-side customs, child rearing, social networking, traditional gestures, magical beliefs, and many other aspects of local folk culture. Because religious conversation so thoroughly penetrated everyday life, the trial testimony revealed many aspects of local custom. For example, in one of the Inquisitorial transcripts, we learn from villager Vuissane Testanière:

> At the time when the heretics dominated Montaillou, Guillemette "Benete" and Alazaïs Rives were being deloused in the sun by their daughters. ... All four of them were on the roof of their houses. I was passing by and heard them talking. Guillemette "Benete" was saying to Alazaïs, "How can people bear the pain when they are burning at the stake?"
>   To which Alazaïs replied, "Ignorant creature! God takes the pain upon himself, of course!"

From this and similar records, Le Roy Ladurie concluded that delousing—picking lice from the hair—was an important social ritual, was always conducted by a woman, and was often but not always practiced on a male lover, and that a favorite site for delousing and gossiping in Montaillou was on the flat rooftops of the village houses.

The interpenetration of official and folk belief found in Montaillou also existed in urban areas. French cities produced an abundant civilian architecture, which, along with Church monuments, provided an extensive surface for the inscription of the motifs, themes, and legends of folk culture. The cities of France were richly adorned with an iconography that was both symbolic and functional. For instance, the referential language of street signs is an expression of folklore. Saints and the emblems of their martyrdom signaled shops and tav-

Medieval walls and castle still dominate the French town of Chinon, Anjou. (Adam Woolfitt/ CORBIS)

erns to passers-by, such as St. Lawrence and his grill for rotisseries, St. Catherine and her razor-laden wheel for barbers or potters. The corner pillars of houses, beams, lintels, and fountains all offer traces of a folk culture in which the saints coexist with the Wild Men; mermaids; the misogynist Bigorne, who feeds on harried husbands, and Chicheface, who feeds on good wives; the Four Sons Aymon on their horse Bayard; the bear doing the morris dance; the dragon; and the man who wants to shoe a goose.

Such was the lively and colorful late-fifteenth-century world of François Villon, the quintessential Parisian poet. His work reflects not only his Sorbonne education but also his active participation in urban folklife. Villon's poetry features not the enchanted forests of courtly romance but the taverns, brothels, and even prisons of late-medieval Paris. His often painfully realistic characters include thieves, prostitutes, policemen, and of course a full complement of corrupt clerics, who according to Villon assist the husbands of their parishes by giving pleasure to their wives. An important source of the poet's famous irony is the easy coexistence of the sacred and profane, as apparent in Villon's Paris as in his poetry. In the compact universe of the medieval city, iconography, myth, and custom weave a complex texture of signification that underpins folk life.

As the representations described above suggest, medieval French folklore knew many supernatural or supranatural beings. The most prominent may have been the devil himself (Satan, Sathanas, Lucifer), often personified as the Master Builder who commandeers bridges and steeples in particular and puts sinners to sleep "with his viola." Others include dwarfs like the famed Oberon, elves such as the later Pacolet, giants and ogres from Geoffroy à la Grande Dent to Gargantua, mermaids or "serpent women," Wild Men and Women, fairies and ghosts, and the premier magician Maugis, cousin to the Four Sons Aymon, who was protected by the magical horse Bayard. We might include what Nicole Belmont calls verbal beings: bogey men whose mere name frightens children—for instance, the Barbo or Babou (thirteenth century), subject of a rich 1982 essay by Jacques Berlioz, who shows its link to a werewolf called Barbeu.

Many French folk narratives are associated with particular places. Place names are witness to important legendary figures whose names are attached to hills and mountain passes. Among them stand out figures from the chansons de geste: Roland, the ill-fated nephew of Charlemagne, or the horse Bayard, mount of the Four Sons Aymon.

Places all over France are connected to stories of the supernatural. Gervase mentions the high tower of the castle of Livron near Valence, still called the devil's tower in the nineteenth century, which does not tolerate a night watchman and mysteriously deposits any intruder at morning down in the valley, or the rock of the Annot castle, in the same region, which can be easily moved by the little finger but not the whole body. Other localities are attached to legends concerning historical figures, such as Pepin the Short, father of Charlemagne, slaying a lion at Ferrières-en-Gatinais, represented on a capital of the twelfth-century church. Numerous legends concern the fairy-mermaid Melusine, a serpent-tailed woman who is linked to the origins of the noble family of Lusignan, from whom Eleanor of Aquitaine descended, and to the regional histories of Poitou.

(One English legend identifies the serpent-tailed woman as Richard I's mother, although no legends go so far as to claim that Eleanor herself was half serpent.)

Other legendary beings seem not to be connected with a particular locale. The Wild Hunter is known through numerous local traditions: Hellekin, a figure of Germanic origin first documented by Ordericus Vitalis, was reputed to ride down lonely roads followed by hordes of noisy, disheveled ghosts, who played dissonant metallic music and seized any unfortunate passerby. The Wild Man spawned an entire family in the decorative arts of the Middle Ages; they appear on tapestries, engraved chests, and coffers. In festive folk traditions, the Wild Man—sometimes conflated with the bear—was a frequent figure in costumed Carnival celebrations. In female form, the Wild Woman is linked to fear-producing beliefs in children and to populations of wild animals.

In short, every area of folklore as we know it in the West has been represented in the French Middle Ages and invites continuous unearthing of what the French call the "archaeology of knowledge."

Literature and Folklore

Folklore and folk culture have provided the inspiration and context for much of France's most memorable literature, including *lais*, romances, ballads, and chansons de geste. The *Chanson de Roland* tells of a disastrous battle, which actually occurred at Roncevaux in 778, in which the Moors surprised and annihilated the rearguard of Charlemagne's army, led by Roland. The story of his final stand was probably passed down through heroic songs performed in French by *jongleurs* until the time of the First Crusade (1096–1099). When the *Chanson* as we now know it was written down, around 1100, Roland was the ideal hero for French knights, who had been inspired by the idea of fighting the Muslims in the Holy Land. This may be the reason that the *Chanson* was put into literary form and began a long tradition of Roncevaux legends.

The figure of the *jongleur* plays an important role in the *Roman de Silence*, an unconventional thirteenth-century romance. In this story, a beautiful, aristocratic girl is disguised as a boy and trained for knighthood. Because the king has decreed that women cannot inherit property and her parents have no sons, they resolve to pass her off as a male and raise her as they would raise a son. As the girl grows up, Nature and Nurture begin to argue over her proper condition, but Nurture, with the help of Reason, exerts power over the young Silence, and the ruse works. Nevertheless, Silence lives in constant fear of discovery, and she worries that even if the law changes, she possesses no skills that would enable her to survive as a woman. She therefore assumes another disguise and leaves her parents with a troop of *jongleurs*, from whom she resolves to learn their trade. Minstrelsy was one of the few professions open to women, and if she mastered it she could always support herself. Difficulties naturally ensue, the most delicate of which begins when the disguised Silence enters the royal court, and the queen, believing her to be a boy, tries to seduce her. When Silence refuses her advances, the queen accuses "him" of rape, a charge that Silence can, of course, prove false, but only by revealing who she really is. The "happy" ending, which troubles some modern readers, includes the execution of the queen and the marriage of Silence to the king, solving her inheritance problem.

Nature, the reader is encouraged to assume, will enable her to live as a woman from this point forward.

Strong female characters, good and evil, appear in the late-twelfth-century *lais* of Marie de France, who claims to have derived her poems from Breton oral traditions. For instance, her *lai* of *Bisclavret* features a werewolf similar to Barbeu. The beginning of *Bisclavret* finds the title character happily married to a beautiful woman. Although she loves him, she insists on knowing why he is absent from home for three days every week; the worst she can imagine is that he is seeing another woman. When he reveals that he goes to the forest, sheds his clothes, and becomes a werewolf, she is horrified and ceases to love him. With the help of another man, who wants her to become his mistress, she follows Bisclavret to the forest and steals his clothes. Without them he cannot regain the form of a man, and she is able to live with her lover while Bisclavret remains a beast in the forest.

After a year or so the king, on a hunt in this forest, sees a wolf that bows before him. Flattered, the king adopts him and takes him back to the palace, where his docility makes him a great favorite. He attacks no one—except a certain knight and his lady, who, of course, turn out to be his wife and her lover. Puzzled by this selective fierceness, the king subjects the lady to torture until she reveals what she did to her husband. Fortunately, she still has the clothes. Bisclavret regains his former shape, and the scheming couple is exiled.

Marie's *lais* are known for their lively style and economy of words—*Bisclavret* is not much longer than the summary above. An example of the opposite approach is the work of Marie's contemporary, Chrétien de Troyes, who like Marie based much of his work on Celtic legendary traditions. Chrétien is known for his creative Arthurian romances, which are as elaborate and highly developed as Marie's *lais* are efficient and concise. Like Marie, Chrétien makes use of magic and the supernatural. For instance, *Yvain, ou Le chevalier au lion* (The Knight with the Lion) includes the figure of the Wild Man, along with a magic spring, a magic ring, an evil giant, and a salve that cures madness (prepared by none other than Morgan le Fay).

Yvain initially sets out to find the magic spring to avenge the humiliation of his friend, who was put to flight by its owner. As his friend tells him, if one pours some of the water from the spring onto a nearby slab, such a tempest ensues that no animal can stay in the forest. The owner, angry at the wreckage of his forest, comes out ready to fight, and he is too big and strong for most knights to withstand. Yvain, however, fares better than his friend. He mortally wounds this knight, whom he pursues into his castle. The castle's portcullis comes down, killing Yvain's horse and trapping Yvain inside. In the manhunt that follows, Yvain is saved from capture by Lunette, maid to the lady of the castle. Lunette reminds Yvain that she once visited Arthur's court and that of all the knights, only Yvain treated her with courtesy. In gratitude, she makes him invisible and offers to let him escape. However, Yvain hesitates to return to court without proof of his exploit, and when he sees the knight's beautiful widow, Laudine, he no longer wishes to escape. Yvain realizes that wooing the widow of the man he has killed will be no easy matter. Therefore, Lunette does the wooing for him, and she prevails quickly. Meanwhile, Arthur, believing that Yvain has been killed, brings an army to avenge him, but by the time his forces arrive at the spring, Yvain is lord of the castle.

The story might have ended happily at this point, but Yvain's old friend Gawain criticizes his retirement from athletic chivalry, including jousts and tournaments. Reminding Yvain of his reputation, Gawain persuades him to leave home for a while. Laudine consents to this, giving Yvain a ring that will protect him from harm as long as he is true to her, which means, among other things, returning to her within a year. Yvain, enjoying the sport and the company of his old comrades, loses track of the time and overstays his leave. When he realizes that he has incurred eternal banishment from Laudine's presence (and an emissary of Laudine's comes to take back the ring), Yvain goes mad. He lives as a wild man in the woods until he is found and cured with Morgan's salve. After regaining his wits Yvain vows to regain his wife. Before he can do so, he must meet a number of challenges, including killing a giant and rescuing Lunette from the stake. Lunette once again applies her considerable verbal talents to the reconciliation of her mistress with Yvain. Again she prevails, and the romance ends happily.

Like Chrétien's other romances, *Yvain* not only borrows magical elements from Celtic tradition but adapts them to his particular audience, the northern French aristocracy of the late twelfth century, which included a large proportion of bachelor knights, landless young warriors who stood little chance of marrying well or acquiring castles and lands. Yvain is himself a bachelor knight, attached to a royal court but apparently landless, whose sheer skill at arms allows him to gain a fairy-like lover and the rulership of an otherworldly realm. Chrétien, in bestowing Yvain with wife and lands, creates an ideal compensation fantasy for the bachelor knights in his audience. Like the master narrators of oral tradition, even this most refined of medieval French writers crafts his poems to embody the unofficial values and aspirations of his community.

See also: Chanson de Geste; *Chanson de Roland*; Charlemagne; Chrétien de Troyes; Courtly Love; Fairy Lover; Guinefort, Saint; Marie de France; Mermaid; Romance; William of Orange

References and further reading: The miracles and rites of French kings are discussed in M. Bloch, *Les rois thaumaturges* (1924), translated by J. E. Anderson as *The Royal Touch: Sacred Monarchy and Scrofula in England and France* (1973). For the folk calendar and rituals of the city, see F. Canadé Sautman, *La religion du quotidien: Rites et croyances populaires de la fin du moyen âge* (1995). For the traditions of Guinefort, see J.-C. Schmitt, *The Holy Greyhound: Guinefort, Healer of Children since the Thirteenth Century,* trans. M. Thom (1983); for Montaillou, see E. Le Roy Ladurie, *Montaillou: The Promised Land of Error,* trans. B. Bray (1978), quotation above from page 141. G. Duby, *The Chivalrous Society,* trans. C. Postan (1977), describes the social conditions of the bachelor knights of the late twelfth century.

See also J. Berlioz, C. Bremond, and C. Velay-Vallantin, *Formes médiévales du conte merveilleux* (1989); M. Jeay, "Savoir faire: Une analyse des croyances des 'Evangiles des Quenouilles,'" *XVe Siècle* 10 (1982); J. Le Goff, *Time, Work, and Culture in the Middle Ages,* trans. A. Goldhammer (1980); C. Gaignebet and D. Lajoux, *Art profane et religion populaire au moyen âge* (1984); R. Vaultier, *Le folklore pendant la Guerre de Cent Ans d'après les lettres de rémission du trésor de Chartes* (1965); P. Walter, *Mythologie chrétienne: Rites et mythes du moyen âge* (1992).

—*Francesca Canadé Sautman*

Funeral Customs and Burial Rites

Ceremonies and rituals performed after death to aid the soul of the departed and to give comfort to the living.

Funeral rituals are a rich source of information on folk beliefs surrounding the human body, social identity, and life after death in the Middle Ages. St. Augustine, in a famous passage in his tract on the care of the dead, suggested that funeral ceremonies are "rather solaces for the living than furtherances to the dead"—a sentiment that no doubt contains an element of truth. Medieval funerals operated as markers of social status, and their ritual structure afforded elements of psychological therapy for the living participants. It is also possible that many of the ritual forms, though nominally Christian, were dictated by long-standing superstitions regarding vampires, evil spirits, and vengeful ghosts. At the same time, it should not be forgotten that most medieval customs were predominantly religious in purpose, aimed at helping the soul of the deceased in its journey to the next world.

Funeral customs are best characterized as *rites of passage*. In Arnold van Gennep's classic formulation, they comprise rituals of separation (preliminal), transition (liminal), and incorporation (postliminal). For the medieval Christian, this ritual process embraced (1) the separation of the soul from the body, (2) a transitional phase during which the soul's fate was decided, and (3) the soul's eventual incorporation into heaven. A similar pattern awaited the body: separated from the land of the living by death, the corpse underwent a liminal stage during which it was prepared for burial, before submitting to postliminal rites of incorporation in the cemetery.

Unlike modern Western attitudes, however, which focus on death as a rupture rather than a passing, medieval society afforded more significance to rites of transition and incorporation than to those of separation, reflecting the close ties between living and dead in this period. The emphasis on passage and transformation also reflects a loss of certainty in the period regarding the fate of the human soul. Whereas the Christian communities of Roman antiquity tended to celebrate death as the passage of the triumphant soul to celestial bliss, by the early Middle Ages salvation no longer seemed assured. Humankind's fallen condition required penitence, and death rituals consequently focused increasing attention on the state of the dying person's soul as it passed from one world to the next. In the years before 900 a complex of prayers, gestures, and actions emerged that formed the basis for a rite of passage that was to see the vast majority of Christians from deathbed to grave for many centuries thereafter. Although such rituals were as yet largely confined to the cloister, they became generally available to most members of the laity by the twelfth century.

From Deathbed to Funeral

The first stage in the traditional medieval death ritual began in the last hours of life. When the family, doctor, or friends sensed that death was near, it was their duty to call for the priest. After performing mass in church, the priest would solemnly transport the consecrated host to the home of the sick person. His ministrations began by holding a crucifix before the face of the dying person to provide comfort and to drive away demons. After testing their faith, extreme unction was administered (anointing with holy oil), followed by the sacrament (called the *viaticum*, Latin for "one for the road"). In the fifteenth century printed instruction manuals on the art of dying well (called *Ars moriendi*) became popular in Western Europe, and illustrated versions contain a final woodcut depicting the deathbed ritual. *Moriens* (the dying man) still grasps a lighted candle, supported by the cleric who conducts the last rites. The soul escapes from the body, to be caught by angels above, while angry demons seethe with disappointment on the floor below.

The onset of death was tested by various methods, such as holding a feather or mirror in front of the mouth to determine whether a person was still breathing. Middle English lyrics recounting the signs of death listed the visible indications that might be perceived:

When the head trembles,
And the lips grow black
The nose sharpens
And the sinews stiffen
The breast pants
And the breath is wanting,
The teeth clatter
And the throat rattles,
The soul has left
And the body holds nothing but a clout.

After death, the first action was to lay out the body and wash it. The corpse remained in the location where death had taken place, usually at home. If the body was to be kept in the house overnight, a wake, or "night watch," might be organized and candles might be lit around the corpse. In her will of 1434 the London widow Margaret Ashcombe requests "two tapers to stand at my head while my body resteth in my house of dwelling." Lit candles and tapers were commonly depicted around bodies awaiting burial in medieval manuscript illuminations, and though conventionally understood in Christian contexts as representing the "light of faith," these possibly fulfilled an apotropaic function by warding off evil spirits.

Before the body could be moved, it had to be appropriately dressed in a shroud or winding sheet. In the early Middle Ages the body was usually exhibited uncovered on a bier, both at home and on its way to the cemetery. However, by the thirteenth century in northern Europe, it was commonly sewn in a shroud and enclosed in a coffin. Once covered, the corpse might also have been laid out on a hearse. Unless the departed was wealthy, the coffin was usually only for the purpose of conveying the corpse from the place of death to the graveside, so that a reusable coffin and a public hearse were normally standard parish equipment. *Herse* is a French word signifying "harrow," and the fifteenth-century hearse simply took the form of an iron stand, with harrow-like spikes adapted as candle holders.

Once the corpse had been properly prepared, the next stage in the funeral ritual was the procession. This was a symbolic journey with both social and religious significance. Usually made up of priests, monks, friends, and relatives, it was also followed (if the deceased was wealthy) by a group of poor people who would pray for their superior's soul. At the front of the procession or at the church a bell might be sounded: this "passing bell" announced the passing of the soul into the next world, frightened off devils, and requested the prayers of those who heard it ring; sometimes it also indicated the social status of the departed by the number of tolls. The funeral ceremony was thus an important status symbol for the rich, an outward sign of the power and prestige of the deceased and the family to whom he or she belonged. But it also functioned on an eschatological level, generating prayers for salvation and providing an opportunity for good works; the poor were crucial elements in funeral pageantry and were usually rewarded with small gifts of alms in return for their attendance.

The religious function of the funeral procession is demonstrated by the fact that it was accompanied by the recitation of verses from the *Ordo defunctorum* (Office of the Dead), a collection of prayers and hymns modeled on the monastic timetable of hours. The office comprised two major components: first, the evensong of the dead known as the *placebo* (after the opening word of the service, from Psalm 116:9) and, on the next morning, the *dirige* (the opening word of Psalm 5:8, from which the English word "dirge" derives).

Depending on the status of the deceased, a funeral sermon might be delivered. An important death presented an ideal opportunity to remind the living of the transitory nature of life, and John Mirk started his sermon for burial with a salutary *memento mori*: "Good men, as ye all see, here is a mirror to us all: a corpse brought to the church." In addition, the deaths of the wealthy might be accompanied by funeral feasts (which are sometimes mentioned in wills).

Rituals of Mourning

During the funeral ceremony participants would often wear specific outfits to express their grief. In the later Middle Ages mourning dress was subject to strict sumptuary laws. The restrictions imposed by these laws guaranteed that dress was used to define and enforce social distinctions. The strict regulations of Margaret Beaufort, mother of Henry VII of England, make this clear. Issued in 1495–1510 these dictate the etiquette of mourning dress to be worn by each rank. Those of "greatest estate" had the longest trains, held by train bearers; they were also permitted the lengthiest tippets (thin, narrow attachments to the hood). In contrast, chambermaids were to have "noe manner of tippetes" at all. Books of hours reflect similar sentiments: the late-fifteenth-century *Grimani Breviary* contains a full-page miniature depicting a funeral ceremony, at the base of which is a burial scene clearly demarcating social boundaries. The chief mourners wear the deepest mourning and longest tippets, and the young boy at the front (possibly heir to the deceased) wears a tippet that extends from his hood to the back of his heels.

During the fourteenth century black became the predominant color of mourning for the wealthy, reviving the classical traditions of ancient Greece and Rome. Before this time black was probably not the norm. The Bayeux Tapestry shows Edward the Confessor's shrouded corpse being carried to Westminster Abbey on a bier by men wearing ordinary colored clothing. However, a glance at illustrations of the Office of the Dead in fifteenth-century books of hours

The death of Edward the Confessor as portrayed in the eleventh-century French Bayeux Tapestry. (Gianni Dagli Orti/Corbis)

confirms that black was the most popular color of mourning in northern Europe in the later Middle Ages, at least for the well-to-do. Indeed, in 1451 a wealthy testator commanded that the church at Somerby by Brigg be put into mourning and that "the priests array the altars and over sepulchers with black altar cloths."

Black's associations with death are ancient. Its oldest meanings are predominantly negative: darkness and night, evil and misfortune, the dark depths of hell and the unknown. Its use is also possibly connected with a deep-rooted dread of ghostly return, since it purportedly renders human beings invisible to spirits and thereby protects them from harm during the period of mourning, which corresponded to the length of time during which the corpse was thought to be dangerous. In addition, black was the color of the ascetic life, and Benedictine monks were known as *nigri monachi* (black monks) by the eleventh century. Lepers were required to wear gray or black in the fourteenth century, symbolizing the fact that they were "dead to the world." Significantly, living lepers were sometimes separated from society with elaborate funeral-like rituals: the diseased individual was led to the church chanting the penitential psalms of the funeral service, and a requiem mass was performed before the leper was taken to the cemetery to be sprinkled with a spade of earth. Thus, the color black had a long tradition of marking certain members of society off from others through its associations with humility, penance, and death.

Other than the adoption of mourning dress, grief was expressed through various bodily signs. The history of gestures in the Middle Ages is difficult to gauge, for the very reason that body language is inherently folkloric—passed down from generation to generation by ritual repetition rather than textual transmission. Nevertheless, cautious use of visual representations and textual anecdotes allows a degree of insight into the medieval language of emotion. Evidence suggests that control over one's emotions was revered for much of the Middle Ages, and uncontrollable gestures were connected with sin. Violent acts of grief such as wailing, tearing of the hair and beard, the clawing of the face and breast, and the kissing of the dead were condemned by early Church Fathers, such as John Chrysostom, who described the lamentations of women at funerals in the fifth century as "diabolic trickery." However, by the thirteenth century the appearance in art of apocryphal scenes such as the Lamentation over Christ testifies to a greater emotional tendency in art and religion. Normally in such contexts male figures, when they appear, are models of self-restraint and stoical resignation, whereas the female mourners perform dramatic acts of grief. The gender polarity is repeated in funeral and burial scenes in books of hours, which commonly depict exclusively male mourners and are consequently free of violent gesticulation. It should be stressed that manuscript images represent ideals, not social realities, and they cannot be taken as direct evidence of everyday folkloric practice, although they are clearly related.

The dead body awaiting burial was subject to various folkloric beliefs, including the idea that the corpse of a murder victim would bleed to reveal its killer. When the duke of Burgundy was present at the funeral of the duke of Orléans in 1407, dressed in black and "showing very great mourning, as it seemed," legend has it that spectators saw blood flow from the corpse, indicating foul play; it transpired that the duke of Burgundy had indeed ordained the murder.

Cemeteries and Burial

The burial of the shrouded body marked the next stage in the ritual process. The corpse was blessed in the cemetery before burial to ward off demons. Visual images of interment in manuscripts do not usually depict the presence of mourners, only a priest and his assistant. Graveyard scenes show people at their most desolate, abandoned by fellow humans and God. This reflects the liminal status of the unburied corpse—neither of this world nor yet of the next. Nowhere is this sense of desolation more striking than in the *Rohan Book of Hours* (c. 1420), where the dying man of *Ars moriendi* illustrations is famously transported to the cemetery, his naked corpse laid out on the ground amid skull and bones, as St. Michael and Satan battle it out over the fate of his soul—a surreal juxtaposition of deathbed rituals with the desolation of the grave.

Burial was one of the seven corporal acts of mercy, and it is depicted in one of the painted glass roundels from Wygston's House, Leicester (c. 1500) representing the theme. These portray a shrouded cadaver being lowered into a freshly dug grave, bones all around. A priest touches the corpse with a cross as it enters the grave, and clasps a sprig of hyssop with which he sprinkles holy water. The symbolism of hyssop relates to Psalm 51:7, "Purge me with hyssop, and I shall be clean." The widow is also in attendance, and behind the priest stands the benefactor who holds a lit candle and a rosary.

In ancient Mediterranean cultures the dead were buried outside the precincts of the living in burial complexes, or *necropoli* (cities of the dead). However, unlike Jews and pagans, for whom contact with corpses was strictly taboo, Christians regarded the bodies of martyrs as sacred and holy—intercessors between living and dead. This eventually gave rise to the burial of the sainted dead within the city walls, in basilican churches, so that between the fourth and sixth centuries the creation of holy sites dedicated to "the very special dead" completely transformed the urban topography of pagan antiquity. The desire to be buried *ad sanctos* (near the saints) led to the eventual admission of the dead bodies of the whole Christian populace into the communities of the living.

Grave goods are not normally discovered in Christian graves, with the exception of members of the Christian hierarchy such as clerics, bishops, and kings, who were buried with the insignia of rank. A good example is Archbishop Walter de Gray (d. 1255), whose tomb in York Minster was opened in 1968. His coffin contained a pastoral staff, ring, chalice, paten, and fragments of fabric. Such adornments were probably worn "in readiness to meet Christ." In contrast, the bodies of normal people were usually buried naked in the shroud, and excavations of Anglo-Saxon cemeteries indicate that pagan-style burials, in which the body was clothed and buried with grave goods, ceased in England during the early eighth century. Notable exceptions include pilgrim burials, such as the one discovered at Worcester Cathedral, where the body was found complete with boots, coat, staff, and scallop shell.

By the later Middle Ages the orientation of graves was consistent: head points west, feet east, in anticipation of resurrection. Excavations of cemeteries for criminals, however, suggest different orientations: at St. Margaret in Combusto, Norwich, "where those who have been hanged are buried," bodies were buried east-west, north-south, or south-north, and some were thrown into the grave facefirst (an example of the phenomenon of *widdershins*, or ritualistic reversing). Such treatment suggests that old ideas died hard regarding the life of the body after death. Indeed, excavations of Anglo-Saxon cemeteries from the seventh century suggest a transition period when pagan practices still lingered among ostensibly Christian communities: superstitious behaviors, from decapitating corpses to providing pagan amulets, suggest that people had their doubts about the power of the new religion over the potentially revenant dead who had been denied traditional pagan burials.

R. C. Finucane has shown how the different forms of burial accorded to various social groups reaffirmed "the secular and spiritual order by means of a corpse." The ceremonial burial of kings was poles apart from the disrespect shown to criminals; the enshrinement of saints in the holiest part of the church contrasted wildly with the refusal of Christian burial to heretics, excommunicates, pagans, Jews, and unbaptized infants. Women who died in childbirth and suicides were also technically condemned to burial outside the perimeter of the churchyard for most of the Middle Ages, though in practice it seems that these regulations were rarely adhered to. Strict punishment of suicides after death, which could entail stakes through the heart and burial at crossroads, was only strictly enforced in the late fifteenth century.

The Legend of the Three Living and the Three Dead, *a thirteenth-century fresco located in the Monastery of St. Benedict, Subiaco, Italy. (Corbis/Archivo Iconografico, S.A.)*

After the church, the medieval cemetery was the most sacred place in most towns and villages, and if it was polluted by bloodshed, no one could be buried there for months or even years after. A special ceremony had to be performed— usually consisting of public penance by the perpetrator—to remove the pollution.

Burial grounds were also important social spaces, used for games, markets, and even the pasturing of animals. This reflects the close ties between living and dead in the Middle Ages. In the twelfth century, according to the *Chronicle of Jocelin of Brakelond,* on Boxing Day (December 26) there were gatherings in a cemetery in Bury Saint Edmunds: there were "wrestling bouts and matches between the Abbot's servants and the burgesses of the town; and from words they came to blows, and from buffets to wounds and bloodshed." By way of punishment the people involved were stripped naked and scourged, and the abbot "publicly forbade gatherings and shows in the cemetery."

Remembrance

Commemoration of the deceased marked the final stage in the funeral ritual. Strictly speaking, "funeral" in the Middle Ages did not denote a single event pinpointed in time but a process that might be drawn out over weeks or even years. The section of the Office of the Dead known as the "dirge" continued to be recited at the week, month, and year anniversaries of a person's death, and a requiem mass might be performed for a period after burial, according to the individual wishes of the deceased. This continued performance of the requiem mass stimulated the foundation of chantries, which, while of direct benefit to the soul of the deceased in purgatory, also allowed the bereaved to be constantly involved in the welfare of the dead.

For those who did not have the means to pay for the endowment of a chantry, the parochial bederoll served a similar purpose, listing members of the parish for whose souls prayers were to be said. That this form of remembrance was not beyond the means of the poor is suggested by the fourteenth-century poem *St. Erkenwald*, which states: "Yet plenty of poor people are put in graves here / Whose memory is immortally marked in our death-lists."

The wish to attract intercessory prayer also affected the design of tombs, which were often erected in the same space as chantry chapels. The exact function of tomb iconography is a matter of some controversy. Whereas Erwin Panofsky argues that tombs were concerned primarily with looking forward to the afterlife and promoting the rank and family name of their inhabitants, Philipe Ariès sees after the eleventh century "a return to the individuality of the grave," speaking of the stark contrast between the later period and the anonymity of the early Middle Ages, where only the graves of saints and very great persons were identified.

See also: Blood; *Memento Mori;* Purgatory; Spirits and Ghosts

References and further reading: The literature on funeral customs and burial rites employs a variety of general explanatory models. For an apotropaic interpretation, emphasizing the fear of revenants and the undead expressed by burial practices, see B. S. Puckle, *Funeral Customs* (1926), a wide-ranging survey that, though dated and opinionated, still has its uses for folklorists. P. Barber, *Vampires, Burial, and Death* (1988), presents more-up-to-date research in the area (though his material, like Puckle's, is largely postmedieval). C. Daniell, *Death and Burial in Medieval England, 1066–1550* (1997), takes a more theological line, attempting to relate burial practices (as evidenced by testamentary and archaeological evidence) to changes in Christian belief surrounding the afterlife, as does F. S. Paxton, *Christianizing Death* (1990), which provides the most comprehensive survey to date of the liturgical aspects of death rituals as they developed before the ninth century. The latter, however, should be used with caution in discussions of popular practice, describing as it does ideals more than lived actualities. Paxton also applies and contextualizes the anthropological schema of A. van Gennep, *The Rites of Passage* (1960), which affords a useful structural model of funeral rituals.

P. Brown, *The Cult of the Saints* (1981), investigates the impact of the cult of martyrs on death and burial, as well as the progressive incorporation of the dead into the societies of the living, in the first centuries of Christianity. P. Ariès, *The Hour of Our Death* (1981), is a rich source for the study of cemeteries, deathbed rites, and tomb iconography; see also R. C. Finucane, "Sacred Corpse, Profane Carrion: Social Ideals and Death Rituals in the Later Middle Age," in *Mirrors of Mortality,* J. W. Whaley, ed. (1981), which analyzes the symbolic content of burial rites for different social groups. For a review of funeral provisions in late-medieval wills, see C. Gittings, *Death, Burial, and the Individual in Early Modern England* (1984), and for chantries, see G. H. Cook, *Medieval Chantries and Chantry Chapels* (1947), and E. Duffy, *The Stripping of the Altars* (1992). The *Ars moriendi* is comprehensively outlined in M. C. O'Connor, *The Art of Dying Well* (1942).

P. Binski, *Medieval Death* (1996), and M. Camille, *Master of Death* (1996), provide lively introductions to depictions of death and burial in medieval visual culture; a detailed survey of representations of burial in manuscript imagery can be found in G. K. Fiero, "Death Ritual in Fifteenth-Century Manuscript Illumination," *Journal of Medieval History* 10 (1984), and memorial iconography is afforded in-depth treatment in E. Panofsky, *Tomb Sculpture* (1964). An extensive study of medieval funeral attire remains to be written, but good starting places include L. Taylor, *Mourning Dress* (1983), and P. Cunnington and C. Lucas, *Costumes for Births, Marriages, and Deaths* (1972). For an account of mourning gestures in painting, see M. Barasch, *Gestures of Despair in Medieval and Early Renaissance Art* (1976), and for the significance of the color black, see J. Harvey, *Men in Black* (1995).

—*Robert Mills*

Games and Play

Pastimes either planned or spontaneous, operating in a space and time set apart from the routine, subject to their own rules, and involving any or all of the elements of mental or physical competition, display, or imitation.

Like our modern word *play*, the Latin word *ludus* (play) and its vernacular equivalents, including the word *game*, could refer to a wide range of activities in the Middle Ages: a seasonal festival, a theatrical drama, a board game, an outdoor sport, a joke, or almost any form of amusement.

Throughout the Middle Ages games were both condemned and defended. Preachers frequently discussed idle pastimes as part of the deadly sin of sloth. Late-medieval woodcuts show demons encouraging gamesters to play dice, and sermons and educational treatises warn against overindulging in summer games and other entertainments. Monarchs, religious authorities, and town officials issued numerous prohibitions of games, sometimes mandating severe penalties such as imprisonment and even death. Yet there is ample evidence that people continued to indulge in traditional pastimes despite urban and clerical bans, and arguments for the psychological and social benefits of play are found throughout the period. For example, the fifth-century monk John Cassian recorded a story comparing the human mind to a bent bow, which must occasionally be released to avoid its becoming lax and ineffective. In 1444 a Parisian cleric similarly defended the Feast of Fools, an annual ceremony that parodied the religious service. After likening devout Christians to wine barrels about to burst with the pressures of piety, he argued that play was an essential release valve: "We permit folly on certain days so that we may later return with greater zeal to the service of God."

Medieval games—as the historian Thomas S. Henricks puts it, "who gets to play what with whom before whom (and in what ways)"—can tell us a great deal about social relations in the Middle Ages. Some games were limited, by custom or by strict regulation, to participants of a certain age, gender, or social level. For example, noblemen competed against one another in exclusive jousts and tournaments, where entry depended on status. On the other hand, many games were enjoyed by a large portion of medieval society. Men and women, monarchs and peasants alike, indulged passionately in dice games, whose popularity is attested by accounts of court cases, records of gambling debts, and the large number of dice found at archaeological sites.

Just as important as who played certain games were the social functions these games performed for participants and spectators. Leisure pastimes could reinforce social hierarchies, a role that the historian Mervyn James has posited for the Corpus Christi celebrations of medieval English towns, in which citizens processed in order of status. Or games could seemingly turn social hierarchies upside down, as did Hocktide, a spring celebration that involved women pursuing and capturing men. Some pastimes, such as annual football matches between neighboring villages, could regulate potentially deadly rivalries, but games could also cause tensions to erupt in violence. In the 1260s in London a man killed a woman during a quarrel arising from a game of chess, and in Basel in 1376 Carnival celebrations caused a riot. Thus, although games occurred in a time and space separated from the everyday (a holiday afternoon, a field temporarily given over to sport), they could also reinforce or even amplify the everyday conflicts and bonds of the medieval community. In fact, games were sometimes used as symbolic representations of society: medieval scholars wrote chess moralities in which each social class (pawns, knights, king, and so on) performed its own particular function in a common battle against the devil.

Village and Urban Games

Village and urban games and festivities most frequently occurred on Sundays and holidays, particularly during the Carnival season (the days preceding Lent) and during the spring and summer months. In his account of London life written around 1180 William Fitzstephen lists numerous carnival and warm-weather diversions: young men occupied themselves with football, horse racing, cockfighting, mock battles, leaping, archery, wrestling, stone throwing, and javelin throwing; young women occupied themselves with dancing. Fitzstephen also mentions winter games: bull and bear baiting, ice skating, and ice tilting (mock combat using poles). These pastimes, along with many others, were enjoyed not only in twelfth-century London but throughout medieval Europe.

Competitive games added to a sense of community, and whole villages or urban neighborhoods might turn out to support the participants. In England annual football matches took place between neighboring villages by at least the fourteenth century, and in the fifteenth century married and unmarried men played against one another at weddings. Medieval football (an ancestor of soccer) involved two teams, of unspecified and sometimes quite large size, attempting to move a ball across a boundary. Judging by court records, the game was loosely organized and often brutal. Though it provided an alternative to (and may have even developed from) unregulated fighting, it sometimes led to riots, accidental deaths, and even homicides.

Bowls (*boules*), another ball game, was exceedingly popular, especially in France. In a common version, competitors tried to throw their balls closest to a target, either a stake or a smaller ball, while at the same time attempting to knock their opponents' balls away. Variants of bowls eventually evolved into modern croquet and bowling.

In addition to competitive games, holiday festivities in the Middle Ages included such other forms of play and spectacle as mumming, theatrical performances, processions, puppet shows, acrobatics, minstrelsy, performances of trained animals, and elections of mock rulers.

Medieval villagers and townspeople also engaged in more sedentary pastimes, both indoors and outdoors. Men and women played dice, backgammon (or tables), morris (or merels), and—to a lesser extent—chess. Morris, an expanded version of our tic-tac-toe, involved creating rows of pieces and capturing the opponent's rows. Wooden morris boards survive from the tenth century, and morris boards have been found scratched into the floors of cloisters and watchtowers. Card games became popular only in the late fourteenth century.

Almost all medieval games involved gambling, with both participants and spectators wagering on the outcomes. Money was the most common wager, though *boules* games in France were frequently played for wine. Dice, the quintessential betting game, was repeatedly and unsuccessfully banned. Some gaming laws were more concerned with cheating and swindling than with gambling or the game itself: in medieval Hungary those found using fixed dice could be punished by being dunked in hot water or having a die struck through their palm.

Medieval authorities occasionally mandated participation in village and urban games, a command blurring the line between work and play. During the Hundred Years' War the king of England ordered that men making less than a certain income practice archery during their free time. To ensure cooperation, many other holiday pastimes, such as handball and football, were banned under pain of imprisonment. At the same time the king of France also promoted archery practice and prohibited popular games such as dice and *boules*. In the minds of these rival monarchs, the safety of their realms depended on the control of village pastimes.

Courtly Games

The perceived link between play and military prowess was made even clearer in the case of courtly pastimes. Furthermore, just as village games could contribute to camaraderie and a sense of local identity, so some courtly games were a way for noble men and women to confirm their membership in the aristocracy.

Hunting was one such elite sport; it was thought to refine military skills and noble virtues. Kings and noblemen hunted on restricted land—the most extensive was the king's forest established by William the Conqueror in England—and had exclusive rights to certain prey, such as the stag and the boar. Trespassers and poachers could be severely punished. Interestingly, poaching itself became a risky and prestigious game for the lower classes, who were legally permitted to hunt only vermin, such as wolf, fox, and badger.

Another activity important to upper-class identity was chess. The game penetrated Western Europe sometime before the year 1000, probably through the Islamic cultures of Spain and Sicily, and is first recorded among churchmen. After early and unsuccessful attempts by Church officials to control its popularity, chess spread to lay society through the monasteries, schools, and universities of the twelfth century. Although chess was played in towns and villages as well as in noble homes, the mastery of chess remained a sign of courtly refinement for noblemen and -women. Manuscript illuminations depict chess games in gardens, and medieval romances portray chess as a typical aristocratic pastime.

Despite these examples it is often difficult to draw a clear distinction between high and low culture in the Middle Ages. Nobles and peasants observed the same religious holidays and frequently attended the same celebrations. Entertainments such as minstrelsy, mumming, dancing, and dramatic performances were enjoyed both in towns and at the royal court. Furthermore, many courtly pastimes differed from village ones only in the playing space and in the quality and availability of specialized equipment. Tennis, a game that originated in France and swept Europe during the fourteenth century, is a good example: while the upper classes played with expensive rackets on standardized courts and used an elaborate scoring system, the lower classes played handball—an earlier version of the game—in streets and fields. Even the elaborate tournaments of medieval knights were mirrored in the sword-and-buckler play of the towns and villages.

Children's Games

Like children of other time periods, medieval children of all classes engaged in imitative and competitive play, sometimes involving special toys. As spectators or participants, children were fully involved in the festive life of their communities, and in their play they copied not only the work but also the leisure activities of their elders. For example, the game of marbles—whose popularity is demonstrated by the hundreds of marbles uncovered at archaeological sites— was probably a miniaturization of the adult game of bowling.

Children's Games (1560), a famous painting by Pieter Brueghel the Elder, depicts more than 80 children's games, many of which date to the Middle Ages. Medieval manuscript illuminations show infants being amused with rattles and

Children's Games; *sixteenth-century oil painting on oak wood by Pieter Brueghel the Elder.* *(Erich Lessing/Art Resource, NY)*

toddling with wheeled walkers and older children playing with balls, tops, hob-byhorses, whistles, drums, cymbals, hoops, jump ropes, kites, and marbles.

Some toys, such as dolls, were designed for imitative play and reflected the world that medieval children grew up in. Archaeologists in France and Germany have discovered small clay knights, women, and animals dating from the thirteenth century, along with tiny clay vessels that might have been toy dishes. Figures of knights on horseback and other military toys were probably used to fight mock wars and tournaments. An illustration in a twelfth-century German manuscript shows two children manipulating toy knights with strings, and in 1383 the young Charles VI was given a wooden cannon to play with.

Like adult games, children's games could involve an element of violence. In hoodman-blind, a medieval version of blindman's bluff, the child who was "it" was "blinded" by a hood and tried to catch the other children, who hit at him or her with their own knotted hoods. Children also engaged in animal sports, hunting small game with child-sized crossbows, and holding their own cockfighting matches. On Shrove Tuesday, the day before Lent, medieval English schoolboys brought their cocks to school, where the birds would fight to the death.

See also: Carnival; Festivals and Celebrations; Fools, Feast of; Harvest Festivals and Rituals; Masking; Puppets and Puppet Plays; Sword Dance

References and further reading: J. Huizinga, *Homo Ludens* (1950), is an influential analysis of play in culture; M. James, "Ritual, Drama, and Social Body in the Late Medieval Town," *Past and Present* 98 (1983), relates medieval festivity to social integration. G. Olson, *Literature as Recreation in the Later Middle Ages* (1982), examines medieval theories of recreation. Recent surveys of medieval games include T. McLean, *The English at Play in the Middle Ages* (1983); T. S. Henricks, *Disputed Pleasures: Sport and Society in Preindustrial England* (1991); J. Carter, *Medieval Games* (1992); and A. C. Reeves, *Pleasures and Pastimes in Medieval England* (1998). R. Hutton, *The Stations of the Sun* (1996), and the essays in M. Twycross, ed., *Festive Drama* (1996), discuss seasonal holidays. The volumes of the REED (Records of Early English Drama) series (beginning in 1979) contain valuable primary sources for medieval England. P. Burke, *Popular Culture in Early Modern Europe* (1978), focuses on a later period but includes some medieval pastimes. R. Vaultier, *Le folklore pendant la Guerre de Cent Ans* (1965), examines games mentioned in French legal documents, while S. Petényi, *Games and Toys in Medieval and Early Modern Hungary* (1994), discusses Hungarian documents and artifacts. Studies of specific pastimes include J. Cummins, *The Hound and the Hawk* (1988); R. Eales, *Chess* (1985); R. McConville, *The History of Board Games* (1974); N. Elias and E. Dunning, "Folk Football in Medieval and Early Modern Britain," in *The Sociology of Sport*, ed. E. Dunning (1971); A. Fraser, *A History of Toys* (1966); and W. Tauber, *Das Würfelspiel im Mittelalter und in der frühen Neuzeit* (1987). Though somewhat outdated, J. Strutt, *The Sports and Pastimes of the People of England* (1801), and E. K. Chambers, *The Mediaeval Stage*, 2 vols. (1903), remain valuable resources.

—*Karen Bezella-Bond*

Garden of Eden

The earthly paradise mentioned in the Bible where God created Adam and Eve, forbidding them to eat of the Tree of the Knowledge of Good and Evil; and when they did so, from which they were banished, condemned to lives of hardship and eventual death.

LAPSVS HVMA=
NÎ GENERÍS ∴

Hans Baldung Grien, Adam and Eve. *(German woodcut, 1511; National Gallery of Art, Washington, Rosenwald Collection)*

The idea of an earthly paradise that still existed in faraway lands was both believed literally and accounted for geographically throughout the Middle Ages. The Garden of Eden—along with the Elysian Fields, the Happy Isles, and the kingdom of Prester John—was often found on medieval maps, although various cartographers differed in their placement of these sites. This medieval belief was primarily nourished by three major attitudes: nostalgia for a lost earthly paradise, the expectation of a kingdom of happiness to be reestablished on earth as a kind of New Eden and lasting a millennium, and the hope of a heavenly Paradise as the reward of the Christian faithful.

Even before Christianity, sacred gardens had been part of other religions as well. The Sumerian myth of Enki, the *Epic of Gilgamesh,* and ancient Mesopotamian and Persian religions all mention gardens containing magical trees and overflowing with plants and water. However, none of these gardens contains such a Tree of Knowledge. By Greco-Roman times the ideas of golden ages and Elysian Fields or Happy Isles were sometimes combined in literature. By the early-medieval period these mythical places had been adopted by Christian culture, which blended them with the concept of an actual Garden of Eden. Medieval philosophers and theologians expounded on such specifics of chronology as when the earthly paradise was created, how much time passed between the creation of Adam and the creation of Eve, and how much time lapsed between Eve's creation and the expulsion from Eden.

Medieval depictions of Eden in art and literature focused especially on the temptation, the Fall, and the expulsion. In the fifteenth-century book of hours known as the *Très riches heures* of Jean, duke of Berry, a full-page illumination (folio 25v) follows the conventional iconography, showing Adam and Eve innocently and openly nude before the Fall, Eve accepting the forbidden fruit from a devil who is half woman and half serpent, Eve offering the fruit to Adam, God judging them while they try to cover their nakedness with their hands, and finally their being driven, now clothed with aprons of leaves, from the garden by a red angel. In a stained glass window in Canterbury Cathedral Adam appears digging with a spade to signify his need to labor for food as one of the consequences of the Fall.

Though both official and popular Christianity stressed the banishment from Eden, there remained a hope for regaining that earthly paradise. By the central to late Middle Ages, expeditions sent east into Asia and west across the Atlantic with the aim of discovering this earthly paradise were often conducted in conjunction with enterprises involving trade, exploration, and conquest. Medieval cartographers placed Eden variously on the far edge of the Asian continent, on an island in the middle of the Atlantic or Indian Ocean, or in the far north or far south.

See also: Books of Hours; Mythography; Prester John; Travel Literature
References and further reading: An excellent overview of this material is J. Delumeau, *History of Paradise: The Garden of Eden in Myth and Tradition* (1995).

—*Bradford Lee Eden*

Gargoyles

Stone, marble, or (rarely) metal waterspouts found on medieval ecclesiastical and secular buildings.

From the late twelfth century onward gargoyles served to drain rainwater from roofs and direct it away from walls. Their practical function was usually masked by decoratively carving the gutter's top surface and by making the exit hole correspond to an anatomically correct hole on the figure's body. Though gargoyles are generally carved as whole sculptures, less frequently they consist of two halves fit together, as seamlessly as possible, around the central gutter (e.g., at Laon Cathedral, c. 1210).

Generally overlooked in art history studies, gargoyles are occasionally cited in research on single folkloric themes. Gargoyles can be considered only in part a kind of medieval marginalia: situated on the upper edges of tall walls, they bear comparison to manuscript margins' decorations, misericords, keystones, and other elements adorning the peripheries of buildings, books, and furniture; yet the subjects that carvers and architects chose for gargoyles overlap only slightly with the subjects depicted in other medieval marginalia. It is also difficult, given the present state of research, to identify thematic relationships among gargoyles belonging to the same building. Thematic studies have been limited to isolated figures or sometimes to types of gargoyle. Particular care must be taken when making a folkloric interpretation of gargoyles, as those that appear in published studies constitute only a small percentage of the actual total, and there is great uncertainty about their chronology. Furthermore, postmedieval restorations (for example, Eugène-Emmanuel Viollet-le-Duc's restoration of Notre-Dame in Paris in 1845–1864) have drastically changed the original appearance of certain gargoyles and replaced others altogether, so that many of the most famous "medieval" gargoyles were in actuality carved long after the Middle Ages. The literature on gargoyles seldom refers to such restorations. An attempt at a thematic classification can therefore be no more than a working hypothesis until art history research provides surer grounds for interpretation.

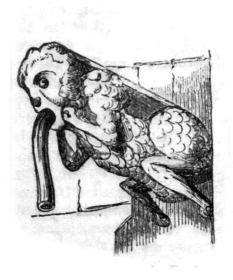

Animal-inspired waterspout on St. Alkmunds Church, Derby, circa 1450. (Archive Photos)

Gargoyles frequently appear in animal form. There are animals belonging to real species native to Europe, dogs being the most popular (the sculptures on the cathedrals of Laon in France and Mechelen in Belgium are particularly noteworthy), but goats, donkeys, cows, pigs, and birds also abound. Among the most popular nonnative species are lions (for example, the thirteenth-century figures, largely restored, on the eastern end of Rheims Cathedral or the fourteenth-century compositions on Saint Mary's Church, Over, Cambridgeshire) and monkeys (on the Hauptmarkt fountain in Nuremberg or the fourteenth-century monkey-like beings at Vincennes castle). Particularly common are fantastical species, such as

*Gargoyle as a caricature of a nun on Horsley
Church, Derbyshire, circa 1450. (Archive Photos)*

dragons and unicorns. Medieval
bestiaries, which provide moralizing
and allegorical descriptions of both
real and imaginary animals, provide a
good key to the basic symbolism of all
these species. Motifs overtly recalling
specific folkloric themes seem to be
more rare: for example, the folktale
motif of the animal musicians (motif
B297.1), which appears as a sow with
a harp at Notre-Dame-de-l'Épine,
France (sixteenth century).

Hybrid animal types are especially
common: creatures constructed of
parts of different animals, like the thirteenth-century bird with four legs on
Burgos Cathedral, Spain, or the
figures at Ely cathedral. Particularly common are four-legged animals equipped
to fly: cows (Utrecht, Netherlands), dogs (Milan, Italy), fish (Lier, Belgium),
lions (den Bosch, Netherlands), and goats (Mechelen, Belgium) all appear with
wings. According to some interpretations, these composite creatures have an
overtly negative, if not a precisely diabolical, significance, representing confusion and disharmony.

Along with nonhuman animal hybrids, there are hybrids composed of human and nonhuman parts. Only seldom do these partly human gargoyles represent creatures known from classical and medieval mythology, that is, such figures
as sirens, centaurs, mermen (Milan), or harpies (e.g., Brussels town hall, sixteenth century). More often they appear as "disordered" combinations. Many
of these grotesque creatures display features—such as horns, pointed ears, and
fangs—belonging to the iconography of the devil, and they have frightening
expressions; see the fourteenth-century gargoyles of the church of Saint Ouen
in Rouen or the gargoyles on the facade of the twelfth-century church of Saint
Martin in Laon.

Fairly common are images of human beings covered with scales or hair,
identifiable as Wild Men or as their close relatives, Green Men—for example,
the gargoyle apparently converted into a well spout in the courtyard of the
Hôtel de Cluny in Paris. The Wild Man, especially, is a pervasive folkloric figure in other contexts; it appears often in festivals, pageants, and carvings as well
as in the form of gargoyles.

Human beings are rarely represented as physically handsome. A few such
good-looking gargoyles are found on the thirteenth-century facade of Salisbury
Cathedral, the fourteenth-century cathedral of Freiburg im Breisgau, and the
thirteenth-century church of Saint Ursin in Troyes. More often the human figure undergoes various deformations. These can consist of a grotesque alteration
of the face or of other parts of the body, resulting in general somatic ugliness, or
of gestures considered indecorous because they are exceedingly expressive,

overtly mocking, or obscene. Among the first we find expressions of terror or rage; among the second, figures pulling their mouths to grotesque widths or sticking out their tongues. Among the most famous obscene creatures are the men exposing their anuses and apparently defecating—for example, outside the cathedrals of Autun (thirteenth–fourteenth centuries) and Freiburg im Breisgau (fourteenth century).

Because of their pronounced ugliness, these figures have been seen as general depictions of sin and its punishment or as representations of particular sins. This latter hypothetical interpretation is perhaps based on a reading of the gargoyles' nakedness or of certain gestures the gargoyles eternally assume—for example, touching their throats with their fingers in a gesture that could be interpreted as representing the deadly sin of *gula*, or gluttony. Sometimes gargoyles are seen as generic representations of vice—vice embodied in the physical deformity of the human figure, a sort of "reverse image" of the well-ordered harmony of creation. Moreover, the deformed human figure in gargoyles would be a reminder of punishments awaiting the sinner after death; thus, such figures would have been seen by contemporaries as damned souls, changed into hideous stone figures and forbidden from entering the church.

There are many more interpretations of monstrous gargoyles, which are based on the relationship between the inside and the outside of the building: that these are apotropaic demons keeping guard over the church or diabolical beings or worldly temptations waiting outside the church.

The apparently scatological gargoyles—for example, the defecating men at Autun and Freiburg—have generally been interpreted as functioning apotropaically (that is, to ward off evil) or simply as being gestures of mockery. They have been related to the many similar examples known from medieval folklore and iconography. Yet more complicated interpretations have seen these figures as conveying initiatory meanings related to ritual anal presentation and kissing.

More clearly connected to folklore are rare complex scenes, such as that of a woman copulating with a goat (a well-known embodiment of the devil)—an act commonly attributed to witches throughout the last centuries of the Middle Ages and beyond—at the church of Notre-Dame-de-Marais in Villefranche-sur-Saône (France, sixteenth century). There is also a group apparently representing a deer-hunting scene, transposed in a vertical sequence at Freiburg im Breisgau Cathedral, that evokes not only representations of hunting from Roman art but also episodes of medieval literature, folktales, and hagiography. Consider as well the male figure carrying a fool on his shoulders at Saint-Germain-l'Auxerrois in Paris (fifteenth century).

It is also a difficult task to establish thematic connections between the gargoyle and the sculpted console that sometimes supports it because the two are not always contemporaries. This is the case with the facade of Poitiers Cathedral (thirteenth century) or with Saint-Père-sous-Vézelay (fourteenth century).

Even if we concede the difficulty of evaluating medieval gargoyles as a repertory of folkloric themes, we can still see them as an expression of a certain medieval taste for deformity and the grotesque—terrifying and comic at once. This taste has been much examined in a large variety of studies of medieval culture. Meanwhile, great care should be taken in interpreting gargoyles as a space freely given to sculptors' imagination on the margins of Gothic buildings—buildings that are otherwise carefully mapped out to the last detail. In approaching gargoyles, we should follow the lead of those who have studied the grotesque figures of manuscript marginalia and consider the degree of conventionality of certain themes, the possible existence of a tradition internal to the genre that probably carried far more weight than is presently thought. Such a tradition certainly had its roots in what we call popular culture, but precisely detecting and classifying its themes and their significance and origins seems a particularly difficult undertaking, at least for the moment

See also: Green Man; Iconography; Manuscript Marginalia; Mermaid; Misericords; Wild Man; Wild Woman

References and further reading: The latest contribution on gargoyles is J. R. Benton, *Holy Terrors: Gargoyles on Medieval Buildings* (1997), which provides examples, images, an introduction to the main interpretative problems, and a bibliography but lacks a systematic distinction between medieval gargoyles and modern restorations. Although geographically limited, L. B. Bridaham, *Gargoyles, Chimères, and the Grotesque in French Gothic Sculpture* (1930; rpt. 1969), is a still extremely useful repertory, with careful differentiation of original from restored pieces. For a strictly architectural and art-historical study, a basic reference remains E.-E. Viollet-le-Duc, *Dictionnaire raisonné de l'architecture française* (1854–1868), s.v. "gargouille." More recently, see M. Camille, *Images on the Edge* (1992). N. Kenaan-Kedar, *Marginal Sculpture in Medieval France* (1995), gives a vast catalog, but the book suffers from ideological interpretations that are too rigidly formalistic. For a cultural approach of greater breadth, J. Baltrusaitis, *Réveils et prodiges* (1960), remains unsurpassed. In general there is a sort of scholarly reluctance to include gargoyles in treatments of subjects that would naturally consider them; consider their very limited treatment in F. Klingender, *Animals in Art and Thought to the End of the Middle Ages* (1971), or in C. Gaignebet and J.-D. Lajoux, *Art profane et religion populaire au moyen âge* (1985).

—*Chiara Piccinini*

Gawain [French Gauvain]

Nephew of King Arthur and a paragon of Round Table chivalric virtues.

Some scholars speculate that the character of Gawain is linked to that of a Celtic solar deity (given that his strength sometimes waxes and wanes with the energy of the sun) or with the Irish hero Cú Chulainn. However, he first appears in Arthurian literature in the early twelfth century as Walwanus, a warrior and kinsman of Arthur in the chronicles of Geoffrey of Monmouth, *Historia regum Britanniae* (History of the Kings of Britain).

By the time he appears in France in the mid-twelfth-century *Roman de Brut* of Wace, Gauvain (to use the French version of his name, appropriately, here) has become an exemplar of courtliness. Chrétien de Troyes portrays him as a model for his central heroes, Erec, Lancelot, and Yvain. Although he begins these romances in a position of preeminence, his role in many romances becomes secondary when he is surpassed by the central hero. Gauvain becomes associated with certain flaws, especially a tendency toward dalliance with female admirers. Gauvain's worldliness disqualifies him from the spiritual quest for the Grail in Chrétien's *Le conte du Graal* and its continuations. In the later

Grail romances, particularly the Vulgate cycle, Gauvain's wantonness and other faults are increasingly apparent. Though Gauvain is the hero of other French romances, such as *La mule sans frein* (The Mule without a Bridle) and *Le chevalier à l'épée* (The Knight of the Sword), his dignity is undercut by humor in these works.

Gawain remains popular in Arthurian literature throughout Europe. In Germanic cultures he is a less flawed and more exalted hero. He has a major role in German romances, including Wolfram von Eschenbach's *Parzival* and Hartmann von Aue's *Erec*. Heinrich von dem Türlin gives him the central role in *Diu Crône* (The Crown), where he finally succeeds in the Grail quest. The Middle Dutch *Roman van Walewein* offers further evidence of his widespread appeal.

Late-medieval English romances seem to retain an awareness of Gawain's reputation for dalliance, as the hero is tempted by a lady in *Sir Gawain and the Green Knight*, and he weds or beds a variety of uncourtly maidens in the tail-rhyme romances *The Wedding of Sir Gawain and Dame Ragnell, Sir Gawain and the Carle of Carlisle*, and *The Jeaste of Sir Gawain*. Nevertheless, in these tales Gawain proves loyal and monogamous. Here, as in the alliterative romances *The Awntyrs off Arthure* and *Golagras and Gawaine* and in the final books of Malory's *Le Morte Darthur*, Gawain emerges primarily as a warrior supremely devoted to his uncle Arthur and other members of his family.

Thus, medieval romance presents two Gawains, reflecting two distinct cultural perspectives. The French Gauvain serves as the flawed foil for greater knights, while the Germanic Gawain upholds values of warrior prowess and

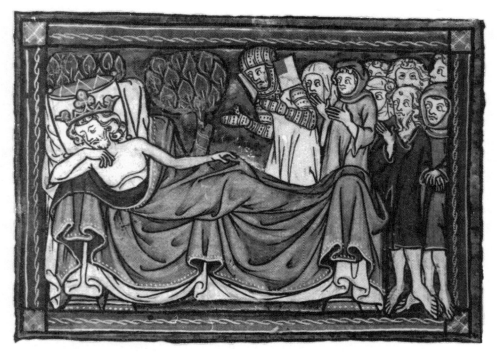

Arthur tarries at the Castle of Dover after sending the body of Gauvain to Camelot and before going to fight Mordred. (Reproduced by courtesy of the Director and University Librarian, the John Rylands University Library of Manchester; French MS 1, fol. 255v)

tribal loyalty. Gawain particularly excels in such nonnoble creations as *Gawain and Ragnell,* where his courage far exceeds Arthur's—an indication that Gawain probably served as a model for England's less exalted social groups as the Middle Ages drew to a close.

See also: Arthurian Lore; Loathly Lady; Romance; *Sir Gawain and the Green Knight*
References and further reading: In *Gawain in Old French Literature* (1980) K. Busby presents a comprehensive analysis of Gawain's role in French romance. E. Brewer offers useful English translations of the episodes that make up the sources and analogs of *Sir Gawain and the Green Knight* in *From Cuchulainn to Gawain* (1973). The English Gawain romances are brought together in T. Hahn, ed., *Sir Gawain: Eleven Romances and Tales* (1995). *Diu Crône* is available in an English translation, *The Crown,* by J. W. Thomas.

—*Cathalin B. Folks*

Geoffrey of Monmouth (c. 1090–1155)

Anglo-Norman writer whose *Historia regum Britanniae* (History of the Kings of England, c. 1138) professed to present a continuous historical narrative of the kings of Britain from the eponymous Brutus, great-grandson of Aeneas, to the Britons' loss of sovereignty to the English following the death of Cadawallader in 689 C.E.

Geoffrey traces the fortunes of the "ancient Britons," the forefathers of the Welsh, Cornish, and Bretons, through a succession of some 120 kings and queens over a period that extends from the sack of Troy to the seventh century. Brutus, son of Silvius, grandson of Aeneas's son Ascanius, together with his followers, flees the sack of Troy and, exiled from Rome, spends years living in Greece and wandering the Mediterranean Sea and southern Gaul before settling on the island of Albion, which is renamed Britannia. Geoffrey's narrative moves swiftly over the period of British hegemony and gives vivid accounts of wars, conquests, invasions, and civil discord. But the central figure in the history is Arthur, and the account of his antecedents and reign takes up almost half the story. The wars with the English and Arthur's temporary success—ultimately undermined by his betrayal by his nephew Modred and the resulting civil war, in which Arthur is killed—prove to be the turning point in the narrative. The years following Arthur's passing are years of final decline, and Geoffrey brings the book to a close quickly.

Geoffrey claimed to have translated his history from "an ancient book in the British language," which his friend Walter, the archdeacon of Oxford, had brought out of *Britannia* (which can mean either Wales or Brittany). But the strong thematic structure of the *Historia* (which plays recurrently on the relationship between Britain and Rome) and its firm composition (which varies periods of internal strife, wise rehabilitation, and foreign threats and which gives some prominence to the role of women leaders) preclude our taking the book to be a translation of an old Welsh or Breton chronicle. Its literary qualities and historiography suggest, rather, that its context is to be found in twelfth-century English historical writing, but that Geoffrey's book, unlike his contemporaries' work, is largely an imaginative narrative, a "prose epic" rather than a *historia*. As such, it can be read at different levels—as an outrageous forgery, a satire of contemporary historians (especially William of Malmesbury and Henry of Huntingdon), or a "British" version of the Anglo-centric histories being produced—but in terms of content it is a pastiche made up of material from a variety of sources: the Bible, Bede, *Historia Brittonum* (History of the Britons), and British legendry.

As with any other composed literary work, it is not easy to trace the *Historia*'s sources precisely, as Geoffrey freely used and adapted his reading, his general culture, and contemporary ideas. There is no doubt that he drew upon popular folkloric elements, but these may differ significantly in their status as sources and in the way in which they were utilized.

Some episodes are popular elements that Geoffrey appears simply to have taken from the general stock of themes and stories that were familiar to him and that he used in his own narrative context. Thus, the sea monster that attacks Northumbria and is killed by Morvidus need not have had any such specific existence prior to the *Historia*. The claim that Albion was inhabited by giants before the coming of Brutus may be not traditional but, rather, Geoffrey's adaptation of Genesis or perhaps of Ovid's *Metamorphoses*. If so, Corineus's combat with the most notable of these giants, Gogmagog, is not traditional but a reflection of the popularity of Cornish wrestling. Brutus himself had received a prophetic dream vision of his coming to Albion when he offered a sacrifice to the goddess Diana before sleeping in front of the altar on the skin of a hind. Dream visions during sleep on an animal skin are part of medieval folklore, but they have a wider context in medieval dream literature and belief, and Brutus's dream is another example of Geoffrey's use of contemporary themes (or of a literary source such as *Aeneid*, Book 7) to give verisimilitude to his account. Geoffrey includes a number of other prophetic dreams in the *Historia* (though not occasioned by any divinatory practice), and it is interesting that Geoffrey displays a degree of skepticism about their significance.

Other popular themes, taken either from literary or general oral sources and used by Geoffrey for his own purposes, are fraternal discord, donning an opponent's arms to deceive an enemy, and disguising oneself as a servant to gain access to an enemy to kill him (often by poison).

Geoffrey has used Welsh legendry whenever he could and within the limits of his own knowledge. His prime source appears to have been *Historia Brittonum*. His account of the coming of the Saxons under Hengist and Horsa, their duping of Vortigern, and the "treachery of the long knives" is an elaboration of the Nennian narrative, which appears to have been an established traditional legend with a number of popular themes. It came to Geoffrey, however, from a literary, not an oral, source. Part of the narrative is an account of Vortigern's tower and its sinking foundations. Vortigern's sages advise the king that the blood of a boy born without a father must be sprinkled on the foundations. Geoffrey draws on popular beliefs—that the boy was born of a nun and an incubus—to elaborate the account, and, in one of his favorite ploys, he gives the boy the name Merlin or Myrddin (instead of Nennius's Ambrosius) so that he may be eponymously associated with Caerfyrddin (modern Carmarthen), which could be popularly understood as "stronghold of Myrddin." From Nennius, too, comes Geoffrey's descriptions of two lakes possessing remarkable natural features. These form part of Nennius's list of *mirabilia* (marvels) and derive from popular tradition. Geoffrey, however, uses them to enliven his narrative and gives them an Arthurian context. Geoffrey's knowledge of Arthur's early campaigns comes from Nennius, but he has also some independent information about the king: his special weapons, the shield Prydwen, the lance Ron, and the sword Caliburnus, and his closest followers and family, Guinevere, Kay, Bedivere, Gawain, and Modred. Geoffrey also knows of a traditional tale about the passing of Arthur to the Isle of Avalon after the battle of Camlan, though he is careful not to prophesy his return. This section of the Arthurian narrative is given its own introductory paragraph, which may suggest that Geoffrey knew of it as a particularly significant episode in the legend of Arthur.

Geoffrey has a unique account of the begetting of Arthur. The love-stricken Uther Pendragon comes to Ygerna and seduces her in the shape and form of her husband Gorlois. Forms of this story are found elsewhere; for example, the myth in which Jove sleeps with Alcmene in the form of her husband Amphitryon and begets Hercules; or the late-Irish story of the begetting of Mongan by Manannán mac Lir in the form of Fiachna. The same plot may underlie the shapeshifting of Pwyll and Arawn in the First Branch of the Welsh Four Branches of the Mabinogi. Whether the tale of the begetting of Arthur is traditional or Geoffrey's creation cannot now be established.

Other examples of Welsh historical legendry that Geoffrey does not appear to have drawn from literary sources, but that are reflected in Welsh texts, are the role of Cassivelaunus (in Welsh, Caswallawn) in the reception of the Romans, and the story of Maxentius (in Welsh, Maxen Wledig), Conanus Meriadocus (in Welsh, Cynan Meiriadog), and the founding of Brittany.

Apart from his personal use of nonspecific popular elements and his knowledge of Welsh historical legendry, Geoffrey has a few examples of what may be genuine folk narratives, embellished and adapted to his own purposes. One such tale may be the story of Lear and his daughters; another may be the ruse by which Hengist, offered as much land as a hide might cover, cuts the skin into a single thong to mark the bounds of his citadel, thereafter called "Thanceastre." This may be a genuine etymological tale (though "Thanceastre" has not been identified), but a similar story is found in *Aeneid* Book 1 about Dido and Carthage. The story of the removal of Stonehenge (Giants' Dance) from Ireland to Salisbury Plain has no clear parallels (though the idea of stones with medicinal properties is familiar). Their actual removal is accomplished by Merlin's skill and contrivances, not by his magic, but that Geoffrey should have envisaged the transporting of such a huge monument from one part of Britain to another is striking in view of the now accepted opinion that these massive stones were somehow moved from Pembrokeshire. Whether some story about the erecting of Stonehenge was current in the twelfth century cannot be confirmed, but Geoffrey's account is intriguing.

Geoffrey has other giants—*ogres* is a better term—whose stories appear to be unreconstructed folktales. The fierce monster of Mont-Saint-Michel sank ships with rocks and devoured their crews and raped and killed Helena, niece of the king of Brittany. He is challenged by Arthur and slain in single combat. Arthur may not have been the original hero, but it seems probable that Geoffrey is drawing on a local folktale that explained the name of a small adjacent island, Tombelaine, as *Tumba Helene* (the tomb of Helen). After killing this monster, Arthur recalls an earlier combat on Mount Arvaius with the giant Ritho, who had demanded the king's beard, promising to make it the prized part of his cloak of royal beards. Arvaius was taken by Welsh translators to be Eryri, Snowdonia (in north Wales), and they render the giant's name as *Rhita* or *Rhica*. The tale is not found prior to the *Historia*, and at least some of the later Welsh stories about Rhita Gawr (the giant) owe something to Geoffrey, but the story of *Culhwch and Olwen* has an episode in which Arthur seeks the beard of the giant Dillus Farfog (Dillus the bearded) to make a leash for one of his hounds. In Welsh law and folk custom, beards were symbols of status and vitality, and Geoffrey's story fits a Welsh cultural context very well. Both of these giant stories portray an Arthur less sophisticated than the Norman king-emperor characteristic of the *Historia* but more like the leader found in early Welsh poetry, and they may be genuine pieces of folk narrative.

Geoffrey of Monmouth does not appear to have drawn heavily on popular tradition. He intended his history to be readable but acceptable, and it does not contain many fantastic episodes. His use of popular elements is judicious and is intended to enliven his narrative.

When trying to determine the relationship between the *Historia* and folk tradition, it can be just as confusing to consider texts compiled after Geoffrey as to consider his possible sources. The *Historia* was so well received that it became in effect the official history of Wales and influenced subsequent views of history and tradition. As a result it is very difficult to determine whether an item that first appears in the *Historia* and then in later texts existed orally before Geoffrey, was passed as literary text from Geoffrey to the later sources, or passed from Geoffrey into oral tradition, whence it was picked up by later writers. Sometimes one can discern folklore in the translations of the *Historia*, in which translators-copyists have changed or added to Geoffrey's work in accordance with the story as they knew it. The most striking example of this is the addition of the story of *Lludd and Llefelys*, in which the wise Llefelys advises his brother Lludd on how to rid the Island of Britain of three plagues that infest it.

See also: Arthur; Arthurian Lore; Brutus; Lear, King; Maxen Wledig; Merlin; Myrddin; Nennius

References and further reading: See J. S. P. Tatlock, *The Legendary History of Britain* (1950), especially ch. 14; C. Grooms, *The Giants of Wales* (1993), for Rhita; L. Thorpe, "Le Mont-Saint-Michel et Geoffroi de Monmouth," in *Millénaire du Mont Saint Michel* (1967); S. Piggott, "The Sources of Geoffrey of Monmouth: The Stonehenge Story," *Antiquity* 15 (1941); B. F. Roberts, *Cyfranc Lludd a Llefelys* (1975), and "Historical Writing," in *A Guide to Welsh Literature*, ed. A. O. H. Jarman and G. R. Hughes (1976).

—*Brynley F. Roberts*

George, Saint (d. 303?)

An early martyr, probably a Roman soldier, reputedly killed in 303 C.E. at Lydda (Palestine); later, the patron saint of England.

All further stories told of St. George are unhistorical. Beginning in the sixth century, he was regarded as a patron of the Byzantine army, but to Western Europe he was only a minor figure until a reported vision of him before the capture of Antioch in the First Crusade was taken as a sign of victory. A military and aristocratic cult rapidly developed. His feast day (April 23) was made a holiday in England in 1222, Edward III chose him as patron of the Order of the Garter in 1343, and Henry V invoked him at Agincourt; by the close of the Middle Ages he was regarded as the patron saint of England and a model of chivalry. He was also the patron of Venice, Genoa, and Portugal and was venerated in Germany as one of the "Fourteen Holy Helpers." In postmedieval times his cult declined steadily, and in its calendar reforms of 1969 the Catholic Church reduced his ranking from that of a "universal" saint to an optional local one.

Early accounts (Greek, of the sixth century) concentrate on his martyrdom; for eight days he miraculously survived various tortures, including being speared, scourged, forced to run in red-hot shoes, broken on a wheel, thrown into quicklime, and poisoned, but he was finally beheaded. Later Latin texts multiply the tortures to extend over seven years, interspersed with equally astounding miracles. But it was the tale of his combat against a dragon that ensured his popularity. This tale first appears in the *Legenda aurea* (The Golden Legend), compiled by Jacobus de Voragine in the thirteenth century. It tells how George came to a pagan city whose inhabitants, terrorized by a dragon from a nearby lake, were forced to feed it a human being daily; the lot had fallen on the king's daughter, but George pierced the dragon with his spear, bound it with the princess's girdle, and led it into the city before beheading it. All then became Christians.

The dragon fight was a popular subject for icons and paintings. George's deeds and his prolonged martyrdom are also shown in a series of murals in the cathedral of Clermont-Ferrand and the chapel of San Giorgio in Padova (Padua, Italy), and a set of sixteenth-century windows in the parish church of Saint Neots (Cornwall).

In England in the late Middle Ages his feast day was celebrated by processions in many major towns, including Leicester, Coventry, Reading, and King's Lynn, as well as in many smaller places. A magnificently dressed rider impersonated the saint, and an effigy of the dragon was paraded and "slain." Though ostensibly religious in intent, these events were also occasions for displays of communal pride by guilds and civic officials and for popular delight in pageantry; some therefore survived the Reformation as civic events, transferred to some other date. One of the best documented took place at Norwich from 1408 onward, organized by the local St. George's Guild; after the Reformation it became a Mayor's Show, in which saints or religious symbols were forbidden but the dragon was still allowed "to show himself, for pastime." The last of these dragon effigies, known as "Snap" and made in about 1795, can still be seen in

St. George [right], England's patron saint, bearing a cross on his shield and his tunic, stands next to Edmund Crouchback. (Bodleian Library, Oxford, MS Douce 231, fol. 1r)

the Castle Museum at Norwich. It is made of painted canvas over a wooden frame, designed to rest on the shoulders of a man walking inside it; its neck can retract, shoot out, and turn, while its iron-clad jaws are opened or snapped shut by a cord.

A versified charm preserved in a fifteenth-century manuscript shows that St. George was not only the patron saint of fighting men but could also be invoked as a protector against more homely evils—and, interestingly, that he was thought of in chivalric imagery as "Our Lady's knight." Anyone whose horses are "hag-ridden" (i.e., suffering from night sweats, ascribed to being ridden by a supernatural witch) is instructed to

> Take a flynt stone that hath an hole thorow it of hys owen growynge, & hange it ouer the stabill dore, or ell [else] ouer ye horse, and writhe this charme:
>
>> In nomine Patri &c. [the words recited in a blessing or
>>   when making the sign of the cross]
>> Seynt Jorge, our ladys knyght,
>> He walked day, he walked nyght,
>> Till that he fownde that fowle wyght [foul creature];
>> And when he her fownde,
>> He her beat and her bownde,
>> Till trewly ther her trowthe sche plyght [gave her word]
>> That sche sholde not come be nyght
>> With-inne vij rode [seven rods] of londe space
>> Ther as Seynt Jeorge i-namyd was.
>> In nomine Patri &c.
>
> And wryte this in a bille and hange it in the hors' mane.

The legend of George was remodeled after the Reformation, first in Spenser's *Faerie Queene*, where, as the "Red Crosse Knight," he represents the struggle of Protestant truth against popish error, and later by Richard Johnson in 1596 in a popular work, *The Most Famous History of the Seaven Champions of Christendome*. Johnson strips the Christian elements from the lives of the patron saints of seven countries, replacing them by chivalric and magical adventures imitated from medieval romances. George is born to noble English parents but is stolen soon after birth by an enchantress, whose power he eventually outwits. Not only does he save Sabra, the king of Egypt's daughter, from a dragon, but after further adventures he encounters a second dragon (in England) and kills it, but himself dies from its poison and is buried in Windsor Chapel. This patriotic and secularized story proved immensely popular, and together with Spenser's work ensured George's continued status as patron of a Protestant England.

See also: Dragon; Saints, Cults of the

References and further reading: The charm quoted in the text appears in the manuscript MS Bod. Rawlinson C 506 f. 297. There are entries for George in all reference works on saints, whether alphabetical or calendrical; older editions are more tolerant of legendary material than current ones. For detailed studies, see H. Delahaye, *Les légendes greques des saints militaires* (1909); G. J. Marcus, *St George of England* (1939); and I. H. Elder, *George* *of Lydda* (1949). For English folk customs on St. George's Day, both medieval and postmedieval, see A. R. Wright and T. F. Lones, *British Calendar Customs*, vol. 2: *England* (1938).

—*Jacqueline Simpson*

Geraint ab Erbin [Geraint, Son of Erbin]

Hero of the medieval Welsh romance *Geraint and Enid*, one of the three Welsh stories related in some way to romances by Chrétien de Troyes, in this case *Erec et Enide*. (The other two Welsh romances are *Historia Peredur ab Efrawg*, related to Chrétien's *Perceval*, and *Owain*, related to Chrétien's *Yvain*.)

Geraint is the subject of an early (c. 1100) Welsh poem that praises his valor in battle, most especially at Llongborth (perhaps Langport in Somerset), where he appears to have been killed. The poem claims that Arthur was present at the battle, and in later Welsh tales Geraint figures in lists of Arthur's courtiers. The royal pedigrees of Dumnonia (present-day Cornwall and Devon) name Geraint, and he may therefore have been a historical personage. Geoffrey of Monmouth manipulated these genealogies to provide a pedigree for Arthur, and this is the source for the claim in *Geraint and Enid* that Geraint and Arthur are cousins. Geraint's southwestern connections are further established by the frequent occurrence of the personal name in the records and genealogies of Dumnonia.

See also: Chrétien de Troyes; Owain; Peredur, Son of Efrawg
References and further reading: See R. Bromwich, *Trioedd Ynys Prydein* (1978), and P. C. Bartrum, *A Welsh Classical Dictionary* (1993).

—*Brynley F. Roberts*

Gerald of Wales (c. 1146–1223) [French Gerald de Barri, Latin Giraldus Cambrensis]

Norman-Welsh scholar (educated in Paris; taught canon law), cleric (archdeacon of Brecon; twice rejected as bishop of St. Davids, for whose independent status he ardently fought), royal clerk (in the court of England's Henry II), ecclesiastical reformer, and monarchical critic.

Gerald wrote some 20 books presenting his arguments, his philosophies, and accounts of his travels and in the process recording innumerable items of folklore—oral, customary, and material—much of it in an autobiographical context and deriving from personal experience.

Certain of Gerald's books are marked by their inclusion of folklore. *Topographia Hibernica* (Topography of Ireland, 1188) draws on materials gleaned during two trips to Ireland: in 1183, accompanying his brother to recover family lands, and in 1185–1186, accompanying Prince John and then staying on for his own studies. The book treats nature lore (the crane responsible for guarding the flock holds a stone in its upraised foot so that if it dozes off the falling stone will wake it; barnacles on logs turn into birds), migratory legends (a lake resulting from a well overflowing when momentarily left uncapped), saints' legends (a duck belonging to St. Colman cannot be cooked; St. Ninnan banishing fleas from a certain village), material culture (hooded capes and trousers made of wool; the reins and crooked sticks used to guide horses; midwives not swaddling infants or shaping their limbs but, rather, letting nature take its course), music (fast, lively airs on harp and timpani), and customs (ritual union of a king with the land through intercourse with and ingestion of a white mare). *Itinerarium Cambriae* (Journey through Wales, 1191), which reported a journey with Archbishop Baldwin of Canterbury in 1188 to enlist volunteers for the Crusades, and *Descriptio Cambriae* (Description of Wales, 1194) detail a similar range of items, including nature lore (how beavers escape hunters), material culture (techniques for leading plowing oxen, fishing with coracles, design of reaping knives, foodways, communal beds made from rushes and covered with a *brychan*, a woven, usually woolen coverlet), music (on harp, pipe, and *crwth*—a stringed instrument—and singing in multipart harmony), and customs (young people celebrating St. Eluned's feast day by singing and miming work forbidden on Sunday). In addition to saints' legends (a boy sticking to St. Davids Church when he would have defiled it, dogs refusing to shelter in St. Caradog's cell until invited by him, St. Curig's staff healing those who offer proper payment at his shrine) and *memorates* (first-person accounts of supernatural experiences), such as the tale of the child named Elidyr who claimed to have been taken to a beautiful underground otherworld by two tiny beings, the *Descriptio Cambriae* also contains historical anecdotes, such as the tales of birds bursting into song in recognition of Gruffydd ap Rhys ap Tewdwr as rightful ruler of the land, or of Henry II testing Merlin's prophecy that an English king who had conquered Ireland would die upon crossing the stone known as Llech Lafar; Henry crossed and lived.

Gerald's descriptions of Ireland and Wales, fraught with an outsider's view of native and therefore perceivably primitive cultures, reflect his own peculiar cultural status and expectations as a member of Marcher society, the product of intermarriage combining the lines of Welsh princes and Norman aristocracy, trained in Paris at the center of urban, urbane Europe, and employed in the English court. When he looked at the Irish he recognized some of the qualities of the "noble savage," but he also saw a culture devoid of the hallmarks of civilization—settled agriculture, cities, industry, commerce, and the preferred form of Christianity—and he accepted all his culture's stereotypes of the "barbarian."

He traveled to Ireland, the western edge of the known world, expecting to find wonders comparable to those of the East. His readiness to accept marvels, combined with his failure to understand the full cultural context of everything he learned, meant he was not always able to assess the accuracy of his material, making him appear ingenuous at times. Nevertheless, his descriptions, if not always his interpretations, are considered generally reliable, and he did attempt to write rounded ethnographies, describing a people by recording various interrelated aspects of their lives: their appearance, environment, history, customs, entertainments, warfare, and daily practices.

In both Ireland and Wales, where he was only a little less the outsider, Gerald proved a keen and curious observer providing otherwise lost information and simultaneously revealing bits of his own folk culture and belief system. He displays, for example, a fascination with and acceptance of prophecies, and he shows himself an able manipulator of folklore. He uses the story of Meilyr, for example, to denigrate a rival author: Meilyr would be relieved of his demons whenever St. John's Gospel was placed in his lap but be immediately overcome by the demons when touched with Geoffrey of Monmouth's *Historia regum Britanniae* (History of the Kings of Britain), a book that in Gerald's opinion was filled with falsehoods. Gerald also drew extensively on folk traditions about St. David to support his fight for metropolitan status for the see of St. Davids.

When Gerald writes about the Church he writes as an insider, although still from the position of one observing the strange behavior of the "locals." As an archdeacon (the "eye" of the bishop) Gerald would have been responsible for discipline, spotting irregularities, border disputes, and other assorted problems; as someone trained in the Roman Church, he would have had difficulty accepting some of the vestiges of ecclesiastical custom of the earlier "Celtic" Church. Accordingly, in addition to tales of Christian marvels, he also repeats narratives critical of ecclesiastical misbehavior and hypocrisy, especially when involving his personal villains, the monks. Gerald's *Gemma ecclesiastica* (The Jewel of the Church, 1197), for example, draws many exempla from patristic, classical, and hagiographic writings (which were themselves ultimately drawn from oral tradition), but it also records many oral narratives: exempla about images of Jesus or the Virgin Mary bleeding when struck, fabliaux about various monks and clerics sexually tempted by women, anecdotes involving incubi and succubi (male and female sexual predators), and contemporary legends about spiders accidentally drunk in the sacramental wine crawling out through the drinker's toe, arm, or tonsure. *Speculum ecclesiae* (A Mirror of the Church, 1220), with a more embittered and critical tone for the monastic orders, contains contemporary anecdotes and fabliaux about lax morals of monks, gluttony and love of drink, and covetousness. *De jure et statu Menevensis ecclesiae* (The Rights and Status of St. Davids, 1218) includes, along with its accounts of conversations with Pope Innocent III and other prelates, narratives such as the ribald tale of the stolen horse shown to be a gelding upon examination.

See also: Celtic Mythology; David, Saint; Exemplum; Folklore; Geoffrey of Monmouth
References and further reading: Gerald's works appear in Latin in J. S. Brewer, J. F. Dimock, and G. F. Warner, eds., *Giraldi Cambrensis opera*, 8 vols., in the Rolls Series; significant English translations include J. J. Hagen, trans., *The Jewel of the Church* (1979); L. Thorpe, trans., *The Journey through Wales and the Description of Wales* (1978); and J. J. O'Meara, trans., *The History and Topography of Ireland* (1951). Biographies and interpretations include B. F. Roberts, *Gerald of Wales* (1982); R. Bartlett, *Gerald of Wales, 1146–1223* (1982); and T. Jones, "Llên-gwerin yn 'Nheithlyfr' Gerallt Gymro," in *Mân Us* (1949).

—*Elissa R. Henken*

German Tradition

The folkloric culture of the West Germanic peoples.

Medieval folk tradition and its customary transmission in Germany were the result of thousands of years of development. Thus, both the tradition and its

lines of transmission consist of many highly varied elements, of diverse historical and cultural origins. This great diversity manifests itself in many folkloric
forms, including sacred and secular rituals, life-cycle customs, magical beliefs,
folk wisdom, folk medicine, sayings about the weather, and both the written
and oral traditions of märchen, legends, saints' lives, proverbs, riddles, jokes
and anecdotes, folk sayings, and beliefs about ghosts and demons, angels and
saints, and witches and devils. In addition, it manifests itself in material culture
in the forms of houses and settlements, utensils and tools, the material products
of religious and secular folk art, clothing, costume, and food. All of these have
undergone thousands of years of development, shaped by many and various intellectual, cultural, material, and socioeconomic influences. Stemming from a
variety of sources, these elements of folklore differ widely even in their respective ages.

Even today the various tribal divisions of the German people continue to
play a fundamental role. For almost 2,000 years the Germanic homeland consisted of the north German plains, the region of lower Saxony between the Ems
and the Elbe Rivers. Expanding to the south and west, West Germanic tribes
settled lands originally inhabited by Romano-Celtic peoples; migrating to the
east, they took over Baltic and Slavic territory. Despite the fragmenting effect
of centuries of territorial movements, traditional tribal divisions remained intact even at the end of the Middle Ages: Bavarians, Swabians (Alemanni), and
Franks occupied the South; Wesphalians and Lower Saxons, the North; Saxons, central Germany; and Frisians, the North Sea coast. This geographic and
tribal diversity played a fundamental role in determining traditional German
folk culture at least up to World War II.

In the Middle Ages tribal differences were reflected in the very layout of
fields and villages. Fields were worked according to the three-field system of
crop rotation—that is, every year the soil was prepared for a different crop. In
the north German and lower Alpine regions single farms predominated, while
Franks and Hessians preferred to settle close together in villages. During the
Middle Ages nearly every region developed its own characteristic type of house;
for example, the *Hallenhaus*, a type of longhouse popular in lower Germany; the
two-story Swabian *Einhaus*, built on a stone foundation; and the typical
Schwarzwald, or Black Forest house, which like the other two house types provided lodging for both people and livestock, but which unlike the others contained a wall to separate the animals from the people.

Within village society the smith and the shepherd have played special roles
since time immemorial. In the eyes of the common people they possessed mysterious powers to heal sick cattle or to recover stolen livestock. Bee culture was
common on the outskirts of the villages, where wild bees were smoked out of
their hives in order to get the honey. Villagers drove swine into the forest to
fatten on acorns. Charcoal was produced in forest kilns. Peasants mowed grain
with sickles and cultivated spelt, millet, flax, and poppies along with rye to
increase self-sufficiency. Clothing was strictly regulated, especially in the cities,
where every level of society—peasant, middle class, nobility, or clergy—possessed its own particular costume that made it instantly recognizable. During
the eighteenth century regional variations in costume developed from the more
formal urban models and gradually reached rural areas.

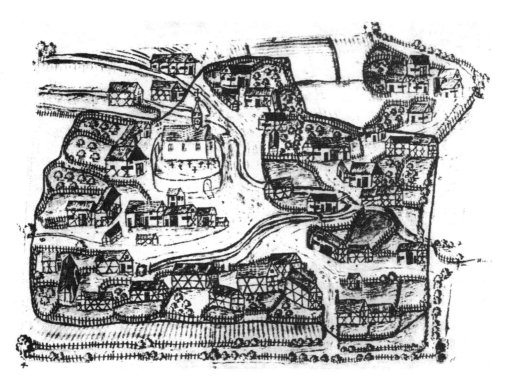

The village of Heudorf, near Constance, 1576. A church is near the center. A fence surrounds the village and its gardens. (Reproduced from Werner Rösener, Peasants in the Middle Ages, Urbana and London, 1992)

Celebrations and customs also underwent changes over the course of centuries. The first major turning point was the Christianization of the German tribes in the eighth century. Christian missionaries, especially St. Boniface among the Frisians and St. Columban, St. Gall, and St. Pirmin in the South, declared the Germanic gods to be *unhold* (*hold* meant "friendly" or "good-natured"; thus the negative *unhold* was roughly equivalent to "diabolical"). Ideas and concepts that sprang from tribal and folk origins were animistic and presumed that natural occurrences, as well as the fate of the individual, were governed by supernatural powers. Those powers could in turn be influenced by resorting to magical and, especially, religious means. There is surely no people that does not populate its world with supernatural beings, which serve the function of explaining the unexplainable in human life. The oldest documentary evidence of German folk custom, after the *Germania* of Tacitus (c. 100 C.E.), is the so-called *Indiculus superstitionum et paganarum* (Letter Concerning Superstitions and Pagan Practices), written in 743 C.E. but only rediscovered in a manuscript in the Vatican in 1652. It originated during the period of the conversion of the Saxons and contains brief descriptions of stone- and tree-worshipping cults, magical spells and predictive sayings, traditions honoring the dead, annual ritual fires, image magic (charms), and vegetation cults. The manuscript bears witness to a syncretic blending of heathen cult forms with those that are, on the surface at least, Christian. Vestiges of such customs and magical beliefs have continued essentially into modern times: fires lit to celebrate the winter and summer solstices, stone- and spring-worshipping cults on sites of Christian pilgrimage, and even the Christian tradition of relics. Many such customs were preserved, if in modified form, into early modern times—for example, ringing bells and intoning blessings during storms and employing other blessings to ensure good weather.

The various genres of folk narrative are attested only in the later Middle Ages. The oldest documentation is found in the jokes and student songs of the *Cambridge Song Manuscript*, a Latin collection copied by an Anglo-Saxon hand about 1059. Alongside sacred songs, the manuscript contains comic poetry originating on German, English, and French soil. Toward the end of the Middle Ages can be found numerous collections of humorous tales, intended primarily for casual amusement. Often they present stereotypical characterizations ridiculing unfaithful wives, unscrupulous innkeepers, greedy merchants, miserly bourgeois, and fat, naive peasants. Also common in these stories is the mockery of the lower orders of the clergy, lecherous village priests, and mendicant friars. These tales possess parallels in the Italian *novella* tradition, in Boccaccio for example, as well as in Chaucer, demonstrating how commonly medieval tales crossed national boundaries.

Texts of exempla and sermons from the Middle Ages are also excellent sources of popular humor, saints' lives, fables, märchen, and legends. By injecting anecdotal, edifying, and cautionary tales into his sermons, the preacher sought to instill Christian precepts in the faithful as he engaged their interest by entertaining them.

Medieval comic tales, with their didactic, moralizing, and religious functions, constitute an exceptionally rich source for cultural history, providing information on the acceptable and unacceptable folk customs of the time and illuminating the ways of life of various levels of society, from the clergy to the peasant and the mercenary soldier. A further source of folk narrative is provided by the so-called *Gesta Romanorum* (Deeds of the Romans, 1342), a collection of tales, legends, and anecdotes recorded by priests and later translated into all the European languages, disseminated throughout the Continent for entertainment and edification.

In medieval times written and oral transmission were already interacting in mutually enriching ways, although heroic legends such as those of the Nibelungs, Alexander, and Roland, which were fixed early on in written form, possessed very few parallels in popular oral tradition. It was not until the beginning of the nineteenth century that märchen and legends were first collected and written down. Famous as pioneers in this endeavor, the brothers Jacob and Wilhelm Grimm published the first edition of their *Kinder- und Hausmärchen* (Children's and Household Tales, better known as *Grimms' Fairy Tales*) in 1812, followed by their extensive collection, the *Deutsche Sagen* (German Legends), in 1816 and 1818. They drew the märchen predominantly from the contemporary oral tradition, while for the legends they utilized the widest-ranging written sources: chronicles, travel literature, sermons and exempla, topographical and statistical works, classical works, medieval manuscripts, and calendars.

Most German folk legends had been transformed over the centuries by Christianity. This Christianization of legendary material occurred in two phases.

In the first phase, *interpretatio Christiana* (Christian interpretation), which occurred during the period of the conversion of the Germanic tribes, their gods and sacred objects were reinterpreted as the works of the devil; the "heathen" beliefs and magic practices and rituals, such as those preserved in the above-mentioned *Indiculus superstitionum*, were the most affected. The second phase began in the twelfth century with the development of the concept of purgatory as the "third realm" between heaven and hell. It is scarcely possible to comprehend the Western medieval transmission of legendary material without recognizing the importance of the Christian doctrine of purgatory, which was first fixed as a dogma toward the end of the twelfth century. Priestly logic demanded that there be a place that would serve as the abode of those deceased persons who were not to be consigned directly to hell but who were also not so free of (original) sin that they could be accepted immediately into heaven. Thus, they conceived of a temporary residence, a place where souls of the sinful atoned for venial sins and were purified. Picturing their suffering powerfully stimulated the fantasies of the faithful. Many legends tell of apparitions of those tortured souls seeking redemption. As a tangible or visible sign of their existence they might leave behind an imprint of a hand, stamped in fire on wood or other surfaces. Such signs persist into present times, strengthening the popular conception of poor sinners as worthy of mercy and deserving help through the donation of masses, offerings, and prayers. A Christian ethos manifested itself not only in the obligation of almsgiving but also in the doctrine that words of forgiveness from survivors can help the newly deceased find salvation.

Alongside legends of the dead, which were rooted primarily in the popular religious conception of the tortured soul, Christian motifs are also found in the legends of sin and its punishment. One of the earliest of these is the tale of the dancers of Kölbigk, mentioned around 1075 in the chronicle of the monastery of Hersfeld: during the Christmas matins (morning prayers) of the year 1012, 16 men and women dance in the cemetery by the church. As the pastor admonishes them to take part in the matins, they ridicule him. In response he places a curse on them, requiring them to dance for the entire coming year. Eventually their dancing feet dig a deep trench in which they stand up to their hips. At the end of the year Bishop Heribert of Cologne releases them from the curse, at which point most of the dancers either die or become incapacitated. The tale is based on an epidemic of dance mania that under priestly influence was turned into a moralizing exemplum. Diffusion of the story during the Middle Ages was aided by the fact that travelers and beggars claimed to have been participants in the blasphemous dance and produced petitions that reinforced their claims by stating that the tale was an actual account of their experience.

Among the oldest legends that we know, even from pre-Christian times, are those concerning the crossing of the dead into the world beyond, already attested by Procopius of Caesaria (sixth century). They originate from a concept of a kingdom of the dead separated from the world of the living by a body of water. These legends turn up in nineteenth-century tradition as does the story of subterranean beings or dwarfs crossing a river at nighttime; the ferryman cannot even see his passengers and notices that they have filled his boat only as it sinks. This tale belongs to a body of legendry that transmits knowledge of the beyond. The souls of the dead are ferried over to the Isles of the Dead, which, according to Procopius, is Britain. The author maintains, "These events are verified by statements of the people of that region." The narrative undoubtedly points to archaic strata of popular belief that have not yet been Christianized.

A similarly ancient tale is that of the Wandering Soul (the legend of Guntram), told by the Langobardian historian Paulus Diaconus in his *Historia Langobardum* (History of the Lombards, 787–797). According to the story, the Franconian king Guntram takes a rest while out hunting and falls asleep. A servant attending the king watches as a small creature, probably a snake, crawls out of the king's mouth and attempts to cross a small stream flowing nearby. The servant lays his sword across the stream, enabling the creature to crawl over and disappear into a mountain. After a short while, it returns and slips back into Guntram's mouth. On awakening the king tells of a dream in which he crossed a river on an iron bridge, reaching a mountain where he found wonderful treasures. Excavations in the mountain across the stream turn up a quantity of gold. This story, which Paulus Diaconus wrote down toward the end of the eighth century, is the oldest written documentary evidence of the concept of the separable soul. The story of a man's wandering soul, or alter ego, taking on animal form presents relics of an archaic and very widespread belief that has an extensive oral and literary tradition and was even included by the Grimm brothers in their legend collection.

The monk Notker the Stammerer of St. Gall (d. 912) tells of a goblin that steals wine for the bishop. When he permits the barrels to run empty, the bishop curses him and flogs him unmercifully. The goblin screams, "Woe is me, that I lost the bottle of my godfather." Stories of goblins are also told by Thietmar of Merseburg (975–1018) in his chronicle, which states that in the year 1017 he and other residents of his monastery actually experienced these supernatural events. The pious bishop recognizes the goblins to be ungodly demons and attributes the events to his lack of success in converting the Saxon populations: "Moreover, it is not surprising to see such a sign and wonder in these regions. For the inhabitants seldom go to church and care nothing of the visits of their pastor. They worship their own household gods and sacrifice to them, believing they can be of help to them."

For centuries the Roman Church waged intense war with werewolves and Wild Women, fairies and witches, norns and goblins. But its struggle with the belief in spirits and magical concepts, all deeply rooted among the populace, made scarcely an impression on the popular attitudes and conceptions of the surrounding world. Again and again one is astonished to see the range of sources upon which German narrative tradition draws. Sometimes individual motifs, such as the Polyphemus motif from the *Odyssey* or the Sisyphus motif, separated from their ancient narrative framework, reemerge in the tales of a completely different culture, in this case that of Alpine legends. Polyphemus complains to his cyclopean companions that "Nobody" has wounded him (Odysseus assumed the name "Nobody" to trick the Cyclops), but the other Cyclopes retort that they can do little for someone who has hurt himself and decline to come to his aid. In the analogous German legend, a forest demon is caught in the crook of a tree by a clever peasant who gives as his name "Did It Myself"; when the demon's fellows rush to his aid and ask who trapped him, he can only answer "Did It Myself." In another tale, similar to that of Sisyphus, a shepherd who let a cow fall to its death must spend his afterlife forever hauling the cow back up the mountain, only to have it slip from his hands and fall back down just before the goal is reached. It is of course difficult to establish solid theories about the transmission of such motifs from antiquity or from the East. The interrelationships have not been sufficiently investigated and are not always even clear, owing to a lack of knowledge of intervening stages in the process of transmission. For now, we can only state that such motifs can derive from other cultures and earlier epochs and can live on into the present.

See also: Eulenspiegel; Legend; *Nibelungenlied;* Peasants; Tannhäuser; Wolfram von Eschenbach

References and further reading: A rich source of information about German folk beliefs, from antiquity to the Middle Ages and into early modern times, remains J. Grimm, *Deutsche Mythologie,* 4 vols. (1835), translated into English by J. S. Stallybrass as *Teutonic Mythology* (1883; rpt. 1966). An excellent translation of the Grimms' *Deutsche Sagen* is D. Ward, trans. and ed., *The German Legends of the Brothers Grimm,* 2 vols. (1981). The only study of folk belief that limits itself strictly to the Middle Ages is W.-E. Peukert, *Deutsche Voksglaube des Spätmittelalters* (1942). A good treatment of the Middle Ages, emphasizing both cultural history and folklore from the point of view of the historian, is A. Borst, *Lebensformen im Mittelalter* (1973). H. Achterberg, in his *Interpretatio Christiana* (1930), treats the transformation of pre-Christian beliefs by the Christian missions to the Germanic peoples. In a much more thorough and theoretical manner, D. Harmening juxtaposes medieval beliefs with the Christian faith: *Superstitio: Überlieferungs- und theoriegeschichtliche Untersuchungen zur kirchlich-theologischen Aberglaubensliteratur des Mittelalters* (1979). A representative edition of the German-language oral narrative tradition, complete with notes and commentary, is L. Petzoldt, *Deutsche Volkssagen,* 2nd ed. (1978); see also Petzoldt's *Historische Sagen,* 2 vols. (1975–1977) and his *Kleines Lexikon der Dämonen und Elementargeister,* 2nd. ed. (1995). Medieval sermon exempla are examined for the folk narrative material in E. Moser-Rath, *Dem Kirchenvolke die Leviten gelesen: Alltag im Spiegel süddeutscher Barockpredigten* (1991). A representative sampling of German comic narratives can be found in L. Petzoldt, *Deutsche Schwänke* (1979), which provides an outline of their literary history as well as notes. Two older but still important treatments of German folklore that have much to offer are A. Spamer, *Die deutsche Volkskunde,* 2 vols. (1934), and W. Pessler, *Handbuch der deutschen Volkskunde,* 2 vols. (1936). A more recent but less comprehensive treatment is R. W. Brednich, *Grundriss der Volkskunde: Einführung in die Forschungsfelder der Europäischen Ethnologie* (1988). A recent edition of the *Cambridge Song Manuscript,* provided with notes and facing-page English translations, is J. Ziolkowski, ed. and trans., *The Cambridge Songs (Carmina Cantabrigiensia)* (1994).

—*Leander Petzoldt*

Giants

Monstrous supernatural beings in Scandinavian mythology; also, the subject of local legend throughout medieval Europe, represented in medieval pageants, and appearing in many medieval romances and more recent folktales.

The fullest picture of giants in northern mythology is found in Old Norse literature. In the mythological poems of the Icelandic *Poetic Edda,* they are in conflict with the gods and are represented as an older race of beings, who know of the beginning of the worlds. Even Odin, wisest of the gods, consulted the giant Vafthrudnir when he wished to discover hidden knowledge. In the thirteenth-century *Prose Edda* of Snorri Sturluson the world was said to have been formed from the body of an ancient giant, Ymir, from whom both giants and gods were descended after he was slain by the creator gods.

The giants, who dwelt in Jötunheim (literally, Giant World), were dangerous neighbors to the gods in Asgard, and Frigg warned her husband against making a visit to Vafthrudnir, because if Odin could not outdo the giant in a riddle contest he could be destroyed. The enmity between gods and giants was like that between gods and Titans in the mythology of ancient Greece, and Thor, with his mighty hammer and power over the lightning, defended the gods from the threat of cold, darkness, and sterility.

The giants are sometimes called "frost giants." Their aim was to carry away Freyja, goddess of fertility, as well as the golden apples that gave the gods perpetual youth, and the sun and moon, thereby causing the return of chaos. Surviving myths show the constant threat the giants posed to the gods. They sought to obtain Thor's hammer, the weapon they feared most, or else to lure him unarmed into Jötunheim. One giant, Hrungnir, made his way into Asgard, but was slain by Thor in a duel. Another giant built a wall around Asgard, but demanded Freyja and the sun and moon as payment, so Loki prevented him from completing his work, and he was slain.

Myths recounting Thor's, Odin's, or Loki's entrance to the realm of the giants are found in some of the earliest surviving poems from pre-Christian Iceland, and some are illustrated in carvings considerably older than the literary sources. One such journey, ending with the battering to death of the giant Geirröd and his two daughters after they attempted to destroy Thor, was known to Saxo Grammaticus, the thirteenth-century Danish historian.

A long comic tale of about the same date in the *Prose Edda* relates how Thor was humiliated when he visited the hall of the huge giant Utgard-Loki, skilled in deceptive magic. Thor only discovered too late how he had been hoodwinked, but he had terrified the giants by his divine strength. When Thor went fishing for the Midgard serpent, he was accompanied by a sea giant, Hymir, who was so frightened when Thor hooked the monster that he cut the line at the crucial moment of the catch. Thor went to the hall of the giant Thrym to recover his stolen hammer, disguised by Loki as the goddess Freyja, coming to be wed, and once he got his hammer back he slew the giant and all the wedding guests.

Odin overcame the giants by disguise and cunning rather than by brute force, and a famous and possibly ancient myth relates how he recovered the magic mead of inspiration, which the giant Suttung had taken and kept within a mountain. In serpent form, Odin crawled through a crack in the rock and then made love to the giant's daughter in return for three drinks of mead. He emptied the three vessels that held it and flew back in the form of an eagle, to vomit up the precious liquid when he reached Asgard. In another tale Loki rescued the stolen golden apples, along with the goddess Idun, and flew off in bird form, pursued by the giant Thjazi in the form of an eagle, but the gods prepared a fire that singed the giant's wings when he flew into Asgard, and he was slain by Thor.

Thus, it can be seen that a number of early and powerful myths are concerned with the struggle of gods against giants to preserve the culture that they had created, until the end comes at Ragnarök. In this battle the giants at last gain entrance to Asgard, accompanied by the monsters that also threaten the gods, and by the treacherous Loki, sometimes represented as a giant. In the final battle both gods and giants perish, while the earth is destroyed by fire and sinks into the sea. But it is fated to rise again from the cleansing waters, to be ruled by the sons of the gods in a new age.

A different relationship between supernatural beings is indicated by marriages between the gods and the daughters of giants. In the poem *Skirnismal* (The Lay of Skirnir), Skirnir woos the fair maiden Gerd on behalf of Frey; she is the daughter of a giant in the underworld and can only be reached by a long and perilous journey. Skadi, daughter of the giant Thjazi, married the god Njord, although the marriage failed because she belonged to the world of mountains and he belonged to the world of the sea.

These northern giants possess a certain power and dignity not retained in later medieval literature. There are traces of a powerful giant race among the

Illumination depicting King Harold and the giant, from Flateyjarbók, an Icelandic manuscript from the end of the fourteenth century. (Corbis/Werner Forman)

Germans. Weland, known to the Anglo-Saxons as a supernatural smith and associated with an ancient burial mound on the Ridgeway in southern England, was a member of a family remembered in heroic poetry. His father was the giant Wade, remembered in English local tradition, and his son was the famous hero Widia. In the romances and folktales, however, giants appear as powerful but rather stupid unnamed beings who wreak havoc in the land, capture maidens and imprison them in their castles, feast on human flesh, and hurl stones and boulders about the landscape. They are overthrown by valiant knights or deceived by intelligent young heroes. In postmedieval folktales the giant's wife often assists the hero by concealing him from her husband, as in the widespread tale of "Jack the Giant-Killer."

Much local tradition throughout Europe associates giants with impressive ruins or spectacular rocks and hills, while long mounds may be known as their graves. The Anglo-Saxons described the ruins of Roman buildings as the work of giants, as in the poem *The Wanderer*.

The builder of Asgard was a giant, and there are many later legends of two giants flinging stones or a shared hammer from one to the other as they made roads or piled up rocks, and sometimes the giant's wife helped in such operations, carrying stones in her apron until the strings broke. Dropped stones or loads of earth were said to account for certain hills and isolated boulders. Sometimes the giant in such legends was transformed into the devil, but many giants survived in local tradition. They were particularly popular in Cornwall, and according to Geoffrey of Monmouth this was the case as early as the twelfth century.

Local giants of postmedieval legendry were by no means always hostile figures; many were remembered with affection, and humorous tales were told of them. Some seem to have been local men of outstanding size and strength rather than supernatural figures. Tom Hickathrift is still remembered in East Anglia, where a long piece of granite in a churchyard is identified as his grave and columns of broken memorial crosses are declared to be his candlesticks. He is recalled as a friendly neighborhood giant, whose great exploit was that of overthrowing another giant by using the wheel of the wagon he had been driving as a shield and its axle as a weapon. A similar tale is told of another Tom, known as the Hedger, a Cornish giant remembered as a man of great strength, eight feet tall. Their powers, however, were liable to increase in popular tradition; Tom Hickathrift was said in a rhyme to devour church and steeple, and all the people, and still remain hungry, and his name was used to frighten naughty children.

A custom that kept giant figures alive in popular imagination was that of carrying giant figures in procession in various towns and cities; they were regarded with pride and affection by the townspeople. Most of the English processional giants were destroyed at the Reformation, but one survives at Salisbury. Originally 14 feet high, he is supported on a light wooden frame that can be carried by a succession of men, and he was provided with new clothes from time to time. He was the pageant figure of the Guild of Tailors, mentioned in their records as early as 1570, and was known as St. Christopher since the Middle Ages. He was brought out on June 23, St. John's Eve, and July 15, the eve of St. Ogmund's festival, and he still appears on such special occasions as the Silver Jubilee of Queen Elizabeth II.

Two London giants housed in the Guildhall are figures carved in wood, now known as Gog and Magog; in Tudor times they were Gogmagog and Corineus, from Geoffrey of Monmouth's twelfth-century account of the giants of Britain. Earlier still, they were Samson and Hercules. They welcomed Philip of Spain when he married Queen Mary in 1554 and saluted Elizabeth I from Temple Bar when she became queen in 1558. There are also references to two giants welcoming Henry V in 1415 after his victory over the French in the battle of Agincourt. The present figures replaced eighteenth-century ones—14 feet, 6 inches high—burned in the London Blitz. They were successors to an older pair, destroyed in the Great Fire of London.

Processional giants have fared better in continental Europe and flourished in the Netherlands, Belgium, and northern France, where many are still paraded at festivals. Some are accompanied by dragons and monsters of various kinds, like the Salisbury Hob-Nob, a horse-like figure with snapping jaws that might tear the clothes of people in the crowd.

The folklore of giants is a mixture of horror and comedy, with the latter element predominating. Tales of a local giant getting the better of a villain or of a powerful but simple giant overcome by a quick-witted young opponent are popular because they are amusing. The various landmarks and objects associated with giants are shown to children and thus keep their memory alive. Jesting tales of their exploits, however, are still told among adults, as well as among children, and so it must have been in medieval times.

See also: *Anglo-Saxon Chronicle;* Burial Mounds; Eddic Poetry; English Tradition: Anglo-Saxon Period; Geoffrey of Monmouth; Scandinavian Mythology; Snorri Sturluson's *Edda;* Thor

References and further reading: Accounts of giants in Old Norse literature and of the myths in which they appear are given by H. R. E. Davidson in *Gods and Myths of Northern Europe* (1964) and *The Lost Beliefs of Northern Europe* (1993). For Weland, see H. R. E. Davidson, "Weland the Smith," *Folklore* 69 (1958). Giants in European folklore are discussed by J. Simpson in *European Mythology* (1987). A useful account of Cornish giants is given by B. C. Spooner, "The Giants of Cornwall," *Folklore* 76 (1965), and E. Porter provides information about Tom Hickathrift in "Folk Life and Traditions of the Fens," *Folklore* 72 (1961), and *The Folklore of East Anglia* (1974). Processional giants in northern France are discussed in *Cités en fête,* issued in 1992 by the Musée National des Arts et Traditions Populaires. For the Salisbury giant, see H. Shortt, *The Giant and Hob-Nob,* rev. by J. Chandler, issued by the Salisbury and Wiltshire Museum (1988), and for the giants in the London Guildhall, see J. Westwood, *Albion: A Guide to Legendary Britain* (1985). No thorough study of giants has yet appeared, and it seems as if one is needed.

—*Hilda Ellis Davidson*

Gildas (c. 495–c. 570)

British cleric, Welsh saint, and author of the earliest surviving history of Britain.

Born, it is believed, in the northern British kingdom of Strathclyde, Gildas probably trained in the Church in south Wales and may eventually have settled in Rhuys in Brittany. He is credited with giving essential impetus to the monastic movement in Wales through his writings and his own religious activities. He wrote *De excidio et conquestu Britanniae* (On the Ruin and Conquest of Britain,

c. 547) and probably a penitential, and he is the subject of a ninth-century Breton *vita* (saint's life) and a twelfth-century Welsh *vita* compiled by Caradog of Llancarfan. Gildas both preserved traditional lore and was the subject of it, appearing as a character in both secular and hagiographic tradition.

In *De excidio*, composed principally as a diatribe against the excesses and improprieties of his society and its rulers, secular and ecclesiastical, Gildas relates in an introductory section the history of Britain—its founding, conquest by Rome, and conflicts with the Saxons. Gildas's application of the biblical notion of history as a record of God's dealings with peoples (*gens*) and his interpretation of Britain's losses to the Saxons as God's chastisement of the people's waywardness and sin are his own, but his history, the earliest extant written history of the British, appears to be based on oral history. Though his history has very few specific dates or names, it does include report of the "supreme ruler/proud tyrant" (*superbo tyranno*), identified in later texts as Vortigern, who invited the Saxons into the land and whose name could be interpreted as "supreme ruler"; reference to a decisive British victory at Badon Hill (later associated with Arthur); and contemporary anecdotal criticism of the British king Maglocunus (Maelgwn Gwynedd) for killing his uncle the king, listening to the praises of poets, and incestuous union with his nephew's wife. *De excidio* is significant in medieval folklore not only for the hints of oral tradition it contains but also as the first link in a chain of histories that laid out the Welsh national historical myth with its understanding that the British once ruled the whole island and will one day do so again.

In the *vitae*, in eleventh- and twelfth-century genealogies, and in the eleventh-century prose tale *Culhwch and Olwen*, Gildas is depicted as one of many (20, 21, or 24) sons of Caw, a king (and possibly giant) in Scotland. Gildas is associated with Arthur through his brothers. According to his Welsh *vita*, Gildas's brother Hueil kept harassing Arthur until the king was finally forced to kill him. Gildas imposed a penance on Arthur, and the two made peace with each other. The conflict of Hueil and Arthur seems to be a well-established tradition that reappears later in Welsh texts. In *Culhwch and Olwen* Hueil's stabbing of Arthur leads to a feud between them, and in Elis Gruffudd's chronicle (c. 1530), Hueil again wounds Arthur, this time after stealing his mistress, and the whole affair ends when Arthur beheads Hueil. Caradog's *Vita Gildae* also reports the earliest abduction tale about Gwenhwyfar (Queen Guinevere). When Arthur lays siege to Glastonbury where Melwas is holding Gwenhwyfar, Gildas intercedes and effects the safe return of Gwenhwyfar. Gildas is probably a late addition to this Arthurian tale, either as a foil to subdue Arthur or in the role of an existing character, perhaps the wise intermediary, but this provides a good example of how a figure can be incorporated into an already existing oral tradition, either for political reasons or because of his own increased importance.

Another example where Gildas is drawn into another's tradition involves St. David. According to several of St. David's *vitae* and to *Vita Gildae*, Gildas was unable to preach in the presence of the unborn David, a sign that all would give way before David, who would become the preeminent Welsh saint.

Other traditions about Gildas include relatively common hagiographic motifs of healing, raising fountains, driving off or confining birds through prayer, and causing thieves to stick to the ground, but he is specially noted for making bells (given specifically to St. Brigid, St. Cadog, and St. Illtud) and writing books (the *De excidio* and a splendid, miracle-working copy of the Gospels).

See also: Arthurian Lore; *Culhwch and Olwen*; David, Saint; Geoffrey of Monmouth; Maelgwn Gwynedd; Nennius

References and further reading: See Gildas, *The Ruin of Britain and Other Works*, ed. and trans. M. Winterbottom (1978); H. Williams, ed. and trans., *Gildas*, Cymmrodorion Record Series (1901); M. Lapidge and D. Dumville, eds., *Gildas: New Approaches* (1984); and E. R. Henken, *Traditions of the Welsh Saints* (1987). Elis Gruffudd's chronicle is found in the National Library of Wales, manuscript 5276D.

—Elissa R. Henken

Glastonbury

A town in southwest Britain and a medieval community of Benedictine monks housed at Glastonbury Abbey, famous for its legendary history.

According to chronicle evidence, Glastonbury existed as a Christian religious site by the seventh or early eighth century. In the time of the Domesday Book it was the wealthiest monastery in England. Glastonbury's legends are best understood within medieval contexts of the veneration of saints and saints' relics. The earliest surviving traditional stories have origins external to the community and date from the late tenth to the early twelfth centuries. In these stories Glastonbury is commonly assigned a pre-Saxon origin, often linked to the "old church" dedicated to the Mother of God. Associated Celtic saints include Patrick, the apostle of the Irish; David of Wales; and Indract, described as the martyred son of an Irish king. The most extensive hagiography is related to St. Dunstan, tenth-century abbot of Glastonbury and later archbishop of Canterbury.

Around 1120 Eadmer of Canterbury addressed a furious letter to the community, attempting to suppress a rumor that Dunstan's relics had been moved from Canterbury to the abbey during the Danish invasions of the previous century. Perhaps ten years later Glastonbury's own traditions were recorded by William of Malmesbury, a noted historian from another Benedictine monastery some 40 miles away. William wrote a *Life of St. Dunstan* for the abbey, without repeating Eadmer's gossip. A second work, *De antiquitate Glastonie ecclesie* (The Early History of Glastonbury), was so heavily altered in the thirteenth century that William's original composition is unrecoverable.

However, references to Glastonbury's legends were added to later revisions of William's *Gesta regum Anglorum* (Deeds of the Kings of England). Two traditions relate to early Christianity: one associates Glastonbury with the Venerable Bede's story of Lucius and Eleutherius, set in the second century. The other credits Christ's own disciples with Glastonbury's foundation; William further speculates that St. Philip's first-century mission to Gaul (present-day France) might have extended to Britain. Both stories reference the church of the Mother of God, St. Mary's, believed by William to be the oldest church in England. The work reaffirms the traditional Celtic associations, giving accounts of Patrick,

Glastonbury's late-twelfth-century Lady Chapel, built on the site of the "old church." (Courtesy of Deborah Crawford)

David, and Indract. Gildas is mentioned, as are the Irish saints Brigid and Benignus. William describes two old monuments or pyramids in the monastic cemetery and records the legible lettering; he identifies some names as those of the community's pre-Saxon abbots. Arthur is mentioned, but not in connection with Glastonbury. He is presented as a warrior, not a king, an individual worthy of true history rather than false tales. A later statement indicates that Arthur's burial site is unknown, resulting in legends of his return.

Around 1191 Gerald of Wales documented the sensational discovery at Glastonbury of the grave of "King Arthur" and his wife, Guinevere. Gerald, an aristocratic churchman with access to royal circles, also wrote a second account some 25 years later. He credits the recently deceased Henry II of England with instigating the search. The actual excavations and construction of an impressive new marble tomb had taken place under the aegis of the new abbot of Glastonbury, Henry of Sully, nephew of Richard I. Abbot Henry showed Gerald the evidence, a giant shinbone, supposedly taken from the grave, and a cross naming the occupant as Arthur, buried in the "Isle of Avalon." Gerald claims to speak for the monastic community and its traditional history: Arthur was a saintly king, devoted to St. Mary's Church, and a generous donor; he is praised in the abbey records, and the pyramids are his memorials. Gerald's contentions, however, do not match Glastonbury's own stories, told earlier by William of Malmesbury and retold later in the mid-thirteenth-century revision of the *De antiquitate*.

The altered *De antiquitate* continues earlier emphases in Glastonbury's tradition, the early or apostolic origins of St. Mary's Church, and the abbey's associations with Celtic saints, particularly Patrick. Older speculations are presented as certainty, and new details are added, based on a "Charter of St. Patrick" not known to William of Malmesbury. St. Dunstan is still a central figure, and the rumors of Eadmer's time are finally addressed from Glastonbury's perspective. Lengthy passages detail the legend of the removal of Dunstan's body from Canterbury, and the reported recovery of the relics following the abbey fire of 1184. The only feature reminiscent of Gerald's claims is a short summary, identified in the text as the Arthurian tale of Ider/Yder, presenting Arthur as a royal donor to the monastery. St. Mary's Church and the pyramids are not associated with Arthur. The finding of Arthur's grave is recognized and dismissed in half a sentence. But the Arthurian link has permitted a tentative, single-sentence incorporation of St. Joseph of Arimathea into the story of apostolic origins and the repetition of the "Isle of Avalon" motif. Late-thirteenth-century marginal notes and short insertions add perhaps three more Arthurian references.

The mid-fourteenth-century retelling of the abbey's legendary history comes from John of Glastonbury's *Cronica sive antiquitates Glastoniensis ecclesie* (The Chronicle of Glastonbury Abbey). In this version, the stories of Patrick have been augmented and expanded with new legendary material. Dunstan is no longer a central character. Glastonbury's stories of early Christianity have acquired an extended definition and detail through the association with St. Joseph. The striking additions, a crusader's legend, material from an apocryphal Gospel, and a Celtic bard's prophecy, are related to the saint. References to Arthur are given a less prominent place. However, a document confirming Glastonbury's privileges, under the name of Henry II, lists Arthur among the kings who have granted such privileges in the past. This document was also incorporated into Adam of Domerham's late-thirteenth-century work, the *Historia de rebus gestis Glastoniensibus* (History of Deeds Performed at Glastonbury).

The earlier Glastonbury legends are a set of interwoven saints' stories, centering on the "old church" and associations with early Christianity, Celtic saints, and the monastery's beloved Dunstan. The end of the twelfth century probably marks a period of external intervention in the development of the tradition, the introduction of contemporary aristocratic fascinations with Arthurian romance. A majority of scholars have judged that the discovery of Arthur's grave was fraudulent. Other scholars have pointed to royal involvement and to the political value of undercutting the story of Arthur's future return, a potential folkloric focus for Welsh resistance to English rule. Additionally, it appears that Gerald of Wales did not speak for the monastic community and its traditional history. If the community was promoting a "cult of Arthur" based on the discovery, there is no evidence in the mid-thirteenth-century legends. The emphasis is on Glastonbury's established saints.

Royal expediencies and perceptions of history may have created significant additions to Glastonbury's legends, but the monastic community ultimately reshaped those materials to its own concerns. Arthurian romance, through its association with St. Joseph of Arimathea, provided a way to reinterpret, elucidate, and enrich the traditional stories linking Glastonbury to early Christianity in Britain.

See also: Arthur; Gerald of Wales; Joseph of Arimathea, Saint
References and further reading: The best general study is J. Carley, *Glastonbury Abbey*, rev. ed. (1996). Relevant archaeological information is discussed in P. Rahtz, *Glastonbury* (1993). Latin texts and English translations are found in J. Scott, *The Early History of Glastonbury* (1981), and J. Carley, *The Chronicle of Glastonbury Abbey* (1985). Additional Latin texts are provided in W. Stubbs, *De gestis regum Anglorum*, Rolls Series (1887–1889), and *Memorials of Saint Dunstan*, Rolls Series (1874), containing the "B" *Life of Dunstan*, Eadmer's letter, and William of Malmesbury's *Life of Dunstan*; T. Hearne, *Historia de rebus gestis Glastoniensibus* (1727); A. W. Wade-Evans, "*Vita Sancti Dauid*," in *Vitae sanctorum Britanniae et genealogiae* (1944); and M. Lapidge, "The Cult of St. Indract at Glastonbury," in *Ireland in Early Mediaeval Europe* (1982). For a translation of Eadmer's letter, see R. Sharpe, *The Archaeology and History of Glastonbury Abbey* (1991). Excerpts from Adam of Domerham are paraphrased in English by H. F. Scott Stokes, *Glastonbury Abbey during the Crusades* (rpt. 1993). The Latin texts of the various accounts of the finding of Arthur's grave are included in R. Barber, "Was Mordred Buried at Glastonbury?" Appendix A, in *Arthurian Literature* 4 (1985). English translations of the accounts by Gerald of Wales are found in L. Thorpe, trans., *The* Journey through Wales *and* The Description of Wales, Appendix 3 (1978).

—*Deborah Crawford*

Godiva, Lady (d. 1067)

Arguably the most famous citizen of Coventry, known for her legendary naked horseback ride through the town's streets, covered only by her body-concealing long hair, an incident that has made her an instantly recognizable figure of medieval folklore.

The ride was provoked when, on behalf of the citizenry of Coventry, Godiva importuned her husband Leofric to lower taxes, and he promised to do so only if she rode naked through the town. Her long hair allowed Godiva to fulfill her husband's "impossible task" or ultimatum and thus intercede for the citizens while still protecting her wifely chastity from the shame of revealing her nakedness to the public.

Although Godiva and Leofric are historically documentable figures (he died in 1057; she died in 1067), her ride was not mentioned in records concurrent with Leofric's eleventh-century earldom of Coventry. Contemporary chroniclers Florence of Worcester and Roger of Hoveden merely report that this Anglo-Saxon earl and his wife enjoyed a shared reputation for piety and charity, and William of Malmesbury notes Godiva's special devotion to the Virgin Mary. The earliest narration of her ride through the streets of Coventry occurs in Roger of Wendover's early-thirteenth-century chronicle *Flores historiarum* (Flowers of History), produced at the Abbey of St. Albans nearly two centuries after the purported event. Another similar account occurs in the mid-thirteenth-century *Flores historiarum*, reputedly by Roger's successor at St. Albans, Matthew Paris. Both Roger and Matthew begin by attesting the various endowments to religious houses made by the earl and his wife, and they continue the tradition of Godiva's devotion to the Virgin Mary.

According to these thirteenth-century chroniclers, who provide the most detailed versions of the Godiva legend, Godiva spoke to her husband about Coventry's citizens' disgruntlement with high taxes he had imposed, begging him, in the name of Christ and his mother the Virgin Mary, to release his people from these onerous financial burdens. Angered by his wife's insistence on an issue that was against his financial interests, he forbade further discussion. When she continued imploring him on behalf of the people, he promised to lift the taxes only if she would ride naked through Coventry's marketplace. She loosened her long hair, "veiling" her naked body from public view "except for her beautiful white legs," and rode, accompanied by a pair of knights, through the town's center. Leofric then upheld his pledge and canceled the high tolls.

Both accounts indicate that Godiva's ride took place immediately after her argument with Leofric, while the entire town was assembled in the marketplace. Matthew Paris's version differs from Roger's by placing the outcome in a more hagiographical framework. Matthew attributes the fact that Godiva's nakedness was not seen by the townsfolk to a miracle, and he views the town's deliverance from taxation as a divine sign. Later medieval chroniclings of the legend reduce the tale to its essentials, briefly covering how the town got financial freedom and leaving the time frame between Leofric's challenge and Godiva's ride vague.

The abbreviated account in the fourteenth-century *Polychronicon* by Chester-based Ranulf Higden adds a new detail, perhaps derived from oral versions of the now-spreading legend: despite Godiva's ride horses were still subject to Leofric's tolls. Higden's popular history was a source for other chroniclers writing throughout the fourteenth and fifteenth centuries, which may account for the inclusion of the Godiva legend in Henry Knighton's *Chronicon*, John of Tynemouth's *Historia aurea* (Golden History), John Brompton's *Chronicle*, and the *Chronicle* of John Hardyng.

By the fifteenth century Godiva's ride had eclipsed any other events in Leofric's reign. Local reference to the story began in the fourteenth century when a stained glass window was erected in Coventry's Holy Trinity Church, honoring Godiva and Leofric and bearing an inscription saying that Leofric made Coventry toll-free for his wife. Faced with the threat of an increased toll on wool in 1495, the Coventry townsfolk nailed a verse to the door of a local church reminding all of how "Dame Good Eve" once made Coventry toll-free and calling for similar freedom now from the wool custom. In the sixteenth century Coventry celebrated a mass in her honor, and in later centuries her picture was placed in St. Mary's Guildhall, processions were held in her honor, and she became an important feature of the annual St. Michaelmas town fair. In the seventeenth century another element was added, the story of the town tailor, Peeping Tom, who wanted to see Godiva's nakedness as she rode by but was blinded when he looked at her.

The power of the symbols and images that inform Godiva's legend are more significant than questions of its historical accuracy. Godiva, called Dame Good Eve by fifteenth-century inhabitants of Coventry, incorporates the sometimes contradictory aspects of three powerful and archetypal female figures from medieval hagiographical or religious symbolism: Eve, the Virgin Mary, and Mary Magdalen. Her nakedness and the importuning of her husband suggest the shame of Eve, the most negative female stereotype in medieval iconography, at the Fall in the Garden of Eden. Her intercessory function as spokesperson for the oppressed citizenry of Coventry suggests the special object of Godiva's devotion and her probable model, the Virgin Mary, in her role as intercessor for or mediatrix between all humans and her son Christ. Godiva's long, body-concealing hair suggests Mary Magdalen, a reformed penitent and patron saint of prostitutes, whose medieval iconography depicted her naked body completely concealed by her long, luxuriant hair. The Virgin Mary and Eve were antithetically opposed in medieval biblical typology: Mary was the "new Eve" who through her role in the Incarnation of Christ canceled Eve's sinful legacy to humanity. The unreformed Mary Magdalen recapitulates Eve's sensuality and sinfulness; the reformed Magdalen's ultimate attainment of grace and sanctity in the life of an anchorite also reverses Eve's sinful fall while at the same time suggesting affinity with her namesake, the Virgin Mary.

In every respect, Lady Godiva, or Dame Good Eve, literally embodies the saintly models of the two Marys, her avowed patroness Christ's mother and Mary Magdalen, who also covered her naked body with long hair. In medieval typology, both Marys were "good" versions of postlapsarian Eve, rendering Godiva another Good Eve for her transgressive but sanctified ride through the marketplace to attain financial freedom for the oppressed people of Coventry. Many visitors are drawn to present-day Coventry by Godiva's legend. As they exit or enter the train station in the heart of the commercial center, they encounter a larger-than-life equestrian statue of Godiva's ride, which attests Godiva's past and, through increased tourism, ongoing importance to the market economy of Coventry.

See also: Mary Magdalen, Saint; Virgin Mary
References and further reading: For overviews of the legend and folklore of Godiva, see
    H. R. E. Davidson, "The Legend of Lady Godiva," *Folklore* 80 (1969), and K. L. French,
    "The Legend of Lady Godiva and the Image of the Female Body," *Journal of Medieval
    History* 18 (1992). On Leofric's historical reign and contemporary and later chroniclers'
    reports of the incident of Godiva's ride, see *Anglo-Saxon Chronicles*, ed. and trans. G. N.
    Garmonsway (1953); Florence of Worcester, *Chronicon exchronicis*, ed. B. Thorpe, vol. 1

(1848); Roger de Hoveden, *Annals*, ed. H. T. Riley, vol. 1 (1853); William of Malmesbury, *Gesta pontificum Anglorum*, ed. N. Hamilton (1870); Roger of Wendover, *Flores historiarum*, ed. H. Coxe, vol. 1 (1841); Matthew of Westminster, *Flores historiarum*, ed. H. R. Luard, vol. 1 (1890); Ranulf Higden, *Polychronicon*, ed. J. R. Lumby, vol. 7 (1879); H. Knighton, *Chronicon*, ed. J. R. Lumby, vol. 1 (1889); *The Chronicle of John Hardyng*, ed. H. Ellis (1812); and *The Coventry Leet Book*, ed. and trans. M. Dormer, 2 vols. (1907–1908). On the conflation of Godiva with the figures of the Virgin Mary, Eve, and Mary Magdalen, see M. Miles, *Carnal Knowing: Female Nakedness and Religious Meaning in the Christian West* (1989); also, M. Warner, *Alone of All Her Sex* (1976).

—*Lorraine K. Stock*

Gododdin, Y [The Gododdin]

Welsh poem ascribed in its original form to the poet Aneirin (fl. c. 600) and found in thirteenth-century manuscript *Book of Aneirin* (Cardiff Central Library).

The text as found in the manuscript consists of 103 stanzas, some of which are found in variant forms, and it is clear that the poem existed in more than one version. Many of the stanzas mourn the death in battle of individually named warriors of the war band of the Gododdin (the earlier Votatini tribe) around modern-day Edinburgh. Some 300 in number, they had been feasting for a full year at the court of Mynyddog Mwynfawr the king but were annihilated in a disastrous foray against Deira and Bernicia at Catraeth, usually taken to be Catterick in Yorkshire. There is no historical record of the battle (nor of the king), and the circumstances for the composition of the poem must be inferred from the text itself. The poem shows mature literary skills and is a classic example of the ethos of heroic verse. There is some evidence for a written version of the poem in the ninth century, but it is clear that the extant text contains later accretions to whatever may have been first composed. The extant text also provides evidence that the poem was a highly regarded part of the curriculum of bardic training, and medieval poets refer to it both as a model to be emulated and as an element in bardic contests. The poem was part of an active literary tradition from its first composition, so that it is not surprising that narrative features in the text should show folkloric developments. Typical of "the epic of defeat" (a martial tale celebrating the heroes of lost battles) is the comment that only the poet, "on account of his fair song," and three others escaped from the battle; another stanza claims that there was only one survivor.

The poem has always been ascribed to Aneirin, named in the *Historia Brittonum* (History of the Britons) as one of the British poets who "flourished" in the time of Ida of Northumbria (c. 558–570). The text, however, has some indications of the development of the historical poet into a saga character. One stanza refers to his being imprisoned and rescued or ransomed with gold, silver, and steel. This allusion to imprisonment in an underground cell has been interpreted as being a reference to the custom (attested in Irish literary tradition) of inspired bardic composition in a darkened room.

Later Welsh tradition gives to Aneirin the role of a sage and seer, attributing to him gnomic and prophetic verse. Another stanza in *The Gododdin*, obviously later than the original poem, refers more explicitly to Aneirin's violent death as the result of a blow; this is again referred to in two related triads, which note the killing of "Aneirin of Flowing Verse, Prince of Poets," by Heidyn son of Enygan as one of the three unfortunate assassinations of the Island of Britain, and as "one of the three unfortunate hatchet-blows of the Island of Britain." The narratives that developed around the poem and its author are not as well recorded for Aneirin as for his contemporary, the poet and prophet Taliesin, but that the historical and folkloric personae were becoming merged in his case also cannot be doubted.

See also: Nennius; Taliesin; Triads of the Island of Britain
References and further reading: I. Williams, *Canu Aneirin* (1937); K. Jackson, *The Gododdin* (1969); A. O. H. Jarman, *Aneirin: The Gododdin* (1988); P. K. Ford, "The Death of Aneirin," *Bulletin of the Board of Celtic Studies* 34 (1987); R. Bromwich, *Trioedd Ynys Prydein* (1978); P. C. Bartrum, *A Welsh Classical Dictionary* (1993).

—Brynley F. Roberts

Golem [Hebrew "body without soul"]

Homunculus or anthropoid; a human-like creature created by mortals using mystical or technological means.

In the ancient cultures that once flourished in the areas of present-day Egypt, China, and Greece there is much evidence attesting to traditions of statues that became animated. Well known is the statue of a woman created by Promotes, which was called Veritas (Truth), and the one created by his apprentice, which was called Mendacio (Lie); both became living creatures. In these ancient traditions the creation of anthropoids was connected to the worship of idols and to the need to prove that these objects of worship are not only material objects but also have life of their own. In a Jewish tradition of late antiquity, Enosh, a grandson of Adam, was asked to demonstrate how God had created the first man. He took dust and water, shaped out of it a form of a man, and blew life into its nostrils. But Satan entered into it, and people started to worship it as God. This was the beginning of idolatry.

The word *Golem* appears only once in the Hebrew Bible (Psalms 139:16), where it refers to the creation of the first man. Later interpretations of this text, especially in the Talmudic literature, present the Golem as one stage in the 12-hour process through which God created Adam (Babylonian Talmud tractate Sanhedrin 38b; Midrash Genesis Rabbah 24:2). The affiliation of the Golem with the creation of Adam continues to be one of the most widespread traits in Jewish traditions throughout medieval and later periods.

Another important element of the Golem traditions is the function assigned to the mystical book *Sefer Yetzira* (Book of Creation) in the process of its creation. This small and most influential Hebrew composition was created in late antiquity, and it presents the letters of the Hebrew alphabet as the foundation God's deeds—the creation of the world and of human beings. According to this composition God created Adam by means of the letters of the alphabet; thus, the mystics could imitate God's manipulation of the letters and create a man in the same way. Thus, *Sefer Yetzira* became the most important source of magic knowledge used in the attempts to create humans in late antiquity and in the Middle Ages.

The most influential passage in the Babylonian Talmud (tractate Sanhedrin 65b) tells of the learned Rava who created a Golem as an intellectual practice; it was returned to dust. Other rabbis, while studying *Sefer Yetzira*, on every Sabbath eve used to create a calf and then eat it. Such legends, which medieval Jews accepted as factual, were the proof that proper knowledge of the practices described in *Sefer Yetzira* is the key for the mystery of creating humans, and so it was studied in depth and followed intensively by magicians and mystics.

Almost all Jewish mystical and magical trends of the Middle Ages connected the creation of the Golem to their systems and practices. From a folkloristic point of view, the narrative traditions developed by and around the German Pietists of the twelfth to thirteenth centuries are of special significance. The Pietists' interest in all magical aspects of everyday life and their deep beliefs in the possibility of changing reality by means of mystical practices involved them deeply in attempts to create humanoids. In the cycles of legends told about the central figures of the movement—Rabbi Samuel the Pious and his son Rabbi Judah the Pious—they participate deeply in the creation of the Golem. A typical legend is that of Rabbi Elijah of Chelm, a folk healer and mystic of the sixteenth century. He

> made a creature out of matter and of form and it performed hard work for him for a long period, and the name of *'emet* was hanging upon his neck, until the Rabbi saw that the creature of his hands grew stronger and stronger. ... R. Eliyahu the master of the name was afraid that he would be harmful and destructive. He quickly overcame him and removed the name [*'emet*] from his neck, and it turned to dust.

This narrative appears in many and various forms in Hebrew manuscripts and early prints, which attests to its popularity in oral and written traditions. It also raised, for the first time explicitly, the moral question of the legitimacy of repeating the most important deed of God—the creation of man—for personal benefit. As in the Talmudic legends mentioned earlier, when the Golem was created as an intellectual exercise, as an act of pride, or for personal benefit (to be eaten or to serve the master), it gets out of hand, becomes dangerous, and has to be eliminated.

The most popular Golem legends, which connect him to the sixteenth-century Rabbi Judah Löw of Prague (the Maharal of Prague), attempted to resolve the moral dilemma of creating the Golem. The legends appear only in late sources of the eighteenth to nineteenth centuries, but they started much earlier as oral local legends of the Jewish community of Prague and were adapted quickly in the folklore of many Jewish communities, and ultimately by general, non-Jewish folklore and popular culture as well. According to these legends, the great scholar and mystic Rabbi Löw created the Golem, following the ancient Jewish practices, in order to save the Jews of Prague from the blood libels they were accused of at that time. The Golem, an invincible creature that no weapon or fire can harm, was used by the rabbi as the only soldier and guard of the Jewish community. After the danger passed, Rabbi Löw took him to the attic of the Altneuschul—the ancient synagogue of Prague—and there removed the sacred name from him (as Rabbi Elijah of Chelm had before), and the Golem became a pile of dust that exists in the closed attic of the synagogue to this very day.

The message of these legends is that one can exceed the limits of one's humanity and imitate God only when one does so for a moral cause. Any other motivation, such as pride or greed, leads to punishment. This cycle of legends was developed in the late nineteenth century, and it reflects attitudes and concerns of Jewish culture of the time, but its roots and beliefs are earlier and can throw light on the folklore of the Golem in the Middle Ages.

See also: Jewish Tradition; Judah the Pious; Magic; Magic Manuals

References and further reading: Good surveys of the development of the legend of the Golem in Jewish traditions are G. Scholem, "The Idea of the Golem," in *On the Kabbalah and Its Symbolism* (1965); B. L. Sherwin, *The Legend of the Golem: Origins and Implications* (1985); and M. Idel, *Golem: Jewish Magical and Mystical Traditions on the Artificial Anthropoid* (1990). These studies concentrate their attentions mainly on the mystical and Kabbalistic aspects of the myth and rarely deal with the folkloristic aspects. On the idols as living creatures, see K. Müller, "Die Golemsage und die Sage von der lebenden Statue," *Mitteilungen der schlesischen Gesellschaft für Volkskunde* 20 (1919). On Enosh and the origin of idol worship in rabbinic sources, compare S. D. Fraade, *Enosh and His Generation* (1984). On the Golem of Rabbi Löw of Prague and modern traditions of Jewish folklore, see A. Goldsmith, *The Golem Remembered, 1909–1980* (1981), and E. Yassif, *Judah Judle Rosenberg: The Golem of Prague and Other Tales of Wonder* (1991; in Hebrew).

—Eli Yassif

Grail

An object sought by King Arthur's knights in perhaps the most famous quest in legend and literary history.

The grail is almost invariably associated with nourishment or feasting and is generally capable of producing any desired food or drink; its power often sustains life itself. At first a mysterious object with certain marvelous properties, the grail was soon transformed by writers into a sacred object associated with Christ's death and with the Church's sacraments.

The word *grail* itself (Old French *graal*, derived from Latin *gradalis, gradalem*) originally meant simply a serving dish or platter and had no religious or other special significance. It was first given a specialized meaning by Chrétien de Troyes in his romance *Perceval, ou Le conte du Graal* (Perceval, or The Story of the Grail, c. 1190). Perceval, a guest in the Fisher King's castle, witnesses a strange procession that includes a mysterious bleeding lance and a grail radiating light and set with precious stones. Much later in the story, he and we learn that the grail is a "very sacred object" and that it is associated with a genital wound that has disabled both the Fisher King and, by extension, his land. Chrétien informs us that the grail contains a single Mass wafer that sustains the life of the king's father. By neglecting to ask about the grail, Perceval fails to restore the king's and the land's health, and his failure necessitates a quest to find the grail and ask the appropriate question. Chrétien's romance is incomplete, and thus it is left to later writers both to define the grail further and to bring the quest to a successful conclusion.

The Welsh romance *Peredur*, related to Chrétien's romance, features a platter that is an obvious analogue of the French author's grail, but it is not designated by that name: it is called simply a *dyscyl* (platter). In addition, it contains not a Mass wafer but a human head, reflecting perhaps the John the Baptist story as much as a pagan myth. It was once assumed by some scholars that the Welsh text was Chrétien's model, but *Peredur* probably dates from the thirteenth century, and it is more likely that the two romances had a common source.

In Chrétien the grail is, as noted, a wondrous and marvelous object, but it is not yet the Holy Grail that it would soon become—the chalice of the Last Supper and the vessel in which Christ's blood was collected after the Deposition. That identification was made soon after Chrétien by Robert de Boron, in his *Joseph d'Arimathie* (Joseph of Arimathea, c. 1200). Robert thus completed the refashioning of the mysterious grail into the Holy Grail, a symbol of Christ's real presence. He also offered a fanciful etymology for the word *graal*, deriving it from French *agréer* (to please) because of its ability to provide pleasure.

At about the same time, several authors continuing Chrétien's romance further develop the theme of the bleeding lance, identifying it as the spear of Longinus and leading to the association of both Grail and Lance with the mass. Both objects also play a central role in Wolfram von Eschenbach's great romance *Parzival* (c. 1200), but Wolfram writes of a Grail that is neither a platter nor a chalice but, rather, a stone. Identified as *lapsit exillis*—a puzzling term that suggests "fall" and "exile"—this Grail is guarded by Templars. The castle's king, Anfortas, suffers from a wound in the groin but is kept alive by the Grail. He can be released from his suffering only by a youth who will ask the appropriate question about his condition. That youth, Parzival, initially fails to make the inquiry and must undergo chivalric tribulations and religious renewal before he can return to the castle to heal Anfortas.

Despite Wolfram's innovation, the Grail remained, for most writers, the chalice associated with the Last Supper. A major development of the Grail theme occurs in the vast French Lancelot-Grail (or Vulgate) cycle, composed between about 1215 and 1235. Consisting of five interconnected romances, the cycle relates the history and prehistory of the Grail (the vessel from which Christ and his disciples ate the paschal lamb) and that of the Arthurian world. In the fourth of the Lancelot-Grail romances, *La queste del saint Graal* (The Quest for the Holy Grail), the quest is preceded by the mysterious appearance of the Grail at Arthur's court. The vessel enters the castle (without being carried) after a thunderclap and a great light; accompanied by a wonderful fragrance, it moves through the room producing the food and drink most desired by each person there.

Although some manuscripts identify Perceval as the Grail knight, that role generally falls instead to Lancelot's son Galahad, the only knight who, perfect and pious, is spiritually qualified to achieve a full Grail vision after transporting the Grail to the holy city of Sarras. In *La queste del saint Graal*, the final Grail vision is a mystical experience during which the figure of Josephus, the first

luure de   messire

The Grail appears to Galahad in the Perilous Seat and the knights of the Round Table. (Paris, BN MS Fr. 120, fol. 524v)

Christian bishop, conducts the Grail mass; the latter is a literal transubstantiation in which Christ himself appears and speaks to Galahad and his companions. Galahad dies immediately afterward, and the Grail is taken up into heaven.

These and other French sources inspired numerous writers and were translated or adapted into a number of languages. The most notable was Sir Thomas Malory, whose *Le Morte Darthur* (completed in 1470) largely established the model for the Grail and other Arthurian themes in modern literature and art. The Grail itself is the same object for Malory that it had been for the Vulgate authors: the cup used at the Last Supper. Malory, however, alters the rigorous moral test that in the French version had ultimately excluded all but Galahad. In the process Malory appears to be offering hope of accomplishment to any Christian person of proper virtue and devotion.

Perhaps curiously, the medieval Church remained silent on the subject of the Grail and the quest, and it is largely in the postmedieval period that speculation has flourished about the object itself, its origin, and its possible survival and location. In popular lore a number of objects—a wooden cup in Wales, a green bowl in Genoa, and so on—have been identified as the Grail. In addition to seeking sources or prototypes of the Grail itself, scholars have investigated in detail possible models for the procession in which the Grail appears. Theories are numerous and complex but inconclusive. The major approaches can roughly, if simplistically, be divided among Christian, ritual, and Celtic theories: in the first, the objects in the Grail procession (in Chrétien's romance) are considered to be related to the liturgy and perhaps in particular to the St. John Chrysostom mass.

The theory of ritual origin, most popularly associated with the work of Jessie Weston, hypothesizes that a link exists between the Fisher King story and the Eastern religions (of Attis, Osiris, and Adonis) associated with death and rebirth. Related theories tie the story of Perceval to that of the Egyptian god Horus. In general the ritual theories attempt to link fertility or vegetation rites to the idea of a Waste Land that lies sterile until its king is healed by circumstances or actions (such as the asking of a particular question) related to the Grail.

The names most closely linked to the theory of Celtic origin are doubtless Roger Sherman Loomis and Helaine Newstead; they and others sought Celtic analogues of numerous themes and motifs from Grail romances. One of these theories connected the Fisher King (named Bron in Robert de Boron's work) with the Welsh hero Bran the Blessed, who in legend was wounded by a poisoned spear. The Grail itself, with its capacity for producing abundant food and drink, is seen as a representation of a magical cauldron of plenty (or cornucopia), of which many exist in Celtic legend.

During the late twentieth century yet another theory has received a great deal of popular exposure, though without gaining any significant scholarly acceptance. That is the Holy Grail–Holy Blood theory, the notion that the Grail is associated with (or simply is) the bloodline of Christ, a notion sometimes tied into suggestions that the Cathars were—and that a secret society still may be—the Grail's guardians.

See also: Arthurian Lore; Chrétien de Troyes; Joseph of Arimathea, Saint; Peredur, Son of Efrawg; Wolfram von Eschenbach

References and further reading: Grail studies are nearly uncountable, though a good many of them are popularizations or highly eccentric treatises concerning the Grail's existence or its psychological, mystical, or New Age appeal. As a result, prudence and discernment are essential. Highly recommended is D. Mahoney, ed., *The Grail: A Casebook* (1999), which has an informative introduction and some 20 essays concerning Grail origins and literary (and other) representations of the Grail. In addition, *Les romans du Graal dans la littérature des XIIe et XIIIe siècles* (1956) offers a collection of important earlier essays on French and German Grail texts, as well as on the question of origins. The origins of the object and of the legend have been the subject of the majority of serious Grail studies in the past. The most widely known of those may well be J. Weston's *From Ritual to Romance* (1913), but it is not a reliable work of scholarship. Far more scholarly, but expressing an uncompromising commitment to Celtic hypotheses, are the works of R. S. Loomis, including *The Grail: From Celtic Myth to Christian Symbol* (1963). D. D. R. Owen, in *The Evolution of the Grail Legend* (1968), offers a useful study of the Grail as a Christianization of an object whose origins are Celtic. J. Frappier's "Le Graal et la chevalerie," *Romania* 75 (1954), discusses the synthesis of religion and chivalry found in early Grail romances.

—Norris J. Lacy

Grain Miracle

Legend associated in the Middle Ages with the Virgin Mary and a variety of female saints, who, by passing through or around a field, cause grain that has just been sown to grow miraculously to its full height.

Examples of the grain miracle legend appear in writings, paintings, and sculpture throughout the Middle Ages and beyond. Sometimes the legend is associated with the Virgin Mary. Carrying the child Jesus, she flees toward Egypt with Herod's soldiers in pursuit and passes by a man in the act of sowing seeds (or sometimes plowing his field). The Virgin instructs the farmer that if soldiers come looking for her, he should tell them that he saw a woman pass by while he was sowing. As soon as Mary leaves, the freshly sown seeds sprout and grow tall. Immediately Herod's soldiers arrive and ask the farmer if he has seen a mother and child pass by. He answers, "Yes, when I first began to sow this seed." Assuming the seed had been sown months before, the soldiers turn away, and Virgin and Child are spared.

When the basic plot is adapted to a female saint, she is typically a virgin who is fleeing a would-be rapist. This tale appears as a featured event in the lives of early-medieval saints—Radegunda (French, sixth century), Macrine (French, ninth century), Walpurga (English and German, eighth century), and Milburga (English, d. 715)—whose veneration is associated with the agricultural cycle. For example, in England in the eleventh century, Radegunda's feast day was observed on February 11, the day "the birds begin to sing," as spring and the plowing season begin. Similarly, a fourteenth-century story about Milburga relates how she kept the peasants' fields free from geese and worms during sowing season and in this way preserved the crop from predators. Thus, the virgin saints associated with the grain miracle can be seen as grain protectresses.

These legends have roots in the magico-religious ideas going back to the Bronze Age and are manifest in diverse goddesses worshipped among disparate agrarian peoples of the Mediterranean. There is archaeological, textual, and art-historical evidence that points to the ongoing veneration, in a variety of cultures, of a female figure propitiated by special rites when the ground was first "awakened." It was at this time, before the seed was placed in the "belly" of the earth, that the land was "purified" and an earth mother goddess was invoked as protectress of the grain. One of the earliest pictorial examples of this vegetation protectress is found on a pithos (a large earthenware jar for storing grain) from the ninth century B.C.E. in Crete. This goddess, riding atop her cart, arrives to promote the growth of vegetal life in the spring.

The concept of a grain protectress is found in pagan Roman and Celto-Germanic agrarian cultures as well. Textual accounts from the Roman world describe the *Feria sementiva* (Seeding/Planting Festival), celebrated in the very early spring when the new agricultural cycle began. Ovid (*Fasti*, 1.655–704), Tibullus (2.1.5.–8,) and Virgil (*Georgics*, 1.337–350) describe a seeding festival that invoked the mother goddess of grain. Participants asked her to provide abundant growth and to protect the fields. The ritualized enactment of this ceremony included a purification rite and a sacred circuit around the fields, a circuit that was to provide a barrier against any evil spirits that could harm the grain.

The festivities associated with *sementiva* persisted well into the Christian era, as peasants were reluctant to abandon customs so intimately connected with the growth of vegetation and therefore with the sustaining of life. In the Germanic north as well as in Romano-Celtic Gaul, literary and art-historical evidence reveals the imagery of a grain protectress who promoted crop fertility by her symbolic passage through the countryside. In his *Liber in gloria confessorum* (Book in Praise of the Confessors) Gregory of Tours (538–594) supplies a description of the statue of the earth mother goddess of sowing venerated by the

Franks. He describes how she was drawn around in a cart to enhance the prosperity of the fields but reports that when the cart got stuck, the people turned away from her and converted. This Christian text provides an example of how the early spring seeding ritual was taken over by the Church so that it could redirect peasant veneration from the pagan earth mother goddess to early-medieval female saints.

See also: Brigid, Saint; Peasants; Virgin Mary
References and further reading: See P. Berger, *The Goddess Obscured* (1985); P. Boglioni, ed., *La culture populaire au moyen âge* (1979); J. N. Coldstream, "A Protogeometric Nature Goddess from Knossos," in *Bulletin of the Institute of Classical Studies, London* (1984); M. Gimbutas, *The Goddesses and Gods of Old Europe* (1982); J. Le Goff, *Pour un autre moyen âge* (1977); and R. Manselli, *La religion populaire au moyen âge* (1979).

—*Pamela Berger*

Green Man

The somewhat whimsical name for what are less romantically termed "foliate heads"—carved faces (usually male) from whose mouths foliage emerges.

A variant type is a human face formed of foliage, framed by hair depicted in a foliate manner, as found, for example, in Villard de Honnecourt's famous mid-thirteenth-century sketchbook. Unfortunately, much nonsense has been written about these motifs—precisely the sort of thing that has given the study of folklore a bad name in academic circles—and some of it by scholars who should have known better. M. D. Anderson, for example, sees them as relics of pre-Christian tree worship, personifications of the spirit of the tree, and makes the inevitable reference to *The Golden Bough*. Highly dubious comparisons are regularly made with the attested druidic reverence for the oak and with folk customs, such as the Jack of the Green (a character in postmedieval May Day pageants, who dressed in greenery and sometimes took on the appearance of a walking tree), first attested in the late nineteenth century, or with other exotic cultures. Extremes of idiocy are reached by those writers who plot the occurrences of the popular pub name "The Green Man" as if this reflected the former prevalence of a pre-Christian tree-worshipping cult.

Conventionalized leaves emerge from the mouths of stone capital heads as early as the Norman period in England (e.g., at Kilpeck) and are also found in contemporary Continental sculpture. By the later Middle Ages, however, the motif is preeminently an English decorative taste, enjoying great popularity in sculptural media and especially common on roof bosses, corbels, and misericords. In fact, heads emerging from or above stylized acanthus leaves can be found in Roman sculpture (as on the third-century B.C.E. so-called Jupiter columns at Cirencester and elsewhere). By the eighth century the "inhabited vine-scroll" populated by tiny human (and animal) figures frolicking in or battling against the tendrils of the foliage has become a decorative commonplace.

See also: *Sir Gawain and the Green Knight*
References and further reading: The person mainly responsible in modern times for the relics-of-tree-worship theory was Lady Raglan, "The 'Green Man' in Church

Architecture," *Folklore* 50 (1939). See also R. O. M. Carter and H. M. Carter, "The Foliate Head in England," *Folklore* 78 (1967); R. Judge, *The Jack in the Green: A May Day Custom* (1977); O. Lauffer, "Geister im Baum," in *Volkskundliche Gaben* (1934); R. Sheridan and A. Ross, *Grotesques and Gargoyles* (1975); K. Basford, *The Green Man* (1978); W. Anderson, *Green Man, the Archetype of Our Oneness with the Earth* (1990); and M. Harding, *A Little Book of the Green Man* (1998).

—Malcolm Jones

Griffin [Griffon, gryphon]

A fabulous winged creature with an eagle's beak and lion's body.

Bird mammals existed in the lore of Mesopotamia and other ancient cultures, but the medieval griffin was chiefly inherited from Greco-Roman art and literature. The classical griffin originated in oral travelers' tales from Scythia first recorded by Herodotus, Pliny, and other ancient writers. Griffins were believed to live in remote deserts of central Asia, where they guarded gold, made nests on the ground, and preyed on horses, deer, and humans. Although travelers in the Middle Ages continued to describe griffins as real fauna of Asia or India, no author ever claimed to have seen a live griffin.

By late Roman times griffins had come to be associated with Nemesis, goddess of divine retribution. By 500 C.E. the classical griffin's strength, ferocity, and guardianship over gold were integrated into Christian imagery. Medieval bestiaries drew on Greco-Roman natural histories to describe the enigmatic griffin's appearance and behavior, and the creature assumed layers of ambiguity, fantasy, and symbolism. Medieval additions to the griffin legend included eggs of agate, the ability to fly, tremendous strength, and magical powers.

Griffin designs decorated a wide range of secular and religious objects of the Middle Ages: caskets, jewelry, tapestries, game pieces, coats of arms, manuscript margins, architectural details, and liturgical lamps. The variety reveals how versatile the motif could be for elites and ordinary folk alike. For example, ornate Italian and English chests for precious jewels and valuables were often adorned with griffins, recalling their traditional role as defenders of gold. Griffins also stood guard on elaborately carved coffins and saints' reliquaries. On the other hand, a series of plain bronze griffin buckles (Byzantine, eighth–tenth centuries C.E.) were definitely not luxury items; art historians believe that these everyday items warded off evil spirits for less affluent wearers. In the complex symbolism of bronze lamps cast in fantastic griffin shapes and decorated with crosses and other Christian symbols, the griffin represented violence and temptation subdued by the Church.

The griffin's exotic nature suited the bizarre zoology of Romanesque and Gothic art. Along with other real and imaginary fauna, griffins abounded on cathedrals and monasteries from Italy to Ireland. Naturalistic griffins are included in Adam and Eve's earthly paradise on ninth-century French ivories, and the border of the Bayeux Tapestry (c. 1100) teems with griffins. Some scholars argue that the griffin's popularity in European art and architecture must have been influenced by the development of bestiaries, but it is more likely to be evidence of the continuous survival of a very ancient cross-cultural tradition, as Asian, Middle Eastern, and African decorative goods and beliefs were integrated into medieval Europe.

Compilers of bestiaries provided a vivid illustration and appended a Christian allegorical meaning for each creature. Greed and bloodthirsty antipathy toward humans were the griffin's standard "moral" traits. Yet the rich tradition of griffins and their composite, dualistic nature meant that they were never simply purely evil monsters; they could also be seen as vigilant guardians, relentless avengers, and even gentle protectors.

The griffin was a natural emblem in heraldry. The earliest griffin coat of arms, attested in 1167, was that of Richard de Revers, earl of Exeter. The griffin device became especially prevalent in the 1400s and accounts for the many Germanic and English family names derived from the word *griffin*. One ingenious explanation for the origin of medieval griffins proposes that it is the result of an early instance of the heraldic process of dimidiation, in which the left and right halves of two different coats of arms (in this case, an eagle and lion) are conjoined by a diagonal bend (diagonal band from upper right to lower left) or vertical pale (stripe). The result would be an eagle-headed lion. But as we have seen, griffins preceded heraldry by millennia.

A depiction of a griffin woven into the border of the eleventh-century French Bayeux Tapestry. (Bild Archive/Foto Marburg)

Numerous medieval romances describe fierce griffins carrying off strong men: *Herzog Ernst* (c. 1180–1220) and *Kudrun* (c. 1230) are two German examples. Medieval traditions associated griffins with Alexander the Great (356–323 B.C.E.). In some versions, the ambitious Alexander harnesses four flying griffins to carry him aloft to triumph over the heavens, but God forces the heathen conqueror back to earth. In the early fourteenth century, Griffin symbolism inspired a very different climax in Dante's *Divine Comedy*, in which the triumphal chariot of the Church is drawn by a Sacred Griffin. Its golden head and wings represent Christ's divinity, and the red-and-white limbs signify the Savior's earthbound nature. The Sacred Griffin restores the Tree of Knowledge, withered since the Fall, and returns to heaven.

People expected to learn more about mysterious griffins in travelers' lore about faraway lands. Marco Polo (1254–1324) identified the griffin with a monstrous bird of Madagascar. According to another highly popular fourteenth-century work, the *Travels of Sir John Mandeville*, one griffin was as strong as eight lions and 100 eagles, able to carry a horse or two oxen to its nest. The talons were so huge they served as drinking cups. Around this time so-called griffin's claws (typically, polished ibex or rhinoceros horns or the tusks of extinct mammoths) elaborately set in gold and encrusted with gems began to circulate in Europe. These claws, as well as griffin "feathers" and "agate eggs," were alleged to reveal the presence of poison, confer magical power, and cure blindness and infertility.

Prehistoric fossils may have influenced the griffin's image. In 1993 I proposed that the ancient Scythian-Greek legend was inspired by observations of the remains of beaked, egg-laying, quadruped dinosaurs about the size of lions. These well-preserved skeletons and nests with petrified eggs are ubiquitous along the caravan routes through the central Asian deserts where gold has been mined since the Bronze Age. Continued sightings in the Middle Ages of fossils along the Silk Road (a trade route stretching from China to the Middle East) would perpetuate the tale, and souvenir bones, horns, and eggs would convince European travelers of the griffin's existence. This scenario has been generally accepted by paleontologists and classicists, but other cultures' bird-mammal folklore also nourished medieval European beliefs about griffins. As scholars of many fields have shown, in the Middle Ages the venerable griffin was a powerful multicultural image of great age, depth, and profound symbolic potential.

See also: Bestiary; Fossils; *Mandeville's Travels*
References and further reading: For a well-illustrated study of griffins from the ancient Middle East to the present, see J. Nigg, *The Book of Gryphons* (1982). The relationship between dinosaur remains and griffin folklore is set forth in A. Mayor and M. Heaney, "Griffins and Arimaspeans," *Folklore* 104 (1993), and A. Mayor, ch. 1 of *The First Fossil Hunters* (2000). In his discussion of the archaic griffin's transition to medieval Christian iconography, W. Bartscht emphasizes its age-old duality in religious symbolism and in romances: see "The Griffin," in *Mythical and Fabulous Creatures*, ed. M. South (1987). G. Bliss, "Griffins in Medieval Art," in *Survival of the Gods* (exhibition catalog, List Art Center, Brown University, 1987), stresses the survival of pagan traditions in the Christian adaptation of the ancient griffin image from Greco-Roman, Byzantine, and Islamic sources. Bartscht and Bliss offer valuable bibliographies on the medieval griffin. P. Lum,

"Senmurv and the Gryphon," in his *Fabulous Beasts* (1952), places the griffin in the context of bird-mammal lore of other cultures, but some of his interpretations are dated. Cryptozoologist P. Costello, *The Magic Zoo* (1979), asks what the griffin meant in various mythological contexts and provides a history of attempts to identify the griffin as a real animal.

—*Adrienne Mayor*

Guinefort, Saint

A greyhound celebrated in thirteenth-century legends and rituals near the French city of Lyons.

Although the name St. Guinefort was also applied to several human figures (notably Guinefort of Pavia, Italy), it is the dog that has become the focus of folkloric interest because its story and cult were unusually well documented and have been studied at length by Jean-Claude Schmitt.

The legend and cult of the greyhound came to ecclesiastical attention through Stephen of Bourbon (c. 1180–1261), a Dominican friar attached to the convent of Lyons, whose descriptions are recorded in a treatise left unfinished at his death. Stephen heard the legend and testimony concerning the cult about 1250 in the course of preaching against sorcery and hearing confessions in the diocese of Lyons. Many women confessed that they had taken their children to St. Guinefort. They related this legend about the holy dog:

> The greyhound Guinefort belonged to a lord and lady, who one day left their baby boy in the care of a nurse. When the nurse left the baby unattended, a huge serpent entered the house. The faithful greyhound killed the serpent and tossed its body a safe distance from the infant. But when the nurse returned to the house to find the cradle upset and cradle and dog covered with blood, she shrieked; the lord entered and instinctively slew the dog with his sword before finding the baby unharmed.

This narrative of the faithful dog is a widespread exemplum and legend type, classified as B331.2 in Stith Thompson's *Motif-Index*. The tale is recorded in no fewer than 11 Latin versions written throughout the late Middle Ages and in many more-recent accounts. Perhaps the most famous variant is the story from which Thompson takes his title: "Llewellyn and His Dog," in which a Welsh prince kills his faithful dog Gelert before discovering that the hound has saved his child from a snake. Although the earliest recorded Gelert narrative dates only to 1800, a manuscript illumination dated 1484 pictures the prince of Wales with a helmet surmounted by a cradle in which a greyhound stands—this iconographic flourish, unique in medieval heraldry, is taken as evidence that the story of Llewellyn and his dog was well established in Britain by the end of the Middle Ages.

The French version, however, is of particular interest because it bears evidence of oral circulation among a peasant population. Unlike the numerous elite versions of the exempla collections, the folk story recorded by Stephen has no appended moral. It is also the most economical account, mentioning, for example, one female servant assigned to the infant instead of the two or three women mentioned in exemplum accounts. Schmitt interprets this narrative economy both as an indication of a tale streamlined through the process of oral narration and as an indication of a peasant's view of a noble household, in which one servant is more than enough to mind the manor.

The importance of Stephen's narrative extends well beyond its possible indications of peasant narrative styles because the friar proceeds to contextualize the legend by explaining how village women used it as a justification for their healing rituals. His account continues:

> Discovering the loyalty of the dog, the people of the household threw it into a well near the manor house, heaped stones upon the grave, and planted trees nearby. After the manor fell into abandon, peasants, preserving the memory of the dog's heroics, began to honor it as a martyr. They made the grove and grave the site of a ritual in which mothers would take their ailing infants. Under the guidance of an old woman, they brought offerings of salt and other things to the grove, removed their babies' swaddling clothes and hung them on bushes, drove nails into the grove's trees, and passed their naked babies between two trees. The mother would toss the child nine times between the trees into the arms of the old woman, invoking the "fauns of the forest" (i.e., the spirits of the woods) to take the ailing child and to replace it with a healthy one. Then the child was placed naked on a bed of straw between two lit candles and left alone. If the child was alive when the mother returned, she plunged it nine times into the waters of a nearby river, which action was supposed to ensure that the child would be healthy.

This complex ritual contains many elements—such as purification by fire and water—that have been documented not only in the Middle Ages but also among French peasantry into relatively recent times. The significance of the trees as agents in the healing process, for example, evokes a religious practice documented in the region of the Guinefort cult in 1158: a shrine containing the relics of St. Taurinus, when set at the foot of an oak tree, instantly cured a paralytic. The tale and the ritual, read together, offer unusually rich testimony of a living legend complex through which peasants used narratives to explain their ritual activities. The ritual itself reflects a belief in changelings: the ailing infants brought to Guinefort's grove were apparently believed to be not human children but spirit children that had been substituted for babies. The ritual was designed to induce the spirits to take back the substitute children and to return the human babies.

As an orthodox churchman, Stephen regarded this cult practice as misguided and demonic. His account emphasizes that he had the remains of the dog disinterred and the grove destroyed by fire. As Schmitt points out, Stephen's response is patterned according to a major topos in ecclesiastical folklore, a narrative pattern in which a holy man visits the site of a cult and debunks the central cult figure. Both the peasant women and Stephen of Bourbon could thus be said to be acting according to ostention—the process through which people use legend as a script for their own actions. The women used the story of the greyhound, as Stephen used saints' lives, as inspirations to guide their own activities.

See also: Doghead; French Tradition; Legend
References and further reading: The major study of the Guinefort legend and ritual is J.-C.
Schmitt, *The Holy Greyhound: Guinefort, Healer of Children since the Thirteenth Century*,
trans. M. Thom (1983). S. Baring-Gould retells several of the medieval versions of
"Llewellyn and His Dog" in *Curious Myths of the Middle Ages* (1961).

—Carl Lindahl

Guy of Warwick

Hero of romance, legend, and history, popular from the thirteenth-century
Anglo-Norman poem, with international repute by the fifteenth century, widely
known during the Renaissance and to the present day.

Guy's story combined chivalric high sentiments and dedication to preserving order in this world with the idea of withdrawal from worldliness to serve
God in expectation of union in eternity; these combined ideals help render
Guy such an appealing hero. His story, which celebrates chivalric ideals and
recognizes their real limitations, has been adapted across the centuries to reflect
current religious, social, and political values. The composite romance has attracted a wide audience and includes many traditional elements that persist in
increasingly abbreviated versions of the original long narrative.

A Saxon of the tenth century, in the reign of Athelstan, Guy begins life as
a steward's son, receives knightly training, and falls in love. In order to win
Felice, daughter of Rohalt, earl of Warwick, he achieves fame as the finest knight
by winning tournaments, assisting many in distress, becoming a sworn companion of the earl Terri, and slaying the Irish dragon in Northumberland. Forty
days after their marriage, and the begetting of a son Reinbrun, Guy has a moment of religious understanding that leads him to forsake his worldly seeking
and dedicate himself to God.

He begins a second series of adventures as a pilgrim knight in the Holy
Land, where he slays the pagan giant Amorant. As a pilgrim champion, announced to Athelstan by an angel, Guy defeats Colbrond, the Saracen giant of
Anlaf, king of the Danes. Refusing public honors, Guy retires to Warwick to
live as a hermit. He is reunited with Felice, who has performed many deeds of
charity in his absence, only moments before he dies. Felice soon follows, and
they are buried in Lorraine.

Heralt d'Ardern, Guy's mentor and friend, goes to Africa and finds Reinbrun,
who had been stolen when a boy. After Reinbrun rescues one of his father's old
companions from a fairy knight and encounters Heralt's son Aselac, all return
home. The poem's prologue and epilogue identify Guy as an ideal figure, worthy
of emulation.

The original Anglo-Norman romance *Gui de Warewic* (12,926 lines) was
written for a baronial society that sought respectability through ancient lineage
and a sense of belonging in a conquered land. The first romancer drew upon the
historical characters of Athelstan and William Marshall, the hagiography of St.
Alexis, the exploits of William of Orange, and episodes and stylistic traits of
Chrétien de Troyes. There are two complete fourteenth-century translations
into Middle English romance and one in French prose. Peter Langtoft intro-

duced Guy into history as the savior of Britain in his *Chronique d'Angleterre* (Chronicle of England), translated into Middle English by Robert Mannyng of Brunne in 1338. Here, Guy's victory over Colbrond gives the account of Athelstan an emphasis analogous to the Anglo-Saxon poem *The Battle of Brunanburh*. Guy's place in history as the savior of England expands with chroniclers like Gerald of Cornwall and Henry Knighton, and his exemplary character is deployed in *Speculum Gy de Warewyke* and as a subject for sermons in the Latin *Gesta Romanorum* (Deeds of the Romans), where Tale 172 combines episodes from the romance to make Guy an example of constancy.

Pictorial representations most frequently show Guy as the slayer of giants and dragons (Taymouth *Hours* and Smithfield Decretals, a Gloucester misericord, a mazer [large drinking cup]), apt icons for the favorite medieval English hero, whose fame at times exceeded that of Arthur and Robin Hood. Guy shares traits with the later English folktale hero Jack the Giant Killer, and with St. George, the patron saint of England.

Illuminations in the fourteenth-century Smithfield Decretals give evidence of popular, oral tradition; they depict Guy slaying giants and dragons, as well as the Dun Cow, a local folk episode that becomes part of written texts only in the sixteenth century.

With the increasing influence of the Beauchamp earls of Warwick in the fifteenth century, Guy continues in *Chronicles* of Thomas Rudborne and John Hardyng and a poem of John Lydgate. He is featured in the *Rous Rolls* and *Beauchamp (Warwick) Pageants*, in which Guy is recognized by the Soldan's lieutenant in the Holy Land. At Guy's Cliffe, already tied to the legend because of a cave where Guthi's (Guy's) prayer is carved in Roman and Saxon runic characters, a larger-than-life statue is carved from the rock. Richard de Beauchamp modeled his life on Guy, and his funeral effigy emulates his ancestor. There is a less sophisticated Middle English romance and a short metrical romance, *Guy and Colebrande*. Guy's international repute is evident in a Celtic *Irish Life of Sir Guy of Warwick*; *Gydo und Thyrus*, a German retelling and romanticizing of the tale from the *Gesta Romanorum*; and the frame story of William of Warwick in Joan Martorell's *Tirant lo Blanc* (begun 1460, pub. 1490).

The legend of Guy of Warwick contains many traditional elements found in medieval romances and saints' lives, as well as later oral folktales; these are among the most common motifs: proud princess rejects low-born suitor (L100), knight becomes hermit (*P56), husband in disguise visits wife (K1813), winning of a princess (Blanchflour) in a tournament (H331.2), sworn brotherhood (P311), false steward (Morgadour; K2242), slaying of giants (*F531.6.12.6), fight with dragons (B11.11), decision of victory between armies through single combat (*H217.5).

See also: George, Saint; Romance
References and further reading: Motifs preceded by an asterisk in the final paragraph of this entry are from G. Bordman, *Motif-Index of the English Metrical Romances* (1963).

The most comprehensive study of *Guy* is V. B. Richmond, *The Legend of Guy of Warwick* (1996); see also the earlier discussion in her *The Popularity of Middle English Romance* (1976). L. Hibbard, *Medieval Romance in England* (1924), discusses some folkloric elements; D. Mehl, *The Middle English Romances of the Thirteenth and Fourteenth Centuries*

(1967), is a helpful survey, as is W. R. J. Barron, *English Medieval Romance* (1987). Three recent studies of romance include analyses of *Guy of Warwick* that reflect current literary theory: S. Crane, *Insular Romance* (1986); C. Fewster, *Traditionality and Genre in Middle English Romance* (1987); and A. Hopkins, *The Sinful Knights* (1990).

—*Velma Bourgeois Richmond*

Gwynn ap Nudd [Gwynn, Son of Nudd]

King of the otherworld, later king of the fairies, in Welsh folklore.

His name suggests his mythological origins. *Gwyn* (white) is frequently associated with otherworld figures, and Gwynn's father, Nudd, who sometimes has the epithet *Llaw Ereint* (Silver Hand), is cognate with Irish Nuadha Airged "silver hand or arm," king of the otherworld race, the Tuatha Dé Danann. Both the Welsh and Irish names are etymologically related to Nodons, a god, to whom dedications have been found in a Romano-British temple at Lydney Park, Gloucestershire. A tale about Gwynn ap Nudd is outlined in *Culhwch and Olwen*, a Welsh story dating from about 1100 in its surviving form. Gwynn had abducted Creiddylad, daughter of Lludd, from Gwythyr ap Greidiol, to whom she was to be married. Arthur reconciled Gwynn and Gwythyr, decreeing that they should do battle for her each May Day until Doomsday, when the victor on that day should have the right to claim her.

Gwynn's Irish counterpart is Finn (Fionn), who is, however, the husband who loses his wife Grainne to the young Diarmaid, with whom she elopes on the night of their wedding feast. The Welsh and Irish tales are obviously analogous stories of love triangles and elopements (or abductions), though the roles of Gwynn and Finn have been reversed. In the Irish story, Diarmaid and Grainne take refuge in a clearing in a wood but succeed in escaping when Finn and his men surround them. A similar episode may be referred to in a fragment of Welsh folklore conserved in a fourteenth-century Latin treatise condemning soothsaying: the author notes the foolish actions of those who call upon the king of the spirits and his queen ("ad regem Eumenidium et reginam eius") saying, "Gwynn ap Nwdd qui es ultra in silvis pro amore concubine tue permitte nos venire domum" [Gwynn ap Nudd, (you) who are yonder in the forest, for the love of your mate, permit us to enter your dwelling]. *Culhwch and Olwen* assigns a special place to Gwynn as a huntsman, and there are other references to his horsemanship and hunting skills. He later appears in Welsh folklore as the leader of *cŵn Annwn* (hounds of Annwfn), the devil's pack hunting their prey of doomed mortals. The shift from king of Annwfn to king of the fairies or of the devils and the identification of Annwfn with hell are found in *Culhwch and Olwen*, where Gwynn is described as he "in whom God has set the spirits of the devils of Annwn lest this world be destroyed."

Gwynn's hellish associations are expressed unequivocally in the sixteenth-century *Life of St. Collen*, wherein the subjects of Gwynn, "the king of Annwfn and the fairies," are dismissed as merely devils. The saint visits Gwynn's court on Glastonbury Tor, "the fairest castle he had ever seen." He is not deceived, however, and he makes the illusion disappear by pouring holy water over the gathering. Both late-medieval poets and later folklore stress the fairy aspects of

Gwynn's legendry, focusing on the stories of his leading unwary travelers into his marshes and pools and causing them to lose their way on the misty hills, and the more gloomy, frightening features of Gwynn's character disappear.

See also: Annwfn; Celtic Mythology; *Culhwch and Olwen;* Fairies; Wild Hunt
References and further reading: See I. Foster, "Gwyn ap Nudd," in *Duanaire Finn,* part 3, ed. G. Murphy (1953); B. F. Roberts, "Gwyn ap Nudd," *Llên Cymru* 13 (1980–1981); P. Mac Cana, *Celtic Mythology* (1970); and R. Bromwich and D. S. Evans, eds., *Culhwch and Olwen* (1992).

—*Brynley F. Roberts*

Hamlet

Protagonist of a Danish legend.

The principal source for the medieval legend is the biography composed in Latin by Saxo Grammaticus around 1200 as part of his *Gesta Danorum* (History of the Danes; 3.6.1–4.2.2). Other accounts are found in Danish annals and in Icelandic literature. His name appears in such forms as Amleth, Amblet, Amlæd, Ambluthe, Amblothæ, Amlóthi, and Ambáles but never as Hamlet, a similar-sounding but etymologically unrelated English name that Elizabethan playwrights adopted when they reworked the medieval Danish story for the tragic stage.

According to Saxo, Amleth's father and uncle were corulers of the Danish peninsula of Jutland, but the latter grew envious of the former, openly slew him, and wed his widow Geruth. Sitting at the filthy hearth and carving wooden crooks for no obvious purpose, Amleth played the fool so that his uncle would not take him seriously as a potential avenger. Suspecting that Amleth's apparent folly might conceal cunning, the king's men subjected him to a series of tests. First they brought him together with a beautiful woman in a secluded spot to see if he would have sexual relations with her; Amleth did so, but only after eluding his spies. Next they brought him together with his mother in her bedroom to see if he would speak openly with her; again Amleth did so, but only after slaying the eavesdropper. When eventually the suspicious king dispatched him to Britain with two escorts and a runic letter instructing the British monarch to put him to death, the youth secretly rewrote the letter during the voyage, calling upon the king to execute the escorts and to give his daughter in marriage to Amleth. Returning to Denmark just as the king's men were celebrating the funeral, Amleth plied them with drink, tied them up, and set fire to the king's hall. Amleth became ruler of Jutland and went on to have other adventures before eventually falling in battle.

The narrative is enlivened with a good deal of humor, especially in the hero's punning responses to the interrogations of the king's men by means of which Amleth manages to tell the truth while cheerfully maintaining an appearance of imbecility.

The other major treatment of the Hamlet of tradition is the Icelandic *Ambáles Saga*, a romantic saga of the sixteenth or seventeenth century, composed at a time when evidently the story still circulated in Icelandic oral tradition. There is little trace of the oral story after this work.

Numerous scholarly attempts have been made to discover the origin of the Hamlet legend or the etymology of the hero's name on the assumption that they contain the key to understanding the story. These attempts have not found a consensus, although they have called attention to various other legends that resemble that of Hamlet, whether closely or distantly. In my opinion, the Scandinavian legend of Hróar and Helgi (also called Harald and Halfdan) and the ancient Roman legend of Brutus are so similar to the Hamlet legend that a genetic connection must be assumed. If this is correct, the Hamlet legend is one of several realizations of an old migratory legend.

Saxo's work was first published in 1514. Later in the century the Frenchman François de Belleforest retold the story of Amleth in a popular collection of tragic stories, *Histoires tragiques*, and soon afterward there was an English play, now lost, on the subject. Around 1600 Shakespeare reworked the story for the company to which he belonged.

See also: Scandinavian Mythology

References and further reading: W. Hansen, *Saxo Grammaticus and the Life of Hamlet* (1983), contains a full discussion of the Hamlet story and its analogs from the earliest evidence through Shakespeare. For the text of Saxo, see *Saxonis gesta Danorum*, 2 vols., ed. J. Olrik and H. Raeder (1931–1957), and for the minor Danish texts, see E. Jörgensen, *Annales Danici Medii Aevi* (1920), and M. Lorenzen, *Gammeldanske kröniker* (1887–1913). The Icelandic materials are fully treated in I. Gollancz, ed. and trans., *Hamlet in Iceland* (1898).

—*William Hansen*

Harp

Musical instrument consisting of strings—framed in wood—that are plucked by the artist.

The European harp of the early Middle Ages is distinguished from the ancient Mediterranean harp by its three-part construction of sound chest, string arm, and column, which together create a triangular frame. The origin of this Western frame harp is uncertain; various sources credit its creation to either Irish, Anglo-Saxon, or Norse cultures. Scholars must rely on the visual arts in researching the medieval harp, for there are no extant instruments that predate 1400 C.E. A tenth-century Anglo-Saxon manuscript is cited as the earliest example of a frame harp in an English drawing. The continental European Utrecht Psalter, written and illustrated between 816 and 835, depicts David the psalmist with a frame harp. Sometimes David carries an ancient Greek lyre, and this has led to some confusion as to whether the Latin *cithara* refers specifically to the frame harp. The ambiguity is also reflected in several Germanic languages, in which the verb "to harp" meant "to play a stringed instrument" and did not necessarily describe the Western harp. Depending on the time and place, the harp was called by many names—*hearpe, cythara, cruit, chrotta, rottae, lyre,* or *telyn*—but whether these names referred exclusively to the frame harp continues to be debated.

The harp is described as the "joywood" or "gleewood" in *Beowulf*, and it is the singing and harp music that maddens the monster Grendel and leads to

Grendel's attacks on Hrothgar's hall. The discovery of the Sutton Hoo ship burial in Suffolk, England, provided archaeologists with the remnants of a stringed instrument. However, a 1969 reconstruction of the Sutton Hoo instrument resembles more a rounded lyre than the triangular frame suggested by the name *hearpe* or *harpa*.

In the Norse sagas not only do harpers play songs of heroes, but heroes themselves play the harp. Gunnar, a hero of the thirteenth-century Icelandic *Völsunga Saga*, displays great skill as a harper. When thrown bound into a snake pit, he plays a harp with his toes. Witnesses find the performance better than most performers could accomplish playing with their hands. Gunnar's music charms all but one of the poisonous snakes to sleep; that one snake eventually kills him.

Other major harper heroes of medieval traditions include Tristan and Orpheus. In Gottfried von Strassburg's romance, *Tristan* (c. 1210), the famous

Tristan harping before King Mark, from a decorative tile in Chertsey Abbey, England, circa 1260–1280. (The Trustees of the British Museum)

lover astounds King Mark's court by playing the harp in "Breton style" so well that "many who stood and sat there forgot their own names." Orpheus, the famous musician of classical tradition, is transformed into a minstrel king in the fourteenth-century Middle English romance, *Sir Orfeo*. Orfeo's wife, Dame Heurodis (i.e., Eurydice), is abducted by the king of the fairies, and Orfeo follows her to the otherworld, where he plays the harp so enchantingly that he induces the fairy king to relinquish her.

Traditionally, gatherings of the early Irish Parliament, or *Feis*, at Tara, County Meath, were followed by minstrelsy and harping in the banquet hall. According to legend, St. Ruadhan cursed the gathering in 560 C.E. and the harp was mute thereafter, as Thomas More related in his poem "The Harp That Once through Tara's Halls." Early Irish ecclesiastics, such as St. Kevin and St. Columba, are reported to have played the Irish *cruit*, and Alfred the Great was said to have disguised himself as a harp player in order to enter the Danish camp. St. Aldhelm, the eighth-century bishop of Sherborne, played his harp at a bridge crossing and then preached a sermon to the crowd that gathered. In 1183 Gerald of Wales, court chaplain to Henry II, wrote in praise of the musicians he had heard in Ireland, and he states that both Wales and Scotland were influenced by the Irish harpers.

The harper was singled out from earliest times for special recognition in northern Europe, and especially in the Celtic-speaking areas of the British Isles. The harpist was accorded the status and privileges of the highest-ranking commoner in society. The harper's chief function was to accompany the poet's recital of panegyric poetry, and the harpist was given a place of honor beside the poet, although the harpist was not of noble birth. Harpers were also liable to persecution because of their association with nationalist feeling. The Welsh harpers were persecuted after the conquest of Wales by Edward I in 1284. Although one of the most magnificent surviving Irish harps dates from around 1500 (now in the National Museum of Ireland), Irish harpers were placed under threat of death by the mid-1500s. By 1600 the harping tradition was almost extinct in Ireland although harping still continued in isolated areas throughout the Celtic world. The harp itself continued to evolve into the frame-pedal harp familiar to most people today, but harping as a pastime associated with the communal merriment of the early Middle Ages had ceased by the early seventeenth century.

See also: Cædmon; Folk Music and Folksong; Minstrel
References and further reading: An excellent overview of the history of the frame harp can be found in R. Rensch's *Harps and Harpists* (1989). *The Harp* (1969), also by Rensch, provides additional information on the harp as it has been represented in literature and art. Other useful sources for the medieval harp include G. Reese, *Music in the Middle Ages* (1940); J. Montagu, *The World of Medieval and Renaissance Musical Instruments* (1976); and W. Matheson, ed., *The Blind Harper* (1970). The tenth-century Anglo-Saxon manuscript cited above is *Cædmon's Metrical Paraphrase of Scripture History*, now housed in the Bodleian Library, Oxford (MS. Junius II); its association with the seventh-century Saxon poet Cædmon dates from only the seventeenth century. For harp traditions connected with Orpheus, see J. B. Friedman, *Orpheus in the Middle Ages* (1970).
—Cynthia Whiddon Green

Harrowing of Hell

A widespread and popular narrative relating what Christ did after his Crucifixion and before his Ascension into heaven.

According to a myth circulated in the Middle East, a deity goes to the underworld and conquers its prince. Motivated by the belief that Christ also descended into hell during the three days after his death, early Christian

Christ treads Satan underfoot and lances him while leading the souls of the just out of the mouth of hell. From the French Miniatures of the Life of Christ, circa 1200. (Pierpont Morgan Library, MS M. 44, fol. 11v)

communities added it to the topography of the hereafter to which Jesus had descended after his death. Even so, it is only between the fourth and eighth centuries that this idea became an obligatory part of religious faith and was taken up in the creeds. The place of the descent into the underworld—limbo— was referred to as *limbus patrum* (borderland of the fathers), as the Fathers of the Old Testament dwelled there (cf. *limbus puerorum* [borderland of unbaptized children]). Especially important here would be the apocryphal Gospel of Nicodemus (third to fifth centuries), a widely popular "eyewitness account" that describes how Christ breaks open the gates of Hades and has the prince of the underworld bound. Then he leads Adam, Eve, and the other righteous souls of the old covenant out of limbo. In the early phase of the Reformation there was embittered discussion as to whether or not Christ himself had also experienced the sufferings of hell during this descent into the underworld.

In visions of the hereafter, in scholarly literature, and in religious poems and prayers, the descent of Christ into limbo is scarcely found as a separate theme. Limbo, however, did appear frequently in Romanesque and Gothic representations of the life of Christ (e.g., on Lent cloths); it was commonly portrayed as the jaws of hell, with the souls contained therein, and was held open by a pillar to which Christ had bound Satan. Limbo also appeared as a prison or a burning fortress.

The descent of Jesus into hell was present in the general consciousness mainly through Easter plays. The devils' fear of God's arrival, their attempts to keep some of the souls for themselves, and their later efforts to repopulate hell were expressed in thoroughly burlesque scenes. The gratitude of the released souls, whom Christ leads into heaven, was forcefully depicted. For all of them, including the innocent, had been previously handed over to the devils to be tortured. Although an authority such as Pope Gregory the Great had believed that the righteous among the Fathers had been held in confinement in a darkened cell without being tortured, the Middle Ages frequently made no distinction at all between torture in the real hell and torture in this limbo. This can be clearly seen in the wording of religious drama. Thus, for example, Jesus says to the devils in the so-called Easter play of Muri (mid-thirteenth century), as he liberates the souls from limbo, "You have destroyed them in a wretched and horrible fashion through the fire and fierce agonies of hell." And the souls reply that they called for the Savior "in the fierce agony of hell." Judas, Annas, Caiaphas, and Herod, however, must remain there forever.

See also: Dante Alighieri; Hell; Purgatory

References and further reading: Standard works on the subject include J. Kroll, *Gott und Hölle* (1932), and E. Kunstein, "Die Höllenfahrtsszene im geistlichen Spiel des Mittelalters," Ph.D. diss., Cologne (1972). For the apocryphal Gospel of Nicodemus, see H. C. Kim, *The Gospel of Nicodeme* (1973); A.-E. Ford, *L'Evangille de Nicodème* (1973); and Z. Izydorczyk, *The Medieval Gospel of Nicodemus* (1997). On the iconography, see H. M. v. Erffa, *Ikonologie der Genesis I* (1989); G. Schmidt, *The Iconography of the Mouth of Hell* (1995); and M. Herzog, *Descendit ad inferos* (1996).

—Peter Dinzelbacher

Harun al-Rashid (763 or 766–809) [Haroun al-Raschid, Harun ar-Rashid]

ᶜAbbasid caliph who ruled Baghdad from 786 to 809 C.E., when the city was at its cultural and commercial peak, and who subsequently became a major figure in Arabic storytelling traditions.

As ᶜAbbasid leader, Harun al-Rashid led the pilgrimage nine times during his reign and led Muslim troops against the Byzantines. He is perhaps best known in Western tradition as the caliph who presented Charlemagne with an elephant. In Baghdad the caliph surrounded himself with poets, musicians, and scholars. Harun's era has thus come to represent both the golden age of ᶜAbbasid rule and its attendant decadence and luxury.

Developing parallel to the historical record of Harun al-Rashid's character and accomplishments was a flourishing legend tradition, both written and oral. In addition, Harun al-Rashid, his wife Zubaida, and his vizier Jaᶜfar figure prominently in the *Thousand and One Nights*. Even historians such as al-Masᶜudi (896–c. 956) relied heavily on anecdotes and stories when describing him, and it is now widely agreed that what is known about Harun is largely derived from fiction and legend. The folk traditions of Harun al-Rashid tales are based loosely on actual events and circumstances, but the popularity of the fictional accounts has allowed them to subvert the authority of even the most reliable historical records.

One series of legends and tales about Harun al-Rashid concerns his relationship with Jaᶜfar the Barmaki. The Barmaki (also known as the Barmecides) had been for generations advisers to the ᶜAbbasid caliphs. Harun's execution of his adviser and boon companion Jaᶜfar in 803, however, substantially lessened the Barmaki's influence over the ruling family. Jaᶜfar's political influence had become a threat to the caliph's authority, but the more prevalent story was of romantic intrigue. Popular legend has it that Harun married his sister ᶜAbbasah to Jaᶜfar so that he would not have to be without either of them. While Harun purportedly saw the marriage as platonic and chaste, Jaᶜfar and ᶜAbbasah had other ideas. Many women's tales (*amr al-mar'ah*) tell this version of events, and although most historians rejected the story, they continued to include it in their histories of the ᶜAbbasid caliphate as evidence of the ruler's fiery temper.

Tales also attribute to Harun a social nature, despite the fact that he moved out of Baghdad to a country estate as soon as it was politically expedient. Harun al-Rashid's reputation as wine drinker—wine was forbidden to Muslims—and party-goer persisted largely due to his patronage of Abu Nuwas (d. c. 810), a poet famous for wine songs. Like his relationship with Jaᶜfar, Harun's friendship with Abu Nuwas was inconsistent. He paid the poet handsomely but imprisoned him several times as well. Harun al-Rashid's erratic behavior led to numerous tales of a caliph who drank and who would then feel remorse and punish his party companions. Legends indicate that the caliph tolerated unlawful drinking, and tales in the *Thousand and One Nights* show him participating in these illicit activities. The popularity and supposed credibility of these accounts led the historian Ibn Khaldun (1332–1406) to attempt to rehabilitate Harun al-Rashid's reputation. A caliph as renowned for his piety and as interested in theology as Harun al-Rashid was could not, reasoned later historians, also participate in drinking and revelry.

Harun al-Rashid's distrust of his advisers and his intellectual curiosity are well documented. Storytellers, aware of these traits, also endowed the caliph with insomnia and composed tales of him wandering the streets of Baghdad in disguise in order to monitor the activities of his subjects. The night wanderings of Harun al-Rashid are not a commonplace of the histories but are widely accepted as part of his biography. In the *Thousand and One Nights* he is depicted as rash and adventurous, often getting himself into trouble, and certainly not acting with the dignity expected of the commander of the faithful. In "The Porter and the Three Ladies of Baghdad," he almost loses his life because he speaks out inappropriately at a party, and in "The Slave Girl and Nur al-Din," he climbs a tree to investigate an illicit affair taking place in one of his palaces. These incidents are typical of the way in which Harun is depicted in the *Thousand and One Nights*. A discerning Ja'far often accompanies him on his journeys in order to temper the caliph's impulsiveness. In these stories, too, Ja'far patiently suffers Harun's wrath.

The importance of Harun al-Rashid to medieval folklore extends beyond his role as subject of legend. Harun's reign was also the golden age of 'Abbasid storytelling, and many of the medieval Arab tales still extant were recorded during his reign. In both oral and written forms, the stories of the 'Abbasid period have perpetuated and enhanced the reputation of Harun al-Rashid as ruler and patron of the arts.

See also: Arabic-Islamic Tradition; *Thousand and One Nights*
References and further reading: Many Arab histories of the 'Abbasid period have been
    translated into English, and many make reference to or accept as fact various legends. Al-
    Mas'udi, *The Meadows of Gold: The Abbasids*, trans. P. Lunde and C. Stone (1989), and al-
    Tabari, *The 'Abbasid Caliphate in Equilibrium: The Caliphates of Musa al-Hadi and Harun
    al-Rashid*, trans. C. E. Bosworth (1989), written in the tenth century, are the closest in
    time to Harun al-Rashid's rule. Ibn Khaldun, *The Muqaddimah*, trans. F. Rosenthal (1969),
    reinterprets Harun's reign. H. Haddawy, *Arabian Nights* (1990), and R. Burton, *A Plain and
    Literal Translation of the Arabian Nights Entertainment* (1885), include fictional tales of
    Harun al-Rashid. Commentary on these treatments may be found in D. Pinault, *Story-
    Telling Techniques in the Arabian Nights* (1992), and R. Irwin, *The Arabian Nights: A
    Companion* (1994).

—Bonnie D. Irwin

Harvest Festivals and Rituals

Events, feasts, and performances marking the culmination of the agricultural year.

The Labors of the Season

The end of the agricultural year in medieval Europe was an incredibly busy period for rural workers. From roughly the beginning of August through early November there were the multiple tasks of cutting, drying, and storing animal fodder; harvesting grain for human consumption; and processing this grain by threshing, winnowing, milling, and storing or brewing. The harvest stubble was then grazed by domestic beasts and fowl, outlying herds were driven in, and a portion of the livestock was slaughtered and preserved by smoking or in brine. In particular areas there was the special case of grape harvesting and wine production as well. Naturally the time frames for these many activities and their attendant festivals of thanksgiving would vary greatly from the Mediterranean regions to the northern realms of Scandinavia and Scotland.

Harvest Celebrations

Celebrations at the end of the reaping of rye, wheat, barley, and oats are no doubt as old as agriculture itself. Sir James Frazer and the Cambridge School of comparative religion made much of early modern European harvest rituals in the interest of establishing connections with an aboriginal worldview and particularly with an all-pervading Corn Spirit. This numen (that is, spiritual force) would be represented and indeed concentrated in the last standing stalks of the field. Sickles might be thrown at them until they fell, or the last stalks might be trampled into the earth, indicating an accreted and dangerous power in this unharvested remnant. German folklore has a *Roggenmuhme,* or harvest bogey woman, for example. The last sheaf particularly had to be removed in special ways and was especially honored and woven into anthropomorphic or abstract shapes that might have any number of local designations: "harvest doll," "kern baby," "old man," "cripple goat," or "harvest queen" (which British antiquarians liked to identify with the Roman goddess of grain, Ceres). Such practices appear to be pan-European. Poland, for instance, has both a *pszenna baba* (old wheat woman) and a *dziad* (old man). The figure is brought out of the fields in triumph, usually on a decorated "hock cart," to serve thereafter as a focus for festivities. These large anthropomorphic figures are evidently the ancestors of the decorative "corn dollies" hung up in individual houses in more recent times in Britain and elsewhere. The fundamental notion of the dying and reviving god was thus thought to be very much alive in rural Europe up to the Industrial Revolution and even beyond. Such early modern folksongs as "John Barleycorn" were quite self-conscious celebrations of this very Corn Spirit. Such perennialist notions were widespread in late-nineteenth- and early-twentieth-century scholarship, for example, in the work of Heino Pfannenschmid.

While a connection to the Corn Spirit remains an attractive, even a logical thesis given the general conservatism of the rural people, there is very little in the way of hard evidence to corroborate it from the early-medieval period. To be sure, one can argue, as did Maire MacNeill in her magisterial study *The Festival of Lughnasa,* that in the ultraconservative west of Ireland there was a real continuity with the pagan Celtic past in the bonfires on mountaintops on the first day of August. These celebrate the first fruits and, obliquely, the ancient solar and fructifying deity Lug (Lugh). Elsewhere in the British Isles the day is Lammas (from the Anglo-Saxon *hlafmaesse,* "loaf-mass") and lacks this pagan coloration. There are intriguing hints in the medieval record for England, however. William of Malmesbury passed along a bit of Anglo-Saxon lore that appears to be the remnant of an etiological myth for the arrival of agriculture in the North: the magical child Sceaf (Sheaf) was said to have arrived off

Scandia asleep on a sheaf of grain in an oarless boat. He would later become an ancestor of the Anglo-Saxon kings. And what are we to make of this report from the reign of King Stephen (1135–1154) by the chronicler William of Newburgh?

> At harvest-time, when the harvesters were busy in the fields gathering crops, two children, a boy and a girl, emerged from these ditches [Wolfpittes, near Bury Saint Edmunds]. Their entire bodies were green, and they were wearing clothes of unusual colour and unknown material. As they wandered bemused over the countryside, they were seized by the reapers and led to the village.

The green children refuse all human food until they are given newly shelled beans, upon which they subsist until they learn to eat bread. Having then learned "our language," they describe their twilight homeland across a wide river, a typical description of Faerie (the fairy realm). Is this an embroidered account of the discovery of actual feral children, or is it a garbled account of an archaic harvest ritual translated into legend form? It could be either, but it may well be that the Corn Spirit, here as in the William of Malmesbury passage, is peeking through as a palimpsest in the records of elite culture.

An unbroken chain of celebratory harvest practices going back to the Neolithic is certainly possible for much of medieval Europe, but throughout the region these customs were altered by at least a certain degree of Christian influence, which no doubt varied widely from region to region. Thanksgiving for the harvest is of course biblical as well, and we must imagine a range of practices, some more pagan in feel, some perfectly Christian and acceptable even to many of the Reformed, like the more recent display of the fruits of the harvest in church, or the tamer harvest wreaths and simply decorated sheaves.

In the special case of wine production, it seems that medieval practice had little or no connection with or recollection of Dionysus comparable to the Corn Spirit phenomenon, probably because of the dominating influence of monasticism in the spread of viniculture in the early-medieval period. Early Modern images of the reveling Bacchus in wine-drinking cultures are clearly popular reflections of Renaissance learning. Medieval viniculture, by contrast, was under the patronage of such demure saints as the martyr St. Vincent in France or the pope St. Urban in German-speaking areas.

If we can extrapolate backward from more recently documented folk practices, all the end-of-labor celebrations, the singing of the "harvest home," the thanksgiving and conspicuous feasting, the final rounds of fairs and parish gatherings known as church ales must certainly have occasioned a high degree of revelry and afforded opportunities for creating solidarity between the owners and the workers of the land in the central Middle Ages. (The visual record of harvest time when it emerges—in the illuminations of aristocratic books of hours, for example—invariably shows the work of the season and little of the celebration.) Although there might be local practices, such as the two principal reapers being designated Harvest Lord and Harvest Lady, harvest festivals do not seem to have developed very strong rituals of inversion, mock kingdoms, and so forth. They might be extremely egalitarian, but they were not quite fully carnivalesque in spirit.

Robert Herrick, a poet of the seventeenth century, probably gives us the best window on earlier harvest celebration in his "The Hock-cart, or Harvest Home," dedicated to the earl of Westmorland:

> Come forth, my Lord, and see the Cart
> Drest up with all the Country Art.
> See, here a *Maukin*, there a sheet,
> As spotlesse pure, as it is sweet:
> The Horses, Mares, and frisking Fillies,
> (Clad, all, in Linnen, white as Lillies.)
> The Harvest Swaines, and Wenches bound
> For joy, to see the *Hock-cart* crown'd.
> About the Cart, heare, how the Rout
> Of Rurall Younglings raise the shout;
> Pressing before, some coming after,
> Those with a shout, and these with laughter.
> Some blesse the Cart; some kisse the sheaves;
> Some prank them up with Oaken leaves:
> Some crosse the Fill-horse; some with great
> Devotion, stroak the home-borne wheat:
> While other Rusticks, lesse attent
> To Prayers, then to Merryment,
> Run after with their breeches rent.

While Herrick might have been influenced by classical descriptions of revelry here, there are many valuable close observations of contemporary rural celebration in the passage: the white linen caparisons for the horses; a female image (the *Maukin*) made of the last sheaf, and particularly the festival behaviors of the folk. The poem's expression of a high-spirited agricultural piety is probably quite accurate. Later folkloric descriptions mention liberally drenching the cart and revelers with water and occasional cross-dressing, which could also be archaic features of the ceremony. After this passage Herrick describes a massive feast given by the lord of the manor in which the agricultural tools are freely toasted by the laborers: "the Plough . . . your Flailes, your Fanes, your Fatts . . . the rough Sickle, and crookt Sythe, / Drink frollick boyes, till all be blythe."

Harvest was the period for adjusting manpower needs as well. As feudalism broke down, and especially after the Black Death, when agricultural laborers became a more fluid commodity, the old quarter days for rent payments (Michaelmas in England and Martinmas in Scotland, for example) would also mark the time for renegotiating arrangements of employment and securing winter quarters. Harvest feasts thus served as earnest or severance pay for this new rural working class. In Yorkshire, for example, these "mell suppers" would become foci for dramatic sketches and class satire. But again, such developments nowhere approached the rich theatricality of the Christmas season or the days of Carnival.

Christian Feasts of Harvesttime

Rituals and celebrations during the harvest season, then, varied in time from region to region, and indeed from crop to crop, but were fairly consistent in their celebratory form and content. Particular feasts in the Christian liturgical calendar served to fix some features of the seasonal celebration to specific dates. The Western Church's Feast of the Archangel Michael on September 29 arose from a Roman Church dedication in the sixth century, but it also approximated the autumnal equinox. As conqueror of the fallen angels, Michael would be an ideal protector against the forces of darkness at the time when day began to lose out to night. His cult places were usually on high ground and often overlooked the sea-lanes, as with Mont-Saint-Michel in Normandy and Mount Saint Michael in Cornwall. Mountaintop St. Michael fires were common, especially in Germanic-speaking territories. Michaelmas was more prosaically a quarter day in England, but it was also the prime time to dine on geese fattened on the post-harvest stubble. The Michaelmas goose, often sold at special "goose fairs," was often relegated to St. Martin's Day (November 11) in other parts of Europe. Special large loaves, such as the St. Michael's Bannock of the Isle of Skye, are also characteristic of the archangel's feast day and of the season in general.

Michael's function as psychopomp (guide of souls to the otherworld) in medieval culture is more properly represented a month later in the joint feasts of All Saints' Day and All Souls' Day (November 1 and 2), festivals instituted by the Church in the ninth century to appropriate the two pre-Christian festivals—Celtic and Germanic—celebrating the new year. These pagan festivals, and particularly the Celtic Samhain, marked the dying of the earth into itself and were powerful periods of liminality when the dead—and assorted spirits—were likely to intersect with the now sedentary, and hopefully well-provided-for, human population. Particularly archaic elements clustered at this turning of the year, especially in regions of Celtic influence. There were large bonfires with their attendant sports, such as leaping the fire and scattering the firebrands. All Hallows' in Celtic territories also marked the first appearance of masked performers with their village perambulations and Mischief Night acts of chaos. It is not too difficult to see in these guisers prophylactic impersonations of ancestors or otherworldly figures. "Punkies," hollowed-out turnips with carved features and candles inside, carried on high poles (ancestors of the American jack-o'-lanterns), may have been another way of representing these liminal personages. Indoor games of prognostication were also common to the season—predicting how one would fare during the year, ones' future love life, and so on—and might well have been a degeneration of darker and more serious divination practices. These often involved fruits of the harvest, such as apples.

Church influence on the All Hallows' period can be seen in such practices as "souling" or "soul-caking" in Britain and elsewhere, in which a begging procession sings (to some degree as surrogates for the departed souls) and receives money or a special bread, the "soul cake." Bell-ringing for the departed souls was another widespread practice, documented by Roger Vaultier for fourteenth-century France. We can see in the harvest festivals a general movement of wider and wider inclusion, from celebrating the land laborers at the harvest home to incorporating even more marginal elements of society—the beggars, the homeless, the "poor souls"—at the gate of November. The two halves of the festival, the pagan and Christian, thus served simultaneously both to placate the elemental or chthonic forces and to honor the unseen members of the universal Church. The Church's control over this process was by no means complete. Indeed, it could be argued that Halloween became one of the most resistant of the "pagan" festivals originally appropriated by the Church. In America the holiday, after generations of confinement to children, is rapidly growing among the adult population in a carnivalesque direction. In the case of the Mexican Los Dias de Muertos (Days of the Dead) we can see another example in which a different pagan inlay breaks uproariously though the Church's solemn festivals of the saints and souls.

The onset of winter was also a time for particular attention to domestic animals. In Bavaria the feast of the animal patron St. Leonard (November 6) marks the last processional "riding" of the year and the blessing of the horses against the winter season. Elaborate decoration of herd animals is common in Alpine regions in the earlier events of the *Almatrieb* or *Kuhreihen* (cow dances), which brought the stock down from their high summer pastures. Some herd animals were so honored in the harvest season, but others were subject to blood sports in conjunction with their slaughter for meat, particularly in November, known as the "blood" or "slaughter" month in all the Germanic languages. "Goose pullings" involved riding under a suspended goose with the intent of pulling off its head. Village-wide bull-runnings were not confined to the Iberian Peninsula in the Middle Ages: they could be found as far north as Lincolnshire. From early Norman London to late-medieval Würzburg, combats between wild boars were also common holiday fare during the late harvest season.

Martinmas (November 11) was the final harvest festival. "Inter festum S. Michaelis et S. Martini venient cum toto ac pleno dyteno" [between the feasts of St. Michael and St. Martin they sing harvest home] reads a medieval record from Hedington in Oxfordshire. In many parts of Europe the day signaled the slaughtering of animals (cattle, pigs, and geese especially) that were not to be kept over the winter. It was also a common date for broaching the new wine in France and central Europe. The surplus meat, the perishable innards, and the new wine afforded another opportunity for conspicuous feasting. The Martinmas carouse, particularly in the German-speaking areas, laid more emphasis on verbal arts (drinking songs, comic tales, and so on) than did earlier harvest feasts and in this respect was more like a winter revel. As with the "poor souls" of November 2, the famous icon of the "Charity of St. Martin" (in which St. Martin splits his cloak to share it with a naked beggar) served to underscore obligations downward to the underprivileged at the onset of winter, especially the obligations to share harvest and slaughter largesse. Since Merovingian times Martin's feast also marked the beginning of the penitential season of Advent. Martinmas thus served as a kind of brief Carnival to this lesser Lent.

See also: Advent; Festivals and Celebrations; Samhain
References and further reading: See J. G. Frazer, *The Golden Bough: The Roots of Religion and Folklore* (1981); *The Complete Poetry of Robert Herrick*, ed. J. M. Patrick (1968), quotation

above from page 141; M. MacNeill, *The Festival of Lughnasa: A Study of the Survival of the Celtic Festival of the Beginning of Harvest* (1982); H. Pfannenschmid, *Germanische Erntefeste im heidnischen und christlichen Cultus, mit besonder Beziehung auf Niedersachsen* (1878); J. M. Russ, *German Festivals and Customs* (1982); R. Vaultier, *Le folklore pendant la Guerre de Cent Ans d'après les lettres de rémission du Trésor des Chartes* (1965); and M. W. Walsh, "November Bull-Running in Stamford, Lincolnshire," *Journal of Popular Culture* 30 (1996).

—*Martin W. Walsh*

Havelok

Legendary king of England and Denmark whose story survives in Anglo-Norman and Middle English sources and is depicted on the thirteenth-century municipal seal of Grimsby, Lincolnshire.

The earliest mention of Havelok occurs in an 816-line passage of Geoffrey Gaimar's legendary history, *L'estoire des Engleis* (History of the English; c. 1135–1140). Possibly derived from Gaimar, *Le lai d'Havelok* (c. 1190–1220) presents the story in 1,112 lines, in a form reminiscent of the *lais* of Marie de France. Among other surviving accounts, the fullest is the Middle English *Havelok the Dane* (c. 1280–1300), a verse narrative of 3,002 lines, preserved in a single nearly complete manuscript. In all versions, the English king Athelwold (Adelbriht in the Anglo-Norman versions) dies, leaving his young daughter Goldborw (Argentille) heir to his throne and in the protection of a treacherous regent, who hopes to usurp her title by marrying her to a seemingly baseborn kitchen knave. In Denmark, the young Havelok's father has similarly left him in the care of a usurping regent, who gives Havelok to his man Grim to be executed. Through magical signs, Grim recognizes Havelok as the heir and escapes with him to England, where they found the port of Grimsby. Havelok finds work in the kitchen of Goldborw's regent, who unknowingly marries the two dispossessed heirs. The two go to Denmark, where the royal retainer, Ubbe (Sigar Estal), eventually recognizes Havelok and helps him to defeat the usurper and assume his throne. The royal couple return to England, defeat the English usurper, and become rulers of England as well.

Various attempts have been made to associate these events with historical figures. Havelok has been linked to Anlaf Cwaran, son of Sigtrygg, a Scandinavian king of York from c. 925. The names Havelok and Anlaf may be related, and Cuaran is the false name under which Havelok serves as scullion in Gaimar and the *lai*. The two have otherwise little in common, and the identification in the English version of a märchen-like plot structure and more than 50 folktale motifs suggests how thoroughly traditional retellings have transformed any historical core. An important witness to the legend's oral circulation is Robert Mannyng, whose *Chronicle* (c. 1338) reports a lack of written sources and states that Havelok's story is being told by "uneducated men" in English. Mannyng describes the story as "still current" in Lincolnshire. The presence of Grim, Havelok, and Goldborw on the Grimsby seal testifies to the thirteenth-century circulation of the eponymous founding legend.

The English poem is commonly thought to derive from the Anglo-Norman versions, but no definitive verbal parallels exist, and it may be that the English poet's primary source was local Lincolnshire tradition. According to Mannyng, "men say" that a stone still lying in Lincoln Castle was thrown farthest by Havelok, an incident also present in the English but not the French versions. In the seventeenth century Gervase Holles recorded variants of the legend collected from the townspeople of Grimsby. Like most of its bearers, Holles expresses his belief in the story.

See also: Romance
References and further reading: The Middle English Havelok manuscript is Laud Misc. 108, Bodleian Library. The standard edition of the English poem is G. V. Smithers, ed., *Havelok* (1987); its introduction discusses the poem's presumed Anglo-Norman origin. A. Bell has edited *Le lai d'Havelok* (1925) and Gaimar's *L'estoire des Engleis* (1960). Folkloric investigations include G. Bordman, *Motif Index of the Middle English Metrical Romances* (1963); B. Rosenberg, "The Morphology of the Middle English Romance," *Journal of Popular Culture* 1 (1968), which associates the poem with märchen structure; and N. M. Bradbury, "The Traditional Origins of *Havelok the Dane*," *Studies in Philology* 90 (1993), which argues for local legendary influence.

—*Nancy Mason Bradbury*

Hell

An underworld place of punishment for those dead who had led wicked lives.

The descriptions of hell in classical literature (Virgil, *Aeneid* 6) were seen as poetic fictions in the Middle Ages, and like those of the Germanic and Celtic traditions they played a rather minor role in Christian beliefs concerning the hereafter. Considerably more important was the biblical tradition, and even

Hell-mouth, a fifteenth-century German woodcut. (J. de Teramo, The Book of Belial, *Augsburg, 1475; Dover Picture Archives)*

Demons in hell, torturing the damned, from a fifteenth-century manuscript of a French translation of St. Augustine's City of God. *(Giraudon/Art Resource, NY)*

more important was the tradition of the Apocrypha, above all the Apocalypse of Saint Peter and the *Visio Pauli* (third century) with their lengthy descriptions of the punishments of the hereafter.

According to general medieval opinion, hell was created by God in the center of the earth especially for those angels who, under Lucifer's guidance, had fallen from God. For that reason in many legends (e.g., about Theodoric the Great) volcanoes were considered entrances to the underworld. Occasionally it was thought, however, that one could locate special regions of hell also on the surface of the earth. In the legend of St. Brendan, for example, we hear of islands whose cliffs are burning or where gigantic forges are housed, where the souls of the sinners are tortured in perpetuity. There were also local traditions about specific hellish regions, as numerous place names for particularly desolate regions demonstrate in all of Europe. That the distinction between hell and purgatory was not always clear often becomes evident, for example,

Satan tortures the damned while he himself is roasted on a grill. From the Très Riches Heures du duc de Berry, *Burgundy, early fifteenth century. (Giraudon/Art Resource, NY)*

when it is stated in the *Prick of Conscience* concerning hell, purgatory, and limbus that "Alle thes places me mai helle calle, / For hei beth y-closed withinne the eorth alle" [All these places men may call hell, for they are all enclosed within the earth].

Today it is surprisingly little known that the Church Fathers and teachers of Christianity, from late antiquity to the early modern period, considered it an established fact that by far the greatest part of mankind is predestined by God for hell. The most influential of the Church Fathers, St. Augustine (d. 430), formulated this in writing: because of original sin, mankind became a *massa damnationis* or *massa damnata*, a throng foreordained to hell, from which only very few are pardoned by the mercy of God. All others are "predestined," that is, designated in advance, "to perpetual death," "to perpetual ruin," "into the eternal fire." This teaching was transmitted to the people through sermons. Johannes Herolt, a popular German preacher of the fifteenth century, calculated that of 30,000 dead, only 2 attain salvation and only 3 may atone for their sins in purgatory; all 29,995 others are damned. According to Church lore it was completely clear: *extra ecclesiam nulla salus*—outside of the Catholic Church there is no salvation. The Council of Florence (1438–1439) declared unequivocally: "The souls of those who die with a mortal sin, or even only with original sin, descend immediately into hell, where they are, however, punished with different types of tortures." Since only baptism redeems one from original sin, the fate of all non-Christians, including unbaptized Christian children, was thereby sealed. The latter were thought to be in eternal darkness in a limbo, *limbus puerorum* (literally, a borderland of children). Neither did the Church recognize the circulating legends in which a heathen such as Emperor Trajan was freed from hell through the prayers of Pope Gregory I or a man who murdered his son, such as the father of St. Odilia, was freed from hell by the prayers of his daughter.

In hell an accumulation of the most unimaginable tortures exists in perpetuity. In the vision of the English layperson Ailsi (died c. 1120), for example, hell is an infinitely large house in which the souls are bound with red-hot chains on that part of the body with which they sinned. The lawyers, advisers, liars, flatterers, slanderers, and all similar people are fastened with chains of fire through their tongues. Other souls are cooked in lead, pitch, and brimstone baths and liquefied into nothing; they take shape again, however, for further tortures and go from one torment to the next. In addition, there are hundreds of similar depictions of hell from monks and laypersons, as well as from famous female mystics, such as Hildegard of Bingen, Birgitta of Sweden, or St. Frances of Rome. These fantasies were proliferated through the sermon and were captured in the plastic and graphic arts.

While the representations of hell prior to the central Middle Ages intensively occupied the intellectual upper stratum, at that time primarily monks, the average believers were for the most part not yet exposed to them in detail. Not until they were confronted with Romanesque art, with its depictions of the Last Judgment on churches, outside on the west facade and inside on the arches and walls, and with the increased rigor of the sermons, primarily by the friars of the early thirteenth century, were the people more intensely injected with the fear of hell. Even when the form given to hell or to the jaws of hell in the depictions of the Last Judgment referred to the eternal dungeon at the time of the resurrection of the bodies, one still did not imagine this place differently. The representation of hell, for example, that the sculptor Erhard Küng (d. 1507) created for the tympanum of the cathedral in Bern shows the damned hung on hooks by their widely stretched-out tongues while they hopelessly attempt to pull up their legs, which are being burned from below by leaping flames. A monk and a prostitute are forged together with a heavy chain; a demon crushes the monk's penis with tongs. A naked pope still wearing his tiara is pushed head over heels by a biting devil into the abyss of hell, and so on.

The citizens of every medieval city were confronted daily with these and similar scenes in public spaces. And in how many churches was hell not also painted behind the high altar, so that persons doing penance there had their fate before their eyes in the event that they concealed a sin! Religious drama brought the jaws of hell to life on the stage through Easter plays and Last Judgment plays; usually, as in Gothic art, these terrible jaws were given the form of a lion's mouth, which could be opened and closed through a mechanical apparatus, in which it thundered and out of which fire shot forth. An analysis of pictures and texts available to the common people shows that the fear of hell occupied the Christians of the Middle Ages significantly more than the pleasure of anticipating heaven.

See also: Dante Alighieri; Harrowing of Hell; Purgatory
References and further reading: Scholarly accounts of the development of ideas and representations of hell include J. Baschet, *Les justices de l'au-delà: Les représentations de l'enfer en France et en Italie, XIIe–XVe siècles* (1993); A. Bernstein, *The Formation of Hell* (1993); R. Cavendish, *Visions of Heaven and Hell* (1977); C. Davidson and T. Seiler, eds., *The Iconography of Hell* (1992); P. Dinzelbacher, *Die letzten Dinge: Himmel, Hölle, Fegefeuer im Mittelalter* (1999); *Enfer et paradis*, Les cahiers de Conques 1 (1995); P. Jezler, ed., *Himmel, Hölle, Fegefeuer: Das Jenseits im Mittelalter* (1994); L. Kretzenbacher, *Legendenbilder aus dem Feuerjenseits* (1980); M. Landau, *Hölle und Fegfeuer in Volksglaube, Dichtung, und Kirchenlehre* (1909); J. Mew, *Traditional Aspects of Hell* (1903); G. Minois, *Die Hölle* (1996); D. D. R. Owen, *The Vision of Hell: Infernal Journeys in Medieval French Literature* (1970); D. Stuart, "The Stage Setting of Hell," *Romanic Review* 4 (1913); H. Vorgrimler, *Geschichte der Hölle* (1993).

—*Peter Dinzelbacher*

Hispanic Tradition
The folkloric culture of the peoples of the Iberian Peninsula.

Numerous aspects of Spanish and Portuguese folk literature and folklore are well documented in medieval sources, though there are many gaps in our knowledge, gaps that can only be very partially filled by analogous evidence from postmedieval traditions. Lyric poetry, epic, ballad, drama, folktales, proverbs, riddles, folk speech, legends, music, children's rhymes and games, folk belief, cookery, and material culture are substantially attested and will be discussed in this entry.

History, Context, Worldview

Before the Roman conquest—a gradual process not completed for some 200 years (214–219 B.C.E.)—the Iberian Peninsula was inhabited by numerous peoples of diverse origin and unrelated linguistic affiliation, about whom, in many cases, we know relatively little. Pre-Roman Iberia can be seen as two distinct regions. On the one hand, the southern and eastern coasts, from the Pyrenees to the Portuguese Algarve, had long been receptive to commercial contacts and cultural exchanges and early on saw the establishment of trading posts and even foreign colonies along their shores. On the other hand, the less accessible center, west, and north attest to a complex of tribal societies bitterly opposed to outside intervention. The southern coasts were occupied by the Tartessians; their land and capital, Tartessos (of unknown location, but possibly near the mouth of the Guadalquivir), corresponds to the biblical Tarshish, whence, every three years, ships came to King Solomon: "Bringing gold and silver, ivory and apes, and peacocks" (2 Chron. 9:21). Along the northeastern coast lived Iberians, who gave their name to the entire peninsula, as well as to the Ebro River. Both peoples spoke non-Indo-European languages. The southern coasts and the Balearic Islands were colonized by Phoenicians at an early date (1100 B.C.E.), while the east and northeast saw the establishment of numerous Greek trading posts. The Carthaginians, colonizers of what is now Tunisia and heirs to Phoenician language and culture, occupied the southern coasts and the Balearics during the fifth through third centuries B.C.E. These three eastern Mediterranean colonial initiatives left various place names (Cadiz, Alicante, Cartagena) but otherwise had no effect on modern Hispanic languages. The center and north-northwest were inhabited by a linguistically diverse population: pre-Indo-Europeans on the one hand and various consecutive invaders from central Europe on the other: Indo-European pre-Celts, proto-Celts, Celts (Celtiberians), and some early Germanic peoples. The Lusitanians, one of the pre-Roman peoples of Portugal and western Spain, were probably, at least in part, of Celtic origin. The various dialects of Basque represent the only modern survival of Spain's pre-Indo-European language stock. Basque, which in medieval times extended south to the environs of Burgos and east along the Pyrenees as far as Andorra, has given a number of loanwords to Castilian and, to a lesser extent, to the other languages and has perhaps also influenced Castilian phonology. Basque, for its part, has accepted a massive lexicon of borrowings from Latin and from medieval and modern Spanish. Basque is probably distantly related to the Caucasian languages (though rival origin theories compete for serious consideration). Gradual Romanization established a form of colloquial, or "vulgar," Latin as the common language, except for the Basque-speaking regions and possible pre-Roman speech islands that may have persisted into the early Middle Ages. Hispanic Latin was somewhat archaic by comparison to more central and more innovative areas of Romania (Gaul and Italy), and it embodied a substantial number of pre-Roman loans in its lexicon and morphology.

Like other regions of the Western Roman Empire, Iberia experienced massive invasions by various Germanic peoples during the early years of the fifth century C.E.: Suevians occupied Galicia in the northwest; Visigoths came to control all other areas and eventually, after defeating the Suevians (585), the entire peninsula; Alans (Iranians associated with the Germanic migrations) were soon annihilated by the Visigoths; their remnants joined the Vandals, who, after briefly settling in southern Spain (perpetuating their name in Andalusia), elected to cross to North Africa to found a powerful Vandal kingdom in Tunis. The Visigothic presence on the peninsula lasted from 413 until the Islamic invasion of 711 C.E. When they reached Hispania, the Visigoths had already experienced many years of association with Roman language and culture; many were probably bilingual in Gothic and Latin, and the Gothic language was doubtless already fighting a losing battle for survival. Even so, Gothic has given Spanish and Portuguese many loanwords (often referring to war and to material culture), as well as numerous personal names and place names. When they arrived in Spain the Visigoths were already Christians, but their Arian creed contrasted with the Hispano-Romans' Catholicism. Motivated more by political expediency than religious sentiment, Recared I, together with many of his subjects, converted to Catholicism in 587, but religion did not play the all-important role within the value system of Visigothic Hispania that it was to have in Hispanic life in subsequent centuries.

Hardly 80 years after the death of Muhammad (632 C.E.), the armies of a victorious, rapidly expanding Islam had swept across North Africa and stood at the Straits of Gibraltar, on Hispania's southern threshold. In 711 an expeditionary force of 7,000 men, made up mostly of Berbers and a few Arabs and commanded by a Berber warrior, Tariq ibn Ziyad (whose name is remembered in *Gibraltar* [*Jebel Tariq*, or "Tariq's mountain"]), crossed the straits and defeated the forces of Roderick, the last Visigothic king. In 712 Tariq was joined by the Arab governor of North Africa, Musa ibn Nusayr, with a mostly Arab army of 18,000 men. Within 6 years the entire peninsula, except for a narrow northern fringe along the Cantabrian coast and the Basque Pyrenees, was under Muslim control. These momentous events and the subsequent eight centuries of Christian Reconquest are the two most important factors in medieval Hispanic history and were crucial in shaping the distinctive character of Hispanic peoples, leaving a significant imprint on essential features of their culture. Spain and Portugal during the Middle Ages were complex, multiethnic, tri-religious societies in which Christians, Muslims, and Jews lived side by side and interacted, influencing each other's cultures. As the Reconquest gradually moved southward, the Christian north came to be divided into a number of small, independent, rival regions, none strong enough to prevail against the Muslim south. From east to west, Christian Hispania consisted of Catalonia, Aragon, Navarre, the Basque area, Castile, Asturias-Leon, and Galicia, each with its separate language and its distinctive culture—distinctions that persist to the present day. Medieval Spaniards thought of themselves in religious rather than in national terms. The adjective *español* is a borrowing from Provençal. The frontier society that evolved out of the Muslim Conquest and the Christian Reconquest comprised a variety of ethno-religious minorities. In the Muslim south many descendants of Goths and Romans had accepted Islam but were initially thought of as a distinctive group, while others maintained their Christian faith and were known as *mozárabes* (Arabized). Christians, Muslims, and

Christians and Moors at war in Spain, from a thirteenth-century manuscript. (Cantigas de Santa Maria, Monastery of the Escorial, Madrid)

Jews all spoke as their everyday language the archaic Mozarabic dialect, a highly conservative form of Ibero-Romance, while Arabic was the language of government and literature. As the Christian kingdoms slowly advanced southward, a large Muslim population came to live under Christian domination. These conquered Muslims were called *mudéjares* (Arabic for "those allowed to remain"); after the Reconquest was completed in 1492—followed by their forced, though superficial, conversion to Christianity—they were known as *moriscos* (Moorlike). Along the changing *frontera* between Christian and Muslim territory there lived a small, culturally flexible, and religiously ambivalent group known as *enaciados* (from two Arabic terms meaning "stranger; deserter; turncoat" and "distant, removed"), whose livelihood—as scouts, messengers, smugglers, spies, and translators—depended essentially upon the peculiar circumstances of a frontier society. In the late fourteenth century many Spanish cities witnessed violent anti-Jewish pogroms, leading to a progressive decline in the Jewish communities and culminating in the exile of all unconverted Jews in 1492. Consequently, the late Middle Ages and the sixteenth century saw the formation of yet another ethno-religious minority, *conversos* (or *marranos*), Jews who had converted to Christianity (and their descendants). The medieval Hispanic symbiosis of Christians, Muslims, and Jews is reflected in numerous cultural exchanges: the rich poetic tradition developed in Muslim Spain and creatively imitated by Hispanic Jews undoubtedly patterned its distinctive stress-syllabic metrics on Hispano-Romance models, as opposed to classical Arabic poetry. One of the Hispano-Arabic poetic genres was the strophic colloquial Arabic *zajal*, which was also used in Castilian compositions of the late Middle Ages. Several Hispano-Christian institutions were doubtless patterned on Islamic models: the pilgrimage to the tomb of St. James in Galicia, initially conceived as a means of spiritually uniting all the peninsular Christian peoples (and ultimately a major cultural link between Hispania and the rest of Europe), was surely suggested by the Muslim hajj, the pilgrimage to Mecca. The Spanish military orders, which combined war-like and religious functions, were probably based (like their crusader counterparts in Palestine) on the analogous Muslim institution of the *ribat*, border monastery fortresses manned by religiously in-spired warriors devoted to the territorial expansion of Islam. Indeed the Recon-quest itself can be seen as a response to the Muslim holy war (jihad). Hispano-Arabic gave to medieval Spanish, Portuguese, and Catalan numerous place names and an abundance of lexical borrowings—pertaining especially to agriculture, architecture, commerce, science, war, and material comforts—many of which continue in modern use. Particularly striking are semantic calques, which attest to the syncretic character of medieval society: Old Spanish *casa*, like Arabic *dar*, comes to mean both "house" and "city," while *correr*, on the model of Arabic *gha-wara*, means not only "to run" but also "to pillage." Such Spanish expressions as *Esta es su casa* (This is your house), said to welcome a guest, *Hasta mañana, si Dios quiere* (Until tomorrow, if God wills it), and *Que Dios te ampare* (May God protect you), said to avoid giving alms, all have exact Arabic counterparts. The religious totalism of Spanish Islam, combined with similar values in medieval Christianity, was to leave its distinctive mark on Spanish Catholicism.

See also: Arabic-Islamic Tradition; James the Elder, Saint; Jewish Tradition
References and further reading: See S. G. Payne, *A History of Spain and Portugal*, 2 vols. (1973); A. H. Oliveira Marques, *History of Portugal*, 2 vols. (1972); L. Vicens Vives, *Approaches to the History of Spain* (1970); R. Menéndez Pidal, ed., *Historia de España*, 26 vols. (1954–1968); E. A. Thompson, *The Goths in Spain* (1969); G. Jackson, *The Making of Medieval Spain* (1972); J. F. O'Callaghan, *A History of Medieval Spain* (1975); J. N. Hillgarth, *The Spanish Kingdoms*, 2 vols. (1976–1978); A. MacKay, *Spain in the Middle Ages* (1977); B. Reilly, *The Contest of Christian and Muslim Spain* (1992), and *The Medieval Spains* (1993); W. Montgomery Watt and P. Cachia, *A History of Islamic Spain* (1967); L. P. Harvey, *Islamic Spain, 1250–1500* (1992); Y. Baer, *A History of the Jews in Christian Spain*, 2 vols. (1961–1966); and P. Díaz-Más, *Sephardim: The Jews from Spain* (1992). Reappraisals of Muslim and Jewish contributions include A. Castro, *The Structure of Spanish History* (1954), and *The Spaniards* (1971); M. R. Menocal, *The Arabic Role in Medieval Literary History* (1987); on peoples, languages, and loanwords, see R. Lapesa, *Historia de la lengua española*, 9th ed. (1981).

Lyric Poetry

Hispanic lyric poetry is first documented in brief Mozarabic-dialect stanzas, known as *kharjas* (Arabic for "exit"), appended to learned compositions in clas-sical Arabic and Hebrew, written by Muslim and Jewish poets from the elev-enth to the fourteenth centuries. The exact nature of the *kharjas* has inspired heated polemics, but numerous agreements in style, themes, metrics, and for-mulaic diction between the Mozarabic *kharjas* and later lyric genres—Castilian *villancicos* (peasant songs) and Portuguese *cantigas d'amigo* (lovers' songs)—as-sure us of the *kharjas*' ultimately traditional character, though known texts have doubtless been distorted by the learned context to which they were adapted. The *kharja* "What shall I do, Mother? My lover is at the door" embodies not only the same protagonists and the same situation, but also the same á-a asso-nance as a *villancico* documented in the early 1600s: "Gil Gonzalez is knocking at the door. I don't know, Mother, if I should open it for him." Thematically the *kharjas* are extremely limited: most are attributed to amorous girls who lament the absence or faithlessness of their lovers. The *villancicos* and *cantigas d'amigo*, usually represented as women's poetry, are thematically much more variegated, covering a rich panoply of topics and perspectives. Surviving medieval lyrics are only a vestige of what once existed: Catalan Jewish wedding songs have uniquely survived in two fifteenth-century Hebrew-letter manuscripts. Competitively improvised lyric poetry can be substantiated in tenth-century Hispano-Arabic and later on in Castilian. Funeral dirges were sung in Castilian and almost certainly in the other languages as well. Doubtless various lyric genres have been totally and irretrievably lost.

References and further reading: See R. Hitchcock, *The Kharjas* (1977); S. G. Armistead, "A Brief History of Kharja Studies," *Hispania* 70 (1987); J. M. Sola-Solé, *Corpus de poesía moizárabe* (1973); and A. Jones, *Romance Kharjas in Andalusian Arabic Muwashshah Poetry* (1988). For *villancicos*, see J. G. Cummins, *The Spanish Traditional Lyric* (1977); on *cantigos d'amigo*, F. Jensen, *The Earliest Portuguese Lyrics* (1978); M. E. Schaffer, "The Galician-Portuguese Tradition and the Romance Kharjas," *Portuguese Studies* 3 (1987); for *kharjas* and *villancicos*, R. Menéndez Pidal, *España, eslabon entre la Cristiandad y el Islam* (1956); M. Frenk Alatorre, *Las jarchas mozárabes y los comienzos de la lírica románica* (1975); for other medieval lyric genres, J. Riera i Sans, *Cants de noces dels jueus catalanes* (1974); S. G. Armistead, "La poesa oral improvisada en la tradicion hispánica," in *La décima popular en la tradicion hispánica*, ed. M. Trapero (1993); a comprehensive and authoritative collection is M. Frenk Alatorre, *Corpus de la antigua lírica popular hispánica (Siglos XV a XVII)* (1987).

Traditional Heroic Poetry

In Castilian traditional heroic poetry was devoted to various national themes, as well as to numerous Spanish adaptations of Old French chansons de geste. Only three epics have survived in poetic form: the *Cantar de mio Cid* (Poem of the Cid), *Las mocedades de Rodrigo* (The Cid's Youthful Adventures), and *Roncesvalles* (a Spanish adaptation of the *Chanson de Roland*). All three survive in unique, incomplete copies. A number of other narratives, both national and French, can be partially reconstructed on the evidence of chronicle and clerical adaptations, ballad derivatives, and lyric references. There were undoubtedly also epic poems in Aragonese and Catalan, though they survive only in chronicle prose. A thirteenth-century Portuguese parody echoes the *Chanson de Roland*, suggesting that the epic circulated in Portugal either in Old French or in a Portuguese adaptation. The *moriscos* also cultivated heroic prose narratives in their distinctive Spanish dialect, following Arabic models. Debate concerning the essentially traditional or learned nature of medieval epic has generated an ongoing polemic between advocates of traditionalism and individualism.

See also: *Cantar de mio Cid*; Chanson de Geste; *Chanson de Roland*
References and further reading: See E. de Chasca, *The Poem of the Cid* (1976); J. J. Duggan, *The Cantar de mio Cid* (1989); M. Harney, *Kinship and Polity in the Poema de mio Cid* (1993); J. Horrent, "Un écho de la Chanson de Roland au Portugal," *Revue des langues vivantes* 14 (1948); M. de Riquer, *Les gestes catalanes: Història de la literatura catalana*, 2nd ed., vol. 1 (1980); for individualist and traditionalist perspectives, see C. Smith, *The Making of the Poema de mio Cid* (1983); R. Menéndez Pidal, *La épica medieval española*

(1992); S. G. Armistead, "The *Mocedades de Rodrigo* and Neo-Individualist Theory," *Hispanic Review* 46 (1978), and "From Epic to Chronicle," *Romance Philology* 40 (1986–1987).

The Hispanic Ballad

With origins in fourteenth-century Castile, the Hispanic ballad (romance) soon spread to all areas of Spain and Portugal. It was sung in Spanish, Portuguese, and Catalan and by Christians, Muslims, and Jews. We have a few Castilian ballads in fifteenth-century manuscripts, and many were selectively printed in sixteenth-century chapbooks and poetry collections. There is less evidence from Portugal, though it is still very substantial, existing in a few sixteenth-century manuscript copies and in many contemporary allusions. There is much less from Catalonia, though the very first ballad text preserved is in a mixture of Spanish and Catalan (1421). We have indirect evidence that ballads were sung by exiled *moriscos* in Tunis, while substantial modern documentation from Sephardic Jewish communities in North Africa and the Balkans abounds in medieval text-types and assures us that the ballad genre *(romancero)* was cultivated by all Hispanic peoples, regardless of religion. The ballads originated as fragments of epic poems. Numerous epic-based songs were printed in the sixteenth century, and some survive in the modern tradition, but the eight-syllable assonant ballad verse was also used early on to compose historical and novelesque narratives having nothing to do with the epics. The genre is characterized by great diversity of themes and postmedieval pan-Hispanic diffusion; it has survived, from its medieval origins to modern times, in essentially all communities where Hispanic languages are spoken.

References and further reading: See R. H. Webber, ed., *Hispanic Balladry Today* (1989); R. Menéndez Pidal, *Romancero hispanico*, 2 vols. (1953); S. G. Armistead, *Judeo-Spanish Ballads in the Menéndez Pidal Archive*, 3 vols. (1978); M. da Costa Fontes, *Portuguese and Brazilian Balladry*, 2 vols. (1997); for *morisco* evidence, see S. G. Armistead, "Spanish Romances in Tunisia in 1746," *Neophilologus* 63 (1979); for early Judeo-Spanish citations, S. G. Armistead and J. H. Silverman, "El antiguo romancero sefardí," *Nueva revista de filologa hispanica* 30 (1981). The individualist-traditionalist polemic also extends to the ballads: see C. Smith, "On the Ethos of the *Romancero viejo*," in *Studies of the Spanish and Portuguese Ballad*, ed. N. D. Shergold (1972); S. G. Armistead, "Neo-Individualism and the *Romancero*," *Romance Philology* 33 (1979–1980). An authoritative collection is R. Menéndez Pidal and M. Goyri, *Romancero tradicional de las lenguas hispánicas*, ed. Diego Catalán et al., 12 vols. (1957–1985; ongoing).

Popular Drama

With its close connection to liturgy, popular drama is surely the least exclusively oral of medieval folk-literary genres. Vernacular religious drama is poorly documented in Castilian, with the twelfth-century *Auto de los Reyes Magos* (The Three Kings) as the lone testimony from before the 1400s. By contrast, there is evidence of a rich medieval liturgical drama in Catalonia. Previously unnoticed documentation has recently emerged for Portugal. Though they have not come down to us, there must also have been other, secular types of popular representations, such as the scandalous *juegos de escarnios* (games of mockery), condemned in laws compiled by Alfonso the Wise (late thirteenth century). Popular religious dramas, heirs to the medieval tradition, have survived down to the present in various regions of the Hispanic world.

References and further reading: See R. B. Donovan, *The Liturgical Drama in Medieval Spain* (1958); J. P. Wickersham Crawford, *Spanish Drama before Lope de Vega*, 2nd ed. (1968); F. Laitiro Carreter, *Teatro medieval* (1986); and S. L. Robe, "The Relationship of *Los Pastores* to Other Spanish American Folk Drama," *Western Folklore* 16 (1957).

Folktales

Folktales as such cannot be documented, but there are numerous compilations of exempla (moralistic stories) in Castilian. Though many have a long written ancestry, going back to Latin and Arabic sources, others doubtless were drawn from oral narrative, and in some cases their structure agrees with that of folktales current in modern tradition. Some can be shown to have been orally transmitted from Hispano-Arabic origins. Golden Age Spanish literature (sixteenth and seventeenth centuries) attests to a rich corpus of traditional stories and anecdotes, many of which undoubtedly began to circulate in medieval times.

References and further reading: See R. E. Marsan, *Itinéraire espagnol du conte médiévale (VIIIe–XVe siècles)* (1974), and J. England, "The Structure of the Short Story in *El Conde Lucanor*," in *Juan Manuel Studies*, ed. I. Macpherson (1977). For Arabic stories, see C. Wallhead Munuera, "Three Tales from *El Conde Lucanor*," also in *Juan Manuel Studies*.

Late-thirteenth-century Spanish manuscript illumination of a falcon hunt from Alfonso the Wise's Las Cantigas. *(Gianni Dagli Orti/Corbis)*

Proverbs

From the very beginning proverbs have been incidentally cited in such literary works as the Castilian epic, clerical poetry, and historical and didactic prose writings. They are also an essential part of other genres: proverbs became songs and songs became proverbial; particularly apposite ballad lines came to be used as proverbs and proverbs were absorbed into ballad narratives; and stories were based on proverbs and their lessons became proverbial. Proverbs are also frequently cited in Portuguese, Catalan, Hispano-Arabic, and Hispano-Hebraic writings. They continue to be a vital and dynamic part of Hispanic folkspeech today, as they have been for centuries. The first systematic collections date from the fifteenth century, and numerous lengthy compilations, embodying much medieval material, were brought together in the 1500s and 1600s. Some proverbs can be traced to Middle Eastern sources: "El polvo de la oveja, alcohol es para el lobo" [The dust of the sheep is balm to the eye of the wolf]. Many proverbs first recorded in the 1400s are still in modern use: for example, "Cria cueruo e sacarte ha el ojo" [Nurture a crow and it will pluck out your eye], and "Más vale paxarillo en la mano, que buytre volando" [A little bird in the hand is worth more than a vulture flying].

References and further reading: See E. S. O'Kane, *Refranes y frases proverbiales españolas de la Edad Media* (1959); G. Correas, *Vocabulario de refranes y frases proverbiales* (1627), ed. L. Combet (1967); and C. Sullivan, "Gender Markers in Traditional Spanish Proverbs," in *Literature among Discourses*, ed. W. Godzich and N. Spadaccini (1986). For proverbs and stories, see S. G. Armistead, "Un congénere para el Exemplo VIII del *Conde Lucanor*," *Dicenda* 7 (1987), and M. E. Barrick, "The Dust of the Sheep," *Proverbium* 9 (1967).

Riddles

Though there are no medieval riddle collections per se, medieval oral riddles can be documented in Castilian in various literary sources. Some are picked up by proverb compilations, as in the following postmedieval example from Hernán Núñez (1555): "Cien dueñas en el corral, todas dicen un cantar—Que es cosa y cosa de las ovejas" [A hundred ladies in a pen, all sing the same song—A riddle about sheep]. The following riddle, traditionally concerning the sun, was given a new, pious interpretation and published in *Dámaso de Ledesma* (1605): "Que es cosa y cosa, que pasa por el mar y no se moja?" [A riddle: What passes through the sea and doesn't get wet?] (no. 414). Eastern Sephardic Jews had a substantial riddle tradition. About half the repertoire is of Turkish or Balkan origin, but other examples can be traced to peninsular analogs, and thus some at least may predate the 1492 exile. We lack early documentation from Portugal. There is a short fifteenth-century Catalan list, which, however, seems more literary than oral.

References and further reading: See H. Goldberg, "Riddles and Enigmas in Medieval Castilian Literature," *Romance Philology* 36 (1982–1983). On Hernán Núñez, see F. C. R. Maldonado, ed., *Refranero clásico español* (1960); on *Dámaso de Ledesma,* see J. de Sancha, ed., *Romancero y cancionero sagrados* (1855). On Sephardic riddles and their diverse origins, see S. G. Armistead and J. H. Silverman, "Adivinanzas judeo-españolas de Turquia," in *Philologica hispaniensia* (1983), and M. Viegas Guerreiro, *Para a história da literatura popular portuguesa* (1978).

Folkspeech

Medieval texts abound in conventional phrases, often binary in structure: *en invierno y en verano* (in winter and in summer, i.e., "always"); *ni de dia ni de noche* (neither by day nor by night, i.e., "never"); *nin en yermo y nin en poblado* (neither in uncultivated land nor in populated places, i.e., "nowhere"); *moros y christianos* (Moors and Christians, i.e., "everyone"); *grandes y chicos* (grown men and youngsters, i.e., "everyone"); *de voluntad y de grado* (with goodwill and willingly); *non vale un figo* (it's not worth a fig). Just as Middle English used binary expressions combining Anglo-Saxon and Norman French synonyms (*huntynge* and *venerye*), so—particularly in *morisco* texts—we find Spanish-Arabic doublets such as *sunna i regla* (doctrine and law). Traditional comparisons, such as *commo un bravo leon, ... oso ravioso, ... lobo carnicero* (like a wild lion, ... a raging bear, ... a ravening wolf), occur in heroic poetry and respond as much to traditional formulaic diction as to colloquial usage. Curses and insults—some startlingly severe—are well attested in medieval law books. Francisco del Rosal documents many contemporary expressions that probably differ little from late-medieval counterparts.

References and further reading: See F. del Rosal, *La razón de algunos refranes*, ed. B. B. Thompson (1976), and for negative expressions, E. L. Llorens, *La negación en español antiguo* (1929). Some modern folk comparisons doubtless perpetuate medieval antecedents; see S. L. Arora, *Proverbial Comparisons and Related Expressions in Spanish* (1977).

Legends

Medieval texts are replete with legends: the Goth Teodomiro, lacking warriors, puts women holding reeds on the battlements of Murcia to deceive the Muslim invaders. At Covadonga the Moorish arrows shot at Asturian defenders miraculously turn back against the attackers. King Ramiro II of León, betrayed by his Muslim queen, ties her to an anchor and throws her into the sea, thus explaining the Portuguese place name Fozde-Ancora. The city of Zamora supposedly derives its name from the founders' encountering a black cow (*vaca mora*) at the location of the future town and shooing it away, using the exclamation *aza!* (scat!). The birth of King James I of Aragon is connected to the traditional motif of the substitute bed partner. Some legends are surely of Islamic origin: King James I, just like ʿAmr ibn al-ʿAsi, the seventh-century conqueror of Egypt, orders his tent left standing because a swallow has nested atop the tent pole. Legends often form part of epic narratives, but they need not be used to explain their origin: Spain's betrayal to the Muslims; Fernán González's purchase of Castile; the Cid's illegitimate birth.

References and further reading: On Teodomiro, see C.-E. Dubler, "Los defensores de Teodomiro," in *Études/Levi-Provençal*, vol. 1 (1962); on Covadonga, R. Menéndez Pidal, *Reliquias de la poesia épica española*, 2nd ed. (1980); on King Ramiro, R. Menéndez Pidal, *De primitiva lírica española y antigua épica* (1951); on Zamora, J. Gil de Zamora, *De preconus hispanie*, ed. M. de Castro y Castro (1955); on King James, F. Delpech, *Histoire et légende* (1993); on the nesting swallow, S. G. Armistead, "An Anecdote of King Jaume," in *Cultures in Contact*, ed. D. Hook and B. Taylor (1990); on Spain's betrayal, R. Menéndez

Pidal, *Reliquias* (1980); on Fernán González, L. P. Harvey and D. Hook, "The Affair of the Horse and Hawk," *Modern Language Review* 77 (1982); on the Cid's birth, S. G. Armistead, "Dos tradiciones épicas," *Nueva revista de filología hispánica* 36 (1988).

Music

Many medieval tunes were notated. Alfonso the Wise's vast late-thirteenth-century Galician-Portuguese compilation, *Cantigas de Santa Maria* (Songs of Holy Mary) embodies a rich assemblage. The presence of Arabic and Jewish elements is hotly debated. The music of St. James pilgrim songs has survived in medieval Catalan notations, as have transcriptions of *cantigas d'amigo* by the Galician minstrel Martin Codax and *cantigas d'amor* (love songs) by the Portuguese King Dom Dinis (the latter brought to light, in a dramatic discovery, only in 1990). A good number of ballad and lyric tunes are also available, particularly in the massive *Cancionero musical de Palacio* (Palace Song Book); others, subjected to the polyphonic tastes of sixteenth-century court composers and guitar masters, must be approached with great caution if viewed as authentic medieval witnesses. No Hispano-Arabic music was notated, but a good number of medieval songs are still sung in North Africa, and their music doubtless also originated in the Middle Ages. We know a good deal about musical instruments from contemporary allusions and iconography. Their designations, reflecting the eclectic character of the music itself, embody a mixture of Western and Arabic terms. A tenth-century penitential gloss (*Glosas silenses*) warns against participating *ena sota* (Latin *in saltatione*), which corresponds etymologically to the *jota*, a modern Aragonese folk dance—allowing us a rare glimpse of some sort of ritualized dance or mime, involving disguise in women's clothing, grotesquely painted faces, and the brandishing of bows (and arrows?), spades, and similar implements. There are other medieval allusions and iconographic representations of dances, but little detailed description. For the Golden Age (sixteenth and seventeenth centuries) we are better informed, though many—but surely not all—patterns may have changed. Central to medieval music and its performance were professional minstrels (Spanish *juglar*; Portuguese *jogral* and *segrel*; Catalan *joglar*), a diverse, multilingual, and widely traveled company that included Christians, Muslims, and Jews. Some journeyed abroad, and at home they were joined in providing entertainment by numerous foreign colleagues, especially from Provence but also from northern France, Italy, Germany, Flanders, England, Scotland, Bohemia, and even Cyprus.

See also: *Liber Sancti Jacobi*

References and further reading: See G. Chase, *The Music of Spain*, 2nd ed. (1959); R. Stevenson, *Spanish Music in the Age of Columbus* (1960); I. Fernandez de la Cuesta, *Manuscritos y fuentes musicales en España: Edad Media* (1980); J. Snow, *The Poetry of Alfonso X, El Sabio* (1977); I. J. Katz and J. E. Keller, eds., *Studies on the* Cantigas de Santa Maria (1987); J. Ribera, *Music in Ancient Arabia and Spain* (1929; rpt. 1970); H. Anglés, *Cancionero musical de palacio* (*Siglos* XV–XVI), 2 vols. (1947–1951); G. Morphy, *Les luthistes espagnols du XVIe siècle*, 2 vols. (1902); D. Devoto, "Poésie et musique dans l'oeuvre des vihuelistas," *Annales musicologiques* 4 (1956); and B. M. Liu and J. T. Monroe, *Ten Hispano-Arabic Strophic Songs in the Modern Oral Tradition* (1989). For minstrels, see R. Menéndez Pidal, *Poesía juglaresca y orígenes de las literaturas románicas*, 6th ed. (1957).

Children's Rhymes and Associated Games

A Spanish counting-out rhyme—*De vna, de dola, de tela, canela*—was printed in 1596 and may well be of medieval origin, as more certainly is a cumulative song about the consecutive aggressions of dog-cat-rat-spider-fly, probably alluded to in Fernando de Rojas's *Celestina* (1507) and indisputably attested in an early-seventeenth-century citation (Gonzalo Correas). An illumination in Alfonso's *Cantigas* depicts boys playing a medieval form of baseball, and Catalan children's games are nicely illustrated in a fifteenth-century book of hours. Rodrigo Caro's learned treatise, comparing mid-seventeenth-century games with their classical analogs, doubtless also documents medieval practice.

References and further reading: See G. Armistead and J. H. Silverman, "A Neglected Source of the Prolog to *La Celestina*," *Modern Language Notes* 93 (1978); J. E. Keller, "Daily Living … in King Alfonso's *Cantigas*," *Kentucky Foreign Language Quarterly* 7 (1960); R. Caro, *Días geniales o lúdicros*, ed. J.-P. Etienvre, 2 vols. (1978).

Folk Belief and Custom

Elements of pre-Christian mythology survived into medieval times (and indeed, to the present): the huntress Diana lives on in the *xanas*, supernatural denizens of springs, caves, and forests. Orcus, god of the classical underworld, came to be seen as Death personified, known in medieval Spanish as Huerco. The mysterious Elpila, alluded to in the *Poem of the Cid*, may be a Germanic elf. Juan Ruiz's *Libro de buen amor* (Book of Good Love; 1330–1343) refers to *mozas aojadas* (girls affected by the evil eye) and Ibn Quzman in the twelfth century likewise mentions the evil eye. Beliefs in magic, witchcraft, auguries, the flight of birds, and other practices are well attested. There are various references to soothsayers (*adevinos*). Folk medicine, popular prayers, and incantations (*ensalmos*) can be documented or inferred from sixteenth-century and modern examples, just as a rich corpus of modern agricultural rituals surely embodies much medieval material. A modern Judeo-Spanish rain prayer agrees exactly with an early seventeenth-century counterpart: "Agua, O Dio. Que la tierra la demanda" [Water, O God! The earth requires it]. Francisco del Rosal's late sixteenth-century compilation doubtless records many medieval beliefs and customs.

References and further reading: For *xanas* and Huerco, see J. Corominas and J. A. Pascual, *Diccionario etimológico castellano y hispánico*, 6 vols. (1980–1991); for Elpha, R. Menéndez Pidal, *En torno al* Poema del Cid (1963); for witchcraft, J. Caro Baroja, *The World of the Witches* (1965); on folk medicine, prayers, and *ensalmos*, C. Crews, "One Hundred Medical Recipes in Judeo-Spanish of ca. 1600," *Revue des études juives* 126 (1967); on Judeo-Spanish prayers, see S. G. Armistead and J. H. Silverman, "A Judeo-Spanish Prayer," *La corónica* 19, no. 1 (1990–1991). Such texts, considered heretical, are amply attested in Inquisitional records, for example, S. Cirac Estopañár, *Los procesos de hechicerías en la Inquisición de Castilla la Nueva* (1942). For agricultural rites, see E. Casas Gaspar, *Ritos agrarios* (1950), and J. Caro Baroja, *Ritos y mitos equívocos* (1974); on rain prayer, S. G. Armistead, "Judeo-Spanish Traditional Poetry in the United States," in *Sephardim in the Americas*, ed. M. A. Cohen and A. Peck (1993).

Cookery

Ruperto de Nola's *Libro de guisados* (Cookbook) was translated into Castilian and printed in 1525, from a Catalan original probably written in Naples in the

1470s. It thus reflects eastern peninsular usage, offering detailed instructions for preparing *caldo lardero de puerco salvaje* (fatty wild boar's broth), *escabeche de conejos* (marinated rabbits), *gato assado como se quiere* (roast cat as you like it), *lobo en pan* (breaded wolf), *morena en parrillas* (grilled moray eel), and *potaje de calamares* (squid stew), among a host of other delicacies. Medieval cookbooks catered to the tastes of royalty and the high nobility, and aside from the generally traditional character of medieval society, we should be cautious about seeing these recipes as folk cookery. There is similar aristocratic information for Portugal. We are also well informed about Hispano-Muslim cuisine, for which, among other sources, there is a thirteenth-century treatise. Abstention from (or willingness to eat) pork products was very much on people's minds in Christian Spain. Ruperto de Nola's recipe for *berenjenas a la morisca* (*morisco* eggplants)—still famed in Cervantes's time as a typical *morisco* dish—insists on the use of olive oil rather than bacon grease. The fifteenth-century *converso* poet Antón de Montoro laments that despite attending mass, crossing himself, saying the credo, and eating bowls of fatty pork and half-cooked bacon, he has never been taken for a Christian. Inquisitional records tell of individuals denounced for refusing to eat pork. A *morisca* and her family come to grief because of their distinctive and obviously Muslim eating habits: "They ate couscous with their hands, rolling it into little balls like the Moors do." Juan Ruiz's *Libro de buen amor* documents the word *adefina* (from Arabic *dafana*, "to cover"), showing that the classic Hispano-Jewish stew (*adafina*), still eaten on the Sabbath by modern Sephardim, was also enjoyed in the Middle Ages.

References and further reading: Ruperto de Nola's medieval cookbook is *Libro de guisados*, ed. D. Pérez (1929); another edition is *Libro de cozina*, ed. C. Iranzo (1969). See also S. G. Armistead and R. Dean, "Jottings from a Monastic Kitchen," *La corónica* 13 (1984–1985); A. H. Oliveira Marques, *Daily Life in Portugal in the Late Middle Ages* (1971); D. Waines, "The Culinary Culture of al-Andalus," in *The Legacy of Muslim Spain*, ed. S. K. Jayyusi (1992); L. Cardaillac, *Morisques et chrétiens* (1977). On *adafina*, see S. G. Armistead, "Américo Castro in Morocco," in *Américo Castro: The Impact of His Thought*, ed. R. Surtz, J. Ferrán, and D. P. Testa (1988); M. Joly, "A propósito del tema culinario en la *lozana andaluza*," *Journal of Hispanic Philology* 13 (1989).

Material Culture

Medieval iconography and modern analogs suggest what rural houses must have been like. Some types, such as the modern northwestern *pallozas* (round thatch-roofed houses), even perpetuate premedieval patterns. Medieval furnishings were sparse and austere. Items implying comfort and luxury—including the words for "pillow" and "bedspread"—in several cases have Arabic names. In the realm of dress—about which we know a great deal, thanks to iconography (though mostly in reference to the nobility)—and fabrics, Hispano-Muslim and northern European products competed in popularity. In the twelfth- to thirteenth-century Castilian pantheon of Las Huelgas, Catholic kings, queens, princes, and princesses were buried in luxurious Hispano-Muslim robes and rested on pillows decorated with ornate Koranic inscriptions. In fifteenth-century Burgos stylish ladies were still dressing in Moorish garb. We have substantial knowledge of medieval agriculture and of the implements and technologies it involved, many of which can be traced to Middle Eastern origins.

References and further reading: See O. Marques, *Daily Life in Portugal* (1971); C. Bernis Madrazo, *Indumentaria medieval española* (1956); M. Gimson, *As Pallozas* (1983); R. Dozy, *Noms des vêtements chez les arabes* (1845); M. Gómez-Moreno, *El panteón real de las Huelgas de Burgos* (1946); on Moorish dress in fifteenth-century Burgos, see A. Castro, *The Structure*, ch. 5 (1954), and T. F. Glick, *Irrigation and Society in Medieval Valencia* (1970), and *Islamic and Christian Spain in the Middle Ages* (1979).

—*Samuel G. Armistead*

Homosexuality (male)

Condition and behaviors most often referred to in medieval texts as *sodomy* and *the sin against nature*.

Such terms derive from moral theology and canon (church) and civil law and suggest freely willed actions, almost always without any modern notion of sexual orientation as a genetic or psychologically fixed condition. Contemporary scholars of the Middle Ages will use all of these terms in qualified ways, adding on occasion the more theoretically tendentious *gay* or *queer*.

Whatever the term, there is plenty of evidence of homosexual male activity in the Middle Ages. Yet paradoxically, medieval discussion of male-male relations is characterized by intentional silence, rumor, and innuendo. These form part of a largely negative strategy of canon and civil law against homosexuality that intensified from the beginning of the twelfth century. More neutral medical writings on homosexuality were less widely known or applied. At the same time, same-sex desire seems to have its own literature, particularly in the earlier Middle Ages.

The problem with the so-called sin against nature or sodomy (a name derived from the story of the destruction of Sodom in Genesis 19) is that authorities were often divided about what it actually comprised. Often no clear explanation of it existed. Law codes and penitential manuals (handbooks for priests hearing confession) may condemn sodomy but may either not explain exactly what it is or even warn priests not to explain it, lest repenting sinners become tempted. M. Jordan notes that no other sin or class of sinners was treated in such a contradictory manner.

More rumors abounded about sodomy than outright depictions of it. A type of rumor-insult has a number of documented sources, such as in certain Galician Portuguese poems. Much further north, the rumor-insult warranted peculiar attention over centuries in Scandinavia. The major god Odin accuses the trickster god Loki of being a "lactating cow" and a passive homosexual (*argr*), an insult also associated with cowardice. By contrast, some sources also depict Odin drinking the semen of hanged men in order to regain or replenish masculine power. In later Norse culture even an accusation of effeminate homosexuality (as in *Njal's Saga*) could result in permanent outlawry (i.e., lifetime banishment).

In the urban centers of Europe priests and students were commonly thought to practice sodomy. Walter Map, who studied in Paris in the twelfth century, decried the prevalence of sodomy there. Certain kings were believed to be sodomites or known to have same-sex lovers (such as Frederick II of Sicily and

Edward II of England), and the late-eleventh-century court of the Norman English king William Rufus was criticized for its fashionable, long-haired young male retinue. More ominous were the rumors that began with Justinian's *Corpus juris civilis* (The Body of Civil Law), which held that sodomy was responsible for famines, plagues, and earthquakes. Peter the Chanter declared that when the Virgin Mary gave birth to Jesus, all of the sodomites in the world died instantly. Greed for the wealth of the Templar Knights as well as rumors of sodomy led to the arrest of all Templars in 1307.

Such intolerance drew in no small part from the writings of St. Paul in the New Testament and especially of such early Church Fathers as Augustine, who regarded all nonprocreative sex as sinful. Augustine opposed same-sex activity, though not with detailed articulation. But the connection between theological pronouncement and actual practice varied according to time and circumstances. Scholars such as John Boswell argue that intolerance against sodomy grew out of social anxiety rather than ecclesiastical repression; others adjust this thesis by accentuating the Church's complicity. D. F. Greenberg sees the rise of intolerance as part of a struggle between Church and state for lands and wealth; to put up a united front in the process, the Church reinforced the discipline of both married and "sodomite" clergy. Greenberg does point out that an increased focus on sacramental theology emphasized the purity of priests.

Intolerance can also be traced at least in part to theology and canon law. Before the eleventh century most canon law on sodomy was relatively mild, calling for only temporary excommunication for offenders. With increased attention in penitential manuals for confessors and the invective of antisodomites such as Peter Damian (who seems to have invented the term *sodomy*), penances for sodomy increased. Compared to other sexual sins, sodomy received the most severe penalties (as much as 7–15 years of penance).

Moral theologians and canonists appealed to the developing notion of the "natural" that received greater definition by the later eleventh century. Arguments from nature were seldom based on observation but relied, rather, on the Stoic and Aristotelian writings that became more available in the twelfth century. Sodomy, for example, was considered particularly "unnatural" since it was believed that not even animals engaged in it (except for male hyenas, who were believed to change their sex to suit male partners). Gratian's code of canon law, completed circa 1150, condemned as unnatural the inappropriate, nonprocreative use of the sex organs, including sodomy, fornication, adultery, and incest. In the thirteenth century St. Thomas Aquinas developed a hierarchy of four major categories of unnatural sexual sin: masturbation, bestiality, homosexual sodomy, and heterosexual sex not directed toward procreation (for example, coitus interruptus).

Civil law in Byzantium, developed by Justinian, instituted the death penalty for sodomites, though there was apparently no popular support for such punishment. Other than the Visigothic penalty of castration for sodomy, Western European civil law did not impose serious penalties until after the eleventh century. Charlemagne's edicts against sodomy and unnatural acts contained no actual penalties, only an appeal for repentance. In the later Middle Ages, Greenberg argues, pressure from middle classes in autonomous towns of the

Low Countries, Germany, and northern Italy led to harsh municipal laws; in 1260 Orléans called for castration, amputation of the penis, and burning at the stake.

Both ecclesiastical and civil control had become more organized and centralized by the later Middle Ages, and both sources of repression linked various marginal groups together: sodomites, heretics, witches, Muslims, Jews, and usurers. Heretics were often assumed to be sodomites. In fact, the word *bougre* (either from the Bulgarian source of the Catharist heresy or from heresy opponent Robert le Bougre), ancestor of the modern word *bugger*, was not only applied to heretics but also to the usury and deviant sexuality they were believed to promote. Heretics appear with usurers and sodomites in the literature of the period, notably in the Circles of the Violent in Dante's *Inferno*.

In contrast to condemnation in theology and secular authority or literature, medical writings presented a dispassionate description of the causes and nature of same-sex desire or activity. The *Problemata* (attributed to Aristotle) speculates that men desire passive homosexuality because retention of semen in the anus requires friction of the anus to release it. Later in the Middle Ages the widely circulated *Canon of Medicine* by Avicenna dismisses earlier physiological explanations, proposing a cure of beating, fasting, and imprisonment that is penal rather than medical. Jordan notes that Albertus Magnus (c. 1200–1280) had access to medical writings by Avicenna (980–1037) and other sources, yet he used them selectively and omitted medical explanations of sodomy when it was convenient to do so.

It is possible, nonetheless, to speak of a homoerotic literature in the Middle Ages. From the Carolingian era (late eighth century) and for the next few centuries homosexual erotic poetry can be found, though it is not clear how widespread this poetry was even in learned, most likely urbanized ecclesiastical circles, and some scholars have argued that medieval writers are echoing classical Latin rhetorical commonplaces rather than actual feelings. In the twelfth century a debate poem pitting Ganymede against Helen weighed the merits of loving boys or women. Aelred of Rievaulx, a twelfth-century Cistercian, encouraged a tender, singular affection for other monks that was based on his theological premise, "God's friendship," and referred to John and Jesus as "married."

Saints' legends include negative exempla—for example, the martyrdom of the beautiful young Pelagius, who resisted the sexual advances of an evil caliph. On the other hand, stories of paired saints, such as the martyrs Sergius and Bacchus (d. 290), express such a passionate and exclusive devotion that they have recently been interpreted as lovers. J. Boswell, in *Same-Sex Unions in Premodern Europe*, has studied rites of brotherhood in Greek and Slavonic texts, suggesting cautiously that they might have had an erotic meaning under certain circumstances. (Indeed, some Slavic peoples were notable for a relative lack of concern about homosexuality well into the early modern period.)

Boswell's thesis, however qualified, remains controversial among other scholars. But as with the study of sexuality in general in the Middle Ages, a certain amount of speculation is inevitable. The inconclusiveness of sources and the dialectic of rumor, silence, punishment, and class-based popular literature continue to make medieval homosexuality a fertile field for the approaches of folklorists.

See also: Knights Templar; Lesbians; Sexuality

References and further reading: Information on medieval homosexuality is summarized in the *Encyclopedia of Homosexuality*, ed. W. R. Dynes (1990). Book-length studies by M. Goodich, *The Unmentionable Vice* (1979), and J. Boswell, *Christianity, Social Tolerance, and Homosexuality* (1980), examine attitudes about and both prohibitions and expressions of male-male desire in the Middle Ages. Though Boswell's work has received much lively criticism, it remains a significant point of departure for scholarship. More circumspect, but still controversial among some scholars, is Boswell's *Same-Sex Unions in Premodern Europe* (1994), which studies the rituals of "making brothers" in various Eastern Orthodox traditions and considers what such rituals could have meant for relationships of same-sex eroticism. D. F. Greenberg's *The Construction of Homosexuality* (1988) includes a lengthy chapter on "Feudalism" and attempts to explain social reactions to same-sex desire in the context of Church-state political struggles. R. I. Moore's *The Formation of a Persecuting Society: Power and Deviance in Western Europe, 950–1250* (1990) illuminates the development through the earlier period of the Middle Ages toward linking persecutions of marginal groups in Europe. J. A. Brundage's *Law, Sex, and Christian Society in Medieval Europe* (1987) charts sexuality from Roman law and mores to mid-twelfth-century canon law. Three books of essays that include a wide variety of information of particular interest to folklorists across medieval cultures are J. E. Salisbury, *Sex in the Middle Ages: A Book of Essays* (1991), and V. Bullough and J. Brundage, *Sexual Practices and the Medieval Church* (1994), and *Handbook of Medieval Sexuality* (1996). M. Jordan's *The Invention of Sodomy in Christian Theology* (1997) claims a modest scope—the creation of the term *sodomy* and its incoherence as a moral and theological category—but this short monograph will certainly become an essential theoretical text for future research.

—*Graham N. Drake*

Hungarian Tradition

The folkloric culture of the Hungarians, who settled in their present-day country and converted to Christianity in the tenth century.

Before the tenth century, during their wanderings from the East, from the southern Russian steppes, and to the Carpathian basin, the originally Finno-Ugric Hungarian language and culture were subjected to Turkic, Iranian, and later Slavic influences. Slavic influence continued to play an important role during the centuries of settlement and afterward, together with later Italian, French, and German impact. During the eleventh to thirteenth centuries, pre-Christian religion and culture coexisted with Christian culture, and popular culture with "pagan" roots went through a process of Christianization. We cannot really speak of folklore as separate from an also primarily oral popular culture. In the thirteenth and fourteenth centuries, aspects of pre-Christian culture and poetry survived in the traditions of rural populations rooted in agriculture and animal husbandry. At the same time, the traditions of the peasantry gradually integrated into the framework of Church culture, merging with and transformed by newly arrived European literary and folkloric influences. New medieval European genres and forms developed and spread in Hungarian folklore; most of these genres only incidentally contained archaic, pre-Christian features.

Although the Latin literature of the Church was present from the beginning of the period, most of the potential written sources for the study of medieval folklore were destroyed in wars and migrations in the Middle Ages and in later times. Surviving sources allow us only an indirect view of oral folklore from occasional notes and allusions by royal chroniclers and monastic historians, the folkloric elements of sermon literature, chance remarks by travelers, and surviving data of urban, semifolkloric genres. At the same time, certain elements of modern folklore that are archaic or probably of medieval origins, linguistic evidence, and, sometimes, analogs of European lore preserved in medieval literature also make it possible to infer the existence of a genre or a work of art in Hungary at the time. The primary sources for the study of popular religion, rites, and beliefs are Church regulations, laws, notes, and prohibitions of certain "pagan" rites.

Religion

Probable traditions in the pagan religion of ninth- and tenth-century Hungarians, some of which were later assimilated into Christian mythology and cults, include a god of the sky and a creator deity (which were assimilated in the Bogomil Christian beliefs of the dual creation of the world), a goddess of childbirth and fate, nature spirits, a weather demon (dragon), helpful and harmful spirits, and demons of diseases. Linguistic evidence points toward the existence of cults of bears and wolves. The pantheon of gods and demons survived partly in beliefs eclipsed by Christianity and partly in myths and legends. Some of these narratives later merged with apocryphal etiological Christian legends related to the Old and the New Testaments, which were also widespread in folklore. Royal laws and linguistic data hint at the activities of magicians, diviners, and healers, and we have linguistic evidence for the existence of a *táltos* (shaman) during the Hungarian settlement period. The ancient Hungarian shaman continued to exist in a form and with a function similar to those of the mediators of the Christian Slavs. Driven to the periphery by the Christian clergy, his main task became the securing of agrarian fertility.

As for cult activities, very early sources give information about the sacrifice of a white horse to the god of the sky. However, the cult of the dead and the sacrifices to the dead have survived to the present in an altered form. Originally a propitiatory sacrifice, the funeral feast had become a memorial charity feast by as early as the first centuries of Christianity. The rites of church culture, the cults of saints, dead heroes, holy places, and relics imbued with Christian symbolism and the Christian forms of communication with the otherworld, visions, and apparitions quite soon gained a central position in folklore.

One of the most important forms of the folklore surviving from the pre-Christian times was the "magical poetry" that accompanied individual and collective magical rites. Incantations were used to heal, to ward off diseases, and to bring abundant harvests or good luck to the house. The folkloric incantations merged with the official formulas of benediction and exorcism used by priests and monks; thus, the texts contain pagan magical elements to drive away sickness as well as Christian elements of prayer and blessing. The first known Hungarian written example, the "Incantations of Bagonya," dates from 1488.

Related to magical poetry is a specific, archaic, paraliturgical verse form of prayer. Its existence in the Middle Ages can be inferred from some stylistic elements of modern texts, but examples are known from twelfth-century Italy and Germany as well. It is characterized by free rhythm, lack of stanzas, a recitative performing style, and contents that differ from the topics of official prayers: the magic defense of the individual and the home, the magical enforcement of salvation, or apocryphal elements of the Passion of Christ.

Rites, Plays

We have no information on the rites of the shepherds' feasts, probably held in the spring and fall. All our medieval data refer to calendar holidays. From the beginning of the Middle Ages, collective rites and related rite songs (magic poetry) were part of the rituals of Christian holidays, or at least they were related to Christian calendar holidays. Due to the links with Byzantium in the first centuries of the Hungarian kingdom, some of the holiday rites have Byzantine, Orthodox, or Slavic parallels. Later elements show characteristics that are predominantly central European, related to Western Christendom. Among the agrarian population, the holidays of the winter and summer solstices (St. Lucy's Day, December 13; Christmas; St. Stephen's Day, December 26; New Year's Day; Midsummer or St. John's Day, June 24) as well as the spring holidays (Palm Sunday, Whitsun) were accompanied by magic words influencing the fertility of animals, crops, and families. These were sung by processions of groups wearing animal or demon masks. The *regösének* (*regös* song) of the winter solstice and the *szentiváni ének* (Midsummer Day song) had certain elements that referred to the solstice and a cult of the sun (deer masks with astral symbols, lighting bonfires). The main themes of spring rites, performed with green twigs, were the expulsion of winter/death (cf. central and Eastern European *morena*) and the bringing in of reviving vegetation. The racing tournaments and king-making games at Whitsun contained elements of initiation into adulthood. Festival songs often contained Christian references related to the day in the calendar (e.g., Midsummer Day's songs invoked St. John the Baptist). Pre-Christian motifs of fertility magic were now complemented by genres and motifs of love poetry, itself just developing in Europe. *Párosítók* (pairing songs) were performed at ceremonial rites and weddings, and nonliturgical religious poetry such as the *Certamen* (Contest of Flowers) were sung at Midsummer, while moralities and allegorical plays were enacted in carnivals. Some elements of the customs of reciting greetings by masked men at Carnival time were connected to world-turned-upside-down symbolism. In the celebration of carnivals, a custom taken over from Italy and Germany, motifs of the lay popular theater of medieval Europe were present: contests, tournaments, sword dances, and *moresca* (morris dances).

In the genre of the church drama, we have data on the activities of liturgical singing groups, performing students, craft guilds, and confraternities, as well as performances in towns, where the ordinary citizens also participated at Christmas and Easter with songs in the vernacular (eleventh- to thirteenth-century Corpus Christi processions included *tableaux vivants*). At Christmas there were *betlehemezés* (Nativity plays); at Epiphany, *tracti stellae* (star-plays); and at Easter *ludi paschalis* (Easter plays). Toward the end of the Middle Ages villagers were probably also performing folkloric plays (e.g., the *Quem quaeritis*, which later became a separate Easter play). Folkloric variants of *betlehemezés* were accompanied by shepherds' plays and shepherds' dances in which the performers wore animal-shaped masks. The folklore forms preserved archaic, pre-Christian European musical material (recitatives, forms of cries, twin-bar structures). Important genres were the musical greetings of students on various holidays, which were based on plain chants of the liturgical repertoire, and the ceremonial *recordation* where carols were sung (e.g., on St. Blaise's Day—February 3).

As for the folklore of rites of passage, we can infer musical material connected to weddings and funerals. Beside love songs (pairing songs preserving the memories of magical "pairings" of marriages), traces of religious dramas connected to wedding feasts (e.g., the "Wedding of Cana") are discernible. The rites and textual and musical materials of funerals are mainly of church origin, with the exception of the *sirató* (lament). The lament genre flourished throughout the Middle Ages. Performed by women, it was connected to several elements of the funeral rites, and repeated parts alternated with improvised lyrics.

Music, Dance

We have data not only on music as an accompaniment for ritual and liturgical forms but also on instrumental music performed at revels by Hungarians on foreign raids. Individual players of various instruments are mentioned in several sources. From the end of the Middle Ages we consider data on musicians at fairs, weddings, and dance parties; wandering musicians in villages and towns; court musicians; and even wandering Hungarian musicians in other parts of Europe. Probable instruments included the *furulya* (whistle), a horn-like instrument, and a one-sided drum. The Hungarian *hajdu* dance was already popular in Poland before 1500. In the court of the prince of Milan in the fifteenth century a dance "after the Hungarian style" is mentioned. Some of the more modern forms of dances offer hints about the nature of late-medieval dances. Shepherds' dances and skipping dances are somewhat undeveloped in form and genre. Lads' dances, old dances in pairs, and girls' roundels performed at Lent are more elaborate.

Lyric Poetry, Songs, Hymns

In addition to the "flower songs," a new medieval genre, the "dawn song" (French *aube*; German *Tagelied*), in which lovers recall their night spent together, was known in Hungary as well. Dance songs, drinking songs, swineherds' songs, goliardic poetry, *nefanda carmina* (cursing songs), and mocking songs were probably also known at this period. Wandering minstrels and, especially, itinerant students had an important role in performing and spreading these songs. Besides performing theatrical plays and epic poetry, students had another function as singers of holiday and family greetings: performing satirical and parodic genres.

Popular hymns came to Hungary with the Gregorian style. The chants, translated from Latin to Hungarian, appeared first as tropes within the liturgy and later as independent forms sung on church or lay communal events, holidays, and family feasts (e.g., Christmas and Easter carols, Holy Thursday hymns, songs to the Virgin Mary, lamentations of the Virgin Mary). Musically they represented the style that had become universally popular in Europe by the fourteenth century.

Epic Poetry

Epic poetry continued the traditions of pre-Christian times and the first centuries after the settlement of Hungarians. Although no lyrics survive, the content of these songs can be reconstructed from thirteenth- and fourteenth-century chronicles. Important topics include the "Legend of the Wondrous Stag" (Kézai's *Chronicle*, *Illustrated Chronicle*) about the origins of the Hungarian people. In the legend, Hunor and Magor (the personifications of the Onogur and Magyar ethnic names) arrive in their new land while chasing a stag. The motif of stag hunting and the name of the *progenitrix ünő* (female stag) suggest a totemic heritage. The motif of intercourse with a male bird of prey appears in the "Legend of Álmos," the totemic origin myth of the first royal family. The Christian version of the legend of the Wondrous Stag is related to St. Stephen, the first Hungarian king: the stag, wearing a cross between its horns, leads the Hungarian people into their new homeland and converts its pursuer, the pagan hero. The story of the killing of Prince Álmos, who led the Hungarians into the Carpathian basin, suggests a system of dual rulership and the sacrificial murder of the king. According to the story of the "Country Bought for a White Horse," the Hungarians bought their new land from the Slavic peoples already living there; this is a well-known theme in more-recent Hungarian folklore. Several chronicle tales recount the feats of the heroes conquering the new land and the adventures of the first kings—for example, the conflict between King Endre and his brother, Béla, when the latter had to choose between the crown and the sword. Other legends center on exploits of the chieftains leading Hungarian raids on the West—for example, how the short Botond killed a Greek giant, or how the chieftain Lehel, by blowing his horn at the scaffold, made the German emperor who had ordained his execution become his servant in the otherworld.

Many earlier songs concerned the eleventh-century king St. László. Stories about him became legends, and scenes from these legends often appear on the frescoes of fourteenth-century Romanesque churches. The most important motifs include the mythical, invulnerable hero wrestling; the king releasing the girl carried away by a Cumanian warrior; and the motif of "searching for lice on the head of the king," known from the Bluebeard story cycle.

These song cycles centered on individual heroes contained in motifs with Asian (that is, Mongolian) parallels (e.g., mythical combats), as well as common European folklore motifs of heroic tales and Christian legends.

After the thirteenth century ancient Hungarian epic poetry partly integrated into the emerging Latin literature and into the court epic tradition, which began to develop in Hungarian in the thirteenth and fourteenth centuries. At the end of the twelfth century and in the first half of the thirteenth century, French chansons de geste and romances—including poems about Troy and Alexander the Great—began to spread among the top layers of Hungarian cultural life, but presumably written examples have all been destroyed.

Certain themes of the declining heroic epic lingered on in a new, late-medieval genre, the ballad, which became fashionable and displaced the heroic epic songs from Hungarian culture. The ballad came from France to Hungary through cultural relations with thirteenth-century Anjou and through French-

Walloon settlers moving into Hungary in the thirteenth and fourteenth centuries. Ballad topics include love tragedies, adultery, incest, conflicts between
husband and wife or between children and parents, child murder, and social
antagonism. We also know of some humorous ballads and legendary religious
ballads, the latter showing a close connection with apocryphal legends and ancient mythological topics (e.g., songs to the Virgin Mary, Jesus looking for shelter, the girl carried off to heaven). Some ballads continue the Hungarian heroic
epic tradition, containing Eastern European Turkic and Caucasian elements
(e.g., the ballad of Izsák Kerekes, containing the motif of a magical sleep before
battle, or the ballad of "The Walled-Up Wife"). Although Western European,
especially French, influence has a strong mark on the musical material, the
tunes of the ballads primarily bear medieval Hungarian and some archaic
presettlement characteristics.

The other important developing epic genre in the Middle Ages was the
tale. We do not know when the shift from heroic epic to heroic tale took place,
or whether it took place at all, but part of the European wealth of tales already
well documented at the time must have been known in Hungary. Codices written in Latin and later in Hungarian, as well as sermons, sometimes refer to
legends and tales related to the Golden Legend. For instance, we know of the
tale of "Truth and Falsehood" (AT 613) from the records of a fifteenth-century
preacher, who got it "from the mouth of the folk." Heroic tales probably preserved some pre-Christian Eastern themes: celestial bodies obtained by a
demiurge (creator god), voyages to the realms of the dead, and the like.

See also: Baltic Tradition; Finno-Ugric Tradition; Slavic Tradition, East
References and further reading: There is no comprehensive work covering the whole of
medieval Hungarian folklore, but there have been numerous articles on particular
approaches or contents and volumes of studies dealing with the question from various
aspects but not covering all areas. An example of the latter is a collection of articles
incorporating the latest research on folk poetry genres and religion of the ninth and tenth
centuries, focusing on the legacy of pre-Christian religion, mythology, epic poetry, song,
and dance: L. Kovács and A. Paládi-Kovács, eds., *Honfoglalás és néprajz* (1997), especially
the essays by V. Voigt, L. Vargyas, I. Katona, L. Felföldi, and É. Pócs. A volume covering
the whole of the Middle Ages but dealing mainly with religion and folk belief is É. Pócs
and V. Voigt, eds., *Ôsök, táltosok, szentek* (1996), with studies by V. Voigt, P. Tóth, P.
Veres, M. Hoppál, and É. Pócs. Equally comprehensive studies concerning ethnological
and linguistic approaches to the popular culture in the settlement period are V. Diószegi, *A
sámánhit emlékei a magyar népi műveltségében* (1958); L. Vargyas, *Keleti hagyomány—nyugati
kultúra* (1984); and D. Pais, *A magyar ősvallás nyelvi emlékeiből* (1965). On the possibilities
of the continued existence in the Middle Ages of archaic poetry and heroic epic songs and
their forms, see Gy. Király, *A magyar ősköltészet* (1921); Gy. Kristó, *Ôsi epikánk és az Árpád-
kori íráshagyomány* (1942); and V. Voigt, "Hôsepika," in *A magyar folklór*, ed. G. Ortutay
(1979). This same work contains chapters by I. Katona on lyric poetry. A comprehensive
literary reference work devotes separate chapters to medieval textual folklore: T. Klaniczay,
ed., *A magyar irodalom története*, vol. 1 (1964). A historical survey of Hungarian textual
folklore that also takes medieval aspects into consideration is I. Katona, *Historische
Schichten der ungarischen Volksdichtung*, Folklore Fellows Communications 194 (1964). An
important comprehensive work on the ballad genre with the medieval history of its origin
and spread is L. Vargyas, *A magyar népballada és Európa*, vols. 1 and 2 (1976). The chapters
by L. Vargyas, Zs. Erdélyi, and É. Pócs in the new general reference work *Magyar Néprajz
V. Népköltészet*, ed. L. Vargyas (1988), also give an overview of medieval data on the

folksong, archaic prayer, and incantations. A literary history also dealing with the medieval aspects of dramatic plays and festive rites is F. Honti, *Az eltűnt magyar színjáték* (1940); an analysis of folklore history also examining medieval aspects of popular dramatic plays is T. Dömötör, *Naptári ünnepek—népi színjátszás* (1964). The general work by Z. Kodály, *A magyar népzene* (1937), includes the history of Hungarian folk music in the Middle Ages. The general reference work on the history of Hungarian music has a separate chapter and detailed overview of medieval folk music, with a summary of the latest research findings: L. Dobszay, B. Rajeczky, and J. Szendrey, "Középkori népzenénk," in *Magyarország zenetörténete*, vol. 1, ed. B. Rajeczky (1988).

—*Éva Pócs*

Icon

Originally, a Greek Orthodox Christian painted image portraying a sacred person or event. In current usage the term has acquired new significations, which mainly stress its function as an active, powerful, autonomous symbol in cultic phenomena.

In early Christianity, icon veneration was originally proper to some Gnostic sects, such as that of Carpocratians (first–second centuries), and to individual syncretic worshippers, such as the Roman emperor Alexander Severus (c. 208–235). Among Orthodox believers, the presence of icons is witnessed sporadically from the second century on and was apparently restricted to private, nonliturgical locations. The custom of displaying apotropaic portraits of one's holy patron in domestic interiors, over the entrance of shops, and also on one's clothes was already widely diffused in the fourth and fifth centuries in the East and in Italy. The earliest image to become the proper center of a cultic phenomenon was a bronze marble group in Paneas (actually Baniyas, Syria) representing Christ and a woman at his feet. Although some scholars believe it to be an ancient statue of Asklepios, reinterpreted as one of the Savior, earlier traditions described it as a votive and thanksgiving image displayed in a public space. Progressively, however, it became the focus of pilgrimage, and the grass growing by the feet of Christ's statue was thought to be health giving. By the sixth century its translation into a chapel sanctioned its newly gained status of miraculous image.

The attitude of Church officials toward icon veneration remained ambiguous through the pre-iconoclastic period. While officially condemning their use as an idolatrous practice, the ecclesiastical hierarchy gradually admitted icons into sacred buildings. Mostly originating in Palestinian traditions bound to the Holy Land and its sacred places and relics, painted tablets representing holy persons and events became more and more present in Byzantine churches. In great part, however, these were offerings displayed as *ex-votos* that had no proper liturgical function. Ancient sources that mention icons as tokens commonly displayed in sacred buildings, and especially in relation to the liturgical space, appear only sporadically—for example, in Abraham bar Lipeh's seventh-century *Nestorian Book of Offices*. By the early Middle Ages, many ambiguous and semi-magical functions were attributed to images. Not infrequently, icons were asked to cast down enemies, to operate as judges in juridical and economic questions, or even to find a spring of water. In the sixth century there appear images "not made by human hands," such as the famous "mandylion" (a cloth bearing the imprint of Christ's face), which was venerated as a relic in the Syriac town of Edessa.

In the two phases of the politically motivated iconoclastic controversies (726–787 and 815–843), the Greek Church was forced to formulate an unambiguous doctrine on icon veneration. While rejecting the iconoclastic party's arguments by affirming the principle that veneration was not directed to the object itself but to the sacred person represented in it (the prototype), the defenders of images devoted themselves to regulating the laity's devotional practices and to shaping a standard way of paying homage to images by involving them in the liturgical calendar and by attempting to standardize the iconographic types of sacred portraits and scenes. In the posticonoclastic period, images of holy persons were identified by inscriptions bearing their names and by symbolic details defining their merits as martyrs, ascetics, or doctors of the Church. Relic-like and miraculous images were not absent, but they were mostly confined to monasteries and other ecclesiastical institutions, or they were involved in the emperors' rituals and symbolic apparatuses, as in the case of the palladial icons (i.e., icons serving the function Pallas Athena had in earlier times) of Our Lady of Blachernae and the Hodegetria in Constantinople.

Nonetheless, though forced to oppose iconoclastic arguments, icon defenders had legitimated a whole group of legends and traditions concerning miracles shown by or through sacred images. The histories of the Edessan mandylion, the relief "not made by human hands" of Mary in Lydda, or the bleeding icon of Christ in Beirut would long exercise their influence in constructing the sacred aura of religious images both in Byzantium and the medieval West. The diffusion of the legend of St. Luke as a painter who produced an icon of the Virgin Mary was at the origin of several attributions of sacred images to the hand of the Evangelist through the Middle Ages.

Although the Latin Church did not generally make use of icons in the early Middle Ages, there were exceptions in Italy and southern Gaul, where Eastern influence was strong. Rome inherited from the period of Byzantine domination several cultic phenomena centered on sacred images, such as those of the Savior in Sancta Sanctorum or that of the Virgin in St. Maria Maggiore. From the tenth century on, the diffusion of Byzantine traditions pertaining to miraculous images influenced the emergence of iconic miracles in Marian literature, which were to become more and more present in the twelfth and thirteenth centuries after the direct contacts between Westerners and Eastern Christianity during the Crusades. In addition, an autonomous appearance of images started in the tenth-century Frankish kingdom, where important cult places were provided with statue-like reliquaries containing relics of venerated saints. The earliest one known to us is that of St. Foy in Conques. The practice of veneration was gradually transferred from the treasured relics to their figural containers, a process that culminated in the twelfth century. By then the focus of veneration had reversed: believers made statues more venerable by introducing relics or other sacred objects into their inner hollows.

"The Holy Mandylion," Byzantine, circa 950. Genoa, Church of San Bartolomeo degli Armeni. (Courtesy of Hans Belting)

From the eleventh to the fifteenth centuries the attribution of painted images to St. Luke became widely diffused in Rome, mostly in monastic and Mendicant churches, where every order pretended to have its own original portrait of Mary. Assimilated to the holiest relics in the city, their celebrity was diffused by pilgrims' tellings and pious literature. From the late thirteenth century on, other Italian communes, such as Spoleto, Florence, and Bologna, claimed to possess an original icon by St. Luke, which was venerated as a palladial object. In the following centuries important towns throughout Europe (including Venice, Regensburg, Liège, Prague, Brno, and Madrid) perpetuated such claims.

Both statues and two-dimensional images increasingly became the main foci of sacred places and phenomena, mainly in Marian shrines, along with the growing devotion to the Blessed Virgin in the twelfth through the fifteenth centuries. The twelfth-century Romanic wooden statue of the Virgin of Montserrat (Catalonia) was probably produced as an accessory implement for a flourishing Marian cult related to a sacred mountain and a health-giving spring, but step-by-step it acquired a central function in the related pilgrimage and devotional practices. The most ancient cult images to appear in Tuscany consisted of relic-related or relic-like objects, such as the Volto Santo in Lucca (a reliquary including relics of Christ's passion) or the image "not made by human hands" in a monastery near Pisa. From the end of the thirteenth century on, sources mention images creating new cultic phenomena through a miraculous epiphany: in the 1280s the veneration of the Virgin of Or San Michele in Florence started after a miracle in the public granary, while such icons as Our Lady of Cigoli or the Madonna of Impruneta in the countryside near Florence became the main foci of important local pilgrimages.

Nonetheless, miraculous or publicly venerated icons played only a restricted role among religious images in the later Middle Ages. Objects such as painted crosses, crucifixes, and images of the Virgin and the saints in different artistic media played an increasingly important role as accessories for rituals, processions, and paraliturgical actions, such as religious dramas. As such, many had no fixed locations in churches but could be used in the particular solemnities of the liturgical year. Even so, some images could be directly connected to the main altar or to the space of the celebrants, such as the painted crosses hung on or over the barrier separating the clergy from the congregation during the mass, which frequently displayed iconographic themes related to personal eschatology and salvation. Devotion paid to such images was frequently a consequence of the laity's desire for a deeper involvement in the soteriological meaning of the liturgical action. In the thirteenth century their use as tokens for prayer and other devotional practices became widely diffused in lay confraternities and among private worshippers, who mostly imitated habits already proper to monks and friars. Painted portraits of sacred patrons progressively became standard elements of late-medieval house furniture and also started to be diffused in such extraliturgical places as on the corners of buildings or at the crossroads in towns as well as in the countryside. Images came more and more frequently to express the new instances of a nonliturgical, laity-bound devotional piety, which mainly flourished in late-medieval urban milieus. In extraordinary cases images could

"The Blessed Virgin Painted by St. Luke," Byzantine, twelfth century, Spoleto Cathedral, Italy. (Courtesy of Hans Belting)

also play extraordinary roles: in the Italian penitential movement of the Bianchi (1399–1400), who lacked a real spiritual leader, a charismatic function was attributed to crucifixes and Marian paintings.

The sixteenth- and seventeenth-century reformers' view that icon veneration was an idolatrous practice inherited from ancient paganism has produced a lengthy debate. The idea that image cults were a hallmark of "popular" and "primitive" religion and a kind of fetishistic practice was current in books by positivist scholars and by early exponents of the phenomenology of religions, such as G. Saintyves in 1911. Some scholars, such as E. De Martino, writing in

1959, adopted a no less static view in interpreting images as media by which Church hierarchies were able to exert their symbolic dominion on the religion of the lower classes. E. Kitzinger, in his frequently cited essay "The Cult of Images in the Age before Iconoclasm," still interpreted holy images as strongholds of popular culture progressively admitted by churchmen. Against Kitzinger's view, Peter Brown has recently proposed that icons were phenomena directly bound to holy men's cults in late antiquity.

Long conditioned by a misleading conception of popular religion, scholars have seen icon veneration and cults as originally serving nonliturgical but unnecessarily class-bound functions. Famous miraculous images were seldom identified as objects originating among lower classes or in agricultural communities; on the contrary, their birthplaces seem usually to have been urban milieus or important monastic institutions. Analogously, only in relatively few cases did an icon constitute the actual main focus of a cultic or pilgrimage phenomenon or play a somewhat magical or idol-like role; instead, they should be interpreted as media through which worshippers might more easily attain a sacred benefactor's protection and help. No holy force or energy was necessarily felt to be inherently present in the images. Rather, a sort of confusion between the real object and what it signified was enhanced by believers, who performed ritual acts in front of icons as if they were directed to really present persons.

In the later Middle Ages, widely diffused public devotion often led to an image being seen as miraculous; in such cases a standard picture or statue was given a symbolic meaning that was no longer restricted to individual worshippers' piety; on the contrary, the picture or statue came to express the religious feelings of a whole community. In this sense, Victor and Edith Turner, interpreting Christian image cults from an anthropological point of view, have ranked them among "liminal" phenomena; since images are ambiguous symbols, whose ideological (theological) referents are combined with sensory and emotional ones, believers often tend to transform their meanings by involving them in a social group's life.

See also: Relics; Saints, Cults of the; Votive Offerings

References and further reading: E. Kitzinger's frequently cited essay "The Cult of Images in the Age before Iconoclasm" (1954; rpt. in his *The Art of Byzantium and the Medieval West*, 1976) still provides the fullest description of image cults and practices in early Christianity and the central Middle Ages; further evidence and bibliographies may be found in H. Belting's *Likeness and Presence* (1993). On Byzantium, see the essays by A. Kazhdan, H. Maguire, G. Dagron, N. Oikonomides, and N. Patterson Ševčenko collected in *Dumbarton Oaks Papers* 44 (1991). Theologians' attitudes and doctrines about icon veneration are analyzed by M. Barash in *Icon* (1992), while S. Sinding-Larsen's *Iconography and Ritual* (1984) is devoted to liturgical uses of images in the West; for a descriptive text about devotional practices involving sacred images in the later Middle Ages, see H. Van Os, *The Art of Devotion in the Late Middle Ages in Europe, 1300–1500* (1994). The history of cult icons in medieval Rome is best outlined by G. Wolf, *Salus populi Romani* (1990), while a survey of the history of icons attributed to St. Luke is contained in M. Bacci's *Il pennello dell'Evangelista* (1998); insights on the "images not made by human hands" are provided by the essays collected in H. Kessler and G. Wolf, eds., *The Holy Face* (1998). Methodological reflections and monographic studies may be found in two recent miscellaneous books: F. Dunand, J.-M. Spieser, and J. Wirth, eds., *L'image et la production* du sacré (1991), and J.-C. Schmitt and J. Baschet, eds., L'image, fonctions, et usages des images dans l'Occident médiéval (1996). See also V. Turner and E. Turner, Image and Pilgrimage in Christian Culture (1978).

—Michele Bacci

Iconography

Conventional, symbolic representations in the visual arts, conveying information of interest to folklorists in almost every conceivable artistic medium, in monuments of "high art" as much as in humbler media such as lead badges and biscuit molds.

While the modern distinction between the religious and the secular is not valid for the Middle Ages themselves, it is nevertheless of practical use in discussing medieval iconography here, especially as, historically, nonreligious imagery has been neglected. The exceptions have been those categories of secular iconography that pertain to the aristocratic strata of medieval society (e.g., Arthuriana and other romances of chivalry, such as the Charlemagne and Alexander cycles).

Scholars have adequately surveyed the illustration of fables (e.g., in the borders of the Bayeux Tapestry), of beast epics (especially that of Reynart), and of the fauna of the Bestiary and "monstrous races" (insofar as these last have entered the popular consciousness). However, such ready-made collections of folkloric material are the exception. For the most part there is no substitute for combing the published catalogs of the various categories of artifacts, and there is still much of interest to be extracted from them. Nor, indeed, is there any substitute for original observation and research: of all the areas of medieval studies, this is perhaps the least well quarried.

Badges, Seals, and Molds

Religious folklore and popular Christianity, especially the lore of saints, have received considerable attention in recent years, particularly via the evolving study of "pilgrim badges." Colorful folktales are summarized in such lead images as the devil being conjured into the boot held by the Berkshire "saint" John Schorn, or the greyhound badges inscribed "Bien aia qvi me porte" [May he who wears me have good luck]. This auspicious phrase probably alludes to the cult of the French greyhound, St. Guinefort, invoked to protect infants. The same little lead souvenirs commemorate other equally remarkable saintly deeds— for example, the miracle through which St. Werburg miraculously contained geese within their wattle pen; unlike such proverbial fools as the Wise Men of Gotham, who sought in vain to pen the cuckoo, the saint as a "fool for Christ's sake" achieves the folly. Even the organizers of St. Thomas Becket's cult did not disdain from issuing a lead memento in the form of their saint's initial at the center of a four-leaf clover, a classic example of the "reinforcement" of a religious amulet by a secular good luck charm. The festivities of popular religion are also alluded to in such fifteenth-century badges as the crowned plows that commemorate the festival of Plow Monday.

The lead badges of secular content have perhaps an inordinate degree of importance for the study of popular attitudes, because sexuality, in particular, is rarely so explicitly expressed in any other medium. The Salisbury badges (fourteenth and fifteenth centuries) include milkmaids celebrating May with their vessels piled on their heads some three centuries before such dances are recorded in writing. A holly sprig is plausibly interpreted to be an allusion to the folk game played between the partisans of holly and ivy (this game can be inferred from contemporary carols). Lovers' badges embody a mixture of popular and more courtly motifs. Prominent are hearts and flowers—especially the quatrefoil (four-leafed) flower known as the "truelove"—bearing such inscriptions as "herte be true" and "veolit in may lady." A unique Dutch badge depicts the arm of a lover who literally "wears his heart on his sleeve." Miniature openwork purses in which imitation "coins" are trapped are doubtless "good luck charms" to attract (monetary) fortune. One inscribed *grommerci* (thank you) bears comparison with the fifteenth-century carol refrain, "Gramercy my own purse." The ape who stands on a fish and urinates into a mortar that he simultaneously works with a pestle is perhaps a satire on the dubious ingredients used by apothecaries. Religious satire is certainly present in the badge of the fox friar who preaches to the geese, his intentions made clear by the dead goose tucked out of sight under his belt.

Unlike lead badges, personal seals were not available to the humblest pockets, but by the later Middle Ages they had descended quite far down the social scale from the earliest royal and aristocratic types. There is a frequent use of the rebus to represent the owner's surname—for example, a ginger jar above the words *grene ginger*, the seal of John Grene (1455), confirming the medieval delight in punning humor. Other seals refer to folktales. Despite its Latin motto, "Te waltere docebo cur spinas phebo gero" [I will teach you, Walter, why I carry thorns on the moon], the seal of Walter de Grendon (c. 1330), depicting a hooded man bearing a double bundle of thorns hanging from a stick over his shoulder inside a crescent moon, with a little dog at his feet in front of him and two stars, alludes to the popular notion of the Man in the Moon, banished there for gathering firewood on a Sunday. There seems no obvious reason why Walter chose this seal for himself; how much more appropriate it would have been for Richard Moneshine, whose seal is dated 1394. Other motifs include the world-turned-upside-down theme of the hare riding the hound, popular on fourteenth-century seals.

The stone and earthenware molds in which biscuit and cake dough were formed had assumed a degree of complexity by the later Middle Ages, especially in Germany, and, like seals, they frequently combine text and image. An inventory made in 1521 of molds mostly dating from the previous decade and belonging to one Claus Stalburg of Frankfurt will serve both as a representative list of such popular imagery, in its mixture of the sacred and the profane (including erotica), and also as a timely reminder that the iconographic record is not necessarily dependent on the survival of the images themselves.

The 40 molds enumerated bear 52 representations, including Pyramus and Thisbe; St. Christopher; Romulus and Remus; the Death of Lucretia; the Baptism of Christ; Venus and Cupid; the fabliau of the widow's son killed by the

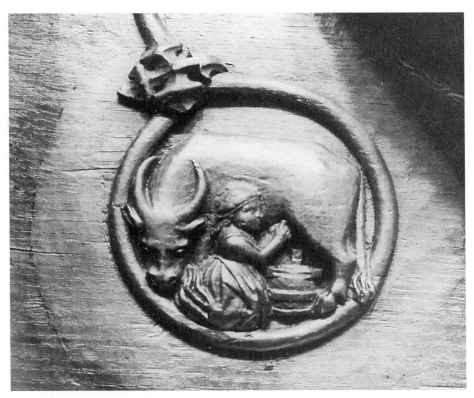

Milking the Bull: an adynaton, or impossibility, of the sort commonly depicted in medieval folk iconography. (Misericord supporter, Beverley Minster, Yorkshire, 1520; photograph by Malcolm Jones)

king's son's horse, and the king's sentence on him; women and fools playing; a young man and a woman on a bed; a peasant and wife threshing hens out of eggs (a proverbial Gothamesque folly); an old man with a young woman, the folly of whose unequal relationship is pointed out by both the presence of a fool and a swarm of hornets who sting the man; three naked women fishing; Christ's Passion; a morris dance; a fool in a basket being dragged along by an old woman; a young woman who offers a hermit a love potion; Samson and Delilah; Adam and Eve; and a peasant trying to force an outsized caltrop into a sack (showing incidentally that this design must derive from a woodcut in the enormously influential early printed book *Das Narrenschiff* [The Ship of Fools, 1494]).

Images in Cloth, Wood, and Stone

Tapestry and embroidery remain two of the most valuable media for the study of secular art, but—because of their costliness—the themes they illustrate seem to reflect the aristocracy's taste for the tales of chivalry or courtly love; many subjects are now only known to us through inventories: Sir John Fastolf (d. 1459) owned a bench covering of "a man scheyting at j blode hownde" [a man shouting at a bloody hound], which looks very like an illustration of the tale "Llewellyn and His Dog" (motif B331.2), in which a dog saves a child from a snake and is seen leaving the child's room with blood on its mouth; a man, thinking the dog has killed the child, kills the dog before discovering his error. If this image indeed refers to the tale, it significantly predates the German wood-cuts illustrating the story, which appeared in the 1530s.

The humbler painted cloth—the "poor man's tapestry"—is perhaps of greater relevance, as it reflects more popular taste; unfortunately, however, very few survive. Once again, though, the evidence of inventories is of help here: particularly interesting is the mention of "a paynted cloth of Robyn hod" hanging in the parlor of Robert Rychardes of Dursley (Gloucestershire), according to an inventory taken in 1492. Even erotica seem to have appeared in this relatively transient medium, for according to an inventory of the effects of a Brussels official who died in 1505, among the four secular pictures he owned were two paintings on cloth representing *amoureusheyden* (lovers or loving). Upon her death in 1448 Alice Langham of Snailwell, near Newmarket, left her son a cloth painted with the history of *King Robert of Sicily*, a pious romance; in 1463 John Baret of Bury Saint Edmunds left his nieces "the steyned cloth of the Coronacion of Oure Lady" and another one featuring the "Seven Ages of Man." The latter was no doubt a far humbler version of the "VII Aages" tapestry series that Jean Cosset of Arras produced for his lord in 1402. It was perhaps familiarity with such stained cloths that led Sir Thomas More "in his youth … in hys fathers house in London" (c. 1490) to devise "a goodly hangyng of fyne paynted clothe, with nyne pageauntes, and verses over of every of those pageauntes" on the same Ages of Man theme. The poet John Lydgate (d. c. 1450) similarly "deuysed" a "peynted or desteyned [stained] clothe for an halle a parlour or a chaumbre … at the request of a werthy citeseyn of London." This cloth is of particular iconographic interest, for it depicted the satirical misogynistic motif of the mythical beasts "Bycorne," who grows fat on a diet of submissive husbands, and "Chichevache," who grows skinny preying on faithful wives. Chivalric themes were also represented in the late fifteenth century: one of the members of the Clarel family of Aldwarke in South Yorkshire bequeathed to the Church of All Saints in Rotherham a stained cloth depicting the celebrated joust between Anthony Woodville and the Bastard of Burgundy, which took place before Edward IV at Smithfield in 1467.

Although it survives for the most part in ecclesiastical contexts, sculpture in wood and stone contains much of folkloric relevance. In wood it is misericords, in particular, that are of interest to us. In stone the primary sites of interest are roof bosses, capitals, and corbels. The roof bosses are fascinating both because of their location—in this respect, they are similar to misericords—and because they are not easily visible. Their carvers seem sometimes to have been granted considerable license, perhaps because the roof bosses were rarely seen. Bosses, in particular, make use of phallic imagery and scatology and illustrate exempla (e.g., the Clever Daughter at Exeter) and other popular motifs (e.g., the preaching fox and the bagpiping pig at St. Mary's, Beverley; a doghead at Bristol). They also attest such folk amusements as "gurning" (making ugly faces) through a horse collar (Lacock, Wiltshire). At Meavy (Devon), a mouse emerges from one ear of a human (?) head, while its tail is visible in the other; perhaps this image is a humorous portrait of some "empty-headed" local.

Individual capitals and corbels reflect the same range of imagery: the Aesopic fable of the ass who tried to imitate his master's lapdog was carved on a capital at Westminster Hall as early as circa 1090 (it does not appear again in English art until the late-fifteenth-century Reynard woodcuts). Proverbs are also illustrated in stone, especially in late-fifteenth-century Flemish art.

One of a series of bas-reliefs decorating the Brussels town hall depicts the man who is so churlish that he cannot bear to see the sun shining in the water as well as on him! In addition to its being represented appropriately in snow, this is one of more than 100 proverbs illustrated in Pieter Brueghel the Elder's famous painting *Netherlandish Proverbs* (1559). This work represents the culmination of the late-medieval enthusiasm for proverbs and their representation in the arts; the late-fifteenth-century French illustrated *Proverbes en rimes* (Rhymed Proverbs) manuscripts are but one manifestation of this interest.

Snow, Metals, Printing, and Illuminations

Snow was undoubtedly the most ephemeral sculptural medium, however! It seems incredible that any record of such spontaneous sculpture should survive, and yet we know that a *danse macabre* (dance of death) was made at Arras in 1434. Moreover, a 400-line poem published in Brussels in 1511 describes in some detail the fascinating series of sculptures made throughout the city during the hard winter of the previous year. These include Christ and the woman of Samaria; a preaching friar with a dripping nose; a cow "manuring" the ground; Adam and Eve; St. George rescuing the princess from the dragon; Cupid with drawn bow atop a pillar; Roland blowing his horn; Charon's ferry; a *mannekin-pis* (pissing mannequin) whose rosewater "urine" fell straight into the mouth of a gaping man below; a mermaid; a fool and his cat washing its bottom; a unicorn resting its head in a virgin's lap; the King of Friesland (Freeze-land); a tooth-puller; the Man in the Moon; a woman naked but for a rose held before her genitals (cf. the symbolism of the flower in the *Roman de la rose* [Romance of the Rose]); an armed merman; a man astride a keg of real beer; and two motifs from the extremely popular late-medieval power of women topos: Sardanapalus, with his head in Venus's lap, and so "unmanned" by her that he is portrayed with distaff in hand (Hercules is much more common in this role), and Aristotle ridden by Phyllis, brought to grief by her *quoniam* (genitals) as the text has it.

Bronze statues would have been visible to the populace in such public media as tomb sculpture, candelabra, and fountains: fools from each medium, respectively, exemplify the motifs of whipping a snail in order to make it go faster (a Gothamite folly found also on a Bristol misericord), standing foolishly with finger in mouth, and wearing only one shoe.

Because of their taste for depicting everyday urban life, aristocrats' metalwork (known to us mostly from inventories) sometimes includes motifs of folkloric interest. One such example is an enameled goblet owned by Louis d'Anjou with the figure of a knight handing a lady up some steps; at the top of the steps there was a blind beggar, together with his dog, holding a basin and the inscription: "Donnez au povre qui ne voit" [Give to the poor man who cannot see].

Another example is the table ornament enameled with all the various street cries of Paris (inscribed on banderoles held by the traders).

Wall paintings are another vast area of interest, and those late-fifteenth-century examples still extant in the Swedish churches of Osmo, Tensta, and Kumla, among others, are perhaps of greatest value to students of medieval folklore. Subjects include a witch's familiar, a "milk hare" draining a cow of its milk (Osmo), and the antifeminist exemplum of the devil who is so afraid of an old woman (who has succeeded in splitting up a married couple where all his efforts had failed) that he dare not hand her the pair of shoes that are her reward; instead, he holds them out to her on the end of a stick (there are several examples of this image). World-turned-upside-down subjects can also be found, such as the ox butchering the butcher (Tensta), and hares capturing the hunter (Kumla). Woodcuts and engravings make their appearance in the late Middle Ages. Although they often illustrate works of interest to the folklorist, they rarely possess a value independent of the text. At times, however, one can gain valuable insights into the popular attitudes of the period by examining such motifs as the one on the title-page cut to *Neu Layenspiegel* (New Mirror for Laymen; Augsburg, 1511), where the young witch copulating with a man is shown "unnaturally" on top.

A 1479 woodcut of a schoolroom, in a book published in Augsburg, shows one of the pupils wearing an ass's head—an actual contemporary punishment for dunces. This piece reminds us of the proverbial stupidity of that animal, according to medieval (and indeed, later) popular belief. Compare this with a marginal scene in the Rutland Psalter (English; c. 1260) that depicts two monks quarreling—the one who is about to draw his dagger says to the other (in mirror writing), "Tu es asin[us]" [You are an ass].

The earliest broadsheets extant are equally valuable. There is the French sheet published by Guy Marchant (Paris; c. 1495), in which the monstrous cow Chicheface—who lives off faithful wives—complains that there are so few that it is reduced to the skinny state in which the artist has drawn it. Other examples are given by the German spinning sow, which is also pressed into the service of antifeminism, and the fragmentary English sheet of King Henry VI, venerated as a saint, being adored by kneeling supplicants who pray to him to ease their wounds; it shows the little votive limbs hanging up at the shrine left as offerings. Of equal interest is the German woodcut (c. 1420–1440) of St. Gertrude, plagued by mice as she spins. Similarly, the early woodcut *Pestblätter* (plague sheets) invoke the protection of various saints against a more serious plague.

Images depicting those beliefs and practices that some religious authorities condemned as superstitious even before the rise of Protestantism (apart from the pilgrim badges discussed above) are to be found in all types of saints' lives. Many "religious" scenes in miniatures and paintings offer important opportunities for students of medieval folklore. "The Reviling of Christ before the Crucifixion," for instance, is a most valuable record of contemporary (insulting) gestures: the tongue out, the mouth distorted by the fingers, the "fig" gesture, the teeth flicking, the goitered appearance of the torturers. Scenes of hell are similarly valuable as a source of motifs of demeaning popular punishments (e.g., barrowing).

A twelfth-century manuscript illustrating the life of St. Amand depicts a blind woman whose sight is mysteriously restored once she takes an axe to the tree she had worshipped before she was converted by the saint. The artist has depicted two very human-looking heads representing the tree spirits in the top of the tree. On a happier note, newborn babies are sometimes accompanied by a seemingly irrelevant stork in attendance (e.g., the cradled baby in the border of the "Judgment of Solomon" page in the *Hours of Catherine of Cleeves*).

There are many other categories of decorative material that are not considered here—among them, stained glass, ceramics (including floor tiles), ivories, the so-called *Minnekästchen* (love caskets), the earliest woodcut playing cards, and pictorial graffiti.

See also: Cockaigne, Land of; Cuckold; Fool; Manuscript Marginalia; Misericords; Phallic Imagery; Sheela-na-Gig; World Turned Upside Down

References and further reading: Nothing could more eloquently reveal "The State of Medieval Art History" in the particular area with which we are concerned here than the fact that H. Kessler's essay of the same name, *Art Bulletin* 80 (1988), affords this topic less than a paragraph out of 20 pages!

Anything by Joan Evans—for example, *Pattern* (1931) or *Art in Medieval France* (1948)—is worth reading. This author commanded a range of knowledge that is seemingly no longer available to English scholars, who have been overtaken in this by German and Dutch scholars.

Little known but extremely valuable is Stammler's bibliographical essay "Schrifttum und Bildkunst im deutschen Mittelalter," in *Deutsche Philologie im Aufriss,* 2nd ed. (1962). Similarly, the *Reallexikon der deutschen Kunstgeschichte* is an invaluable aid, of much wider relevance than its title would suggest, and far more reliable than many of the current single-volume dictionaries of art and symbolism. One excellent discussion of popular iconography relevant to our period, despite its title, is F. Sieber's *Volk und volkstümliche Motivik im Festwerk des Barocks* (1960).

For proverbs, see M. Jones, "The Depiction of Proverbs in Late-Medieval Art," in *Europhras 88: Phraséologie contrastive,* ed. G. Gréciano (1989), with bibliography. Many proverbs are also illustrated in L. Röhrich's magisterial *Grosses Lexikon der sprichwörtlichen Redensarten,* 2nd ed. (1991).

In a trilogy of articles published in the journal *Folklore,* under the general title "Folklore Motifs in Late Medieval Art," M. Jones attempts to survey particular iconographic themes: "Proverbial Follies and Impossibilities," *Folklore* 100 (1989); "Sexist Satire and Popular Punishments," *Folklore* 101 (1990); and "Erotic Animal Imagery," *Folklore* 102 (1991).

For the iconography of gesture, see F. Garnier, *Le langage de l'image en moyen âge* (1982), and J.-C. Schmitt, *Gestures* (1984), and for gesture in a particular context, R. Schmidt-Wiegand, "Gebärdensprache im mittelalterlichen Recht," *Frühmittelalterliche Studien* 16 (1982).

For a representative selection of the lead badges—whose importance is increasingly coming to be recognized—see especially B. Spencer, *Pilgrim Souvenirs and Secular Badges* (Salisbury Museum Medieval Catalogue, Part 2, 1990). For the Dutch material, see H. J. E. Van Beuningen and A. M. Koldeweij, *Heilig en profaan: 1000 laat-middeleeuwse insignes* (1993). For the French badges now in the Musée de Cluny, see A. Forgeais, *Collection de plombs historiés trouvés dans la Seine* (1862–1866).

A fascinating collection of German biscuit molds is discussed by F. Arens in "Die ursprüngliche Verwendung gotischer Stein- und Tonmodel," *Mainzer Zeitschrift* 66 (1971). The revised and expanded version of K. Varty's *Reynard the Fox* (1967) is an indispensable research tool.

R. S. Loomis and L. H. Loomis, *Arthurian Legends in Medieval Art* (1938), is now supplemented by A. Stones's excellent "Arthurian Art since Loomis," in *Arturus Rex,* vol. 2, ed. W. Verbeke et al. (1990). This volume contains a very full bibliography. In addition to this, there is L. Lawton, "The Illustration of Late Medieval Secular Texts with Special Reference to Lydgate's 'Troy Book,'" in *Manuscripts and Readers in Fifteenth Century England*, ed. D. Pearsall (1983). Also useful is A. Martindale, "Painting for Pleasure: Some Lost Fifteenth-Century Secular Decorations of Northern Italy," in *The Vanishing Past*, ed. A. Borg and A. Martindale (1981). For the Tirol, see J. Weingartner, "Die profane Wandmalerei Tirols im Mittelalter," in *Münchener Jahrbuch der bildenden Kunst*, N. F. 5 (1928).

H. J. Raupp's *Bauernsatiren* (1986) is an extremely valuable study of the depiction of the peasant in medieval art and much more besides. The latest book by the Dutch cultural historian H. Pleij, *De sneeuwpoppen van 1511: Literatuur en stadscultuur tussen middeleeuwen en moderne tijd* (1988), treats a similarly generous range of popular imagery that uses the extraordinary snow sculptures made in Brussels in 1511 as its starting point. C. Gaignebet and J.-D. Lajoux, *Art profane et religion populaire au moyen âge* (1985), contains many fresh and fascinating images. Its text, however, should be treated with caution, since it is a work firmly rooted in the French "mythological" tradition.

C. J. P. Cave pioneered the study of *Roof Bosses in Medieval Churches* (1948). Aquamanili are handsomely illustrated in P. Bloch, *Aquamanilien: Mittelalterliche Bronzen für sacralen und profanen Gebrauch* (1981). For another important type of domestic bronzeware (the shallow dishes with stamped decoration), see H. P. Lockner, *Messing: Ein Handbuch über Messinggeräte des 15–17 Jahrhunderts* (1982).

The late-medieval art of Switzerland is particularly rich in folkloric themes. The tapestries discussed in W. Wells, "Vice and Folly in Three Swiss Tapestries," *Scottish Arts Review* 8 (1961), are good examples of nonaristocratic creations depicting such motifs. W. Muschg and E. A. Gesler, eds., *Die schweizer Bilderchroniken des 15/16 Jahrhunderts* (1941), discusses a genre of illustrated manuscripts containing much of interest to folklorists. Another interesting work is the extraordinary *Bayerische Bild-Enzyklopädie*, published by E. Chojecka (1982). Yet another genre not considered above is the "performance art" of the carnival float, of which the Nuremberg *Schembartlauf* is a particularly fine and well-documented example; see especially H. U. Roller, *Der Nürnberger Schembartlauf* (1965).

For painted glass of a mainly nonreligious type, see E. von Witzleben, *Bemalte Glasscheiben* (1977). For the iconography of religious folklore, see the works on lead badges referred to above and, especially, G. Jaritz, "Bildquellen zur mittelalterlichen Volksfrommigkeit," in *Volksreligion im hohen und späten Mittelalter*, ed. P. Dinzelbacher and D. R. Bauer (1990).

—Malcolm Jones

Inns and Taverns

Establishments selling wine and sometimes lodging, food, and ale, located mainly in England.

Although the distinction between inns and taverns was sometimes blurred in the Middle Ages, inns offered lodging to their customers but taverns did not, and inns were generally larger in size and served customers of a more elite class than taverns. Inns first arose in England in the twelfth and thirteenth centuries, and by the fifteenth century inns were a prominent feature of the medieval town. Late-medieval inns were very large, capable of housing between 200 and 300 guests, and their facades extended across wide sections of a town's main thoroughfare. Although innkeepers sometimes brewed their own ale and beer, they primarily served wine. At an inn a guest would also be served elaborate meals including several courses of meat and fish. Taverns began to appear sometime in the twelfth century. By the fourteenth century the number of taverns had increased significantly, though they were mostly concentrated in England's southern counties. Taverns had expanded in size, often encompassing several rooms, and were the main social centers of urban life. Late-medieval taverners, especially those that were also vintners, were oftentimes prominent members of society. Most taverns served no beverages other than wine, and, indeed, some scholars believe that during certain parts of the Middle Ages taverners were prohibited from selling ale. Since the price of wine was very high throughout the Middle Ages, taverns were frequented only by the middle to upper classes; even when the cost of wine was at a relative low during the thirteenth century, it was still not affordable for the lower classes, and after England's loss of Gascony during the Hundred Years' War the cost of wine soared. Some taverns also sold food, but only basic and simple meals; elaborate feasts were only to be had at inns.

As roads improved and more and more Christians began to go on pilgrimages to visit shrines containing holy relics, abbeys and monasteries began to establish adjacent hospices in which they offered shelter for pilgrims and other travelers for two or three nights. The abbeys and monasteries required no fee from their guests, but a gratuity for the guest-master, the elder monk or friar who supervised the hospice, was expected from those who could afford it. Eventually inns arose along merchant routes and pilgrimage ways to ease the crowding of monasteries and to offer travelers the option of longer stays. Located on the main road of the town, inns were also more convenient for the traveler than were the abbeys and monasteries, which were usually far from the main roads. Inns served traveling clerics and wealthy wool merchants as well as pilgrims, and they offered their guests entertainment as well as food, drink, and lodging: the communal rooms in the lower level of the inn would often be filled with players, acrobats, jugglers, and mummers. The innkeeper's obligation to entertain his guests, it is thought, is related to the emphasis on entertainment at abbeys and monasteries, where monks entertained the travelers with music, singing, and storytelling at the guest-master's request.

The earliest ancestors of taverns were the *tabernae* (small shops or booths) that sold drink alongside the Roman roads in the Anglo-Saxon period. The *tabernae* were identified by a long pole (later termed an "ale-stake") outside the front door; a vine or evergreen branch hanging from the top of the pole indicated that the shop sold wine as well as ale. The green branch or bush was supposed to be suggestive of ivy leaves, the symbol of Dionysus, the Roman god of wine. It has been conjectured that the symbols of the pole and the bush were adopted from the Romans, who probably introduced early *tabernae* along with the roads they constructed in the 100 years after Julius Caesar's invasion of England in 55 B.C.E. We know that taverns proper first arose sometime before 750 C.E., because it was approximately then that Ecbright, archbishop of York, issued Canon 18 forbidding priests from eating or drinking in taverns.

Ecbright's was the first of many such regulations established as the number of inns and taverns rose. In 1175 Archbishop Richard decreed that clerics might stop at taverns if their travels necessitated it but that they could not do so only for pleasure, and in 1195 Archbishop Walter ordered that priests should abstain from taverns and public drinking. That the prohibition was repeated suggests that priests and clerics were frequent patrons of taverns. In 1329 a civic proclamation in London ordered that "whereas misdoers, going about by night, have their resort more in taverns than elsewhere, and there seek refuge and watch their hour for misdoing, we forbid that any taverners or brewers keep the door of his tavern open after the hour of curfew." Moreover, lawmakers of fourteenth-century London were as wary of taverners themselves as they were of their customers, for in 1311 they issued a charter dictating that taverns must always have their wine cellar doors open, so that customers might see their wine being drawn, to ensure that it was not being watered down. In the later Middle Ages Taverners and Innkeepers assizes, such as those passed in Coventry in 1474, restricted the profits that could be made on wine. Fifteenth-century London taverns were prohibited from selling drink on Sundays until high mass had ended, but inns, interestingly, were exempt from this rule. H. A. Monckton suggests that the exemption "is an interesting example of the way in which inns attempted to give their guests the same sort of freedom which they could enjoy in the privacy of their own houses," but perhaps, I would suggest, the exemption also reflects the higher social status of the inn's patrons.

There is evidence that some taverns offered what were considered objectionable forms of entertainment: John Wycliffe, the fourteenth-century theologian and reformer, condemned the habits of clergymen who idled their time in taverns among "strumpets," and in 1393 London magistrates reported that "many and divers broils and dissensions [arose] by reason of the frequent ... consorting with common harlots at taverns." Gambling with dice and cards was common at many taverns, and by the later Middle Ages backgammon had become a popular tavern game.

Taverns consisted of several rooms, usually on the ground floor of a building with a wine cellar on the same floor. Some taverns also had kitchens where simple meals were cooked; if there was no kitchen a taverner might order food for his customers from a neighboring cookhouse. Inns were generally much larger buildings. They had their kitchen, parlors, stabling, halls, and communal rooms on the ground floor and guest chambers on the first and second floors. Most inns conformed to one of two architectural styles: the courtyard style, in which the inn surrounds a courtyard and has galleried upper floors accessible by stairs on either side of the courtyard, or the gatehouse style, in which the courtyard is at the rear of the inn. Because players often performed in the inn courtyard while guests watched from the galleried upper floors, it is thought that the courtyard-style inn suggested the design of early modern theaters like the Globe, where higher-class patrons seated behind the balustraded galleries watched performances on the stage below.

Inns and taverns had elaborate and interesting signboards whose pictures symbolized their establishment. A signboard might portray a bush, representing the wines of Dionysus, or the heraldic shield of the family on whose land the inn was, or certain animals (lions, bulls, greyhounds, or white harts) that represented the crests of different kings of England. Some signboards represented trades and vocations, aligning the inn or tavern with a certain trade organization; for example, a sign might portray a wheat sheaf to represent the Bakers' Company or three compasses to refer to the Carpenters' Company.

One of England's most famous inns is the Tabard in Southwark, built about 1304. The Tabard is known to many as the initial meeting place of the pilgrims in Chaucer's *The Canterbury Tales*, and in the late Middle Ages it was a well-known point of departure for pilgrimages. In *The Canterbury Tales* the inn creates a community out of a disparate group of people. Chaucer's contemporary, John Gower, provides a less favorable portrayal of a drinking establishment in his *Mirour de l'omme* (Mirror of Man). Gower describes a taverner who deceives his customers by allowing them to sample fine-quality wines and then selling them poor-quality or watered-down bottles of wine instead. The deceitful taverner also bandies about the exotic names of different kinds of wine while serving ladies, inciting them to drink more by pretending to give them samples of these different wines while really selling them several glasses of the same cheap wine.

See also: Pilgrimage; Wine

References and further reading: For general information about inns and taverns in medieval England, see the first five chapters of H. A. Monckton, A *History of the English Public House* (1969), and the first two chapters of P. Clark, *The English Alehouse* (1983). Monckton's book is especially good for its account of civic and religious regulations concerning inns and taverns. P. Haydon, *The English Pub: A History* (1994), offers little information about inns and taverns that cannot be found in the two books just cited, but it provides some excellent photographs and illustrations of such well-known medieval inns as the Tabard in Southwark and the Angel in Grantham. For good illustrations of the architecture of medieval inns and taverns as well as a concise history of the Roman and Anglo-Saxon *tabernae*, see M. Jackson, *The English Pub* (1976). M. Brander, *The Life and Sport of the Inn* (1973), offers a nicely illustrated account of the games and entertainment offered by medieval inns and taverns in different regions of England. The "Entertainment" and "Travel" chapters of E. Rickert, *Chaucer's World* (1948), provide documents from civic records, personal accounts, and literature that offer information about the role of inns and taverns in late-fourteenth-century England. L. Wagner's two books, *London Inns and Taverns* (1924) and *More London Inns and Taverns* (1925), provide detailed histories of individual establishments as well as a full description of the hospices run by monasteries and abbeys. For an in-depth account of the history and symbolism of particular inn and tavern signboards, see M. Christy, *The Trade Signs of Essex* (1887). W. C. Firebaugh, *Inns of the Middle Ages* (1924), is a narrative history of the medieval inn that helpfully includes some information about inns in France and Germany as well as England, but it is rendered problematic because of its dated and inaccurate perception of the Middle Ages.

—*Tara Neelakantappa*

Investiture [Investiture of the Fief]

A symbolic act performed in the ceremony of vassalage in northern Europe to effect the creation or transfer of a property right.

In France and the Low Countries especially, investiture usually followed at once the first two parts of the ceremony: first, the act of doing homage, or the self-surrender of the kneeling vassal to his lord, in which the vassal, hands clasped in the lord's, promised to be the lord's man; and, second, the pledging of fealty, of faith to the lord, which gave the assurance of fidelity, demonstrated that the homage had been done freely and uncoerced, and prepared the way for the oath on holy relics or the Bible, whose purpose was as much to reassure the lord of the vassal's faith as to remind all present, including the lord, that the reciprocity of the established vassalage was now a mutual obligation under God's protection.

The most precise example of investiture cited by historians discussing the feudal ceremonial of vassalage appears in Galbert of Bruges's *The Murder of Charles the Good* in the account of the rendering of homage and fealty to Count William of Flanders in 1127. After describing how the nobles had done homage and sworn fealty to the count, Galbert introduces the act of investiture as he says "the count [then], with a wand which he held in his hand, gave investiture to all those who by this compact had promised loyalty and done homage and likewise had taken an oath." F. L. Ganshof offers a variant—but no less instructive—example of the act of investiture in the vassalage ceremony from Jean Bodel's twelfth-century *Chanson des saisnes* (Song of Enfeoffment), in which Charlemagne, after receiving homage and fealty from Bernard of Montdidier, enfeoffs, that is, invests, his new vassal by presenting him with a standard.

Always a symbolic act, investiture was performed in one of two ways, as indicated by the two examples cited above. In the first, the lord, having accepted the homage and fealty of his man, conferred the fief while holding an object—such as a ring, a scepter, or a wand—to represent the act of vesting, as in the case of Count William's investiture of the nobles whose homages had just been received. The object in this sort of investiture was retained by the lord, and if it was of little value, as was sometimes the case, it was formally broken after the ceremony.

In the second way investiture was performed, as Charlemagne's enfeoffment of Bernard illustrates, the object held by the lord was conveyed to and kept by the vassal himself, as its purpose was to represent that which was vested. In this case, as a symbolic representation of the fief, the object might be a stalk, a piece of straw or the *festuca*, or a banner. An instructive visualization of this type of object, known informally as the *Landrecht* (land right), appears in a German manuscript: a king conveys a scepter to a bishop and an abbess, suggesting a different kind of fief than that represented by three standards or banners conveyed to three laymen standing across from the ecclesiastics, on the other side of the lord who is seated in the center of the picture.

Marc Bloch indicates that many embellishments of the symbolic object, representing either the act of vesting or the thing vested itself, were introduced over time by lay and ecclesiastical investitures alike. Charles du Fresne Du Cange identifies 98 symbolic objects in all.

The symbolic object, whether retained to represent the act of vesting or conveyed to represent that which was vested, implied the lord's concession to bestow on the vassal the *seisin*, or possession, of the fief. Two things were usually meant by this bestowal of *seisin*, especially in earlier instances of the rite. First, the *usufruct*, or the right to the enjoyment and advantages of a property or of any other type of fief, short of destroying or wasting its substance, was conveyed to the vassal before all present and thereby secured so long as the vassal remained his lord's man. Second, having acquired the usufructuary right in the fief, the vassal's useful or profitable "possession," or more precisely, "holding" of the fief—that is, his *dominium utile* as opposed to the lord's *dominium directum*, or direct or straight possession of the fief—was protected now and in the future against invasion. Though necessary for obvious reasons, this protection eventually led to a blurring of the distinction between *seisin* and the idea of possession under Roman law, a blurring that makes its first appearance in documents beginning with the fourteenth century.

Bloch points out that the rite of investiture had to be repeated when a fief was renewed and that the lord could not refuse the investiture of a natural heir, though such a concession was rarely accorded freely. In Germany, where joint heirship prevailed well into the twelfth century, collective investitures often took place. Lay investiture of clerics continued, too, until its prohibition in 1075 by Pope Gregory VII, marking the beginning of a nearly half-century-long struggle between the Church and the state.

See also: Knight; Rites of Passage
References and further reading: While much has been written on the ceremonial of vassalage, the most useful place to begin to understand investiture is with C. Stephenson's *Medieval Feudalism* (1942) and J. Le Goff's *Time, Work, and Culture in the Middle Ages* (1980) for basic principles and terminology and with F. A. Ogg's *A Source Book of Medieval History* (1908) for pertinent, translated examples of the rite from charters, cartularies, and so on. That done, the next step is to turn to M. Bloch's *Feudal Society*, 2 vols. (1961), and F. L. Ganshof's *Feudalism*, 3rd ed. (1964), for detailed discussion and analysis of nuance and distinction. Indispensable at this point, too, is M. Bloch's essay on types of the rupture of homage, "Les formes de la rupture de l'hommage dans l'ancien droit féodal," in *Mélanges historiques* (1963). Finally, C. du Fresne Du Cange, ed., *Glossarium mediae et infirmae Latinitatis*, 12 vols. (1884), should be consulted for sources and examples not found in other treatments of the subject; Du Cange presents the 98 objects used in investiture ceremonies, which are listed in Appendix 1(A) of Le Goff's *Time, Work, and Culture in the Middle Ages*.

—*Liam Purdon*

Irish Tradition

Medieval Irish tradition, reflected in an enormous corpus of literature produced in Latin and Irish by the literati in the period from the sixth to the seventeenth centuries C.E.

In this article, the intimidatingly large load of information about a wide range of folkloric genres presented by medieval Irish literature of this period will be divided into smaller corpora, and an indication will be given of what kinds of "folklore" or data useful to folklorists can be gleaned from them.

First, let us consider the roots of and motivating factors behind the remarkable literary productivity of medieval Ireland, for without a sensitivity to the agenda of Irish writers, the folklorist, like the Celticist, is liable to underestimate the cultural value of this literary evidence. While we have no incontestably fifth-century vernacular literature surviving from Ireland (in general, I should note, the dating of Irish texts is a hazardous and risky business), given the sophistication of the earliest attested literary Irish it is reasonable to assume that the project of rendering a written form of the native language using the Latin alphabet was launched shortly after the introduction of Christianity in the fifth century. (This project was arguably already afoot in the pre-Christian development of *ogam*, a system for writing Irish, primarily for inscriptional purposes, that was based on the sounds represented by the Latin alphabet.) The invention of a written vernacular, or of what scholars call "Old Irish" (essentially the literary language of pre-Viking Ireland, evident in texts whose original production can be dated to between the sixth and ninth centuries), took place in the setting of the scriptoria, that is, copy rooms, of the monasteries and churches of Ireland and of those ecclesiastical institutions on the Continent established by peripatetic Irish clerics. These scriptoria, however, were not insulated, strictly "religious" environments. Rivaling the courts of local kings (whose family members were in many cases deeply implicated in the religious life), monasteries became the major political, social, and cultural centers of medieval Ireland, and the perspectives of the producers of early Irish literature clearly reflect this centrality and the monasteries' interdependence with the secular world around them. Early on in the history of Irish Christianity its representatives made peace (easy or uneasy, depending on which scholar is consulted) with some key "native" institutions that had played (and with this new rapprochement with, or co-optation by, the Church continued to play) key roles in the transmission of tradition. These institutions included kingship, whose possessors patronized the Church and in turn could at least in theory turn to churchmen for the preservation (in written form) of traditions that validated their kingship; the localization of religious cult, which, translated into Christian terms, generated the extraordinary proliferation of saints in early-medieval Ireland, along with their cults' intimate associations with particular monasteries or churches and federations of such units; and poetry, whose practitioners were dramatically reinvented within the Christian milieu, with the result that the *fili* ("one who sees," the standard word for "poet" in Irish, designating a figure whose range of expertise and functions extended far beyond the composition or performance of poetry) became a staple member and welcome guest of the monastic community.

Thus, while their religious orientation and strong interest in the literatures of early Christianity and the classical world may have diminished or affected their sympathy for certain aspects of their native culture, the learned producers of early Irish literature were by no means cut off from their society (or at least, not from the upper echelons of their intensely hierarchical society), and literary composition, like the project of devising a written form of the vernacular, was clearly motivated at least in part by a desire to record current, receding, and past oral traditions and in "capturing" them in writing to reformulate their authority in terms of new cultural poli-

The Ogham stone inscribed with Ogham characters, which still stands near Colaiste Ide, county Kerry, Ireland. (Probably fifth–seventh century C.E.; *Werner Forman/Art Resource, NY)*

tics. While it would be going too far to describe medieval Irish literature as ethnography, it nevertheless contains a strong impulse to preserve as well as to create. Even if in many cases texts present us with invention or reinvention rather than preservation of tradition, they provide us with valuable clues as to what tradition was supposed to be like.

We actually do have Latin compositions that were probably written in Ireland in the fifth century, but these hardly constitute "Irish literature," although they did wield considerable influence. The texts in question are the *Confessio* (Confession) and *Letter to Coroticus* attributed to Patrick, a missionary to Ireland celebrated in legend in oral and written tradition down to the present day. In his tantalizingly brief references to the Irish, among whom he lived as a slave before he returned to convert them, the Briton Patrick mentions some "pagan" customs of interest to a folklorist, such as the sucking of the breast as a traditional sign of supplication and the offering of a portion of one's food to supernatural forces in order to turn away evil. Scholars of Patrician legend little appreciate the fact that the very narrative framework that Patrick constructs for his life by way of the personal experience narratives he strings together in the *Confessio* is folkloric, evoking the "heroic biography" pattern studied by many scholars, notably Tomás Ó Cathasaigh.

Beyond Patrick's own writings, some of the earliest literature to have survived from Ireland are the saints' lives written in Latin in the seventh century. Chief among these are the lives of Patrick written by Muirchú and Tírechán, the life of Brigid by Cogitosus and some other early Latin lives of this popular female saint, the life of Columba written by Adomnán, and the account of the voyage of Brendan, possibly authored by a non-Irishman. In these texts, which to some extent exerted an influence on Continental hagiography as well, we have the earliest attestations of certain legends that live on in the oral traditions of twentieth-century Ireland and Scotland, such as the stories of Patrick's reviving the wicked pagan's bull and Brigid's loss and miraculous recovery of her eye, as well as of important elements of saints' cults alive and well in the present day, such as the importance of wells for healing and of elevations for pilgrimage. In his introduction to a collection of Latin lives of the saints, Charles Plummer cataloged the "pagan" elements and other matters of ethnographic interest to be found in these texts, as did Whitley Stokes in his introduction to an edition and translation of the Irish saints' lives from the Book of Lismore.

Constituting, at least in some of their more archaic layers, our earliest corpus of vernacular literature from Ireland are numerous law tracts, which cover a wide range of topics, including the maintenance and curing of the sick, the procedures of satire, the rituals of contract, and beekeeping. Fergus Kelly's massive study of early Irish farming, based primarily on the law tracts, shows how many of the "folkways" of medieval Ireland can be reconstructed on the basis of these difficult texts, which have proven invaluable to linguists and cultural historians alike. The legal aphorisms with which these tracts are peppered clearly constitute an important subgenre of proverb, and the occasional references to narratives provide us glimpses of the multiformity of the storytelling repertoire, as well as witnessing to the function of story as paradigm and precedent.

Complementing and clearly closely connected to the secular law tracts in Irish (produced and elaborated upon by Irish legal specialists throughout the medieval period) are surviving collections of ecclesiastical legislation in Latin or Irish—such as the *Law of Adamnán*, whose preface presents a bizarre account of what Daniel Melia has described as shamanic initiation—and penitentials (the genre is an Irish invention), which catalog sins that in many case pertain to folk custom and belief.

While poems surviving from the Old Irish period (including the many poetic passages in the law tracts) typically evince their learned origins and in some cases even represent innovative extensions of the poetic function, these texts, and their prose introductions or frames, offer valuable clues as to particular oral performative genres and ritual activities, such as inspired prophetic utterance (e.g., the archaic, or archaized, *roscada* attributed to characters in heroic saga), keening or lamenting the dead (e.g., Bláthmac's poem on the death of Christ), work songs (e.g., *Tochmarc Étaíne* [Wooing of Étaín]), and lullabies (e.g., the poem to the baby Jesus attributed to St. Íte). The genre of praise poetry, the basic product of the poet operating outside the scriptorial milieu but perhaps deemed subliterary by the producers and guardians of literature, is only rarely represented, or only indirectly, in the earliest manuscripts, except for the purpose of demonstrating metrical forms in learned tracts on such matters. Although most medieval Irish prose tales also include poetry, and poetry often comes equipped in manuscripts with a prose introduction that sets up the premise, poetic language and prose obviously serve different ends, and the marked language of poetry is typically more embedded in particular ritual or social situations. (This is not to say that prose tales or their performance in medieval Ireland were not sensitive to context—see, for example, the epilogues to the late Middle Irish *Altrom Tige Dá Medar* [Fosterage of the House of Two Cups] and to the parodistic *Aislinge Meic Conglinne* [Vision of Mac Conglinne].)

For only a few secular tales have incontestably Old Irish versions survived; a marked number of these have to do with encounters with the (non-Christian) otherworld, such as the *Immram Brain* (Voyage of Bran), which tells of marvelous transmarine realms and beings encountered by the Odysseus-like Bran and his crew, and the cycle of stories about the legendary Ulster king Mongán, who leads a curious double life as both mortal and supernatural being. These narratives affirm the venerability of the beliefs widely attested in modern Irish and Scottish folk traditions that the otherworld presents a mirror-image (although often with some crucial difference) of this world and that a human who travels to an otherworld will experience, like Rip van Winkle, a dislocation in time—a theme most vividly exploited in the Middle Irish tale *Echtrae Nerai* (Nera's Supernatural Adventure).

It was during the period between and including the tenth and twelfth centuries, in the phase of the literary language referred to as Middle Irish, that the bulk of the surviving literature of medieval Ireland was produced, at least in its original form. This is an era of ambitious literary undertakings, including the compilation of the *Lebor Gabála Érenn* (Book of the Invasions of Ireland), commonly referred to as the masterpiece of Irish pseudohistory, that is, the attempt of the literati to construct a history comparable to existing Continental literary models that would fit native Irish traditions about the past into a larger "learned" (including biblical) historical framework. In fact, this pseudohistorical project, including such other ancillary texts from this period as the *Cath Maige Tuired* (Battle of Mag Tuired) (an account of the ambivalent relations between the Tuatha Dé Danann, one of the primeval invading peoples of Ireland, and the demonic Fomorians [Fomoire], would-be possessors of the island) and the *Suidiugud Tellaig Temrach* (Settlement of the Territory of Tara), comes close to mythography, along the lines of what Hellenistic authors such as Apollodorus and the medieval Icelander Snorri Sturluson fashioned out of their own traditions. The introductory passages of Middle Irish tales from the so-called Ulster cycle (which I discuss below), such as the *Serglige Con Culainn* (Sickbed of Cú Chulainn) and the *Mesca Ulad* (Drunkenness of the Ulstermen), make it clear that the Tuatha Dé Danann and other residents of the *síd* ("otherworldly dwelling," the standard term in both early and later Irish for the sites of the supernatural) constituted the pantheon or recipients of the worship of the pre-Christian Irish. Perhaps not surprisingly, it is to these later texts that we have to turn to find some (occasionally dubious) indication of who the gods and goddesses of the ancient Irish were, and what stories were told about them, instead of to the earlier saints' lives, which are in general tight-lipped or dismissive about just what it was that Christianity was replacing (although the word *síd* is to be found in the text of Tírechán's *Life of Patrick*, a rather conspicuous vernacular import into the Latin text).

Arguably the most intriguing pieces of evidence provided by Middle Irish literature to the student of traditional narrative are the tale lists, one of which is embedded in a narrative text. These purport to be inventories of the storytelling repertoire of the *fili*. (The poet in Irish tradition, as in Welsh tradition, is assigned the function of storyteller or guardian of narrative lore.) Among the repertoire the list presents us with approximately 200 titles, of which only a fraction is actually represented in the surviving literature. Of particular interest in these lists is the organization of the narrative material according to generic titles that index the main action or event in the story—such as *aithed*, "elopement"; *aided*, "violent death"; *táin*, "cattle raid"; *togail*, "destruction"; and *serc*, "love." Conceptualizing stories in terms of what happens in them is a traditional procedure also in evidence in the titles actually assigned to narrative texts in manuscripts, although the latter also feature a different taxonomic principle, commonly used by scholars of medieval Irish literature as well, whereby stories are organized on the basis of their cast of characters or setting. The twelfth-century manuscript known as the *Book of Leinster*, for example, contains, among many other items, not only a recension of the *Táin Bó Cúailnge* (Cattle Raid of Cooley), the massive centerpiece of the Ulster cycle of stories having to do with Cú Chulainn, Conchobor, Fergus mac Roig, and other heroes associated with Ulster of a particular era, but several additional stories from this cycle as well. Moreover, some of the titles assigned to narrative texts by scribes (e.g., *scéla*, "news [about]") do not highlight a particular action or event at all but, instead, function as the equivalent of "other" among responses to a multiple-choice question. Still, there is much of narratological value to be gleaned from these designations of "native genres," whether or not they stem from popular or learned tradition, and the studies of Vincent A. Dunn and Daniel Melia show that examining medieval Irish narratives grouped according to their designations uncovers key recurring structural patterns.

It has often been asked whether the Ulster cycle of tales (which in the historical arrangements of medieval Irish scribes comes after the primeval period of what scholars would call the "mythological cycle," featuring the successive invasions of Ireland, but before the periods of the kings' cycle and the Fenian [Fianna] cycle discussed below) reflects an earlier, Iron Age phase of Irish society and culture, comparable perhaps to the civilization of the ancient Continental Celts. The archaeologist James Mallory has demonstrated that the artifacts and technologies on display in the Ulster cycle do not point to any one era but, rather, form a synthesis of the contemporary and the anachronistic. Dating problems aside, these texts contain a wealth of information about traditional dress, foodways, crafts, and medicine. The stories themselves supplied Hector Munro Chadwick and Nora K. Chadwick with an important Celtic pillar for the construction of their idea of a Heroic Age perpetuated in epic, even though the application of the term "epic" to the Ulster tales is problematic. Still, given details such as Cú Chulainn's divine paternity (some of our texts make him out to be the son of Lug, one of the great gods of the Irish as well as the Continental Celtic pantheon); the barely sublimated supernatural qualities of important players such as Medb, the queen of Connacht; and the larger-than-life quality of the characters in general, including Conchobor, the king of Ulster, one could reasonably set these tales alongside the Homeric and Indo-Iranian epics as reflecting an Indo-European tendency (studied most productively in the Irish context by Elizabeth Gray) to transpose the mythological dramas of the gods onto the level of heroes and heroic tale.

Another compelling question that has been asked about these texts is: by whom or in whose interests were the literary compositions featuring Ulster tales (which, one should note, often feature non-Ulster characters and places) produced or collected? Various theories having to do with the political, familial, and cultural agendas of medieval Irish literati and their ecclesiastical and secular patrons have been proposed. Doubtless also contributing to the seeming popularity of these narratives and characters in pre-thirteenth-century Irish literary tradition, which was based primarily outside Ulster, is their otherness. Perhaps playing a role comparable to that of stories about cowboys and Indians in modern U.S. culture, these tales about the struggles between the heroes of Ulster and those of Connacht and the other parts of Ireland simultaneously evoked nostalgia from the audiences of medieval Ireland and satisfied their appetite for the exotic.

An intriguing miscellany of texts having to do with kings, reigning from the pre-Christian era to the eighth century, is also to be found in the corpus of Middle Irish literature. Examples include the *Togail Bruidne Da Derga* (Destruction of Da Derga's Hostel), *Fled Dúin na n-Géd* (Feast of the Fort of the Geese), *Cath Almaine* (Battle of Allen), and *Aided Muirchertaig meic Erca* (Death of Muirchertach mac Erca). While this kings' cycle has nothing like the recurring cast of characters that we find in the mythological or Ulster cycle, and the kings in question are from various parts of Ireland, there is a certain thematic consis-

The High Cross at Monasterboice, Ireland; late ninth century. (Photograph by John McNamara)

tency to these tales, which typically dwell on the difficult, often deadly deci-sions kings have to make. The assertion of historicity that often informs these tales (which sometimes find their way into annalistic literature as well) and their cautionary overtones (the message that kings should not overstep their bounds, and the morbid glee evident in the depictions of what happens to them when they do) remind the folklorist of the legend, a genre to which these texts are clearly indebted. Worth mentioning in connection with the kings' sagas are the numerous references in a variety of texts to the rituals and ideology of kingship, including the genre of wisdom literature putatively addressed by traditional figures of authority to kings or kings-to-be—for example, the Old Irish *Audacht Morainn* (Testament of Morann) and the Middle Irish *Tecosca Cormaic* (Instructions of Cormac)—and a list of the prohibitions (*geisi*) placed upon the king ruling in the ancient site of Tara. (The motif of the *geis* survives into modern Gaelic heroic tales.)

A Middle Irish masterpiece that deserves a separate mention in a survey of this kind is the *Aislinge Meic Conglinne* (Vision of Mac Conglinne); though it is a parody (or perhaps precisely because it is a parody), it sheds light on all the folkloric features of medieval Irish literature that have been mentioned so far, including the legendry and cult of saints, stories of the deeds of heroes and the perils of kingship, generic distinctions among narratives, the performative contexts of prose and poetry, and the inclusion of ethnographic detail as a stylistic device. Additionally, the author has provided us with an extraordinary inventory of foods and food preparation to go along with the text's over-the-top verbiage, setting up in effect a fascinating equation between food and words as parallel items of social exchange. The figure of Mac Conglinne himself—his gluttony, avarice, craftiness, and gift of the gab—is worthy of inclusion in any rogues' gallery of Greatest Tricksters, and the text's allusions to other "vulgar" characters of story like Mac Conglinne, and to the class of roving performers/ rhymesters/satirists whose ranks the clerical student Mac Conglinne joins at the beginning of his adventures, provide us with a glimpse of types of popular entertainment and entertainers at a considerable remove from the learned and perhaps old-fashioned repertoire and persona of the *fili* usually featured in literature of this period. Other Middle or Early Modern Irish texts that intimate this wider world of performance and performers are the *Loinges Mac n-Uislenn* (Exile of the Sons of Uisliu), the famous story of Derdriu, a storyteller's daughter whose beauty and poetic voice provoke a testing of gendered power structures; *Tromdám Guaire* (Heavy Hosting of Guaire), in which the whole array of the medieval Irish entertainment profession is comically and embarrassingly on display; and the *Buile Shuibne* (Frenzy of Suibne), the account of a truly offbeat poet.

Folklore is to be found not only in the great narrative compositions of Middle Irish literature. Rife with bits of lore—including popular belief and custom, traditional explanations of the origins of names, proverbs, and allusions to narratives mentioned nowhere else in the corpus—are learned compilations such as the *Sanas Cormaic*, commonly known as *Cormac's Glossary*, the *Cóir Anmann* (Fitness of Names), the *Triads*, and the *Auraicept na n-Éces* (Scholars' Primer). In *Cormac's Glossary*, for example, we find a famous description of the mantic rite known as *imbas forosnai*, "the great knowledge that enlightens," and other techniques for obtaining esoteric knowledge. An invaluable resource for scholars researching Irish place names and the traditions associated with them is the voluminous *Dindshenchas* (Lore of Places), which exists in both poetry and prose. Even though many of the etymologies and etiologies presented herein are the products of learned invention, this compilation constitutes the apex of the pervasive medieval and modern Irish fascination with toponymy.

Also redolent of this fascination are the earliest major texts that have survived from medieval Ireland having to do with the adventures of Finn (Fion, Fionn) mac Cumaill and his hunting-warring band (*fian*, often referred to in the plural, *fianna*). (Marie-Louise Sjoestedt, Kim McCone, and others have argued that Finn and his men derive from the Indo-European complex of ritual and myth having to do with the *Männerbund*, an ancient initiatory institution for young men, which is also reflected in, for example, the "Wild Huntsmen" legends and beliefs to be found among other Western European peoples.) Unlike the Ulster heroes and kings who figure in most earlier narrative compositions, Finn the *rígfhénnid* ("chief *fénnid*," i.e., member of a *fian*) and his comrades range freely over Ireland, exhibiting a remarkable familiarity with and freedom in all of its wildernesses, which constitute their turf. The knowledge and love of the landscape regularly exhibited by the so-called Fenian heroes go hand in hand with the literary compulsion to account for place names and to record antiquarian lore, as is evident in the medieval masterpiece of Fenian literature, the *Acallam na Senórach* (Dialogue of the Ancients), in effect a frame tale, whose earliest recension probably dates from the twelfth century. St. Patrick plays a starring role in the *Acallam*, in which the missionary saint meets the miraculously surviving members of Finn's *fian* and, like a folklorist or oral historian, coaxes them to tell him and his scribes all that they know about the past, particularly their own. The ancient Fenian heroes, particularly Caílte and Oisín, the son of Finn, oblige Patrick happily and provide him with a veritable archive of lore, including stories and poems, Fenian and otherwise. The *Acallam* is one of the most popular (that is, widely copied and redacted) texts of the later medieval and early modern period. Like another Fenian composition from the twelfth century or later, the *Feis Tighe Chonáin* (Feast of Conán's House), it demonstrates the centrality of the trope of dialogue to the medieval Irish literary project—the conceit that literature is produced as the result of a conversation, sometimes made possible by supernatural intervention, between "contemporary" and "ancient" interlocutors, or a conversation among just the "ancients" that is recorded for posterity. This stereotypical casting of literature as the product of fieldwork is especially suggestive in its application to these and the other Fenian texts that start to appear in profusion in the twelfth and later centuries, since quite possibly Fenian story actually was a literary import from more popular traditions. (Stories about the Fenian heroes were collected from the Gaelic-speaking storytellers of Ireland and Scotland, and even of Nova Scotia, well into the twentieth century.)

Not only did the Fenian tradition contribute a new source of story to medieval Irish literature, but it also provided a context for a heretofore uncharacteristic use of poetic language in Irish literature—namely, to tell a story in a style and form that can be described as "balladic." The earliest surviving Fenian *laídi*, "lays," are to be found in the twelfth-century *Book of Leinster*, and these are of a piece with the Fenian narrative poems to be found in later manuscript collections, such as the sixteenth-century *Book of the Dean of Lismore* from Scotland and the seventeenth-century *Duanaire Finn* (Finn's Songbook), based on Irish sources. The singing of such "ballads," featuring the adventures of Fenian or other heroes, was still attested in Gaelic-speaking areas in the twentieth century. More study of these poetic texts, both medieval and modern, and of their composition in terms of formula, theme, and story pattern (as these are used in the scholarly examination of oral epics and ballads) is in order.

The *Acallam* represents more than the infusion of Fenian tradition into the literary realm. In its agenda of reevaluating the past and in its insistence on the necessity for Irish Christian learned culture to take on the responsibility of recording that past, the text (especially with its "gimmick" of the saint interviewing pre-Christian heroes) adumbrates a period of transition and retrenchment. In the period between the eleventh and thirteenth centuries, many forms of literary production, and many of the families devoted to literary pursuits that had developed in the monastic milieu of early-medieval Ireland, moved, or were moved, out of the ecclesiastical establishment under pressure from reforms within the Irish Church. Literature and its preservation became primarily secular affairs under the patronage of nobles, although the writing of religious literature, and literary activity within the religious milieu, continued as well. In the wake of this cultural shift from church to court, and also in the wake of the twelfth-century Anglo-Norman incursion into Ireland (a presence that was to have profound implications for Irish history), Irish literature became more open to a wider array of external influences, including the chivalric literature of France and England. (The Anglo-Norman invasion also brought with it Gerald of Wales, whose writings on Ireland and the Irish in the twelfth century provide us with an outsider's view of a wide range of native customs and beliefs.) The so-called romantic tale, one of the literary forms that developed during the Early and Classic Modern Irish period (1200–1700), reflects the impact of the Arthurian story and other streams of Continental courtly literature on the Irish storyteller and his scribal counterpart, although these romantic tales (which often feature Fenian heroes or other figures from the Irish narrative repertoire) also repackage existing native story elements and plots. Alan Bruford has argued that the virtuosically performed hero tale of modern Irish and Scottish Gaelic storytelling tradition is in most cases a direct descendant from the literary romantic tale or from other literary sources, but this argument has not been universally accepted. On the basis of the evidence, it is equally if not more reasonable to view the relationship between Gaelic oral and literary stories as in general the same as that between the chicken and the egg. Kevin O'Nolan's work, comparing the formulaic language and style of romantic tales and other late-medieval literary compositions with those of modern Irish storytellers, demonstrates just how complex the relationship between "written" and "spoken" forms of narrative performance continued to be throughout the medieval period and down to modern times.

See also: Beltane; Brigid, Saint; Celtic Mythology; Patrick, Saint; Samhain; Scottish Tradition; Ulster Cycle; Welsh Tradition

References and further reading: There are numerous studies of the various aspects of the Irish tradition; some of the most important are L. Bieler, ed. and trans., *The Irish Penitentials* (1963); C. Bowen, "A Historical Inventory of the *Dindshenchas*," *Studia Celtica* 10/11 (1975/1976); A. Bruford, *Gaelic Folk-Tales and Mediaeval Romances: A Study of the Early Modern Irish "Romantic Tales" and Their Oral Derivatives* (1969); J. Carney, *The Problem of St Patrick* (1961), and *Studies in Irish Literature and History* (1955); H. M. Chadwick, *The Heroic Age* (1912); L. De Paor, trans., *St. Patrick's World: The Christian Culture of Ireland's Apostolic Age* (1993); M. Dillon, ed. and trans., "The Taboos of the Kings of Ireland," *Proceedings of the Royal Irish Academy* 44 (1951); D. N. Dumville and L. Abrams, *Saint Patrick*, A.D 493–1993 (1993); V. A. Dunn,

Cattle-Raids and Courtships: Medieval Narrative Genres in a Traditional Context (1989); P. K. Ford, ed., *Celtic Folklore and Christianity: Studies in Memory of William W. Heist* (1983); E. A. Gray, ed. and trans., *Cath Maige Tuired: The Second Battle of Mag Tuired* Naas (1982); E. A. Gray, "*Cath Maige Tuired*: Myth and Structure," *Éigse* 28 (1981) and 29 (1982–1983), and "Lug and Cú Chulainn: King and Warrior, God and Man," *Studia Celtica* 24/25 (1989/1990); A. Harrison, *The Irish Trickster* (1989); F. Kelly, *Early Irish Farming* (1997), and *A Guide to Early Irish Law* (1988); B. Lambkin, "The Structure of the Blathmac Poems," *Studia Celtica* 20/21 (1985/1986); P. Mac Cana, *Celtic Mythology* (1970; rpt. 1983), and *The Learned Tales of Medieval Ireland* (1980); K. McCone, *Pagan Past and Christian Present in Early Irish Literature* (1990); D. MacManus, *A Guide to Ogam* (1991); J. P. Mallory, ed., *Studies in the Táin* (1992); D. F. Melia, "Law and the Shaman Saint," in *Celtic Folklore and Christianity: Studies in Memory of William W. Heist*, ed. P. K. Ford (1983), "Remarks on the Structure and Composition of the Ulster Death Tales," *Studia Hibernica* 17/18 (1977/1978), and "Some Remarks on the Affinities of Medieval Irish Saga," *Acta Antiqua Academiae Scientiarum Hungaricae* 27 (1979); K. Meyer, ed. and trans., "The Instructions of King Cormac mac Airt," *Todd Lecture Series* no. 15 (1909), and "The Triads of Ireland," *Todd Lecture Series* no. 13 (1906); G. Murphy, *Duanaire Finn: The Book of the Lays of Fionn*, vol. 3, Introduction and Notes (1953); G. Murphy, trans., *Early Irish Lyrics* (1998); J. F. Nagy, *Conversing with Angels and Ancients: Literary Myths of Medieval Ireland* (1997), "Orality in Medieval Irish Narrative: An Overview," *Oral Tradition* 1 (1986), and *The Wisdom of the Outlaw: The Boyhood Deeds of Finn in Gaelic Narrative Tradition* (1985); Gerald of Wales, *The History and Topography of Ireland,* trans. J. J. O'Meara, rev. ed. (1982); J. J. O'Meara, trans., *Navigatio Sancti Brendani: The Voyage of Saint Brendan* (1994); S. Ó Catháin, *The Festival of Brigit: Celtic Goddess and Holy Woman* (1995), "*Echtrae Nerai* and Its Analogues," *Celtica* 21 (1990), "Oral or Literary? Some Strands of the Argument," *Studia Hibernica* 17/18 (1977/1978), and "Place and Placename in *Fianaigheacht,*" *Studia Hibernica* 27 (1993); T. Ó Cathsaigh, *The Heroic Biography of Cormac mac Airt* (1977); K. O'Nolan, "Homer and Irish Heroic Narrative," *Classical Quarterly* 63 (1969), and "The Use of Formula in Storytelling," *Béaloideas* 39/41 (1971/1973); C. Plummer, ed., *Vitae Sanctorum Hiberniae,* 2 vols. (1910); A. Rees and B. Rees, *Celtic Heritage: Ancient Tradition in Ireland and Wales* (1960); M.-L. Sjoestedt, *Gods and Heroes of the Celts,* trans. M. Dillon (1949); E. M. Slotkin, "Folkloristics and Medieval Celtic Philology: A Theoretical Model," in *Celtic Folklore and Christianity: Studies in Memory of William W. Heist,* ed. P. K. Ford (1983); C. Watkins, "Indo-European Metrics and Archaic Irish Verse," *Celtica* 6 (1963), and *How to Kill a Dragon: Aspects of Indo-European Poetics* (1995).

—Joseph Falaky Nagy

Italian Tradition

The folkloric culture of the Italian peninsula, Sicily, and Sardinia.

Medieval Italian traditions are complex because they reflect the historical developments of peoples with diverse backgrounds. The Italian peninsula, Sicily, and Sardinia were densely populated even before the foundation of Rome in 753 B.C.E. and the almost contemporaneous beginnings of Greek colonization of southern Italy in the eighth century. (This area of Greek colonization came to be called *Magna Grecia,* "Greater Greece.") Both the Romans and the Greeks faced obstacles and challenges to their future hegemonies posed by these prior inhabitants as they contended with them for land, trading outposts, and control of the seas. Some of these peoples left their names upon the lands wherein they dwelled (e.g., the Etruscans [Tuscany], the Bruzi [Abruzzi], the Veneti, the Italici). Groups such as the Ligurians and the Sabines, who have had their names recorded by Cicero and Virgil, are remembered for their fierceness and for their conflicts with the Romans. Contention sometimes led to

outright war with these prior inhabitants: the Etruscans were admired and emulated by the Romans. Etruscan expansion toward the coast, however, provoked
a war with the Cumans (Greeks), even though the Greeks at Pitekoussai, on
the island of Ischia, had originally maintained peaceful trading contacts with
Etruscan centers and regions with metal ores. During the course of their descent
into the peninsula the Celts pushed back the Ligurians and the Etruscans. The
Phoenicians, predecessors of the Greeks in Sicily and of the Romans in Sardinia,
were linked to the adversaries of the Romans in the Punic Wars.

Not only bellicose divisions but also cultural ties emerged from contacts
among the peoples of the peninsula, Sicily, and Sardinia. The Archaeological
Museum of Palermo recently offered an exhibit of Punic (Phoenician) Palermo,
the fruit of an ongoing excavation. Sardinia was colonized by the Carthaginians
(Phoenicians) prior to the arrival of the Romans, during the Second Punic War
(219–201 B.C.E.). A Punic inscription at Bithyia is dated as late as the third
century C.E. The word *zippiril*, Sardinian for *rosmarino* (rosemary), is an example
of such influence. Sardinia is unique, for it was under the cultural influence of
peoples such as the Greeks and the Berbers.

Other groups also left traces of their culture in Italian tradition. Consider a
story from Boccaccio's *Decameron* (7,1) that mentions the custom of placing a
donkey's head in the vineyard or field for fertility purposes and for warding off
evil; this practice derives from Etruscan funeral rites and rituals, which have
left a profound mark. In Magna Grecia, Neapolis (present-day Naples), originally founded by the Greeks, retained its Greek traditions despite its later conquest by Rome and thus provided the Romans with a nearby place in which to
learn Greek philosophy, art, literature, and religion.

Medieval popular traditions are dominated by Christianity and by an element of popular religion that includes both regional and national customs.
Children in Sicily, the Veneto, and certain other regions of Italy receive gifts
on St. Lucy's Day, December 13; another such occasion is the night of November 1. St. Lucy's feast comes during the same time as the winter solstice, and St.
Lucy is thus associated in popular tradition with (spiritual) light. In the Middle
Ages her cult became so popular that she became the distributor of gifts to
children, along with Baby Jesus, St. Nicholas, and the Befana (the good Epiphany
witch). It is quite plausible that Lucy was, therefore, the Christian version of
the goddess Aurora.

Also because of her association with light, St. Lucy became the patron saint
of eyesight and eye diseases. Even Dante Alighieri adopted her as his protector
because he suffered from bad eyesight, and he made her a symbol of illuminating grace (*Inferno* 2:100). St. Lucy's remains were transported from Syracuse,
the city of her martyrdom, to Constantinople by the Byzantine general Maniace
(1038–1042) as a symbol of his victory over the Sicilians. They are presently in
the Church of San Geremia (St. Jeremiah) in Venice. Present-day formulas and
invocations to St. Lucy for cures for eye diseases and for finding lost objects go
back to the Middle Ages.

Only under the rule of Odoacer (beginning in 476 C.E.) could one begin to
speak of the Italian peninsula as "Italia"—a name that originally pertained only
to the region now known as Calabria. The name was given to the whole penin-

sula under Romulus Augustulus, whom Odoacer deposed. With this event the Western Roman Empire ceased to exist, and thus began the Middle Ages. Odoacer was defeated by the Ostrogoth Theodoric, who ruled from 493 until 526 and brought with him a vast number of immigrants. Justinian I, emperor of the Eastern Empire in Constantinople (Justinian the Great, whose greatest achievement was his *Codex*, a collection of all ancient laws and the commentaries of great jurists), sent two of his generals, Belisarius and Narses, to reconquer the Italian province (553 C.E.).

An important factor during this period is the emergence and independence of the Western Church, aided by the foundation of Western monasticism, although politically Italy was still under the influence of the Eastern Empire. This process of Westernization continued with the domination of the Lombards, a people who had settled in Hungary and then moved rapidly into the Italian peninsula. Their king, Alboin, entered Pavia *nulli lesionem ferens* (without causing any injury), as a savior, to the relief and acclaim of the local population. Pavia became the capital of the new kingdom (572 C.E.). Pope Gregory the Great succeeded in converting the Lombards (680 C.E.). This domination lasted until 774 C.E., but it had little influence on culture or customs, for the Lombards absorbed the Roman influence of the conquered people, especially under the rule of Theodolinda and Alboin.

On the other hand, the Lombards brought some technical and agricultural innovations, a small patrimony of influences on laws and family life, and a number of legends and proverbs formed around the figures of their leaders—particularly around Alboin and his wife Rosamund. The latter avenged her father's death by killing Alboin, who had given her wine to drink from a cup made of her father's cranium. A variation of this motif inspired Boccaccio's tale of Ghismunda and Tancredi (*Decameron* 4, 1). The linguistic influence of the Lombards was mainly felt on words related to war and the military: *castaldo* (king's steward), *sperone* (spur), *guerra* (war), but many localities besides Lombardy bear names of Lombard origin. There is no Lombard literature, but Paulus Diaconus is their major historian. His *Historia Langobardorum* (History of the Lombards) describes the migrations, deeds, legends, and adventures of this people.

One of the glories of the Lombards is the monastery of St. Colombanus at Bobbio, which was built with the support and assistance of this Germanic people. It became a center of learning and piety. An account of the Lombards is also found in *The Golden Legend* of Jacobus de Voragine in the story of the pope St. Pelagius. And in *Origo gentis Langobardorum* (Origin of the Lombards), by a certain Theodaldus, one also finds an account of the origin and the legends of this people.

The Lombards occupied most of the North, but cities such as Venice and Ravenna were never under their control. They were engaged mostly in warfare and agriculture, but only landowners could be in the army. They left their mark on the physiognomic traits of the population: they were physically a strong, tall, and fair people. In the Genoese dialect, the word *lambardan* means a tall, strong, graceless person. The word *langubardu* is an astacus—a type of crustacean with scissor-like claws—a creature with which the Genoese chose to associate the Lombards. The word *fara*, which means ownership by a collective group or lineage of a group, was the Lombard name for the partition of occupied land. There are several towns in Abruzzi bearing this toponym: for example, Fara San Martino, Fara Filiorum Petri. Collective kin groups known as *consortes* were part of this system, a tradition that resulted in the clan known as in Dante's time as *consorteria* (cabal).

The Lombards did not succeed in expelling the Byzantines from the southern part of the peninsula. In this they were opposed by the pope, who received in recompense the territory of Sutri (728), which made the Church a temporal power. The Lombard kings' attempt to conquer all of Italy caused the ruin of their monarchy, which was soon replaced by the Frank invaders under Pepin (754).

The well-developed and highly organized society of the Franks bears no comparison to that of the previous Barbarian invaders. Charlemagne established the *Regnum Italicum* (Kingdom of Italy) in 781 C.E. and became Holy Roman emperor in the year 800. The Frankish reign lasted until 963, when Otto the Great, emperor and king of Germany, came to Italy to depose the last Frankish king, Berengar II. During this time Venice was allowed to become more independent, and the Duchy of Benevento remained autonomous with a large territory.

Under Frankish rule the form of government remained largely unchanged. Dukes were replaced by counts and marquis. The principle of *faidus* (feuds) prevailed over the private vendetta, which, however, was legal in cases of homicide, rape, abduction, or adultery. Among the elite there was a notable increase in literacy. There was no development of vernacular literature. Two figures, however, stand out: Paulus Diaconus, the author of the above-mentioned *Historia Langobardorum*, and Peter the Grammarian—eminent intellectuals of the Carolingian Renaissance. In Italy, commerce, including the importation of goods and slaves, increased by way of seaports such as Genoa and Venice. Under the Franks, military subscription was obligatory. Service was based on the amount of land owned. Beginning with Otto the Great, the Kingdom of Italy was ruled by the German emperor, who was also king of Italy. From Charlemagne's time Italy was divided in three parts: the Kingdom of Italy, comprising all of the northern and central part; the papal state, consisting mostly of Latium; and the Duchy of Benevento, including Abruzzi, Campania, and the rest of southern Italy.

One historical event that left its mark on the culture and civilization of southern Italy was the Arab invasion of Sicily, which culminated in the capture of Palermo in 831. The first Arab invasion took place in 652, followed by others in 669, when the Arabs entered Syracuse, and they soon afterward seized the island of Pantelleria, which they used as a base from which to raid the entire southern Italian coast. In 740 Habib ibn Ubaidah laid siege to Syracuse. From this date onward Arab incursions continued periodically until 827, when, at the instigation of a Byzantine governor, the Arabs moved decisively to conquer Sicily and established Palermo as their capital.

The Arabs remained in Sicily for almost two centuries, during which time they created an Arab Sicily with a distinct culture and civilization. They did not stop there; they seized Brindisi, Taranto (837–838), and Bari (841) and even threatened Rome (846). Indeed, all of Italy was threatened by an invasion. Arab influence penetrated every aspect of life, especially in Sicily, because of the length of their rule. Arab influence can be found in popular songs and musical rhythms, in poetry, in folktales, and in legends. A character well known in Sicilian folktales, Giuffa, is of Arab origin. He is the typical wise fool. An Arabic Andalusian traveler of the twelfth century, Ibn Jubayr, gave a colorful account of Arab Sicily.

The Arab domination of Sicily and parts of southern Italy lasted well into the eleventh century—Palermo fell to Robert Guiscard in 1072—and transformed the island culturally and economically. The local Arab-Sicilian dynasty, called the Kalbite—made up of wise administrators, artists, and poets—began to disintegrate around 1060, and various cities such as Palermo, Syracuse, Trapani, and Noto were under the rule of local emirs. Rivalries eventually led some of these local rulers to invite the Normans to intervene. Messina fell to the Normans in 1061; Castrogiovanni in 1064; Palermo in 1072. Ibn al Ward, the emir of Syracuse, briefly reoccupied some cities until 1091, when Roger of Hauteville became great count of Sicily and Calabria, thus setting down the foundation for a kingdom that would last until the nineteenth century, through different dynasties and royal houses. As a result, it created the great divide between north and south that is still a threat to the unity of Italy today. The Normans absorbed and adopted the Byzantine-Arab civilizations. They created a modern state that was unified and culturally diverse. They perfected methods of administration, such as the Arab *dohuana,* from which the term *dogana* (customs) derives. The Norman period was a splendid time for the cultural and economic development of Sicily—diverse in languages, cultures, architectural styles, and traditions. A city such as Palermo, where Latin, Arabic, Italian, Greek, French, and English were spoken, represented an image of enlightenment and cultural splendor that was later to be maintained by the Houenstaufen dynasty, in the person of Frederick II.

The cultural force of the Arab presence in Sicily and southern Italian territories, such as the Emirate of Bari, must not be underestimated. The oral transmission of legends, myths, tales, music, and poetry was to become enormously important. Equally important were stories from the East such as the *Thousand and One Nights,* the *Disciplina clericalis* of Petrus Alfonsi, *The Seven Sages,* and *The Book of Kalila and Dimna.* These stories were being transmitted in written and oral form and they filtered through to the earliest collection of Italian tales, *Novellino* (end of the thirteenth century), and to Boccaccio's *Decameron* (c. 1349–1351). Holy Roman Emperor Frederick II (d. 1250) would later become a major cultivator of Arab culture and learning; his own treatise on falconry owed much to Arab texts. The poetry developed at his court in Palermo, the *Scuola Siciliana* (Sicilian School of Poetry), was undoubtedly influenced by the songs and poetry of the Arabs. The art of the Sicilian School, which was to become the first Italian school of poetry, was exported to Tuscany and the rest of Italy and transformed by poets such as Guittone d'Arezzo (d. 1294) of the Tuscan-Sicilian School, Guido Guinizelli (d. 1276), Dante Alighieri (d. 1321), and Guido Cavalcanti (d. 1300) of the *Dolce Stil Nuovo* (Sweet New Style), in which courtly love and Averroistic elements can be traced and in which the image of woman was elevated almost to the level of divinity.

St. Francis of Assisi preaching to the birds, from Matthew Paris's Historia Major, *circa 1240 (Corpus Christi College, Cambridge, MS 16, fol. 66v; reproduced from Elizabeth Hallam,* Four Gothic Kings, *New York, 1987)*

Figures such as Leonardo Fibonacci (the inventor of the *liber abaci*) and Michael Scot lived at Frederick's court, directly absorbing the Arab influence. Scot was a famous astronomer and alchemist (see Dante's *Inferno* 20:115–117) to whom many prophecies were attributed, including one, related by the chronicler Salimbene of Parma, about the future of some Italian cities. During the period of Arab domination, poetry was a major cultural endeavor, especially under the Kalbite dynasty: the best-known Arab-Sicilian poet is Ibn-Hamdis (d. 1132). In contrast to the three centuries of Byzantine domination, the two and a half centuries of Arab political rule created a resurgence of both the countryside and the cities from earlier squalor and misery. Agriculture, for instance, underwent a significant development. The Arab rulers were tolerant toward Christians and Jews, and so the cultures and the customs of the people became enriched and diverse. This influence is to be found in every aspect of life: personal and place names, customs and usages, popular beliefs, sayings, linguistic expressions, urban structures of old quarters, markets, squares, food, and clothing. The Palatine Chapel in the Royal Palace of Palermo (constructed 1132–1140) is an example of Arabic and Byzantine art coexisting at the time of Roger II (c. 1130).

Arab civilization enriched the entire peninsula through the powerful political force of the Kingdom of Sicily. In the early part of the thirteenth century Italian cities underwent rapid economic development, as the power of the communes offset the central hegemony of the emperor. Economic progress brought about cultural enrichment and a definite imprint on folk culture in every aspect of life. The creation of guilds and corporations, architectural activity, the rise of the cities—all had a great effect on all aspects of daily life: clothing, festivals, saints, feasts, popular literature, music, dance, the calendar as a whole. We might consider specific items such as births, weddings, funerals, and feasts. In his *Antiquitates*, Ludovico Antonio Muratori attempted to reconstruct these popular traditions by recording fashions in dress, nuptials, spectacles, and games and by studying such sources as chronicles and legislation from the period of the Barbarian invasions. In speaking of Odoacer, whom he praises, Muratori states that there have been Barbarians much more prudent and clean than the Romans and the Greeks. He considered mimes and historians popular poets.

Life-Cycle Traditions

Rites of passage attended major transitions in the life cycle. Birth, an event accompanied by a great many rituals, was centered around the infant's baptism. It was a sin to kiss an infant before he or she was baptized. The midwife carried male infants to church on her right arm, females on her left arm. Upon returning home, she would recite the formula "You gave me a pagan; I bring back a Christian." The godfather threw confetti—a symbol of plenitude whose origin probably goes back to the Roman practice of giving *sacra natalicia* (holy birthday) gifts. This was followed by a banquet or refreshments to celebrate the presence of a new member of the community.

There was also a rite of purification for the mother, derived from the Hebrew tradition, especially from the story of Mary's Purification, celebrated on the day of Candelora, so called because of the custom of distributing candles, which, according to popular piety, offer protection against such calamities as bad weather (Candlemas, February 2). This feast day coincided with the Roman rite of the Lupercalia (during the course of which nearly naked priests struck women, attempting to render them fertile) and the days of purification called Iunio Februata.

The custom of singing *ninne-nanne* (lullabies) to infants is of Roman origin. In the Middle Ages such poems were thought to have been sung to the Infant Jesus by the Virgin Mary. Dante records a lullaby in a verse, *"colui che mo' si consola con nanna"* (*Purgatory* 23:111), as a custom to placate children. First Communion and Confirmation are connected to rites of passage in primitive and ancient religions. The colors used for the vestiary were also significant: Arnold van Gennep indicates that in France pink and red were for males, and white and light blue were for females, these being the colors of the Madonna. These colors were later inverted in Italy. In Dante's time baptisms were registered in a parish with little balls or fava beans: black for males, white for females. The same colors were later used for balloting during the Councils of the Republic: black, yes; white, no.

Various wedding rites and customs derived from Eastern (Indian) and Roman rites, such as the groom crossing the threshold without touching it with his feet. The bride's veil and apron were red, according to Roman customs. The banquets—their duration and the foods served—were also traditional. In Florence the first banquet lasted three days; the second was held eight days later at the bride's house. The dance was both a sacred ritual and a symbol of fecundity.

Death and funeral rites often followed ancient customs. For example, the custom of placing a rock or stone under the deceased's pillow goes back to the Romans and their veneration of the god Terminus; it meant that the person may have violated the boundaries of the land marked in stone. The *corrotto*, the mourning and lamentations held by relatives, friends, or even professionals, is derived from funeral customs of ancient origin, as depicted in Homer or on Egyptian or Etruscan tombs. Among the Romans, professional mourners were called *prefiche*. Though Christianity sought to eliminate this custom, it endured, especially in the southern regions and on the islands. Similarly, the custom of placing a coin in the mouth of the deceased is also of very ancient origin, the idea being that the deceased would pay for his or her journey with this coin. In certain regions of Italy a friend or a neighbor, the *consolo*, would arrange the banquet after the funeral rites. This Roman custom survives to this day. On the Day of the Dead, All Souls' Day, it was customary to eat chickpea soup—an ancient funeral dish derived from the Romans and Greeks.

Feasts and Festivals

In medieval Italy special attention was given to expressions of popular piety for particular favors received by patron saints. Several saints were especially popular for the protection they could afford: St. Lucy (eyes), St. Agatha (breasts), St. Blaise (throat), St. Anthony (animal protection), St. Julian (hostels, hospitaliers), St. Christopher (travelers), St. Joseph (carpenters), St. Amedeus (hair stylists), St. John (printers), St. Eligius (blacksmiths), St. James (hatmakers), and many others. Many saints and their feasts are associated with pagan deities. Others are tied to rural life, such as St. John the Baptist (flowers and fruits, June 24), the feast of Mary's Assumption (harvest, August 15), St. Bartholomew (eggs, butter, cheese, August 25; also a feast of eating and drinking), and St. Nicholas (water, bread, gifts, December 6).

Every guild or *compagnia* had a pageant, a theatrical representation, or a procession. Pilgrimages to Rome, Jerusalem, Santiago de Compostela, and San Michele in the Gargano (Apulia, modern Puglia) were popular and were a source of many legends, traditions, folksongs, special clothing, and income. The Via Francigena connected Apulia to Rome and to Lucca and then split—toward Liguria, to southern France, on to Galicia (to the shrine of St. James)—or toward the northeast via Bologna, Piacenza, and the northern countries.

The Milky Way, in popular culture, was called Il Cammino di San Giacomo (St. James's Way). In Sicilian and Calabrian folklore St. James's Way was the conduit through which the dead continued to communicate with the living.

Medieval alchemists used the word *compostela* in the phrase *campus stellae* (field of stars) as the primary matter joined with the stars. St. James was thus the patron saint of alchemists.

The number of local pilgrimage shrines was stunning, and each one had its own color, customs, and rites, such as St. Paul of Galatina, in the Salento region of Apulia, sacred to people who have been bitten by tarantulas, snakes, and spiders. The *tarantolati* (the victims of tarantulas) executed a ritual dance that would free them from the tarantula bite (June 29). The belief in the efficacy of relics of saints (as in Boccaccio's *Decameron* 1:10 and 6:10) was common in such practices.

Among the popular feasts, special notice must be given to the Carnevale (Carnival). A burlesque character personifying Carnevale was playfully "put to death" in public after a period of pleasures and dissipation. At his side was Old Lady Quaresima (Lent). Carnevale season usually began on January 17 (St. Anthony's feast day) or on February 2 (Candelora or Candlemas). The departure of the Carnevale character could be enacted in various ways: via a parody

The facade of Orvieto Cathedral. (John Heseltine/Corbis)

of a funeral, for example, or through the burning of a straw man. The contrast between Carnevale and Quaresima became part of the early literary tradition, as in Guido Faba's epistle, *De Quadragesima ad Carnisprivium* (thirteenth century). Lorenzo de Medici's "Trionfo di Arianna" is one of the most celebrated *Canti Carnascialeschi* (Carnivalesque Songs). Carnival was celebrated with masks and pageants, accompanied by popular dances. Most famous were those held in Florence, Venice, and Rome. In Bologna there was a battle between Carnival, on a big horse, and Lent, on a small one. A summer carnival took place in some regions of Italy: in the Tuscan town of Barga, near Lucca, there remains a summer carnival in which the *maschere* (costumed characters) satirically poke fun at the establishment. Summer carnivals also took place on the feasts of Corpus Christi (June 8) and of St. John the Baptist (June 24).

In Verona and Ivrea (Piedmont region) there were two of the oldest forms of the Carnival. In the version at Ivrea people wearing red berets would rush to watch a *belle muliera* (beautiful woman) who would free the population from the abuses of the feudal lord. In Sicily the names *lu nannu* and *la nanna* stood for the Old Man and his Wife who were sacrificed because they represented fun and joy being taken away. This departure provoked the funeral lament called *ruculiamentu* in Sicily and *corrotto, repito,* and *vocero* in other regions. This lament is a parody of the funeral lament of the *prefiche* present in Sardinia, Corsica, Abruzzi, and Campania.

Feasts, festivals, games, and pageants all served the human need for cleansing rituals in response to the miseries of war and plagues on Italian soil. Of course, carnivals incurred the wrath of clergymen, such as St. Bernardino of Siena (d. 1444) and Girolamo Savonarola (d. 1498), and even of Erasmus during a visit to Siena in 1509. Calendimarzo and Calendimaggio (the Kalends of March and May—that is, March 1 and May 1) are especially famous for the many rituals, rites, dances, bonfires, and country feasts that preceded and followed labor in the fields. There was a custom called *incantate,* in which the peasants harvesting wheat would yell insults at people. Every religious feast of major importance in the liturgical calendar provided a special ritual or representation for the popular imagination, through sacred drama, songs, popular tableaus, or elaborate dramatic processions of the Passion of Christ. Magical practices, amulets, rituals, and formulas were very common.

The popular religion easily replaced ancient gods with the saints venerated by Christendom. Symbols such as the cross, liturgical expressions, and ejaculations (very short prayers, often only phrases) became amulets, magical formulas, and talismans. The cruciform sign present in many cultures became the amulet of Christians, who transferred to it the power and protection needed against the maleficent practices and incantations of magicians, witches, and devils.

Dances and Games

Very popular dances included the *ballo a tondo* (a type of round dance), also called *ridda* or *ruota* (wheel), and the *tresca* mentioned in Dante's *Inferno* (7:24; 14:40–42; 16:19–27). In *Paradiso,* however, the dances are the slow, calm type of religious dances sanctioned by the Church. Both Dante and Boccaccio list a number of musical instruments common in their times: harp, pipe, cither, guitar, horn, gig, lyre, lute, tuba, and instruments *ad archetto* (bowed), such as the crotta, rebeck, and viella. Collections of tales such as *Ii Piovano Arlotto* (a type of country cleric and merry priest), Sercambi's *Novelle*, and the works of other *novellieri* (short-story writers) such as Sacchetti, Bandello, Masuccio Salernitano, and others are a rich source of folklore. In Boccaccio's *Decameron* (8,2) a peasant character named Monna Belcolore (Lady Beautiful Color) displays knowledge of songs, dances, and instruments. She is described as being able to play the tambourine, dance a reel or a jig, and sing notoriously spicy songs. Indeed, songs and dances are scheduled at the end of every day of the *Decameron*. The rich folkloric tradition in Italy during the Middle Ages is intrinsically tied to other European countries bordering the Mediterranean. As neighbors, they form a shared world of beliefs and ways of life—a treasure still affecting today's world.

See also: Arabic-Islamic Tradition; Carnival; Dante Alighieri; *Decameron*; Saints, Cults of the

References and further reading: See L. Allegri, *Teatro e spettacolo nel medioevo* (1990); G. Pitre and S. Salomone-Marino, eds., *Archivio per lo studio delle tradizioni popolari*, vols. 1–23 (1888; rpt. 1967); P. Burke, *Popular Culture in Early Modern Europe* (1978); F. Cardini, *Magia stregoneria: Superstizioni nell'occidente medievale* (1979), *Il giorno del sacro*, *Il libro delle feste* (1983), and *Il medioevo in Toscana* (1989); A. Cattabiani, *Calendano. Le feste. I miti. le leggende e i riti dell' anno* (1989); G. Cocchiara, *Storia del folclore in Europa* (1954); G. G. Coulton, *Life in the Middle Ages: Folk-Lore and Superstition* (1928); C. Gaignebet, *Le Carnaval* (1974); E. Giancristoforo, *Tradizioni popolari d'Abruzzo: La loro genesi*, vol. 1: *Religion* (1995); F. Heer, *The Medieval World* (1962), and *The Intellectual History of Europe*, vol. 1 (1968); J. Le Goff, *Medieval Callings* (1990), and *The Medieval Imagination* (1988); H. Pirenne, *Economic and Social History of Medieval Europe* (1967); D. P. Rotunda, *Motif-Index of the Italian Novella in Prose* (1975); J. C. Schmitt, *Medioevo superstizioso* (1992); J. de Voragine, *The Golden Legend*, trans. W. G. Ryan (1993); A. van Gennep, *Manuel de folklore français contemporain* (1937; rpt. 1972); and C. Wickam, *Early Medieval Italy* (1989).

—*Giuseppe C. Di Scipio*

James the Elder, Saint (first century C.E.)
[Latin *Jacobus*, Spanish *Santiago*]

One of the 12 Apostles of Jesus Christ.

From the New Testament we know that James was a fisherman and was nicknamed Boanerges (Son of Thunder). He was the first of the apostles to be martyred, by Herod Agrippa I, in the year 44 C.E. Any details about his activities after Christ's death and before his own and his subsequent miraculous works are speculative. Yet around this figure wound an intricate story that became codified in about the twelfth century. Its development incorporated elements from folk traditions that include boat burials, stone cults, and Celtic religious rites. The legend of James became intertwined with Christian explication, commingling ecclesiastical motives and historical circumstance.

The saint's biography is in some respects a series of tenuously connected tales, several of which exist in multiple versions. His legend can be loosely divided into three parts: activities before his death; burial, the tomb's later discovery, and resultant pilgrimage to the site; and the saint as Matamoros.

The standard *vita* begins after Pentecost and places James on the Iberian Peninsula to preach and convert. He gained only a handful of disciples in the northwest region of Spain called Galicia. Returning to the Holy Land, he passed through Zaragoza. There, in her only miraculous appearance while she was still alive, the Virgin Mary commanded him to build a church to commemorate her son. As proof of her identity she brought with her the pillar on which Christ had been flagellated (hence the origin of a common Spanish name for a woman, Pilar). A later tale relates that, further on his journey, the saint stepped on a thorn and was unable to remove it. The Virgin sent angels to help. A chapel near Lérida commemorated this event.

After his beheading St. James's body was placed in a boat, which miraculously landed at Iria Flavia (modern Padrón) on the northwest coast of the peninsula. James's few converts pulled his body ashore, but having no tomb ready, they laid it on a stone, which miraculously conformed to hold the saint's body. The saint's disciples asked the area's pagan Queen Lupa for permission to bury him. She was adamantly opposed, giving the disciples impossible tasks to perform in exchange for her permission. The best known of these was to yoke two wild oxen to their cart. When the oxen saw the saint's body, they immediately walked tamely to the cart to be yoked. The saint was buried.

Nothing is said about the next seven centuries. The tomb was not discovered until about 814. One version of its discovery relates that shepherds guarding their flocks saw a particularly bright star, which they followed to a hidden burial place. Bishop Teodomiro was consulted, the tomb was opened, and the body of St. James was recognized. A small church was erected there, followed by another, larger shrine. The area around the chapel had probably been inhabited in the pre-Roman and Roman eras, but its development is inextricably linked to the saint's cult. Its name, Santiago de Compostela, attests to this close relationship. Yet even the etymology of *Compostela* has been variously interpreted as *campo stela*, "field of stars" or "pretty site."

This biography was made even more complex when Santiago took on a militaristic role in Spanish history. In the year 711, the *musulmanes* (Spanish *moros*) from Africa invaded and conquered nearly all of the Iberian Peninsula. In time, the few Christian holdouts in the northern mountains began skirmishes to push south, initiating the famous Spanish Reconquest (completed in 1492). At a place called Clavijo in about 850, in a battle designed to end an onerous yearly tribute of 10 or 100 or 1,000 (depending on the version) virgins, from the sky descended a knight on a white horse wielding a sword against the Moors: Santiago, now named Santiago Matamoros (Moor-slayer).

People were already visiting the shrine of the saint's burial place for cures, devotion, and prayer. But now political and devotional motives merged. When Santiago aided the Christians in their fight against the Moors, the political rulers acknowledged their debt by increasing donations, both monetary and territorial. Pilgrimage to Compostela became popular, reaching its high point in the twelfth century.

Pilgrims to Santiago's tomb in Compostela returned home with a scallop shell as symbol of having journeyed there, perhaps because St. James returned to the peninsula from the sea or perhaps because in an early miracle attributed to him he saves a man from drowning in the sea. Confraternities (religious groups of lay people) dedicated to St. James were common in communities throughout Western Europe. They aided pilgrims and often held local festivals on the saint's day.

Localized belief in the saint's powers is evidenced by numerous shrines and chapels named in his honor throughout Europe. The saint is represented throughout most of northern Europe as a pilgrim, with the wayfarer's attributes of staff, satchel, hat, and long cloak and a scallop shell as his identifying mark. Within the Iberian Peninsula he is widely represented as Matamoros as well, generally in a white tunic, astride a white horse, wielding a sword and crushing Moors beneath the horse's hooves.

The *vita*, now long and multifaceted, apparently evolved slowly during its first few centuries. The earliest records linking St. James the Apostle to the Iberian Peninsula began appearing in the seventh century, but they may be later interpolations. The English monk Aldhelm of Malmesbury (d. 709) wrote a clear reference to St. James's having preached in Spain, and several other authors did likewise in that and subsequent centuries. The twelfth-century *Liber Sancti Jacobi* (Book of Saint James) codified his legend for Christianity and made evident the importance of making a pilgrimage to his tomb. The mixture of ecclesiastical and popular beliefs was generally accepted as true throughout the Middle Ages, although the history was not made official Church doctrine until 1884. For the most part, it was not until the Reformation and the Protestant movement that skepticism was heard or broadly written. Even the nucleus of his identity as Matamoros is questioned, since both the tribute and the battle are now debated by historians, but it was an aspect of the saint's legend that was not contested until recently.

See also: Hispanic Tradition; *Liber Sancti Jacobi*; Pilgrimage; Saints, Cults of the
References and further reading: M. Dunn and L. Davidson, *The Pilgrimage to Santiago de Compostela: A Comprehensive Annotated Bibliography* (1994), annotates over 2,900 works about the pilgrimage to Compostela, both modern and medieval. H. Davies and M. Davies, *Holy Days and Holidays: The Medieval Pilgrimage to Compostela* (1982), explains motivations for medieval pilgrimage and offers a view of the pilgrim to Compostela; L. Vázquez de Parga et al., *Las peregrinaciones a Santiago de Compostela* (1949; rpt. 1992), is the standard history. J. Van Heerwarden, "Saint James in Spain up to the Twelfth Century," in *Wallfahrt kennt keine Grenzen*, ed. L. Kriss-Rettenbeck and G. Mohler (1984), explains the early development of the legend of the saint and his relationship to Spain. F. López Alsina, *La ciudad de Santiago de Compostela en la alta Edad Media* (1988), traces and compares information about Compostela as it developed in the twelfth century; M. Stokstad, *Santiago de Compostela in the Age of Great Pilgrimages* (1978), focuses on the state of the city of Compostela in the twelfth century. F. Grundfeld, "The Road to Santiago," *Reporter* 34, no. 1 (1966), although somewhat touristic, has interesting information about folklore along the route; W. Starkie, *The Road to Santiago: Pilgrims of St. James* (1957), has been a great stimulus for the modern pilgrimage. His personal narrative has several folkloric stories, but it is unannotated; C. Hohler, "The Badge of St. James," in *The Scallop: Studies of a Shell and Its Influences on Humankind*, ed. I. Cox (1957), speaks to the use of the scallop shell in the pilgrimage and on pilgrimage art; F. Romero, "La leyenda de la reina Lupa en los montes del Pindo," *Cuadernos de estudios gallegos* 34, no. 99 (1983), details the region's folkloric beliefs about the pagan queen, including the beliefs that her tomb is filled with gold and that earth from around it can cure the sick. H. Peake, "Santiago: The Evolution of a Patron Saint," *Folklore* 30, no. 3 (1919), and H. Howes, "The Cult of Sant-Iago at Compostela," *Folklore* 36 (1925), offer interesting insights into the use of the ancient folk traditions in the legend. The most recent study of the history and culture of this pilgrimage, with recountings of folk stories told in villages along the route, is D. Gitlitz and L. Davidson, *The Pilgrimage Road to Santiago: The Complete Cultural Handbook* (2000).

—*Linda Davidson and Maryjane Dunn*

Jesus Christ

Believed by Christians to be the Son of God and the second person of the divine Trinity.

New Testament accounts of Jesus' career are well known. The canonical Gospels (Matthew, Mark, Luke, and John) should not be classified as biographies as the term is conventionally understood: they are, rather, works of theology, even though they are based on the life, work, and death of Jesus of Nazareth. Nonetheless, all but the most die-hard modern skeptical scholar would concede that the narratives are based on historical events.

Historically based though they may be, these Gospels only relate disparate events; none of these narratives provides a complete picture of Jesus' life. The Gospels describe his birth; then, they relate an incident that occurred when he was 12. After another gap, he is encountered being baptized by John the Baptist before embarking on a ministry of possibly three years' duration, during which he is reported to have taught many people, to have traveled around Palestine accompanied by a core of 12 disciples, to have performed many miracles, and then to have been arrested in Jerusalem, ultimately tried by the Romans and crucified. The Gospels end with reports that Jesus was raised from the dead and with accounts of his post-Easter appearances.

After his death and Resurrection, the one who in the Gospels is the proclaimer becomes the one who is proclaimed by his followers. The rest of the New Testament outside the Gospels is concerned with the founding and growth of the Church. Groups who were converted and followed Christ's teaching encountered many social, administrative, and theological troubles because the new religion was breaking away from its Jewish roots and heritage. The Acts of the Apostles and the Epistles, principally those written by or in the name of Paul, enable us to plot the growth of Christianity and its problems in the first century.

Normative Christianity thereafter used the New Testament writings as its foundation documents, and by the fourth century, the Church, East and West, had agreed on the canon of Christian scripture. Events in Jesus' life were made the centerpieces of Christian celebration and worship as the liturgy developed and as ecclesiastically approved lectionaries were adopted. Jesus' teaching was meditated upon and preached about by influential patristic writers. Church councils deliberated about his person, and especially about his relationship to God. Popular piety accepted at face value the events and teachings attributed to Jesus by the Evangelists.

Other writings, particularly those of the second century, attempted to build on the New Testament Gospels and to plug perceived gaps in the biographical details about Jesus as seen within the Gospels of Matthew, Mark, Luke, and John. The so-called apocryphal Gospels are full of imaginative details about Jesus, particularly concerning his formative years; very few details in them are likely to be historical. Some Gospels, such as the influential second-century Protevangelium of James, relate stories about Jesus' ancestry. Others tell stories of his boyhood. The Arabic Infancy Gospel has a cycle of stories in which Jesus performs many miracles during the Holy Family's sojourn in Egypt.

Another of these early apocryphal writings, the Infancy Gospel of Thomas, has various episodes set in Jesus' childhood: he works in his father's carpentry shop, runs errands for his mother, and astounds his schoolmasters. In addition to such stories, the Infancy Gospel of Thomas relates several miracles in which Jesus, almost an enfant terrible, performs various destructive acts on those who vex him. Bizarre as some of those stories are, they nevertheless reflect an orthodox tendency in early Christianity to emphasize Jesus as a real flesh-and-blood human born of a woman and brought up as a normal child, albeit one with divine power over life and death.

That emphasis conflicts with several "heretical" interpretations, especially Gnostic and Docetic. Those interpretations of Jesus gained in popularity in the second century and threatened the traditional, orthodox view by denying him an actual physical existence during his ministry and by stressing only his supernatural nature. Believers who were determined to defend orthodox teaching had to counter such heretical interpretations. The apocryphal tradition—superstitious, uncritical, and magical though it may appear to sophisticated modern minds and castigated as it was by ecclesiastical authorities determined to concentrate attention on only the New Testament writings—nonetheless had an enormous influence on subsequent writings, art, and devotion and assisted in preserving the teaching about the physical ministry of Jesus of Nazareth.

However, in one influential apocryphal text, the second-century Acts of John, part of the narrative (especially the chapters normally numbered 87–105, known from only one manuscript) seems to have been contaminated by Gnostic ideas. Jesus' earthly body is described there in mystic terms. It is not unchanging but, rather, capable of adopting varying guises—an old man or a youth; bearded or clean-shaven; short or towering. His body is sometimes solid, sometimes immaterial and incapable of leaving even a footprint on the earth (Acts John 89, 93). Here, Jesus himself describes his Crucifixion as being that of only a phantom body, the "real" Jesus being distanced from these events (Acts John 97, 101).

What therefore ultimately emerged in writings about Jesus were two often diametrically opposed pictures: one, the Incarnate Messiah; the other, the divine Son of God. Both pictures, of course, may be found even within the New Testament writings themselves, but distortions of both are to be seen throughout Christianity and Christian writing. Christian theological thinking has had to try to explain, resolve, or reconcile many such contradictions. Christian art likewise is divided between pictures of Jesus as Pantocrator (Ruler of All) or with a nimbus and those that locate him in naturalistic scenes as a man among mankind. Popular belief in general has tended to focus on his well-known miracles—healings, exorcisms, and especially such nature miracles as the feeding of the 5,000 or the walking on the water—but Christian devotion also emphasizes his role as eternal and risen, at one with God, and as the eventual inaugurator of the End Time, when he is to reappear in glory.

Inevitably, it was the biblical accounts of Jesus' deeds and preaching that motivated orthodox Christian devotion, practice, and teaching throughout subsequent centuries. Until the radical *Lives of Jesus* in the nineteenth century and recent publications of liberal scholarship, uncritical readers of the Bible accepted the New Testament's portrayal of Jesus as teacher, healer, and Savior. The additional, apocryphal, stories of his infancy and boyhood had a limited impact.

There is, however, one popular nonbiblical story about Jesus that was used in medieval folklore; namely, Jesus' descent to the underworld. The belief that Jesus preached to the departed in the period between his death on Good Friday and his Resurrection on Easter Day and led the faithful out of Hades and into Paradise may have been based on a particular interpretation in 1 Peter 3:19; however, in its developed form it is found in the second half of the Gospel of Nicodemus, probably composed in the fifth to sixth centuries. The scene, known as the Harrowing of Hell, was performed by the saddlers in the York cycle of medieval mystery plays. The Christian credal statement, "He descended into hell" is evidence of the influence of this tradition.

See also: Christmas; Grain Miracle; Harrowing of Hell; Joseph, Saint; Joseph of Arimathea, Saint; Mary Magdalen, Saint; Peter, Saint; Pilate; Virgin Mary

References and further reading: Many of the most influential later legends about and sayings attributed to Jesus are to be found throughout collections of early Christian apocrypha, such as J. K. Elliott, *The Apocryphal New Testament* (1993), and *The Apocryphal Jesus: Legends of the Early Church* (1996), and W. Schneemelcher, *Apocryphal New Testament*, 2 vols., ed. R. McL. Wilson (1991, 1992). Works on the Jesus of history, such as A. Schweitzer, *The Quest of the Historical Jesus* (1954); G. Bornkamm, *Jesus of Nazareth* (1960); and C. H. Dodd, *The Founder of Christianity* (1971), may now be read alongside studies of Jesus' Jewishness, such as E. P. Sanders, *Jesus and Judaism* (1985), or G. Vermes, *Jesus the Jew* (1973).

—*J. K. Elliott*

Jewish Tradition

The beliefs, customs, verbal traditions, folk arts, and folklife shared by communities belonging to the Jewish faith.

One of the most pervasive concepts shaping the lives and culture of medieval Jews was that of *galut* (diaspora), the sense that Gentile hatred and Jewish sins had robbed the Jewish people of their glorious past and precipitated the disaster of their dispersion and degradation. Jewish communities of the Middle Ages thus shared a lack of sovereign territory and a powerful yearning for an irretrievable time.

Medieval Jews were divided into two main groups: those communities living under the peoples of Islam, from Yemen in the East to Spain and Morocco in the West, and those Jews living in Christian realms, from the Byzantine Empire to England. There had been Jewish communities in Egypt and Babylonia since biblical times, and in Europe Jewish settlements antedated the Roman Empire. Jewish collective memory, however, identified the dispersion with the two great destructions of Jerusalem: that of the first temple, in biblical times, and that of the second temple, carried out by the Romans in 69 c.e. Though the destruction of the second temple was accompanied by the destruction of the remnants of Jewish political existence in Palestine, paradoxically, this violent and futile act created the conditions for the flowering of European Jewish culture. Historians agree that the Jewish Middle Ages began with the invasion of Palestine by Muslim armies and the establishment of the Muslim states in the mid-seventh century. These events separated the Jewish communities of the newly emerged Muslim world from those of the Christian realms and laid the foundations of medieval Jewish social, religious, and cultural life.

Although separated geographically, the Jewish communities maintained a close relationship across the cultural divide between East and West. This made both the communities and their folklore ideal mediators between Arab and Christian cultures. Books were translated from Arabic into Hebrew and thus entered Europe via Jewish culture; Jewish travelers, emigrants, and wandering scholars spread customs and narrative traditions from Europe to the East and back.

Hebrew and Jewish Concepts of Tradition

A core question in any study of medieval Jewish folklore concerns language. Hebrew was the sacred tongue, the main language of the ancient sources, yet during this period it was not a "living" language, as it was not used for ordinary communication. Jews communicated among themselves and with their neighbors in Arabic or in the European vernaculars. By the central Middle Ages Jews had developed their own vernaculars: Judeo-Arabic, Judeo-German (Yiddish), and Judeo-Spanish (Judizmo, Ladino). These initially modest means of oral communication developed into full literary languages. Further complicating this situation is the fact that though Hebrew was not a "living" language, neither was it "dead." For Jews, one consequence of the East-West divide was the necessity of arriving at a means of communication. Ancient customs and traditions (the daily prayers and yearly rituals conducted in Hebrew) provided the only common tongue.

The availability of Hebrew enabled local communities to host students who journeyed to Iraq to study in Torah academies, helped merchants trading in the East, and allowed emissaries traveling in Europe to raise money for the poor of the Holy Land. If an author wished his book to be read by Jews everywhere, he had no choice but to write in Hebrew. This state of affairs puts Jewish folklore of the time in an awkward perspective: the language of everyday Jewish life was the local vernacular; their folklore was undoubtedly created and transmitted in the vernacular as well. Yet almost all Jewish folklore of the Middle Ages was set down in documents written in Hebrew. Tales of all genres, magic formulas, descriptions of rites and customs, and travelers' accounts all appear in Hebrew. This aspect of the preservation of Jewish traditions bears comparison to the complex relations between Latin and the vernacular dialects in medieval Europe.

But the similarity ends when the different social status of the two languages is considered. Latin was the preserve of the learned elite; teaching it to only a few safeguarded the authority of the Church. While most Europeans of the period were illiterate, literacy in Hebrew was a religious imperative for Jews. Every male Jewish child between the ages of three and five attended school, where he learned to read and write Hebrew and acquired a basic understanding of the Bible and the Mishnah (Oral Law). This primary education enabled Jewish males to read prayers during synagogue services and to understand the reading of the Bible. The practice of educating children "democratically" was the reason that the balance of oral and written traditions in Judaism was different from the balance between those traditions in the surrounding culture. Folkloric documents—including collections of tales, lists of folk cures, and magic practices—were written to be read by a literate audience, not to be recited orally or read aloud by storytellers or preachers. This gave the Hebrew folkloric document a different character from that of its counterparts in other medieval cultures. The written document was not only a means of preserving folklore but a folkloric item in itself.

A basic concept of medieval Judaism was *shalhelet ha-kabbalah* (the chain of tradition); that is, each generation is one link in a long chain starting with the giving of God's word to Moses, who transmitted it to Joshua, and Joshua to the Elders, and the Elders to the Prophets (Mishnah Avot 1:1), and on and on to the learned rabbis of the Middle Ages. This ultraconservative model of tradition presented every cultural asset as having originated fully formed in the ancient past, and it impeded the emergence of new cultural creations and patterns of life. Yet medieval Jewish culture did produce new texts, customs, and traditions, circumventing this formal barrier with the aid of another basic concept: *minhag* (local custom). When ancient, formal law clashed with the needs of medieval life or thought, local custom—the folkloric practice common in the local community—was permitted and became part of the official law. *Minhag*, as the vehicle for the renewal of traditions, was a powerful tool; it was the chief instrument of change in the social and economic life of medieval Jews, in the development of new liturgical and ritual forms, and in the creation of new narratives. From the folkloric perspective, *minhag* bridged the gap between the learned, official religion and folk culture. It also opened a door between distinct Jewish folk cultures, allowing customs and beliefs to pass through, to gain currency in other communities, and ultimately to be recorded in legal documents.

Absorption of Foreign Traditions

Official Jewish culture eventually absorbed many newly created or originally foreign folk customs pertaining to life and year cycles. One example is the custom of the "night watch," wherein a week-old male infant is guarded the night before his circumcision to forestall any demonic kidnapping attempts. Another is the breaking of the glass beneath the bridal canopy, originally a typical deterrent against demons who might otherwise endanger the marriage. The official religion, after banning this practice as part of idolatrous, pagan cults, transformed it into a symbolic ritual recalling the grief over Jerusalem's destruction. In performing *kapparot* (expiation), one symbolically transfers all of one's sins to a fowl and then sacrifices it on the eve of Yom Kippur (Day of Atonement). Also belonging to this category are certain dances performed by men and women during marriage festivals, and many death customs, such as placing a rock on a grave, tossing grass behind one's back before leaving the cemetery, or the family of the deceased taking a different route home so as not to be followed by the dead man's soul.

Medieval rabbis deliberated over these customs and dozens more and, acknowledging their folkloric or non-Jewish origin, rejected them as *darkei akum* (idolatrous) or immoral. Ultimately, however, common practice prevailed, and rabbinic authority had to accept local customs through the agency of *minhag*. Talmudic literature, central to the cultural activity of the preceding period and to a great extent of the Middle Ages as well, is an all-encompassing creation. It incorporates most of the period's cultural components: scriptural commentary and medicine, law and astronomy, linguistics and historiography, liturgical poetry and geography—all in the course of a single, unbroken, and largely undifferentiated discussion.

By the height of the Geonic period (Iraq-Babylonia, eighth and ninth centuries), a tendency had evolved to create special works on law, Hebrew grammar, Jewish philosophy, liturgical poetry, and historiography. This significant cultural phenomenon, known as the separation of disciplines, was connected to a parallel development in Arabic culture during the first centuries of Islam. The first Hebrew anthologies of folk narratives—which preserve information on the creation and spread of the rich folk traditions among Jewish communities—

belong to that time, place, and cultural milieu. Although the collections of medieval Hebrew folktales were, with few exceptions, anonymously composed, research has established that two of the earliest, namely the *Midrash of the Ten Commandments* and the *Alphabet of Ben Sira*, were created in the eighth to ninth centuries and originated in the region of Iraq-Persia.

Talmudic and midrashic activity (that is, the creation of commentaries on the Scriptures), so dominant in late antiquity, continued unchecked by the development of folkloric anthologies in the Middle Ages. Midrashic works such as *Midrash Genesis Rabbati* (Provence, eleventh century), *Yalkut Shimoni* (Germany, thirteenth century), *Midrash ha-Gadol* (Yemen, thirteenth century), and *Yalkut ha-Makhiri* (Provence, fourteenth century) continued to zealously preserve the literary frameworks of the past. These midrashic anthologies belong to the first type of medieval Jewish folkloric traditions, those based in antiquity that lived on into the Middle Ages. These archaic midrashic works are folklorically less interesting, however, than the medieval folk-narrative anthologies, much of whose content (about one-third) originated in talmudic-midrashic literature. Though drawn from the writings of the past, many of these tales reappear in the later works not as verbatim variants but in new versions. This is another indication that the midrashic folktales were told orally in the Middle Ages and refashioned, as are all folkloric works, in order to express not only the old norms but also, and more important, the contemporary concerns of the narrating society.

The second type of medieval Jewish folkloric tradition involved borrowing from neighboring cultures. Here the experience of the diaspora—the essence of Jewish life in the Middle Ages—left its deepest marks. Every Jewish community of the period, from England to Yemen (and perhaps even further east), was a cultural minority among Christians or Muslims. The demands of daily life, economics, politics, and cultural debates necessitated close ties between Jews and their neighbors, and naturally the greater cultural influence was exerted upon the minority. Jewish religious restrictions nevertheless kept Gentile customs and traditions from encroaching too deeply, and Jewish life remained separate and "other."

The omnipresent confrontation between ancient, sacred traditions and local, non-Jewish folklore was an unavoidable feature of daily life and the major shaping influence on medieval Jewish folklore. The folklore anthologies of the period exhibit this conflict by presenting narratives originating in sacred talmudic literature alongside non-Jewish erotic *novelle* or demonological tales. The folk *novella* "Crescentia" (AT 712), the demonological tale about the marriage to a she-demon (motif F302), both originating in Christian or Arabic folklore, appear in the Oxford manuscript collection of tales of the twelfth century alongside the midrashic tales of Rabbi Akiva, Hillel the Elder, and the destruction of Jerusalem. Another important feature of the borrowing process is the translation of folkloric compositions into Hebrew (and later in the Middle Ages into Yiddish and Judeo-Arabic). The principal medieval frame tales and romances—including *Kalila wa-Dimna, Tales of Sendebar, Thousand and One Nights, Romance of Alexander, King Arthur and the Round Table, The Romance of Antar, The Prince and the Hermit (Barlaam and Josaphat)*, and the knightly romance

Amadis de Gaula—were translated into Jewish dialects and became a part of the Jewish culture of the period. The Judeo-Spanish ballad was one of the most important literary-folkloric creations of the period. Spanish Jews adopted oral poetic narratives (*romanceros*), recited them in their own Judeo-Spanish dialect, and made them part of Jewish culture. After the expulsion from Spain (1492), Jews scattered in the Balkans, Turkey, Morocco, the Netherlands, and Palestine continued to see these ballads as part of the cultural heritage and collective memory from their beloved *Sefarad* (Spain). They continue to perform them to this very day.

Both the borrowing of non-Jewish folk traditions and the translation of folkloric compositions are more culturally complex than the revision of older Jewish traditions because the newer materials had to undergo a process of Judaization. The inclusion of international folk narratives in the collections of folktales or the translation of whole compositions into Hebrew was never merely technical; rather, it transformed the borrowed traditions in ways that were sometimes superficial, at other times profound. Some changes were linguistic, and others involved the inclusion of Jewish customs and rituals or the rejection of non-Jewish ones. Scripture and Talmud were quoted, references were made to events from Jewish history, and sometimes the whole structure of a tale was altered to make it correspond to Jewish moral and religious norms.

In his introduction, the translator of the *Romance of King Arthur* (1279) explains why he, a pious Jew, occupied himself with such trifles as Gentile romances:

> I attempted the translation of these conversations for two important
> reasons: The first was the preservation of my physical well-being. . . . The
> second and most important reason for my translation was that sinners will
> learn the paths of repentance and bear in mind their end and will return to
> God, as you will see in the conclusion [of the story].

He went beyond translating to reconstruct the romance so that this "sin and punishment" pattern, so important to him as a medieval Jew, would become the narrative focus of the Hebrew version. The synthesis between non-Jewish narrative structures and Jewish cultural norms was not without consequences. In most stories belonging to this type, there is a sharp tension between the pagan, Christian, or Muslim narrative models and Jewish religious and social norms. This tension, inseparable as it was from the mentality of medieval Jews, is one of the most important characteristics of Jewish folklore of the time.

The main folk narrative genres of late antiquity lingered in the Middle Ages, but with diminished popularity. For example, the main narrative genre in the talmudic-midrashic literature was the rewritten biblical story, in which the original tale was expanded and reworked to suit the new generation's cultural and political interests and literary tastes. These creations of the preceding age were the main building blocks of the medieval midrashim (plural of midrash). Medieval Jews, however, preferred those rewritten biblical narratives that embodied the literary and cultural values peculiar to their own day. *Divrei ha-Yamim Shel Moshe* (The Chronicles of Moses; tenth–eleventh centuries) is one such narrative. The story is constructed as a heroic epic, narrating the life of Moses from birth to death as a sequence of heroic deeds, in the best literary tradition of the Middle Ages. Even so, all the narrative blocks upon which this epic tale is built are taken from talmudic literature, thus strengthening the tendency to synthesize traditional material with the new form. Another interesting narrative of the same period is *Midrash va-Yissa'u* or *Milhamot Bnei Ya'akov* (The Wars of the Sons of Jacob), which recounts the wars waged by the tribes, the sons of Jacob, against the Canaanite peoples, after the rape of their sister Dina. The wars are typical knightly fights, using the same norms, strategies, feudal mores, and weapons as those of the chivalric romances. Yet here, too, most of the narrative materials are taken from the apocryphal *Testaments of the Twelve Tribes,* written during the second temple period. Another type of medieval rewritten biblical story is *Sefer ha-Yashar* (The Book of Right Deeds). It retells biblical stories from the Creation to Joshua's conquest of the Land of Canaan. The stories are expanded and written in elevated Hebrew style, with much emphasis on dialogue, dramatic situations, and pathos. The short, condensed biblical tales are transformed into expanded *novelle,* in the best literary style of the late Middle Ages.

The dominant narrative genre in medieval Jewish traditions, as in those of Christian culture, was the exemplum. This genre also possessed roots in ancient Jewish traditions, as evidenced both in talmudic literature and the Christian New Testament. The first Hebrew tale collection of the Middle Ages, the aforementioned *Midrash of the Ten Commandments,* was constructed as a series of exempla, in which folktales illustrate the importance of observing each biblical commandment, the punishments for transgressions, and rewards for obedience. Another important medieval collection of exempla is the *Hibbur Yafeh min-ha-Yeshu'ah* (An Elegant Composition Concerning Relief after Adversity), written in the eleventh century by Rabbi Nissim ibn Shahin of Kairouan of Tunisia (it is one of the few Hebrew narrative works of known authorship). That Rabbi Nissim, a leading religious authority of the day, should have published this work in the contemporary Jewish-Arabic dialect and busied himself with folkloric material is one of the clearest indications that the dichotomy between "learned" and "folk" culture in the Middle Ages was indistinct. The tales are set in a rhetorical context. Each chapter focuses on a central norm, and in each of them the teacher explains its importance and offers the story as validation. Most of the tales had roots in Arab culture and were adapted to suit Jewish norms and lifestyles, giving rise to that characteristic tension discussed above. One of the earliest Christian exempla collections, the eleventh-century *Disciplina Clericalis* (Clerical Discipline), by Petrus Alfonsi, should be considered part of the same Jewish tradition. Petrus Alfonsi (known as Mose Sefardi before his conversion from Judaism) was familiar with Judeo-Arabic folk traditions and used them to express his Christian values and ideas, thus becoming one of the first Christian writers to use folktales as exempla. The influence of Jewish narrative traditions upon one of the central cultural creations of medieval Europe is clear and evident here.

The most important collection of Jewish exempla is *Sefer Hasidim* (Book of the Pious) by Rabbi Judah ben Samuel he-Hasid (the Pious) of Regensburg (twelfth or thirteenth century). *Sefer Hasidim* is a collection of pietistic norms directed toward the "good people" of the Jewish communities—those few

Hasidim willing to accept Rabbi Judah's extreme religious standards. Some 400 short stories are scattered throughout this voluminous code of rules. Most are presented as personal experiences of either Rabbi Judah himself or of reliable authorities, and each of them illustrates or reinforces one of Rabbi Judah's rulings. The didactic function of these short stories is stressed: "That is why *Sefer Hasidim* was written: so that its readers would know what to do, and what ought to be refrained from." Thus, each tale emphasizes a lesson in the terrible punishments suffered by sinners and the great rewards enjoyed by the righteous.

The stories abound with vampires, *strigae* (witch-like beings that sucked the blood of children), seducing demons, witches assuming the shape of cats, and the evil powers of the underworld. The appearance of these medieval German folkloric figures in *Sefer Hasidim* is evidence of close relations between Jews and their non-Jewish neighbors on the folk-cultural level. It is also noteworthy that a leading social figure, Rabbi Judah, the founder of a new religious movement, intensively utilized non-Jewish folkloric traditions to advance his political and moral goals. His use of exempla is similar to that of his Christian contemporaries.

In addition to being a narrator of folktales and the creator of a collection of exempla, Rabbi Judah he-Hasid was also the hero of a hagiographic cycle. Like the rewritten biblical tales and the exempla, legends of the rabbinic sages were a part of ancient traditions. Indeed, legends of Jesus had belonged to this genre of Jewish folklore and initiated Christian folklore's hagiographic tradition. The chief distinction between Jewish and Christian medieval hagiography is that Judaism never envisioned sainthood as an established norm. Medieval Jewish saints were those leading Jewish sages (writers, biblical commentators, philosophers, moralists, poets, mystics) whose deeds the people found worthy of retelling—in realistic or miraculous mode. These saints fulfilled community expectations in safeguarding them from their cruel and dangerous neighbors. Saints' legends appear often in the Jewish literature of the period: in biblical commentaries and legal tracts, moral treatises, and mystical writings. Yet purely hagiographic collections are few. The eleventh-century *Megilat Ahima'az* (The Scroll of Ahima'az) is the first known to us. A rhymed family history from southern Italy, it recounts 200 years of deeds by the leading family members. The patriarchs of the family constantly confront non-Jews, especially kings and religious leaders, and perform various miracles to protect their family and community from evil.

It is only in the late Middle Ages, however, that we find the full-fledged hagiographic collections concerning the most renowned Jewish luminaries, Rabbi Shelomoh ben Itzhak (Rashi), Maimonides, Rabbi Abraham ibn Ezra, and Nahmanides among them. The main collection is in the form of a historiographic work: the mid-sixteenth-century *Sha'shelet ha-Kabbalah* (The Chain of Tradition), by Gedaliah ibn Y'hya. The links of his "chain" are the sages from ancient times to the sixteenth century. He relies heavily on oral folk traditions ("as told to me by the elders of that community") and on other ancient collections of tales. It is clear that such folk traditions were the basic data for the construction of the legendary biographies of many of the Jewish saints of the Middle Ages. The same century gave rise to the collections of another hagiographic cycle—that of Rabbi Judah he-Hasid and his father Rabbi Samuel he-Hasid—in Hebrew and Yiddish traditions. The legends collected in this cycle, like those collected by Gedaliah ibn Yahya, were undoubtedly a product of medieval rather than sixteenth-century notions. They had been transmitted orally and recorded by folk writers either in the original dialects (Yiddish, Judizmo) or in Hebrew. This cycle had an important impact on all later Jewish hagiography, as it laid the model for the European *Hasid* (i.e., the charismatic, religious, wandering miracle worker) who appears mysteriously wherever he is needed to guard a Jewish community in distress. The narrative models established by these late-medieval legends of saints formed the basis of Jewish folklore in the sixteenth and seventeenth centuries, and they indicate the importance of medieval Jewish traditions for all later Jewish culture.

See also: Arabic-Islamic Tradition; Golem; Hispanic Tradition; Judah the Pious; Judith; Lilith; Passover Haggadah; Purim

References and further reading: General histories of medieval Jews, with emphasis on culture and folklife, include S. W. Baron, *A Social and Religious History of the Jews: The Middle Ages*, vols. 3–9 (1959–1965); C. Roth, *The World History of the Jewish People: The Dark Ages* (1966); H. H. Ben-Sasson, "The Middle Ages," in *A History of The Jewish People*, ed. H. H. Ben-Sasson (1976); and K. Stow, *Alienated Minority: The Jews of Medieval Latin Europe* (1992). The first to study the relationships between Jewish and Christian magical beliefs and customs was M. Güdemann, *Geschichte des Erziehungwesens und der Cultur der abendländischer Juden während des Mittelalters* (1880). Other studies are I. Abrahams, *Jewish Life in the Middle Ages* (1896), and J. Trachtenberg, *Jewish Magic and Superstition* (1939). The following works deal with Jewish rituals, beliefs, and customs in different periods, but the Middle Ages is their main topic: H. Schauss, *The Jewish Festivals* (1938), and *The Lifetime of a Jew* (1950), and H. Pollack, *Jewish Folkways in Germanic Lands* (1971). The most influential study of the cultural impact of medieval Jews as mediators between the Eastern, Muslim culture and Christian Europe remains M. Steinschneider, *Die hebräischen Übersetzungen des Mittelalters und die Juden als Dolmetscher* (1893). Studies of folk literature and tale collections include J. Dan, *The Hebrew Story in the Middle Ages* (1974), and E. Yassif, *The Hebrew Folktale* (1994). On local customs (*minhag*) and their relation to the learned, official traditions, see D. Sperber, *Jewish Customs: Origins and History* (1990), and I. M. Ta-Shma, *Early Franco-German Ritual and Custom* (1992). Some of the main collections of tales were translated to English in D. Stern and M. J. Mirsky, eds., *Rabbinic Fantasies* (1990), and M. J. Bin-Gorion, ed., *Mimekor Yisrael: Classical Jewish Folktales* (1990). Medieval European romances in Jewish culture were discussed by J. Dan, "Hebrew Versions of Medieval Prose Romances," *Hebrew University Studies in Literature* 6 (1978), where references to English translations can also be found. The two main collections of exempla were published and studied by W. M. Brinner, ed. and trans., *An Elegant Composition Concerning Relief after Adversity* (1977), and I. G. Marcus, *Piety and Society: The Jewish Pietists of Medieval Germany* (1981); see also T. Alexander-Frizer, *The Pious Sinner* (1991). On the *Disciplina Clericalis* as Jewish-Eastern folklore, see E. Hermes, trans. and ed., *The Disciplina Clericalis of Petrus Alphonsi* (1970). On the field of Yiddish folktales, see J. Maitlis, *The Exempla of Rabbi Samuel and Rabbi Judah the Pious* (1961), and S. Zfatman, *The Jewish Tale in the Middle Ages between Ashkenaz and Sepharad* (1993). The major medieval Jewish fables (thirteenth century) were studied as comparative folklore by H. Schwarzbaum, *The Mishle Shu'alim* [Fox Fables] *of Rabbi Berechiah ha-Nakdan* (1979). The basic collection of Judeo-Spanish ballads is S. Armistead, *El romancero Judeo-Español en el archivo Menéndez Pidal* (1978); see also S. Armistead, "Recent Developments in Judeo-Spanish Ballad Scholarship," *Studies in Jewish Folklore* (1980). A bibliography of the main studies of medieval Jewish folklore is included in E. Yassif, *Jewish Folklore: An Annotated Bibliography* (1986).

—Eli Yassif

Jews, Stereotypes of

The medieval Jew as popularly imagined—following the *New Oxford English Dictionary*'s definition of "stereotype" as "a preconceived, standardized, and over-simplified impression of the characteristics which typify a person" or group, emphasizing here such popular conceptions rather than the various accusations that were made about alleged Jewish actions.

From the early Middle Ages Jews were clearly linked with the twin realms of Satan and sorcery. Their link with the former, evident already in the Gospel of John (8:44) and Revelation (2:9, 3:9), was greatly emphasized by John Chrysostom of Antioch, who late in the fourth century asserted that "the souls of the Jews and the places where they congregate are inhabited by demons" and that "the Jews do not worship God but devils." During the course of time, as Robert Bonfil has noted, "the tendency to connect the Jews with the devil became a fundamental and persistent aspect of Christian attitudes toward Jews and Judaism."

In the twelfth century Peter of Blois, who was born in minor French nobility but served as deputy to the archbishops of Canterbury for two decades, linked the Jew's demonic character with a host of other "annoying" traits: "For the Jew is always inconstant and shifty," he wrote in his *Contra perfidiam Judaeorum* (Against the Treachery of the Jews). "At times he affirms, at times he negates, he quibbles about the literal meaning, or he refers all matters to the times of his own messiah, that is, of the Antichrist. After the manner of the devil his father, he often changes into monstrous shapes." In thirteenth-century Spain the Dominican priest Raymond Martini, who was an accomplished student of rabbinic literature, asserted in his *Pugio fidei* (Dagger of Faith) that it was the devil who had blinded the Jews to the true (allegorical) meaning of the Mosaic commandments. Martini also argued in his widely circulated polemical work that it was Satan who returned them, "by some demonic miracle" to observing those commandments (such as circumcision and the Sabbath) that God himself had clearly intended to nullify through Roman persecutions.

The association between the Jewish messiah and anti-Christ mentioned by Peter of Blois had been made as early as the ninth century by Rabanus Maurus, archbishop of Mainz. In the central Middle Ages such leading scholastics as Thomas Aquinas and Albertus Magnus subscribed to the view that anti-Christ would be born in Babylon to the tribe of Dan, that he would proceed to Jerusalem where he would be circumcised, and that after persuading the Jews that he was their messiah he would rebuild the Temple and organize a vast army of conquest. Paradoxically, another notion developing during the same period in European Christendom was that Jews were cowardly and effeminate, so effeminate, in fact, that Jewish men as well as women menstruated monthly.

The popular legend of Theophilus, the oldest Latin version of which dates from the ninth century, but which probably originated in sixth-century Anatolia and later served as the basis for the story of Faust, explicitly linked the Jews, the devil, and the magical arts. Theophilus, who "sought not for divine but human glory," made contact with a Jewish sorcerer, who in turn took him to the devil. Similarly, several medieval versions of the Passion play presented the Jews of Jerusalem, instigated by Satan, as working their most potent charms against

Jesus. At the Church's Council of Béziers in 1255, attended by King Louis IX, it was decreed that "Jews should desist from usuries, blasphemies and sorceries." And in Matthew Paris's account of the ritual murder of "little Hugh of Lincoln," whose body was found in the same year, 1255, we read that the Jews had "disemboweled the corpse, for what end is unknown; but it was said to practice magical arts."

During the later Middle Ages, with the popularization of the ritual murder accusation across Europe, different theories emerged as to why Jews needed Christian children or their blood, some of which were reflected in the "confessions" attributed to the Jews themselves. In the spring of 1475, after the dead body of a 2-year-old boy named Simon was found in Trent, a 25-year-old local Jew "explained" under torture that his coreligionists needed Christian blood since "if they don't use blood they'll stink." This, of course, was an allusion to the old myth of the *foetor judaicus*, which allegedly disappeared automatically on the administration of the waters of baptism. Scholars have pointed to a late-sixth-century poem by Venantius Fortunatus, composed after the Jews of Clermont were forcefully converted in 576 after attacking a former coreligionist who was baptized on Easter/Passover of that year, as the earliest source alluding to the alleged sweetening of the Jewish stench through baptism.

A number of later medieval legends repeat this stereotype. One, reported early in the thirteenth century by Caesarius of Heisterbach, told of a Jew of Louvain whose daughter, after her baptism, suddenly became aware of a foul stench emanating from his body when he came to rescue her from the Cistercian convent into which she had been placed. In 1401 the city council of Freiburg petitioned Duke Leopold to expel the Jews, who were believed to constitute a danger since "every seven years all Jews must obtain Christian blood," which

An English manuscript depicts the persecution of the Jews in thirteenth-century London; like the two figures in the center, Jews were legally required to identify themselves by wearing two strips of yellow cloth on their garments. (British Library, London, MS Cotton Nero D.ii., fol. 183v)

they either ingest or smear upon themselves. This was done, it was claimed, "for the prolongation of their lives, and particularly from a desire not to stink, for when they lack this blood they stink so foully that no one can remain near them." Yet there were, in time, also some learned Christian skeptics. Martin Luther, in his 1523 essay "That Jesus Christ Was Born a Jew," advised that Jews be dealt with kindly and instructed through Scripture concerning the truths of Christianity. "If, however, we use brute force and slander them," he asked, "saying that they need the blood of Christians to get rid of their stench and I know not what other nonsense of that kind … what good can we expect of them?"

There were indeed various kinds of "nonsense" circulating in German-speaking lands during the late fifteenth century about the Jewish "need" for Christian blood. In 1476 a Jew "confessed" in Regensburg that his coreligionists drank Christian blood and smeared it on their unleavened bread as a prophylactic against leprosy, and in Baden, in the very same year, another Jew "admitted" that they used Christian blood in order to alleviate the wound of circumcision—a confession first heard in Endingen some seven years earlier. This explanation was later recorded during a 1494 investigation of an alleged ritual murder in Tyrnau (now in the Czech Republic), whose Jews also allegedly explained that both Jewish men and women had found Christian blood an effective means of alleviating their menstrual cramps!

The myth of male Jewish menstruation, as I. M. Resnick has recently shown, goes back as far as the thirteenth century, to Jacques de Vitry, bishop of Acre (in Palestine), who wrote in his *History of Jerusalem* that as a divine punishment for having killed Jesus, the Jews had become "weak and unwarlike, even as women." Moreover, he added, "it is said that they have a flux of blood every month," God having "smitten them in the hinder parts and put them to perpetual shame." A similar assertion was made around the same time by Caesarius of Heisterbach, who included in his *Exempla* a number of stories concerning Jewish girls who were attracted to Christian men. In one of these the girl explained to her prospective "date," a nephew of the bishop of London, that her father watched her so carefully that they could meet only "on the night of the Friday before your Easter." Caesarius provided an interesting explanation: "For then the Jews are said to labor under a sickness called the bloody flux, with which they are so much occupied, that they can scarcely pay attention to anything else at that time."

This theme reappeared later in the thirteenth century in the writings of the Dominican Thomas of Cantimpré, who also claimed that Jews, both male and female, suffered from a bloody flux, which, as in the case of Caesarius, may have referred to hemorrhoids rather than menstruation. Thomas's special contribution, however, was to claim that Jews believed this "flux" to be curable only with Christian blood. "It is hence quite evident," he added, "that according to custom, Jews shed Christian blood in every province they inhabit. It has certainly been established that every year they cast lots in each province as to which community or city should produce Christian blood for the other communities."

In 1943 the American rabbi and scholar Joshua Trachtenberg wrote that "the only Jew whom the medieval Christian recognized was a figment of the imagination." These bold words contain no small measure of truth, although they are perhaps less persuasive today than when they were first published—precisely a decade after Hitler's rise to power. The rise of Nazism in Germany and its catastrophic consequences led to much scholarly inquiry into the dark history of what today would be called Europe's "construction of the Jew." Trachtenberg's *The Devil and the Jews*, which carried the telling subtitle *The Medieval Conception of the Jew and Its Relation to Modern Anti-Semitism*, was preceded during the 1930s by important discussions of these issues by the British scholars James Parkes and Cecil Roth.

The latter, whose 1938 essay "The Medieval Conception of the Jew" was clearly echoed in the subtitle of Trachtenberg's book (and later, in one of the chapter titles of Guido Kisch's *The Jews in Medieval Germany*), advanced the thesis that Jews were seen by medieval Christians as being fundamentally different, in both body and mind, from other human beings: "There were numerous natural signs," he wrote, "which clearly indicated to the popular mind that the Jews were a race apart, cursed for all eternity." Similarly, Trachtenberg asserted that for medieval Christians the Jew was not quite human, but rather "a creature of an altogether different nature, of whom normal reactions could not be expected."

By contrast, Guido Kisch, himself a refugee from Nazi Germany, was sharply critical of historians, both Jewish and Gentile, who sought, anachronistically in his view, to present the medieval perception of the Jew in racial terms. "Race," he stated unequivocally in 1949, "was no factor in the medieval attitude toward, and legal treatment of, the Jews." Kisch's position, however, was not widely adopted. In 1978, four decades after the appearance of Roth's influential article, Lester Little was able to state confidently that during the eleventh to thirteenth centuries European Christians regarded Jews "as inferiors, as some class of subhuman beings. They wrote tracts to prove the point, extended the argument with pictorial and plastic representations, and fixed the point by law."

It is perhaps appropriate to quote, in conclusion, the ringing words with which Roth concluded his twice-reprinted 1938 essay: "It is possible to acquit the ordinary man of the Middle Ages of unreasoning cruelty in his relations with a people whom he was encouraged to consider in so distorted a light; but not our own contemporaries, who revived an equally preposterous conception in this ostensibly enlightened age."

See also: Blasons Populaires; Blood; Magic

References and further reading: A pioneering article, still of value, is I. Loeb, "Le juif de l'histoire et le juif de la légende," *Revue des études juives* 20 (1890). Important work was done in the 1930s and 1940s by J. Parkes, *The Conflict of the Church and the Synagogue* (1934); C. Roth, "The Medieval Conception of the Jew," in his *Essays in Memory of Linda R. Miller* (1938), reprinted in his *Personalities and Events in Jewish History* (1953) and again in J. Cohen, ed., *Essential Papers* (1991); J. Trachtenberg, *The Devil and the Jews: The Medieval Conception of the Jew and Its Relation to Modern Anti-Semitism* (1943); and G. Kisch, *The Jews in Medieval Germany*, ch. 12 (1949; rpt. 1970). A good collection of classic and recent articles may be found in J. Cohen, ed., *Essential Papers on Judaism and Christianity in Conflict* (1991). For a synthetic treatment of the image of the Jew in the Middle Ages with a good bibliography, see S. W. Baron, *A Social and Religious History of the Jews*, vols. 5, 11.

Valuable articles and monographs include L. Little, *Religious Poverty and the Profit Economy in Medieval Europe*, ch. 3 (1978), reprinted in Cohen's *Essential Papers*; R. Bonfil, "The Devil and the Jews in the Christian Consciousness of the Middle Ages," in *Antisemitism through the Ages*, ed. S. Almog (1988); R. Po-chia Hsia, *The Myth of Ritual Murder: Jews and Magic in Reformation Germany* (1988), and *Trent 1475: Stories of a Ritual Murder Trial* (1992); I. M. Resnick, "On the Roots of the Myth of Jewish Male Menses in Jacques de Vitry's *History of Jerusalem*" (pamphlet), International Rennert Guest Lecture Series (Bar-Ilan University), no. 3 (1998). The best source collection of Christian attitudes, high and low, is H. Schreckenburg, ed., *Die christlichen Adversus-Judaeos Texte und ihr historisches Umfeld*, 3 vols. (1982–1994). The most recent collection of articles on Christian attitudes to Jews and Judaism is J. K. Cohen, ed., *From Witness to Witchcraft: Jews and Judaism in Medieval Christian Thought* (1996); especially valuable on stereotypes are the articles by Hsia, Foa, and Marcus.

—*Elliott Horowitz*

Joan of Arc, Saint (1412?–1431)

French war heroine and popular religious figure, canonized in 1920.

Joan's triumphs—the liberation of Orléans (May 8, 1429) from the English and the crowning and anointing of the Dauphin Charles VII in Rheims (July 17, 1429)—and her pathetic trial and death at the stake made her a legend in her own time.

Coming from a 17-year-old "maid" (she liked to call herself *La Pucelle*), her deeds seemed supernatural. She was worshipped and feared, and was finally condemned as a heretic in Rouen on May 28, 1431. Her judges could not forgive her for her loyalty to the saints—Michael, Margaret, and Catherine—who had appeared to her and instructed her since she was 13. Led by the archbishop of Beauvais, Pierre Cauchon, clerics from the University of Paris could only consider such a denial of Church authority with suspicion. One consequence of their mistrust was their determination to demonize her; in this way they were also opportunely undermining Charles VII's legitimacy.

The customs that Joan shared with the other youngsters in her village of Domrémy—the dances, the picnics around the Fairy Tree on the second Sunday of Lent, the stations of the cross at the healing fountain—offer us intimate views of late-medieval village ritual. Testifying at her trial, Joan described the Fairy Tree:

> There is a tree called the Ladies' Tree, and others call it the Fairies' Tree, near which there is a spring of water; and I have heard tell that those who are sick and have the fever drink the water of this spring, and ask for its waters to recover their health. . . . It is a big tree called beech from which fine Maypoles are made. . . . Sometimes I went out with the other girls and by the tree made garlands . . . for the image of Our Lady of Domremy; I have seen the girls put such garlands on the tree's branches and sometimes I myself put some on.

At Joan's rehabilitation hearing in 1450 many of her fellow villagers added their testimony to enrich this portrait of festive life. Yet at her trial in 1431 such information had been used by her accusers exclusively as evidence of diabolical idolatry.

Even Joan's most sacred and religious actions could be interpreted as magic: for example, her frequent reception of communion, which was seen as a misuse of the Eucharist, or the power emanating from her virginal body. The questions she was asked at her trial demonstrate her judges' concern about her healing powers, her alleged use of a mandrake, and the nature of the sign that allowed her to recognize the dauphin in a crowd of nobles when she met him for the first time. Other controversial points were her miraculous discovery, at the chapel of Saint Catherine de Fierbois, of the sword she bore in battle; her banner with the representation of God holding the world and of her two female saints displayed on it; and her ring, engraved with the words "Jesus Maria."

Joan could not completely deny that a cult had developed around her, for people had tried to touch her ring or her hand, venerated images of her, and celebrated masses in her honor. She was recognized as the miraculous female savior who had come from an oak wood in Lorraine, an extraordinary apparition that had been announced by a prophecy widely attributed to Merlin.

In spite of the solitary nature of her visionary experience and the publicity of her condemnation, Joan of Arc was a figure of her time. She takes her place in a line of female prophets, among them Catherine de La Rochelle, who tried to compete with her. And around 1440 another similar figure, Claude des Armoises, was sponsored by Joan's brothers. They exhibited Claude as Joan, dressed as a man, and fighting as a warrior as she had done.

Joan's male attire is all the more important inasmuch as the accusation of apostasy against her was based on her dress. Joan's clothing crystallized her transgression of the accepted canons of womanly behavior and gave rise to the more general discomfort generated by the blurring of fundamental categories.

See also: French Tradition; Saints, Cults of the; Woman Warrior
References and further reading: There is no accurate translation into English of the trial or of the rehabilitation. For the trial, in French, see P. Tisset and Y. Lanhers, *Procès de condamnation de Jeanne d'Arc* (1960–1970); in English, see W. P. Barrett, *The Trial of Joan of Arc* (1932), and W. S. Scott, *The Trial of Joan of Arc* (1956). For the rehabilitation, in French, see P. Duparc, *Procès en nullité de la condamnation de Jeanne d'Arc* (1977–1986); in English, see excerpts in R. Pernoud's *Retrial of Joan of Arc* (1955). For biographical data, see R. Pernoud, *Joan of Arc* (1962), quotation above of Joan's trial testimony from pages 21–22; and for the legendary aspects, see F. Gies, *Joan of Arc: The Legend and the Reality* (1981); M. Warner, *Joan of Arc: The Image of Female Heroism* (1981); and A. L. Barstow, *Heretic, Mystic, Shaman* (1986). On her afterlife, see N. Margolis, *Joan of Arc in History, Literature, and Film: A Selected Bibliography* (1990).

—Madeleine Jeay

Joseph, Saint

Husband of the Virgin Mary and putative father of Jesus.

Although the two genealogies of Jesus found at the beginning of the Gospels of Matthew and Luke were originally traced through the carpenter Joseph, the betrothed of his mother Mary, it is quite clear from the New Testament's birth narratives that Joseph is only the putative father of Jesus, Mary's conception of Jesus having been achieved through divine intervention. Modern critical biblical scholarship has invested much energy into discussing the historicity of the accounts of Jesus' birth, the alleged typology (the idea that Old Testament characters foreshadow those of the New Testament) with Joseph's patriarchal namesake in the Old Testament, and the apologetic motives behind the Gospels as a whole. Christian theology meanwhile continues to debate the significance of the virginal conception of Jesus and in effect to ignore Joseph.

The biblical accounts of Jesus' birth and the postbiblical elaborations of them, notably in the second-century apocryphal Gospel, the Protevangelium of James, portray Joseph as a loyal husband, accepted publicly as the actual father of Jesus. But in the apocryphal tradition Joseph is given an increasingly important role. He makes the Holy Family a complete and recognizable unit: a number of legends, notably in the Arabic Infancy Gospel, have Joseph prominent in several stories concerning the flight to and sojourn in Egypt. In the Infancy Gospel of Thomas he acts as a normal father, overseeing Jesus' education, working with him in the carpenter's shop, and even reprimanding him. Some medieval art was inspired by these domestic scenes.

In the Protevangelium Joseph is given an important monologue (P J 18), in which he describes how all of nature was put into a deep sleep at the moment of Jesus' birth. The Joseph of the Protevangelium is no mere village carpenter but a building contractor, whose work takes him away from home for months at a time. More significantly, he is portrayed as an elderly widower with grown-up children from an earlier marriage. As a consequence of this, we see the development of portrayals of Joseph as a buffoon in later medieval mystery plays, where he is an old man with a young wife, almost a caricature cuckold, and thus a comic character.

The details about Joseph's previous marriage, found in the Protevangelium and in later legends dependent on it, served to satisfy those Christians who were perplexed by the references in the New Testament to Jesus' siblings alongside the teaching about Mary's virginity. Describing these siblings as Jesus' half brothers and half sisters helped preserve the developing doctrines that Mary was a perpetual virgin.

In contrast to stories elsewhere, including the traditions within the New Testament itself, in which Joseph appears as a relatively inconsequential character, we find in the fifth- to sixth-century *History of Joseph the Carpenter* a lengthy narrative, mostly put onto Jesus' lips, telling of the death of Joseph at a great age. Such a narrative, which enjoyed great popularity, especially in the East, acted as a counterpart to the many apocryphal legends about Mary and her death. The stories about Joseph served to enhance his reputation and ensure subsequent devotion to him, leading to his canonization. As St. Joseph he came to be revered as the patron saint of workers and of a good death. Christian tradition thus eventually made him more than merely the foster parent of Jesus or the husband of the Virgin Mary.

See also: Christmas; Jesus Christ; Saints, Cults of the; Virgin Mary
References and further reading: Many of the legendary stories about Joseph, especially those that had an impact on medieval imagination and interpretation, are to be found in J. K. Elliott, *The Apocryphal New Testament* (1993), and a selection appears in his *The*

Apocryphal Jesus: Legends of the Early Church (1996). A different English translation of many of the texts is also to be found in W. Schneemelcher, *New Testament Apocrypha*, ed. R. McL. Wilson, 2 vols. (1991, 1992).

—*J. K. Elliott*

Joseph of Arimathea, Saint

A follower of Christ who came forward to ask for Christ's body after the Crucifixion.

Pontius Pilate, the Roman administrator of Judea, granted his request. Joseph gave the body an honorable burial in a rock-cut chamber tomb. The story is told in all four Gospels (Matt. 27:57–61, Mark 15:42–47, Luke 23:50–56, and John 19:38–42). Joseph was apparently a person of some prominence, for he is described as a rich man or a Jewish council member.

Joseph's fame in legend rests on his association with Christ's death and burial. Later legend also featured three related figures from the biblical accounts: Mary Magdalen, the Pharisee Nicodemus, and an anonymous soldier who had pierced Christ's side with a spear during the Crucifixion (John 19:31–37).

By the end of the fourth century, the biblical information about Christ's death was extended through an apocryphal Greek composition: this work and derivative forms were later known as the Gospel of Nicodemus. The Latin translation has fifth-century origins. An imprisonment of Joseph of Arimathea was an early part of the story; the Gospel also gave a name, Longinus, to the soldier of the Crucifixion account. The Gospel of Nicodemus enjoyed great popularity during the Middle Ages. It appeared in a range of vernacular versions before the end of the thirteenth century: Old English, Middle Irish, Old French, Occitan, Old Norse, and Middle High German.

Joseph also appears as a minor figure in Old French chansons de geste. *Le couronnement de Louis*, from the first half of the twelfth century, describes how Nicodemus and Joseph removed Christ's body from the Cross, and placed it in a tomb. Longinus is also mentioned, as "Longis." These references are based on popular tradition rather than the biblical accounts. In the poem, Mary Magdalen is identified as the woman who anoints Christ at the house of Simon; the Last Supper and the betrayal of Christ also occur at the same location. In contrast, the New Testament describes the woman as Mary, the sister of Lazarus (John 11:1–2, 12:1–8, Mark 14:3–9), and gives other locations for two of the three events (Luke 22:7–23, John 18:1–12).

In the late twelfth century other chansons de geste present Joseph as a knight who served Pilate for seven years and requested Christ's body in payment for his services. This characterization is repeated in two works of the Old French Crusade cycle, *La chanson de Jérusalem* and *Les chétifs* (The Captives). Both mention the soldier Longis. The latter poem names yet another figure from ecclesiastical history, Judas Maccabaeus (1 and 2 Macc.).

Despite these developments, the story of St. Joseph of Arimathea probably would have remained a lesser feature of popular tradition had not his name become associated with Arthurian romance beginning around 1200. The link was probably established through a process of identifying Arthurian objects with holy relics from the East. The *Perceval* of Chrétien de Troyes had previously introduced the bleeding lance and the mysterious grail. The anonymous *First Continuation of Perceval* extended Chrétien's unfinished composition. Most of the manuscripts of this latter work identify the bleeding lance as the spear that pierced Christ's side; two also name Longis. An interpolation, found in more than a third of the manuscripts, describes the grail as a relic of the Holy Blood, brought by Joseph and Nicodemus to Britain. A second interpolation, found less often, presents the sword of Montesclaire as the sword of Judas Maccabaeus, again brought by Joseph of Arimathea. Through its Arthurian connections the grail was already linked to Britain. Once the grail had been defined as a relic of Christ's blood, the addition of St. Joseph would have been a natural reflex, given his role in the Scripture and in popular tradition.

Robert de Boron's verse romance *Le roman de l'estoire dou Graal* was written at approximately the same time as the *First Continuation*. It also identifies the grail as a relic of the Holy Blood. Two motifs, an imprisonment of Joseph and the saint's possession of the grail, are used to tie together three largely unrelated segments. The first is a review of biblical history, repeating popular traditions such as those about Mary Magdalen and Simon's house. Again, Joseph appears as a paid soldier of Pilate. The second follows the general outline of *La venjance Nostre Seigneur*, another twelfth-century chanson de geste, associated with the Veronica legend. In the final segment, developed from a limited number of Arthurian motifs, members of Joseph's family will take the grail to the "Avaron" of the West, presumably the Arthurian Avalon.

At the midpoint of the thirteenth century St. Joseph was tentatively incorporated into the much older traditional legends of Glastonbury Abbey in southwest Britain. Some 60 years earlier, around 1191, Gerald of Wales had reported the finding of King Arthur's grave at Glastonbury, which he identified as Avalon. By the middle of the fourteenth century, Joseph had become a favored saint of the monastery, but without the grail.

The complex elaborations of the stories of Joseph survived side by side with traditions closer to the saint's pre-Arthurian role, as demonstrated by the fifteenth-century manuscripts of English mystery plays. The *Crucifixion* drama of the Towneley Plays presents Joseph as a servant of Pilate and includes the figures of Nicodemus and "Longeus," or Longinus. The second *Passion Play* of the N-Town manuscript also features the three: it shows little innovation above a detail also found in medieval art, the provision of ladders for Joseph and his fellow disciple.

See also: Glastonbury

References and further reading: An analysis of the Joseph and Glastonbury legends appears in the journal *Folklore*: D. Crawford, "St Joseph in Britain: Reconsidering the Legends" (1993–1995), and "The Ghost of Criticism Past" (1996). A discussion of the figure of Joseph is found in the "Saints" chapter of J. Carley's *Glastonbury Abbey*, rev. ed. (1996). For the apocryphal biblical material, see Z. Izydorczyk, *The Medieval Gospel of Nicodemus* (1997). The relevant chansons de geste are published in E. Langlois, ed., *Le couronnement de Louis* (2nd. rev. ed. 1925; rpt. 1984); N. Thorp, ed., *La chanson de Jérusalem* (1992); and G. Myers, ed., *Les chétifs* (1981). L. Gryting gives a synopsis and an edition of *La venjance Nostre Seigneur* (1952). See also W. Roach, ed., *Perceval*, rev. ed. (1959), and the *First Continuation* (1949–1955; rpt. 1965, 1970). W. A. Nitze's edition of *Le roman de l'estoire dou Graal* (1927) has also been translated into English in J. Rogers, *Joseph of Arimathea:*

A *Romance of the Grail* (1990). R. O'Gorman's *Joseph d'Arimathie* (1995) includes a more recent edition of Robert de Boron; the notes and bibliography provide a wealth of information. In some instances, the textual editing should be approached with caution.

—*Deborah Crawford*

Judah the Pious (c. 1150–1217) [Judah ben Samuel he-Hasid]

German Jewish religious leader, mystic, and storyteller, generally considered the founder of the *Hasidei Ashkenaz* (German Pietists) movement, and the main author of its founding composition, *Sefer Hasidim* (Book of the Pious).

Judah he-Hasid is the author of many books on Jewish philosophy and mysticism, commentaries on the Hebrew Bible, and books on Jewish prayers and religious morals and education. Like many of his contemporary European Christian authors, Judah he-Hasid can be considered an amateur ethnographer. He had immense interest in storytelling, in supernatural beings and events, and in out-of-the-ordinary beliefs and customs—and an interest in recording them in writing. As in the case of his Christian contemporaries, the main drive behind his ethnographic work was undoubtedly mainly religious. His immensely interesting work, *The Tractate "He Has Made His Wonderful Works Be Remembered,"* recently discovered, sheds much light upon his motives for these activities. The title of this work is taken from a verse in Psalms (111:4). In his special interpretation, it expresses the idea that God's power is revealed in this world through unusual and unnatural phenomena. In this tractate, Judah the Pious describes dozens of phenomena that have no rational explanation, attesting to his great interest and constituting a great contribution to the understanding of medieval folklore. In his opinion, all these phenomena are the ultimate proof of the existence of God and of his control of this world. In his many writings, most of which are still only in manuscript form, he describes *strigae* (witch-like beings that sucked the blood of children), monsters, vampires, revelations of heavenly voices, the dead coming back to this world, supernatural healing, outstanding dreams, magic practices, various demons, and many more. All these he ties to one, all-inclusive theological system, but they should be considered also a major contribution to the study of medieval European folklore.

The most interesting contribution of Judah he-Hasid to Jewish folklore is in the field of folk narrative. In his theological, mystical, and interpretive works, he included dozens of stories as integral parts of his theoretical discussion. Judah the Pious's extreme moral values did not allow him in any way to invent stories and treat them as "fictions." He heard all these stories and recorded them from "reliable folk," and so they constitute important evidences of folk and oral traditions in the Jewish communities of medieval central Europe.

The founding text of the German Pietist movement that Judah established (or rather, hoped to establish, without great success) was *Sefer Hasidim*. In this large composition, Judah the Pious reveals his religious, moral, and social convictions, which he considers the foundation of a new and revolutionary trend within traditional Judaism. This trend is outstanding for the extremity of its religious and moral values, which verge on asceticism (which is prohibited in Judaism)—hence pietism. Judah attempted to promote these new ideas and insights by way of tales. Thus, *Sefer Hasidim* includes hundreds of stories of many types and themes. Since all these tales function as vehicles for promoting religious and moral values, they all should be considered as exempla—actually one of the major contributions to the creation of European exempla in the peak of the period of its creation—which has not yet been acknowledged by the students of this genre.

Among the exempla included in *Sefer Hasidim*, there is one remarkable group of stories—about a quarter of the more than 400 tales—that are outstanding and innovative, even in comparison with the rich body of Christian exempla. These are short, condensed narratives in which the main *dramatis persona* is the *Hakham* (wise man)—the leader of the religious community—to whom people come for advice in intimate matters, personal, social, or economic; the stories thus reveal very important and telling details about daily life in Judah's time. There was no way that Judah the Pious could know about such intimate matters unless he himself was the *Hakham*, unless he himself recorded these hundreds of cases brought before him as religious leader. These exempla, in which the saint himself is the narrator of the tales as well as their main hero, are of great importance for the study of medieval exempla.

In the fifteenth and sixteenth centuries hagiographic tales about Judah the Pious started to appear in manuscripts and early books in Hebrew and in Yiddish cycles. The cycles began with the exceptional figure of Judah's father, Rabbi Samuel, whose pietism and deeds presaged the miraculous birth of the real hero, Judah the Pious. In these tales Judah is depicted as the backbone of the Jewish community, as its guard against its Christian enemies, as the ultimate Jewish sage, fluent in all the branches of religious and secular science, a master of magical knowledge and practice. The main sources of these saint's legends attest to their origin and spread in the Yiddish language—the spoken vernacular of the Jewish communities of central Europe, northern Italy, and, later, Eastern Europe. This proves that Judah the Pious became one of the central heroes of Jewish folklore at the close of the Middle Ages and the dawn of early modern times.

See also: Exemplum; Golem; Jewish Tradition

References and further reading: General surveys on the German Pietist movement and the place of Judah the Pious in it include I. G. Marcus, *Piety and Society: The Jewish Pietists of Medieval Germany* (1981), and I. G. Marcus, ed., *The Religious and Social Ideas of the Jewish Pietists in Medieval Germany: Collected Essays* (1986; in Hebrew). On the narrative and folkloric aspects of *Sefer Hasidim*, see J. Dan, *The Hebrew Story in the Middle Ages* (1974; in Hebrew); T. Alexander-Friezer, *The Pious Sinner: Ethics and Aesthetics in the Medieval Hasidic Narrative* (1991); E. Yassif, "Entre culture populaire et culture savante: Les exempla dans le *Sefer Hasidim*," *Annales: Histoire, Sciences Sociales* 49 (1994). *The Tractate "He Has Made His Wonderful Works Be Remembered" by R. Judah the Pious*, has been published by I. Ta-Shema in *Kovetz Al-Yad* 12 (1994). On his theological principles, see J. Dan, *The Esoteric Theology of Ashkenazi Hasidim* (1969; in Hebrew).

—*Eli Yassif*

Judith [Hebrew *Yehudite*, Latin *Iudith*]

First depicted in the Greek Apocrypha as the pious Jewish widow who seduces and cuts off the head of the Assyrian general Holofernes with his own sword and returns triumphant to Bethulia.

Central to the tale of Judith is God's use of a faithful woman to intervene in history. Judith's great beauty and felicity, as well as her prayers and purity, all contribute to this triumph. While many scholars agree that the apocryphal text appears to allude to the revolts of Judas Maccabaeus in 164–161 B.C.E., the range of speculations as to its date of composition extends from as early as the period of the Jews' return from Babylonian exile in 538 B.C.E. to as late as the Roman rule of Herod Agrippa I in 40 C.E. The book contains many historical inaccuracies and anachronisms, and it is believed by most scholars to have been a popular legend or parable composed to maintain the nationalistic spirit of the Jews. The text was not included in the Hebrew Bible, but the Jewish community maintained the Judith legend in its oral tradition until it was recorded in the Middle Ages in the form of midrash.

Midrashim, or homilies, dating from the tenth or eleventh century recalling and elaborating on Judith's heroism, were read in the synagogue during Hanukkah, the Feast of Dedication. *Yehudite*, the Hebrew for Judith, translates as the "Jewess," and the midrashim are often themselves compilations of narratives recounting the heroism of Jewish women. One midrash gives to the high priest Yohanan's daughter, an unnamed young woman newly married and thus obligated to have intercourse with Jerusalem's Greek viceroy, the role of leading Judah's men in a revolt in which the viceroy is decapitated. This act inspires the widow Judith to decapitate the Greek king. Thus, young bride and widow act in conjunction to preserve the Israelite women from rape and to save the city from invasion. In another midrash we are presented with Judith, a virgin (*betulah* in Hebrew) who slays Seleukos, a conquering Gentile king of Jerusalem. In this version Judith states that she is "impure," or menstruating, and she is granted permission to perform a ritual immersion and to move freely about the camp. It is under this cover that she first escapes the king's advances and later is able sneak past the guards with his head.

In the tenth-century Anglo-Saxon poem *Judith* the poet constructs a Judith figure who is a conflation of a saint and an Anglo-Saxon heroine. It is generally believed that the poem was sung at banquets given by kings and nobility. Of interest to scholars are the radical changes the poet makes to the apocryphal biblical account. Judith's sexuality and seductive powers are written out of the narrative. Judith's faith endows her with the strength to slay Holofernes; however, the fact that a woman has slain Holofernes is not emphasized. Both Christian and pagan elements are added to the poem: a prayer in which Judith invokes the Trinity is included, as is a battle in which the Hebrew warriors triumph over the Assyrians. It is only after the army triumphs that Judith is celebrated by her people. The tale has been compared to medieval hagiography because Holofernes' lust and malice turn to folly, and Judith's chastity and faith are instrumental in sending Holofernes to a Christian hell.

Popular ballads preserved and retold the apocryphal account of Judith's adept manipulation of Holofernes' desire. According to Edna Purdie, the Early Middle High German *Judith* (or *ältere Judith*), dating from about the eleventh century, was probably sung by a *Spielmann*, a type of wandering balladeer. The action of the poem is located in Bathania, which resembles a medieval German town. Central to the drama is Holofernes' immediate and overwhelming desire for Judith and Judith's active manipulation of this desire. It is Judith and not

Holofernes who suggests a *Brutlouf*, a kind of feast that often signals the enemy's impending defeat in Germanic tales. After Judith steals Holofernes' sword, she prays on behalf of the town. It is the intervention and direction of an angel that is emphasized at the conclusion of the ballad rather than Judith's faith or action.

In late-medieval literature Judith comes to represent a certain ambivalence toward women assuming political power. She also represents the potential of love and desire to bring down men of might. Christine de Pizan extols Judith's power and wisdom in *The City of Ladies* and argues that Judith's story supports the inclusion of women in the political sphere. In "The Tale of Melibeus" Chaucer uses Judith to portray Good Counsel, while in "The Monk's Tale" he depicts Holofernes as a great man seduced by a clever woman. In an effort to warn men against the power of love, Petrarch portrays Holofernes alongside Samson in his poem "Triumph of Love."

See also: Jewish Tradition

References and further reading: E. Purdie, *The Story of Judith in German and English Literature* (1927), while incomplete, is the only bibliography available. Purdie surveys 103 versions of the Judith story in German and English literature, beginning with the ninth century, and extensively discusses the treatment of the story; L. A. Callahan, "Ambiguity and Appropriation: The Story of Judith in Medieval Narrative and Iconographic Traditions," in *Telling Tales*, ed. F. C. Sautman, D. Conchado, and G. C. Di Scipio (1998), explores the conflicting medieval constructions of Judith in text and iconography as well as the narrative's folkloric elements; M. Stocker, *Judith: Sexual Warrior* (1998), includes a substantial discussion of political, religious, and literary representations of Judith in the Middle Ages; B. H. Mehlman and D. F. Polish, "A Midrash for Hanukkah," in *Conservative Judaism* (1982), offer a rare translation of a medieval midrashic compilation of Judith narratives; M. Griffith, ed., *Judith* (1997), is a critical edition of the Anglo-Saxon poem that includes an in-depth discussion of Christian and pagan influences.

—*Sandra H. Tarlin*

Knight

A member of a social class with roots in the eleventh century; a heroic figure in romance and chronicle.

The English word *knight* comes from the Old English *cniht*, meaning "young man" or "warrior." In Anglo-Saxon England to be a young man was almost by definition to be a warrior. In Germany at that period the situation was much the same, and the German *knecht* applied to the same broad category. Before the twelfth century these terms applied to farming men as much as to the nobility.

Knighthood in the form we now recognize it began in France in the ninth century and flourished throughout Europe in the twelfth and thirteenth centuries. The French word for knight is *chevalier*, which (like the Spanish *caballero* and the Italian *cavaliere*) literally signifies one who fights *à cheval* (on horseback). The designation of a "horseback" warrior indicates the formation of a noble warrior class, distinct from the farmer foot soldiers who, now defined by their work instead of their role in warfare, came to be known as peasants.

In the chaos that followed the collapse of the Carolingian Empire, mounted warriors were among the few authorities in France, and though they would defend the peasants against outside attacks, they were oppressive rulers. They ruled by force of arms and got most of what they wanted through violence—robbery, assault, torture, or rape. They fought one another constantly, struggling for wealth and power and pursuing personal vendettas. They did not become a well-defined class with a code of courtesy until two centuries later.

In the eleventh century, with what is often called the medieval peace movement, these brave but ruthless warriors began to be defined as upholders of the law and protectors of the weak. Many were beginning to tire of living in a state of continual war and to wish for the security that a measure of peace might bring. The Church, whose unarmed officers were often victims of their violent attacks, brokered the first agreements to limit personal war and reduce the targets of violence. The Peace of God, arranged by various French Church councils in the late tenth and early eleventh centuries and achieved with immense difficulty, outlawed attacks on unarmed peasants, clerics, and other helpless victims. Once the warrior chiefs agreed to this measure, they found themselves in the position of working together to enforce it. Since few others had either the might or the authority to do so, warriors had to police one another and to control the unregenerate robber barons among them. Thus, the ideal of a brotherhood of warriors, united to enforce justice, came into being. The Truce of God (beginning c. 1040), which limited personal war to certain days of the week, enjoyed less success because most warriors were not yet ready to obey it. What helped solve that problem was the crusading movement, which, beginning in the late eleventh century, effectively redirected the chevaliers' blood lust away from one another and toward the Muslims in the Holy Land.

Around this time an elite, somewhat unified class of mounted warriors began to call themselves knights. The original purpose of the High Order of Knighthood, as it developed through the Peace of God and the Crusades, was best articulated by the English cleric John of Salisbury in 1159:

> What purpose does ordained knighthood serve? To protect the church, to
> battle against disloyalty, to honour the office of the priesthood, to put an
> end to injustice towards the poor, to bring peace to the land, to let his own
> blood be spilled for his brothers, and, if necessary, to give up his own life.

When a young man who qualified for knighthood came of age, he went through an increasingly elaborate ceremony, whose most important feature was the transfer of arms, especially the sword, usually from an older knight to the young initiate. When the young man received the sword, he vowed to use it for appropriate purposes, as defined by his role as *justicier,* including the defense of Holy Church, as well as the weak and helpless, including widows, orphans, and the poor. In the early days, after presenting the sword the older knight would strike the candidate across the face. In the later Middle Ages this blow—known as "dubbing"—developed into a light, symbolic touch on the shoulder with the flat of the sword. Originally, however, it was a hard slap or even a box to the ear, which the young man had to take without flinching or retaliating.

As the dubbing ceremony developed, and with the Peace of God and the Crusades, the making of a knight began to acquire the character of a religious ritual. During the eleventh century medieval writers began to speak of "ordaining" instead of simply "making" a knight. By the twelfth century the blessing of the sword had become an essential part of the ceremony, and newly ordained knights were receiving their arms directly from the hand of a cleric. In the late Middle Ages the religious component increased. Candidates began to hold vigils the night before their dubbing and to pray over their armor in preparation for their knighting.

From this creative fusion of Christian and warrior ethos came the code of conduct that we know as chivalry. At the height of its influence, from the mid-twelfth to the late thirteenth centuries, the chivalric ideal had manifested itself in three distinct types. All are distinguished by firm loyalty, but they differ in the objects of their loyalty. The oldest type is the *miles Christi* (soldier of Christ). Born of the crusading movement and represented in literature by Galahad (among others), the *miles Christi* was defined by his devotion to God and the Church. This was the ideal that John of Salisbury described. It also inspired the founding of the military religious orders, such as the Templars and Hospitallers, and it gained influence as the importance of these orders increased. The second type, which developed somewhat later, exemplified ideal knighthood as a feudal institution: the "warrior knight" is always ready for battle, not for God but

There foloweth the fyrth boke of the noble and worthy prynce kyng Arthur.

How syr Launcelot and syr Lyonell departed fro the courte for to seke auentures, & how syr Lyonell lefte syr Launcelot slepynge & was taken. Caplm. j.

None after that the noble & worthy kyng Arthur was comen fro Rome in to Englande, all the knyghtes of the rounde table resorted vnto þe kyng and made many iustes and turneymentes, & some there were that were good knyghtes, whiche encreased so in armes and worshyp that they passed all theyr felowes in prowesse & noble dedes & that was well proued on many. But in especyall it was proued on syr Launcelot du lake. For in all turneymentes and iustes and dedes of armes, bothe for lyfe and deth he passed all knyghtes & at no tyme he was neuer ouercomen but yf it were by treason or enchauntement. Syr Launcelot encreased so meruaylously in worshyp & honour, wherfore he is the first knyght þ the frensshe booke maketh mencyon of, after that kynge Arthur came from Rome, wherfore quene Gueneuer had hym in grete fauour aboue all other knyghtes, and certaynly he loued the quene agayne aboue all other ladyes and damoyselles all the dayes of his lyfe, and for her he

A page from Malory's Morte Darthur, *printed in 1529 by Wynkyn de Worde. (North Wind Picture Archives)*

for his lord or king. In literature, the knights of the Round Table, who never refuse a challenge and undertake quests for the glory of King Arthur, are warrior knights. The third type, with whom most modern readers are familiar, is the lady's knight, sometimes called the gallant knight. The lady's knight, represented by Chrétien de Troyes's Lancelot, Erec, and Yvain, among others, incorporates another ideal, that of idealized, "courtly" love, in which the lover stands in quasi-feudal or even quasi-religious subjection to the lady. In this respect the gallant knight mimics the other two types. All his brave deeds, which the lady inspires, are for her glory rather than the glory of God or king. The extent to which this noble (courtly) ideal influenced the real conduct of knights toward women is, of course, a matter of some debate. While no one claims that knights consistently treated women with the reverence depicted in courtly literature, it would be equally absurd to assume that the gallant ideal had no influence at all. Noble women particularly, who were part of knightly society, exerted considerable power and were entitled to the respect of their husbands' retainers.

Social Context

The word *miles*, usually employed in medieval Latin to signify a knight, originally had no class implications. However, as already mentioned, from the ninth century forward warfare was dominated by trained mounted warriors, who furthermore assumed the cost of arming themselves as well as breeding and training their horses. Because of the time and expense involved, only those with considerable landed wealth could fight on horseback. By the eleventh century knighthood became synonymous with landed nobility, and *miles* therefore came to signify a member of the ruling class.

Because the idea of knighthood developed before the nobility had been defined as a legal class, the qualifications for it underwent some evolution. When the dubbing ritual began, any knight could perform it and thereby "make" another knight. However, in the twelfth century the French "knightly class" (knights and descendants of knights) became concerned about an increasingly wealthy group of urban tradesmen who might acquire the means to become chevaliers and therefore the social equals of the old nobility. Knighthood had become an important part of what separated them from the rest of society, and those who wished to keep it an exclusive club changed the law to the effect that only a man whose father or grandfather had been a knight could become one himself. *Miles* by this time had strong class connotations and had come to replace *nobilis* as the preferred term for what was now a ruling warrior class. By the later Middle Ages nobility throughout continental Europe meant the hereditary right to be knighted, whether or not one exercised that right.

In England, however, the legal definition of knighthood developed differently. Because of the small number of knights in Norman England and the imperial ambitions of the Plantagenet kings who succeeded the Normans in 1154, as many military captains as possible were needed. Therefore, the royal government began "distraint of knighthood" (i.e., requiring anyone whose land yielded a certain income to formally accept knighthood and the military obligations it entailed). Thus, knighthood in England came to be defined by income, rather than birth, as it was in the older Continental systems.

The everyday life of knights is difficult to reconstruct, since literature tends to focus on the important events rather than the daily routines. Chivalric romances create the impression that a typical knight's life consisted of a string of adventures, courtly festivals, and amorous intrigues. Given the responsibilities that we know knights had—to be available to serve their lords and administer their own estates—this image cannot be accurate. Nevertheless, some of the common features of romances—the young knight leaving the court to seek adventure, the quest for spiritual salvation, and sublimated, idealized, "courtly" love—may have had a basis in the realities of knightly life.

Only one son could inherit the father's land and castle, and even before the establishment of strict primogeniture that son was normally the eldest. Younger sons were often not permitted to marry because the establishment of several sons as heads of households would mean dividing the estate. The sons who did not inherit the castle frequently went to live in the lord's castle, where they lived in dormitory-like arrangements with other knights in the lord's service. With a large number of restless, competitive, hot-headed young warriors living in close proximity, tensions were inevitable, and many of the journeys, hunts, and formal displays of prowess, such as jousts, in which knights participated may have been designed to manage this tension. In addition, newly made knights were often sent on tours for as long as two years, probably for the purpose of spending some of their youthful enthusiasm before they entered the lord's service. When romances refer to a young knight leaving the court to seek adventure and prove his manhood, they may be referring to this practice.

The quest for the Holy Grail has a real-life analog in the Crusades. Prior to the crusading movement, laypersons generally sought salvation indirectly by donating to a religious community, in exchange for which the monks would pray for his soul. The new definition of *miles Christi* that emerged during the Crusades gave warriors a way to obtain salvation for themselves while practicing their own profession. The great Cistercian promoter of the Crusades, Bernard of Clairvaux, wrote with pride of the many criminals and potential criminals who, through the crusading movement, had become soldiers of Christ. It is surely no coincidence that the most famous of the French prose Grail romances, *La queste del saint Graal*, was written by a Cistercian monk at the height of the crusading movement.

Finally, the much-debated phenomenon of courtly love may be explicable in the context of numerous rival warriors living in the same castle. A modern reader may have difficulty seeing why it might actually be in the interest of the lord of the castle to have the knights who resided there desire his wife. However, the lady in courtly literature is often unattainable, and this fact does not prevent the knight from loving her. On the contrary, it increases his passion and allows his idealized image of her to remain intact. More important from the lord's point of view, it had the potential to inspire young men to great feats of arms—for the glory of the lady, but certainly also to the advantage of the lord. The lady of the castle was a natural object for the admiration and even devotion of the many unmarried young men who benefited from her munificence. Because the rules of courtly love demanded irreproachable knightly conduct in the lover, it could also limit the violence resulting from rivalries off the battlefield. Knights did occasionally succeed in absconding with the wives of their lords, but this was uncommon, and the benefits to the lord of inspired but well-behaved soldiers may have been worth the risks.

The Role of Chivalric Ideals in the Life of the Nobility

The extent to which the chivalric code governed the conduct of actual knights has been the subject of much controversy. No one, of course, would claim that knights consistently lived up to their vows. Perfect knights are almost as rare in literature as they must have been in life, and numerous antichivalric texts attest to the failure of knights to live up to their own code of conduct. The question is whether this code ever had an application to real life and when, if ever, it ceased to have one. In other words, was the knightly code ever a practical guide to handling real situations, or was it entirely the stuff of romances, festivals, and courtly displays? Lee Patterson has outlined the three major positions that scholars have taken on this subject, and they follow a rather unusual pattern: instead of becoming more skeptical over time about the usefulness of chivalry, they become less so. First, Johan Huizinga argued that chivalry was always an act and only got its practitioners into trouble when they tried seriously to live by it. For Huizinga the only difference between the chivalry of the fifteenth century and chivalry at its "height" (in the twelfth and thirteenth centuries) is that in the later period the nobility could no longer pretend to take it seriously. Thus, chivalric displays became more elaborate and stylized—more obviously play-acting. Later, Arthur Ferguson softened this position by claiming that chivalry did at one time have a practical purpose, but that it ceased to have one in the later Middle Ages because of political and social changes that were in the process of transforming medieval Europe into Renaissance Europe. Finally, Malcolm Vale argued that the chivalric code continued to be of practical use through the end of the Middle Ages. He cited the importance that heavy cavalry continued to have in warfare and the influence of chivalric values on later codes of conduct. Most scholars agree that the knightly code continued to affect the values, if not the conduct, of the aristocracy in Europe long after the end of feudalism and that even in modern times it retains its power as an ideal.

See also: Chrétien de Troyes; Courtly Love; Investiture; Knights Templar; Romance; Tournament

References and further reading: M. Bloch's *Feudal Society*, trans. L. A. Manyon (1961), remains an essential source on knighthood as a feudal institution; see also J.-P. Poly and E. Bournazel, *The Feudal Transformation, 900–1200*, trans. C. Higgitt (1991). In addition, G. Duby has written several useful studies on knighthood and daily life in the Middle Ages. In *A History of Private Life*, trans. A. Goldhammer, vol. 2, (1988), he gives a detailed description of communal life in a medieval castle. In *The Chivalrous Society*, trans. C. Postan (1977), Duby explains the development of knighthood and the transformation of the European aristocracy into a social class with a code of courtesy. He explores the meaning and purpose of medieval marriage in *The Knight, the Lady, and the Priest*, trans. B. Bray (1983). This book also provides exceptional detail about the daily lives of women, as Duby places aristocratic marriage in its political and social context. Finally, in *William Marshal: The Flower of Chivalry*, trans. R. Howard (1985), Duby shows how both the ideals and the social realities of knighthood applied to the case of an actual knight. H.-W. Goetz, *Life in the Middle Ages*, trans. A. Wimmer (1986), provides a helpful overview of knighthood as an institution, as well as the culture and living space of knights from the seventh to the thirteenth centuries. On the application of chivalric ideals to knightly life, especially in the late Middle Ages, J. Huizinga's *Autumn of the Middle Ages*, trans. R. J. Payton and U. Mammitzsch (1996); A. Ferguson's *Indian Summer of English Chivalry* (1960); and M. Vale's *War and Chivalry* (1981) continue to be good sources. In *Chaucer and the Subject of History* (1983), L. Patterson gives a balanced appraisal of how chivalric ideals and realities applied to literature; his chapter on Chaucer's knight contains a good discussion of knighthood in general.

—*Leigh Smith*

Knights Templar

An order of religious knights similar in origin to such other groups as the Knights of Saint John (Hospitallers) and the Teutonic Knights.

The Knights Templar were one of several organizations, or orders, of religious knights that developed in the Holy Land during the era of the Crusades. However, the Templars became the best known through their spectacular successes—and also through the even more spectacular nature of their demise. In the last years of the eleventh century Western Europeans under the leadership of Godfrey of Bouillon had waged the First Crusade, which culminated in the recapture of Jerusalem, in 1099. By the second decade of the twelfth century the Knights Templar had developed informally into a group of French knights dedicated to protecting pilgrims traveling on the dangerous highway between the port of Jaffa and Jerusalem. Under their leader, Hugues de Payens, the Knights received the patronage of King Baldwin II of Jerusalem and were granted quarters near the site of Solomon's Temple. The Knights professed chastity and obedience to the Patriarch of Jerusalem; they would eventually, with papal permission, assume a white garment emblazoned with a red cross.

At the Council of Troyes in 1128 the Templars received official Church recognition and the attention of Bernard of Clairvaux. In *De laude novae militiae* (In Praise of the New Military Order) Bernard devised a rule for the Templars. *De laude* answered the thorny question of how a religious order, traditionally barred from shedding blood, could bear the sword. Bernard argued that the religious knight "is the instrument of God, for the punishment of malefactors, and for the defence of the just. Indeed, when he kills a malefactor, this is not homicide but malicide—the destruction of evil. Consequently, by carrying out such an act, the knight is accounted Christ's legal executioner against evildoers."

A bull published by Pope Innocent II in 1139 made the Templars solely answerable to the Holy See. The order grew in numbers and was organized into ten provinces stretching from Jerusalem to Hungary to Portugal.

Over the course of the next two centuries the Templars became involved in crusader conflicts with the Muslim kingdoms surrounding Jerusalem. The Templars' aid to King Louis VII of France during the Second Crusade in 1147 exemplifies the nature of such entanglements. Templar fortresses and manors were built not only in the Middle East and in Saracen-threatened Spain but also in Cyprus and in many parts of Europe. In 1291 the Templars formed part of the Christian forces defeated at Acre, the last major Christian stronghold. After the fall of Acre the order moved its headquarters to Cyprus.

Though individual members committed themselves to poverty, the wealth of the Templars grew through donations by benefactors. With their increasing wealth, Templars became personal bankers to various rulers. Henry II of England entrusted the Templars with the money paid in recompense for Archbishop Thomas Becket's murder. The Templars lent funds to Louis VII for the Second Crusade, and eventually the Templar headquarters in Paris became the de facto royal treasury of France.

Inevitably stories of Templar arrogance in the face of their visible wealth tainted the reputation of the order. William of Tyre instigated clerical opposition to the Templars at the Third Lateran Council in 1179. William claimed that the Templars had sold an Egyptian convert to Christianity to the Egyptian authorities for a huge sum of money. It was also alleged that the political terrorists known as the Assassins had been on the verge of converting to Christianity, but the Templars had intervened, lest they lose tribute money from the Assassins. Pope Innocent III cited the order for pride and for abuse of papal exemption in 1207. In 1265 Pope Clement IV echoed the accusations of pride. Similar complaints were lodged against the Hospitallers. Despite an uncooperative rivalry that emerged at times between the Templars and the Hospitallers, prominent knights such as Ramon Lull of Catalonia called for a union between the two military orders for the purpose of advancing the faith against Islam more effectively.

The long-standing relationship between France and the Templars was strained by King Philip IV's increasing opposition to papal influence within his realm. While many Templars (including the grand master, Jacques de Molay) were French, and the order provided crucial financial services to the French crown, the Knights owed their final allegiance to the pope. The king desired greater control over the appointment of bishops and control of Church property, and he had also put pressure on Clement V to establish a residence in Avignon, which was not actually part of the kingdom of France but was closer to Philip's sphere of influence than to Rome.

It is not completely clear which of the king's inclinations toward the Templars played the larger part in motivating his final drastic action against them: whether he was moved by the piety he professed as befitting the most Christian king of France or driven by his desire for a possible transfer of Templar properties to France's guardianship and enrichment. Irrespective of his motives, however, on the morning of October 13, 1307, the king's officers arrested members of the Templars throughout France.

The "supremely abominable crimes" of which they were accused included denial of Christ, obscene ritual kisses, homosexual acts, and idolatry. By the following year these charges had been formalized and expanded into 127 articles, including among them new charges alleging their disbelief in the sacraments, the practice of lay absolution, the existence of sinister secrets, and rampant greed. Surviving depositions show the Templars admitting to such behaviors as spitting and urinating on the cross and kissing their brethren not only on the mouth (a standard part of the Templar reception ceremony) but also on the lower back and anus.

It was further alleged that they were being encouraged to commit sodomy (one knight claimed three encounters with Jacques de Molay him-

Seal used by the Knights Templar. (British Museum)

self in a single night), to worship and adore cats and a certain other idol, and to desecrate the host at mass. Though it was never discovered, this other idol was said by some to have been a head—perhaps that of Hugues de Payens himself. Accusations of witchcraft, sodomy, and heresy were linked in the popular imagination at this time; Catharist heretics and Jews were victims of denunciations broadly similar to those leveled at the Templars.

Pope Clement V was skeptical of the charges; however, he eventually commissioned papal inquiries to hear confessions. The zealous Philip IV urged other kings to arrest and interrogate the Templars in their jurisdictions, but such monarchs as Edward I of England and Juan I of Aragon displayed even more skepticism and delay than did the pope. Torture was not permitted under English or Aragonese law, and it took the intervention of the pope to implement it. Most of the confessions on record were probably made under torture or the threat of it, for in places where torture was slow in coming or nonexistent, few confessions were extracted. Although defenders came forward among the Templars in France, in 1310, 54 Templars were burned at the stake for their alleged crimes. At the Council of Vienne in 1312–1313 the pope finally suppressed the order. Jacques de Molay and other Templar leaders were executed by burning in 1314, even though they persisted in adhering to their retractions of their original confessions of guilt. Their property was to be dispersed to the Hospitallers (except in the Iberian kingdoms), but what transfers took place were diminished by delay and by the expenses demanded by the French crown and others.

A sometimes outlandish interest in the Templars began to develop in the eighteenth century, particularly in France and Germany. In these countries the Templars were connected with the developing legends of Freemasonry, and they were seen as champions of a secret and benevolent wisdom in the face of ecclesiastical corruption. Complex nineteenth- and twentieth-century conspiracy theories (such as that of the Abbé Barruel) have placed the Templars in a conspiratorial chain of esoteric knowledge stretching from the Manichaeans to the Jacobin-led Freemasons of the French Revolution. The legends of the Templars have far outgrown their relatively brief historical involvement in the faith and politics of Western Europe.

See also: Homosexuality (male); Knight; Witchcraft
References and further reading: General information about the Knights Templar can be found in studies that ultimately focus on the actual trials and depositions of the Templars: E. Burman, *Supremely Abominable Crimes: The Trial of the Knights Templar* (1994), and M. Barber, *The Trial of the Templars* (1978). Barber's work elucidates the many variants of accusation and confession with some extensive passages of comparative folkloric study, particularly about the "Templar head." For the history of alleged practices of magic in the Middle Ages, see R. Kieckhefer, *Magic in the Middle Ages* (1989). The Templars appear briefly in the larger context of witches and other persecuted minorities—heretical, sexual, or otherwise—in J. Richards, *Sex, Dissidence, and Damnation: Minority Groups in the Middle Ages* (1991). P. Partner deals briefly with the medieval history of the Knights Templar and their dissolution; he then concentrates on later attitudes to the Templars, including attempts to link them to the Temple of Solomon and to Gnosticism and the incorporation of these ideas into Freemasonry: *The Knights Templar and Their Myth* (1987); the quotation in the text from Bernard of Clairvaux is on page 8. Partner's work becomes an uneasy

diatribe in its final pages, but this should not detract from the usefulness of his study. S. Dafoe also attempts to refute the connections between the Templar accusations and Freemasons in *Unholy Worship* (1998).

—*Graham N. Drake*